# Nationalist Mobilization and the Colla̤ρ̤_ _ʲ the Soviet State

This study examines the process by which the seemingly impossible in 1987 – the disintegration of the Soviet Union – became the seemingly inevitable by 1991, providing an original interpretation not only of the Soviet collapse, but also of the phenomenon of nationalism more generally. Probing the role of nationalist action as both cause and effect, Beissinger utilizes extensive event data and detailed case studies from across the USSR during its final years to elicit the shifting relationship between pre-existing structural conditions, institutional constraints, and event-generated influences in the massive nationalist explosions that brought about the collapse of the Soviet Union. As Beissinger demonstrates, the "tidal" context of nationalism – that is, the transnational influence of one nationalism upon another – is critical to an explanation of the success and failure of particular nationalisms, the ability of governments to repress nationalist challenges, why some nationalisms turn violent, and how a mounting crescendo of events can potentially overwhelm states, periodically evoking large-scale structural change in the character of the state system.

Mark R. Beissinger is Professor of Political Science at the University of Wisconsin, Madison and former director of its Center for Russia, East Europe, and Central Asia. He is author of the book *Scientific Management, Socialist Discipline, and Soviet Power* (1988) and numerous articles and book chapters, as well as co-editor of the books *The Nationalities Factor in Soviet Politics and Society* (1990) and *Beyond State Crisis? Postcolonial Africa and Post-Soviet Eurasia Compared* (2002).

## Cambridge Studies in Comparative Politics

*General Editor*

Margaret Levi    *University of Washington, Seattle*

*Associate Editors*

Robert H. Bates    *Harvard University*
Peter Hall    *Harvard University*
Stephen Hanson    *University of Washington, Seattle*
Peter Lange    *Duke University*
Helen Milner    *Columbia University*
Frances Rosenbluth    *Yale University*
Susan Stokes    *University of Chicago*
Sidney Tarrow    *Cornell University*

*Other Books in the Series*

*Continued on page following Index*

*For Jonathan and Rebecca*

# Nationalist Mobilization and the Collapse of the Soviet State

**MARK R. BEISSINGER**

*University of Wisconsin, Madison*

CAMBRIDGE
UNIVERSITY PRESS

CAMBRIDGE UNIVERSITY PRESS
Cambridge, New York, Melbourne, Madrid, Cape Town, Singapore,
São Paulo, Delhi, Dubai, Tokyo, Mexico City

Cambridge University Press
32 Avenue of the Americas, New York, NY 10013-2473, USA

www.cambridge.org
Information on this title: www.cambridge.org/9780521001489

First published 2002

*A catalog record for this publication is available from the British Library*

*Library of Congress Cataloging in Publication data*
Beissinger, Mark R.
Nationalist mobilization and the collapse of the Soviet State: a tidal approach to the study
of nationalism / Mark R. Beissinger.
p.   cm. – (Cambridge studies in comparative politics)
Includes bibliographical references and index.
ISBN 0-521-80670-4 – ISBN 0-521-00148-X (pb.)
1. Soviet Union – Politics and government – 1985–1991.   2. Nationalism – Soviet
Union.   3. Soviet Union – Ethnic relations – Political aspects.   I. Title.   II. Series.
DK288 .B45   2001
320.54′0947′09048–dc21          2001025404

ISBN 978-0-521-80670-1 Hardback
ISBN 978-0-521-00148-9 Paperback

# *Contents*

# Illustrations

# *Tables*

# *Acknowledgments*

This project began in 1988 as the Soviet Union was first enveloped by large-scale protest; it concluded thirteen years later in a world largely unimagined at its inception. Indeed, in the course of this investigation what began as a comparative study of protest among multiple nationalities within a single country ended up as a cross-national study of nationalist mobilization within fifteen countries (or more, depending on who does the counting). Not only did the object of research transform, but my approach to the subject necessarily altered as well. I learned a tremendous amount throughout this project – not only from the object of my study, but also from the many colleagues who graciously shared their ideas and expertise with me. I have no excuse for the prolonged production other than the empirical and theoretical aspirations contained herein.

A project of this scope would have been impossible without the assistance of many organizations. Two grants from the National Council for Soviet and East European Research and one from the National Science Foundation allowed me to create the event databases on which this study is based. The International Research and Exchange Board (IREX) and Fulbright-Hayes afforded me field opportunities for gathering materials for the book. A fellowship from the Woodrow Wilson International Center for Scholars gave me the opportunity to begin pulling this enormous mass of material together into manuscript form. The Graduate School of the University of Wisconsin-Madison on several occasions supplied critical supplementary support, and the university generously provided a sabbatical to finish the writing. The Davis Center for Russian Studies at Harvard University also partially supported the final phases of my work. To all these organizations, I express my deep appreciation.

I am grateful as well to the many individuals – too numerous to name – who aided my research in the former USSR and at *Arkhiv samizdata* at Radio Liberty, but in particular, I would like to thank Sergei Markov, Maria Rozeriunova, Sergei Grigoriants, and Mario Corti for their special assistance. Jeffrey Gayton, Daniel Geller, Terry McKenna, Rob Moser, and Kate Weaver provided able research assistance in compiling and coding the event data. Pranas Ciziunas and Dean Wilson furnished additional support during my term at the Wilson Center. Kate Graney and Ed Schatz acted as a critical audience for many of the arguments in the book. Jonathan Cebra and Mitch Pickerel aided in the statistical analysis of the event data. Unless otherwise noted, all statistical analyses were performed using the 6.0 version of STATA.

Throughout this project I was fortunate to receive outstanding input and feedback from many colleagues. Doug McAdam, Sidney Tarrow, and Charles Tilly were particularly helpful at various stages of the project and were kind enough to share portions of their collaborative work on contentious politics. Charles Franklin, Jason Wittenberg, and Susan Olzak gave excellent advice concerning the proper statistical methodologies to employ; obviously, they bear no guilt for my mistakes in the application of these methods or in the interpretation of the results. I received many useful comments and suggestions during presentations at Wisconsin, Cornell, Princeton, Stanford, Berkeley, Harvard, Duke, Michigan, Chicago, and the University of Illinois, as well as at the Wilson Center, the Institute for State and Law in Moscow, and numerous conferences and professional association meetings. It would be impossible to name all the colleagues whose questions or suggestions are somehow represented in the final product. Among those not already named whose comments, input, or support proved especially useful were Donna Bahry, Nancy Bermeo, Rogers Brubaker, Valerie Bunce, Jane Burbank, Timothy Colton, John Hall, Stephen Hanson, Kathie Hendley, Donald Horowitz, Michael Kennedy, Anatoly Khazanov, Herbert Kitschelt, Mark Kramer, Ruud Koopmans, David Laitin, Scott Mainwairing, Dick Merelman, Alex Motyl, Diana Mutz, Norman Naimark, Dieter Rucht, Michael Schatzberg, Ron Suny, Roman Szporluk, Larissa Titarenko, Bernie Yack, and Crawford Young. For critical readings of the final manuscript I would like to express my special thanks to Valerie Bunce, Stephen Hanson, David Laitin, Ed Schatz, and Crawford Young.

Portions of several chapters draw on materials previously published. Parts of several chapters appeared in: "How Nationalisms Spread: Eastern

## Acknowledgments

Europe Adrift the Tides and Cycles of Nationalist Contention," *Social Research* (Spring 1996), pp. 97–146; "Nationalisms That Bark and Nationalisms That Bite: Ernest Gellner and the Substantiation of Nations," in John Hall, ed., *The State of the Nation: Ernest Gellner and the Theory of Nationalism* (Cambridge, UK: Cambridge University Press, 1998), pp. 169–90; and "Event Analysis in Transitional Societies: Protest Mobilization in the Former Soviet Union," in Dieter Rucht, Ruud Koopmans, and Friedhelm Neidhardt, eds., *Acts of Dissent: New Developments in the Study of Protest* (Berlin: Sigma Press, 1998), pp. 284–316 [published in the United States by Rowman and Littlefield Publishers]. An earlier version of Chapter 6 appeared in "Nationalist Violence and the State: Political Authority and Contentious Repertoires in the Former USSR," *Comparative Politics*, vol. 30, no. 4 (July 1998), pp. 401–22. I thank the publishers for permission for publication of these revised materials in this volume.

Finally, my wife Margaret and our two children Jonathan and Rebecca endured this project with the warmth and affection that has typified our family. I dedicate this book to our wonderful children – in awe of the miracles that they and our family are.

# 1

## *From the Impossible to the Inevitable*

... we travel abroad to discover in distant lands something whose presence at home has become unrecognizable.

   Michel de Certeau, *The Practice of Everyday Life*

On May 18, 1991, two Soviet cosmonauts blasted off from the Baikonur cosmodrome for a routine four-month mission aboard the Mir space station. While aloft in weightlessness, below them one world died and another was born. By the time they returned to Earth, they no longer knew whether the country that had dispatched them still existed and to which state they and their spacecraft belonged.

The shattering of the Soviet state was one of the pivotal transformations of the twentieth century. It fundamentally altered the world in which we live, provoking an end to half a century of communist domination in Eastern Europe, breaching the Cold War division of the planet, and prompting new disorders with which the twenty-first century will long grapple. But the breakup of the USSR also presents us with many paradoxes that challenge our understanding of politics. The Soviet Union was a nuclear superpower with global commitments and a seventy-four-year record of survival – a polity which had endured two devastating wars, several famines involving millions of deaths, the mass annihilation of its own citizens by its rulers, and a social revolution that brought it into the industrial world. It was a state which launched the first human into space, whose founding political ideas inspired millions throughout the world, and which was widely regarded by many social scientists as a model of successful transition to modernity. From 1988 to 1991 that state exploded, largely under the pressure of its ethnic problems.

1

The disintegration of the Soviet Union was also one of the most notoriously unanticipated developments of modern history. Had Western experts been polled in 1987, the near-unanimous opinion would have been that the dissolution of the USSR was highly unlikely, if not impossible. Indeed, some prominent experts refused to recognize the demise of the USSR even after it happened! As Jerry Hough later recalled about the period, "[t]he flow of events was so rapid and so unexpected that no one had time to step back and reflect upon what had transpired. Observers tended to retain their interpretations of events even after they had been proved incorrect and to combine them with interpretations of later events in contradictory ways."[1] Those few experts who before 1988 had entertained the possibility that the Soviet Union might disintegrate as a result of its nationality problems largely did so for the wrong reasons, believing that the breakup would be precipitated by a Muslim uprising in Central Asia.[2] In reality, Central Asia played little role in the entire affair and was conspicuous for its quiescence. Western experts on ethnicity fared no better. In a book of essays written in 1990 and published in 1992 in which leading theorists of nationalism and ethnicity were asked to place the ongoing upheavals in the USSR into a comparative perspective, not a single author anticipated the imminent breakup of the country, and many openly argued against the idea that the Soviet Union was disintegrating.[3]

---

[1] Jerry F. Hough, *Democratization and Revolution in the USSR* (Washington, DC: Brookings Institution Press, 1997), p. 3.

[2] Hélène Carrère d'Encausse, *Decline of an Empire* (New York: Newsweek Books, 1980). Even Richard Pipes, who in 1984 correctly concluded that the Soviet Union was facing a "revolutionary situation," did not predict the breakup of the USSR, but thought that the likely outcome of crisis was reform. As he wrote: "There is no likelihood that the Soviet government will voluntarily dissolve the Soviet Union into its constituent republics, but genuine federalism of some sort, with broad self-rule for the minorities, is not inconceivable; it calls only for making constitutional fiction constitutional reality. Such a step would go a long way toward reducing the ethnic tensions that now exist." Richard Pipes, "Can the Soviet Union Reform?" *Foreign Affairs*, vol. 63, no. 1 (Fall 1984), p. 58.

[3] Alexander J. Motyl, ed., *Thinking Theoretically About Soviet Nationalities: History and Comparison in the Study of the USSR* (New York: Columbia University Press, 1992). Among those who argued that the breakup of the USSR was unlikely were Ernest Gellner, Crawford Young, Donald Horowitz, David Laitin, and Michael Hechter. Anthony Smith, Paul Brass, and Kenneth Minogue expressed no opinion on the issue, while only John Armstrong and S. N. Eisenstadt noted the "uncertain" future of the USSR. In an article written on the eve of the August 1991 coup, David Laitin similarly decried "the unjustifiable assumption" that the USSR was on a course toward dissolution; after the August coup, a postscript was added in which Laitin confessed that recent events had made "the image of a rotting empire, discredited in . . . [the] essay, seem intuitively correct." David D. Laitin, "The National Uprising in the Soviet Union," *World Politics* (October 1991), pp. 139–77.

## From the Impossible to the Inevitable

Although many of the accusations against Sovietologists for their defects of vision are deserved, they must be understood in context: Even the vast majority of Soviet dissidents in 1987 (including most non-Russian dissidents) could not imagine the collapse of the USSR.[4] Before 1990 the breakup of the Soviet Union remained outside the realm of the conceivable for the overwhelming mass of Soviet citizens, irrespective of ethnic background.

This book is about the disintegration of the Soviet state – and specifically, about how within a compressed period of history the seemingly impossible came to be widely viewed as the seemingly inevitable, turning a world once unthinkingly accepted as immutable upside down. Ironically, though few thought it possible only a few years before it happened, the prevailing view of Soviet disintegration today is that the breakup was inevitable – the manifestation of inherent qualities of the Soviet state and of processes set in motion long before the actual events which brought it about. Often underlying assertions of the structural predetermination of Soviet disintegration is an implicit teleology, defined by Isaiah Berlin as the assumption that history contains an inherent logic, nature, or purpose beyond control of the individual that is revealed in the movement of history itself. Berlin argued that teleological explanation obfuscates the role of human action in the history that we make and takes as the goal of explanation the *ex post* revelation of the essential character of things which makes the present unavoidable. As Berlin asserted, in teleological reasoning "[w]e are plainly dealing not with an empirical theory but with a metaphysical attitude which takes for granted that to explain a thing . . . is to discover its purpose. . . . Teleology is a form of faith capable of neither confirmation nor refutation by any kind of experience; the notions of evidence, proof, probability and so on, are wholly inapplicable to it."[5]

Several types of teleological explanations predominate in scholarly and folk accounts of the collapse of the Soviet state. Some authors, such as Martin Malia, assert that the total disintegration of the Soviet state was inherent in the very logic of Leninism because its totalitarian essence bred an incapacity to reform. As Malia puts it, "the intrinsic irreformability of communism is no longer a question of opinion; it is now a matter of

---

[4] Writing in 1969, Andrei Amalrik was one of the few who foresaw the breakup of the USSR along national lines, although he believed it would be precipitated by a war with China, not by internal reform. See Andrei Amalrik, *Will the Soviet Union Survive Until 1984?* (New York: Harper and Row, 1970), pp. 62–65.

[5] Isaiah Berlin, *Historical Inevitability* (London: Oxford University Press, 1954), pp. 12–17.

historical fact."[6] Malia's is not a probabilistic explanation of Soviet collapse. It is rather an essentialist understanding. Yet, if this were true and
the breakup of the USSR was inevitable, why did so many come to believe
only a short time before its collapse that the Soviet state was fundamentally stable? It was widely argued on the eve of *glasnost'* that Soviet institutions had achieved a degree of broad-based legitimacy within the Soviet
population, irrespective of the national context within which Leninism
appeared, and that persuasive methods of rule had replaced state-
sponsored intimidation.[7] In retrospect, Soviet legitimacy was an illusion,
but at the time seemed real enough to inspire the decisions of Gorbachev
and others to introduce *glasnost'* in the first place. As one Western expert
on Soviet nationalities issues put it at the time, *glasnost'* was above all "an
expression of confidence in the legitimacy of the Soviet system" and "a
recognition that the pretense of infallibility is no longer necessary to
command popular allegiance and support."[8] This popular support eventually faded in the wake of the subsequent onslaught of events. Nevertheless, Gorbachev's reforms cannot be accounted for by arguments which
view the disintegration of the Soviet state as emerging only from the
system's inherent logic, for why should a system whose very logic doomed
it to failure give rise to the confidence that seemed to underlie political
liberalization? The very fact that Soviet leaders risked liberalizing reform
tells us that something critical is missing from explanations of Soviet collapse that make reference only to the "logic" of the system.

There is also the fundamental problem of how the Soviet state came to
be recognized as irreformable – that is, how its irreformable quality
became the "historical fact" that Malia observes. Obviously, when viewed
from the present, the past contains no contingency in the sense that it took
place. The choices embodied within it are irreversible and buried in
history's immutability. But as Marc Bloch described the way in which we

[6] Martin Malia, "Leninist Endgame," in Stephen R. Graubard, ed., *Exit From Communism*
(New Brunswick, NJ: Transaction Publishers, 1993), p. 60. For a critique of what he called
this "essentialist" argument, see Alexander Dallin, "Causes of the Collapse of the USSR,"
*Post-Soviet Affairs*, vol. 8, no. 4 (1992), pp. 279–302.

[7] See, for instance, Peter Hauslohner, "Politics Before Gorbachev: De-Stalinization and the
Roots of Reform," in Seweryn Bialer, ed., *Politics, Society, and Nationality: Inside Gorbachev's
Russia* (Boulder, CO: Westview Press, 1990), pp. 41–90.

[8] Gail Lapidus, "State and Society: Toward the Emergence of Civil Society in the Soviet
Union," in Alexander Dallin and Gail W. Lapidus, eds., *The Soviet System in Crisis* (Boulder,
CO: Westview Press, 1991), p. 140.

should approach history, "[w]hen the historian asks himself about the probability of a past event, he actually attempts to transport himself, by a bold exercise of the mind, to the time before the event itself, in order to gauge its chances, as they appeared upon the eve of its realization."[9] In this case, several years before the events in question, they seemed highly improbable to most participants and observers. Did the Soviet state break apart because it was inherently incapable of survival, or do we now see it as having been incapable of survival precisely because the Soviet state broke apart? In history winners take all, including the explanation of their own victory. As daunting as the structural obstacles to reform were (a subject about which many scholars, including myself, wrote well before the events of the late 1980s), ultimately the argument of the fundamental inevitability of Soviet collapse can only be meaningless, since any judgment concerning the inability of the Soviet state to survive cannot be extracted from the very events which caused the Soviet Union to disintegrate in the first place. As Berlin noted, teleological explanation cannot be proved or disproved; it rests rather on faith. In this instance there are good reasons to inject some doubt into teleology's faith. The fact that within a relatively short but very intense period of history the idea of the disintegration of the Soviet state moved from the wholly unimaginable to the completely inevitable within the popular mind – both within the USSR and outside – does not breed confidence in ascriptions of the Soviet collapse solely to an inherent logic of Leninism, for this fails to explain how such a tremendous transformation in attitudes toward the state took place within such a short period of time.

Similar problems beset other widely accepted explanations of Soviet disintegration. It is commonplace to argue that the Soviet Union broke apart because it was an empire. From this perspective Soviet collapse was inevitable – determined perhaps even as far back as the creation of the Soviet state – due to the inherent imperial quality of Bolshevik rule.[10] In this view, all empires are destined to disappear in a world in which national self-determination has become the accepted norm, and because the Soviet Union was an empire, it too could not escape its preordained fate. A similar

---

[9] Marc Bloch, *The Historian's Craft* (New York: Vintage Books, 1953), p. 125.

[10] See, for instance, Hélène Carrère d'Encausse, *The End of the Soviet Empire: The Triumph of Nations* (New York: Basic Books, 1993); Alexander J. Motyl, "From Imperial Decay to Imperial Collapse: The Fall of the Soviet Empire in Comparative Perspective," in David Good, ed., *Nationalism and Empire* (New York: St. Martin's Press, 1992), pp. 15–43.

dilemma confronts these arguments: Did the USSR collapse because it was an empire, or is it now routinely referred to as an empire precisely because it collapsed? A sudden profusion of empire imagery accompanied the demise of the USSR. On the eve of *perestroika*, relatively few observers employed a discourse of empire to depict the nationality problems of the USSR. Crawford Young expressed the attitude prevailing at the time toward the use of the term "empire" to describe the Soviet Union:

States perceived in international jurisprudence and dominant political discourse as colonial have been dismantled, but this imagery – however serviceable as cold war lexicon . . . is unlikely to govern the unfolding dialectic between the central institutions of the Soviet state and its non-Russian periphery. . . . [A]lthough there is an undeniable element of "exceptionalism" to the Soviet case, it belongs on balance in the contemporary universe of polities founded on the doctrinal postulates of the "nation-state," and is therefore susceptible of interpretation according to the same empirical inferences as other members of the contemporary body of states.[11]

Throughout the Cold War the dominant image used by scholars to describe the Soviet Union in its internal dimensions was that of state rather than empire. To be sure, the countries of Soviet-dominated Eastern Europe (and to a lesser extent, the Balts) were frequently referred to as "captive nations." But the imperial analogy was only occasionally extended beyond this to cover the multinational character of the Soviet state. Rather, as the Soviet Union collapsed, it came to be widely recognized as a multinational empire. In this sense, the real issue that needs to be explained is how a polity once almost universally construed as a state came to be universally condemned as an empire. The critical question that those interested in understanding the disintegration of the Soviet state need to answer is not whether the Soviet breakup was inevitable, but rather how it came to be widely viewed as inevitable by a population that, only a short while before, could barely imagine such an outcome.

Teleological explanation violates one of the fundamental attributes of social causation: Causation always flows through the beliefs and actions of individuals, even if the actions produce unintended results. Indeed, teleological explanation can be defined as "the attribution of the cause of a historical happening neither to the actions and reactions that constitute the happening nor to concrete and specifiable conditions that shape or constrain the actions and reactions but rather to abstract transhistorical

---

[11] M. Crawford Young, "The National and Colonial Question and Marxism: A View from the South," in Motyl, ed., *Thinking Theoretically*, pp. 91, 97.

processes leading to some future state."[12] Whether this be some inevitable march toward freedom and democracy, the unavoidable requirements of modernization or the market, or the unfolding drama of national self-determination, teleological explanation celebrates the determination of structure over agency. It is one thing to talk about the effects of structure – that patterning of social interaction which constrains, facilitates, or defines human behavior – in probabilistic terms and as factors conditioning choice. But teleological explanation is not probabilistic. It views the actions of individuals as epiphenomena of structure, as if the human actions involved in the collapse of the USSR were not intentional but mere reflections of a larger logic or moving hand operating outside the individual.

In all the ink that has been spilled concerning the demise of Soviet communism, the serious task of probing the causal interaction between structure and agency has not yet been tackled. It is true that a great deal of attention has been focused on Gorbachev's personal role in bringing down the Soviet state,[13] and a considerable literature has emerged on individual nationalist movements that were instrumental in fostering change.[14] Others, by contrast, have placed emphasis on the institutional, economic, or social structural conditions which prepared the way for both Soviet liberalization and the eruptions of nationalist mobilization that precipitated the Soviet collapse.[15] Whereas the first group of authors focuses almost

[12] William H. Sewell, Jr., "Three Temporalities: Toward an Eventful Sociology," in Terrence J. McDonald, ed., *The Historic Turn in the Human Sciences* (Ann Arbor, MI: University of Michigan Press, 1996), p. 247.

[13] For a few of the many works on Gorbachev's impact on events, see Archie Brown, *The Gorbachev Factor* (Oxford: Oxford University Press, 1997); Hough, *Democratization and Revolution*; Mark Galeotti, *Gorbachev and His Revolution* (New York: St. Martin's Press, 1997); Martin McCauley, *Gorbachev* (New York: Longman, 1998); Robert G. Kaiser, *Why Gorbachev Happened: His Triumph and His Failure* (New York: Simon & Schuster, 1991). The Russian-language literature is also enormous.

[14] Among the numerous English-language works, see Rasma Karklins, *Ethnopolitics and Transition to Democracy: The Collapse of the USSR and Latvia* (Baltimore, MD: Johns Hopkins University Press, 1994); Rein Taagepera, *Estonia: Return to Independence* (Boulder, CO: Westview Press, 1993); Alfred Erich Senn, *Lithuania Awakening* (Berkeley, CA: University of California Press, 1990); Alfred Erich Senn, *Gorbachev's Failure in Lithuania* (New York: St. Martin's Press, 1995); Jane Dawson, *Eco-nationalism: Anti-Nuclear Activism and National Identity in Russia, Lithuania, and Ukraine* (Durham, NC: Duke University Press, 1996); Taras Kuzio and Andrew Wilson, *Ukraine: Perestroika to Independence* (London: Macmillan, 1995); Jan Zaprudnik, *Belarus: At a Crossroads in History* (Boulder, CO: Westview Press, 1993).

[15] Valerie Bunce, *Subversive Institutions: The Design and the Destruction of Socialism and the State* (Cambridge, UK: Cambridge University Press, 1999); Philip G. Roeder, *Red Sunset: The*

exclusively on a specific individual or movement and fails to probe larger relationships of social causation which might have conditioned action, the latter group largely eschews in-depth analysis of the actual actions which brought about the collapse, treating these as the logical manifestations of particular institutional designs or social processes set in motion well before the events in question occurred. As one review of the literature concluded, social scientific explanations of the collapse of communism have tended to be excessively deterministic.[16]

Still others view the Soviet collapse as largely unrelated to the mobilizational explosions that rocked the Soviet state in the *glasnost'* years – as a realignment of control within the ruling elite or as a process of the appropriation of the state's resources by bureaucrats due to a loss of confidence in central institutions.[17] Obviously, nationalism was both a cause of and a consequence of the declining institutional coherence of the Soviet state brought on by *glasnost'* and failed institutional reform. But in a period of revolution, insurrection, and major upheaval in which hundreds of thousands took to the streets on a daily basis, explanations that focus solely on elite maneuverings or on the bureaucratic appropriation of state resources lack a ring of authenticity. They ultimately cannot account for why the Soviet state ended by disintegrating into national pieces as opposed to merely undergoing regime change. They fail to address how the seemingly impossible – the breakup of the Soviet state – became the seemingly inevitable. Indeed, much of the appropriation of resources by bureaucrats occurred as the future prospects of the state declined.

Closely related to the interplay between structure and agency in the disintegration of the Soviet Union is their broader relationship within the study of nationalism. For the USSR was brought down in large part by a remarkable explosion of nationalist mobilization and the impact that mobilization had on the ways in which both Russians and non-Russians thought

*Failure of Soviet Politics* (Princeton, NJ: Princeton University Press, 1993); Ronald Grigor Suny, *The Revenge of the Past: Nationalism, Revolution, and the Collapse of the Soviet Union* (Stanford, CA: Stanford University Press, 1993); Rogers Brubaker, "Nationhood and the National Question in the Soviet Union and Post-Soviet Eurasia: An Institutionalist Account," *Theory and Society*, vol. 23 (1994), pp. 47–78; Moshe Lewin, *The Gorbachev Phenomenon* (Berkeley, CA: University of California Press, 1988); David Lane, *The Rise and Fall of State Socialism* (Cambridge: Polity Press, 1996).

[16] See Stathis N. Kalyvas, "The Decay and Breakdown of Communist One-Party Systems," *Annual Review of Political Science*, vol. 2 (1999), pp. 323–43.

[17] Hough, *Democratization and Revolution*; Steven L. Solnick, *Stealing the State: Control and Collapse in Soviet Institutions* (Cambridge, MA: Harvard University Press, 1998).

about the Soviet state. The study of nationalism in recent years has under-gone a paradigm shift. Scholars have increasingly come to appreciate the ambiguous, arbitrary, and constructed character of nationalist claims and the shifting, embedded, and overlapping nature of cultural identities. This book does not seek to overturn this consensus, but consciously attempts to build on it by pushing our understanding of nationalism in a direction which, I believe, deserves greater attention if observers are to avoid making the same types of mistakes in other contexts that were made with respect to Soviet collapse. Empirically, its central task is to elicit the process by which the unthinkable about nationhood becomes the seemingly inevitable. Theoretically, it seeks to carve out an answer by focusing on nationalist action as both cause and effect.

As with the study of Soviet collapse, the structure/agency debate so prominent within other areas of social science has rarely been interrogated within the study of nationalism. A large number of works seek to uncover the origins of nationalism, assuming that by understanding origins, one thereby understands the universal essence of the phenomenon. Most scholars regard manifestations of nationalism as the logical consequence of a particular social interest or identity position embedded by prior history or emerging out of the impact of broader social forces. Structure, not agency, looms heavily in their interpretations. Many theories are plainly teleological, portraying nationalist conflicts as the realization of an unfolding national spirit, universal norms of self-determination, or the logic of industrialism.[18] The idea that identities could be defined in the context of agency or that nationalism is both a structured and structuring phenomenon has not received sufficient attention.

Most studies understand nationalist action as merely an externalization of nationalist ways of thinking brought into being well before the onset of nationalist action. Miroslav Hroch, for instance, focused attention on what he termed Phase B in the development of nationalism (the period of patri-otic agitation), calling it "the most important phase," largely ignoring how and why the emergence of nationalist elites leads to the rise of mass national movements (Phase C). Although Hroch noted that "Phase B was not necessarily destined to pass over into Phase C," his assumption was that nationalist action is not worth intensive examination, since what

---

[18] For a discussion of the teleological and functionalist aspects of Ernest Gellner's theories, for instance, see John Hall, ed., *The State of the Nation: Ernest Gellner and the Theory of Nationalism* (Cambridge, UK: Cambridge University Press, 1998).

occurs during Phase C is largely determined by the ways in which national identities are formed prior to action.[19] Liah Greenfeld takes this position to an extreme, arguing that "the character of every national identity was defined in the early phase" of the formation of national identity, when *ressentiment* took hold within elite segments of society. "Its effect, in the political, social, and cultural constitution of the respective nations, as well as their historical record, are attributable to this original definition which set the goals for mobilization, not to the nationalization of the masses." To be fair, Greenfeld loosens the jaws of history somewhat, adding that the origins of nationalism do not "*completely* shape its social and political expressions" or determine the conduct of nations. They only create "a predisposition for a certain type of action, and a probability that, in certain conditions, such action will take place."[20] But the questions of how and under what circumstances predispositions are translated into action remain unaddressed. Is there a direct relationship between certain nationalist predispositions (and ultimately the structural factors which lie behind them) and the ways in which people contest the nation? Why are some predispositions translated into action and others not? Can predispositions change in the context of translation in action? And moving still further away from the thought-to-action paradigm, can predispositions themselves emerge and form as a result of or in the context of action?

These are not idle questions. Rather, they engage the very epistemologies and ontologies that lie behind our knowledge of nationalism (and for that matter, many other political phenomena as well). The discursive shift in the study of nationalism that now dominates scholarly inquiry has raised questions about the thought-to-action paradigm by shedding light on the roles played by states and nationalist intellectuals in inventing standardized languages, national histories, and national traditions. Both primordialism and instrumentalism – the former focusing on identities as the product of sticky emotional attachments, the latter focusing narrowly on identities as mere expressions of self-interest – reflect a kind of structural determinism in which action flows logically from structurally determined

[19] Miroslav Hroch, *Social Preconditions of National Revival in Europe: A Comparative Analysis of the Social Composition of Patriotic Groups among the Smaller European Nations* (Cambridge, UK: Cambridge University Press, 1985), pp. 22–24.

[20] Liah Greenfeld, *Nationalism: Five Roads to Modernity* (Cambridge, MA: Harvard University Press, 1992), pp. 22–23, 25.

10

identities and interests. By contrast, constructivism has shown how the acts of representing nationhood through the written word and other communications media and of dividing political space through boundary definition and other classificatory schemes have been critical in shaping the ways in which nations are "imagined." But constructivism has generally not interrogated the ways in which collective action itself may be constitutive of nationhood.

In developing such a perspective, I focus on the role of the contentious event in the politics of nationalism. Rogers Brubaker has argued that "a theoretically sophisticated eventful perspective on nationness and nationalism is today urgently needed." As he puts it, "We have a large and mature developmentalist literature on nationhood and nationalism" that "traces the long-term political, economic, and cultural changes that led, over centuries, to the gradual emergence of nations." Other works focus on nationhood as a stable property of groups rather than a relational variable over time. But nationhood, he says, is not a constant. It is a temporally defined way of thinking and behaving. Such ways of thinking and behaving, Brubaker argues, do not merely develop. They also happen. An important strand missing within the literature on nationalism, Brubaker observes, is a perspective which allows the possibility of thinking of nationhood "as something that suddenly crystallizes rather than gradually develops, as a contingent, conjuncturally fluctuating, and precarious frame of vision."[21]

This is not to say that the events associated with nationalism have not been studied. On the contrary, a plethora of works have focused on the events surrounding specific nationalist conflicts around the world. But there is a difference between the study of nationalist events and the "eventful" study of nationalism.[22] An "eventful" perspective places time and action centrally in its analysis and seeks to probe the relationship of action to subsequent outcomes, controlling for the influence of other factors. More than that, it implies that nationalism needs to be understood not only as a cause of action, but also as the product of action. This recursive quality of human action – the fact that action can function as both cause and effect – and the significance of this for the study of nationalism are the central theoretical issues this book seeks to address.

[21] Rogers Brubaker, *Nationalism Reframed: Nationhood and the National Question in the New Europe* (Cambridge, UK: Cambridge University Press, 1996), p. 19.
[22] The term itself comes from Sewell, "Three Temporalities," pp. 245–80.

## Structural Facilitation, Institutional Constraint, and Contentious Event

Anthony Giddens' notion of the "duality of structure" (that is, structure as intrinsic to the world of action and vice versa) provides a necessary starting point for any discussion of the recursive quality of action and the role of agency in the rise of nations.[23] But there are differences in the approach which I take. Like Giddens, I am interested in the processes by which particular social practices (in this case, the practices of nationhood) come to be reproduced or modified over time. I accept as well Giddens' basic notion that structure is implicated in action and action in the formation and reproduction of structure. This book does not, however, draw explicitly on structuration theory. This is because I find the critique of Margaret Archer persuasive: In trying to dissolve what he sees as the false dichotomy between structure and agency, Giddens actually elides the two, thereby in effect destroying the analytical utility of both.[24] Indeed, as many critics have pointed out, Giddens is ultimately forced to reintroduce the very duality he seeks to abolish and to "bracket" the impact of one in order to talk concretely about the other – a practice which itself suggests a kind of temporal sequencing. As I am interested in elucidating the structural and conjunctural factors which might accelerate or constrain agential influence, structuration theory provides a collection of powerful metaphors for understanding these relationships, but it does not provide an adequate analytic tool, for by treating structure and agency as fully coterminous, structuration theory cannot distinguish ontologically and methodologically between the two. In line with his emphasis on structure as medium and outcome of action, Giddens also overemphasizes the enabling dimensions of structure and downplays the degree to which order limits and conditions human action.

A more reasonable position would distinguish between three interactive dimensions of structural influence on action: pre-existing structural conditions; the constraints imposed by institutions; and the impact of action itself on subsequent action.[25] I use the term "pre-existing structural

---

[23] See Anthony Giddens, *Central Problems in Social Theory: Action, Structure, and Contradiction in Social Analysis* (Berkeley, CA: University of California Press, 1979).

[24] Margaret S. Archer, *Realist Social Theory: The Morphogenetic Approach* (Cambridge, UK: Cambridge University Press, 1995), p. 65.

[25] Giddens draws a similar distinction between structure and order, but reserves the former term for "rules and resources" and the latter for the patterning and repetition of action.

conditions" to refer to one dimension of structural influence on action: to the accumulated resources, established patterns of behavior, or norm-delineated conditions which facilitate action through their presence. Here, I accept Giddens' point that agency is inherent in the creation of structure and that structure always exercises some degree of influence over agency. But I delimit this form of structural influence on action by the words "pre-existing" and "conditions" to reflect the fact that these influences are, in the Durkheimian sense, givens of social life that, at any specific moment, confront the individual and influence the probability of his or her successful action, though in turn these conditions may subsequently be affected by the consequences of those actions. At the moment of action, for instance, the individual has no control over the level of development of the society in which he or she acts, the extent to which it is culturally plural, the geographic location of its boundaries, its past history, or other such conditions. These conditions – the products of past agency – are embedded in social reality, though they clearly affect the resources and expectations which people bring to bear in action. Structure understood in this sense aids action when it is present. But successful action in the absence of any single pre-existing structural condition is not necessarily excluded; it is merely made harder. Thus, pre-existing structural conditions facilitate rather than preclude. Their influence occurs probabilistically through their cumulation and, though operative across time, is most strikingly visible spatially across individuals or social situations, since at any given moment the cumulation of structural advantage makes it more likely that some rather than others will be capable of acting with success.

A second level of structural influence on action occurs through the orderliness of institutions. Institutions constrain and otherwise positively define the ways in which agents pursue their interests through their power to instill regularity and predictability in social affairs and to preclude alternative ways of acting. The regularity and predictability of institutions derive from the ways in which they define and enforce rules and marginalize the actions of those who would challenge them. It is this which gives institutions many of the nomothetic qualities that the new institutionalism has at times observed – that is, by enforcing rules on society,

See J. D. Mendoza, "Ontological Security, Routine, Social Reproduction," in Christopher G. A. Bryant and David Jary, eds., *Anthony Giddens: Critical Assessments*, vol. 2 (New York: Routledge, 1997), p. 271.

institutions establish behaviors and expectations that flow around those rules and that are rulelike, so that the logic inherent in rules or in their subversion becomes the logic inherent in human behavior. Unlike pre-existing structural conditions, the definition and enforcement of order and the predictability of institutions are not supposed to be probabilistic phenomena; rather, institutions aim to shape social reality actively and to insert certainty into the outcomes of social life by rewarding those working within the rules, punishing or marginalizing those who do not, and instilling a sense of "normality" and belief in the impossibility of alternatives. In imposing a national order on populations, for instance, states have reproduced specific conceptions of nationhood by physically marginalizing those who would advocate alternative bindings of political authority, rewarding those who accept a given definition of nationhood, and socializing populations to accept a particular understanding of nationhood as their own. They have reproduced nations in part through the very regularity of the state's operations and the expectations which this regularity generates that the national order championed by the state could not be otherwise. But there are particular conditions under which uncertainty is injected into the operation of order. That uncertainty also varies spatially, but is usually most conspicuous in its temporal effects on action – for example, in the ways in which the opening and closing of opportunities alter the sense of possibility for contesting a political order.[26]

A third level of structural influence on action emerges from action itself and from what I refer to throughout this book as "events." I understand events as contentious and potentially subversive acts that challenge normalized practices, modes of causation, or systems of authority.[27] Hannah Arendt defined "events" as "occurrences that interrupt routine processes and routine procedures,"[28] thereby capturing the essential notion that

---

[26] Sidney Tarrow, *Power in Movement: Social Movements and Contentious Politics*, 2d ed. (Cambridge, UK: Cambridge University Press, 1998).

[27] My definition borrows heavily from Sewell, but Sewell uses the term primarily in the sense of "a chain of occurrences that durably transforms previous structures and practices." William H. Sewell, "Historical Events as Transformations of Structures," *Theory and Society*, vol. 25, 1996, p. 843. My definition includes not only those disruptions which successfully transform a given order, but also those which attempt to do so but fail. This latter category is critical for any systematic attempt to engage historical counterfactuals.

[28] Hannah Arendt, *On Violence* (New York: Harcourt Brace and Company, 1970), p. 7. Michel Foucault called events "the locus of chance reversal." Indeed, Foucault's work has at times been called a "philosophy of the event." See Charles C. Lemert and Garth Gillan, *Michel Foucault: Social Theory and Transgression* (New York: Columbia University Press, 1982), p. 4.

events are purposeful forms of action whose perpetrators aim to transform rather than to reproduce, to overturn or alter that which, in the absence of the event, others would take for granted. In this sense, events are distinguished from the routinized and the normal, as well as from actions that uphold an ongoing system of authority, for what makes an action an "event" is in part "its contrast with the ongoing order of things and its disruption of that order."[29] An event is part of a larger contention, a conjuncture when those who seek to disrupt the naturalized find the opportunity and will to act.

As Larry Griffin has noted, events are "imbued with sociological import because it is *in* and *through* their unfolding that we see the collision of social structure and social action."[30] Not all events are made equal. Some, as William Sewell notes, wield a "transformative power that goes beyond such obvious political effects as redistribution of power or reshaping of political strategies," altering "the cultural meanings or significations [of] political and social categories" and "fundamentally shap[ing] people's collective loyalties and actions."[31] Others fail to exercise much of an impact at all or are barely noticed. The absence of an event cannot be taken to mean the absence of challenge, but only the absence of perceivable challenge. Usually any challenge capable of being perceived is preceded by a protracted series of small and often unnoticed acts of subversion that are diffuse, disaggregated, and sometimes ambiguous. Many of these diffuse acts remain concealed from public observation – the famous "hidden transcripts of resistance" described by Scott.[32] In other instances, acts of dissent may gain notice as events. Nevertheless, there is always a social quality to an event. An event requires not only the existence of two contending categories of agents (those who uphold a given order and those who challenge it), but also a third set of participants – those who observe. As opposed to diffuse acts of hidden resistance, the desired presence of this

[29] Marshall Sahlins, "The Return of the Event, Again: With Reflections on the Beginnings of the Great Fijian War of 1843 and 1855 between the Kingdoms of Bau and Rewa," in Aletta Birsack, ed., *Clio in Oceania: Toward a Historical Anthropology* (Washington, DC: Smithsonian Institution Press, 1991), p. 45. A similar use of the term "event" can be found within physics and geology.

[30] Larry J. Griffin, "Temporality, Events, and Explanation in Historical Sociology: An Introduction," *Sociological Methods and Research*, vol. 20, no. 4 (May 1992), p. 413.

[31] William H. Sewell, Jr., "Collective Violence and Collective Loyalties in France: Why the French Revolution Made a Difference," *Politics and Society*, vol. 18, no. 4 (1990), p. 548.

[32] James C. Scott, *Domination and the Arts of Resistance: Hidden Transcripts* (New Haven: Yale University Press, 1990).

larger audience lends a spectaclelike quality to an event and, as we shall see, provides it with much of its transformative power. An event in this sense invites the "observer" to become agent: to affirm the transcendence of a prior series and the ascendance of its alternative, even at the very moment when the prior order continues to function and its alternative has freshly emerged.[33] In this way, the event potentially throws into sharp relief the complex issues of compliance, loyalty, and identity that underlie any order, but which, in the absence of the event, are not ordinarily subject to contemplation.

Most important for understanding the politics underlying events is the fact that events and the contention over identity which they represent are not distributed randomly over space and time. Their appearance is structured both temporally and spatially. Some populations generate challenges more quickly, more frequently, and with greater effect than others because they are advantaged by more favorable pre-existing structural conditions. Events also cluster temporally in chains, series, waves, cycles, and tides, forming a punctuated history of heightened challenge and relative stability. This clustering of challenging acts in time, well known within the social movement literature, emerges from the constraints which order imposes on action. Splits within ruling coalitions, an opening or liberalization of the parameters of permissible discourse, electoral campaigns, severe stresses on the capabilities of states caused by war, financial crisis, fundamental realignments of forces within a ruling coalition, failed attempts to repress opposition, and the example of analogous challenges elsewhere – all these are widely known to encourage eruptions of political challenge, largely through the altered perceptions of possibilities for contention that accompany them. These conditions make challenge appear possible by providing the political space necessary to organize challenges and by weakening potential targets of mobilization. But the temporal clustering of events is not merely due to objective shifts in the balance of forces between those controlling institutions and those challenging them. Rather, the rules by which institutions maintain order create a sense of what

---

[33] E. E. Schattschneider observed that "[e]very fight consists of two parts: 1) the few individuals who are actively engaged at the center and 2) the audience that is irresistibly attracted to the scene. The spectators are as much a part of the over-all situation as are the overt combatants. The spectators are an integral part of the situation, for, as likely as not, the *audience* determines the outcome of the fight. . . . *This is the basic pattern of all politics* [emphasis in original]." E. E. Schattschneider, *The Semi-Sovereign People: A Realist's View of Democracy in America* (New York: Holt, Rinehart and Winston, 1960), p. 2.

constitutes the normal, and therefore what constitutes an "opportunity" to disrupt the normal.[34]

Challenging acts are not only clustered temporally and spatially. They are also linked sequentially to one another across time and space in numerous ways: in the narratives of struggle that accompany them; in the altered expectations that they generate about subsequent possibilities to contest; in the changes that they evoke in the behavior of those forces that uphold a given order; and in the transformed landscape of meaning that events at times fashion. It is a truism that all events are "unique" or "singular," in that they never take place in exactly the same context. Nevertheless, what are seemingly unique occurrences are in fact conceptually linked into a larger, interrelated struggle by those involved in them. This linkage operates across space as well, as a geographically remote challenge can inspire analogous acts within a separate spatial context because actors find it expedient to impart connection to them.

The linkage and clustering of events are central to an explanation of the contingencies that events introduce, for what begins as a challenging act induced and heavily constrained by structure contains the potential to become itself a causal variable in a subsequent chain of actions. As the constraints of order weaken, the clustering and linkage of contentious events themselves can provide a structurelike patterning of action that can gain a particular weight and alter expectations about the possibilities for future action, thereby facilitating further agency. In this way, events can come to act as part of their own causal structure. Events can even affect challenging acts within other fields and arenas of interaction. Some level of influence from pre-existing structural conditions and institutional constraints almost always remains embedded in an event.[35] But a reproducing chain of events can grow to the point that the initial structural influences that played a prominent role in unleashing the series seem buried in the distant past and relatively impotent within the ongoing production of events. What statisticians call "white noise," or a random distribution of events across time, is a situation in which events have become their own structure entirely. White noise is the manifestation of a total breakdown of order, a Hobbesian world in which structure outside of the ongoing

[34] William A. Gamson and David S. Meyer, "Framing Political Opportunity," in Doug McAdam, John D. McCarthy, Mayer N. Zald, eds., *Comparative Perspectives on Social Movements: Political Opportunities, Mobilizing Structures, and Cultural Framings* (Cambridge, UK: Cambridge University Press, 1996), pp. 275–90.
[35] See Sahlins.

17

production of events has become impossible and in which deviance from order itself becomes order. In this context the event becomes normalized and acts as the only standard by which to judge itself. But "white noise" – to the extent that it actually occurs in nature – constitutes a temporary state in social affairs. Not only do those who attempt to disrupt a given order almost always seek to construct a new order (that is, to institution-alize their challenge), but chaos is also a rather exhausting state of affairs because of the arbitrariness and unpredictability that it involves. Even when the construction of a new order through institutionalization remains elusive, uncontrolled processes tend eventually to exhibit recognizable pattern, constituting an alternative form of "order" out of regularities and uneven distribution of resources necessary for reproducing disorder.

The relevance of such an approach to the study of nationalism and to the disintegration of the Soviet state may not seem readily apparent on first reading. But it becomes evident when we contemplate nationalism as a political activity contesting or upholding a particular type of political order. Nationalism would not be the troublesome force it is today were it not for the fact that efforts to define the boundedness of political com-munities engender controversy and evoke challenge. As Ernest Gellner recognized, nationalism revolves around attempts to convert the intrinsi-cally ambiguous and controversial into the conventional and seemingly natural, to impose a normalized order on a much more complex cultural reality.[36] In this sense, nationalism is not simply about imagined commu-nities; it is much more fundamentally about a struggle for control over defining communities, and in particular, for control over the imagination about community. In this contest for the control over imaginations, the event constitutes a critical moment at which the loyalties underlying com-peting claims to nationhood are put to open test.

## Order, Event, and Tides of Nationalism

Understood in its modern usage as a community of people deserving polit-ical self-determination (and frequently, its own state) primarily on the basis

---

[36] As Gellner pointed out, "The central mistake committed both by the friends and the enemies of nationalism is the supposition that it is somehow *natural*. . . . These assump-tions are so much part of the air we breathe that they are generally taken for granted quite uncritically. . . . The theoretical problem is to separate the quite spurious 'national' and 'natural' justifications and explanations of nationalism, from the genuine, time- and context-bound roots of it." Ernest Gellner, *Thought and Change* (London: Weidenfeld and Nicolson, 1964), pp. 150–51.

of its own claims to constitute a community deserving such rights, the nation is a constantly contested terrain seeking recognition as incontrovertible "social fact." Nations are usually imagined by those who press nationalist claims as timeless entities. Yet, ironically the actions of the disciples of the nation are themselves oriented toward turning the nation into a potent category of politics – bringing a shared sense of nationhood into being and creating the social reality imagined by the nation's enthusiasts. In this sense, action is embedded in nationness. Nationalists often speak of the "birth" and "rebirth" of the nation, moments which mark the passage from inchoate and uncertain category to self-conscious community. Ritual reenactment of these moments emerges to validate this passage and to subject society to a continual reaffirmation of the nation's existence, as if the ontological question of whether a nation exists is and can never be fully resolved, but only authenticated through a self-affirming praxis, one of whose purposes is to create the very reality that it claims to reflect.

The approach that I take in this book seeks to capture this role of agency in nationalism by grounding nationalism in an ongoing interaction between a national order and those who seek to overturn or alter that order through the production of disruptive events. The modern state has sought to impose a particular type of political order upon populations – a national order – a peculiarly modern form of political organization, bounded territorially and in terms of membership community, with a fixed set of cultural rules applicable to all. Such an assertion is hardly new.[37] Nationalism deals with high stakes, for in the modern world these are issues that matter. Not only do they concern affective ties of human identity and their relationship to a prevailing system of authority. In a context in which political authority governs territorially, legitimates itself within a membership community, and attempts to play a decisive role in our everyday lives, most people expect that their life chances and those of their offspring are shaped in critical respects by the configuration of the state's territorial boundedness, its membership, and its rules of cultural intercourse. Indeed, what makes nationalism distinct from other forms of contention is *precisely* its focus on this distinct set of political objects – that is, that it raises certain

---

[37] For a sampling of the many works which connect the rise of nationalism with the emergence of a new form of political organization associated with modernity, see Ernest Gellner, *Nations and Nationalism* (Ithaca, NY: Cornell University Press, 1983); Eric Hobsbawm, *Nations and Nationalism Since 1780* (Cambridge, UK: Cambridge University Press, 1990); Anthony Smith, *The Ethnic Origins of Nations* (Oxford: Basil Blackwell, 1986); Brubaker, *Nationalism Reframed*.

issues as opposed to others, even though at times other issues may be implicit or simultaneously raised as well.

Looming large in the state's struggle to impose a national order on populations is what Gellner called the "cultural equipment" of the state: its coercive, material, and normative power. To paraphrase Gellner, states attempt to create, maintain, and normalize their national orders through the gun, the dollar, and the book.[38] They not only aim to marginalize alternative visions of national community, but also to foster internalization of a particular vision of national community to the point of making coercion or reward superfluous. In this sense, states generally seek to fix the boundaries, identities, and cultural rules underlying their operation and to make them appear natural, immutable, and timeless. Returning to our example of the now defunct USSR, the Soviet state excelled at making itself appear immutable and timeless, convincing its own population and even most of the world of the impossibility of challenge, even to the point that its own leaders came to believe that the so-called "nationalities question" had been "solved." Even on the eve of its collapse, the vast majority of those who challenged the Soviet state believed in its permanence, though hoped for fundamental change within it. As the Soviet example shows, there is a strong tendency for individuals to adjust their beliefs to the limits of the possible, accepting a given institutional arrangement as unalterable, natural, and to some extent even necessary precisely because it cannot be changed.[39] Over time under such conditions, dissonant collective memories can grow disrupted, undermined, and potentially supplanted. Some even come to view such arrangements as moral, making the leap from what is to what ought to be. State institutions in this way act as the chief agents for maintenance of the reality and identity that they themselves foster through their control over possibilities, which in turn exercise a powerful limit on the national imagination.

The contentious event within nationalism, by contrast, represents an attempt to contest this order. It is an attempt to disrupt the national arrangements which states impose upon populations, to demonstrate their mutability, and to provide a moment at which individuals are compelled to confront a choice between competing claims over loyalty and identity.

[38] Ernest Gellner, *Plough, Sword and Book: The Structure of Human History* (Chicago: University of Chicago Press, 1988).

[39] Within the rational choice literature, such a causal mechanism is known as "cognitive dissonance reduction." See Jon Elster, *Nuts and Bolts for the Social Sciences* (Cambridge, UK: Cambridge University Press, 1989), p. 4.

It is easy to forget the contention inherent in nationalism when one is ensconced in a state whose territorial and cultural parameters have been subjected to extensive normalization and seem beyond revision, where challenging nationalist movements have been marginalized in the political process, and where a "banal" nationalism has become embedded in everyday discourse in ways that are no longer recognizable.[40] As de Certeau noted, we travel to foreign lands to see better that which we are no longer capable of seeing in ourselves. It is here where the contentious event presses us against the boundaries of our own thinking about nationalism and provides critical insight into the myriad contingencies that, though embedded and long forgotten, make up our own reality.

In this book I argue that the systematic study of events is critical to the explanation of nationalism in a number of respects. First, events are sites at which we would expect to see most visibly the impact of structural influences on nationalism. This is perhaps the traditional way in which events have been understood within the study of nationalism and in social science more generally – as products of pre-existing structural influence. In the event, nationalism is no longer mere representation. Rather, the event tangibly embodies the conflict between self and other that underlies all nationalism and moves that conflict into the world of action. Contentious events are not the only sites at which nationalism assumes concrete form. State policy also transforms nationalism from representation into practice. But like representations of nationhood, state practice is fundamentally an elite rather than a mass phenomenon. It does not seek to test the loyalties of a population as directly as the open contention inherent in the event. As Walker Connor observed, scholars of nationalism have tended to focus on the "musings of elites whose generalizations concerning the existence of national consciousness are highly suspect." By contrast, he contended, nationalism should be understood as "a mass, not an elite phenomenon," although the moment when a sufficient number of people have internalized an identity to cause it to become an effective force for mobilization does not lend itself to easy identification.[41] The event potentially provides

---

[40] Michael Billig, *Banal Nationalism* (London: Sage Publications, 1995).
[41] Walker Connor, "When Is a Nation?" *Ethnic and Racial Studies*, vol. 13, no. 1 (January 1990), pp. 92–103. For an analogous critique of the excessive focus in the study of mobilizational politics on social movements rather than on how they interact with and resonate within society, see Pamela E. Oliver, "Bringing the Crowd Back In: The Nonorganizational Elements of Social Movements," in Louis Kriesberg, ed., *Research in Social Movements, Conflicts and Change*, vol. 11 (Greenwich, CT: JAI Press, 1989), pp. 1–30.

us with such a moment, one in which it becomes possible not only to identify the shifting scope of mass loyalties and commitments to particular
identity positions, but also to distinguish the ways in which pre-existing
structural conditions and institutional constraints affect the manifestation
of those loyalties. Thus, the study of events is useful for testing competing causal claims about structure.

Second, the variety of forms assumed by action within events is important. Indeed, in many respects these action forms are more important to
those attempting to cope with a world consumed by nationalism than representations of nationalism or the specific content of nationalist claims
themselves, and certainly as important to understanding nationalism as
state practice. Our concrete moral judgments concerning nationalism
emerge not from what people think or say about nationhood, but rather
from what agents actually do in the name of the nation – for example,
whether they attempt to resolve issues through elections, demonstrations,
or pogroms. An adequate theory of nationalism must address not only the
question of why we are national, but also why we are national in the ways
that we are.

Third, the spectaclelike quality of the event makes it an important site
of cultural transaction at which national identities are potentially formed.
Here, we begin to move away from the traditional notion of events as mere
products of structure and toward a sense of events having their own independent effect on outcomes. Crowds are one of several sites (like museums,
theaters, monuments, and print media) where claims about nationhood are
put forth and where nations become imaginable and seemingly tangible.
Like the theatrical event, crowds provide "an opportunity to experience
imaginative life as physical presence."[42] The crowd in many ways is a simulated nation. It often views itself and is portrayed by its organizers as the
nation's vanguard. Routinized ceremonial and institutional gatherings can
also breed this kind of identification through the physical presence of
others.[43] What differentiates challenging crowds as symbolic nations from

---

[42] David Cole, *The Theatrical Event: A Mythos, A Vocabulary, A Perspective* (Middletown, CT:
Wesleyan University Press, 1975), p. x.

[43] Scipio Sighele noted the fundamental analogy that exists between parliaments and crowds.
In his view, the state was simply a crowd that had institutionalized itself. J. S. McClelland,
*The Crowd and the Mob: From Plato to Canetti* (London: Unwin Hyman, 1989), p. 178. Ritualized and institutionalized public gatherings are ordered ways of drawing upon the
power of numbers to affect how individuals internalize externally derived claims of
allegiance.

objectified representations of the nation (such as those found in museums or monuments) and from ritualized and institutionalized displays of nationhood (such as official ceremonies) is the degree of uncertainty injected into the outcome of the cultural transaction – the "could have acted otherwise" that Giddens identifies as the hallmark of agency. Whereas the identity represented in the map, museum, and census is already predefined by others, that represented in the contentious event is defined in significant part in the course of action itself. It is this uncertainty of cultural transaction within the event that gives specific events the power to transform. The actions that take place in the course of an event contain the capacity to alter cultural understandings through the altered landscape of meaning that they can create. The backlash effects of repression, the outrage that erupts from intergroup violence, the anger that materializes out of callous government responses to emotionally charged demands – all these contain the potential to transform the opinion climate of politics, to affect the prisms through which individuals relate to authority and to others and therefore understand their identities. Indeed, those who organize or precipitate contentious events often seek to provoke responses from states or other groups that heighten a sense of conflict and identity, so as to drive the engine of history more quickly.

Fourth, the outcome of the contention intrinsic to the event is strongly constitutive of identities. It exemplifies the altered possibilities for imagining one's identity and defines expectations concerning the psychological and material benefits and penalties that accrue to externalizing a particular identity position. Sports have often been viewed as a surrogate for nationalism. But in many ways, the affinity between the politics of identity and the dynamics of team support in sports competition runs still deeper. The cultural categories competing for our allegiances can be compared to the competition among sporting teams for our loyalties. On the one hand, professional baseball teams which consistently win gain huge upsurges in loyalty and attendance, as once marginal fans bandwagon to the cause. This tendency of individuals to share in the glory of success and to identify and associate with winners has been suggested by social psychological experiments.[44] On the other hand, teams which lose consistently lose adherents. Such a team continues to attract a core of die-hard fans whose loyalties run deep, but the allegiances of less committed fans stray toward more viable

[44] Robert B. Cialdini et al., "Basking in Reflected Glory: Three (Football) Field Studies," *Journal of Personality and Social Psychology*, vol. 34, no. 3 (1976), pp. 366–75.

contenders – say, a winning college football team, professional basketball team, or even professional baseball competitor. Some fans lose interest in baseball altogether. Other defectors retain a latent loyalty to their original choice and anxiously await the moment of their team's rebirth.

Although the stakes are enormously higher and the latitude of choice much narrower, something of this same logic holds true for competing and overlapping categories of cultural identity as well. Nothing breeds identity so strongly as success or undermines identity as thoroughly as failure. As Albert Hirschman has noted, "People enjoy and feel empowered by the confidence, however vague, that they *have history on their side* [emphasis in original]."[45] The contentious event is important for understanding nationalism in part because the outcome of the contention represented in the event is one of the means by which people judge the rising or declining fortunes of particular identity positions and therefore make judgments concerning the psychic and material benefits which they are likely to derive from public association with these positions. As we will see, for many individuals the massive reimagining of identities and the transformation of the unimaginable into the inevitable that accompanied the Soviet collapse followed this type of logic.

Fifth, the study of events helps us to understand the ways in which the politics of the possible shapes the politics of identity. Events constitute moments of heightened contention when the choice between competing forms of identity must be made. In the context of the event efforts are usually made to sharpen the confrontation between "us" and "them." These are moments when the opportunity and necessity of choice over cultural allegiances are boldly framed. At times of normalized politics, these choices usually do not present themselves so sharply or so urgently. For most individuals at most times, contesting claims of nationhood cannot and need not be acted on, simply because there is no possibility or necessity to choose among them. Normally, our behavior as "national animals" is highly structured and constrained by the ties that bind us within society and the social order within which we live. As Harrison White observes, "[w]ho 'we' are is all bound up with what 'control' is in [our] social surroundings."[46] In this sense, national identities rest on the

[45] Albert Hirschman, *The Rhetoric of Reaction* (Cambridge, MA: Harvard University Press, 1991), p. 158.
[46] Harrison C. White, *Identity and Control: A Structural Theory of Social Action* (Princeton, NJ: Princeton University Press, 1992), p. 4.

internalization of an externally derived claim over our loyalties, which in turn eliminates the need for reward or punishment. Compliance and the lack of alternative possibility may or may not produce the internalization of belief. But given the discipline that to some degree lies behind all social order, it is only in the context of unusual times – when the normal parameters of social and political life come under challenge and stress and the external constraints that usually bind the behavior of individuals are weakened – that the possibility for acting on alternatives widely exists.

In this sense, contrary to Renan, nations are not really daily plebiscites. Rather, at most times order constrains the possibilities for national imagination and the opportunities for choice. As Elie Kedourie observed, while Renan's description of the nation as daily plebiscite is "felicitous," pointing to how "nationalism is ultimately based on will," nevertheless "a political community which conducts daily plebiscites must soon fall into querulous anarchy, or hypnotic obedience."[47] Rather than daily plebiscite, nations are better understood as punctuated and irregular plebiscites. The timing of these punctuated plebiscites is largely determined by the perceived opening and closing of opportunities to contest an existing order. Like other modes of contestation, the disruptions engendered by nationalism have tended to grow salient in the political arena in defined historical periods – in the context of waves and tides of nationalism in which states and those challenging states openly vie over the boundedness of political communities. Nationalist politics is punctuated by these spikes and parabolas of disruption, a periodic clustering of events that emerge largely as a function of changing perceptions of the possibilities for challenge and the varying resonance of nationalist frames across space and over time. This insight about how the vicissitudes of order alter the context within which the politics of identity plays itself out is central to the arguments I make in this book. The nation may be the largest community to which we pay allegiance when the chips are down. But in politics the chips are not usually on the table. It is only in uncommon circumstances – in the context of the heightened challenge represented by the event – that individuals in large numbers are confronted with the necessity of having to choose between competing cultural allegiances, and this choice usually presents itself within a relatively compressed and tumultuous period of time.

---

[47] Elie Kedourie, *Nationalism* (4th ed.) (Oxford: Blackwell, 1993), p. 76.

In this way, nationalist politics is fundamentally dualistic in character. There is a "quiet" politics of nationalism, a politics in which state institutions remain dominant and the struggle turns around the efforts of states to impose and institutionalize a particular national order, while those who oppose this order prepare for moments when disruption becomes possible. And there is a "noisy" politics of nationalism, precipitated by a perceived opening of political opportunities, in which the political order and its institutions (including the definition of the boundaries of the community) come under direct challenge and contest.[48] In both phases states and challengers contend over the crystallization of identities and the definition of a national order, but on quite different playing fields. The perceived advantage held by one side of the contest alters the strategies and even the goals available to agents.[49] Much of what occurs in the "quiet" phases of nationalism conditions what takes place within "noisy" phases. This is particularly true in the early stages of "noisy" phases, which are heavily structured by what immediately precedes them, though as mobilization progresses this influence gradually tends to recede. In periods of normalized state authority, open contention usually takes the form of disjointed and relatively disaggregated actions. These challenges may be individual or collective. But they are limited in scope, dispersed over time, and marginalized within the larger political process. In phases of quiescence nationalist challengers also tend to frame nationalist issues in diminutive form, as the desirable comes to be shaped by the permissible and the feasible. Nationalist activists who, in a context of loosened state authority, act as ardent advocates of independence often have difficulty imagining independence as a possibility in a context of normalized authority. In 1913, on the eve of the war which gave birth to the Czechoslovak state he founded, Thomas Masaryk stated that "[j]ust because I cannot indulge in dreams of its collapse and know that, whether good or bad, it will continue, I am most deeply concerned that we should make something of this Austria."[50]

[48] By the "quiet" politics of nationalism, I do not mean to intimate that these politics are nonviolent, or even that open acts of revolt do not occur in these phases. Rather, these periods are "quiet" in the sense that challenges to the dominant national order remain marginalized within the political process as a whole, particularly when juxtaposed with what occurs within nationalism's "noisy" phases.

[49] See James DeNardo, *Power in Numbers: The Political Strategy of Protest Rebellion* (Princeton, NJ: Princeton University Press, 1985).

[50] Quoted in H. Gordon Skilling, "T. G. Masaryk, Arch-Critic of Austro-Hungarian Foreign Policy," in Ladislav Matejka, ed., *Cross Currents: A Yearbook of Central European Culture* (New Haven, CT: Yale University Press, 1992), p. 228.

For Masaryk Czech independence had seemed impossible outside of the specific temporal context in which it occurred. In this way, the contrasting terrains of the possible make for fundamentally distinct politics of nationalism.

Finally, contentious events are critical to explaining the recursive capacity of nationalism (that is, the ability of nationalist action to become an element of its own causal structure). As noted earlier, two characteristics of contentious events in particular are central to understanding their recursive power: their clustering in time and their linkage across time and space. Indeed, in a period of heightened challenge events can "begin to move so fast and old assumptions become so irrelevant that the human mind cannot process all the new information"[51] – a phenomenon I refer to in this book as "thickened" history. By "thickened" history, I mean a period in which the pace of challenging events quickens to the point that it becomes practically impossible to comprehend them and they come to constitute an increasingly significant part of their own causal structure. As one Soviet journalist put it in fall 1989, "We are living in an extremely condensed historical period. Social processes which earlier required decades now develop in a matter of months."[52] This heightened pace of contention affects both governing and governed – the former primarily in the state's growing incoherence and inability to fashion relevant policies, the latter by introducing an intensified sense of contingency, uncertainty, and influence from the example of others. What takes place within these "thickened" periods of history has the potential to move history onto tracks otherwise unimaginable, affecting the prisms through which individuals relate to authority, consolidating conviction around new norms, and forcing individuals to make choices among competing categories of identity about which they may previously have given little thought – all within an extremely compressed period of time.

It is the clustering and linkage of acts of contention which impart to nationalism its tidal character. I use the term "tide of nationalism" to refer to multiple waves of nationalist mobilization whose content and outcome influence one another. The word "tide" has many meanings; the *Oxford English Dictionary* cites no less than sixteen definitions, many with further shades of distinction. By using the metaphor of tide, I do not envision an analogy between the politics of nationalist contention and the regular and

---

[51] Hough, *Democratization and Revolution*, p. 316.
[52] *Literaturnaia gazeta*, September 13, 1989.

predictable ebb and flow of water caused by the gravitational attraction of the moon. The word "tide" originally meant an opportune or propitious period of time, which is closer to what I have in mind. By the sixteenth century "tide" in English more commonly came to be applied to the regular rising and falling of the level of the sea (its rising obviously being a propitious time for setting sail). But the word "tide" has often been applied in human affairs to phenomena which rise and fall over time with irregular periodicity (like popular interest, public opinion, or good fortune) and which, for any one individual, are heavily influenced by the actions of others. This association of tides with favorable opportunity and with the influence of the actions of others are the central elements of what I understand as tidal politics.

If water analogies are to be made, the more relevant comparison would be the tsunami or tidal wave. A tidal wave is often described as a "wave train," a series of successive, powerful waves generated by an initial shock of enormous energy (usually the uplifting or subsiding of the ocean floor during an earthquake, disturbing or displacing water). Just as some states are more susceptible than others to experiencing tides of nationalism due to the presence of particular structural preconditions, so too are some ocean basins (specifically, the Pacific) more prone than others to tidal waves due to their more frequent seismic activity. Unlike the everyday shallow water waves created along the shore by wind, which can have a wave length of up to 150 yards, tidal waves occur with irregular periodicity and are unusual in power and effect, with wave lengths of up to six hundred miles and travel speeds of up to five hundred miles per hour. They begin almost imperceptibly in deep ocean as a series of waves typically only a few inches high but extending thousands of meters below the surface to the ocean floor. Little of the energy dissipates as the waves travel across huge distances. As they approach land the structure of the sea floor causes huge volumes of water to push upward, creating waves of enormous height and destructive capacity. Their collision with shore sends additional shock waves back toward the open sea.

The tides of nationalism referred to in this book also emerged with irregular periodicity and grew correspondingly in power and scope in interaction with structural facilitations before crashing on the institutions of the state. But there is a critical difference between the tidal waves of nature and the tides of human affairs fundamental to the arguments of this book. In human affairs the energy of a tide is not transferred kinetically, with an element of compulsion or necessity about it, as one billiard ball imparts motion to another on striking it. Rather, in human affairs the power and effect of tides emerge from the ways in which connections with the actions of others are actively made or used by agents in a mindful way, thereby producing, not merely transferring, motion (a basic attribute of human agency).[53] Tides of nationalism are not produced by a single, initial shock, but rather by the way in which agents forge connections with the challenging actions of others. As we will see, some agents consciously seek to foster tidal influences so as to spread or contain contention spatially and temporally, whereas other agents attempt to ride the tide generated from the actions of others for similarly strategic reasons. But tides also generate strong social pressures toward emulation and conformity through what James DeNardo refers to as "the power of numbers"[54] or what Timur Kuran, focusing more specifically on ethnic politics, has called "reputational cascades." Kuran argues that the interdependencies among individual ethnic behaviors can, at certain thresholds, trigger "a self-reinforcing process by which people motivated to protect and enhance their reputations induce each other to step up their ethnic activities," producing "a cascading of ethnic activity within and across groups." He observes that this cascading quality helps explain why upsurges in ethnic activity can catch both participants and observers by surprise, and why small variations in the characteristics of groups can contribute to much larger variations in aggregate ethnic action.[55] Kuran also notes that this type of cascading behavior can activate similar bandwagoning behavior in other groups, creating what he calls a "superbandwagon" that at times can assume global proportions.[56]

The notion of a tide of nationalism shares similarities with and indeed draws inspiration from the concept of the mobilizational cycle developed by Sidney Tarrow, but is not entirely synonymous with it.[57] Tarrow defines

---

[53] Antony Flew and Godfrey Vesey, *Agency and Necessity* (New York: Basil Blackwell, 1987), pp. 10–12.

[54] DeNardo, *Power in Numbers.*

[55] Timur Kuran, "Ethnic Norms and Their Transformation Through Reputational Cascades," *Journal of Legal Studies*, vol. 27 (June 1998), pp. 623–59.

[56] Timur Kuran, "Ethnic Dissimilation and Its International Diffusion," in David A. Lake and Donald Rothchild, eds., *The International Spread of Ethnic Conflict: Fear, Diffusion, and Escalation* (Princeton, NJ: Princeton University Press, 1998), p. 50.

[57] On the notion of cycles of contention, see Tarrow, *Power in Movement*; Sidney Tarrow, *Democracy and Disorder: Protest and Politics in Italy, 1965–1975* (Oxford: Oxford University Press, 1989); Sidney Tarrow, *Struggle, Politics, and Reform: Collective Action, Social Movements, and Cycles of Protest* (Ithaca, NY: Cornell Studies in International Affairs, 1989);

a mobilizational cycle as "a phase of heightened conflict and contention across the social system" involving (among other features) "a rapid diffusion of collective action from more mobilized to less mobilized sectors."[58] He observed that contention diffuses largely as a response to the successes achieved by others in their efforts to contest the state. As Tarrow noted, protest cycles emerge "through imitation, comparison, the transfer of forms and themes of protest from one sector to another, and direct reaction on the part of those whose interests had been affected by earlier protests."[59] A tide of nationalism in this sense is both contained within and transcends a cycle of contention. Mobilizational cycles typically consist of a great variety of movements espousing many different types of political aims. The protest cycle of the 1960s and early 1970s in the United States, for instance, consisted of movements advocating such varied causes as racial equality, an end to the Vietnam war, protection of the environment, women's rights, gay rights, alleviation of poverty, and socialist revolution, as well as countermobilizations by groups opposed to these causes. Tides of nationalism, by contrast, often emerge out of a larger mobilizational cycle in that they form a powerful stream of substantively related actions among the variety of other streams of mobilization within a cycle. In the Soviet Union, for instance, though nationalism became its dominant theme, the *glasnost'* mobilizational cycle was much more than simply nationalist activity. Democratization, class, and environmental justice constituted autonomous vectors of mobilization – each with its own specific mobilizational frames – that at various times intersected with nationalism. Some mobilizations developed specifically in opposition to the tide of nationalism or with only tangential relation to it. The enormous coal miner mobilizations that shook Russia, Ukraine, and Kazakhstan in summer 1989, for example, had little to do with nationalism, yet certainly were a significant element of the mobilizational cycle. In the Soviet case the tide of nationalism and the mobilizational cycle were thus overlapping but not identical phenomena. As an analytical tool, the concept of a tide of nationalism allows us to interrogate the ways in which competing streams of substantively related actions form and intersect with one

Mark Traugott, ed., *Repertoires and Cycles of Collective Action* (Durham, NC: Duke University Press, 1995); McAdam, McCarthy, and Zald, eds., *Comparative Perspectives on Social Movements*.

[58] Tarrow, *Power in Movement*, 2d ed., p. 142.

[59] Tarrow, *Democracy and Disorder*, p. 223.

another within the context of a mobilizational cycle and why some streams of action resonate more deeply in society than others.[60]

In other respects tides transcend the contours of mobilizational cycles. In Tarrow's original definition, the notion of the mobilizational cycle was applied to the full range of movement activity within a single "social system" (that is, state), the Italian mobilizational cycle studied by Tarrow constituting the paradigmatic case. Yet, the Italian mobilizational cycle was also part of a larger transnational diffusion of particular streams of protest that ultimately encompassed all advanced industrial societies at the time. Tarrow has referred to such transnational flows of contention as "international protest cycles" – the European revolts of 1848 and the New Left in the 1960s being archetypal examples. A tide of nationalism bears similarity to Tarrow's broadened usage of cycle and to Kuran's "superbandwagon." A tide is not only a powerful, substantively related stream of mobilization within a mobilizational cycle, but also a transcultural and transnational phenomenon. Not all streams of mobilization within protest cycles gain this ability to transcend state and cultural boundaries. The notion of a tide of nationalism accentuates in particular the cross-cultural influence of nationalist action on subsequent nationalist action, with the nationalism of one group coming to affect the nationalisms of others both within and across states. In the case of the *glasnost'* tide of nationalism, nationalist mobilization exercised a clear transnational influence that flowed back and forth across cultural and state boundaries. This transnational dimension of nationalism is precisely what makes tides of nationalism periods of potential tectonic change within the state system as a whole, not merely periods of intensified reform or regime change within a single society.

As with the mobilizational cycle, there is a logic to tides of nationalism that emerges from the reverse logic by which state authority maintains national order – that is, the example of successful challenge by one group creates expectations of potential success for further challenge by the same group and by others and sets into motion acts of emulation and bandwagoning. Tides of nationalism, like cycles of mobilization, also contain an inherent structure, as Tarrow describes it, "the broadening of political opportunities by early risers in the cycle, the externalities that lower the social transaction costs of contention for even weak actors, the high degree

---

[60] On this point, see in particular Doug McAdam, Sidney Tarrow, Charles Tilly, *Dynamics of Contention* (Cambridge, UK: Cambridge University Press, forthcoming), Chapter 8.

of interdependence among the actors in the cycle and the closure of political opportunities at its end."[61] The use of the tidal metaphor to study nationalism sensitizes us to the fact that nationalisms are fundamentally cross-cultural phenomena, not merely a collection of individual and isolated stories. They take shape within a context in which the example of one nationalism alters expectations of success or failure in others. This influence accelerates during periods of "thickened" history, as events move at an accelerated pace. The interconnectedness produced by common institutional characteristics, ideologies, modes of domination, or cultural affinities (ironically, factors utilized by authority in "quiet" phases of contention to uphold order) offers opportunities for spreading nationalist contention transnationally in "noisy" phases. Policies or institutional arrangements become lightning rods for nationalist contention in multiple contexts simultaneously when a plausible case can be made that the analogy coheres. Where actors are capable of making such connections plausible, successful nationalist contention in one context, through its example, weakens political order in other contexts by raising expectations among nationalist challengers that state authority can be successfully challenged. As tides of nationalism recede, the renormalization of political order is accompanied by a shift away from mobilized contention toward institutionalized forms of nationalist politics. This institutionalization of identity as politics migrates from the street back to the government office establishes the parameters of "nation building" and national opposition within subsequent "quiet" phases of nationalism.

I do not mean to imply that all significant nationalist mobilization occurs within the context of tides. Nationalist contention of varying scope and scale has been a chronic reality of modern politics. Tides, on the contrary, constitute compact and unusual periods of heightened contention across cultural boundaries. Moreover, not all nationalist events or waves of nationalism broaden into tides. Some are cut short through state repression, cooptation, or the failure of particular frames to resonate within target populations. Whether events build into waves of nationalism and waves into tides depends on those factors which allow challengers to forge connections between prior cases of successful contention and current attempts to disrupt. Here, pre-existing structural conditions and institutional constraints obviously play critical roles. But as we shall see, what I

---

[61] Sidney Tarrow, *Power in Movement: Social Movements, Collective Action and Politics*, 1st ed. (Cambridge, UK: Cambridge University Press, 1994), p. 154.

call tidal influences – that is, the effects emanating from the actions of others – are also critical in explaining how tides come to fruition and the success or failure of particular nationalisms. It is the interrogation of the relationship between pre-existing structural conditions, institutional constraints, and event-specific influences in the production of tides of nationalism that constitutes the central research objective of this book.

As Walker Connor observed, "the history of nationalism underlines the catalytic nature . . . of each actual national movement upon the other movements."[62] Indeed, the modern state has been intermittently subjected to multiple tides of nationalist contention, some of which, when reaching fruition, have brought about large-scale structural change in the character of the state system. The American and French revolutions arguably unleashed the first tide of nationalism, in which nationalist movements from multiple groups within Europe, the Caribbean, and the Americas became engulfed in a struggle to redefine the boundaries of their political communities.[63] The year 1848 was known for many years as "the springtime of nations" in Europe, when, as Kedourie noted, "a great upsurge of nationalist claims and ambitions" burst forth.[64] Other tides of nationalist mobilization swept the Russian, Ottoman, and Austro-Hungarian empires in the 1830s, the 1870s, and the first decade of the twentieth century, while, in the wake of the First World War and the Russian Revolution, new states arose, in Peter Alter's words, "like a wave sweeping across the land between Finland and Yugoslavia."[65] The rise of fascist and militaristic nationalism in interwar Europe and Asia and the wave of decolonization that followed the Second World War similarly represented global tides of nationalism. The *glasnost'* tide of nationalism – like previous tides – was precipitated and accompanied by a sudden upsurge of nationalist claims and ambitions which traversed multiple groups and the boundaries of states and effected large-scale alteration in the structure of the state system.

Although nationalism has at times been spoken of in the language of tides, rarely has it been analyzed as a tidal phenomenon. The exploration of the tidal character of nationalisms in the context of the break-up of the

[62] Walker Connor, "The Politics of Ethnonationalism," *Journal of International Affairs*, vol. 27 (1973), p. 10.
[63] Otto Dann and John Dinwiddy, eds., *Nationalism in the Age of the French Revolution* (London: The Hambledon Press, 1988).
[64] Kedourie, *Nationalism* (4th expanded ed.), p. xii.
[65] Peter Alter, *Nationalism*, 2d ed. (London: E. Arnold, 1994), p. 109.

Soviet state – the ways in which nationalist behavior was influenced by prior nationalist behavior, both within specific nationalisms and between them – constitutes the central theme of the chapters which follow. Essentially, I show how acts which challenge a particular national order can grow to become a significant causal factor in the formation of national identity and behavior. Such an "eventful" accounting of nationalism remains sensitive to time, place, agency, and process; it eschews teleological and deterministic modes of explanation and accentuates the value of historicity in the study of nationalism. Elie Kedourie wrote in an afterword to his well known work on nationalism:

To narrate the spread, influence and operation of nationalism in various politics is to write a history of events, rather than of ideas. It is a matter of understanding a polity in its particular time, place and circumstances, and of following the activity of specific political agents acting in context of their own specific and peculiar conditions. The coherence of contingent events is not the same as the coherence of contingent ideas, and the historian has to order his strategies accordingly.[66]

As will be evident, to elicit the causal role of the event in nationalism is not to cast nationalism into the category of accident. Rather, it is to situate nationalism between the critical choices made by groups and individuals and the broader social and political forces that condition and affect those choices.

## Plan of the Book and Summary of the Arguments

The waves of contentious events that engulfed the former Soviet Union from 1987 through 1991 and precipitated its disintegration provide an excellent opportunity for probing the shifting interplay between preexisting structural conditions, institutional constraints, and agency within nationalism over time. The collapse of the Soviet state constituted one of the most spectacular manifestations of nationalist contestation to emerge in the late twentieth century and deserves the designation of "revolution," both in terms of the characteristics of these events and the outcome which they provoked.[67] Moreover, the disintegration of the Soviet Union was accompanied by immense transformations in political discourse and public perceptions of politics. As noted earlier, a population that could barely imagine the break-up of their country came, within a compressed period

[66] Elie Kedourie, *Nationalism* (4th ed.), p. 139.
[67] Charles Tilly, *European Revolutions, 1492–1992* (Oxford: Blackwell, 1993), pp. 234–35.

of time, to view its disintegration as inevitable. A polity that was once uni-versally recognized as a state came to be universally condemned as an empire. The tide of nationalism that emerged in the USSR during these years transcended Soviet boundaries, moving into East Central Europe and the Balkans in 1989–90, reflecting back into the USSR, and outward once again in connection with the Soviet break-up. But its effects were felt far beyond the communist lands. According to Ted Gurr, two-thirds of all new ethnic campaigns of protest and rebellion in the world during the 1985–2000 period began during the years 1989–93; many of these new conflicts were directly connected with the collapse of the USSR, whereas others were only indirectly affected by it.[68] Ideally, a complete study of the *glasnost'* tide of nationalism would cast a broader net, examining the cross-state dimension of the tide and how the example of nationalist mobiliza-tion in the USSR influenced or failed to influence nationalist struggles in such distant locales as Canada, Croatia, Xinjiang, and Ethiopia. Such a task lies beyond the scope and capabilities of this study, however, and awaits subsequent investigation. Nevertheless, as we will see, the tidal character of nationalist politics was conspicuous in the spread of nationalism within and across cultural groups within the USSR and in the politics that ulti-mately led to the disintegration of the Soviet state.

The great diversity of peoples who inhabited the USSR and the differ-ent responses they exhibited to nationalist messages during this period allow us to probe the variety of relationships between structure and agency in manifestations of nationalism across a variegated population. In 1989 there were 127 officially recognized ethnic groups in the USSR, among which were represented a significant portion of major world religions and language families. These groups were subject to varying degrees of assim-ilation and lived in varied demographic and political circumstances. Though the "lid" was lifted with the introduction of *glasnost'*, not all groups responded in the same way or at the same time. The typical Pandora's box metaphor often used to describe the collapse of the USSR does not hold true, since in quite a number of cases the demons refused to leave the box or only did so under the influence of the actions of others. The variety of outcomes exhibited in the spread of nationalist frames and in the specific forms by which nationalist action manifested itself across this territory makes this an outstanding case (or set of cases) wherein

[68] Ted Robert Gurr, "Ethnic Warfare on the Wane," *Foreign Affairs*, vol. 79, no. 3 (May–June 2000), pp. 52–64.

to probe the interplay between structure and agency in the politics of nationalism.

Some might object that the Soviet state represented an extreme – one of the most repressive dictatorships in modern history – and therefore is ill-suited to probing the relationship between structure and agency. I would contend that exactly the opposite is true. Precisely because political controls were so extensive and exaggerated in the USSR, one can more clearly isolate the effects of altering these constraints on the role of agency than where political constraints operated with less force. Some level of analogous constraint is present in all states, and the dynamics visible within the Soviet case and described in this book manifest themselves to one degree or another within all political contexts. As democratic theory would lead us to expect, under a political process highly open to all sectors of society, political opportunities and constraints imposed by the state should be less significant in structuring the dynamics of contention, and conflict in these situations is more likely to be expressed through institutional channels than on the street. But even within advanced industrial democracies the clustering and linkage of contention across time and space – whether on the streets or within state institutions – are well-established facts. The Soviet state therefore represents in somewhat magnified form the same dynamics of contention one would expect to find in other, less repressive, contexts.

The basic argument of the book is that the disintegration of the Soviet state could not have taken place without the effects of tidal influences of one nationalism on another. Rather than simply being a manifestation of structurally predetermined conditions (the Pandora's box image), the collapse of the Soviet state materialized out of a four-year period of "thickened" history in which events acquired a sense of momentum, transformed the nature of political institutions, and assumed the characteristics of their own causal structure. Within the *glasnost'* tide of nationalism the boundaries of the conceivable altered dramatically; the cross-case influences and unraveling of order that accompanied the tide created opportunities for the expression of nationalist demands which, in normal times, were unthinkable. As we will see, the successful revolts of a number of nationalist movements whose actions were critical to the eventual disintegration of the Soviet state occurred in spite of certain structural disadvantages these movements faced, largely because of their ability to ride the tide of nationalism generated from the actions of others. Indeed, without the

36

effect of tidal forces, the failure of nationalist movements would have been much more frequent than was actually the case. Moreover, the effects of tidal forces on other political actors were also far-reaching. The coercive capacity of Soviet institutions of order was undermined by the multiple waves of nationalist revolt and inter-ethnic violence that enveloped the country, overwhelming the capacity of the Soviet state to defend itself forcefully against destruction. And as tidal forces mounted, they became available for appropriation by established political elites. That once loyal Soviet nomenklatura – the Heydar Alievs, Leonid Kravchuks, Mintimer Shaimievs, and Saparmurad Niiazovs of the Soviet world – could become "fathers" of their respective nations was not a plausible outcome before the onset of the *glasnost'* tide of nationalism. It is an outcome inexplicable by a purely structural explanation of nationalism and without reference to the impact of tidal forces. Thus, a tidal perspective on nationalism is crit-ical for understanding the Soviet collapse for five essential reasons: (1) it allows us to understand how the chances of success facing a particular nationalism were altered by taking advantage of the actions of others; (2) it provides an understanding of the role played by the easing of institutional constraints on nationalism in making nationalist action possible and specific ranges of nationalist thought thinkable; (3) it furnishes us with an understanding of how pre-existing structural conditions came to be translated into actual patterns of nationalist action; (4) it explains how in some cases nationalist movements failed mobilizationally yet nationalism nonetheless succeeded politically; and (5) it allows us to place the causal effect of the individual event back into its proper role in social scientific discourse, thereby avoiding teleological, deterministic, and ahistorical modes of explanation.

The plan of the book is as follows. In Chapter 2 I introduce the *glasnost'* tide of nationalism and its relationship to the larger mobilizational cycle of which it was a part. I examine how the particular structural pre-conditions of the Soviet state in the late 1980s – its institutional and ideological crises, its fusion of state and regime, its submerged sense of ethnic grievance across multiple groups, its overstretch abroad – made the USSR vulnerable to experiencing a tide of nationalism, explaining why nationalism became the dominant stream of mobilization within the mobilizational cycle relative to other streams of mobilization. Chapter 2 also demonstrates how contentious acts in the *glasnost'* period expanded tentatively at first, subsequently growing into a transnational tide of nationalist mobilization, as successful action by one group evoked subsequent efforts by others; how acts of nationalist contention eventually became common-place and constituted a vast tide of disruption, undermining the coherence of political institutions; and how ultimately this contention began to wind down through its partial institutionalization in state structures.

Chapter 3 probes the structuring of nationalist action more systemati-cally through a statistical analysis, showing how shifting institutional con-straints imposed by the state shaped the rise and decline of nationalist contention, and how attempts to organize nationalist challenges to the political order and the resonance of these efforts within target populations were systematically structured across ethnic groups by a series of pre-existing structural conditions, including the level of a group's ethnofederal institutions, its size, its patterns of linguistic usage, and its degree of urban-ization. But Chapter 3 also demonstrates that even when one controls for the influence of these factors, the causal influence of event-specific processes on action – manifest in particular in recursive and cross-case influences – grew in scope and consistency over the course of the mobi-lizational cycle, playing a greater role over time in structuring nationalist action at both the elite and mass levels. The chapter also provides evidence for an underlying structure to tides: Early risers tend to enjoy strong facil-itating structural advantages, but over time this gives way to action by movements characterized by less conducive structural conditions for action, so that late risers depend on taking advantage of the successful example of those who preceded them.

Developing this insight further, Chapter 4 explores the politics of iden-tity change by investigating, through a series of in-depth case studies, the process by which a secessionist identity successfully crystallized across groups during the *glasnost'* period. Moving beyond the primordialist and instrumentalist debates that have dominated the field, I situate the politics of identity change not around whether identities involve enduring emo-tional attachment or are mere derivatives of interest, but rather around how structure and agency interact across an interrelated tide of mobiliza-tion. I show how the uneven distribution of structural advantage located group mobilizational processes temporally across the tide of nationalism and altered the character of identity politics, determining the degree to which the successful mobilization of identity involved a politics of embold-ening in the face of institutional constraints or a politics of persuasion through event-specific processes. The actions of early secessionist risers were heavily constrained by institutions and strongly advantaged by pre-

existing structural conditions, and were thereby dominated by a politics of
emboldening. But, as I show, as the tide unfolded event-specific persuasive processes grew increasingly central to the politics of identity. Nationalist movements from groups with fewer structural advantages around
secession sought to take advantage of the prior mobilizational successes of
other Soviet groups. Over time the example of successful challenge became
a significant resource for changing identities in lieu of the presence of
structural advantage. The crystallization of a Ukrainian secessionist identity, for instance, was inexplicable outside the tidal context in which it
emerged; in this sense, so too is the eventual demise of the Soviet state,
given the central role played by a secessionist Ukraine in the decision
making surrounding the breakup of the USSR.

Chapter 5 elaborates a probabilistic notion of the failure of nationalism
and, on the basis of a comparative analysis of separatist nationalism across
forty groups, demonstrates the ways in which structural advantage, institutional constraints, and tidal effects were implicated in its production.
The failure of separatist nationalism in some contexts was due to the
cumulation of structural disadvantage, which stacked the deck against separatism through the sense of impracticality and outlandishness it instilled,
even without resort to significant institutional constraint. But I also show
that no single feature was associated with the success or failure of separatist nationalism in the USSR and that the structural advantages and disadvantages of groups were cumulative and fungible. Nationalisms could
succeed or fail in the presence of a variety of combinations of structural
factors, and much of what structural influence was about was endowing
groups with advantages in profiting from the actions of others – that is,
providing them with an ability to ride the tide of nationalism. Moreover,
even when separatist movements failed, separatist nationalism often
succeeded in any case due to its strategic appropriation by traditional
nomenklatura elites, largely under the burgeoning influence of tidal
forces.

As I argued earlier, any adequate theory of nationalism needs to explain
not merely the process by which national consciousness crystallizes, but
also variation in the forms of behavior by which populations contest the
nation. In Chapter 6, I explore, through an investigation of the rise of
mobilized nationalist violence, how the concrete forms nationalism
assumed in the *glasnost'* era took shape out of interactive processes. Specifically, I show that large-scale nationalist violence in the USSR emerged
as a phase within a larger tide of nationalist contention, as nonviolent

mobilization in a limited number of cases was transformed into violent mobilization. Within a period of "thickened" history social norms proscribing nonstate violence or violence between segments of the state came to be set aside in certain contexts, and violent action came to be understood as permissible and even moral by large numbers of people. As we will see, the critical contextual variable that allowed such an inversion of social norms to take place was the behavior of the state itself.

In Chapter 7, I examine the failure of the coercive capacities of the Soviet state to contain nationalist revolt, pursuing the questions of why coercion was not deployed in a massive way to prevent disintegration and why, when force was deployed, it proved so ineffective. I probe the failure of the Soviet government's efforts to marginalize nationalist dissent through coercion during the *glasnost'* period as the failure of what I call a "regime of repression" – a set of regularized practices of repression and the internalized expectations that result from these practices about the ways in which authority will respond punitively toward challenging acts. I argue that this internalized pattern of institutionalized repressive practice not only helps to explain why massive force was unlikely to have saved the USSR once tidal forces emerged, but also why the authorities failed to deploy such force in the first place. As I show, not just Gorbachev but also his conservative critics eschewed the use of severe force for defending the Soviet state, largely because they had internalized a certain understanding of how order should be created and maintained. But I also show how the institutions of order were overwhelmed by tidal forces of nationalism, undermining the institutional capacity of the Soviet state to defend itself forcefully.

Finally, in Chapter 8 I return to the issue of the "inevitability" of the Soviet collapse, tracing how a sense of inevitability came to surround the disintegration of the Soviet state during the final year and a half of its existence, focusing in particular on the impact of the tide of nationalism on the ways in which the dominant nationality of the USSR, the Russians, related to the Soviet state. In the end, the USSR was not killed by a single individual or group, but rather by a generalized sense among the very groups that should have been expected to support it that the Soviet state, having exhausted itself in the face of uncontainable nationalist revolt and failed reform, could not be salvaged in usable form. In the wake of four years of "thickened history" and nationalism's tidal onslaught, not only had the unthinkable become the thinkable; it had become the prosaic.

## *Research Strategies and Evidence*

In terms of empirical approach, this study harnesses the advantages of both small-n and large-n research strategies, nesting the former inside the latter. No single research strategy would have sufficed for sorting out the independent effects of pre-existing structural conditions, institutional constraints, and event-specific processes. An argument that the event has an independent causal effect carries little weight unless we simultaneously attempt to explain, and control for, the ways in which events are also manifestations of larger structural relationships. These are not easy relationships to unravel and require multiple methods that allow us to perceive not only the ways in which events are patterned across space and time, but their individual impact on specific actors on the ground as well.

Large-n analysis is useful for identifying evidence of structural influence both temporally and cross-sectionally by analyzing the rise and fall of various forms of contention over time and the patterning of contentious events across groups. When feasible and appropriate, I combine these two modes of analyses in cross-sectional time-series methods and event-history analysis to capture patterns of association across space-time. In probing quantitative patterns of action, however, the problem of endogeneity, caused by the fact that the occurrence of an action changes the probability that another action will occur, must be taken into account. Indeed, this endogeneity – and specifically, the extent to which the event acts as cause or is merely effect – is the central research question this book seeks to address. Linear models assume a direct relationship between structure and action and thereby pretend that agency does not influence subsequent acts of agency. Nonlinear event-count or event-history models, by contrast, are able to take into account these processes of dependence between the occurrences of successive events. Moreover, as we will see, there are ways to test statistically for evidence of the systematic influence of events on subsequent events, and particularly for the influence of processes of recursion and cross-case effects.

The advantage of large-n research strategies is that they can uncover in a sea of action patterns of regularity which are not easily visible through examination of a single case or event. They place an individual event or set of actors into the larger context of which they are a part. But as realist accounts of explanation contend, statistical association and coincidence in timing in themselves do not prove causality; they merely suggest the possibility. Rather, causality assumes that the mechanisms shaping action are clearly specified and that the processes through which these mechanisms generate their effects can be demonstrated empirically.[69] I make extensive use of process tracing through strategically selected case studies exhibiting variable outcomes as a means of tracing the influence of hypothesized causal relationships.[70] In all, case material is presented from the mobilizational records of eighteen nationalities of the USSR. Such qualitative studies not only allow us to examine concretely the constraining and facilitating dimensions of structure as manifested in particular cases, but also to probe the transformative role of specific events, the linkages across events, the ways in which action can become an element of its own causal structure, and the ways in which actions by one group come to influence those of others. In this sense, the endogeneity embodied in the causal role of the event need not be considered an obstacle to understanding that is to be bracketed, but rather needs to be treated as a central object of research.

The fundamental unit of analysis in this study is the contentious event. Although by no means the only method for dissecting contention, event analysis is widely recognized as a tool for studying waves of mobilization. It is essentially a way of tracking over time the rise and fall of particular types of events and the features associated with them. A detailed account of the methods used for deriving event data is provided in Appendices I and II for readers who wish to know more. A short discussion of the rationale for its use and the nature of the data is appropriate at this juncture.

The *glasnost'* era was a very compact and stormy period of history, as most revolutionary upheavals are. It was, as I call it, a period of "thickened history" – a time when events multiplied with great speed and took on a significant causative role of their own. Almost daily for nearly four years new revelations of previously censored material filled the newspapers. Dozens, at times hundreds, of demonstrations, strikes, and mass violent events rocked the country on a daily basis. And the institutional changes which occurred during this period were dizzying. As one social movement activist later wrote about the year 1989, "Europe has not known

---

[69] David Little, *Varieties of Social Explanation: An Introduction to the Philosophy of Social Science* (Boulder, CO: Westview, 1991), pp. 13–38.
[70] See Andrew Bennett and Alexander George, "An Alliance of Statistical and Case Study Methods: Research on the Interdemocratic Peace," *APSA-CP*, vol. 9, no.1 (Winter 1998), pp. 6–9.

a year so packed with events at least since the end of the Second World War."[71] Clearly, time-sensitive methods are required to unpack this kind of compressed history and to place phenomena into their larger spatial and temporal contexts. Event analysis is one method for accomplishing this.

In periods of repression or in an environment in which the possibilities for acting on beliefs are minimal, it is difficult to identify internalized beliefs from the public transcript of behavior. In periods of political upheaval researchers face a very different problem: Public beliefs change so quickly that they are almost impossible to capture. In such an environment public opinion polls merely reflect a frozen moment in time.[72] Even when polls are conducted repeatedly, pollsters rarely frame questions that systematically capture attitudes relevant to a period of momentous change, since issues once beneath the surface of politics become explicit, and the practice of polling is itself affected by the discursive transformations society is experiencing. In the case of the former Soviet Union, no public opinion polls systematically measured the changing attitudes of the Soviet population toward the existence of the USSR during the 1987–91 period. Not until August 1989, well into the mobilizational cycle, was the first countrywide survey of the attitudes of the Soviet population toward secession from the USSR taken. The issue was simply not considered germane by pollsters (both Western and Soviet) until after it had already grown politicized. I have tried systematically to collect information on relevant surveys taken during this period (and a considerable body does exist), but this scattered and disorderly record of public attitudes does not fully capture the dynamics of political change within a revolutionary setting.

By contrast, event analysis was developed precisely as a way of studying periods of rapid historical change. The primary advantage of event analysis is that it is dynamic and temporal. It can help identify the contexts in which people engage in particular forms of collective action and to pinpoint those key moments in which the forms of action and the discourse associated with them shift. Although event data do not in themselves measure beliefs, they can provide (particularly when juxtaposed with other information) insight into the issues that resonate within populations

---

[71] Boris Kagarlitsky, *Farewell Perestroika: A Soviet Chronicle* (London: Verso, 1990), p. 195.
[72] Sidney Tarrow, "'Aiming at a Moving Target': Social Science and the Recent Rebellions in Eastern Europe," *PS: Political Science and Politics* (March 1991), pp. 12–20.

at specific moments in time and into the changing or consistent character of issues over which populations mobilize. Indeed, many of the central theoretical issues which scholars of nationalism engage can be understood as questions about the timing of mobilization, consistency in the demands over which groups mobilize, the relationship of past waves of contention to the wave of contention being studied, and factors which contribute to the presence or absence of mobilization within particular groups.

Through event analysis I have attempted to re-create the waves of mobilization that overwhelmed the Soviet Union, collecting systematic information about 6,663 protest demonstrations and 2,177 mass violent events from January 1987 through December 1992. Demonstrations constituted only one dimension of the multiple forms by which groups challenged the Soviet state during these years. Nevertheless, as the most prevalent and politically salient form of protest activity during this period, they reflect well the changing relationship between the state and its challengers. In addition, I collected information on strike activity, but this proved considerably less accurate and added little not apparent through the analysis of demonstrations. Mass violence was also a significant dimension of mobilization during this period. It was of interest in terms of understanding the factors shaping violent and nonviolent manifestations of nationalism and tended to receive considerable attention among news sources, making for a relatively accurate sampling of events.

The information utilized in this book is not a fully accurate re-creation of the *glasnost'* mobilizational cycle. As Appendix II details, however, from various tests of the data with other records of the time there are reasons to believe it is a reasonably accurate approximation – and indeed, one far surpassing the typical standards for work of this sort. Although the Soviet state collapsed in the wake of the August 1991 coup, I extended the analysis through the end of 1992 (sixteen months after the coup) to avoid problems of right-censoring and to allow study of the impact of the breakup on patterns of mobilization. In addition, information was collected on 185 protest demonstrations and 50 mass violent events that occurred during the 1965–86 period to provide a baseline by which to judge the development of protest mobilization in the *glasnost'* period and to probe relationships between earlier patterns of protest and those of the period under study. One of the advantages of event data is the great flexibility in the ways in which they can be analyzed. They can be aggregated by the characteristics of those who engage in them, the location or territory in which they occur, the types of issues involved, by week or month, or by other criteria. Or they can remain disaggregated and examined through methods of event-history analysis. This flexibility provides for greater reliability of findings.

Just as important, because they are constructed on the basis of thousands of detailed descriptions of protest events, event data also provide the basis for an embedded qualitative research strategy of process tracing, allowing us to probe specific critical events more deeply through the journalist and eyewitness accounts on which the data are based. As with most event analyses, I relied primarily on press-based sources in constructing the data. Over 150 different news sources were examined – 60 in their full press runs during the period under investigation (for a full listing of sources consulted, see Appendix II). In addition, I have made extensive use of the memoirs of movement activists and government officials, published interviews with participants, eyewitness accounts, and the Western and post-Soviet scholarly literature on individual nationalist movements.

My purpose is not to write a history of the collapse of the Soviet Union. That service has been adequately performed by others, although I believe that this analysis does shed light on certain processes ignored in most studies of the collapse. Rather, my main goal is to utilize the Soviet experience to interrogate the shifting roles of structure and agency in manifestations of nationalism over time. I have therefore been selective in the topics and examples on which I focus. I devote relatively little space to the analysis of what I call nationalism's "quiet" phases. The reader should not take this as a sign that I believe this "quiet" politics is somehow unimportant for understanding nationalism. On the contrary, both the theoretical conceptualization I outlined above and the empirical material I present throughout the book emphasize the centrality of this politics for explaining what occurs during "noisy" phases of contention. However, limitations of space and the fact that my focus is on explaining what occurs during "noisy" phases have caused me to confine my discussion to those aspects of the "quiet" politics of nationalism which directly affect politics during periods of heightened contention.

In refocusing the study of nationalism and the Soviet disintegration away from essentialist, deterministic, and reductionist understandings toward one which emphasizes temporality, interconnection, and agency, my purposes are many: to understand why nationalisms emerge or fail at particular junctures in historical time; to elicit the circumstances in which the implicit within politics can become the explicit, thereby transforming

45

identities; to probe how nationalist actions affect one another, periodically building into tides of nationalism that alter the physiognomy of the state system; and to assert the importance of form as well as content in the study of nationalism. Ultimately, it is hoped, such an understanding will help us to grasp how the seemingly impossible can, under certain circumstances, become the seemingly inevitable.

# 2

## The Tide of Nationalism and the Mobilizational Cycle

Certainly all historical experience confirms the truth that man would not have attained the possible unless time and again he had reached out for the impossible.

Max Weber, "Politics as a Vocation"

Not all historical eras are alike. There are times when change occurs so slowly that time seems almost frozen, though beneath the surface considerable turbulence and evolution may be silently at work. There are other times when change is so compressed, blaring, and fundamental that it is almost impossible to take its measure.

Such were the rhythms of Soviet history. When Leonid Brezhnev died in November 1982, Soviet history seemed frozen in time, particularly when viewed in light of the massive upheavals that convulsed the Soviet state during its first thirty-five years of existence. A spirit of stability and normalcy had come to settle upon most of Soviet society in the decades following Stalin's rule, even within the complicated sphere of nationality relations.

Then, in late 1986, the unexpected happened: The longstanding rules constraining freedom of expression in the USSR began to unravel. The French Revolution began as neither a national nor a class struggle, but eventually became both.[1] *Glasnost'* similarly did not begin as a nationalist explosion. It became one. "When *perestroika* began," an Estonian sociologist later observed, "neither its chief architects nor the broad public were prepared for the possible rise of national movements."[2] The first major

[1] Michael Mann, *The Sources of Social Power,* vol. 2 (Cambridge, UK: Cambridge University Press, 1993), p. 167.
[2] K. S. Hallik, quoted in *Pravda,* June 7, 1989, p. 2.

47

eruption of nationalism did not take place until almost a year and a half after *glasnost'* had begun – in February 1988 in Armenia and Azerbaijan – and had nothing to do with the secessionist issues that ultimately pulled apart the Soviet state. Over the course of 1988 and 1989 politics moved increasingly from the government office into the streets, and as this occurred issues of nationalism, once effectively marginalized, pushed themselves stridently into the political sphere. Massive mobilizations encompassed multiple national groups simultaneously, as successful challenge by one group was followed by further challenges by others. At first, most nationalist mobilization centered around demands for freedom of movement, increased autonomy, and linguistic and cultural expression, following closely the liberalizing and reformist spirit underlying *glasnost'*. But over time the demands of newly emerged nationalist movements began to be framed with increasing boldness, focusing in many cases on demands for secession. Enormous demonstrations involving hundreds of thousands appeared in disparate parts of the country. "Rallies, demonstrations. Demonstrations, rallies. . . . And the next weekend it starts all over," a Soviet journalist wrote at the time. "Sometimes it seems as if the whole country has gone to one rally, one demonstration."[3] By fall 1989 the nationalist revolt against the Soviet state had flowed over to the Soviet Union's East European satellites, toppling communist regimes with astounding speed and asserting the national sovereignty of these states vis-à-vis the Soviet empire. In turn, the end of communism in East Europe further radicalized and spread nationalist revolt inside the USSR. Not only had history "thickened," but the outcomes of mobilization in one context had come to influence mobilizational activity in the next. A powerful tide of nationalism had come into being.

This chapter is an introduction to the *glasnost'* tide of nationalism and the mobilizational cycle of which it was a part, examining the questions of why and how a tide of nationalism initially emerged, the evolving place of nationalist contention within the mobilizational cycle, and the effects of this contention on the institutional coherence of the Soviet state. I argue that certain types of states are especially vulnerable to generating tides of nationalism – specifically, large multinational states encompassing several distinct, compactly settled, cultural entities, particularly at moments of regime crisis. In the Soviet and Russian cases, such crises have led to the emergence of tides of nationalism periodically across the twentieth

---

[3] *Izvestiia*, February 22, 1990, p. 1.

century, with varied outcomes. In Gorbachev's USSR liberalization and the growing conflict that it engendered within the central institutions of the Soviet state elicited a burgeoning of challenging acts, which multiplied still further due to the regime's failure to exercise the type of repression routinely applied in the past. I show in this chapter how a tide of nationalism emerged out of this larger mobilizational cycle and quickly came to dominate its agenda. Other types of mobilization besides nationalism – over democratization, labor and economic issues, environmental justice – were present within the cycle and constituted autonomous vectors of mobilization, at times intersecting with issues of nationalism and at times diverging from them. But for a variety of reasons, nationalism gained a particular force and momentum not enjoyed by these other streams. As we will see, the rise of nationalism as the dominant force within the *glasnost'* mobilizational cycle was very much an interaction between pre-existing structural conditions, institutional constraints, and event-specific processes. As institutional constraints eased, challenging acts multiplied, and the successful nationalist mobilization of one group evoked subsequent efforts by others to do the same through processes of analogy and emulation. Ultimately, as challenging acts gained a momentum of their own, they grew increasingly autonomous from the constraints of institutions, even coming to transform the character of the institutions that had once stifled them. With this autonomy events assumed a greater weight in their own causal structure. Eventually, acts of contention grew normalized and constituted a vast tide of nationalist disruption that moved in significant ways according to its own logic.

## Historical Background

In its nationalities sphere, the history of the Soviet state is a history punctuated by periods of heightened contention and periods of relative stability and quiescence. By spring 1918, in the wake of the collapse of the Tsarist state and the Bolshevik seizure of power, the Russian empire had, for all practical purposes, ceased to exist. By then, the Bolsheviks were in control of only the central rump of Russia. The other portions of the empire lay in the hands of rival White forces or a series of weak nationalist movements and proto-governments that had declared themselves independent. Less than three years later, by the end of 1920, a large portion of the lands of the Russian empire had been welded back together into a single political formation through a combination of brute military force, Bolshevik mobilizational capacity, the frailty of nationalist movements and governments, and communist promises of broadranging autonomy.

Throughout its 74-year history the Soviet regime engaged in a massive and frequently forceful effort to impose a particular national vision on a multicultural population. The Soviet state claimed to be an international- ist state, not an ethnic state or empire. Despite their widespread practice of coercion as a solution to the challenges presented by multiethnicity, Soviet rulers consistently attempted to create a civic form of political and cultural allegiance, a sense of patriotism and shared political identity among their Russian and non-Russian citizens. The Soviet regime did much more than simply occupy territories. It waged a massive effort to create a social base for itself and to foster a common sense of community within its multiethnic population – to engage in a particular type of nation- building project. But the thorny question of "whose state?" plagued the Soviet Union from the time of its founding. The answer varied consider- ably over time, but was always inconsistent, ambiguous, and to some degree, contested.[4] Having violently repressed the last vestiges of open secessionism by the mid-1920s, the Soviet government moved to allow a widespread cultural autonomy for its minorities as a way of incorporating non-Russians into the political order. Through the institution of eth- nofederalism, the Soviet state recognized and accepted multiethnicity as a guiding principle of social and political life. The entire population was given formal assignment to specific nationality groups, and a series of eth- noterritorial units were created based on nationality. Native-language schooling and cultural expression within political bounds were encour- aged, and through the policy of *korenizatsiia* (indigenization) non-Russians came to dominate local political leaderships and gained some degree of formal representation in Moscow. Territoriality, political representation, and cultural empowerment were understood by Soviet rulers as necessary

---

[4] For histories of the "nationalities question" (as it was called) in the Soviet Union, see Ronald Grigor Suny, *Revenge of the Past: Nationalism, Revolution, and the Collapse of the Soviet Union* (Stanford, CA: Stanford University Press, 1993); Richard Pipes, *The Formation of the Soviet Union, 1917–1923* (rev. ed.) (Cambridge, MA: Harvard University Press, 1964); Gerhard Simon, *Nationalism and Policy Toward the Nationalities in the Soviet Union: From Totalitarian Dictatorship to Post-Stalinist Society* (Boulder, CO: Westview Press, 1991); Bohdan Nahaylo and Victor Swoboda, *Soviet Disunion: A History of the Nationalities Problem in the USSR* (New York: Free Press, 1989); Terry Martin, *The Affirmative Action Empire: Nations and Nationalism in the Soviet Union, 1923–1939* (Ithaca, NY: Cornell University Press, 2001).

vehicles for cooptation of minorities into a Soviet political community. But they were practices which, it was hoped, would eventually be superseded by a common loyalty to the revolutionary internationalist state. By the late 1920s, however, these permitted political and cultural spaces provided the opportunity for increased nationalist expression and ultimately led to growing cultural conflict within the Communist Party itself, particularly as the Stalinist leadership in Moscow violently imposed a single mode of modernity and social organization on society.

Despite its accommodating practices toward cultural difference in the 1920s, the Soviet state never fully extricated itself from the perception that lurking behind its multicultural policies was an essential Russian dominance. By the mid-1930s and the 1940s, in the midst of Stalin's orgies of violence and the resistance they at times evoked, a more overt though still informal Russianization of the regime was occurring. A once multiethnic but Russified political elite tipped toward disproportionate Russian representation, and a discourse of cultural and political stratification came to be embraced. Forceful incorporation of the Baltic states, Western Ukraine, and Bessarabia (and the attempted incorporation of Finland) reinforced the association of Soviet power with the Tsarist empire. State terror came to be widely practiced as a way of dealing with mutinous nationalities. Yet, this shift toward greater ethnic stratification, coercion, and imperial legitimation was also characterized by inconsistency and ambiguity. Even at the height of glorification of things Russian, Russians were portrayed merely as "elder brothers," not conquerors, and Russian nationalism functioned more as an implicit instrument of rule subordinate to the needs of those in power than a guiding principle of the Soviet state. Russians also suffered tremendously alongside non-Russians in the violence inflicted by the dictator, and despite the millions of victims whose deaths have given rise to charges of genocide, for the most part the imposition of control, not the purposeful destruction of ethnic groups, was the underlying logic of state terror.[5]

---

[5] The closest exceptions were campaigns of state terror and genocide perpetrated against the so-called "punished peoples" in 1943–44. Alongside a massive resettlement program in which significant portions of these populations perished, attempts were made to wipe out all evidence that these peoples ever inhabited their indigenous territories. These entire peoples were assigned to special prison settlements in distant parts of the USSR and their cultural institutions entirely eliminated, primarily to marginalize national resistance to the Soviet state and to punish these groups for their alleged cooperation with Hitler's armies.

51

Expressions of national pride by minorities were strongly discouraged throughout the Stalin era and in the late Stalin era were harshly repressed. But assimilation was not embraced as the dominant mode of nation building under Stalinism. Rather, dual language capability (Russian as the language of "international communication") was viewed as the main medium for fostering a common political identity that was to be overlaid on the individual's fixed attachment to ethnicity. This was interpreted as a biological rather than cultural phenomenon and was formally codified for each individual and emblazoned in the newly introduced passport system. Although attempting to eliminate independent political expression and severely repressing traditional religious and social institutions, Stalin nevertheless recognized a politically circumscribed autonomy for cultural difference. Still, by the time of Stalin's death the reification of the ethnofederal system had proceeded to the point that the hierarchy of units had come to structure the types of cultural and political resources to which groups had access, and minorities without ethnofederal units or living outside those units were no longer considered to have the types of cultural rights they had once been widely afforded in the early Soviet period. The sole exception was the Russians, who, as the dominant cultural group, enjoyed cultural privileges not accorded to others. Migration and population resettlement were frequently employed by Stalin as instruments for normalizing Soviet control, but often this meant in fact the transfer of land, jobs, property, and housing into the hands of Russians and those non-Russians who remained loyal to the dominant order.

At times of severely weakened authority, such as the Second World War, when the Stalinist regime stood on the verge of defeat, Soviet nationhood came under sharp challenge. Many non-Russians remained loyal to the Soviet state during the war, serving in the Red Army against the German invader. But others opted for exit, particularly in the recently acquired territories of the Baltic and Western Ukraine, as well as in Crimea and the Northern Caucasus (where significant numbers, though still a minority, supported nationalist movements allied with and at times organized by the Germans). The Soviet victory over Hitler not only foreclosed this option; it also established the USSR as a major world power and generated an aura of dynamism and success around the Soviet state, thereby fostering considerable patriotic identification with it among Russians and non-Russians. As Merle Fainsod once noted, the Soviet victory in World War II was probably the single most important factor in reconciling the overwhelming portion of the population with Soviet rule.[6]

With the death of Stalin Soviet politics began a protracted evolution toward stabilization and normalization. No longer was mass terror utilized as an instrument of societal transformation or nation building, though the regime consistently continued to suppress public expressions that challenged the dominant national order. Secessionist sentiments remained very much on the margins of Soviet society. Even in those recently conquered and more obstreperous regions such as the Baltic and Western Ukraine, where guerilla resistance to Soviet rule continued well into the 1950s, by the late 1950s and early 1960s secessionist ideas had largely receded into the realm of the seemingly impossible. Opportunities to contest nationhood were ebbing, and a discursive frame established and enforced by the Soviet regime boldly proclaimed that the USSR had "solved" its nationalities problems and had produced "a new historical community – the Soviet people" (*Sovetskii narod*). As one Soviet specialist on nationalities issues later noted, "in practice, the sphere of national relations was removed from criticism and treated as a zone of universal harmony, and that which did not fit into this harmony was simply dismissed and stigmatized as a manifestation of bourgeois nationalism."[7] The international successes of the Soviet superpower reinforced identification of many non-Russians with the Soviet state. The Soviet Union even consciously held itself out as a model for other multicultural countries to imitate.

The Soviet regime exercised a deep cultural impact on its non-Russian inhabitants. After the Soviet collapse it became fashionable to assert that a sense of "Sovietness" never existed within the Soviet population. Yet, in the first years after independence powerful currents of opinion in support of re-creating the Soviet state could be observed among Ukrainians, Armenians, Moldavians, Kazakhs, Belorussians, and others. Obviously, as the eventual collapse of the Soviet state demonstrated, Soviet identity was not strongly embedded in a large portion of the non-Russian population, but neither was it entirely absent. Soviet policy emphasized the possibility of loyalty to both Soviet and nationality categories; it preached the doctrine that these were not mutually exclusive identities, and that no contradiction existed between being a good Latvian and a loyal Soviet.

---

[6] Merle Fainsod, *How Russia Is Ruled* (rev. ed.) (Cambridge, MA: Harvard University Press, 1963), pp. 113, 291.
[7] E. Bagramov, in *Pravda*, August 14, 1987, p. 2.

Many Latvians clearly remained unconvinced, but for the most part non-Russians simply never faced the opportunity or the necessity of choosing between loyalty to the Soviet order and loyalty to one's ethnic identity. With the exception of networks of dissidents in the Baltic and Western Ukraine working on the political margins and continually subject to arrest and harassment, the overwhelming majority of the population considered the possibility of such a choice outside the sphere of the imaginable.[8]

On the surface, the Soviet national order appeared stable in Brezhnev's USSR. As noted earlier, outside observers overwhelmingly believed in the fundamental stability of the regime and in the unlikelihood of Soviet disintegration. Separatist sentiment seemed too geographically confined to the Baltic and Western Ukraine and too politically marginalized to pose much of a threat. The overwhelming coercive instruments in the hands of the Soviet state made national resistance seem futile. And Russian attachment to the Soviet state seemed to rule out the possibility of waging a successful secessionist campaign. Soviet leaders seemed bent on a trajectory of piecemeal adjustment and moderate reform, not the kind of unraveling of control necessary for the staging of national revolts.

Yet, in the practice of everyday life, cultural conflict remained widespread and seemed to grow more salient over the 1970s and 1980s. Diffuse contention took place over such issues as cultural and linguistic expression, religious freedom, the right to return to one's homeland from politically imposed exile, discrimination in the workplace, the distribution of investment between federal subunits, representation of nationalities within elite posts, the right to emigrate, and the territorial boundaries of federal subunits. The discourse of Russian dominance grew considerably more muted during these years. Russian nationalists began to question whether Russians were reaping the benefits from the Soviet regime that a dominant group should expect, and in localities indigenization once again

---

[8] Out of 185 mass demonstrations identified with 100 participants or more that took place in the USSR between 1965 and 1986, only 20 raised the issue of secession, and all of these were located in the Baltic. The largest occurred in Vilnius on October 10, 1977, in the aftermath of a soccer game and included from ten to fifteen thousand participants. Ludmilla Alexeyeva, *Soviet Dissent: Contemporary Movements for National, Religious, and Human Rights* (Middletown, CT: Wesleyan University Press, 1985), pp. 69–71. Before August 1987 only four other secessionist demonstrations mobilized more than a thousand participants: May 18, 1972, in Kaunas; November 1, 1975, in Vilnius; October 1, 1980, in Tallin; and October 26, 1980, in Trakai, Lithuania. In Western Ukraine reports abounded of small-scale acts of separatist resistance and the discovery of underground nationalist organizations well into the 1970s and 1980s. But much of this resistance was highly diffuse.

became the expected norm within the sphere of personnel policy. Efforts by the regime to foster dual language competency and even linguistic assimilation (particularly within non-Russian Slavic populations) accelerated during these years, laying the basis for many of the claims for cultural revival that would later emerge under *glasnost'*. But patterns of demographic and linguistic vibrancy among non-Russians raised growing doubts about the regime's ability to achieve universal Russian-language fluency and therefore integrate non-Russians into a common identity community, at least as such a community had traditionally been conceived. Of course, almost all states in today's world are multicultural to some extent, and all are ethnically stratified. Despite the seriousness and complexity of Soviet nationality issues on the eve of *perestroika*, at the time Soviet ethnic problems appeared to most observers to be significant but hardly unmanageable.

Such was the situation when Mikhail Gorbachev became General Secretary of the Communist Party of the Soviet Union in March 1985. Hardly anyone believed that the USSR was in the midst of a nationalities crisis that would eventually shatter the Soviet state. A sclerotic political system, the declining performance of the economy, the stalemated war in Afghanistan, the deaths of three aging leaders in the course of two and a half years, widespread corruption and scandal within the political elite, a deepening malaise and cynicism within society – all these contributed to a growing conviction among outside observers, as well as among the younger generation of Soviet officials, that, in Gorbachev's words, "a crisis was knocking at the door."[9] But no one within the Soviet elite and few among outside observers conceived of this as a crisis of the Soviet national order per se. Indeed, this confidence in the stability of the Soviet national order was a fundamental assumption behind Gorbachev's efforts to reform the USSR and his decision to embark on the policy of *glasnost'* (openness).

This is not to argue that there were not larger structural conditions that made the Soviet Union vulnerable to the eventual emergence of a tide of nationalism. On the contrary, the tide originated and developed in the USSR and not elsewhere for specific reasons. The institutional and ideological crises of the Soviet state were profound and were bound to find some reflection in the nationalities sphere. The legacy of Stalinist coercion against multiple groups and the limitations on cultural expression – both forbidden zones of discourse in the Brezhnev years – remained

---

[9] Mikhail Gorbachev, *Zhizn' i reformy*, vol. 1 (Moscow: Novosti, 1995), p. 207.

a submerged source of grievance for many, particularly within the intelligentsia. The Soviet Union's aspirations as a world power further magnified its vulnerability to generating a tide of nationalism by establishing a conceptual linkage between the outcomes of external contention over the reach of Soviet power abroad and internal contention over the shape and character of the Soviet state.[10] Moreover, in the USSR the state and the socialist regime were closely fused, in large part because the multinational state was founded by the socialist regime, so a political opening that led to challenges against the regime was likely to politicize issues of stateness.[11] This association between regime and state (for many Soviet citizens, their indistinguishability) was by no means the monopoly of the USSR; it is typical of civic multinational polities around the world – many of which have been susceptible to reconception as multinational empires in the absence of a sense of higher loyalty to and identification with the state that transcends ethnicity, particularly at moments of regime crisis. Indeed, it has been the crisis of the large, multinational state encompassing several distinct, compactly settled, cultural entities which has most often generated tides of nationalism intermittently across modern history. The *glasnost'* era was not the first time a tide of nationalism washed across the Eurasian landmass. In the twentieth century similar upsurges in nationalist mobilization across multiple groups within Russia or its Soviet successor state occurred in 1905, 1917–20, and 1941–44 – whenever state power came under severe strain, as during war or revolution.

Despite the critical roles of the institutional and ideological crises of the Soviet state, the fusion between state and regime, the submerged sense of ethnic grievance across multiple groups, and the Soviet state's overreach abroad, these conditions are nonetheless insufficient for explaining the emergence of a tide of nationalism in the USSR. All groups had suffered to one extent or another during the Stalinist era, had experienced limits on cultural expression, and were subject to the same crises of the state and fusion of state and regime. These conditions help explain why the USSR was vulnerable to generating a tide of nationalism, but they do not explain what actually occurred – the specific actions that constituted the tide, how

---

[10] See Seweryn Bialer, *The Soviet Paradox: External Expansion, Internal Decline* (New York: Knopf, 1986); Jack L. Snyder, *Myths of Empire: Domestic Politics and International Ambition* (Ithaca, NY: Cornell University Press, 1991).

[11] See Valerie Bunce, *Subversive Institutions: The Design and the Destruction of Socialism and the State* (Cambridge, UK: Cambridge University Press, 1999).

it was actually generated, how the politics of the tide played itself out, and the considerable variations with which the tide washed across Soviet society in the *glasnost'* years. Structure alone cannot explain the collapse of the Soviet state. By themselves these conditions were incapable of transforming the unthinkable into the inevitable, to bring about the disintegration of the Soviet state from a position where, even in the presence of these conditions, few thought such an outcome conceivable or possible. For this, one must look instead to the ways in which the *glasnost'* political opening gave rise to an explosion of challenging acts across multiple sectors of society.

## *From Institutions to the Streets*

In light of all that followed, it is difficult to reconstruct the reigning atmosphere within Soviet society in 1985–86 that brought about Gorbachev's decision to liberalize Soviet politics. As Gorbachev later described the situation on the eve of his election as General Secretary:

Problems in the development of the country grew faster than they were resolved. Inertia and paralysis of the forms and methods of management, a loss of dynamism in work, and the growth of bureaucratism – all this brought great harm to our cause. . . . The situation demanded change, but in the central organs, as well as in the localities, a certain psychology took hold that attempted to improve things without changing anything.[12]

Well before Gorbachev's election an atmosphere of impatience had emerged within the younger generation of Soviet officials. "Everything has grown rotten," "we can't go on living this way," "society has to change" – these were the private conversations that those instrumental in defining Gorbachev's program report having with one another in the years preceding *perestroika*.[13] Still, little of this elite-led critique of the existing state of affairs concerned the nationalities sphere per se.

Some vague sense that society had to be included more in the political process and that significant change would have to take place within the Communist Party and Soviet state if the Soviet Union were to overcome

---

[12] *Pravda*, February 26, 1986, p. 2.
[13] See A. S. Cherniaev, *Shest' let s Gorbachevym* (Moscow: Kultura, 1993), p. 10; Eduard Shevardnadze, *Moi vybor* (Moscow: Novosti, 1991), p. 79; Gorbachev, *Zhizn' i reformy*, vol. 1, p. 265; Archie Brown, *The Gorbachev Factor* (Oxford: Oxford University Press, 1997), p. 81.

its "pre-crisis" situation were already present in the thinking of Gorbachev and others at the time of his election.[14] As Gorbachev later admitted, however, the primary purpose of *perestroika* when it first developed as a program in summer 1985 was not liberalization, but rather "to remove everything that was holding back development."[15] Measures were announced to root out mismanagement and corruption in the economy. Gorbachev's infamous campaign against alcoholism (which eventually helped to bankrupt the Soviet state) was launched, and a far-reaching purge began to sweep through the Communist Party apparatus. A campaign for "speeding up" (*uskorenie*) scientific and technological innovation in the economy was announced. At the same time, Gorbachev began to call for "radical reforms" in the economy; according to Gorbachev, these would eventually have resembled a form of market socialism, including liberalization of price setting, turning over ownership of production facilities directly to employees, and some limited room for private entrepreneurship. As Gorbachev has recalled about these early years of *perestroika*, "We talked not about revolution, but *about improving the system*. Then we believed in such a possibility."[16] But already by spring 1986 Gorbachev had grown frustrated with the political and bureaucratic foot-dragging and with what he perceived as a widespread skepticism within Soviet society toward the genuineness of his reforms. As he subsequently observed, by early April 1986

the policy of *perestroika* was encountering huge obstacles, and many took it as the latest campaign, one which would eventually exhaust itself. It was necessary to get rid of these kinds of doubts, to convince people of the necessity of the chosen course. That's how the theme of *glasnost'* appeared.[17]

This course toward drawing society into the reform process took further shape over the summer of 1986 in the wake of the Chernobyl nuclear accident, the enormity of which was at first hidden from the public by Party and state bureaucrats, sparking a debate within the Politburo over the limits of official secrecy.[18]

---

[14] Vadim Medvedev, *V kommande Gorbacheva: Vzgliad iznutri* (Moscow: Bylina, 1994), pp. 29–31; M. S. Gorbachev, *Izbrannye rechi i stat'i*, vol. 2 (Moscow: Politizdat, 1987), pp. 95, 130–31.

[15] Gorbachev, *Zhizn' i reformy*, vol. 1, p. 280.

[16] Gorbachev, *Zhizn' i reformy*, vol. 1, p. 203.

[17] Gorbachev, *Zhizn' i reformy*, vol. 1, pp. 294, 298.

[18] Gorbachev, *Zhizn' i reformy*, vol. 1, pp. 302–4.

As one of his closest advisors has noted, "there was much that was traditional and 'Leninist'" in Gorbachev's initial approach toward *glasnost'*. *Glasnost'* was at first understood by Gorbachev as a policy that was "instrumental from the position of the educational-propaganda influence of the Party, the officially proclaimed vanguard of *perestroika* – with the aim of 'mobilizing the masses' for realizing the new political course."[19] In late June 1986 Gorbachev for the first time raised the issue of *glasnost'* in literature at a meeting with writers. At a meeting of the Politburo he called for activating the public through democratization of local legislatures and granting them real rather than fictive powers.[20] In the fall a series of struggles ensued for control over Soviet artistic unions, eventually leading to the decision to abolish censorship altogether in January 1987. The press began to speak more openly, and in December 1986, in an unambiguous sign of political opening, Andrei Sakharov was released from exile in the closed city of Gor'kii. Gorbachev first publicly declared the new policy of "democratization" in a major speech at the January 1987 plenum of the Party's Central Committee, calling for the introduction of competitive elections on an experimental basis in state and Party organs. Shortly afterward, a large number of political prisoners were released from Soviet prison camps, films and literary works previously banned began to appear with great frequency, and the press rushed headlong into the space opening before it to occupy former "forbidden zones" and to fill in previous "blank spots" in official history. There is no evidence that the new tack toward liberalization was openly opposed by Gorbachev's colleagues within the Politburo at the time. Gorbachev did not believe in 1987 that *glasnost'* meant a loss of control for the Party. Rather, it was to be a shift in the ways in which the Party exercised control. As he noted at the January plenum, "socialist democracy has nothing in common with excessive tolerance, irresponsibility, or anarchy." It was to be combined with discipline and responsibility.[21]

At first *glasnost'* manifested itself almost entirely in the operations of official institutions and channels of the state – in the press, movie theaters, and government offices. Although attempts were made by Party stalwarts to limit the boundaries of open discussion in institutional settings, on

[19] Cherniaev, *Shest' let*, p. 94.
[20] See *Izvestiia*, June 22, 1986, p. 1; V. I. Vorotnikov, *A bylo eto tak . . . Iz dnevnika chlena Politbiuro TsK KPSS* (Moscow: Sovet veteranov, 1995), pp. 102–3.
[21] *Pravda*, January 28, 1987, p. 3.

repeated occasions their efforts failed – at times due to Gorbachev's personal intervention. But already by spring 1987 small groups of hippies, ecologists, Jewish refuseniks, Russian nationalists, and Baltic dissidents began to test the boundaries of the permissible by taking politics to the street, engaging in small-scale demonstrations. For the most part, the police observed but did not interfere.[22] This changed reaction of the authorities to protest created a sense that a new political space had been opened on the streets.

Almost all the protests at this time took place under the banner of *perestroika*, not against the Party. Indeed, Gorbachev portrayed these acts as a positive force for change within Soviet institutions. He told the Politburo in June 1987 that although demonstrations were sometimes disturbing phenomena, the Party "should act so that they do not occur," not by arresting their participants, but rather "by removing those issues that can give rise to an undesirable reaction. We have a whole crowd, a whole army of paid employees whose job it is to resolve those issues for which people are going out on the street, and they are not doing it."[23] In the infamous case of the demonstration by the Russian nationalist group *Pamiat'* (Memory) in Moscow on May 6th, 1987, Moscow party boss Boris Yeltsin agreed to meet with the demonstrators, calling their demands for infusing art with a "patriotic" spirit "justified" and promising to review the possibility of officially registering the organization.[24]

In the summer of 1987 two developments took place that began to give structure to what had previously been isolated acts of protest. The first of these was a concerted protest campaign for the right to return to their homeland by Crimean Tatars, exiled to Uzbekistan by Stalin in 1944 – the first protracted wave of protest in the USSR during these years. The Crimean Tatars had pressed their cause throughout the post-Stalin period, particularly in the late 1960s, when they engaged in an unsuccessful cam-

---

[22] Of the twelve demonstrations with over a hundred participants that occurred from February through May 1987, only one – a *Pamiat'* (Memory) demonstration on May 9 – was harassed by the police (in this instance, due to the embarrassment caused by an earlier meeting between Boris Yeltsin and this radical Russian nationalist group). *Vesti iz SSSR*, 10–14, 1987. Smaller demonstrations were repressed, such as that which was held in Moscow on February 9 by seven Jewish refuseniks in support of Iosif Begun's release. Nevertheless, Begun was released from prison several days later.

[23] Cherniaev, *Shest' let*, pp. 149 50.

[24] *The New York Times*, July 26, 1987, p. E6; Boris Yeltsin, *Against the Grain: An Autobiography* (New York: Summit Books, 1990), pp. 120–21.

paign of demonstrations in Uzbekistan, Crimea, and Moscow. Up to 1986 the Soviet regime had systematically repressed any public discussion of the Crimean Tatar situation. It had even sentenced dissidents raising these issues to psychiatric prison hospitals. By the 1980s the Crimean Tatar national movement had gone into decline – in part due to the arrest of its leaders, in part to "the ineffectiveness of all tactical measures" the movement had deployed in its struggle to gain return to the Crimea.[25] Although memories of Crimea and of the genocide were universally fostered within the Crimean Tatar family, and Crimean Tatars remained a distinctive cultural community in Central Asia, large numbers had begun to plant roots there by the early eighties, and, under the influence of necessity, had lost hope of returning to their homeland.[26] But in early 1987 the release of a number of Crimean Tatar leaders from prison camp and media discussions of the previously unmentionable repressions of Stalin gave rise to new hopes among Crimean Tatar activists about the possibilities for action. In April in Tashkent they drafted a petition to Gorbachev and decided to send a "mass delegation" to Moscow to meet with the Soviet leader. At the end of June members of the "mass delegation" from Krasnodar krai and Uzbekistan began arriving in Moscow. Their representatives were granted a meeting not with Gorbachev, but with Petr Demichev, deputy chair of the Presidium of the USSR Supreme Soviet. Demichev was not sympathetic, but promised to forward their appeal to Gorbachev. Having received no answer from Gorbachev by July 6, 120 members of the "mass delegation" conducted a short but noisy demonstration on Red Square under the banner "Democracy and *Glasnost'* – for Crimean Tatars as well!" Demichev received them once again, this time speaking in Gorbachev's name, promising that the Crimean Tatar issue would be resolved by the end of July. The "delegates" decided not to leave Moscow, however, until they received an answer. In the meantime, a special Politburo commission was created under the leadership of Supreme Soviet Chair Andrei Gromyko to reply to the appeal. A meeting on July 22 between Crimean Tatar representatives and employees of the Central Committee Secretariat left the impression among Crimean Tatars that there was little sympathy for their demands among the members of the commission. On July 23

---

[25] Alexeyeva, *Soviet Dissent*, p. 152.
[26] On the Crimean Tatars in exile, see Brian Glyn Williams, "The Crimean Tatar Exile in Central Asia: A Case Study in Group Destruction and Survival," *Central Asian Survey*, vol. 17, no. 2 (1998), pp. 285–317.

several hundred Crimean Tatar demonstrators once again returned to Red Square, sitting behind a police cordon at the foot of St. Basil's Cathedral, chanting "We want Gorbachev!" and refusing to move until the right to return to their homeland was granted. The novelty of such unrepressed acts of dissent by non-Russians in the very symbolic center of the Soviet state did not go unnoticed in the press or by local residents. Simultaneous acts of protest were carried out in Uzbekistan and Krasnodar krai. The Moscow sit-ins continued unmolested by the police until July 30, when the protesters were rounded up and evicted from the city.[27] But the Crimean Tatar campaign did not end there. Upon return to their homes nationalist activists organized a new wave of demonstrations in September and October in Uzbekistan, Krasnodar krai, and Crimea to coincide with the sixty-sixth anniversary of the formation of the Crimean ASSR. A third wave of protests was carried out in early 1988.[28] As one Crimean Tatar activist later observed, the July 1987 demonstrations were "a Rubicon for the Crimean Tatars." "The process of consolidation of Crimean Tatars in the struggle for their rights reached its zenith," and "even those who considered themselves alien to the national cause were moved onto the path of struggle."[29] More important from the point of view of subsequent events in the USSR, these acts illustrated the new possibilities of street politics for pressing nationalist issues and constituted the first sustained protest campaign within what would become the *glasnost'* mobilizational cycle.

A second development betrayed a growing interrelationship between specifically nationalist challenges and the emergence of a more radical current in the new politics of the street. In February 1987 Gorbachev visited Latvia and Estonia, coming away with the impression that "while the people feel themselves at home in our enormous . . . country," no great enthusiasm for *perestroika* had yet reached the population, largely because of resistance from "the bureaucratism of the bosses."[30] But Gorbachev's

[27] See M. N. Guboglo, S. M. Chervonnaia, *Krymskotatarskoe natsional'noe dvizhenie*, vol. 1 (Moscow: Institut etnologii i antropologii, 1992), pp. 133–39; *Vesti iz SSSR*, 13–22, 1987; 14-4, 1987. On the public reaction to these events among Muscovites, see *The New York Times*, July 26, 1987, p. A3.

[28] See Mustafa Dzhemilev, ed., *Shest'desiat shestaia godovshchina Krymskoi ASSR. Demonstratsii i mitingi Krymskikh Tatar* (London: Society for Central Asian Studies, 1989).

[29] Sh. U. Mustafaev, "Evoliutsiia samosoznaniia – vzgliad iznutri," in A. P. Viatkin and E. S. Kul'pin, eds., *Krymskie tatary: Problemy repatriatsii* (Moscow: Institut vostokovedeniia RAN, 1997), p. 32.

[30] Cherniaev, *Shest' let*, p. 143.

appeals for democratization while he was in the Baltic, the candor with which Stalinism was being discussed in the Moscow press, and the relative tolerance shown to protesting groups in Moscow created a new sense of opportunity for separatist dissidents in the Baltic, some of whom had only recently been released from prison. In July 1986 a small dissident group known as Helsinki-86 and dedicated to achieving Latvian independence sprang into existence in the city of Liepaia. Its leaders were immediately arrested. Their trial was scheduled for January 1987, but, to the surprise of the defendants, the case was suddenly dropped, probably due to the general release of political prisoners then taking place.[31] In May 1987 the group issued a call for a ceremonial laying of flowers at the Freedom Monument in Riga on June 14, the anniversary of the day Stalin exiled thousands of Latvians to Siberia in 1941. The authorities employed various strategies to prevent the demonstration from occurring, even declaring an alternative "Sports Festival" at the monument exactly at the appointed hour. Nevertheless, up to five thousand appeared at the demonstration, with only minor confrontations with the police reported.[32]

The success of the June 14 demonstration in Riga (widely reported in the Soviet press, though in disparaging tones) encouraged a more ambitious challenge – a series of simultaneous demonstrations in all three Baltic capitals to mark the forty-eighth anniversary of the Molotov-Ribbentrop pact on August 23. Links between Baltic dissident and émigré groups allowed for coordination of the event, and foreign radio broadcasts by Voice of America and Radio Liberty (the former no longer jammed as a demonstration of Gorbachev's "new thinking") played a critical role in informing Baltic audiences about the protest.[33] Approximately two thousand demonstrators gathered at protests in Tallin and five hundred in Vilnius, with reports of only minor police coercion – marking the spread of the new street politics throughout the Baltic. In Riga, however, where up to eight thousand participated, several hundred were arrested, fire hoses were turned on the crowd, and a number of people were beaten. Even so, the Latvian Party leadership criticized local authorities shortly afterward for failing to take sufficient measures to prevent the gathering from taking

---

[31] *Vesti iz SSSR*, 1/2–1, 1987; 3–12, 1987.

[32] *Vesti iz SSSR*, 11/12–3, 1987; *Glasnost'*, no. 5 (July 1987), p. 30. Eleven participants were arrested, though all were released. The leader of Helsinki-86, however, was subsequently tried for draft evasion.

[33] *The New York Times*, August 25, 1987, p. A3.

place.[34] Over the ensuing months Baltic separatists organized intermittent acts of public protest (particularly around the symbolic dates of Baltic independence), and the authorities periodically subjected them to arrest and other coercive measures. In none of the Baltic republics did these dissident groupings lead the eventual drives to independence. That role was played by the Baltic popular fronts that emerged in summer 1988 and were, as we will see, movements more closely associated with the authorities. Nevertheless, Baltic dissident movements in 1987–88 were important in making clear the new possibilities of street politics and in linking the Baltic independence movements with one another. In so doing, they fostered the type of transnational influence that was central in making a tide of nationalism.

By September 1987 right and left factions within the Politburo began to crystallize over the direction of political reform, and divisions within the Soviet leadership were for the first time bared to the public.[35] Yeltsin's eviction from the Politburo in October 1987, although due in large part to his erratic personality, nevertheless played into these differences and marked the beginning of open discord within the Soviet leadership. By January 1988 divisions had deepened to the point where "passions boiled" at weekly Politburo meetings over the proper bounds of liberalization.[36] But nationalism had still not erupted in any major sense. It was only in February 1988 that the first major wave of protest to overtake the Soviet Union in the *glasnost'* era materialized, and it assumed specifically national form – the Armenian mobilization over the Karabakh issue in February 1988. The magnitude of these protests and their relationship with acts of contention by other groups were clear evidence that a tide of nationalism was beginning to emerge.

When borders were drawn between Armenia and Azerbaijan with great dispute in 1921, large minorities of Armenians and Azerbaijanis were located inside the titular republic of the other. The Karabakh Armenians were given their own federal subunit, an autonomous province, as a means of delineating their cultural rights. A significant in-migration of Azerbaijanis into Karabakh over the ensuing years diluted the population from 95

[34] *Sovetskaia Latviia*, August 30, 1987, p. 1; *Vesti iz SSSR*, 15/16–3, 1987.
[35] See Yegor Ligachev, *Inside Gorbachev's Kremlin* (New York: Pantheon Books, 1993), pp. 85–86, 105–6. See also Chebrikov's speech in *Krasnaia zvezda*, September 11, 1987, pp. 1, 3.
[36] Gorbachev, *Zhizn' i reformy*, vol. 1, p. 378.

percent Armenian in the 1920s to 76 percent by 1979, and Armenians constantly complained that they were being discriminated against in economic investment and access to Armenian-language media. The issue of Karabakh was raised regularly from the 1920s on through petitions, letter-writing campaigns, official appeals by local party officials, and occasional demonstrations. These efforts were ignored by Moscow, and their initiators were often subjected to persecution by local Azerbaijani authorities.[37] Indeed, the Soviet press portrayed the issue as if it "had been settled once and for all."[38] But the possibilities for contesting the Karabakh issue changed dramatically with the inauguration of *glasnost'*.

In July 1987 Karen Demirchian, longtime first secretary of the Armenian Communist Party, was harshly criticized at a republican Central Committee plenum for tolerating corruption and favoritism. This was understood as signaling an effort by Moscow to undermine Demirchian and to replace him with a reformist leader. Soon, articles appeared in the central press attacking Demirchian. One such piece, on the harmful pollutants emitted by chemical plants in Yerevan, described the local communist leadership as a mafia unconcerned with the health of the population and was widely interpreted as "a maneuver by the central authorities to provoke a popular uprising against the local authorities, which would be the pretext for their removal."[39] By this time ecological demonstrations had already occurred in Tartu, Leningrad, Kazan', and Irkutsk – the beginning of a stream of ecological mobilizations that would at various times intersect with nationalist demands.[40] On September 1, several hundred Armenians demonstrated in front of a polluting synthetic rubber plant, with no attempt by the authorities to repress them. In early October in Karabakh a dispute over the boundaries between an Armenian *sovkhoz* and an Azerbaijani *kolkhoz* in the Karabakh village of Chardokhlu led to local disturbances. Two battalions of soldiers were called in, and one KGB employee was injured while trying to keep order. These events became the occasion for Armenian nationalist activists to politicize the Karabakh issue. In mid-October

---

[37] Levon Chorbajian, Patrick Donabedian, and Claude Mutafian, *The Caucasian Knot: The History and Geo-Politics of Nagorno-Karabakh* (London: Zed Books, 1994), pp. 144–47.

[38] Ronald Grigor Suny, *Looking toward Ararat: Armenia in Modern History* (Bloomington, IN: Indiana University Press), pp. 188–99.

[39] Pierre Verluise, *Armenia in Crisis: The 1988 Earthquake* (Detroit, MI: Wayne State University Press, 1995), p. 84.

[40] See Jane I. Dawson, *Eco-nationalism: Anti-Nuclear Activism and National Identity in Russia, Lithuania, and Ukraine* (Durham, NC: Duke University Press, 1996).

another unsanctioned ecological demonstration attracting up to five thousand participants took place in Yerevan, again with little reaction by the authorities.[41] The following day, a thousand-strong demonstration displaying portraits of Gorbachev and calling for transfer of Karabakh from Azerbaijan to Armenia occurred in Yerevan in solidarity with the Armenians of Chardokhlu. This amplification of demands – from ecology to nationalism – set a pattern that repeated itself in a number of instances in the Soviet Union, as nationalist challengers used the more acceptable issues of environmentalism to probe the limits of the permissible. In this case the demonstration was brutally broken up by the police when demonstrators refused to heed calls to disperse.[42] By this time, however, the rudiments of nationalist social movement organization had begun to emerge.

Demirchian hung on to his post despite persistent attacks. But by January 1988, encouraged by the broadening limits of public debate, the attacks upon Stalinism at the October 1987 Central Committee Plenum, sympathetic statements by several Gorbachev advisors (some of them Armenian) over the Karabakh issue, the retirement of former Azerbaijani party boss Heydar Aliev from the Politburo, and widespread rumors that Moscow intended to look into the problem,[43] the Karabakh Armenians were pressing their claims. As Georgii Shakhnazarov, a Gorbachev advisor and himself a Karabakh Armenian, later noted of those who organized the campaign, "the freedom that loomed on the horizon was embodied in their consciousness primarily by the possibility of uniting with their homeland."[44] In August 1987 the Karabakh Armenians had sent a petition in favor of transferring Karabakh to Armenia to the Central Committee in Moscow. It was signed by seventy-five thousand people. The petition was ignored until an official delegation from Karabakh arrived in Moscow in January 1988 to press the issue. They were promised that their appeal would be reviewed, but in early February a negative answer was crudely relayed from the Central Committee apparatus.[45] This unleashed a co-

---

[41] *Vesti iz SSSR*, 19/20–5, 1987; *Glasnost'*, no. 10, 1987, p. 8. Organizers were merely called into the KGB for "a conversation."

[42] *Vesti iz SSSR*, 19/20–5, 1987.

[43] See Vorotnikov, *A bylo eto tak*, pp. 193–94; Suny, *Looking toward Ararat*, p. 197.

[44] Georgii Shakhnazarov, *Tsena svobody. Reformatsiia Gorbacheva glazami ego pomoshchnika* (Moscow: Rossika, 1993), p. 206.

[45] See Nikolai Ryzhkov, *Perestroika: istoriia predatel'stv* (Moscow: Novosti, 1992), p. 203; *Vesti iz SSSR*, 4–1, 1988. The Central Committee apparatus had received five hundred letters over the previous three years complaining about the situation in Karabakh. See *Soiuz mozhno bylo sokhranit'* (Moscow: Aprel'-85, 1995), p. 22.

ordinated campaign of civil disobedience by Armenians throughout Karabakh, with calls for the local legislature to convene to recognize the territory as part of Armenia. The campaign was organized in part by forces within the local party organization itself.[46] In the meantime, in Yerevan a series of ecological demonstrations were taking place over construction of a new chemical plant on the outskirts of the city. When news of the appeal by the local legislature in Stepanakert for unification with Armenia and its rejection for a second time by Moscow reached Yerevan, the ecological demonstrations quickly grew into manifestations of support for the Karabakh Armenians, attracting up to thirty thousand people. On the night of February 21 anti-Armenian pogroms broke out in the town of Gadrut in Nagorno-Karabakh, injuring sixteen and killing two. Reaction to news of this violence led to enormous demonstrations in Yerevan of up to a million people calling for transfer of the territory to Armenia and physical protection of Armenians living in Karabakh. Demonstrators carried portraits of Gorbachev with the inscription "We believe in you."[47] Even Demirchian came to support the Karabakh cause, pressing the issue before the Politburo. Some analysts suspect that Demirchian, facing pressure for his resignation from Moscow, backed the demonstrators as a way of gaining local support for his retention in office.[48] On February 24 an Organizational Committee for the Issue of the Reunification of Karabakh with Armenia sprang into existence. The following day Gorbachev met with two of its representatives, agreeing to a program of measures proposed by the Committee to strengthen the cultural and economic autonomy of the Karabakh Armenians in exchange for taking the territorial issue off the agenda and calling a halt to demonstrations.[49] By February 27 participation in nationalist demonstrations in Yerevan had dropped sharply, ceasing entirely on February 28. Ironically, precisely as the Armenian mobilization in Yerevan wound down, rallies organized by Azerbaijani refugees from Armenia began to gather on the central square of Sumgait

---

[46] While the leadership of the local party apparatus in Karabakh generally opposed the campaign, one of the main organizers was an *instruktor* of the Nagorno-Karabakh *obkom*. The local party apparatus did not attempt to block the demonstrations, and efforts by Baku to bully the local party *aktiv* into opposing the campaign failed. Gorbachev, *Zhizn' i reformy*, vol. 1, p. 502; Vorotnikov, *A bylo eto tak*, pp. 194–95.

[47] *Vesti iz SSSR*, no. 4–1, 1988; Verluise, *Armenia in Crisis*, p. 86.

[48] Gorbachev, *Zhizn' i reformy*, vol. 1, p. 502; *Ekspress khronika*, no. 52, Dec. 17–24, 1991, p. 6.

[49] See Shakhnazarov, *Tsena svobody*, pp. 205–10.

in Azerbaijan, leading to an orgy of anti-Armenian violence and pushing the conflict toward a new phase. Nineteen eighty-eight later became known among Armenians as "the year when everything was possible."[50]

I have provided a detailed rendering of these early waves of mobilization because careful attention to them reveals much about how streams of mobilization gain a sense of momentum. For one thing, the failure of the regime to prevent specific mobilizational challenges gave rise to new challenges by other groups. Unrepressed mobilizations by Jewish refuseniks and Russian hippies and nationalists influenced the decision of Crimean Tatar dissidents to conduct a protest campaign, which in turn influenced attempts by Baltic dissidents to organize demonstrations, which in turn influenced the behavior of Armenian activists, and so on down the line. Conflict within the leadership of the state and the success of some protest acts evoked a more serious explosion of public expectations – an amplification of demands from relatively benign concerns to issues more directly challenging the parameters of the national order. As the Armenian case also shows, one of the most effective forces for mobilizing populations was violence – through the sense of victimization and activization of ethnic boundaries which it produced.

The institutional contingencies embodied in these early cases of nationalist mobilization loom large. Many of these early protests could easily have been shut down through repression, as the activists who organized them well knew. Alternatively, in the Armenian case, had Gorbachev acceded to the petition of Karabakh Armenians for the transfer of the territory to Armenia, one might well imagine how this could have transformed the entire politics of the issue (demobilizing Armenians, but provoking outrage in Azerbaijan, and subsequently leading to attempts by other groups to change the internal boundaries of the USSR). Because challengers take heart from the example of successful challenge by others, it is hardly surprising that state leaders attempt to maintain national order through the reverse logic, preventing challenges in one field from influencing challenges in other fields. From what we know in retrospect, the Soviet leadership took very seriously the transnational influences that nationalisms have on one another. It viewed the entire affair of Karabakh through the prism of a "domino theory," fearing the encouragement one boundary change might give to other groups. As Gorbachev told the Polit-

[50] Chorbajian, Donabedian, and Mutafian, *The Caucasian Knot*, p. 149.

buro at its July 4, 1988, meeting, "Reviewing boundaries is unrealistic; that would mean going down a disastrous path, and not only in these regions."[51] The Soviet leadership's refusal to accede to demands to transfer Karabakh to Armenia was based on the counterfactual assumption that doing otherwise would have led to an explosion of claims. We will never know whether Gorbachev's assessment was correct, but the subsequent failure of the approach taken raises the question of whether a space for a nonviolent politics of internal boundary change would have altered the course of events. In spite of Gorbachev's attempts to prevent the lateral spread of conflict over internal boundaries, conflict over interrepublican boundaries eventually spread in any case (though as we see in Chapter 6, largely in a violent manner, due in part to the absence of nonviolent alternatives). The linkages among issues and between groups, the ways in which groups looked toward the example of others as a source of comparison, and the modes by which authority maintained order all created a sense of interconnectedness that was critical in giving rise to a tide of nationalism.

## Defining a Tide Within a Cycle

To study any phenomenon is first to delimit its boundaries. But defining the boundaries of a cycle of mobilization and of a tide of nationalism is no simple matter, in part because these are flows of action rather than single events, and their beginnings and ends are necessarily fuzzy. I leave the task of probing the end of the *glasnost'* tide of nationalism for later discussion. My present task is to probe the issues of when cycles of mobilization begin and the relationship of the tide of nationalism to the larger mobilizational cycle of which it was a part.

Understanding the origins of cycles and tides requires an initial look at how contention manifests itself in periods of normalized politics. In "quiet" phases of contention, state institutions utilize their strategic positions to naturalize dominant conceptions of order and to marginalize alternatives. This was starkly obvious in Brezhnevian USSR. The Brezhnev era eventually came to be known in the parlance of *glasnost'* as the "era of stagnation" for its overarching respect for stability and its efforts to normalize the status quo. "Seven times measure and one time cut" – such was the image of propriety Soviet leaders sought to convey concerning the proper modes of policy making. Khrushchev's destabilizing campaigns of de-

---

[51] *Soiuz mozhno bylo*, p. 30.

Stalinization were halted, a pervasive stability in office took hold within the political elite, and the Soviet leadership presented a united and consensual face to society and the outside world. Nascent dissident movements which had emerged during the erratic liberalization of Khrushchev were consistently repressed. Dissent was literally portrayed as madness, as the psychological prison hospital became the symbol of the regime's efforts to infuse a sense of normalcy around loyalty to the existing order.

Yet, in spite of the regime's repressiveness, dissent continued to surface. The history of the Soviet dissident movement is well known. A handful – at most several thousand individuals – bravely brought upon themselves the wrath of the Soviet state through public acts of dissent. The dissident movement in the Brezhnev era was a diffuse opposition largely revolving around actions by individuals and small groups rather than large-scale collective action. Given the great difficulty of organizing large-scale collective action in such a repressive environment, Soviet dissidents favored tactics such as the open letter, the petition, or the hunger strike. Others who inwardly dissented from Soviet policies but did not wish to face reprisal from the regime quietly worked within Soviet institutions or engaged in everyday practices that contradicted the official norms of the system. Figure 2.1 displays the evolving patterns by which challengers contested the state in a period of state dominance. It shows the temporal distribution of 264 mass protest demonstrations and 50 mass violent events during the 1965–87 period for which information was available,[52] as well as information published from Soviet archives on 2,424 convictions on charges of "anti-Soviet agitation and propaganda" during this period.[53] I make no distinction in the figure between particular streams of mobilization, though it should be noted that the majority of the demonstrations (77 percent) and of the mass violent events (64 percent) in the sample concerned issues of ethnonationalism. Thus, even prior to the *glasnost'* opening, mobilizational agendas in the USSR were dominated by issues of nationalism – indicative of deeper structural factors at work that evoked

[52] In focusing on these forms, I do not mean to imply that contentious repertoires were confined to them. Rather, the point is that forms of contention are structured by the opportunities that state institutions present to those who would challenge them. Only demonstrations with one hundred participants or more were included in the analysis.

[53] Political dissent should be understood as having been much broader than simply those convicted of these "crimes." Numerous other articles of the criminal code were used to jail dissenters, some dissenters were declared insane and placed in psychiatric wards, and some emigrated or were forced into exile.

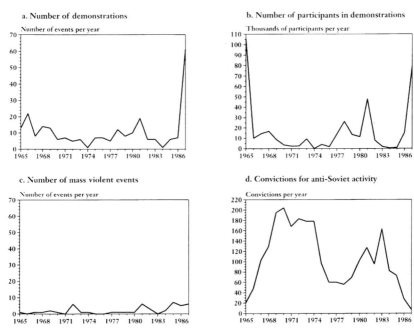

**Figure 2.1.** Demonstration activity, mass violent events, and convictions of dissidents for anti-Soviet activity, 1965–87. (Convictions of dissidents for anti-Soviet activity are defined as convictions for "anti-Soviet agitation and propaganda" or for "deliberately spreading fabrications discrediting the Soviet state and social order." Source: *Istochnik*, no. 6, 1995, p. 153.)

a tide of nationalism. As these figures indicate, mass contention was by no means absent in Brezhnevian USSR. Figure 2.1b shows that the number of persons participating in demonstrations in 1965 most likely exceeded the number of persons participating in 1987, when *glasnost'* was already under way. In 1965, however, the bulk of participation in the thirteen protest demonstrations registered for that year occurred during a single event, the April 1965 demonstration in Yerevan commemorating victims of the Armenian genocide, when one hundred thousand people took to the streets.[54] By contrast, of the sixty-nine protest demonstrations recorded for 1987, the largest demonstration (the ecological demonstration in Kirishi, Leningrad province) involved only ten thousand persons.[55]

[54] See Alexeyeva, *Soviet Dissent*, p. 123.
[55] See *Chelovek i zakon*, no. 7, 1989, p. 33.

71

But the spectacular wave of Armenian protest in 1965 was not part of a mobilizational cycle, for there was no diffusion of mobilization across sectors of society and no compact, iterative chain of attempts to contest the state. In the pre-*glasnost'* period forms of mass contention varied independently of one another. As Figure 2.1c shows, known incidents of mass violence were rare throughout this period; their appearance remained unconnected with patterns of demonstrations.

One can detect temporal variations in collective action across the 1965–87 time span. As Figures 2.1a and 2.1b indicate, somewhat greater demonstration activity occurred in the 1965–68 period, when the dissent unleashed by Khrushchev's removal from office, Brezhnev's retreat from Khrushchev's de-Stalinization efforts, and attempts by a number of nationalities to press rights through street action produced a small clustering of events. This clustering declined in the face of a systematic campaign of repression against dissidents. A similar clustering occurred in the late 1970s and early 1980s – an echo of events in Poland and the somewhat diminished repression against dissent that, as Figure 2.1d shows, was evident during those years. But neither of these clusterings grew into a mobilizational cycle. Participation in them was extremely limited. Acts of contention remained isolated and were rarely repeated, primarily because of the expectation of repression. And these acts remained marginalized within the political process as a whole. Because the regime consistently repressed efforts to contest its policies through protest, and because there were few successful instances of challenge, contention did not spread temporally or spatially through analogy.[56]

In 1987, by contrast, a series of small waves of protest emerged, began to persist, and started to influence one another. The reason is obvious: The easing of institutional constraints due to *glasnost'* altered the boundaries of what was seemingly possible. It thereby gave rise to iterative attempts by dissident groupings to test the political waters through acts of mobiliza-

---

[56] Alexeeva and Chalidze, in an unpublished study of two thousand protest events of all types and sizes during the 1956–83 period, observed a growth in the number of protest acts of all sizes over the course of the Brezhnev era, but a marked decline in the number of participants in such acts, with the sole exceptions of the Baltic and Georgia. Thus, by the early 1980s most of the growth in protest actions that occurred over the previous three decades took place as a result of an increase in small acts of protest, not mass actions. Ludmilla Alexeeva and Valery Chalidze, "Mass Unrest in the USSR," Report No. 19 submitted to the Office of Net Assessment of the U.S. Department of Defense (OSD/NA 85-2965), August 1983, pp. 378–79.

tion and set off a new dialectic of interrelationship between challenging groups. As Figure 2.1a shows, the number of demonstrations in 1987 increased precipitously compared to the previous two decades, marking a clear break with prior patterns of contention. But more significantly, these acts of contention encompassed a variety of groups in distant locations raising disparate types of claims, but who nevertheless were influenced by one another's behavior due to the one attribute they shared in common – prior repression by the Soviet state. In addition to a number of ecological, human rights, pacifist, and Hare Krishna demonstrations, sustained protest campaigns were mounted by Jewish, Crimean Tatar, Latvian, Estonian, and Russian nationalist groups, giving rise by the end of 1987 to attempts to mobilize populations around nationalist issues in Armenia, Belorussia, Tajikistan, and Georgia. In short, already during 1987 the interactive effects of contentious actions across groups had become readily apparent – particularly with regard to nationalist protest.

Some have argued that December 1986 should be viewed as a starting date for the *glasnost'* mobilizational cycle – that is, the Alma-Ata demonstrations and riots of December 17 and 18, when up to ten thousand participants took to the streets in response to the removal of the Communist Party leader of Kazakhstan, Dinmukhamed Kunaev, and the appointment of a Russian in his place.[57] But the Alma-Ata events were in many ways more reminiscent of pre-*glasnost'* protest than they were of subsequent patterns of contention. They illustrate well the difference between events occurring within a cycle and those occurring outside. In the first place, the Alma-Ata disturbances had hardly any effect on or connection with mobilization elsewhere in the former Soviet Union. They lacked movement organization (they were organized spontaneously by a group of students at Kazakh State University), and only two and a half years later did they give birth to a lasting movement.[58] Moreover, the extensive repression that

---

[57] Olzhas Suleimenov, the Kazakh writer, for instance, contended that "the Alma-Ata students and workers were the first in the country to conduct unauthorized meetings" and had been responsible for unleashing the subsequent waves of unrest in the former Soviet Union. *Kazakhstanskaia pravda*, June 10, 1989.

[58] For detailed accounts of what occurred, see Helsinki Watch, *Conflict in the Soviet Union: The Untold Story of the Clashes in Kazakhstan* (New York: Helsinki Watch, 1990); *Literaturnaia gazeta*, in *Foreign Broadcast Information Service, Daily Report: Soviet Union* [*FBIS*], January 5, 1990, pp. 66–69; *Ekspress khronika*, no. 50, December 8–14, 1992, p. 5. The *Zholtoksan* (December) movement was organized in May 1989 by those sentenced for their role in the December 1986 events.

accompanied the Alma-Ata events (up to 2,400 arrested, with 459 injured and 2 dead) effectively subdued further mobilization in Kazakhstan for several years afterward. The Kazakh population did not engage again in significant protest mobilization until June 1989, when thousands took to the streets in the provincial oil town of Novyi Uzen' to carry out violent pogroms against local Meskhetian Turks.[59] The Alma-Ata events of December 1986 lasted only two days and evoked no iterative attempt to contest the state. Nor is there evidence that the student organizers of these protests were inspired to take to the streets by liberalizing change within Soviet institutions, but rather by outrage in response to a contemptible personnel decision by Moscow. They pressed reactive rather than proactive demands.

The beginning of the mobilizational cycle would be better located sometime in the summer of 1987, when iterative attempts to contest the state – particularly by nascent nationalist movements – grew regularized and began to influence one another. We recognize this as the beginning of a cycle only by what subsequently followed: a broadening of challenge to encompass new groups and a growing causal role for the event itself. Challenge had not yet grown normalized at the time and could easily have been shut down. The formation of a mobilizational cycle (and of a tide of nationalism) is heavily dependent on institutional contingencies, though, as we will see, it is not accidental that certain groups rather than others are able to take advantage of those contingencies.

As complex as defining the boundaries of a cycle is defining the boundaries between tide and cycle, for the former is nested within the latter. Cycles of mobilization consist of a series of waves and streams of action which feed off of the connections that agents make with prior mobilizational acts. This production and the active use of linkages across time and space are what impart a sense of momentum to action within a cycle. In this sense, the key to the power of action to reproduce itself within mobilizational cycles is the process by which connections between actions are made. These can occur out of several processes. Contiguity in time or place has often been a powerful factor aiding the production of contention. The heightened pace of prior action – its thickness in time – makes subsequent action more likely by generating bandwagon effects, lowering the institutional constraints to subsequent action, and increasing the possibil-

[59] *Izvestiia*, in *FBIS*, June 21, 1989, p. 52.

*[handwritten: I understand 'tide' but not 'cycle']*

*[handwritten margin note: Bandwagon]*

ity of success.[60] Geographic proximity increases the probability of diffusion through network connections or spillover effects.

But connections are also made between actions on the basis of analogy – that is, on a sense of similarity in the nature of issues, situations, or mobilizational targets. It is here where mobilization gains its power to travel not merely across time within a single spatial context or across contiguous spaces, but often across vast distances between communities with *[handwritten margin note: analogy]* seemingly little in common with one another. These perceived similarities are not givens. They depend in part on the presence of communication *[handwritten margin note: Communicate]* channels and are shaped through acts of framing that define the nature of *[handwritten margin note: framing]* the issues at stake, who is to blame for the situation, and the proposed solution to the problem. The more open media flows of the *glasnost'* period played a critical role in the spatial spread of mobilization by creating the possibility for analogy making. One of the striking aspects of the mobilizational cycle within the Soviet Union was the degree to which specific types of demands spread modularly – that is, within a relatively compressed period of time, similar issues came to be pressed within distant spatial contexts. Specific institutional structures, such as the ethnofederal system or the ministerial structure of the economy, helped to foster this modular spread of contention (the coal-mine strikes of July 1989 and the heightened contention over sovereignty in 1990 being the most striking examples). Moreover, within specific issue areas demands underwent a radicalization over the course of the cycle, from cultural preservation and language revival to sovereignty and independence, from freedom of expression and fair elections to multiparty competition, from improved consumer supply and economic autonomy to the resignation of the government for failure to enact economic reforms. It is here that the sense of thinking about a mobilizational cycle as a series of streams of mobilization around substantively related complexes of issues begins to loom large, for it allows us to investigate more specifically the shifting ways in which movements and populations framed issues over time and how these framings related to one another.

In this respect, nationalism was one of several mobilizational vectors potentially competing for mass allegiance. Within the *glasnost'* mobilizational cycle significant autonomous streams of mobilization – at times unconnected with nationalism, at other times intersecting with it – *[handwritten margin note: Nationalism as one vector]*

---

[60] See Mark Irving Lichbach, *The Rebel's Dilemma* (Ann Arbor, MI: University of Michigan Press, 1998), p. 118.

occurred over democratization, environmental justice, and labor/economic issues. Figure 2.2 tracks the intersection and divergence between ethnonationalist and liberalizing streams of mobilization within the cycle by separating those demonstrations that raised ethnonationalist demands but not demands for regime liberalization from those advocating regime liberalization but not ethnonationalist demands.[61] Figure 2.3 does the same for ethnonationalist and economic streams. As the figures show, there was considerable intersection between ethnonationalist and liberalizing streams of mobilization, in sharp contrast to the near absence of interaction between ethnonationalist and economic streams of mobilization, which remained almost entirely separate. Twenty-four percent of the 6,663 demonstrations in the sample raised both ethnonationalist and liberalizing demands. Despite this considerable intersection, the patterns make clear the dominance of ethnonationalist issues within the cycle: only 16 percent of demonstrations voiced liberalizing demands without raising ethnonationalist demands, whereas 42 percent of the sample consisted of demonstrations that raised ethnonationalist demands but not liberalizing demands. Even more significant, as Figure 2.2 shows, demonstrations that championed regime liberalization but did not raise ethnonationalist demands for the most part gained relatively minor resonance within society, particularly in comparison with demonstrations that were both ethnonationalist and liberalizing or that simply raised ethnonationalist demands. Thus, out of the approximately 102 million participants in the demonstrations in the sample, only 6 percent participated in demonstrations calling for regime transition but not voicing ethnonationalist demands, whereas demonstrations making ethnonationalist but not liberalizing demands accounted for 57 percent of all participants; those voicing both ethnonationalist and liberalizing demands comprised 33 percent. Not only do we see evidence here of the extraordinary mobilizational power of nationalism within the cycle, but also of the significant role played by nationalism in providing regime transition with a social base. The strongest pressures from society for liberalization were precisely those that simultaneously pulled on nationalist tropes.

Similar findings emerge in Figure 2.3 concerning the mobilizational resonance of ethnonationalist issues in comparison with economic issues

---

[61] I have chosen to focus on "ethnonationalist" mobilization (mobilization over nationalist or ethnic demands) in recognition of the porous boundaries between the "national" and the "ethnic" in this period of rapid change.

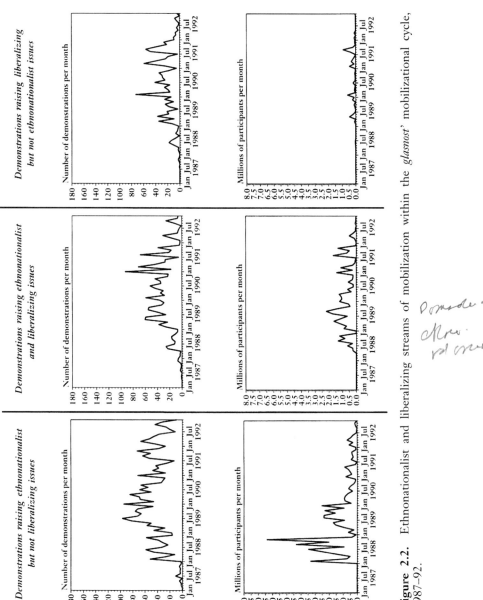

**Figure 2.2.** Ethnonationalist and liberalizing streams of mobilization within the *glasnost'* mobilizational cycle, 1987–92.

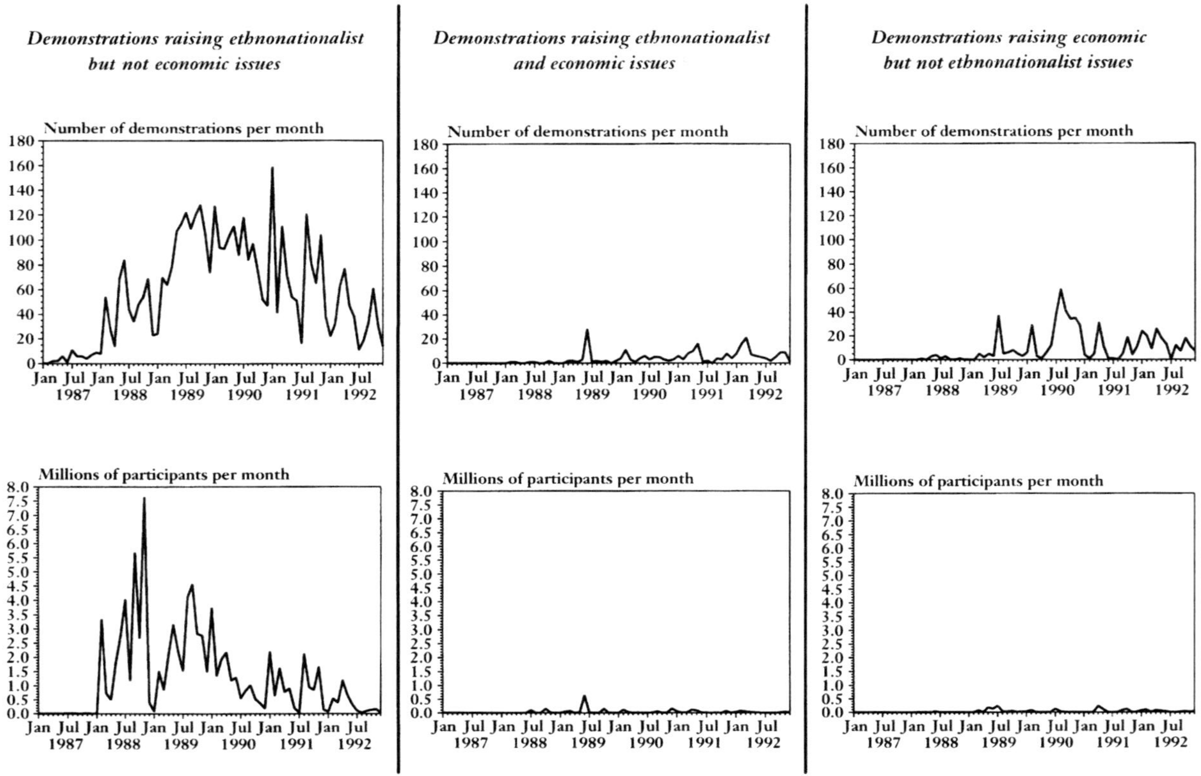

**Figure 2.3.** Ethnonationalist and economic streams of mobilization within the *glasnost'* mobilizational cycle, 1987–92.

– in spite of the marked decline in living standards that occurred during this period. Attempts to mobilize over economic issues were intermittent throughout this period, growing more regular in the second half of 1990 and in 1992 after the collapse of the Soviet state. This was a time of growing economic hardship, economic collapse, and "shock therapy." Nevertheless, demonstrations over economic issues did not gain much resonance within populations and exhibited relatively low mobilizational turnouts, particularly in comparison with demonstrations raising eth-nonationalist issues. With a few exceptions (Belorussia, Eastern Ukraine, Western Siberia, and Northern Kazakhstan) nationalism trumped class as the fundamental frame of mobilization in the USSR during this period – an issue I take up in more detail in Chapter 8.

What allows us, then, to talk about nationalist mobilization in the *glas-nost'* era not merely as a stream but as a full-fledged tide is the unusual force and attraction these issues exercised across multiple contexts and within the cycle as a whole. Clearly, a number of structural conditions characteristic of the Soviet state advantaged entrepreneurs of nationalism over other political entrepreneurs within the mobilizational cycle and even induced entrepreneurs of other causes to express issues within a nationalist frame. Several of these have already been mentioned: the fusion between state and regime; the historical legacy of ethnic grievance across multiple groups; the Soviet Union's ethnofederal state structure; and the Soviet state's overextension abroad. But these facilitating conditions were not the only factors that gave rise to a tide of nationalism. Institutional change and the impact of action on subsequent action exercised strong autonomous influences as well.

### The Diffusion and Normalization of Contention

As the above discussion implies, cycles and tides cannot be defined by a single moment. They emerge as a series of linked chains of events, as prior acts of contention come to influence subsequent acts. An easing of insti-tutional constraints was central to the process by which this initially came about in the USSR, though as contention developed and gained a momentum of its own, these constraints played a diminishing role in the production of events. As we have seen, it was hardly inevitable that the broadened challenges of 1987 and early 1988 would build into a larger mobilizational cycle. With the exception of the Armenian unrest, early mobilizations occurred on a relatively small scale, and the pace of contentious events, though greater than in the previous twenty years, was still relatively slow and manageable. Repressive actions like those used against demonstrators in the 1960s and 1970s were widely expected by most challenging groups in 1987 and 1988, although already by 1986, as Figure 2.1d shows, convictions for anti-Soviet political activity dropped sharply, and in 1987 practically disappeared altogether. Acts of contention gained a tidelike momentum only over the course of late 1988 and 1989 – when it became clear that politics had irretrievably passed into a more openly contentious phase, when the pace of events further "thickened" in time, and massive mobilizations emerged in multiple locations and began to feed off one another. Only then was it clear that contention could not easily be reversed, and politics had moved unambiguously into a phase of open and interrelated challenge.

Again, institutional contingencies – specifically, the intensifying conflict within the Soviet leadership over the pace and purposes of reform – were critical in bringing about this thickened pace of contention. As opposition groups began to test the boundaries of the permissible in late 1987 and early 1988, disputes within the Soviet leadership over the limits of liberalization moved more squarely into the open. Beginning with the October 1987 Central Committee Plenum, which legitimated unbridled discussion of Stalin's legacies, conflict sharpened within the Soviet leadership over the role of *glasnost'* in the media. We have already seen how the early phases of this intraleadership struggle helped to precipitate the massive mobilizations in Armenia in the first half of 1988. Conversely, the events in Armenia and Azerbaijan seemed to confirm the destabilizing possibilities presented by *glasnost'*, raised questions in the minds of Party conservatives about whether *glasnost'* was breeding nationalist revolt and interethnic conflict, and intensified conflict within the leadership over the limits of liberalization. On March 13, 1988, while Gorbachev was on a state visit to Yugoslavia, an article entitled "I Cannot Forsake My Principles" was published in the newspaper *Sovetskaia Rossiia* by Nina Andreeva, a Leningrad chemistry teacher. The article berated Gorbachev's democratization program for destabilizing Soviet society, hinting that camouflaged "cosmopolitan" tendencies (a codeword for Jews) and "left-liberal" intellectuals had captured the Communist Party.[62] Many within the intelligentsia took the article as a sign of the imminent reversal of *glasnost'*. The article, which had been heavily edited within the Central Committee appa-

---

[62] *Sovetskaia Rossiia*, March 13, 1988, p. 3.

ratus, was publicly praised by Central Committee Secretary Yegor Ligachev. At a Politburo meeting at the end of March called to discuss the controversy over the article, a number of Politburo members openly supported its spirit, and Gorbachev privately concluded that "a split was inevitable" within the Soviet leadership.[63] On April 5 *Pravda* published the response of Gorbachev and his aides, who called the article an "anti-*perestroika* manifesto."[64] Ligachev received a reprimand within the Politburo, and the conflict was temporarily papered over. But this open confrontation within the leadership over the limits of liberalization and the possibility of a reversal of *glasnost'* raised by these debates encouraged further migration of conflict from institutions to the streets.

The period before and immediately after the Nineteenth Party Conference of June 1988 marked a watershed in the diffusion of contentious politics in the Soviet Union. The inflated expectations emerging from the political reforms that were to be introduced at the conference, the sense that liberalization remained under serious threat from party conservatives, and the vulnerability of hard-liners in the wake of Ligachev's reprimand all encouraged heightened efforts to challenge the entrenched power of the party bureaucracy. The selection of delegates (which took place in May and June in all localities) to the conference and the efforts of local party bosses to control it (as they normally had in the past) evoked new social movement organizations – the "popular fronts in support of *perestroika*" – in disparate parts of the Soviet Union. These so-called "informal" groups emerged out of the local intelligentsia, many of whom had close connections with their local party organizations and who had grown politicized by the new possibilities for political discourse and action that had materialized over the previous year and a half. Initially, these "fronts" were primarily concerned with the process of delegate selection for the Nineteenth Party Conference. In some localities open nominations for delegates to the conference were allowed, but in most places they remained under the control of the local party apparatus, where opponents of Gorbachev were concentrated. This touched off waves of demonstrations in geographically dispersed locations throughout the Soviet Union in May and June 1988. Small-scale demonstrations took place in Moscow, Leningrad, Kiev, Sverdlovsk, Omsk, Odessa, Irkutsk, Yaroslavl', Krasnoiarsk, Magadan, Kuibyshev, and Tomsk complaining about local Party officials squelching

---

[63] Gorbachev, *Zhizn' i reformy*, vol. 1, pp. 381–90; Cherniaev, *Shest' let*, pp. 203–8, 211–13.
[64] *Pravda*, April 5, 1988, p. 2.

dissent and calling for a more far-reaching democratization of Soviet institutions. But in Estonia, Lithuania, and Latvia (with smaller echoes in Western Ukraine and Moldavia),[65] the creation of popular fronts to protest the delegate selection process quickly flowed over into large-scale separatist manifestations. In Chapter 4 I examine in detail the rise of Baltic separatism in summer and fall 1988 when I discuss the mobilization of identity more specifically; as we will see, the sense of opportunity created by the delegate selection process and the atmosphere following the party conference were critical in the mobilization of Baltic nationalisms.

The Nineteenth Party Conference itself, with its freewheeling debate and its introduction of radical political reforms, was, as Gorbachev later put it, "the real turning point after which *perestroika* took on an irreversible character."[66] It was here that Gorbachev introduced the notion of the "law-based state" (*pravovoe gosudarstvo*), with the goal of holding all officials, from the top to the bottom, subordinate to the law. All party secretaries were to be elected rather than appointed; moreover, they would simultaneously hold the position of chair of their local Soviets, and were they to fail to be elected to their local Soviet, they would be forced to resign their party posts as well. These altered relations of power were to be mirrored at the very top of the Soviet polity, as a new legislature, the Congress of People's Deputies, would be elected partially on a competitive basis. The Central Committee apparatus – the instrument through which successive Soviet leaders exercised their far-flung control over society – was reorganized away from its hierarchical branch departments into a series of six commissions, a reform intended to transform the party bureaucracy from enforcer to consensus builder. "Command-administrative" methods were supposed to be replaced by so-called "political" methods. Ironically, the conference proceedings were dominated by conservative forces, who ruthlessly criticized the press for the "excesses" of *glasnost'*. But the four-day conference considerably widened the parameters of debate by publicly airing the intense conflicts then consuming the country's political elite. Calls for the removal of several old guard members of the Politburo (including President Andrei Gromyko) for their roles in the era of stag-

[65] On the birth of Rukh in L'vov at the time and its connection with the Nineteenth Party Conference, see *Arkhiv samizdata*, no. 37, July 29, 1988 (AS No. 6363), pp. 1–2. On the birth of "The Democratic Movement in Support of *Perestroika*" in Kishinev in summer 1988 as "an expression of frustration with the obstruction of *perestroika* by the republic's bureaucracy," see *Report on the USSR*, vol. 1, no. 8 (February 24, 1989), pp. 30–35.
[66] Gorbachev, *Zhizn' i reformy*, vol. 1, p. 364.

nation mingled with sharp critiques of Stalinism and Brezhnevism, open accusations of bribe taking on the part of several delegates, and a direct confrontation between Ligachev and Yeltsin (then fallen from the party's heights, and already a symbol of resistance to the apparatus). In all these respects, the party conference represented the unambiguous passage to a situation of open political competition, emboldening political expression in ways previously unimaginable. As one activist later reminisced about the atmosphere it created among leaders of the new "informal" organizations, "the situation seemed to favour the most radical undertakings," even reinforcing a sense of confidence "in a swift and easy success."[67]

In the aftermath of the Nineteenth Party Conference, attempts to challenge the Soviet regime proliferated with great rapidity, diffusing across multiple groups and imparting a true tidal character to events. Figure 2.4 provides a temporal analysis of the development of protest among ten nationalities active during the early years of *glasnost'*, placing these activities in the context of some of the major institutional changes associated with the period. As the figure makes clear, in the early years of *glasnost'* shifts in the institutional context of the state were critical in shaping the contours of mobilization. The intermittent and scattered mobilizations of 1987 gave way to an incipient thickening across multiple groups in the first half of 1988. But it is also clear that May/June 1988 constituted a tipping point for the evolution of protest activity among a number of nationalities, specifically the Balts, Georgians, Moldavians, Azerbaijanis, Ukrainians, and Russians. Thus, in response to the opening provided by the Nineteenth Party Conference, protest activity thickened simultaneously among multiple groups.

Beginning at this time challenging groups engaged in a widespread sharing of information, pamphlets, expertise, modes of challenge, and mobilizational frames. By June 1988 representatives of Ukrainian, Armenian, Georgian, Latvian, Lithuanian, and Estonian dissident nationalist movements had initiated contact and established a coordinating committee among themselves.[68] In the summer and fall of 1988 popular fronts along the Baltic model sprang up throughout most of the Soviet Union. In August 1988 representatives of newly formed popular fronts from around

---

[67] Boris Kagarlitsky, *Farewell Perestroika: A Soviet Chronicle* (London: Verso, 1990), pp. 7–8.

[68] *Vesti iz SSSR*, 12–53, 1988; Bohdan Nahaylo, "Representatives of Non-Russian National Movements Establish Coordinating Committee," *Radio Liberty Research Bulletin*, RL 283/88, June 22, 1988.

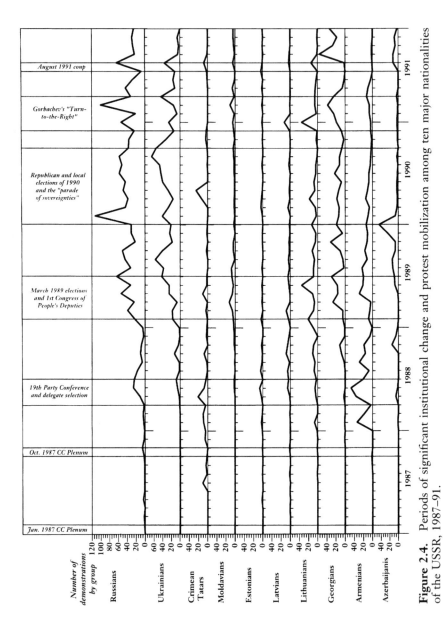

**Figure 2.4.** Periods of significant institutional change and protest mobilization among ten major nationalities of the USSR, 1987–91.

84

the Soviet Union met in Yalta and Leningrad to explore possibilities for cooperation.[69] These groups frequently borrowed their tactics of contestation directly from the successful example of the Balts, relying primarily on the demonstration as a means for mobilizing opinion and disrupting normalized politics. They drew heavily on the programmatic documents of the Baltic fronts, incorporating the anti-imperial paradigm pioneered by the Balts into their own programs, along with specific demands and goals. As one Estonian activist noted in September 1988, interest in the front was "so great that representatives of democratic people's movements from Riga to Novosibirsk have come to us to learn from our experience."[70] Even before the founding congress of the Popular Front of Estonia, the organization had hosted "foreign" delegations from Uzbekistan, Armenia, Moldavia, Leningrad, and Moscow. At the front's founding congress, representatives of emerging social movements from Moldavia, Ukraine, Uzbekistan, Belorussia, Armenia, and Russia were in attendance.[71] By January 1989 nationalist programs and leaflets began to appear in Azerbaijan, copied directly from documents of the Estonian Popular Front, which had themselves been obtained in Armenia.[72] As Algirdas Brazauskas, then First Secretary of the Lithuanian Communist Party, later recalled, in 1989 he frequently confronted complaints from Moscow asking: "What are you doing? Do you want to destroy the Soviet Union? Your Sajudis people are traveling all over – Moldavia, Armenia, Georgia, etc."[73] Nationalism assumed concrete tidal form in the ways in which nationalist paradigms were consciously exported and borrowed transnationally, organizational resources were shared, and challenging groups sought inspiration from the actions of one another. The nationalist revolutions of the USSR were not isolated occurrences, but rather transnational phenomena, gaining force and sustenance from one another's activities.

But Figure 2.4 makes clear that this interactive, transnational tide of nationalist mobilization only began to swell into a torrent of protest over the course of 1989, as a second set of tipping points occurred that caused challenges to the regime to proliferate with great rapidity in diverse parts

[69] *Vesti iz SSSR*, 16–15, 1988.
[70] Quoted in Nils R. Muiznieks, "The Influence of the Baltic Popular Movements on the Process of Soviet Disintegration," *Europe-Asia Studies*, vol. 47, no. 1 (1995), pp. 11–15.
[71] Muiznieks, "The Influence of the Baltic Popular Movements," p. 8.
[72] *Bakinskii rabochii*, January 15, 1989, p. 2.
[73] Algirdas Brazauskas, *Lietuviškos skyrybos* (Vilnius: Politika, 1992), pp. 55–56. I am grateful to Pranas Ciziunas for the translation from Lithuanian.

of the country. The immediate precipitants of these explosions were a series of institutional contingencies and defining events, all of which occurred within a highly compressed period of five months and all of which exercised a countrywide impact on the relationship between challengers and the regime: the campaigns for the March 1989 elections to the USSR Congress of People's Deputies; the Tbilisi massacres of April 1989; the first session of the new legislature in late May and early June; the spectacular miners' strikes of July 1989; and the outbreak of multiple waves of ethnic violence simultaneously in disparate parts of the country. These were institutional changes or events which fundamentally altered the ability of the regime to constrain and marginalize challenge; they represented the increasing autonomy of the event as causal factor in mobilization, the broadening of challenge, and a growing sense of the regime's instability.

The electoral campaigns of early 1989 – the first conducted on a semi-competitive basis in the USSR – became a lightning rod for oppositional mobilization, in part because of the often crude attempts by the party apparatus to control nominations and electoral outcomes, in part because the elections fostered the growth of electoral organization and rallies in support of specific candidates. In the end the Communist Party controlled the new legislature, but there were a number of humiliating defeats that further undermined communist authority. In the Baltic, for instance, Popular Front candidates won almost across the board. Moreover, in a number of major urban centers party apparatchiki failed to gain a sufficient number of votes for election even when running unopposed. The electoral losses suffered by the party generated considerable discontent within the party elite, some of whom preferred retirement to the fire of elections. Communist Party power seemed increasingly vulnerable and on the run.

A second development undermined much of the coercive capacity of the regime to control the streets: the April 9 Tbilisi massacres. I examine these events and their effects in detail in Chapter 7. As we will see, the political backlash from the misuse of force against protesters created a reticence on the part of the authorities to apply force and was a turning point in the ability of the Soviet state to defend itself forcefully from challenges on the streets.

Third, significant mobilizations were triggered in anticipation of and during the first sessions of the USSR Congress of People's Deputies – particularly in Moscow, but in disparate parts of the country as well. The proceedings of the legislative meetings, broadcast live to the country, transfixed the public for days on end and gave particular voice and effect to the regime's critics, who gained a new pulpit from which to spread their message. As Gorbachev's aide, Valery Boldin, related the mood of Polit-buro members during the sessions, "Most of them realized that a door had just been opened and that a motley crowd had burst through it."[74] The newly created Interregional Group of Deputies – combining independent opposition deputies from Russia, Ukraine, the Baltic, and Georgia – proved to be short-lived and was soon made obsolete by the republican elections of 1990. Nevertheless, it demonstrated the ways in which liberal Russian opposition leaders were cooperating with nationalist movements to advance their common interests within the altered institutional environment.

But it was really in the long, hot summer of 1989 that the Soviet regime for the first time appeared to be tottering on the edge. Large-scale demon-strations continued to rack the Baltic and the Transcaucasus, spreading to Ukraine and Moldavia. Indeed, in the wake of the events of the summer of 1989 at least one of Gorbachev's chief advisors came to the conclusion that the partial break-up of the Soviet state – specifically, the departure of the Baltic republics – had become "inevitable,"[75] an opinion increasingly widespread in Moscow over the ensuing months. Within Russia itself a major shift in popular attitudes toward the center was beginning to take shape as well. In July 1989 hundreds of thousands of coal miners in the Kuzbass region of Western Siberia and the Donbass region of Ukraine and Russia, incensed over shortages of soap and other necessities, went on strike, occupying town squares and demanding an improvement in living and working conditions and greater control over their workplaces. I explore the labor-economic stream of mobilization that emerged in summer 1989 in more detail in Chapter 8. Viewed within the larger context of the mobilizational cycle and nationalist tide, the significance of the coal miner strikes was not in the emergence of the strike as a major form of action. From January 1987 through June 1989 Soviet industry had already lost more than twenty-eight million person-days of work to strikes, the vast majority from general strikes over nationalist issues in Armenia, Azerbaijan, and Georgia and by Russians in the Baltic. Nor was the larger significance necessarily in the image of Prime Minister Nikolai Ryzhkov being forced to meet with the miners and to cave in to their demands. The strikes certainly contributed to perceptions of the growing weakness of the

---

[74] Valery Boldin, *Ten Years That Shook the World* (New York: Basic Books, 1994), p. 224.
[75] Cherniaev, *Shest' let*, p. 296.

regime, but their novelty lay in the heightened disaffection from the Soviet state among working class Russians and Russified Ukrainians represented by these events. The highly Russified coal miners of Ukraine should have been among the most ardent of defenders of the integrity of the Soviet state. Yet, in the end these same coal miners voted overwhelmingly to accept Ukrainian independence, largely out of alienation from Moscow's politics. Within Russia itself the rise of a working class opposition gave enormous force to the regime's opponents, who until then had almost entirely consisted of the intelligentsia in Moscow and Leningrad. For the first time the prospect of a base of mass support for the opposition seemed possible within Russian society – which encouraged Russian "democrats" to challenge the Kremlin's power more directly.

Finally, in the summer of 1989 multiple violent conflicts broke out in disparate parts of the Soviet Union. In June intense ethnic violence erupted between Uzbeks and Meskhetian Turks in the Fergana valley, between Kazakhs and Lezgins in the Kazakh oil town of Novyi Uzen', and between Georgians and Azerbaijanis in Georgia's Marneuli district. In July renewed violence in Karabakh between Armenians and Azerbaijanis moved toward more sustained forms of armed combat, Kirgiz and Tajiks fought over land and water rights in the Osh valley, and Abkhaz and Georgians battled each other with automatic weapons on the Black Sea coast as vacationers ran for cover. As I argue further in Chapter 6, sustained ethnic violence in the Soviet Union in 1989 and 1990 was in part triggered by the broader shifts in authority and nationalization of local governments that were occurring throughout the USSR at the time, primarily the result of previous waves of nonviolent mobilization. Thus, violent ethnic mobilization was "rear-packed" within the mobilizational cycle and rose in crescendo as the Soviet Union institutionally came undone. Before mid-1989 nationalist violence had largely been confined to Azerbaijan and Armenia. After the summer of 1989 nationalist violence had grown to the point that it had become a major political force – one which, as we will see, was not only expressive of identities, but very much shaped identities as well.

From mid-1989 to the collapse of the USSR, major protest demonstrations, strikes, and violent interethnic conflicts rocked the country on an almost daily basis. Surveys conducted in 1988 and 1989 by the All-Union Center for the Study of Public Opinion discovered that the level of alternative political activism in the country increased fivefold, whereas participation in Communist Party and official trade union meetings had halved.[76] If, in 1987, demonstrations and strikes were rare and daring endeavors, by 1989 and 1990 they had become an ordinary part of the Soviet political landscape. In Tbilisi on April 8, 1989, the day before the infamous massacres and in the wake of five days of massive demonstrations, tour leaders escorted groups of tourists to the central square of the city, where thousands of protestors were assembled, "since meetings had become a normal aspect of the life of the city."[77] As one journalist observed at the time, "rallies with strikes have become a way of life."[78] Of the massive rally in Moscow on March 28, 1991, in support of Boris Yeltsin and for removal of Gorbachev, in which up to three hundred thousand people participated, journalists reported that these types of events had grown so common that "the people in line outside the McDonald's restaurant, at the very epicenter of the events, stayed put throughout the demonstrations, waiting steadfastly for their hamburgers and Big Macs."[79] This banality of the previously marginal and deviant and its absorption into the fabric of everyday life were reflective of a world in the process of inversion.

Many populations remained untouched by these events. In addition to being structured temporally by institutional constraints and by the surging flow of events, tides of nationalism are also structured spatially, involving certain populations more than others. A number of surveys taken during these years indicated that a minority of the Soviet population as a whole (somewhere between eleven and fourteen percent) ever participated in protest activity. Most protest mobilization during these years was a phenomenon of large cities. Although only fifteen percent of the Soviet population lived in cities with a million inhabitants or more in 1989, forty-one percent of all demonstrations recorded for this study took place in cities with over a million in population, accounting for approximately sixty-nine percent of the total number of participants in demonstrations during these years. Certain territories and ethnic groups remained almost entirely unaffected by the upheavals that consumed the rest of the USSR. As we will see shortly, this variation tells us a great deal about the broader social forces structuring national identity and action. Yet, of the fifty largest

---

[76] Yu. A. Levada, *Est' mnenie! Itogi sotsiologicheskogo oprosa* (Moscow: Progress, 1990), p. 284.
[77] Anatolii Sobchak, *Tbilisskii izlom, ili Krovavoe voskresen'e 1989 goda* (Moscow: Sretenie, 1993), p. 106.
[78] *Rabochaia tribuna*, March 10, 1990, p. 1.
[79] Radio Maiak, in *FBIS*, March 29, 1991, p. 57.

ethnic groups within the Soviet Union, only seven experienced no significant protests during this period (defined here as a demonstration with a hundred or more participants), whereas twenty-six exhibited patterns of protest involving twenty or more significant demonstrations (each with a minimum of a hundred participants). In a number of republics during these years (Armenia, Azerbaijan, Estonia, Lithuania, Latvia, and Moldavia, in particular) acts of protest occurred (sometimes, on multiple occasions) in which more than a third (and in some cases, up to two-thirds) of all urban inhabitants of the republic between ages fifteen and sixty-nine (irrespective of nationality) participated.[80] Here, the crowd as simulated nation approached the actual dimensions of its claimed community.

Particular portions of these populations repeatedly mobilized over a period of several years. Sociologists surveying 446 participants in the February 25, 1990, electoral rally and demonstration in Moscow sponsored by the Moscow Association of Voters (in which up to two hundred fifty thousand people participated) discovered that more than half had participated in other demonstrations in the previous year. A similar survey taken in Moscow the following year, interviewing 891 participants in the March 28, 1991, rally sponsored by Democratic Russia (in which up to three hundred thousand participated) found that more than seventy percent had participated in prior demonstrations, and sixty-three percent had participated in three or more previous demonstrations.[81] Thus, by 1990 in many parts of the Soviet Union demonstration activity had grown regularized to the point that large numbers of people within particular segments of society repeatedly engaged in them. Demonstrations, at least within some microcontexts, had become a normal means for dealing with political conflict. In fact, a survey conducted in March 1991 among 16,857 inhabitants of twenty-four provinces and republics of the RSFSR found that 18.9 percent expressed "a preference" for demonstration activity over other forms of participation as a way of resolving difficult social or political problems.[82]

[80] Were age-specific data available by both nationality and city, they would undoubtedly show that in some localities the vast majority of potential participants did at one time participate in acts of protest.
[81] These unpublished survey results were provided by Yuri Levada and Aleksei Levinson of the All-Russian Center for the Study of Public Opinion.
[82] *Rezul'taty sotsiologicheskogo issledovaniia "Sotsial'no-aktivnye sily Rossii: Usloviia i puti ikh konsolidatsii"* (Moscow: Institut sotsial'nykh i politicheskikh tekhnologii, 1991), p. 72.

The emergence of these protest stalwarts, within a relatively compact time period in a country in which protest activity previously had been infrequent and routinely suppressed, is revealing of the tremendous alterations in consciousness wrought by shifting institutional constraints and events. Within a short period of time populations that previously did not contemplate protest came to embrace these forms of behavior as normal and even preferable under the influence of the example of others. As one author observed about the July 1989 coal strikes, "[b]efore this summer, many miners say, the word 'strike' was not even in their vocabulary."[83] Successful protest brought about further attraction to movements and became a force in altering identities. Boris Kagarlitsky pointed to the impact that a successful protest campaign by the Moscow Popular Front (MPF) in May 1989, at the time of the First USSR Congress of People's Deputies, had on the movement's following. "A large number of people poured into the ranks of the MPF, attracted by the effectiveness of our activity rather than by our ideology."[84] Even children came to imitate the contentious behavior of their parents. In Yerevan several hundred Armenian schoolchildren engaged in a mass burning of their Pioneer kerchiefs and Komsomol membership tickets.[85] In the small town of Tukums Latvian schoolchildren declared a strike in protest against obligatory military training for the Soviet army in their school.[86] In Minsk Belorussian schoolchildren, chanting *"Pe-re-stroi-ka!"* and *"De-mo-kra-ti-ia!,"* carried out a sit-in strike in the halls of their school, demanding that students be given a majority voice on the school council, that they have the right to elect their teachers, and that the school administration be dismissed.[87] In short, from 1989 to 1991 Soviet society experienced what Aristide Zolberg called a protracted "moment of madness,"[88] a time when the social order was turned upside-down, the normal boundaries of political life came undone, and loyalties and affections of individuals were up for grabs. Within a condensed and "thickened" period of history the once unconventional and seemingly impossible had become the ordinary.

---

[83] Lewis H. Siegelbaum, "Behind the Soviet Miners' Strike," *The Nation*, October 23, 1989, p. 451.
[84] Kagarlitsky, *Farewell Perestroika*, p. 140.
[85] *Ekspress khronika*, May 22, 1990.
[86] *Atmoda*, December 18, 1989, p. 7.
[87] *Sovetskaia Belorussiia*, January 22, 1989, p. 3.
[88] Aristide R. Zolberg, "Moments of Madness," *Politics and Society*, vol. 2 (1972), pp. 183–207.

## *The Mobilizational Effect on Institutions*

We have seen that institutional contingencies were key in the politics which gave birth to a mobilizational cycle and tide of nationalism in the USSR. But the tide in turn exercised a profound effect on political institutions. This capacity to alter the very conditions which had allowed it to come into being in the first place was a sign of the tide's growing autonomy and independent causal power.

The tide influenced institutions in multiple ways. One of the characteristic features of periods of "thickened" history is that the pace of events tends to outstrip the movement of institutions and the understanding of leaders (not to speak of outside observers). As Gorbachev described "the essence of the problem" at a special conference on the role of the Communist Party in society in July 1989, "Restructuring in the party is lagging substantially behind the processes taking place in society."[89] Gorbachev, of course, was in significant part responsible for this situation. Yegor Ligachev, among others, noted that "Being late, or reacting too slowly to events, was one of the most characteristic traits of Gorbachev's policies. There were numerous examples, ranging from Nagorno-Karabakh and Lithuania to price reform and economic and financial measures to overtake the crisis. . . . Being too late with concrete practical actions has, in fact, become something of a symbol of perestroika."[90] But it was not simply Gorbachev who proved incapable of comprehending the pace at which change was occurring. Events simply moved far faster than institutions were capable of reacting. Valery Boldin, one of Gorbachev's advisors, later observed: "It became common to hear proposals for measures that would have been meaningful some three or five years earlier."[91] As Gorbachev's press secretary Gennady Gerasimov noted, Gorbachev and his government were so busy that they had little time to rethink the assumptions of their policies in light of altered circumstances.[92]

Certainly, this was true in many policy areas, but, in view of the tide of nationalism and the changes that it wrought, it was most glaringly evident with regard to nationalities issues. Gorbachev and his team of reformers originally envisaged that the issue of center-periphery relations would be

[89] *Pravda*, July 19, 1989, p. 1.    [90] Ligachev, *Inside Gorbachev's Kremlin*, p. 128.

[91] Boldin, *Ten Years That Shook the World*, p. 147.

[92] See Jerry Hough, *Democratization and Revolution in the USSR, 1985–1991* (Washington, DC: Brookings Institution Press, 1997), p. 206.

handled in a second stage of *perestroika*, after the reform of central political institutions.[93] But issues of nationalism quite literally pushed themselves onto the political agenda. In July 1988, when massive nationalist mobilizations encompassed only Armenia and Estonia and secession was not within the realm of the imaginable among most opposition activists, Gorbachev called for the preparation of proposals that would restrict the powers of central institutions over the union republics. A Central Committee Plenum was scheduled for June 1989 for that purpose.[94] But by the time preparations for the meeting had begun, the politics of the street had pushed developments well beyond what anyone could have imagined only a short while before. The meeting had to be postponed several times, and by the time it was held in September 1989, massive secessionist mobilizations had already encompassed the Baltic, Georgia, and Western Ukraine and were beginning to grow widespread in Armenia, Azerbaijan, and Moldova. By this time, the idea of a "renewed" federalism according to the formula "a strong center and strong republics" embraced at the meeting was largely irrelevant and even inflammatory to the rapidly changing situation on the ground. At the end of 1989 Gorbachev continued to cling to the illusion that republican *khozrashchet* (territorial self-accounting, or economic decentralization to the republican level) would somehow satisfy the Balts, even though this demand, which had been put forth by the Balts in 1987 largely as a way of testing the boundaries of the possible, was no longer even on their radar screen by spring 1989.[95] As Eduard Shevardnadze told a Politburo meeting in July 1989:

If we had talked about a transformation [of the federation] two years ago, then this might have been interesting. But by now it is already banal. Some of the boundaries that are trying to be set here are already not boundaries. Psychologically this has the opposite effect. Ordinary things are being posed as if they are innovations, discoveries. This is particularly true with regard to the rights of the republics.[96]

In short, the work of institutions was simply outpaced by the speed and flow of events.

This was evident to Gorbachev as well. In March 1990, after the revolutions in East Europe, the withdrawal of the Lithuanian Communist Party from the CPSU, the declaration of the Second Congress of People's Deputies that the secret protocol of the Molotov-Ribbentrop Pact was

---

[93] Medvedev, *V komande Gorbacheva*, p. 83.
[94] Gorbachev, *Zhizn' i reformy*, vol. 1, p. 399; Cherniaev, *Shest' let*, p. 242.
[95] *Soiuz mozhno bylo*, pp. 68, 75.  [96] *Soiuz mozhno bylo*, p. 62.

invalid, and elections in the Baltic republics that brought secessionist movements to power, Gorbachev publicly recognized that his plan for renewing the federation outlined in September 1989 had already grown "outdated."[97] He dropped the "strong center and strong republics" formula in favor of the idea of an extremely decentralized federalism and of renegotiating the union treaty that had created the USSR in 1922. By this time, however, a number of republics had evolved to the position of favoring a confederal arrangement only, whereas others refused to accept even that, insisting on nothing less than full independence. As Prime Minister Ryzhkov noted, by the end of 1990 "no one needed the Center in any form."[98] Once again, events had outstripped the capacity of institutions to respond.

By the end of 1990 Gorbachev appeared exhausted and increasingly out of touch with the political realities surrounding him. He consistently refused to believe in the seriousness of Baltic demands for independence, maintaining that economically the Balts could not survive independence from the Soviet Union. Even in 1990, after the Lithuanian government declared its independence, he preferred to interpret this mainly as a "symbolic" gesture, believing that the Balts would eventually accept some "special status" within a renewed USSR simply because "they will perish economically if they leave."[99] As he told Helmut Kohl in November 1990:

The nationalists are now feeling that their power is receding. In Lithuania, they have already understood that Landsbergis' line is leading to a dead-end. All the heads of government of the three Baltic republics are sitting either in the USSR Council of Ministers under Ryzhkov or in Gosplan under Masliukov, and they are working toward receiving everything that they need for the economies of their republics for the year 1992. It's fine to engage in demonstrations, of course, but somehow one has to live nevertheless![100]

Similarly, concerning Ukrainian nationalism, Gorbachev believed that "internationalist loyalties are strong among the people," so that separatist demands would go unheeded within the Ukrainian population at large. As

---

[97] *Soiuz mozhno bylo*, p. 95.

[98] Ryzhkov, *Perestroika: Istoriia predatel'stv*, p. 19. See Gail Lapidus, "Gorbachev and the 'National Question': Restructuring the Soviet Federation," *Soviet Economy*, valso ol. 5, no. 3 (1989), pp. 201–50.

[99] Cherniaev, *Shest' let*, pp. 246–51; Gorbachev, *Zhizn' i reformy*, vol. 1, pp. 511, 524–25.

[100] Cherniaev, *Shest' let*, pp. 386–87. As Cherniaev notes, Gorbachev "manufactured soothing conclusions for himself out of real facts" – part of the increasing lack of reality that could be observed in his behavior by 1990–91.

he later admitted, he seriously underestimated the potential that separatist ideas might spread under the combined influence of persistent opposition, alienation from the center, and the example of others.[101] At a Politburo meeting in February 1989, for instance, Gorbachev laid out to his colleagues all the structural reasons why Ukraine and Belorussia were qualitatively different from the non-Slavic republics and were unlikely to succumb to separatist sentiments:

> Here everything is very closely bound up with Russia. Millions of Ukrainians and Belorussians live and work outside their republics. And not only are they recognized within their own republic, but they occupy visible, authoritative positions in society, in production, in administrative and Party organs, and in the cultural sphere. These are large peoples. And given their historically rooted similarity with Russians and the closeness of their languages . . . , it is often difficult to determine who is Russian, Ukrainian, or Belorussian. . . . The Belorussians and Ukrainians themselves do not want their children to attend native-language schools, especially in the big cities.[102]

With hindsight it is easy to fault Gorbachev for the collapse of the USSR and for the many decisions that were or were not made that might have changed the eventual outcome. Dozens of works, both in Russia and abroad, have produced such analyses. Many of these arguments underestimate the tidal force that nationalism had become by 1989–90 and the difficulties of moving institutions with the same speed as events on the ground, especially when institutions themselves were in the midst of being remade and were at the center of contention. Given the emergence of the tide, it is not at all clear that a different leader would have been able to ride events successfully and redirect them toward a viable institutional outcome. Institutional change evoked a tide of nationalism into being; but institutions were quickly outstripped by the dizzying pace of events. Gorbachev's policies often evoked sharp criticism from conservatives within the party, but, as Vadim Medvedev has pointed out, in practically every case the Central Committee voted unanimously in the end to support the Gorbachev line.[103] Had Gorbachev stepped down in April 1989 (when it was first suggested by some of his critics) and another leader come to power, efforts to roll back *glasnost'* would have been likely. But it is not at all obvious that these would have been successful in containing the cross-national tide of revolt, and Gorbachev's removal also would have

[101] Gorbachev, *Zhizn' i reformy*, vol. 1, p. 514.    [102] *Soiuz mozhno bylo*, p. 47.
[103] Medvedev, *V komande Gorbacheva*, pp. 96–97.

precipitated a great deal of protest activity. As we will see in Chapter 7, by mid-1989 efforts at violent crackdown produced their own dysfunctions, furthering the breakdown of central institutions and pushing the process of disintegration forward. The emerging tide of nationalism in the USSR probably could have been cut short by repression in late 1988 and early 1989 before the Tbilisi events and before mass contention had spread widely. But the window of opportunity for successful repression of the tide was much narrower than most analysts make it out to have been – probably a matter of months. Moreover, prior to fall 1988 the dangers posed by the tide to the survival of the Soviet state were not yet fully apparent. Separatist nationalism only came to be recognized by central elites as a danger to the survival of the country by late 1988 and early 1989, but soon afterward the fallout from the Tbilisi massacres, the growing geographic spread of separatist revolt, and the rise of multiple violent conflicts made a forceful response much more problematic.

Alternatively, as some (including one of Gorbachev's chief aides, Anatolii Cherniaev) have suggested, the tide of nationalism could have been cut short through a strategy of cooptation: by allowing the Balts to leave the USSR at an earlier stage in mid-1989, when secessionist consciousness had not yet crystallized elsewhere, and by making clear and enforcing the distinction between the Molotov-Ribbentrop lands incorporated in 1939–40 and the other territories of the Soviet state. But as Cherniaev observed, Gorbachev could not bring himself to the point of letting the Balts go, since he feared the impact this would have on Russians living in the Baltic, the backlash it would cause among Russians within Russia, and especially the encouragement it would give to secessionist challenges elsewhere.[104] Navigating the Soviet state through a tide of nationalism was a ticklish business. Within the shifting political terrain of the tide, actions aimed at cutting short challenges could easily have the opposite effect if carried out in the wrong temporal context or manner, and consciousness of the dangers posed by nationalism was itself a variable. In this respect, assertions by Gorbachev's critics about what should have been done to prevent the Soviet collapse can only be fairly evaluated

---

[104] Cherniaev, *Shest' let*, pp. 325, 339, 374. Writing in 1989, I made a similar argument. See Mark Beissinger and Lubomyr Hajda, "Nationalism and Reform in Soviet Politics," in Lubomyr Hajda and Mark Beissinger, eds., *The Nationalities Factor in Soviet Politics and Society* (Boulder, CO: Westview Press, 1990), p. 320.

by taking into account the tidal context of the times – specifically, how institutions themselves were altered by the rising upsurge of contention and how institutional consciousness and behavior lagged behind the constant onslaught of events.

The tide produced enormous confusion and division within Soviet institutions, making it even more difficult to find institutional solutions to the challenge of holding the Soviet state together. This was true not only of the police and the armed forces, which, as we will see in Chapter 7, were overwhelmed and demoralized by the upsurge of disorder, but even more of the party and state bureaucracies. With the initiation of *glasnost'* the party leadership had grown factionalized into "left" and "right" groupings – in the usage of the times, the former seeking to push liberalization at a faster pace, the latter concerned with the destabilizing effects of liberalization and/or favoring a Russian nationalist agenda. As the country's future began to be called into question in 1989, these factions grew more pronounced, with centrists such as Prime Minister Ryzhkov increasingly leaning toward Gorbachev's critics. Rumors of plots to overthrow Gorbachev circulated widely. All this made it much more difficult to fashion a coherent response to the tide.

The tide created enormous division within Soviet institutions precisely because the boundary between state and society was porous, and the lines of battle frequently crossed the state-society divide. What often allowed challenges on the street to intensify in the first place was the fact that sympathizers of the crowd existed within state institutions. The conflict between Azerbaijanis and Armenians over Karabakh, for example, was not a straightforward confrontation between oppositions and the apparatus. Rather, in both republies unofficial movements received support within party and state institutions. In January 1989 in Azerbaijan, participants in nightly illegal demonstrations in Baku were given food, blankets, and tents from local warehouses (as well as hundreds of thousands of rubles) by officials of state and cooperative enterprises. According to the First Secretary of the Communist Party of Azerbaijan, certain state officials and offices "turned out themselves to be organizers of disorders."[105] In Tbilisi in April 1989 information from closed government and party meetings about how the party leadership intended to break up demonstrations quickly made its way onto the square due to the presence of "traitors" among government

---

[105] *Bakinskii rabochii*, January 15, 1989, p. 1.

officials. As the detailed investigation into these events later revealed, "judging from everything, informers and sympathizers of the demonstrators were plentiful within the Party Central Committee and the Georgian government."[106] In spite of the initial hostile attitude of local party leaderships to them, popular front organizations in each of the Baltic republics received critical support from officials within their respective republican party apparatuses, some of whom subsequently became leaders of these organizations. A. P. Klautsen, first secretary of Riga City Party Committee, noted in July 1988, in the midst of the first major waves of protest in the republic, that the Latvian Communist Party seemed to have "gone underground," led by mass movements rather than leading them and paralyzed by deep splits within its ranks along national and ideological lines.[107]

The pull of alternative movements was particularly strong within the Communist Party rank and file. Party members constituted only eleven percent of the adult population of the USSR during these years, but they supplied a disproportionate number of the activists for nationalist movements. In Estonia, almost half of the 106 members of the leadership of the Estonian Popular Front were Communist Party members. In Latvia, thirty percent of the participants in the founding congress of the Latvian Popular Front were communists, whereas over half of the delegates to the founding conference of Interfront, the movement organized in 1989 to protect the rights of non-Latvians in Latvia, were Communist Party members. At the founding congress of the Ukrainian popular front Rukh in September 1989, 228 (twenty-one percent) out of the 1,109 delegates were communists, and of the 10 members of the ruling secretariat of Rukh elected at the congress, 4 were members of the Communist Party. Similarly, a third of the 35 members of the original organizing committee for the Belorussian Popular Front that formed in October 1988 were communists.[108] A survey of participants in the huge February 25, 1990 demonstration in Moscow discovered that twenty-two percent of those demonstrating so vociferously against the political monopoly of the Communist Party on that day were actually members of the Communist Party.[109] As one poster

[106] Sobchak, *Tbilisskii izlom*, pp. 105–6, 127, 133.
[107] *Sovetskaia Latviia*, January 8, 1989, p. 2.
[108] These figures come from: *Sovetskaia Estoniia*, January 14, 1989, p. 3; *FBIS*, October 14, 1988, p. 49; *Sovetskaia Latviia*, January 26, 1989, p. 1; *Golos*, no. 4, September 17, 1989, p. 2; *Tartuskii kur'er*, October 15–31, 1989, p. 7; *Atmoda*, October 16, 1989, p. 6; *Golos*, no. 5, October 1, 1989, p. 2; *Belorusskaia tribuna*, no. 3, 1989, p. 1.
[109] *Demokraticheskaia platforma*, June 1990, p. 1.

at a mass meeting farcically proclaimed: "Long live the CPSU – the forge of leaders of all opposition movements!"[110]

Obviously, Gorbachev's reforms within the party – his conclusion by February 1988 (well before the tide had gotten under way) that the party was no longer capable of leading *perestroika* to its conclusion,[111] his introduction in July 1988 of competitive elections within the party, his emasculation of the party apparatus in September 1988, and his introduction of a new presidency within the USSR government in late 1989 as a counterweight to the party apparatus – created a great deal of institutional confusion and upheaval and encouraged challenges from and defections to the street. This was not simply the self-interested appropriation of the resources of the state by bureaucrats. Rather, the pull of the street and of nationalist passions in multiple contexts proved greater than the institutional coherence of weakened hierarchy. As we saw earlier, the introduction of competitive elections within state and party organizations in 1989 and 1990 particularly accelerated mobilizational processes in many parts of the country, further undermining party discipline or leading to the isolation of the party from an increasingly active society. In Ukraine, for instance, some local party officials threatened to resign rather than run in competitive elections, where they were likely to face defeat. For others, electoral competition inevitably focused their attention on demands from below rather than on the discipline emanating from party superiors. As the first secretary of Kiev *obkom* complained, "Some communists who are candidates for deputies have fought for great popularity without regard for the Party's charter, Party discipline, or Party ethics . . . [T]o be a member of the Party and simultaneously to pour dirt upon it is, from any point of view, amoral, unprincipled, and, to put it politely, dishonorable."[112] By early 1990 the Lithuanian and Estonian Communist parties had split from the CPSU. The Latvian Communist Party remained Latvian in name only after the departure of nearly all its Latvian members to found an alternative party. In spite of Gorbachev's initial opposition to the idea, pressure for the federalization of the party mounted in the spring and summer of 1990 in response to the transformed institutional situation in republics and localities. New rules adopted at the Twenty-Eighth Party Congress in July 1990 bestowed "autonomous" status on the communist parties of the republics; at the same time, they transformed the party's leadership organs

---

[110] *Rossiiskaia gazeta*, July 25, 1991, p. 2.    [111] Gorbachev, *Zhizn' i reformy*, vol. 1, pp. 413–14.
[112] *Pravda Ukrainy*, May 18, 1989, p. 3.

into territorially representative bodies by making republican party first secretaries ex officio members of the Politburo.

Much of the goal of mobilization was to exercise this type of effect on institutions and their leaderships: to alter longstanding patterns of institutional behavior, to force institutions to function in ways conducive to the aims of alternative movements, and ultimately to appropriate their authority and power. Local party organizations were pulled between the Scylla of keeping their ranks aloof from the influences of the street, thus isolating them from the societies over which they ruled, and the Charybdis of attempting to influence alternative movements through their presence within them but in the process potentially being captured by them. The cross pressures that buffeted the Communist Party as a result of the pull of the street were well summed up by the First Secretary of the Latvian Communist Party in August 1989:

Some advocate "recalling communists from the fronts," failing to understand that by doing so the Party is deprived of the possibility of . . . working broadly with the popular masses. Others believe that the only "pure communists" are those who function within the front and themselves sympathize with it. In essence, they are leading to the dissolution of the Party as a mass political organization.[113]

In a number of cases successful nationalist mobilization led to rapid cooptation of local Communist Party leaderships. Algirdas Brazauskas, First Secretary of the Lithuanian Communist Party, exemplified such an outcome, observing at the September 1989 Central Committee Plenum that "the only way to gain the masses' trust is by becoming deeply imbued with the people's aspirations and interests and by taking radical and resolute political steps. So the familiar slogan 'The party's plans are the people's plans!' now sounds different: 'The people's plans are the party's plans!'"[114] In some instances the party suffered a near-total institutional collapse as a result of the rise of street politics – as happened, for instance, to the Georgian Communist Party in the aftermath of the April 1989 massacres.

As one government official put it, by 1990 in many localities "'meeting' law ha[d] substituted for 'telephone' law."[115] An anecdote reported in the press, of an incident in the city of Volgograd at the height of the republi-

---

[113] *Sovetskaia Latviia*, August 11, 1989, p. 2.    [114] *FBIS*, September 22, 1989, p. 45.
[115] *Pravitel'stvennyi vestnik*, no. 29 (July 1990), p. 12. "Telephone" law was the phrase widely used at the time to describe how the Party apparatus traditionally manipulated legal institutions from behind the scenes.

can and local electoral campaigns, well captures the contested and uncertain lines of authority emerging in Russian cities at the time:

On Monday morning a man approaching middle-age entered the provincial Soviet executive committee building. He looked around and asked the first person he met, "Comrade, where is your chair's office?" "On the third floor. What's your problem?" "I don't have a problem," the man answered, "I've come to work. At the demonstration yesterday I was elected chair of the provincial Soviet executive committee."[116]

For the Soviet leadership, the power of the crowd and the fear that it could instill, already well known to them vicariously from their knowledge of events at the time, was further impressed on them through firsthand experience during the infamous "second wave" of the May Day demonstration of 1990, when a group of twenty-five thousand alternative protesters, chanting slogans of "Down with Gorbachev!," "Down with the Communist Party!," "Down with Socialism and the Fascist Red Empire!," and "Freedom for Lithuania!," subjected them to a barrage of abuse while they were still standing atop the Lenin Mausoleum.[117] In response, Gorbachev's position hardened against cooperation with liberal insurgents within the party, and the Soviet leadership engaged in concrete measures to protect itself from what some within the party hierarchy referred to as "the moral terror" of the crowd.[118] Ironically, a little over a year later in August 1991, much of this same crowd – massed around the Russian White House – would save Gorbachev from these same colleagues when they placed him under house arrest and threatened his life in their aborted attempt to rescue the Soviet state from imminent dismemberment. These were indeed extraordinary times in which normal hierarchies of power were overturned or inverted.

## Summary and Conclusion

We have seen in this chapter through the Soviet example that nationalism is a phenomenon that is highly structured over time. The vicissitudes of order, and the opportunities to contest that accompanied them, produce

[116] *Pravda*, February 17, 1990, p. 3.
[117] Cherniaev, *Shest' let*, p. 344; Vremia, in *FBIS*, May 7, 1990, p. 54.
[118] The phrase comes from a letter written by twenty-nine deputies of the RSFSR Supreme Soviet in March 1991 asking Gorbachev for protection from demonstrators during their attempts to unseat Boris Yeltsin as chair of the body. V. Stepankov, E. Lisov, *Kremlevskii zagovor* (Moscow: Ogonek, 1992), pp. 75, 189.

differing rhythms of nationalist politics – the marginalization of challengers in "quiet" periods of contention and the explosion of contention in "noisy" phases. A number of structural preconditions made the USSR vulnerable to an explosion of nationalism across multiple groups: the institutional and ideological crises of the Soviet state, the fusion of state and regime, the submerged sense of ethnic grievance across multiple groups, and its overreach abroad. But even in the presence of these conditions, the disintegration of the USSR seemed unimaginable and impossible to the overwhelming majority of Soviet citizens. Only under the combined influence of pre-existing structural conditions, institutional change, and massive waves of challenging action did the impossible come to be widely regarded as the inevitable.

As we will see in subsequent chapters, even at the height of mobilizational fervor, some level of influence by institutions on nationalist action remained – at times subtly expressed, as for instance, in the ways in which institutional change influenced the timing and frequency of challenge. In this "noisy" phase of nationalism, as institutions came under stress and lost much of their capacity to constrain, nationalist challenges multiplied and events came to take on a greater causal role of their own – through the influence they exerted over institutions and public beliefs, through the power of emulation unleashed by successful challenge, and through the ability of events to act recursively as part of their own causal structure. Contentious acts gained a tidelike momentum when the pace of events "thickened" and nationalist mobilizations emerged in multiple locations and began to feed off one another. Moreover, challengers consciously sought to foster this tidal quality of nationalism in an effort to spread contention laterally and solidify the legitimacy of their claims through the power of numbers.

We have seen that nationalism is structured over time by the interaction between order and event, but we have also seen some initial evidence that nationalism is structured spatially across groups as well. Not all groups responded alike to the shifts in political order and tidal forces of contentious events precipitated by *glasnost'*; some never engaged in action, and even within groups that did mobilize some segments of the population responded to a greater extent than others. In the next chapter, I explore more concretely the ways in which the tide of nationalism was systematically structured through a complex interaction between pre-existing structural conditions, institutional constraints, and events themselves.

ˣ *Note jumay*

# 3

*Structuring Nationalism*

Human development is a form of chronological unfairness, since latecomers are able to profit by the labors of their predecessors without paying the same price.

Alexander Herzen[1]

Causation necessarily is a complex subject. Any attempt to reduce it either to structural determinism or the complete autonomy of action fails to address seriously the fundamental paradox long ago identified by Marx: that human beings are interactive, communicative animals and therefore conscious creators of their destinies, but that the circumstances in which this occurs are given in part by the past and shape the ways in which we go about doing so.

In the previous chapter we saw initial evidence that three levels of causation operated within nationalism during the *glasnost'* period: pre-existing structural conditions, institutional constraints, and events. The first was most visible in the ways in which nationalism dominated the mobilizational cycle and was structured spatially, as nationalist mobilization encompassed some groups and segments of populations more than others. The second was apparent in the temporal structuring of nationalism, as the opening and closing of institutions altered the politics by which nationalism played itself out and led to a clustering of challenging actions at particular moments in time. The third functioned as both dependent and independent variable, as events became a greater element of their own causal structure within a context of "thickened" history.

---

[1] Quoted in Isaiah Berlin, "Introduction" to Franco Venturi, *Roots of Revolution: A History of the Populist and Socialist Movements in Nineteenth Century Russia* (New York: Alfred A. Knopf, 1960), p. xx.

In this chapter, I explore these three levels of causation and their inter-action more systematically, providing further evidence of their presence, strength, and interrelationship through the ways in which they left their traces on the patterning of nationalist action. In particular, I investigate the reflection of pre-existing structural conditions, institutional con-straints, and events on four fundamental dimensions of nationalist action: who, when, how frequently, and with what resonance.[2] By the time the analysis is concluded, I will also have identified an array of causal factors at work within each category, developed quantitative models explaining variation over time and space in levels of elite and mass nationalist mobi-lization, and identified the changing character of causal relationships over time and the logic underlying these changes. The road to these ends nec-essarily takes us first through separate discussions of the temporal and spatial dimensions of nationalist mobilization – bracketing, in the fashion of Giddens, the influence of one in order to isolate patterns within the other. Eventually this path leads us back toward more realistic explorations of the materialization of nationalism in space-time.

## Nationalism in Time

I begin with a general discussion of the evolution of nationalism in the *glasnost'* era and some of the factors associated with temporal variations in nationalist mobilization. The basis for this discussion is provided in Figure 3.1, which presents pictures of demonstration activity during *glasnost'* and the place of ethnonationalist issues within it based on an analysis of 6,644 protest demonstrations from January 1987 through December 1992. If we understand the number of demonstrations as signifying attempts by nationalist movements to mobilize a target population and participation in demonstrations as reflecting the resonance of those attempts, then Figures 3.1a and 3.1b provide measures of the evolving behavior of move-ment activists across the *glasnost'* period, whereas Figures 3.1c and 3.1d give us portraits of the shifting support for those efforts within target populations.

As Figure 3.1 shows, within the Soviet Union as a whole attempts to mobilize target populations increased steadily throughout 1988 and 1989, rising precipitously to a peak by the first half of 1990. It also confirms

[2] Three other critical questions about nationalist action are addressed elsewhere in the book: over what issues, in what manner, and with what result.

104

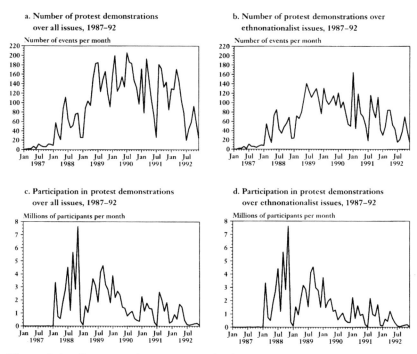

**Figure 3.1.** Demonstration activity in the former Soviet Union, 1987–92.

much of the findings of Chapter 2, showing that throughout this period sudden increases in the number of ethnonationalist demonstrations were temporally connected with larger institutional developments taking place within the state: in the summer of 1988 – the Nineteenth Party Conference; in October-November 1988 – debates over impending reforms to the USSR Constitution (which sparked significant protest campaigns for greater autonomy in the Baltic and Georgia); in spring 1989, with the elections to the USSR Congress of People's Deputies and the opening sessions of the new legislature; in the first half of 1990, with republican and local elections; in the early months of 1991, with the abortive attempts to crack down on challenges to the regime; and in August 1991, with the failed attempt by the State Emergency Committee to seize power. Viewed over time specific state actions and the rhythms of political authority became foci for intensified nationalist activity and gave temporal structure to acts of nationalism.

The sharp but short-lived decline in protest demonstrations in December 1988 and January 1989 was due to the impact of the Armenian earthquake of December 1988, which throughout the former Soviet Union temporarily put an end to efforts to mobilize. This was due not only to the effect of the disaster on Armenian society. It became the occasion as well for a moratorium on protest activities by groups elsewhere out of solidarity with relief efforts and a significant (but ultimately failed) attempt by the regime to stamp out nationalist protests coercively. By the end of 1988 it had taken a natural disaster that killed fifty thousand people, self-imposed restraints by nationalist movements, and a concerted campaign of government intimidation to produce a temporary decline in attempts by challengers to mobilize. By summer 1989, however, the tide of nationalism in the Soviet Union had become self-sustaining, acquiring a momentum and recursive dimension that made challenge increasingly difficult to contain.

The emulative and recursive character of nationalist mobilization is further evident when we view patterns of mass participation in demonstrations. In contrast to the number of demonstrations, which rose steadily over time in the first four years of the cycle, participation was "forward-packed," occurring to a greater extent in the early part of the cycle, peaking in 1988 and 1989, and declining significantly over 1990. On average more than a million people participated in acts of protest over ethnonationalist issues every month from February 1988 through August 1991 (from May 1988 through March 1990 – over two million). In the early part of the cycle, the influence of specific institutional changes on patterns of participation is harder to discern, though many of the peaks and falls of mobilization follow the patterns in Figures 3.1a and 3.1b. In the second half of the cycle the influence of political change on participation emerges more clearly than does its influence on the frequency of demonstrations. As we will see, the general demobilization of participation that occurred in 1990 was largely due to the migration of participation from the streets back to government institutions with the 1990 republican and local elections and the institutionalizing outcomes these elections in some cases produced. By contrast, attempts to mobilize populations continued apace in 1990 and 1991, as an increasingly diverse set of challengers sought to capitalize on the mobilizational successes of early risers, though with less resonance. Thus, prior successes at nationalist mobilization bred an explosion of emulative attempts to challenge the state by nationalist movements, but these efforts met a declining resonance within target populations.

During 1991 partial remobilizations took place in connection with the attempted crackdown in Lithuania in January 1991 and with the August 1991 coup. The sharp drop in mobilization and in elite efforts to organize demonstrations from April 1991 through July 1991 was due to pact politics, in particular, the negotiations between Gorbachev and republican leaders at Novo-Ogarevo, which led to an agreement to halt protest against the Soviet regime among the participating leaders.[3] With the collapse of the Soviet Union, smaller waves of mobilization were unleashed, but by July 1992 participation in demonstrations had largely petered out, even though efforts by challengers to mobilize populations continued apace. The "noisy" politics of nationalism faded as a result of shifts in political authority that brought challengers to power or that made challenge seem increasingly unlikely to lead to success.

## Nationalism in Space

If the above analysis provides quantitative evidence for the systematic role of institutional constraints in shaping nationalist action over time, as well as some preliminary evidence for the effects of event-specific processes such as recursion and emulation, cross-sectional statistical analysis provides evidence for the ways in which nationalist mobilization was structured across space. I now examine some of the ways in which the characteristics of target groups in place prior to the onset of *glasnost'* influenced patterns of mobilization within the cycle. Specifically, I am interested in variations among ethnic groups in patterns of mobilization, and in particular, in the effects on the frequency and intensity of mobilization by an ethnic group of such factors as population size, the ethnofederal system, linguistic assimilation, urbanization, cultural background, prior patterns of mobilization, and the degree to which a group was represented within the Communist Party. The ethnic group here becomes the main unit of analysis – not because I believe ethnic groups are unitary actors, but because I believe that the structural characteristics of target groups are likely to influence the frequency and success of mobilizational efforts by nationalist movements, and that the influence of pre-existing structural conditions is most likely to be visible spatially in the differences in activity across target groups. One could have divided the sample differently, focusing, for instance, on the differences between nationalism in large

[3] See Boris Yeltsin, *The Struggle for Russia* (New York: Random House, 1994), p. 27.

cities versus small localities, republics versus autonomous republics, and so on. We have seen some evidence that these factors did affect the materialization of nationalism spatially. But because ethnic groups (not cities or ethnofederal units) were the targets of efforts at nationalist mobilization, and because other factors such as urbanization or level within the ethnofederal hierarchy were also visible by examining variations in mobilization among ethnic groups, a focus on the ethnic group for understanding spatial differentiation in nationalist action makes sense. Also, given the availability of a number of quantitative measures of independent variables by ethnic group, by using the group rather than territorial entities as units of analysis, it is possible to avoid some of the more egregious forms of aggregation bias inherent in analyzing nationalism on a simple territorial basis.[4]

One of the issues underlying any analysis of the patterning of events across space is that event data can be analyzed in a number of different ways depending on the temporal level at which events are aggregated. Duration data measure the intervals between events, estimating the risk associated with particular characteristics of the units of analysis during the times those units were under risk. Count data, by contrast, analyze the total number of events exhibited by the units of analysis over an aggregated slice of time. Both methods emerge out of the same underlying event processes, but depending on the sample the choice between them can affect the statistical results obtained.[5] Since I am interested here in the overall patterns of mobilization across nationalities, I have chosen to utilize a count model, though the same data were tested using a duration model, yielding analogous findings. For the sake of space, I present only the findings of the event count model.

---

[4] Aggregation bias is a problem when trying to analyze the activity of any collectivity, but is greater when the spatial measurement of variables differs substantially from the spatial boundaries of the research object. Thus, if we are interested in explaining nationalist protest but measure protest spatially by province or republic instead of by ethnic group, our provincial and republican measurements would potentially encompass actions by multiple ethnic groups and therefore be a less accurate measure of the quantity of interest. Similarly, if we were to use republican-level data on income distribution as an independent variable to explain variation in nationalist protests, we would face the problem of the extent to which the republican-level data on income accurately reflects income levels among the groups whose actions interest us.

[5] See James E. Alt, Gary King, and Curtis S. Signorino, "Aggregation Among Binary, Count, and Duration Models: Estimating the Same Quantities from Different Levels of Data," at http://gking.harvard.edu/preprints.shtml.

Table 3.1 displays the results of a negative binomial regression of the total frequency of protest demonstrations over ethnonationalist issues by nationality for forty-seven non-Russian nationalities over the entire January 1987 through August 1991 period.[6] Negative binomial regression models are a type of maximum likelihood estimation typically used in event count models when the dependent variable cannot be negative but varies within a defined range greater than or equal to zero; the assumptions of a normal distribution are violated by such data, since event counts are non-negative, always integers, and often small (at times, zero). Negative binomial regression is an alternative to Poisson models that is appropriate when there is overdispersion in the distribution of events. This is often caused by lack of complete independence between events, so that the occurrence of one event changes the probability that another event will occur – a phenomenon referred to in statistics as "contagion."[7] This parallels neatly the assumptions of this study concerning the causal role played by the event – in the recursive nature of nationalist action, in the processes of emulation that success engenders, and in other event-based effects. Essentially, the negative binomial regression allows us to assume the existence of such processes in the data while exploring the role of cross-sectional influences.[8]

---

[6] The largest fifty groups were chosen as the basis for the sample, though the exclusion of Russians and of other cases of missing data reduced the sample to forty-seven groups. The rationale for treating Russians separately is taken up further in Chapter 8, where I deal specifically with the various forms of Russian nationalism. Suffice it to say here that given the dominant role played by Russians within the Soviet state, Russian nationalism involved a greater degree of variation in terms of goals, thereby posing serious aggregation issues concerning what was being tested. Moreover, some of the variables used here to test the influence of identity processes (in particular, linguistic assimilation) made no sense as applied to the Russians, causing the Russian case to drop out in any case.

[7] For more on the negative binomial model, see J. Scott Long, *Regression Models for Categorical and Limited Dependent Variables* (London: Sage Publications, 1997), pp. 217–50.

[8] Although the theoretical parallels in themselves are good enough intellectual rationale for selecting such a model, as most statistical works on the subject advise, the negative binomial model was tested for its appropriateness by first positing a Poisson model but observing a lack of fit of the data with the Poisson distribution due to overdispersion in the data. In Table 3.1 the extreme statistical significance of the likelihood ratio tests against the Poisson distribution demonstrates that Poisson is not appropriate and that, as a tidal understanding of nationalism would have us believe, a negative binomial distribution is the better choice. The regression parameters in a negative binomial regression model can be exponentiated to produce incidence rate ratios, which measure the likely percent increase or decrease in the expected number of demonstrations from a unit change in the independent variable.

Table 3.1. *Negative Binomial Regression of Total Number of Protest Demonstrations Concerning Ethnonationalist Issues by Nationality (January 1987–August 1991)*[a]

| Independent Variable | Equation 1 | | Equation 2 | | Equation 3 | | Equation 4 | |
|---|---|---|---|---|---|---|---|---|
| | Coefficient | Incidence Rate Ratio | Coefficient | Incidence Rate Ratio | Coefficient | Incidence Rate Ratio | Coefficient | Incidence Rate Ratio |
| Ln population size (thousands), 1989 | 0.658 (4.42)**** | 1.931 | — | — | 0.473 (1.96)** | 1.605 | 0.485 (2.80)*** | 1.624 |
| Dummy variable for union republic | — | — | 1.701 (1.96)** | 5.480 | 0.079 (0.07) | 1.083 | — | — |
| Dummy variable for federal unit lower than union republic | — | — | -0.680 (-0.80) | .507 | -1.134 (-1.35) | .322 | -1.175 (-1.93)* | .309 |
| Linguistic assimilation, 1989[b] | -0.072 (-4.12)**** | .930 | -0.054 (-2.46)** | .948 | -0.074 (-3.18)**** | .929 | -0.075 (-4.50)**** | .928 |
| Level of urbanization, 1970[c] | 0.066 (2.95)*** | 1.068 | 0.077 (3.34)**** | 1.080 | 0.062 (2.81)*** | 1.064 | 0.061 (2.93)*** | 1.063 |
| Number of demonstrations by nationality in pre-*glasnost'* period (1965–86)[d] | 0.057 (0.96) | 1.059 | 0.074 (1.39) | 1.077 | 0.055 (1.01) | 1.056 | 0.055 (1.02) | 1.056 |
| Party membership per 1000 population, 1989[e] | -0.003 (-0.24) | .997 | -0.014 (-1.01) | .986 | 0.001 (0.08) | 1.001 | 0.002 (0.13) | 1.002 |

| | | | | | | | |
|---|---|---|---|---|---|---|---|
| Dummy variable for peoples of traditionally Islamic cultures | −0.328 (−0.65) | .720 | 0.133 (0.25) | 1.143 | 0.058 (0.11) | 1.060 | 0.056 (0.10) | 1.058 |
| Constant | −3.007572 | | .9871567 | | −1.501143 | | −1.530931 |
| Likelihood ratio test against Poisson | $chi^2 = 628.42$**** | | $chi^2 = 1,574.44$**** | | $chi^2 = 576.22$**** | | $chi^2 = 586.52$**** |
| Log likelihood | −167.58772 | | −167.7196 | | −165.8079 | | −165.81028 |
| Pseudo R-square | .1122 | | .1115 | | .1217 | | .1217 |
| Model chi² | 42.38**** | | 42.11**** | | 45.94**** | | 45.93**** |

*Significant at the .10 level   **Significant at the .05 level   ***Significant at the .01 level   ****Significant at the .001 level

*Note:* n = 47 nationalities, excluding Russians.

[a] The sample is derived from an analysis of 5,067 protest demonstrations in the USSR from January 1987 through August 1991 with 100 participants or more, 2,840 of which involved ethnonationalist claims by one of the 47 non-Russian nationalities included in this regression. Z-scores are provided in parentheses, and coefficients have been exponentiated into incidence rate ratios showing the expected rate of change in the number of ethnonationalist demonstrations by a nationality associated with a unit of change in the independent variable.

[b] Proportion of members of nationality not claiming titular language as their native language, 1989. *Source:* 1989 census data.

[c] *Source:* 1970 census data. Subsequent data on urbanization by nationality was not published in the USSR for the full range of groups in the sample.

[d] Based on an analysis of 184 protest demonstrations in the USSR from January 1965 through December 1986 with 100 participants or more.

[e] *Source:* Calculated from *Izvestiia TsK KPSS*, no. 2, 1989, pp. 140–41; no. 7, 1989, pp. 112–13.

111

I tested for the impact of a series of independent variables that, for theoretical and contextual reasons, might have been expected to leave systematic traces on the patterning of nationalist action. These included the population size of a nationality (population size is known in cross-national studies of protest events to be related to the frequency of protest acts),[9] a nationality's status within the Soviet ethnofederal hierarchy (widely argued in the constructivist literature to have structured ethnic protest action in the USSR),[10] its level of linguistic assimilation (a variable capturing critical aspects of identity processes), its degree of urbanization (corresponding to the arguments of developmentalist theories of nationalism),[11] its prior record of mobilization in the pre-*glasnost'* period (as those accentuating the "stickiness" and prolonged character of nationalist conflict might emphasize), the degree to which its population was saturated by Communist Party membership, and Islamic cultural background (these factors being potentially significant politically within the Soviet milieu). Republican ethnofederal status was highly correlated with population size ($r$ = .49) and even more highly correlated ($r$ = .74) with the population variable used in these regressions (the natural log of population size). Yet, there was theoretical justification for believing that both variables were related to the patterning of action across ethnic groups. Several specifications were tested to probe the differential impact of these variables.

Table 3.2, by contrast, reports tobit estimations of the total number of participants in ethnonationalist demonstrations (that is, the resonance of mobilizational efforts within target populations). The tobit model is another maximum likelihood estimation that addresses the issue of nonrandom selection where a variable is censored or truncated at a certain point. In this case, one cannot have participation in a demonstration

[9] See Douglas A. Hibbs, *Mass Political Violence* (New York: Wiley, 1973), p. 25. I used the natural log of the population, as is standard in the literature, to deal with the high variability represented in population sizes.
[10] See Philip G. Roeder, "Soviet Federalism and Ethnic Mobilization," *World Politics* vol. 43 (January 1991), pp. 196–232; Rogers Brubaker, "Nationhood and the National Question in the Soviet Union and Post-Soviet Eurasia: An Institutionalist Account," *Theory and Society*, vol. 23, no. 1 (February 1994), pp. 47–78; Ronald Grigor Suny, *Revenge of the Past: Nationalism, Revolution, and the Collapse of the Soviet Union* (Stanford, CA: Stanford University Press, 1993).
[11] See Karl W. Deutsch, *Nationalism and Social Communication* (Cambridge, MA: The MIT Press, 1953); Ernest Gellner, *Nations and Nationalism* (Ithaca, NY: Cornell University Press, 1983); Miroslav Hroch, *Social Preconditions of National Revival in Europe: A Comparative Analysis of the Social Composition of Patriotic Groups among the Smaller European Nations* (Cambridge, UK: Cambridge University Press, 1985).

without first having demonstrations. By censoring those observations in which no demonstrations occurred, we can estimate whether a particular independent variable increased or decreased participation by populations in ethnonationalist demonstrations given the availability of some opportunity to participate.[12] Six different specifications are tested in Table 3.2. These probe the impact of population size, ethnofederal institutions, urbanization, prior patterns of mobilization, levels of Communist Party membership, and Islamic cultural background on the resonance of mobilizational efforts within populations. The first three equations, however, include data for two outlier cases (Armenians and Azerbaijanis), whereas the last three equations do not (the reasons for their outlier status are discussed below). In addition, Equations 1, 2, 4, and 5 examine variability in the relationship between population size, ethnofederal status, and levels of participation. The inclusion of the number of ethnonationalist demonstrations as an independent variable in Equations 3 and 6 was meant to control the results for the number of attempts by elites to mobilize – which logically should be positively related to the total number of participants in a nationality's demonstrations and could account for their relationship with levels of participation. As Table 3.1 shows, however, this variable was also independently related to a number of the other independent variables in the specification, and therefore the results need to be interpreted with caution.

A comparison of these regressions provides a revealing picture of the broad social forces systematically shaping the spatial manifestation of nationalist mobilization. In all the specifications tested, the degree of linguistic assimilation of an ethnic group was systematically related with fewer events overall, and the level of urbanization was uniformly associated with a greater number of events. Thus, using Equation 1 from Table 3.1, each percentage point of urbanization of a nationality was associated with a 6.8 percent increase in the total number of expected events in which a nationality engaged relative to no change in the degree of urbanization (statistically significant at the .01 level), whereas a 1 percent increase in the linguistic assimilation of a nationality (measured here by the proportion of members claiming the language of another group as their native

---

[12] The interpretation of the parameter estimates in these regressions is straightforward, with a unit change in the independent variable associated with the corresponding change in the expected number of participants per demonstration. On tobit regression models, see Long, *Regression Models*, pp. 187–216.

Table 3.2. *Tobit Estimations of Total Number of Participants in Protest Demonstrations Concerning Ethnonationalist Issues by Nationality (January 1987–August 1991)*

| Independent Variable | Equation 1[a] | Equation 2[a] | Equation 3[a] | Equation 4[b] | Equation 5[b] | Equation 6[b] |
|---|---|---|---|---|---|---|
| Ln population size (thousands), 1989 | 1,143,499 (2.55)** | – | 535,098.4 (1.24) | 560,713.5 (2.55)** | – | –76,166.2 (–0.97) |
| Dummy variable for union republic | –1,309,412 (–0.63) | 2,636,789 (1.76)* | –613,850.4 (–0.34) | –144,558.4 (–0.14) | 1,769,931 (2.45)** | 653,668.8 (1.88)* |
| Dummy variable for federal unit lower than union republic | –774,419.5 (–0.55) | 183,535.7 (0.13) | –219,630 (–0.17) | –403,685.5 (–0.59) | –9,162.4 (–0.01) | 181,265.6 (0.72) |
| Linguistic assimilation, 1989 | –152,013.7 (–3.29)*** | –98,170.1 (–2.34)** | –89,596.5 (–2.00)* | –82,182.1 (–3.51)*** | –54,772.7 (–2.69)** | –19,066.3 (–2.30)** |
| Level of urbanization, 1970 | 30,200.8 (0.73) | 48,059.4 (1.12) | 15,059.8 (0.41) | 36,621.7 (1.80)* | 46,407.1 (2.21)** | 19,443.6 (2.72)*** |
| Thousands of participants in demonstrations by nationality in pre-*glasnost'* period, 1965–86 (squared) | 3,489.1 (12.51)**** | 3,439.4 (11.61)**** | 3,195.4 (12.03)**** | 681.4 (1.10) | 373.3 (0.60) | 291.7 (1.37) |
| Party membership per 1,000 population, 1989 | –8,239.5 (–0.30) | –26,071.4 (–0.95) | –26,689.1 (–1.08) | 7,168.3 (0.50) | 2,648.1 (0.18) | –8,017.6 (–1.52) |

| | | | | | |
|---|---|---|---|---|---|
| Dummy variable for peoples of traditionally Islamic cultures | -1,644,735 (-1.77)* | -1,225,637 (-1.27) | -663,797.5 (-0.75) | -1,537,822 (-3.17)*** | -1,264,858 (-2.54)** | -533,457.5 (-2.95)*** |
| Number of demonstrations raising ethnonationalist issues in which nationality engaged, 1987–91 | — | — | 10,879.7 (2.93)*** | — | — | 10,200.4 (14.40)**** |
| Constant | -5,185,759 | 332,839.1 | -1,735,068 | -3,275,938 | -810,621.9 | 394,590 |
| Uncensored observations | 31 | 31 | 31 | 29 | 29 | 29 |
| Left censored observations at number of demonstrations = 0 | 16 | 16 | 16 | 16 | 16 | 16 |
| Log likelihood | -505.9 | -509.1 | -502.17 | -452.67 | -456.05 | -423.32 |
| Model chi² | 81.29**** | 74.76**** | 88.75**** | 40.04**** | 33.29**** | 98.75**** |
| Pseudo R² | .0744 | .0684 | .0812 | .0424 | .0352 | .1045 |

*Significant at the .10 level   **Significant at the .05 level   ***Significant at the .01 level   ****Significant at the .001 level

*Note:* t-statistics in parentheses.

a For these regressions n = 47 nationalities (excluding Russians).

b For these regressions n = 45 nationalities (excluding Russians), with Armenians and Azerbaijanis omitted as outlier cases.

language) produced a 7.0 percent decrease in the expected number of eth-nonationalist demonstrations that a group experienced relative to no change in assimilation (significant at the .001 level).

These findings are a vivid illustration of how social processes within "quiet" phases of nationalism matter in shaping the ways in which groups mobilize during "noisy" periods of nationalist contention. The role played by urbanization in generating networks of nationalist activists has long been a central assumption within the developmentalist literature on nationalism – though an assumption usually not subjected to so rigorous an empirical test as carried out here. The findings confirm that more urbanized nationalities were considerably more likely to engage in nation-alist action than less urbanized nationalities when the opportunity for action emerged. We saw in Chapter 2 that a disproportionate number of the large-scale demonstrations in the Soviet Union during the *glasnost'* period took place in cities with over a million in population. Thus, urban-ization mattered doubly: Not only did more urbanized nationalities engage in more frequent action than less urbanized groups, but within nationali-ties the more urbanized segments of these populations were significantly more likely to engage in nationalist mobilization than more rural seg-ments. This statistical evidence confirms that the Soviet regime's efforts to modernize, silently and contrary to their manifest purpose, helped to foster the very conditions that eventually undermined control by creating urban national intelligentsias capable of providing leadership to national movements. Modernization subverted the Soviet state not merely by gen-erating a liberal intelligentsia, but even more by generating potential net-works of nationalist mobilizers who, given the opportunity to do so, would organize a torrent of nationalist actions that severely challenged the regime.

One of the central narratives within the academic literature on nation-alism concerns the struggle between assimilating regimes and opposing efforts at cultural revival.[13] Table 3.1 provides statistical evidence that iden-tity processes are important in shaping mobilizational outcomes and that the cultural contestation occurring during "quiet" periods of contention is critical in influencing the ability of would-be nationalists to act in pursuit of shared aims during "noisy" periods. The evidence presented in Table

---

[13] See David Laitin, *Language Repertoires and State Construction in Africa* (Cambridge, UK: Cambridge University Press, 1992).

3.1 does not deal with the resonance of nationalist claims within target populations and therefore does not show that nationalist messages resonated less widely within linguistically assimilated groups than within unassimilated groups (though as shown in Table 3.2, this is true as well). Rather, what the results indicate is that nationalists from groups more highly assimilated linguistically attempted to contest the nation less frequently than did nationalist elites from groups less assimilated. Thus, processes of linguistic assimilation exercised a marked effect on elite behavior by reducing the will and capacity of such elites to engage in contentious nationalist acts.

Table 3.1 indicates, however, that it would be wrong to consider "noisy" periods of nationalism as mere reflections of what occurred during "quiet" periods. When one controls for the effects of other factors, for instance, prior patterns of mobilization (the number of demonstrations in which a nationality engaged during the 1965–86 period) were not autonomously related to the number of demonstrations in which a nationality engaged in the *glasnost'* period (though without controlling for other factors, a statistically significant though substantively small relationship did exist, accounting for only 2.5 percent of the variation in nationalist demonstrations across groups in the *glasnost'* era). The issue is complicated by the fact that prior patterns of nationalist mobilization were also related to population size, urbanization, and linguistic assimilation. Thus, it seems reasonable to assume that the degree of similarity between the pre-*glasnost'* and *glasnost'* patterns of mobilization was largely due to the fact that both were shaped by similar pre-existing structural conditions. In this sense, the *glasnost'* period was not a mere extension of the nationalist conflicts that had occurred in the past. Although clearly what occurred during "quiet" phases influenced what happened during "noisy" phases, distinctive processes also occurred which cannot be entirely accounted for by prior patterns of mobilization.

Some of the more interesting findings from Table 3.1 revolve around the role of population size and the federal system in shaping the frequency of nationalist mobilization. As a number of cross-national studies have shown, for mere demographic reasons one would expect that populations of larger size would be at greater risk of experiencing demonstrations and therefore more likely to exhibit higher levels of protest. The results in Equation 1 provide evidence of the relationship of population size to the overall frequency of ethnonationalist demonstrations by nationalities during the *glasnost'* era. But the influence of group size on the behavior of nationalist elites is more complex than merely the statistical chances of action given the number of individuals in a group. For one thing, the proportion that a group constituted within its federal unit of primary habitation was correlated with population size (r = .42) and even more so with the logged population variable used here (r = .67), so that smaller groups were more likely to be minorities within their territories and would also be expected to be able to marshal fewer political resources in struggling against a dominant regime.[14] Moreover, prevailing international norms since the mid-nineteenth century have favored claims of self-determination by large groups and disfavored those expressed by small groups; recognition of claims to separate statehood has tended to be restricted to groups of considerable size.[15] This alone would be reason enough for smaller groups to have exhibited less capability of engaging in nationalist action. All things being equal, smaller groups had fewer resources available to disrupt the state, were more likely to be outnumbered in their territories, and were less likely to gain recognition for their claims to nationhood, making action seem futile.

In the Soviet case the role played by group size is further complicated by the close association between group size and the ethnofederal system. Population size was part of Stalin's rationale in the assignment of status within the ethnofederal hierarchy, though other factors such as geographic location were critical as well. Over time, assignment to a particular type of ethnofederal unit had consequences for the types of cultural resources available to group members. For instance, a moderately strong negative relationship existed between the level assigned to a group within the ethnofederal hierarchy (treated here as an ordinal variable represented by assignment to a union republic, to a unit lower than a union republic, or to no ethnofederal unit) and the degree of linguistic assimilation of that group (r = −.46). A number of scholars have argued that the rise of nationalism in the former Soviet Union during the *glasnost'* period was in sig-

---

[14] When the proportion of a group within its ethnofederal unit of primary habitation was included in these regressions along with logged population size, it was not statistically significant. When the population variable was dropped, however, the proportion variable was statistically significant, though the degree of variation explained by the regressions dropped substantially. Thus, logged population was a better predictor of mobilization, as it captured much of the variation explained by the proportion variable.

[15] E. J. Hobsbawm, *Nations and Nationalism Since 1780: Programme, Myth, Reality* (2d ed.) (Cambridge, UK: Cambridge University Press, 1990), pp. 30–32.

nificant respects the product of the Soviet model of ethnofederalism. They have contended that, by providing a sense of territoriality for groups that previously lacked a bounded territory, by providing ethnic cultural and educational institutions to specific groups, and by creating a pool of national cadres, ethnofederalism prepared the ground for the *glasnost'* upsurge in nationalism. At least measured in terms of the overall frequency of action by nationalist movements, the findings in Table 3.1 provide some qualified proof for these assertions.

But the key question for identifying the systematic causal role of eth-nofederal institutions in structuring patterns of nationalism in the former Soviet Union is whether their effects can be separated from the very criteria used to create the ethnofederal hierarchy in the first place. This is by no means a trifling issue; it deals directly with the epistemological bases of the new institutionalism which has become so prevalent within political science and sociology in recent years. Institutions, after all, do not emerge out of thin air; they are formed with norms and political criteria in mind and therefore reflect a certain external logic within them. This was certainly true of the Soviet ethnofederal system, which was created in part as a way of preventing groups from seeking secession in the wake of the tide of nationalism that swept through the Russian empire at the time of the Russian Revolution. Emerging norms of self-determination played a significant role in shaping Lenin's thinking about ethnofederalism in the first place, and embedded within these institutions was a logic reflecting the advantages of population size in claims of self-determination. This renders any attempt to isolate the specific impact of ethnofederal institutions on the patterning of nationalist action extremely difficult. In Equation 2 in Table 3.1, for instance, we see evidence that union republican status was a statistically significant factor in increasing the overall number of ethnonationalist demonstrations in which a group engaged. As Equation 3 demonstrates, however, this relationship disappears when we control for population size. This is not to suggest that the very assignment of groups within the ethnofederal hierarchy had no independent effect on the frequency of mobilization by groups; indeed, we will see extensive evidence of its impact below. But because of its close association with ethnofederal status, population size reflects much of the causal influence of the eth-nofederal system on the frequency of attempts to mobilize and is actually a better predictor overall of mobilizational patterns than ethnofederal status, in large part because other factors besides the ethnofederal hierarchy that are related to nationalist mobilization (the probabilities of action

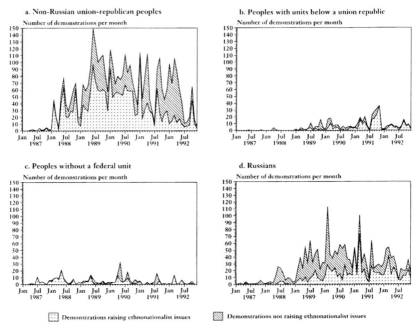

**Figure 3.2.** Ethnonationalist mobilization and the Soviet ethnofederal system.

associated with demographic size, the effects of international norms, and practical power politics) are reflected in the population size variable as well. Thus, a perspective which emphasized the influence of the ethnofederal system on mobilization without taking into consideration the impact of these other factors would be misleading.

At the same time, as Equation 4 in Table 3.1 shows, even when we control for population size, there is a marginally significant relationship (at the .10 level) between whether a group was assigned to an ethnofederal unit below a union republic and lower frequency of ethnonationalist demonstrations overall. This was true irrespective the strength of identity processes (linguistic assimilation) or the urbanized sector of a nationality. Moreover, if we look visually at the distribution of protest acts over time according to group status within the ethnofederal system (presented in Figure 3.2), we find a distinctive temporal pattern among groups with ethnofederal units below the union republican level. Protest actions by non-Russian groups with union republics (and less so, nonnationalist mobilization by Russians) were more or less normally distributed across the mobilizational cycle, and those by groups without a federal unit tended to be concentrated in the earlier portion of the mobilizational cycle. Early mobilization within the cycle was carried out by non-Russian groups with union republics, groups without a federal unit, and Russians. By contrast, action by groups with ethnofederal units below a union republic was largely absent in the early part of the cycle. Their activity grew significantly only in the cycle's second half (as did nationalist action by Russians). In the cases of non-Russian groups with union republics and groups without a federal unit, protest began as predominantly ethnonationalist mobilization and subsequently diversified to other issues. But for groups with units below a union republic and Russians, protest began almost exclusively over other issues and became increasingly ethnonationalist over time – a sign of influence by tidal forces over the course of the cycle.

In short, the assignment of a group to a particular level within the ethnofederal hierarchy did exercise an independent effect irrespective of population size, levels of urbanization, and degrees of linguistic assimilation. But the ethnofederal system acted not only as a facilitating condition; it also acted as an institutional constraint. It was not simply that the ethnofederal system provided linguistic and cultural resources that ultimately brought about the consolidation of nationalist elites and subsequently produced action when the opportunity emerged. Certainly this did occur, as the evidence suggests. But it was also true that institutions constrained and limited the imaginations of some challengers, and only as the norms of sovereignty came undone in 1990 and 1991 under the impact of mobilizations by other groups did mobilization eventually spread to groups with ethnofederal units lower than a union republic. Ethnofederalism structured mobilization as much by providing some groups with the cultural and political resources to challenge the state as it did by limiting the imagination of others concerning what types of actions were appropriate and feasible.

Moving to some of the factors structuring mass participation in ethnonationalist demonstrations, the results in Table 3.2 present a somewhat different picture of mobilizational processes. Equations 1, 2, 4, and 5 demonstrate that, like efforts to mobilize target populations, participation in those efforts was related to population size, the level assigned to a group within the federal hierarchy, linguistic assimilation, and urbanization. But when one controls levels of participation for the number of demonstrations in which a group engaged (Equations 3 and 6), the effects of population size and the ethnofederal hierarchy disappear or become marginally significant, reflecting the fact that these factors affected mobilization largely by influencing the propensity of nationalist elites to organize demonstrations rather than the calculus of target populations concerning whether to participate in them. Ethnofederalism in this respect was much more likely to structure elite rather than mass behavior.

Linguistic assimilation was strongly and relatively consistently related to levels of participation, even when controlling for the number of demonstrations in which a group engaged. In Equation 6, each percentage point of linguistic assimilation was associated with a reduction in a group's level of participation in nationalist demonstrations by approximately nineteen thousand. Moreover, as can be seen from Equations 4 through 6, if one excludes the outlier cases of Armenians and Azerbaijanis from the analysis, urbanization shows a positive statistically significant relationship with mass participation in nationalist demonstrations. This relationship holds true even when controlling for the number of demonstrations in which a group engaged. Urbanization appears to have been key in generating large pools of followers for nationalist collective action, though its influence in Equations 1 through 3 in Table 3.2 is obscured by its close relationship (r = .44) with pre-*glasnost'* patterns of participation (a factor strongly related to Armenian mobilization specifically). As Equation 6 shows, each percentage point increase in the level of urbanization of a nationality produced an increase in a group's overall level of participation in nationalist demonstrations of approximately nineteen thousand, irrespective of the number of demonstrations in which a group engaged. The extremely robust relationship between prior patterns of mobilization in the pre-*glasnost'* period (represented here exponentially) and patterns of participation in nationalist demonstrations in the *glasnost'* period in Equations 1 through 3 and its statistical insignificance in Equations 4 through 6 reflect the fact that one case in particular (the Armenians) displayed the highest levels of protest participation in both the pre-*glasnost'* and *glasnost'* periods.

The relatively recent imposition of national categories by the Soviet regime on much of its Islamic population in the third decade of the twentieth century (and the traditional strength of religious and clan identities within these populations) could plausibly account for the reduced resonance of nationalist frames among Soviet Muslims found in Equations 4 through 6 (when Armenians and Azerbaijanis were excluded as outliers). As we will see, this finding holds up under subsequent investigation. Nationalist movements targeting traditionally Muslim groups in general produced as many nationalist demonstrations as other nationalist movements, at least as might have been expected based on the size of target populations, their ethnofederal status, and their degrees of urbanization and linguistic assimilation. But these efforts did not resonate within target populations so widely as was true of other groups, controlling for the influence of other factors.

Finally, in none of these regressions was any evidence uncovered that the degree of saturation of party membership within a population was related systematically to the frequency or intensity of nationalist mobilization. Nationalities well connected into the regime were just as likely as those more marginalized to engage in nationalist mobilization over the course of the cycle, controlling for other factors. The unmaking of the Communist Party was precisely its inability to find a social base that would have provided a bulwark against the rising tide of nationalism, even among groups which might have been expected to support communist rule based on their overrepresentation within the party. The fact that the degree of overrepresentation of a nationality within the party was not related negatively with nationalist mobilization is a reflection of the extent to which nationalism ultimately penetrated into party institutions and into the party's traditional base of support during this period, undermining the Soviet state from within.

Despite the strong evidence presented here for the influence of pre-existing structural conditions on nationalist mobilization, the significant amount of variance that these regressions leave unexplained (in the demonstration model only 12 percent and in the participation model only 10 percent of the variation at most was explained by the factors examined), the embedded assumption of contagion within these models, and the evidence presented concerning the presence of event-specific processes all point toward the necessity of thinking about nationalist mobilization in the intersection of both time and space, where pre-existing structural conditions, institutional constraints, and event-specific processes collide and interact.

## Nationalism in Space-Time (I): The Temporal Spread of Nationalist Contention

Like all social phenomena, nationalism is fundamentally chronotopic in that it materializes at the conjuncture of time and space. Its study therefore necessitates methods capable of teasing out the ways in which temporal and spatial dimensions interact. The temporal data analyzed above were pooled for the entire country and contain within them many cross-sectional variations at the group level that are concealed by aggregation, whereas the cross-sectional data obfuscate the considerable temporal variations that occurred in group activity. A tide of nationalism is composed of multiple waves of mobilization, each of which feeds in part off the momentum unleashed by prior waves. Through the end of 1989, major waves of nationalist mobilization (each involving some events with more than one hundred thousand participants) swept through Armenia in February 1988, May 1988, July 1988, September to November 1988, May 1989, August 1989, and September to December 1989; through Azerbaijan in May 1988, November to December 1988, and August 1989; Estonia in June 1988, September 1988, April 1989, and August 1989; Lithuania in July 1988, August 1988, October 1988, February 1989, and August 1989; Latvia in July 1988, October and November 1988, March 1989, August 1989, and November 1989; Georgia in November 1988, April and May 1989, and October 1989; Western Ukraine in June 1989 and September to November 1989; and Moldavia in August 1989. Temporal and cross-sectional analyses at the aggregate level are incapable of addressing this chronotopic variation in nationalism across space-time and therefore are unable to capture the ways in which nationalist action in one chronotopic context influenced nationalist action within another.

When Herzen, in the quotation provided at the beginning of this chapter, spoke of the "chronological unfairness" of human history, his concern was not with nationalist mobilization but with the modernization of Russia. But by "chronological unfairness," Herzen had in mind precisely the kind of chronotopic influence of action on subsequent action that is the central theme of this book. He believed that Russia in the mid-nineteenth century was well positioned to learn from the prior mistakes of England and France in the industrialization process through a form of peasant socialism based on the *mir*, or peasant commune. In some ways, the Russian intelligentsia learned the mistakes of English and French industrialization too well; it became obsessed with avoiding them through rejection of the market and fascination with utopian projects of modernization. Because some learn from the actions of others does not mean that they necessarily learn the right lessons. But this type of influence across time and space was an inherent part of the modernization process. Russia eventually profited in myriad ways from the prior actions of early industrializers – perhaps most starkly in its ability to take advantage of technologies and modes of knowledge developed elsewhere. The entire Soviet industrialization process as Stalin described it was an attempt to "Americanize" Soviet society in terms of industrial culture while building state socialism internally.

Much the same "chronological unfairness" occurs within mobilizational cycles. As scholars of social movements well know, cycles of mobilization involve significant variation in the timing of action among groups. Some groups (early risers) engage in action earlier within the cycle than others (late risers). Still others never act at all. The efforts of late risers are likely to be heavily influenced by the successful example of those who preceded them. Though early risers may enjoy more propitious structural conditions facilitating mobilization, they face stiffer institutional constraints than late risers, who, in spite of some of their structural disadvantages, are better positioned to profit from the efforts, mistakes, and successes of those preceding them. This "chronological unfairness" forms much of the basis for the tidal influences exercised by one nationalism on another.

I develop this idea and its consequences in greater depth below and in subsequent chapters. Here, I seek merely to show that the same structural conditions associated with the frequency of nationalist mobilization are also associated with the timing of action by groups within the mobilizational cycle – that is, that nationalism is structured in space-time not only by the opening and closing of institutions, but also by the pre-existing structural characteristics of target groups. My approach focuses on the timing of the first nationalist action by the movements of each group over the course of the cycle. Assigning each day of the mobilizational cycle from January 1987 through August 1991 a consecutive number, I conducted a series of single-failure survival analyses aimed at uncovering the factors associated with the timing of the first action raising ethnonationalist issues by a group within the cycle. Each nationality was treated as the equivalent of an individual at risk of experiencing its first ethnonationalist demonstration at any time in the cycle.[16] The results are presented in Table 3.3.

---

[16] A Weibull regression model was chosen as the most appropriate after engaging in standard tests of model residuals against those of the closest competitors. This involved comparing plots of the Cox-Snell residuals against the opposite of the natural log of the Kaplan-Meier survival estimates. I also compared the log-likelihoods of Weibull and Gompertz models using the Akaike information criterion, which produced a slight preference for the Weibull model over the Gompertz. The appropriateness of the Weibull

Table 3.3. *Weibull Regressions of the Relative Risk of a Nationality Engaging in Its First Protest Demonstration Raising Ethnonationalist Issues (January 1987–August 1991)*[a]

| Independent Variable/Equation | 100 or more participants | | | | | 1,000 or more | 10,000 or more | 20,000 or more |
|---|---|---|---|---|---|---|---|---|
| | Equation 1 | Equation 2 | Equation 3 | Equation 4 | Equation 5 | Equation 6 | Equation 7 | Equation 8 |
| Ln population size, 1989 | 1.301 (1.30) | 1.648 (3.87)**** | — | 1.263 (1.22) | 1.490 (2.90)*** | 1.208 (0.88) | 1.449 (1.37) | 2.567 (2.61)*** |
| Dummy variable for union republic | 2.222 (0.90) | — | 4.908 (2.52)** | 3.632 (1.83)* | — | 4.533 (3.27)** | 6.577 (2.32)** | 11.140 (2.11)** |
| Dummy variable for federal unit lower than union republic | .566 (−0.93) | — | .611 (−0.79) | — | .420 (−1.82)* | — | — | — |
| Linguistic assimilation, 1989 | .956 (−2.26)** | .948 (−3.00)*** | .962 (−2.13)** | .961 (−2.13)* | .946 (−3.06)*** | .941 (−3.28)**** | .918 (−3.13)*** | .896 (−2.72)*** |
| Level of urbanization, 1970 | 1.053 (2.86)*** | 1.057 (3.30)**** | 1.055 (3.01)*** | 1.058 (3.33)**** | 1.050 (2.77)*** | 1.078 (3.90)**** | 1.068 (2.83)*** | 1.114 (3.49)**** |
| Party membership per 1,000 population, 1989 | 1.012 (0.81) | .999 (−0.09) | 1.014 (1.04) | 1.008 (0.57) | 1.010 (0.69) | 1.012 (1.00) | 1.010 (0.63) | .971 (−1.21) |
| Dummy variable for peoples of traditionally Islamic cultures | .463 (−1.40) | .417 (−1.71)* | .514 (−1.24) | .512 (−1.26) | .406 (−1.70)* | .659 (−0.80) | .437 (−1.17) | .027 (−2.89)*** |
| Number of observations | 47 | 47 | 47 | 47 | 47 | 47 | 47 | 47 |
| Number of failures | 31 | 31 | 31 | 31 | 31 | 27 | 20 | 15 |
| Number of days at risk | 1,704 | 1,704 | 1,704 | 1,704 | 1,704 | 1,704 | 1,704 | 1,704 |
| Total analysis times (days) at risk | 51,779 | 51,779 | 51,779 | 51,779 | 51,779 | 56,026 | 63,004 | 66,169 |
| Log likelihood | −40.809045 | −42.930195 | −41.643598 | −41.216057 | −41.213669 | −32.438945 | −20.638234 | −9.443054 |
| Model chi² | 38.17**** | 33.93**** | 36.51**** | 37.36**** | 37.37**** | 44.65**** | 50.54**** | 63.69**** |
| P (shape parameter) | 2.033936 | 1.920254 | 1.991261 | 2.008886 | 2.014092 | 2.425532 | 3.104393 | 4.721127 |
| Z-score for ln P | 4.87**** | 4.38**** | 4.78**** | 4.81**** | 4.74**** | 5.78**** | 6.43**** | 7.185**** |

*Significant at the .10 level    **Significant at the .05 level    ***Significant at the .01 level    ****Significant at the .001 level

[a] Parameters represent hazard ratios, with z-scores for standard errors in parentheses.

Early risers can be understood as those groups which were under greater relative risk of experiencing their first nationalist demonstration, whereas late risers were those under less relative risk.

As the results show, in general the same factors which structure the overall incidence of demonstrations by a group also structure the timing of the initial appearance of nationalist mobilization within the cycle. Early risers tended to be those groups with higher levels of urbanization and lower levels of linguistic assimilation, large in size, and with union republican status. The close relationship between population size and union republican status again makes it difficult to sort out the causal influence of these two factors, but in general the ethnofederal system shaped the timing of nationalist mobilization more consistently than population size – in contrast to the pattern found earlier for the overall incidence of nationalist mobilization. There is also some marginal evidence that autonomous republican status and Islamic cultural background were associated with delayed mobilization within the cycle. The event sample included events with 100 participants or more. But as Equations 6 through 8 show, if the minimal size of the first event is raised to twenty thousand participants, then Islamic cultural background was a statistically significant factor in delaying initial action on this scale (confirming earlier findings that Islamic cultural background did not necessarily reduce the number of ethnonationalist demonstrations overall, but did reduce participation in those demonstrations).

These findings suggest that over the course of a mobilizational cycle contention generally spreads from groups with higher structural facilitation to groups with lower structural facilitation. This is visibly confirmed in Figure 3.3, which presents the Kaplan-Meier product-limit estimates for the failure function (the probability over time that an event has occurred) associated with the first ethnonationalist demonstration in

model's assumption of a monotonically increasing risk of an event is also confirmed by the values of the shape parameters p, which show an increasing risk of an event for nationalities over the course of the cycle that is in each case statistically significant (a p value of 1 would have indicated a flat risk of an event over time, whereas a value less than 1 would have indicated a declining risk over time). The coefficients represent hazard ratios, which in this case measure the risk of the occurrence of the first ethnonationalist demonstration by a nationality relative to the risk of its nonoccurrence associated with a unit change in the independent variable during the days in which a nationality was at risk of experiencing its first ethnonationalist demonstration. See J. D. Kalbfleisch and R. L. Prentice, *The Statistical Analysis of Failure Time Data* (New York: John Wiley and Sons, 1980), pp. 23–24.

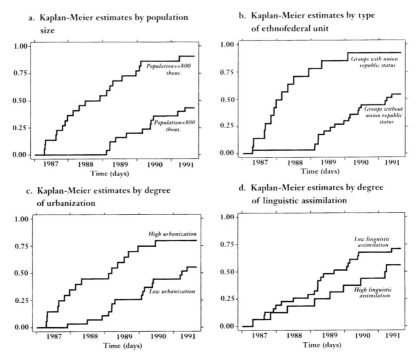

**Figure 3.3.** Kaplan-Meier estimates of the probability of the occurrence of the first ethnonationalist mobilization among forty-seven non-Russian nationalities, January 1987–August 1991.

which a group engaged during the cycle.[17] As is evident from the figure, nationalities with structural advantages (in particular, large size, republican federal status, and high levels of urbanization) were not only more likely to engage in some degree of ethnonationalist protest, but they also tended to engage in earlier mobilization than groups less structurally advantaged. It was not until spring 1989, for instance, that groups smaller than eight hundred thousand in size even began to mobilize on any significant scale (Figure 3.3a). The same was true for the vast majority of groups without union republican status (Figure 3.3b). In both cases, initial

---

[17] The Kaplan-Meier survival function estimates are calculated by taking the probability across all points in time that a case does not experience a failure event within a given population of cases. See D. Collett, *Modelling Survival Data in Medical Research* (London: Chapman & Hall, 1994). The failure function (one minus the survival function) represents the probability that at least one ethnonationalist demonstration by a group has occurred at any given point in time.

mobilizations by the structurally disadvantaged were concentrated in the latter part of the mobilizational cycle. In the case of urbanization (Figure 3.3c) the two step functions show a parallel and even mimicking pattern. A spurt of initial mobilizations by highly urbanized groups in mid-1987 through mid-1988 was followed by a concentrated period of initial mobilizations by less urbanized groups in early 1989, and another spurt of initial mobilizations by highly urbanized groups in 1989 was followed by a second burst of initial mobilizations by less urbanized groups in early 1990. The temporal concentration of initial action by groups sharing similar structural conditions points to a logic underlying the timing of action within the cycle. Movements from groups that were less structurally advantaged were able to exploit the prior actions of the more advantaged within specific temporal contexts as institutional constraints shifted. Figure 3.3d, however, shows a divergent pattern. Differentiation in the timing of action between highly assimilated groups and less assimilated groups emerged only halfway through the cycle in 1989; the differences between the failure functions for highly assimilated and less assimilated nationalities are not statistically significant, and linguistic assimilation only becomes a statistically significant source of differentiation in timing when one controls for the effects of other factors.

Thus Herzen's notion of the "chronological unfairness" of history (latecomers being able to take advantage of the actions of those who precede them) describes well the underlying logic of a tide of nationalism. Structural advantage not only systematically translates into greater frequency of action overall, but into the temporal sequencing of action as well. This structuring of group action across time means that nationalist movements from groups with less robust structural conditions for mobilization are likely to mobilize later than movements from groups enjoying highly facilitative structural conditions. This sequencing of action provides an opportunity for the less advantaged to profit from the example of those preceding them. As we will see below, there is evidence that such cross-group influences were a systematic presence during the *glasnost'* revolution.

## Nationalism in Space-Time (II): The Systematic Effects of Event-Specific Processes

As a final cut, I place the above findings into a single field of play through a cross-sectional time-series (longitudinal) analysis of nationalist mobilization. I show that, even if one controls for the effects of pre-existing structural conditions and institutional constraints on mobilization, event-specific processes (recursion, emulation, and other event-based influences) still account for a significant amount of the variation in mobilization over time and across groups. I also show that the relationship between these three levels of causal influence evolved over the tide, with the causal role of event-specific processes growing in importance relative to institutional constraints and pre-existing structural conditions.

Longitudinal analysis is ideally suited for these purposes. Though requiring some degree of temporal aggregration, cross-sectional time-series regression allows one to view the processes by which mobilization escalates and declines as a result of the influence of both temporal and spatial relationships. I chose aggregation at the weekly level, since this involved minimal temporal aggregation, allowing me to test for influences on processes of escalation and decline that would remain invisible were the data examined at the daily level only, but not overaggregating to the point that temporal causal patterns would be concealed.[18] I developed two longitudinal models: one focused on variation in the frequency of demonstrations; the other explaining mass participation in these demonstrations. Both models analyze mobilization over 237 weekly time periods stretching from January 1987 through August 1991 for fifteen non-Russian nationalities selected out of the larger sample on the basis of their significant records of mobilization, for a total of 3,555 observations.[19] As before, due to the event-count nature of the dependent variable, ordinary least squares was not an option for the demonstration model, and instead a random-effects negative binomial regression model was used.[20] As for the

---

[18] For a similar strategy, see Karen Rassler, "Concessions, Repression, and Political Protest in the Iranian Revolution," *American Sociological Review*, vol. 61 (February 1996), pp. 132–52.

[19] The selection of fifteen groups for longitudinal analysis out of the larger sample of forty-seven was necessitated by the small temporal variation among groups with minimal or no records of mobilization during this period, which would have skewed the statistical results. The groups included were Ukrainians, Belorussians, Uzbeks, Kazakhs, Volga Tatars, Azerbaijanis, Armenians, Georgians, Moldavians, Kirgiz, Lithuanians, Jews, Latvians, Estonians, and Chechens.

[20] On the negative binomial random-effects model, see A. Colin Cameron and Pravin K. Trivedi, *Regression Analysis of Count Data* (Cambridge, UK: Cambridge University Press, 1998), pp. 287–92. For an application to the study of protest events, see Stuart Hill, Donald Rothchild, and Colin Cameron, "Tactical Information and the Diffusion of Peaceful Protests," in David A. Lake and Donald Rothchild, eds., *The International Spread of Ethnic*

participation model, following Beck and Katz I based the model on ordinary least squares with panel-corrected standard errors,[21] particularly since, in accord with my own theoretical assumptions about the recursive effects of nationalist action, I was interested in estimating a dynamic endogenous model that explored processes of serial correlation and cross-case influence rather than a static model that developed standardized corrections for autoregressive processes or panel correlation. Serial correlation in each model was tested for and controlled by adding six weekly lags of the dependent variable.[22] This allowed for modeling some of the recursive processes within the data, thereby engaging a significant theoretical issue and an element of temporal influence identified earlier in qualitative and temporal analyses.

For each model, variables that had proven statistically significant in the previous analyses were included in the specification: population size, union republican federal status (in the demonstration model), linguistic assimilation, urbanization, and (in the participation model) prior mobilizational record and Islamic cultural background. Given that the sample included only fifteen groups out of the earlier sample of forty-seven, not all of these cross-sectional variables should be expected to show statistically significant relationships. Their inclusion in these specifications controls for their differential effects across the groups included in the longitudinal analyses. In addition, three variables were added to control for the effects of

---

*Conflict: Fear, Diffusion, and Escalation* (Princeton, NJ: Princeton University Press, 1998), pp. 61–88. A fixed-effect model was also tested and produced analogous results.

[21] See Nathaniel Beck and Jonathan N. Katz, "Nuisance vs. Substance: Specifying and Estimating Time-Series-Cross-Sectional Models," *Political Analysis*, vol. 6 (1996), pp. 1–36; Nathaniel Beck and Jonathan N. Katz, "What to Do (and Not to Do) with Time-Series-Cross-Section Data," *American Political Science Review*, vol. 89 (1995), pp. 634–47. Beck and Katz provide evidence of the general superiority of OLS estimators with panel-corrected standard errors over GLS estimators through Monte Carlo simulations, particularly for samples with a small number of time observations. Although this was not true of the current sample, Beck and Katz (1996) make a strong argument that GLS leads analysts away from examination of the dynamic qualities of the data and provide evidence that OLS with panel-corrected standard errors provides for consistent estimations.

[22] Since the negative binomial model is multiplicative rather than additive, the natural log of the number of demonstrations was used. See Cameron and Trivedi, *Regression Analysis of Count Data*, pp. 238–39, 294–95. To deal with cases in which the number of demonstrations was zero, 0.5 was added to the demonstration value before taking the natural log. For a similar application, see Hill, Rothchild, and Cameron, "Tactical Information and the Diffusion of Peaceful Protests," p. 76.

shifting institutional constraints on mobilization processes: (1) a dummy variable capturing the influence of electoral campaigns during the six-week period preceding elections for the Nineteenth Party Conference in spring 1988, the Congress of People's Deputies in early 1989, and republican and local legislatures in 1990 and 1991; (2) another dummy variable marking the presence of institutionalizing outcomes, in which nationalist oppositions gained control over republican or local governments or otherwise attained the main goals over which mobilization had taken place; and (3) a political liberalization variable, represented by the time dependency of mobilizational activity, particularly in the early years covered by the model (measured by the week within the mobilizational cycle).[23] As the earlier analysis suggested, greater openness (represented here by the time variable) and electoral campaigns should be associated with heightened attempts to contest (though not necessarily with greater participation), whereas one would expect that institutionalizing outcomes should depress both attempts to contest and participation in demonstrations.

In addition, for the participation model I added a variable marking periods of heightened Armenian-Azerbaijani conflict. As we saw earlier, these cases were outliers in terms of participation. A protracted analysis using dummy variables to explore individual case and period effects indicated that these nationalities showed markedly higher levels of participation in demonstrations than other groups and that much of this heightened mobilization occurred specifically in periods of interethnic violence between the two groups. Why the participation levels of Armenians and Azerbaijanis should stand apart from other groups is not clear. The conflict was particularly intense, but was not the only conflict of this sort to rack the USSR during the *glasnost'* era. It is possible that this very intensity and competition led to bias in the media sources used in constructing the data. Unfortunately, the issue cannot be disentangled easily, but rather

---

[23] In the demonstration model, this was logged to take into account the multiplicative character of the negative binomial regression. I assumed that political liberalization was best conceptualized as a linear time-related process, unmeasurable by any single act and operating generically across all cases. I also assumed that it was likely to be operative during the first years of the cycle. Indeed, when the sample was divided in half, the time variable was positively related to demonstrations and levels of participation during the earlier period (January 1987 through April 1989) but negatively related in the later period (May 1989 through August 1991). For this reason, the political liberalization variable was dropped from specifications dealing with this latter period only. Similarly, no institutionalizing outcomes occurred in the first half of the cycle, so that this variable had to be dropped when analyzing the earlier period only.

than eliminate these important cases from the analysis, I chose instead to include them and to control for the variation which they represented through the inclusion of a time-specific variable marking periods of heightened Armenian-Azerbaijani conflict.

As for providing evidence of the effect of cross-case influences, I have included separate variables for each model: in the demonstration model – the number of demonstrations in which other groups engaged; for the participation model – the number of participants in these demonstrations (in hundreds of thousands). Initial analyses indicated that different processes were at work in the cross-group influences present in the two models. Attempts by nationalist movements to organize demonstrations were more likely to be influenced by the frequency of attempts to mobilize by the nationalist movements of other groups than by levels of participation in these demonstrations, whereas mass participation in demonstrations was more likely to be influenced by levels of participation in the demonstrations of other groups than by the simple number of demonstrations in which other groups engaged. These findings made sense, since they implied that each set of actors compared itself to and monitored an analogous reference set within other groups: movements and populations. I lagged both variables over a six-week period to capture causal direction temporally and to measure the growth and decay of cross-case processes.

Finally, as another event-specific process I included in both models a variable representing the number of mass violent events involving members of the particular nationality. Nationalist violence can have a recursive influence on nationalist mobilization, in that the emotions unleashed by violent nationalist acts against a group can incite further mobilization. By lagging this variable over a six-week period, I again sought to capture causal direction and the growth and decay of the influence of nationalist violence on nonviolent mobilizational activity.

The goals of these analyses were not only to test for the independent and systematic effects of event-specific processes on mobilization, but also to examine how processes of causation evolved over the mobilizational cycle. Toward this latter end, in addition to estimating regression parameters over the entire period, for both models the sample was divided into roughly equal time periods (January 1987 through April 1989 and May 1989 through August 1991) to probe the ways in which causal processes may have altered over time. There are patterns which materialize in the whole but which do not appear in the parts, and this needs to be kept in mind in interpreting the results of the bifurcated sample. Despite these issues, one does obtain from this exercise some sense of the ways in which specific causal influences were concentrated in particular portions of the mobilizational cycle. My assumption was that event-specific processes would grow more pronounced (in terms of the consistency of influence, the size of the effects, and the length of time over which the effects operated) as the cycle developed, and the influence of institutional constraints would lessen over the cycle. Concomitantly, I expected that groups rising within the earlier portion of the mobilizational cycle would rely more heavily on pre-existing structural conditions than on the example of others in generating mobilization, whereas groups rising later, though suffering from greater structural disadvantage, would attempt to compensate for their structural disadvantages by riding the tide generated by previous mobilizers.

The results presented in Tables 3.4 and 3.5 by and large confirm these hypotheses. In Equation 1 of Table 3.4, most of the patterns of pre-existing structural influence found in the earlier cross-sectional analysis hold up when placed into a dynamic temporal model. In the demonstration model, union republican status, linguistic assimilation, and urbanization had statistically significant relationships with weekly rates of demonstrations, whereas population size did not, due largely to its close association with the ethnofederal system and to the elimination of smaller groups from the sample. But the size of the effects also tells a significant causal story: The effect of pre-existing structural conditions was strong, even when controlling for other factors. Thus, in the demonstration model, groups with union republics could expect overall a 60 percent increase in the weekly incidence of demonstrations relative to groups without union republics, even controlling for the effect of population size, assimilation, and urbanization. Every percentage of a group that assimilated linguistically brought about a 1.6 percent decrease in its weekly incidence of demonstrations, and every percent increase in the level of urbanization of a group brought about a 1.8 percent increase in its weekly rate of protest. To place this in perspective, Belorussians, of whom 28.5 percent in 1989 claimed another language besides Belorussian as their native language (mainly Russian) and of whom approximately 43.7 percent were urban, would have experienced a 51 percent decline in the weekly incidence of demonstrations due to their level of linguistic assimilation, though this would have been partially offset by the 44.5 percent increase in the incidence of demonstrations expected as a result of their level of urbanization.

But when we look at how the influence of pre-existing structural conditions evolved over time (Equations 2 and 3 in Table 3.4), we find an erosion of the facilitating effects of structure. During the second half of the cycle a significant weakening occurred in the effects of the ethnofederal hierarchy and urbanization as factors supporting increased rates of protest (the effect of federal institutions practically disappears, and that of urbanization almost halves), whereas the negative effect of linguistic assimilation became stronger. These changes in causal patterns reflected in part the fact that mobilization shifted over time toward groups with less propitious pre-existing structural conditions (for example, less likely to be facilitated by high degrees of urbanization or by union republican ethnofederal status and more disadvantaged by their levels of linguistic assimilation than was true in the earlier part of the cycle). But even among groups with strongly facilitating structural conditions, the influence of structure weakened.

Similarly, in the participation model the patterns of pre-existing structural influence found earlier in cross-sectional analysis were confirmed in our reduced sample (Equation 1 of Table 3.5), with population size, linguistic assimilation, prior mobilizational activity, and Islamic cultural background displaying statistically significant relationships with weekly participation rates, but not urbanization, largely because of its strong association with prior mobilizational activity (when prior patterns of mobilization are excluded from the specification, the urbanization variable grows statistically significant at the .01 level). For the groups included in this panel portion of the analysis (running in size from the nine hundred fifty-three thousand Chechens to the forty-four million Ukrainians), one should have expected weekly participation rates ranging from twenty to thirty-one thousand based solely on variation in population size, holding other variables constant. The expected number of participants in demonstrations based on population size more than doubled over time – in sharp contrast to the lack of relationship of population size and declining influence of ethnofederal categories found earlier in the demonstration model. As these patterns suggest, over time emulative processes spread contention to groups with ethnofederal units lower in the hierarchy, but the resonance of those efforts was still shaped in considerable ways by the normative and power dimensions associated with group size. As was true

Table 3.4. *Negative Binomial Regression of Weekly Count of Protest Demonstrations by Nationality (January 1987–August 1991)*[a]

| Independent Variable | Equation 1 Jan. 1987–Aug. 1991 | | Equation 2 Jan. 1987–April 1989 | | Equation 3 May 1989–Aug. 1991 | |
|---|---|---|---|---|---|---|
| | Coefficient | Incidence Rate Ratio | Coefficient | Incidence Rate Ratio | Coefficient | Incidence Rate Ratio |
| Ln (demonstrations + 0.5), t − 1 | 0.470 (12.46)**** | 1.600 | 0.608 (8.27)**** | 1.836 | 0.390 (9.15)**** | 1.477 |
| Ln (demonstrations + 0.5), t − 2 | 0.132 (3.47)**** | 1.141 | 0.096 (1.27) | 1.101 | 0.118 (2.78)*** | 1.126 |
| Ln (demonstrations + 0.5), t − 3 | 0.089 (2.31)** | 1.093 | 0.036 (0.46) | 1.037 | 0.091 (2.14)** | 1.096 |
| Ln (demonstrations + 0.5), t − 4 | 0.855 (2.25)** | 1.089 | 0.073 (0.87) | 1.076 | 0.081 (1.89)* | 1.084 |
| Ln (demonstrations + 0.5), t − 5 | 0.064 (1.68)* | 1.066 | −0.061 (−0.73) | .941 | 0.064 (1.50) | 1.066 |
| Ln (demonstrations + 0.5), t − 6 | 0.055 (1.51) | 1.057 | 0.105 (1.36) | 1.111 | 0.037 (0.89) | 1.037 |
| Ln population size (thousands), 1989 | −0.040 (−0.70) | .961 | −0.031 (−0.28) | .970 | 0.066 (0.84) | 1.068 |
| Dummy variable for union republican status | 0.468 (2.15)** | 1.597 | 1.693 (3.11)*** | 5.437 | 0.135 (0.57) | 1.144 |
| Linguistic assimilation, 1989 | −0.016 (−2.84)*** | .984 | −0.004 (−0.31) | .996 | −0.022 (−3.52)**** | .978 |
| Level of urbanization, 1970 | 0.018 (4.00)**** | 1.018 | 0.029 (2.77)*** | 1.030 | 0.019 (3.37)**** | 1.019 |
| Dummy variable for period of electoral campaign | 0.205 (2.39)** | 1.227 | 0.226 (1.32) | 1.253 | 0.079 (0.61) | 1.081 |
| Political liberalization (ln week) | 0.865 (9.20)**** | 2.375 | 1.458 (6.87)**** | 4.300 | – | – |
| Dummy variable for period after institutionalizing outcome | −0.403 (−4.70)**** | .668 | – | – | −0.123 (−1.53) | .884 |

| | | | | | | |
|---|---|---|---|---|---|---|
| Mass violent events involving nationality, t − 1 | 0.030 (3.57)**** | 1.031 | −0.004 (−0.15) | .996 | 0.035 (4.08)**** | 1.036 |
| Mass violent events involving nationality, t − 2 | −0.031 (−2.27)** | .970 | 0.002 (0.06) | 1.002 | −0.024 (−1.75)* | .976 |
| Mass violent events involving nationality, t − 3 | −0.007 (−0.52) | .993 | −0.044 (−1.16) | .957 | −0.001 (−0.10) | .999 |
| Mass violent events involving nationality, t − 4 | −0.025 (−1.54) | .976 | −0.028 (−0.59) | .972 | −0.017 (−1.04) | .984 |
| Mass violent events involving nationality, t − 5 | 0.007 (0.60) | 1.008 | −0.036 (−0.72) | .965 | 0.012 (1.01) | 1.013 |
| Mass violent events involving nationality, t − 6 | −0.018 (−1.34) | .982 | −0.054 (−1.07) | .947 | −0.004 (−0.30) | .996 |
| Number of demonstrations by other nationalities, t − 1 | 0.005 (2.53)** | 1.005 | 0.016 (1.77)* | 1.016 | 0.004 (2.10)** | 1.004 |
| Number of demonstrations by other nationalities, t − 2 | −0.007 (−3.17)*** | .993 | −0.016 (−1.92)* | .984 | −0.007 (−3.01)*** | .993 |
| Number of demonstrations by other nationalities, t − 3 | −0.002 (−0.93) | .998 | 0.004 (0.49) | 1.004 | 0.003 (−1.23) | .997 |
| Number of demonstrations by other nationalities, t − 4 | 0.005 (2.43)** | 1.005 | −0.017 (−1.94)* | .984 | 0.006 (2.59)*** | 1.006 |
| Number of demonstrations by other nationalities, t − 5 | 0.001 (0.01) | 1.001 | 0.009 (0.99) | 1.009 | −0.001 (−0.10) | .999 |
| Number of demonstrations by other nationalities, t − 6 | −0.002 (−0.74) | .998 | −0.003 (−0.41) | .997 | −0.001 (−0.62) | .999 |
| Constant | −5.656006 | | −9.951624 | | −1.699547 | |
| t × n | 3,555 | | 1,725 | | 1,830 | |
| Log likelihood | −3,177.0062 | | −899.79094 | | −2,228.2637 | |
| Wald model chi² | 1,060.31**** | | 368.95**** | | 437.89**** | |

*Significant at the .10 level     **Significant at the .05 level     ***Significant at the .01 level     ****Significant at the .001 level.

Note: n = 15 nationalities (excluding Russians); t = 243 weeks.
ª Z-scores in parentheses.

Table 3.5. *Regression of Weekly Count of Participants in Protest Demonstrations by Nationality (January 1987–August 1991)*[a]

| Independent Variable | Equation 1<br>Jan. 1987–Aug. 1991 | Equation 2<br>Jan. 1987–April 1989 | Equation 3<br>May 1989–Aug. 1991 |
|---|---|---|---|
| Participants in demonstrations, t − 1 | .2803647 (6.18)**** | .3401934 (4.21)**** | .1407305 (2.67)*** |
| Participants in demonstrations, t − 2 | .0672512 (1.43) | .0575795 (0.62) | .0801598 (1.50) |
| Participants in demonstrations, t − 3 | .0595728 (1.27) | .0547258 (0.59) | .1044427 (1.96)* |
| Participants in demonstrations, t − 4 | .0079036 (0.17) | −.012046 (−0.13) | .045283 (0.86) |
| Participants in demonstrations, t − 5 | .0645919 (1.37) | .044443 (0.47) | .102464 (1.97)** |
| Participants in demonstrations, t − 6 | .0305788 (0.67) | .0726428 (0.79) | −.0232009 (−0.45) |
| Ln population size (thousands), 1989 | 2,979.2 (3.02)*** | 1,815.4 (1.87)* | 4,161.4 (2.61)*** |
| Thousands of participants in demonstrations, 1965–86 (squared) | 8.4 (2.74)*** | 11.5 (2.17)** | 4.3 (1.87)* |
| Linguistic assimilation, 1989 | −435.5 (−3.86)**** | −433.9 (−2.43)** | −378.3 (−2.78)*** |
| Level of urbanization, 1970 | −14.8 (−0.18) | −13.5 (−0.17) | −10.9 (−0.09) |
| Dummy variable for peoples of traditionally Islamic cultures | −12,110.2 (−3.99)**** | −4,774.7 (−2.08)** | −20,288.0 (−4.39)**** |
| Dummy variable for period of electoral campaign | 8,340.7 (1.15) | 5,048.1 (0.47) | 2,015.9 (0.19) |
| Political liberalization (time dependence) | 75.6 (2.58)*** | 280.8 (2.15)** | — |
| Dummy variable for period after institutionalizing outcome | −19,092.2 (−2.37)** | — | −18,049.4 (−2.82)** |
| Dummy variable for period of heightened Armenian/Azerbaijani conflict | 37,694.8 (2.12)** | 33,635.3 (1.63) | 46,477.2 (1.98)** |

138

| | | | |
|---|---|---|---|
| Mass violent events involving nationality, t − 1 | 3,017.1 (1.02) | −2,778.3 (−0.23) | 4,837.0 (1.99)** |
| Mass violent events involving nationality, t − 2 | −5,026.9 (−1.60) | −12,580.9 (−0.96) | −2,327.7 (−0.94) |
| Mass violent events involving nationality, t − 3 | 745.7 (0.24) | 5,755.2 (0.43) | 16.7 (0.01) |
| Mass violent events involving nationality, t − 4 | −5,129.7 (−1.64) | −12,900.1 (−0.96) | −4,209.6 (−1.69)* |
| Mass violent events involving nationality, t − 5 | 901.0 (0.29) | 206.4 (0.02) | 297.4 (0.12) |
| Mass violent events involving nationality, t − 6 | −1,474.5 (−0.49) | −11,569.1 (−1.09) | 1,021.7 (0.42) |
| | | | |
| Participation by other nationalities (hundreds of thousand), t − 1 | 758.4 (2.42)** | 344.6 (1.08) | 955.9 (2.05)** |
| Participation by other nationalities (hundreds of thousand), t − 2 | −109.0 (−0.32) | −94.9 (−0.31) | −51.5 (−0.11) |
| Participation by other nationalities (hundreds of thousand), t − 3 | −544.6 (−1.58) | −614.1 (−2.04)** | −593.1 (−1.22) |
| Participation by other nationalities (hundreds of thousand), t − 4 | −270.1 (−0.79) | −66.5 (0.22) | −869.3 (−1.77)* |
| Participation by other nationalities (hundreds of thousand), t − 5 | −192.5 (−0.57) | −235.6 (−0.79) | −430.6 (−0.89) |
| Participation by other nationalities (hundreds of thousand), t − 6 | 452.0 (1.45) | 116.5 (0.38) | 712.9 (1.53) |
| | | | |
| Constant | −19,898.9 | −25,991.2 | −10406.8 |
| t × n | 3,555 | 1,725 | 1,830 |
| Log likelihood | −60,250.06 | −53,759.94 | −27,773 |
| Wald model chi² | 295.29**** | 113.02**** | 237.00**** |

*Significant at the .10 level    **Significant at the .05 level    ***Significant at the .01 level    ****Significant at the .001 level.

*Note:* n = 15 nationalities (excluding Russians); t = 243 weeks.

[a] Coefficients represent OLS regression parameters, with panel-corrected standard errors.

for the demonstration model, linguistic assimilation exercised a palpable negative effect on the number of participants. As a result of their high level of assimilation, for instance, Belorussians could have expected approximately twelve thousand fewer weekly participants in nationalist demonstrations than otherwise might have been the case. The negative effect of Islamic cultural background on participation rates in nationalist demonstrations emerges even more clearly in this longitudinal analysis, with Islamic groups exhibiting approximately twelve thousand fewer weekly participants in demonstrations in comparison with other groups, holding all other variables constant. Here again, we see a shift in the types of structural influences that operated over time, with population size and Islamic cultural background growing in consequence during the second half of the mobilizational cycle, and prior patterns of mobilization and linguistic assimilation losing some of their effect on participation. In sum, structural influence was not a constant. Its effects, both in terms of consistency and substance, changed over the mobilizational cycle, as the effects of structural facilitation on action by nationalist movements eroded overall and its effects on participation by target groups remained stable but shifted among various categories of influence.

Turning to the role exercised by institutional constraints, we find quite different influences in the two models. Political liberalization (measured as time dependence) showed a dramatic effect overall (330 percent increase) on the weekly incidence of demonstrations during the first half of the cycle. Yet, the effect on the number of participants, although statistically significant, was substantively quite small (an increase of only 281 participants per week). As these results suggest, generally political liberalization exercised its greatest impact on mobilization through its influence on the efforts of nationalist elites to organize challenging acts rather than on the willingness of populations to participate in these acts. By contrast, in the second half of the cycle institutionalizing outcomes had a more consistent negative effect on participation in protest demonstrations (cutting weekly participation in demonstrations by over eighteen thousand) than on the frequency of efforts by nationalist elites to contest (though when viewed within the context of the entire cycle from January 1987 through August 1991, institutionalizing outcomes led to a 33 percent decrease in the expected number of demonstrations). These results are a statistical confirmation of patterns identified earlier in Figures 3.1 and 3.2, where the number of demonstrations generally continued apace during the latter half of the cycle in spite of the occurrence of significantly reduced mass participation. The results also show that periods of electoral campaigns were associated with a 23 percent increase in the incidence of nationalist demonstrations, but had no statistically significant effect on the number of participants in these demonstrations. Electoral campaigns stimulated challenges from nationalist elites, but did not necessarily lead to heightened mobilization by target populations. Moreover, the effect of electoral campaigns on demonstration activity was more significant in the first half of the cycle than in the second.

Some of the more significant findings emerge when we turn to the effects of event-specific processes on nationalist mobilization. One of the key differences between the demonstration model and the participation model is in the recursive effect of prior mobilization by a nationality on subsequent acts of mobilization by the same group. This was considerably greater in the demonstration model than in the participation model. Thus, the participation model is essentially a one-lag autoregressive process, with every hundred thousand participants generating an additional twenty-eight thousand participants in the following week, but with little recursion beyond this. By contrast, the statistical significance of the lags of the dependent variable in the demonstration model indicates that demonstration activity continued to be associated with subsequent attempts to mobilize up to five weeks later. The decay of the effect was gradual over the six-week period analyzed, suggesting a systematic process at work. Controlling for the effects of other variables, each demonstration increased the expected incidence of demonstrations one week later by 60 percent, two weeks later by 14 percent, three weeks later by 9 percent, and so on. In short, the frequency of attempts by nationalist elites to mobilize was more dependent on riding the inertia generated by prior attempts than was mass participation in these efforts, which on the contrary was a more volatile process.

These results constitute evidence for understanding nationalism as a recursive and emulative process in which prior acts and successes determine in large measure the frequency of subsequent attempts to contest the nation. But it is also significant that for both models recursion was a relatively limited phenomenon in the first half of the mobilizational cycle (a one-lag autoregressive process for both models) and only took on its deepened effect in the second half of the cycle. Even in the participation model there are signs of some sustained influence of participation rates beyond one week in the second half of the cycle, though considerably weaker and less systematic than in the demonstration model. In the emergence of these elongated and consistent autoregressive processes one sees the statistical traces of "thickened history," in which the pace of action exploded and action by members of a target group came to constitute an increasingly significant element of the causal structure of subsequent action by the same group.

The models also provide evidence of the recursive effects of nationalist violence on nationalist demonstrations. In both models, this effect was largely absent in the first half of the cycle, but became a significant factor in the second half, when nationalist violence grew in scope. Thus, each mass violent event involving a nationality was associated with a 3.1 percent increase in the incidence of demonstrations in which that nationality engaged in the week following the event – which for some groups, at particular moments of heightened violence, translated into as much as a 129 percent increase in the incidence of demonstrations in the following week. The negative result for the second lagged week of violence is due solely to its correlation with the first lagged week of the dependent variable and disappears when the latter is dropped from the equations. In terms of participation, the effects of violence were similarly substantial and consistent, with each violent event involving an added 956 participants in the following week. For some groups at particular moments of intense violent conflict, this meant an increase of up to thirty-one thousand participants in the week following an outburst of interethnic violence.

Finally, the effects of cross-case influences are evident statistically in both models as well, though again more visible in the demonstration than in the participation model. Thus, for the entire 1987–91 period each demonstration by a nationality was associated with a 0.5 percent increase in the weekly incidence of demonstrations by another nationality in the following week, controlling for the influence of other factors. Given that the mean weekly number of demonstrations by other nationalities in the pooled sample was twenty (with a low of zero and a high of ninety-two), cross-case influences over a one-week period led to an increase of as much as 46 percent in the weekly incidence rate of demonstrations for some groups at particular moments in time and an average increase of 10 percent, and there is evidence of an additional echo effect after four weeks. Again, further analysis shows that the anomalous negative result for the second lagged week of cross-case influence is due to its correlation with the lagged values of the dependent variable. As hypothe-

sized earlier, the regressions demonstrate that cross-case influences operated more consistently in the second half of the mobilizational cycle than
in the first. This is evidenced by patterns of statistical significance in Equations 2 and 3 in Table 3.4 (in the first half of the cycle, cross-case influences are only marginally significant), as well as by the fact that, in contrast
to the second half, there is no subsequent echo effect of cross-case influence in the first half of the cycle (indeed, the effect in the fourth week was
negative). Thus, cross-case influences on the number of demonstrations
grew more consistent and substantively stronger over time.[24] Similarly,
Table 3.5 shows that cross-case influences on participation in nationalist
demonstrations grew stronger and more consistent during the second
portion of the cycle. No consistent cross-case influence on levels of participation appeared in the first half of the cycle, whereas in the second half
a one-week-after effect is present. The effect of this in the second half of
the cycle was to add as many as thirty-six thousand participants a week to
the demonstrations of some nationalities at particular times, though the
mean weekly effect was only an additional thirteen hundred participants.
Thus, cross-case influences on participation were generally small at most
times, but could burst forth as an important factor attracting participants
to nationalist demonstrations at particular moments when mobilization by
other groups grew significantly.

Table 3.6 summarizes the evolution of causal patterns over time in both
models. As can be seen, event-specific processes grew in influence as the
cycle proceeded, whereas the influence of pre-existing structural conditions and institutional constraints on mobilization either weakened (in the
case of the behavior of nationalist movements) or remained more or less
stable (in the case of target populations). We see here evidence of a particular logic at work. As institutional constraints on mobilization faded,
movements targeting groups with less propitious structural conditions
attempted to mobilize, relying to a greater extent than their predecessors
on the successful actions of others to facilitate their own success. As the
cycle unfolded, events came to take on a greater causal role of their own,

---

[24] Though the incidence rate ratio for the one-week effect in Equation 2 is four times greater
than that of Equation 3 (1.016 versus 1.004), in actual fact, due to the contrasting levels
of mobilization characteristic of each period, the mean one-week effect in both periods
was approximately the same (for the first part of the cycle, a 13.5 percent increase in the
incidence rate, and for the second half of the cycle, a 12.8 percent increase in the incidence rate). But in the second half of the cycle the additional echo effect of cross-case
influences provided an even stronger influence four weeks later.

Table 3.6. *Summary of Shifts in Causal Patterns over Time*

| Type of influence/timing | Early portion of cycle | Latter portion of cycle | Overall direction of change |
|---|---|---|---|
| **Causal Patterns for Number of Demonstrations per Week** | | | |
| Pre-existing structural conditions | Federal status (strong)<br>Urbanization (strong) | Linguistic assimilation (strong)<br>Urbanization (moderate) | Less conducive to mobilization |
| Institutional constraints | Liberalization (strong)<br>Electoral campaigns (weak) | Institutionalization (weak) | Weakened effect |
| Event-specific processes | Recursion (weak)<br>Cross-case influence (moderate)<br>Nationalist violence (weak) | Recursion (strong)<br>Cross-case influence (strong)<br>Nationalist violence (strong) | Strengthened influence |
| **Causal Patterns for Participation per Week in Demonstrations** | | | |
| Pre-existing structural conditions | Population size (weak)<br>Prior participation (strong)<br>Linguistic assimilation (strong)<br>Islamic cultural heritage (weak) | Population size (strong)<br>Prior participation (weak)<br>Linguistic assimilation (moderate)<br>Islamic cultural heritage (strong) | Stability of causal factors with shifting strengths and mixed overall effects |
| Institutional constraints | Liberalization (strong) | Institutionalization (strong) | Shift in causal factors with stable overall strength |
| Event-specific processes | Recursion (weak) | Recursion (moderate)<br>Cross-case influence (moderate)<br>Armenian/Azerbaijani conflict (strong)<br>Nationalist violence (strong) | Strengthened influence |

as recursive, emulative, and other event-based processes assumed a more prominent place in the production of nationalism.

## Summary and Conclusion

In this chapter I tested for the ways in which pre-existing structural conditions, institutional constraints, and event-specific processes left systematic traces on mobilizational activity within the *glasnost'* tide of nationalism. As we have seen, under conditions of loosening institutional constraints, nationalist action came to take on greater causal weight in its own reproduction. This causal role of nationalist action was conspicuous not only in the multiple forms of evidence presented in this and the previous chapter concerning the importance of emulative influences on nationalist mobilization, but also in the existence of a significant recursive dimension to nationalist action. Moreover, as we have seen, event-specific influences in general grew in scope and consistency over the mobilizational cycle, playing a greater role in structuring nationalist action at both the elite and mass levels.

At the same time, we have seen that the "quiet" politics of nationalism shaped nationalist contention in "noisy" phases of contention in multiple and often subtle ways, as the frequency and intensity of nationalist action across groups was influenced by the presence of facilitating structural conditions in place well before the initiation of the mobilizational cycle – conditions such as levels of urbanization and assimilation, population size, a group's status within the ethnofederal system, and its history and cultural background. These were the givens of mobilization that helped give spatial structure to nationalism. We also saw evidence that shifting institutional constraints shaped nationalism temporally, giving rise to the parabola of mobilization and demobilization characteristic of mobilizational cycles. Yet ultimately, nationalism – like all social phenomena – does not exist solely in space or solely in time, but rather in the intersection of the two. And it is here that – through the survival analysis and longitudinal models developed in this chapter – we gained a more realistic and dynamic understanding of nationalism by viewing it within its chronotopic context. As we saw, nationalist movements among early risers tended to enjoy strong facilitating structural conditions, but over time this gave way to action by movements characterized by conditions less conducive for action. In this sense, mobilization for late risers depended to a greater degree than for earlier risers on taking advantage of the successful examples of those who preceded them rather than their given resources and social conditions. By riding the tide of nationalism, some degree of prior structural disadvantage could be mitigated, creating what Herzen called history's "chronological unfairness." As the tide of nationalism evolved, the causal role of the event grew in scope, as later risers with fewer assets but also fewer institutional constraints attempted to take advantage of the successful efforts of those who rose before them. In Chapters 4 and 5 I build on these findings and the logic underlying them to examine the mobilization of identity in greater depth.

# 4

## "Thickened" History and the Mobilization of Identity

A person who changes his viewpoint depending on changes in life rises in the estimation of those around him.

Leonid Kravchuk, April 1991

In May 1987, when *glasnost'* was gathering steam in Moscow but had yet to reach the provinces, I traveled to Soviet Moldavia with my wife Margaret, a fluent speaker of Romanian. Our trip was as Orwellian an experience as I had encountered in my many stays in the USSR. Every minute of our visit was carefully regulated to exclude uncontrolled contact with the population and to ensure our "proper" impressions concerning the loyalties of the local population. We were assigned a multiethnic team to orchestrate our stay: a Moldovan, whose genuine enthusiasm for the achievements of Soviet power (as well as demonization of Romania's connection with Moldavia) surpassed even that of the Russians surrounding him; a Jew, whose scholarly work was far removed from the themes of the visit, but whose suspicious questioning seemed designed to probe the limits of my own Jewish identity; and a Ukrainian, whose main purpose seems to have been to watch over the Moldovan and the Jew. We returned over three years later – in December 1990 – after two years of upheaval in Moldova and a revolution in neighboring Romania. By that time, our Moldovan host had become a prominent leader of the popular front, famous throughout the republic for his fiery nationalist speeches at mass rallies against Moscow's "colonial" policies in the republic; the Jew was in the process of emigrating to Israel; and the Ukrainian had already moved back to Ukraine.

These Moldavian encounters are a metaphor for the massive reimaginings of self that characterized the Soviet Union in its final years and which are the subject of this chapter. Undoubtedly, had public opinion polls asked the question in May 1987, the very idea of Moldovan independence would have seemed absurd to the overwhelming majority of Moldavians. Indeed, aside from the political restrictions that still governed discourse at the time, no one would have thought of asking the question, since it seemed so outlandish an idea. But even in May 1990, after several waves of massive demonstrations, a revolution in Romania, and republican elections which had brought nationalist elites to power, public opinion surveys in Moldova showed that 52 percent of ethnic Moldavians still believed that Moldova should remain a sovereign republic within the USSR rather than become an independent state or be reunited with Romania. Fifteen months later, in August 1991, these same opinion surveys showed that 79 percent of the population of the republic – irrespective of ethnicity – believed that Moldova should become an independent state.[1] "Thickened" history had provided the context for a fundamental transformation of identities which, in "quieter" times, were once believed to be fixed and immutable.

This chapter examines the process by which identities are mobilized and altered within the context of a tide of nationalism. It does so through a comparative analysis of the rise of secessionist consciousness among six Soviet nationalities. I begin by conceptualizing the mobilization of identity as a protracted political process involving an interaction between the creation of structural advantage, emboldening in the face of institutional constraints, and event-generated influences over the uncommitted and over potential defectors. This allows me to talk about various mixes of prior structural facilitation, institutional constraint, and event-generated influences necessary for successful mobilization (that is, mobilization that gains widespread resonance) around a particular identity frame. Such a perspective is useful for understanding how the mobilization of identity evolves over a mobilizational cycle – a subject examined in Chapter 3, but pursued in more fine-grained fashion here with respect to the rise and proliferation of one specific mobilizational frame in particular, that of secession.

Through a series of case studies, I compare the changing process by which secessionist frames emerged and resonated within six target popu-

---

[1] *Obshchestvennoe mnenie: Aktual'nye problemy sotsial'noi zhizni SSR Moldova* (Kishinev: Akademiia nauk SSR Moldova, 1990), p. 54; *Ekspress khronika*, no. 35, August 27, 1991, p. 6.

lations over the *glasnost'* mobilizational cycle. The chapter makes three fundamental points. First, the mobilization of any identity is always an uneven process across a target population involving a mix of prior structural facilitation, the emboldening of supporters in the face of institutional constraints, and the persuasion of those less committed. These latter two processes emerge in the context or aftermath of an event and are what make events such potent sites and instigators of identity change. Some mix of these processes is present in all cases of the mobilization of identity. As we will see, even among early risers within the cycle, who enjoyed the strongest degrees of prior structural facilitation, a significant number of individuals embraced secessionist frames only under the transformative influence of events and the example of action by others.

Second, more than one path or mix can lead to the successful mobilization of identity. When viewed across multiple groups, the roles of prior structural facilitation, institutional constraints, and event-generated influences in structuring mobilization shift over the course of a mobilizational cycle. As we saw in Chapters 2 and 3, on the one hand the mobilization of identity grows more difficult over a cycle due to the diminishing levels of structural facilitation characteristic of late risers. On the other hand, over time the mobilization of identity is facilitated by the unraveling of compliance systems and the "thickened" pace of challenging acts, allowing movements to take advantage of the successful example of others and the increased availability of what Snow and Benford call a mobilizational "master frame" – a frame which, because of its proven potency, tends to be shared across movements.[2] In the Soviet case, it was the anticolonial secessionist frame which gained increasing appeal across cases due to the Stalinist legacy of the Soviet state, international norms advantaging anticolonial movements in gaining recognition for self-determination claims, the prior successes of the frame, and bandwagoning effects. Within a context of "thickened history" event-generated influences grew more significant over time in the politics of identity, leading to distinct patterns of identity politics among early and late risers.

Third, this growing role of event-generated influences over a cycle creates a dependency of late risers on the successes of their predecessors,

---

[2] David A. Snow and Robert D. Benford, "Master Frames and Cycles of Protest," Aldon D. Morris and Carol McClurg Mueller, eds., *Frontiers in Social Movement Theory* (New Haven, CT: Yale University Press, 1992), pp. 133–55.

injecting considerable contingency into the outcomes of identity politics and imparting to them the sense of "cascade" that Timur Kuran observed.[3] Massive identity change in this sense often occurs in clusters across cultural groups, not as a set of isolated and unrelated stories, but as a transnational process, with the final outcome contingent on the outcomes of prior cases.

## The Mobilization of Identity as Political Process

The struggle over identity lies at the core of the contentious politics that constitutes nationalism. As I argued in Chapter 1, through its policies the state seeks to shape the beliefs of its citizens about nationhood in accordance with dominant understandings, to naturalize these understandings, and to present them as inevitable and unalterable. Nationalist movements, by contrast, seek to challenge these conceptualizations and to assert the primacy of alternative bindings. In times of "normalized" politics, official conceptions of nationhood are not easily subject to direct contestation, and nationalist challengers instead prepare for moments when direct challenge becomes possible by attempting to strengthen and implant supporting beliefs, behaviors, and conditions that can act as resources for challenge once the opportunity materializes. In these "quiet" times states and nationalist challengers seek to build structural advantage – to create a reservoir of symbolic capital, to accumulate political resources, and to approximate conditions justifying the application of supportive norms – in order to prevent or facilitate challenges that might emerge in the future. "Noisy" phases of contention are equally critical to identity politics, for it is here that opportunities to put structural advantage to work become more readily apparent to challengers. Tides of nationalist contention are significant sites of identity change in part because they provide a context in which identities and the loyalties that underlie them can be tested and either openly discarded or affirmed. The explosion of open contestation that accompanies a mobilizational cycle provides the opportunity for the assertion of that which lies implicit in times of conventional politics.

But identity politics within the context of "thickened history" is not simply the embodiment of pre-existing structural advantage – the Pandora's Box image that is characteristic of teleological conceptions of

---

[3] Timur Kuran, "Ethnic Norms and Their Transformation Through Reputational Cascades," *Journal of Legal Studies*, vol. 27 (June 1998), pp. 623–59.

nationalism. As Bert Klandermans observed, "On the one hand, the social construction of meaning precedes collective action and determines its direction; on the other, collective action in its turn determines the process of meaning construction."[4] Within a "noisy" phase of nationalist contention, the constraining parameters of politics undergo fundamental challenge, leading to rapidly shifting assumptions about the limits of the possible. This profoundly affects not only the strategic framing of states and movements, but also potentially throws into question the entire array of mass loyalties on which legitimate political order is built. In a period of intensified challenge, specific events and the actions of others also exercise significant effects on identities. In this sense, collective action needs to be thought of as both a dependent and an independent variable with respect to identity.

Social psychologists have noted three fundamental mechanisms involved in the formation of individual beliefs: internalization, compliance, and persuasion.[5] These three mechanisms at the individual level roughly map onto the three broader social processes involved in the mobilization of identity at the collective level: structural facilitation, institutional constraints, and event-generated influences. The creation of structural advantage in identity politics entails in part the creation of relatively durable sets of beliefs resulting from socialization and the gradual formation of symbolic capital. These are the products of the "quiet" politics of nationalism, revolving around efforts by regimes and challengers to build structural advantage in preparation for moments when direct contestation becomes possible. But structural advantage at the collective level can also be generated through the creation of resources and social conditions that facilitate expression of identity. High birthrates, for instance, can lead to large increases in population that could potentially increase the human resources available to a nationalist movement and could eventually support future application of self-determination norms favoring large groups. Structural advantage at the aggregate level may also accrue out of unintended processes. Urbanization, for instance, may take place for reasons only loosely connected with nationalism, but, as we have seen, can have

---

[4] Bert Klandermans, "The Social Construction of Protest and Multiorganizational Fields," in Morris and Mueller, eds., *Frontiers in Social Movement Theory*, p. 82.

[5] These categories are adapted from H. C. Kelman, "Compliance, Identification, and Internalization: Three Processes of Attitude Change," *Journal of Conflict Resolution*, vol. 2, no. 1 (1958), pp. 51–60.

profound effects in fostering the growth of national movements and creating the type of thick networks conducive to nationalist mobilization.

By contrast, compliance involves the formation of beliefs through the imposition of institutional constraints – that is, systems of reward and punishment. Institutional constraints are powerful mechanisms for affecting the ways in which individuals think about their identities, for in times of normalized politics people tend to adjust their beliefs to the boundaries of the permissible and the possible, usually embodied in prevailing systems of incentive and punishment. Both coercion and reward are essential parts of compliance systems. In the Soviet Union, for instance, the unraveling of order was more than simply a decline in the repressive capabilities of the regime, though, as we will see in Chapter 7, this was certainly a part of the process. The decay of authority also involved disruption of those economic incentives promoting cooperation within the existing frame of authority (however weak these might have been at times under state socialism) – a disorder caused in part by the effects of the ethnic mobilization and conflict that had overtaken the country.[6]

The role of compliance in the formation of beliefs is precisely why opportunities are key in the politics of identity. Through disrupting the boundaries of the permissible and the normal, nationalist challengers seek to create conditions allowing people to express ideas which movement activists believe are widely shared but lie repressed beneath the surface of outward behavior due largely to the pressures of public norms and the constraints imposed by institutions. In this chapter, I refer to such politics as "emboldening." Some may question whether emboldening publics to express suppressed identity frames involves an identity change at all, since the formation of beliefs occurs prior to the onset of mobilization. Kuran, for instance, assumes that for the individuals emboldened to act in ways openly challenging the dominant ethnic order, a situation of ethnic "preference falsification" holds, that there is a strong underlying set of "genuine" preferences about identity covered up by the constraints imposed on individuals, and that these preferences are at last revealed under conditions of shifting constraints.[7] This is certainly true for those

---

[6] See, in particular, Prime Minister Ryzhkov's assessment of the role of nationalist conflict in undermining the Soviet economy during these years, in Nikolai Ryzhkov, *Perestroika: Istoriia predatel'stv* (Moscow: Novosti, 1992), p. 319.

[7] See Timur Kuran, "Ethnic Dissimilation and Its International Diffusion," in David A. Lake and Donald Rothchild, eds., *The International Spread of Ethnic Conflict: Fear, Diffusion, and Escalation* (Princeton, NJ: Princeton University Press, 1998), pp. 35–60.

individuals with a strong symbolic attachment to an identity frame. But as the literature on identity has shown, what a "genuine" identity is for many individuals is difficult to define; to varying degrees, ambiguity about identity is a constant presence within all groups. The emboldening of nationalist expression in the face of institutional constraints may involve more than simply "ethnic dissimilation," as Kuran calls it. Rather, for those for whom preferences involve some degree of ambiguity, it may precipitate preference clarification, at least in the sense of movement from a situation of ambiguity to one of certainty. As of the examples below will confirm, the manifest assertion of the implicit and the rejection of the overt are bold acts that usually involve a transformation of consciousness. Such situations are often characterized by those who live through them as an "awakening," "rebirth," or "spiritual revolution" – all terms which suggest a degree of identity change.

The emboldening of expressions of identity in the face of institutional constraints necessarily takes place in the context or aftermath of an event – that is, through occasions which disrupt the normal boundaries of an ongoing order. But it is also greatly facilitated by pre-existing structural conditions. Commitment to an internalized understanding of identity increases the risks individuals are willing to take in pursuit of the values attached to an identity and lowers the effectiveness of opposing systems of authority. Moreover, as the literature on social movements has shown, challenging a compliance system requires resources – networks, skills, funds, facilities, and organization – all of which tend to emerge over a protracted period of time rather than spontaneously at the moment of challenge. Thus, the greater the degree of prior structural advantage around an identity frame that has accrued within a target population, the more robust the institutional constraints (rewards and punishments) needed by authority to prevent an identity frame from being expressed, and the easier it is for an opposition movement to embolden populations to voice suppressed beliefs in the face of potential retaliation. Conversely, fewer resources, weaker internalization of symbolic capital, and fewer supportive norms make it more difficult for a movement to break through a compliance system and to embolden people to express suppressed beliefs, since fewer are willing to risk the threat of retaliation.

In contrast to compliance, in which belief change is induced through the manipulation of rewards and punishments, or its antithesis – emboldening, in which the lifting of constraints becomes the opportunity for the disruption of order and expression of suppressed beliefs – persuasion is a more subtle and variable form of influence exercised primarily over the less committed and over those who could potentially defect from one identity position to another. Rather than a direct relationship between the lifting of constraint and action, under persuasion the individual is led toward a choice that seems in the end to come from within rather than without, although persuasion clearly involves a significant degree of external influence over the individual's reasoning or emotions. Among defectors this choice may be primarily or solely due to strategic calculations emerging from external influences, though the pretense is always made that the decision comes from within. One of the roles of events and of the strategic framing that accompanies them is to induce not merely dissimulation among individuals whose genuine preferences have been concealed, but also preference clarification, genuine preference change, and bandwagoning effects among less committed individuals. Without exercising influence over the less committed and over those cooperating with ongoing authority systems within a target group, most nationalist movements are unlikely to achieve the support necessary for widerspread mobilizational success. The tidal effects of nationalism are in part a form of persuasive influence over the less committed and over potential defectors that emerges out of the concentrated and linked flow of events – not only through the ways in which identities are potentially altered by the transactions of the the event itself, but also through the sense of dynamism and impending outcome which an explosion of contention engenders and the alterations in strategic calculations it generates.

Event-generated persuasive influences can operate in both a positive or a negative fashion. One form of positive persuasion is identification – a relatively unstable attitudinal change that results when people feel linked to an attractive and likeable source of information and come to accept the attitudes and behaviors associated with that source. Such attitudes remain stable so long as the source remains attractive or the belief becomes internalized.[8] The example set by others and a sense of dynamism attached to a movement can exercise powerful persuasive and bandwagoning effects of this sort. They create new opportunities for those sitting on the fence to join, unleash fears of isolation for those who do not, and draw on a natural tendency to identify with success. As Dennis Chong notes, these types of influences are generally the result of prior successful action. "Par-

---

[8] See Kelman, "Compliance, Identification, and Internalization."

ticipation that is motivated by social pressure will slacken if the cause appears to be out of reach, because people will not feel obligated to expend their resources on such an effort; on the other hand, if victory is within grasp and held to be contingent on successful organization, the social pressure on the individual to join will be considerable."[9] Thus, the event creates a contingency surrounding identity for significant numbers of people; the outcome of the event is not determined, but rests instead on the transactions associated with the action itself. But the consequences of that outcome in terms of the identities of individuals can be quite significant. As the quotation by Leonid Kravchuk at the beginning of this chapter illustrates, in the context of "thickened history" individuals are presented with an opportunity to "convert" to new identity frames that, in some cases, they once openly opposed, thereby "rising in the estimation of others." Event-generated persuasion operates in negative ways as well, through the production of widespread repulsion and antipathy toward a particular group or source of authority. Repulsion often lies behind the power of individual events to crystallize opinion around new cultural norms, fundamentally altering the landscape of politics. As we have already seen in Chapters 2 and 3, violence is a particularly potent force for generating negative identification, and some nationalists, knowing this to be the case, at times seek to precipitate such defining events to accelerate the transformation of identities.[10]

Figure 4.1 portrays the politics of mobilizing identity as a combination of the emboldening of supporters and event-generated influences over the less committed under differing conditions of structural facilitation and institutional constraint. It illustrates precisely why traditional scholarly discussions of "primordialism" and "instrumentalism" are often rooted in an irresolvable chicken-or-egg debate. As we compare the ways in which identities crystallize among various groups across a tide of nationalism, the real question becomes not the presence or absence of "sticky" emotional attachments to identity or contextual and interest-based influences on beliefs, but rather the relative mix of pre-existing structural facilitations, emboldening in the face of institutional constraint, and event-generated

---

[9] Dennis Chong, *Collective Action and the Civil Rights Movement* (Chicago: University of Chicago Press, 1991), p. 164.

[10] Fanon, for instance, contended that for the colonized "the practice of violence binds them together as a whole," allowing each individual to form "a violent link in the great chain" of violence, out of which a nation, cemented by "blood and anger," would take shape. Frantz Fanon, *The Wretched of the Earth* (New York: Grove Press, 1968), p. 93.

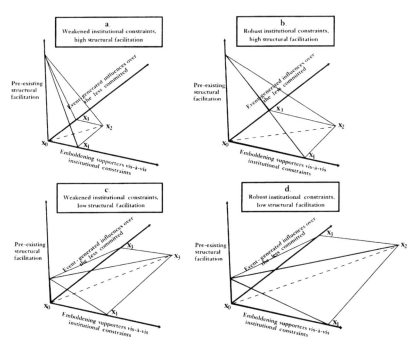

**Figure 4.1.** Pre-existing structural facilitation, emboldening vis-à-vis institutional constraints, and event-generated influences in the mobilization of collective identity.

influences in the mobilization of a given target population. The comparison among these mixes provides the basis for a realistic rather than a reductionist analysis of the mobilization of identity and for transcending the false dichotomy often perpetrated by primordialist and instrumentalist partisans.

Figure 4.1 also presumes that pre-existing structural conditions become causal forces because they are actively *used* by states or movements in the production or prevention of mobilization and that action mediates between pre-existing structural conditions and outcomes. One of the fundamental insights of Giddens is that facilitating structure only becomes facilitating in the process of action itself. This means that pre-existing structural conditions alone can never explain the process by which identities are mobilized, for facilitating structure only gains its effect through action or prevention of action under conditions in which action appears possible. Pre-existing structural conditions affect identity politics in "noisy" phases of contention because they influence the ways in which the emboldening of supporters and event-generated influences on the less committed do or do not occur. Specifically, weaker internalization of symbolic capital around an identity frame, less supportive social norms, and/or lower levels of mobilizational resources raise the bar for both emboldening and event-generated influences, thereby making the mobilization of identity more difficult. Thus, pre-existing structural conditions are critical to determining the ways in which the mobilization of identity occurs, for their presence profoundly affects the mix of emboldening and event-generated influences necessary to mobilize successfully around a particular identity frame. But emboldening and event-generated influences should be regarded as the fundamental engines through which the mobilization of identity occurs, not pre-existing structural conditions, which are more analogous to the fuel and lubrication that power and expedite the movement of the parts. Events can embolden or persuade, but it is in and through events and the discourse that accompanies them that the mobilization of identity takes place.

Figure 4.1 illustrates the trade-offs that exist among these three dimensions of identity mobilization. Point $x_2$ represents the mix of emboldening of supporters and event-generated influences over the less committed necessary for a movement to generate a critical mass within a target population around an identity frame, given a particular combination of prior structural facilitation and the strength of the compliance system. Movements tend to focus their mobilizational efforts primarily on that part of a population most likely to support them rather than on all sectors.[11] Nevertheless, as nationalist movements usually need to gain support among the less committed if they are to achieve mobilizational success, it is useful to think in terms of various mixes of emboldening and persuasion needed for mobilizing a critical mass under differing conditions of structural facilitation and institutional constraints.

My determination in Figure 4.1 of the mix of emboldening and event-generated influences necessary for mobilizing a critical mass is based on the assumption that each variable – pre-existing structural facilitation, emboldening against institutional constraints, and event-generated influences – affects the degree to which other processes must be present for mobilizational success to occur. Strong structural facilitations lower the

---

[11] Gerald Marwell and Pamela Oliver, *The Critical Mass in Collective Action* (Cambridge, UK: Cambridge University Press, 1993), p. 130.

degree of emboldening and event-generated influences necessary to mobilize identities by enhancing the ability of movements to embolden supporters and strengthening influence over the less committed. Obviously, the more robust the institutional constraints backing a particular order, the more central emboldening becomes to mobilization. Thus, the least demanding environment for mobilizing identity is a situation of weakened institutional constraints and high structural facilitation (Figure 4.1a), whereas the most demanding environment is one in which structural facilitation is weak and the system of compliance robust (Figure 4.1d). These variations in the efforts required to mobilize support for an identity frame are represented in each of the figures by the line $x_0-x_2$, which stretches longer as the facilitating conditions for mobilization grow weaker and the compliance systems constraining mobilization grow more robust.

As I argue in the previous chapter, the logic of these relationships drives much of identity politics within a cycle of mobilization. Over time within a cycle, the role of prior structural conditions in facilitating mobilization diminishes, as action comes to encompass groups with less robust facilitating conditions. Moreover, in some (though not all) related contexts, institutional constraints are also disrupted, as spillover effects from persistent challenges to authority affect the coherence of institutions in other cases and raise expectations among challengers from other groups about the ease with which order can be contested. Thus, as time progresses within a cycle, movements tend to face local regimes with less robust institutional constraints, but also with weaker facilitating structures in place.[12] Simultaneously, tidal effects come to play a greater role. The important point to note here, however, is that movements from groups with less robust facilitating structure can still be successful mobilizers, assuming that they are able to "substitute" event-generated influences for the advantages that might have accrued from pre-existing structural facilitation. By taking advantage of the tidal effects produced by the earlier action of other groups or by precipitating other event-specific processes of persuasion, movements can overcome some of the structural disadvantages they face and

---

[12] The exception is cross-state diffusion of nationalism, in which a new series of institutional contexts and structural facilitations is brought into the mix. The Velvet Revolution in Czechoslovakia in November 1989, for instance, resembled Figure 4.1a, whereas the subsequent revolution in Romania a month later resembled Figure 4.1b. Thus, explaining the timing of action is considerably more complex in the cross-state diffusion of nationalism than within a single state due to the variable sets of institutional constraints and structural facilitations which movements in different states confront.

attain a mobilizational success which, in the absence of the tide and based solely on their structural advantages, would have been unlikely.

The process of mobilizing identity for early risers in the Soviet Union (Baltic and Crimean Tatar nationalist movements, for instance) resembled Figure 4.1b – high structural facilitation and robust institutional constraints. This involved a significantly different mix of emboldening and event-generated influences than required by later risers with weaker structural advantages, such as Ukrainian nationalist movements (whose situation was closer to Figure 4.1c – lower structural facilitation and weakened institutional constraints) or Uzbek nationalist movements (where structural facilitation was still weaker and institutional control remained intact, resembling Figure 4.1d). For early risers, the politics of emboldening usually plays a more critical role in the mobilization of identity than for late risers, with event-generated influences a less significant but still palpable dimension. As a cycle unfolds, the successful example of early risers disrupts the compliance systems facing other groups, lowering some of the obstacles that subsequent mobilizers must surmount in order to embolden supporters. At the same time, event-generated influences grow more central to the politics of mobilizing identity, as elites from groups with weaker facilitating conditions seek to emulate the successes of early risers and mobilize tidal effects to their advantage. Obviously, not all – indeed, not even most – attempts to mobilize succeed in the sense of gaining mass resonance. Some never materialize in the first place due to the absence of structural facilitation. Others are cut short through repression or cooptation, whereas in other cases the resonance of an identity frame remains small despite the persistent efforts of nationalists. As we will see in the next chapter, the failure of movements to take advantage of tidal influences often results from the combined effects of weak structural preconditions and robust institutional constraints. But the successful mobilization of identity within a cycle does not follow a single path; rather, it involves shifting mixes of pre-existing structural advantage, emboldening supporters in the face of institutional constraints, and event-generated influences over the less committed, with the latter growing in significance as the cycle evolves.

## Secessionist Mobilization within the Glasnost' Tide of Nationalism

Arguably the most important "master frame" to emerge in the Soviet Union during the *glasnost'* period was the antiimperial secessionist frame

159

that played a central role in the ultimate demise of the Soviet state. In its final years of existence the imperial persona implicit within the Soviet state came to be openly affirmed, as nations claimed their place on the political map of the world. There are a number of reasons why the rise of secessionist consciousness in the Soviet Union provides good cases for exploring the interplay between structural facilitation, emboldening, and event-specific influences in the mobilization of identities. From the point of view of the state and those who support it, the demand for separate statehood is always one of the most radical of demands, akin in many ways to revolution. Unlike other types of nationalist claims (irredentist, integral, imperialist), secession transcends the basic parameters of the polity and threatens the very foundations of existing political order. As such, secessionist movements usually experience severe pressure from the state, and often open repression. In times of a normalized political order, when the state seems unassailable, the expression of demands for separate statehood usually takes a great deal of courage. For the vast majority of people living under such conditions, the pressures of a functioning state are ordinarily so great as to make the possibility of secession appear remote. Even in populations in which there may be widespread beliefs in the desirability of a secessionist outcome, the vast majority of people need to be convinced that such demands can be expressed without fear of reprisal and that gaining independent nationhood is a real possibility before openly affirming the secessionist cause. The rise of secessionist consciousness thus provides an excellent vehicle for probing the politics of mobilizing identity more generally, for it allows us to examine how the changing parameters of the permissible and the possible, pre-existing structuring conditions, and collective action interact in shaping the ways in which people think of themselves and their relationship to the state.

Secessionist mobilization emerged in the Soviet Union as a transnational tidal force, not as an isolated collection of movements, developing first in the Baltic in the summer and fall of 1988 and then spreading in a massive way to Georgia, Armenia, Azerbaijan, Moldova, Ukraine, and even eventually to Russia itself. The diffusion of this antiimperial secessionist frame beyond the Baltic was in part an attempt to capitalize on the prior successes of others. But it was more than this. Baltic popular fronts consciously attempted to reproduce themselves throughout the Soviet Union, out of both philosophical and strategic considerations. As Nils Muiznieks has noted, the leaders of the Baltic fronts "insisted that their own interpretation of self-determination had applicability throughout the Soviet

Union" and "called not only for their own self-determination but also for that of all the titular nationalities of Soviet republics."[13] "There cannot be a sovereign Estonia," Edgar Savisaar noted in October 1988, "if Lithuania, Latvia, and other republics are not sovereign."[14] In this sense, the diffusion of secessionist frames was in part a purposive process. Baltic fronts vigorously organized to extend their influence throughout the Soviet Union by aiding the spread of the master frame they themselves had pioneered. This they did through numerous means: publishing Russian-language newspapers intended for consumption outside the Baltic; dispatching emissaries to engage in agitation or to provide advice about the organization of social movements; hosting "foreign delegations" from other republics and providing nascent social movements with a safe haven from which to operate when they faced repression; and printing newspapers and other materials for social movements from other republics that lacked access to printing facilities. Lawyers from the Latvian Popular Front were sent to Minsk and Tbilisi to aid in the drafting of movement statutes and programs.[15] In all, 210 demonstrations (in which more than 3.9 million people participated) occurred in the Soviet Union from late 1988 through the end of 1991 in which members of one nationality expressed solidarity with the secessionist demands of another. These acts of disruption played an important role at critical moments in the regime's relationship with secessionist movements, as in March 1990 when Lithuania declared independence and was subjected to an economic blockade, or in January 1991 when Moscow attempted its violent crackdown in Vilnius. A conscious strategy of spreading secessionist revolt laterally was pursued, both as an effort to consolidate secessionist movements through the power of the example of others and to weaken the regime, countering its efforts to defuse nationalist organizations. The emergence of a tidal dimension to secessionist nationalism in the Soviet Union was thus part of a strategic politics. Not only did groups contesting official conceptions of nationhood draw freely on the examples of those who had successfully engaged in analogous activity in other parts of the country, but nationalist movements struggled to institutionalize themselves through their own reproduction in other national contexts, symbolized in the slogan often raised at secessionist demonstrations throughout the Soviet Union at the

---

[13] Muiznieks, "The Influence of the Baltic Popular Movements," p. 4.
[14] Radio Vilnius, in *FBIS*, October 31, 1988, p. 50.
[15] Muiznieks, "The Influence of the Baltic Popular Movements," pp. 5–11.

time – "For Your Freedom and Ours!"[16] Nationalist movements have traditionally been considered parochial and inward-looking, lacking empathy and incapable of identifying with others. There is some truth to this characterization, but, as the Soviet example so vividly demonstrates, most nationalist movements are actually transnational in orientation, forced by the exigencies of contentious politics to conceive of their fates as connected with those of others.

One can identify four phases in the development of secessionist mobilization within the USSR as a whole. These are depicted in Figure 4.2, which details various dimensions of mobilizational patterns in favor of secession up through the demise of the USSR. Each of the four phases was characterized by a distinct mobilizational politics in terms of the degree to which nationalists sought to mobilize their populations around secessionist frames, the extent to which these frames resonated within populations, and the number of nationalities targeted by these efforts. In Phase 1 of the development of secessionist mobilization, lasting roughly through May 1988, secessionist frames remained effectively marginalized. Secessionist nationalists, still on the fringes of politics, attempted intermittently to mobilize populations in support of secession, but these efforts were relatively rare and did not find mass resonance. During this period secessionist demands figured prominently in the protest activity of a handful of groups only; secession was visible in the demands raised by activists at demonstrations among five nationalities only, and even here it did not figure among the most frequent demands raised.

Phase 2, lasting from approximately June 1988 to February 1989, represented a period of emboldening among a limited number of nationalities in which the boundaries of the permissible and possible came under challenge. Attempts to mobilize around secessionist frames remained intermittent during this period, but within a few nationalities (the Balts and Georgians) began to resonate more widely and assume a mass character. Nevertheless, during this period secessionist demands were often posed ambiguously, as nationalist movements probed what appeared to be the outer limits of expression by raising demands for sovereignty and autonomy rather than independence. In this period movements were still vulnerable to being shut down by repression, so posing demands

---

[16] The slogan has a long history in the struggle against Russian imperialism. In the early nineteenth century Polish troops under the command of General Henryk Dąbrowski fought alongside Napoleon's armies under the slogan "For Your Freedom and Ours!"

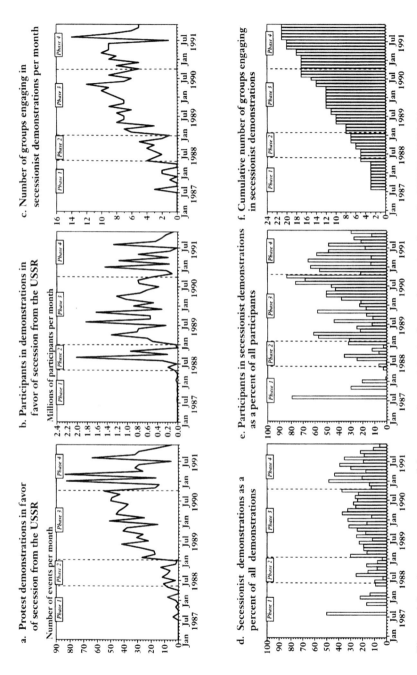

**Figure 4.2.** Aggregate patterns of demonstration activity in favor of secession from the USSR, 1987–91.

163

ambiguously provided some degree of protection. As Figure 4.2e indicates, secessionist frames had relatively minor resonance within the Soviet population as a whole during this time, at least compared to other issues. The number of nationalities engaging in any degree of secessionist protest during these months varied between one and five, and by the end of Phase 2 around January 1989, secessionist demands had made some form of appearance among only two more groups than prior to June 1988. Thus, by January 1989 it still appeared to most within the Soviet elite that the USSR did not face a secession crisis, but mainly a conflict over the redistribution of powers between the center and some of the republics.

It was during Phase 3 (lasting roughly from February 1989 through October 1990) that secession became a dominant political issue in the USSR. From February 1989 the number of secessionist demonstrations began a steep ascent, increasing to five or six times the highest frequencies in Phases 1 and 2. This explosion in secessionist contestation was accompanied by an accelerated diversification of the groups involved, with the number of nationalities experiencing some secessionist protest rising from seven in January 1989 to seventeen by October 1990. February 1989 appears to constitute a sharp break in the incidence, resonance, and lateral spread of secessionist protest, but one is hard-pressed to identify a single event that would explain this altered pattern. What appears to have taken place was a growing boldness in the demands put forward by nationalist elites and a broadened resonance of claims within a number of populations, triggered in part by the prior successes of earlier secessionist mobilization, an increasing sense of the vulnerability of central authority, and a growing alienation from the center's policies. Event-generated influences during this period grew in scope, as the example of earlier risers came to exert a palpable effect on the mobilization of later risers. Secessionist demands came to occupy a dominant place within the protest agendas of multiple groups, and throughout this period the mobilizing power of secessionist demonstrations remained extremely robust, as the goals and symbols of obtaining independent statehood found resonance within growing segments of the Soviet population. The first half of 1990 in particular saw a sharp rise in the number of groups engaging in secessionist protest. During the summer and fall of 1990, at the time of the so-called parade of sovereignties, when federal unit after federal unit went about declaring its "sovereignty" vis-à-vis the center, a significant number of new groups began to mobilize around secessionist demands. The proportion of participants in demonstrations voicing secessionist demands among all participants in demonstrations in the USSR reached 40 to 85 percent every month from May through October 1990. The influence of the communist revolutions in East Europe in fall 1989 and the republican elections of early 1990 seem conspicuous in extending the spread and scope of secessionist mobilization. Phase 3 was also characterized by the institutionalization of a number of secessionist movements within Soviet state structures, leading ultimately to a bifurcation of authority (*dvoevlastie*) and to increasingly bitter disputes over sovereignty. By this time, significant bandwagoning effects were in place, as elites connected with the old system of power began to loosen their ties with the center and play both sides of the fence.

The bandwagoning and bifurcated authority that emerged by the end of Phase 3 led naturally to the more intermittent contestation characteristic of Phase 4. Patterns of secessionist mobilization were shaped in significant ways by the partial institutionalization of secessionist sentiment in republican and local governments, leading to large but more sporadic secessionist mobilizations frequently spearheaded by republican and local state authorities in their struggles with the center over authority. This is evident in Figure 4.2a, for instance, in the sharp decline in the number of secessionist demonstrations that occurred in November–December 1990, February 1991, and April–July 1991 (periods of intensified negotiation over a new union treaty) and the robust remobilizations that occurred in January, March, and August 1991 over the failed attempts by the center to crack down on secessionist challenges. Diversification in the number of groups encompassed by secessionist politics continued during this period, as the impending collapse of the USSR, by this time increasingly obvious, inspired the emergence of new secessionist contenders. In Phase 4, the final phase, persuasive processes emerging out of tidal influences came to play the dominant role in secessionist politics, as the Soviet state grew increasingly incoherent and more visibly on the brink of collapse. In the wake of the wave of declarations of secession following the collapse of the August 1991 coup, protest mobilization in favor of secession from the USSR naturally declined sharply, and with the Belovezhskoe Forest and Almaty agreements to dissolve the USSR in December 1991, the issue died along with the Soviet state.[17]

---

[17] Obviously, many of the successor states were plagued with their own separatist challenges, but the mobilization examined here focused solely on secession from the USSR, not from the union republics themselves. For more on the latter, see Chapter 5.

I turn now to a series of illustrative case studies which trace the successful rise of secessionist sentiment across the cycle, noting the differential ways in which identities altered over the cycle, both within and across groups, through a detailed comparison of the politics of secessionist mobilization. In all six cases examined, secessionist sentiment, once effectively marginalized, ultimately came to resonate widely within populations, lifting nationalist movements to control over the state or causing a fundamental realignment within state institutions. But the process by which this occurred differed significantly across these groups, as tidal influences came to play an increasing role relative to pre-existing structural conditions and institutional constraints.

## Baltic Nationalisms and the Politics of Emboldening and Persuasion

For Balts – the early risers within the secessionist tide – secessionist mobilization was primarily a process of emboldening supporters to express an already latent nationalist frame under conditions of relatively robust institutional constraints and a high degree of pre-existing facilitating structure (Figure 4.1b). Emboldening involved a continuous probing of the limits of the permissible and the possible by oppositional elites. In the Estonian case, for instance, with the exception of largely marginalized dissidents, activists at first pressed within-system demands for autonomy, environmental protection, and reform of language policy, gradually coming to realize the possibilities for a more radical secessionist politics. For some, these more innocuous claims were simply Trojan horses for secession, since they expected that a radical pressing of secessionist claims would precipitate government repression. This ambiguity of aims during the early period in the development of secessionist mobilization blurred "the distinction between official, popular, and dissident-'nationalist'" discourse[18] and ultimately allowed for rapid movement toward more radical secessionist positions. Figure 4.3 shows patterns of mobilization at demonstrations raising secessionist demands among Balts. One of the characteristic features of all three cases of Baltic mobilization (indeed, one that distinguishes Balts from the other groups which we will examine) was the brevity and early location of this equivocal period, when demands for secession were inconsistently and ambiguously pressed.

[18] *RFE/RL Baltic Area Report*, SR/7, July 13, 1988, p. 7.

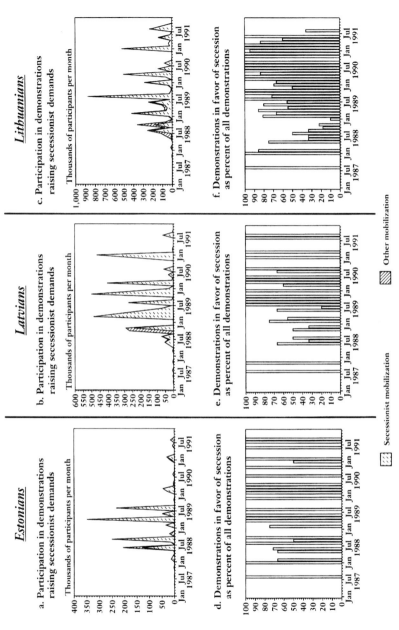

**Figure 4.3.** Demonstration mobilization in favor of secession from the USSR among Balts, 1987–91.

167

This is hardly surprising given the history of Baltic statehood in the twentieth century. Throughout the period of Soviet occupation, Balts continued to share a high degree of symbolic capital over independent statehood, tempered, however, by the seemingly immutable institutional constraints imposed by the Soviet regime. Resistance to Soviet occupation never entirely ceased among Balts, but by the mid-1950s a significant portion of the population had come to accept Soviet rule as an unalterable fact of life. As Rein Taagepera noted, "The awareness of being an occupied country reemerged quickly in the 1980s, but meanwhile, it was buried in the deeper levels of consciousness of most people."[19] Andrejs Plakans concurs, noting that by the late 1960s Latvians "appeared to take Soviet institutions for granted" and viewed Soviet control as "a permanent state of affairs."[20] Dissident movements advocating independence operated on the margins of society. But contention over secession continued. From 1965 through 1986 Baltic dissidents carried out more than thirty-eight major demonstrations throughout the region, twenty-three of which openly espoused independence. In spite of this record of resistance, even as late as February 1988, on the occasion of the seventieth anniversary of Lithuanian independence, Western journalists noted that the dominant mood in the republic was one of "public nonchalance, . . . not a feeling of hostility."[21]

All this changed in the spring of 1988. From late 1986 through summer 1987 a wave of environmental protest gripped the Baltic. This was a time when environmental movements were emerging throughout the USSR, egged on by the Communist Party as a way of attacking the power of the bureaucracy. In the Baltic, outrage over a series of industrial projects was fueled not only by their ecological impact, but also by the large numbers of Russians expected to flock to the region to build and operate them. The indifference of central government agencies to local sentiments became an opening for criticizing the Soviet bureaucracy for its "colonial" style of management.[22] The limits of the permissible were simultaneously attacked from without, as nationalist dissidents pressed a campaign of civil disobedience. Gorbachev's release of political prisoners in late 1986 and early

[19] Rein Taagepera, *Estonia: Return to Independence* (Boulder, CO: Westview, 1993), pp. 89–90.
[20] Andrejs Plakans, *The Latvians: A Short History* (Stanford, CA: Stanford University Press, 1995), p. 162.
[21] Quoted in Alfred Erich Senn, *Lithuania Awakening* (Berkeley, CA: University of California Press, 1990), p. 34.
[22] Taagepera, *Estonia*, p. 122.

1987 infused new groups of nationalist activists into the region. In the second half of 1987 and early 1988, these activists organized a series of demonstrations (known as "calendar demonstrations")[23] on the anniversaries of independence and occupation.

As Figure 4.3 shows, throughout *glasnost'* the Balts exhibited sharply spiked but regular mobilizations around these symbolic dates. This pattern of highly regularized mobilizations is evidence of the widely shared symbolic structure over independence that was in place well before the onset of mobilization. Karklins, for instance, notes the "discipline" characteristic of Latvian protestors and how "knowledge of political anniversaries" facilitated mobilization by reducing the need for formal communication.[24] The strength of embedded understandings reduced the role of movement organization to that of facilitator rather than persuader, blurred the distinction between institutional and noninstitutional politics, and minimized the degree of violence involved in the affirmation of once politically marginalized ranges of discourse. Though emboldening in the face of institutional constraints was a dominant element in the emergence of Baltic separatism, event-specific influences still played a significant role in the process. Indeed, the association, symmetry, and coordination among Baltic nationalisms are evidence of how analogy constitutes a significant element in the mobilization of identity even among groups with strongly embedded beliefs and a high degree of pre-existing facilitating structure. Analogy played a role in the rise of Baltic separatism not because of any cultural affinity among Baltic peoples, but rather because of their similar historical relationship with the Soviet state and their geographic proximity.

The role of official political actors and institutions in the Baltic in transcending state-imposed boundaries of public discourse also points to a widely shared, implicit understanding about nationhood within Baltic populations. We saw in Chapter 2 how secessionist mobilization began in the Baltic in the summer of 1987 as a dissident phenomenon, but remained relatively marginalized. In early spring 1988, however, a ferment arose across the Baltic, led primarily by intellectuals within official institutions rather than by dissidents from outside. In March and April 1988 the Baltic

---

[23] Juris Dreifelds, "Latvian National Rebirth," *Problems of Communism* (July–August 1989), p. 82.

[24] Rasma Karklins, *Ethnopolitics and Transition to Democracy: The Collapse of the USSR and Latvia* (Washington, DC: The Woodrow Wilson Center Press, 1994), pp. 94–95.

intelligentsia, through the official cultural unions that had once suffocated them, began to press for a revision of official history. Their championing of historical truth, attacks on local bureaucrats, and criticism of excessive centralization in Moscow paralleled closely Gorbachev's assaults on the Soviet bureaucracy in 1987 and 1988. Indeed, the popular fronts which sprang into existence in spring 1988 all defined themselves initially as movements for *perestroika*, not for independence, and Gorbachev and other reformers largely interpreted them through the lens of their struggle against bureaucratic domination throughout Soviet life.[25] But bureaucratic and imperial domination were difficult to separate within the Baltic context, where de-Stalinization and democratization were not merely questions of reform, but immediately raised thorny issues about Stalinist deportations and the Molotov-Ribbentrop Pact, and by implication Baltic membership in the Soviet Union. The ambiguity surrounding such words as "territorial self-accounting" and "sovereignty" provided a necessary latitude within which challenging discourse could function.

The crystallization and consolidation of a secessionist consciousness in the Baltic was a process that lasted over two years. It began in Estonia in April 1988 when a joint meeting of the cultural unions expressed its lack of trust in the Estonian Party First Secretary Karl Vaino for failing to defend the republic's interests adequately and called on the Communist Party, at its forthcoming Nineteenth Party Conference, to define the meaning of "republican sovereignty" in the Soviet constitution. Broadcast on Estonian television, such direct criticism was widely interpreted as a signal of Moscow's approval for Vaino's removal. Yet, many at the time refused to believe that anything was about to change; as one Russian correspondent was told by an Estonian acquaintance, "they'll talk a little, they'll have a little row, and then everything will go back to the old rut." But the journalist later commented, "the lock-gates of *glasnost'* had hardly been opened when a powerful rush of popular desires literally splintered apart the doors."[26] On a television program, Edgar Savisaar, an economic planner and one of the authors of a program for "territorial self-accounting" in Estonia, suggested creating "a democratic movement in support of *perestroika*." Two weeks later, a conference organized by the republican party apparatus (also broadcast over television) officially

---

[25] See A. S. Cherniaev, *Shest' let s Gorbachevym* (Moscow: Kultura, 1993), pp. 143–44.

[26] Viktor Shirokov, *Neozhidannaia Estoniia: Politicheskii reportazh* (Moscow: Politizdat, 1991), pp. 62–63.

approved the idea.[27] Within six weeks of its founding the Popular Front claimed a membership of over forty thousand in eight hundred local organizations.[28]

In Lithuania few signs of *perestroika* were visible as late as April 1988.[29] But as in Estonia, Lithuanian intellectuals were gripped by a ferment over de-Stalinization and the revision of official history. When a conservative historian published a letter defending Stalin's deportations, it produced a backlash of opinion, giving voice to a stream of anti-Stalinist expressions in the media.[30] At the end of May, two emissaries from Estonia arrived in Vilnius, sharing information about the organization of the Estonian Popular Front. This coincided with efforts by the republican party leadership to stack the delegates to the forthcoming Nineteenth Party Conference, provoking outrage among reform-minded party members. The result was a stormy meeting of concerned intellectuals in the Lithuanian Academy of Sciences building to discuss the theme "Will We Overcome Bureaucracy?" and the establishment of a "Movement for *Perestroika* in Lithuania," otherwise known as Sajudis. As one delegate at the meeting put it at the time, "We don't have to call it a popular front if that word frightens anyone."[31]

In Latvia ferment within the cultural unions began in March 1988, when the Writers' Union organized a demonstration permitted by the authorities to commemorate the Stalinist deportations in 1949. In imitation of their Estonian colleagues, the Latvian cultural unions held a meeting on June 1 that produced a wide-ranging indictment of Soviet life, including calls for republican sovereignty and official recognition of the truth about Latvia's incorporation into the USSR. But the strength of the dissident movement in Latvia, where up to sixty thousand people participated in "calendar demonstrations" organized by Helsinki-86 in summer 1988, delayed the emergence of mainstream political movements. Only on June 21 did an organizational committee form for the creation of a popular front in Latvia, and even here Helsinki-86 and other dissident movements participated in its creation. Indeed, the regime saw fit to edit the list of

---

[27] *Vestnik narodnogo fronta*, no. 1 (June 17, 1988), pp. 1–2.
[28] *Vesti iz SSSR*, 12–3, 1988.
[29] Georgii Yefremov, *My liudi drug drugu. Litva: Budni svobody 1988–1989* (Moscow: Progress, 1990), pp. 44–45.
[30] Senn, *Lithuania Awakening*, pp. 38–44; *RFE/RL Baltic Area Report*, no. 104 (June 8, 1988), p. 4.
[31] Senn, *Lithuania Awakening*, pp. 56–59.

the front's founders, removing those connected with dissident groups in an attempt to coopt the movement.[32]

In each of the Baltic republics the puncturing of official limits on discourse was a relatively quick affair. In Estonia Vaino's efforts to stack the Estonian delegation to the Nineteenth Party Conference in Moscow evoked an outcry of criticism in the Estonian media. In this situation of ferment, opportunity, and outrage, the annual Tallin song festival took place on June 10, attended by sixty thousand people. The occasion turned into an orgy of nationalist expression, including widespread display of the illegal tricolor of independent Estonia. This was the beginning of the so-called "Singing Revolution" that would echo throughout the Baltic. An institutionalized and officially sanctioned forum provided the cover for a collective display of hitherto forbidden nationalist expressions. A wave of smaller demonstrations rippled through Estonia on June 14, the anniversary of Stalinist deportations in 1941. On June 16 Vaino was removed from office by Moscow; according to some accounts, he had requested military intervention to prevent a mass meeting scheduled for June 17 by the Popular Front – a request Moscow turned down.[33] On June 17 a huge crowd of up to one hundred fifty thousand people, one-tenth of the entire population of the republic, attended a demonstration in celebration of Vaino's removal, pressing further demands for Estonian "sovereignty," the right of the republic to separate diplomatic representation abroad, the enactment of a republican language law, and recognition of the Estonian tricolor as a national symbol.[34] Vaino's successor, Vaino Väljas, openly supported the Popular Front and its demands, including the idea of turning the Soviet Union into a confederation of sovereign states.[35] In September 1988 the Estonian Communist Party endorsed establishment of Estonian as the state language. In response, up to three hundred thousand people (one out of every three Estonians of all ages) gathered in Singers' Field outside Tallin to express their support and to press for "full autonomy" while Väljas sat on the podium in approval.[36] With this, Rein Taagepera writes, "the Singing Revolution reached its grand finale."[37] Not that the revolution had achieved its goal. Nor, as we will see, had a generalized

[32] Dreifelds, "Latvian National Rebirth," p. 84.
[33] Taagepera, *Estonia*, pp. 133–36.
[34] *Vesti iz SSSR*, 12–3. 1988; Hufvudstadsbladet, in *FBIS*, June 23, 1988, p. 29.
[35] *Sovetskaia Estoniia*, September 10, 1988, p. 1.
[36] AFP, in *FBIS*, September 12, 1988, pp. 46–47.
[37] Taagepera, *Estonia*, p. 142.

secessionist consciousness emerged among Estonians by this time. But from September 1988 the history of the Estonian independence movement is primarily an institutional history largely because of the widely shared and highly implicit nature of symbolic capital surrounding independence and the relatively swift transformation in public discourse that overtook local party and government institutions as a result. The capture of local party and government officials by the nationalist cause had evoked a powerful Russian countermobilization by January 1989, when the Estonian government declared Estonian the state language of the republic.

In Lithuania the discursive breakthrough spearheaded by Sajudis was just as swift. Senn has called it a "primordial explosion,"[38] although his own description indicates that considerable attitudinal change accompanied it. As in Estonia, the Lithuanian national awakening was accomplished through a series of demonstrations. The first of these, on June 14, commemorated the victims of Stalinism but attracted only five hundred, considerably fewer than were present at the dissident meeting that followed it.[39] On June 24, Sajudis organized its first major demonstration – a protest of thirty thousand against the procedures by which delegates to the Nineteenth Party Conference were selected. The illegal tricolor of independent Lithuania was occasionally displayed alongside posters of Gorbachev, and the meeting ended with the singing of the forbidden anthem of interwar Lithuania. In the presence of party officials, speakers called on the delegates to the conference to speak out against party privileges, to halt construction at the Ignalina nuclear power plant, and to place the republic's sovereignty on Moscow's agenda.[40] The freewheeling debates at the Nineteenth Party Conference electrified the entire Soviet Union, and on July 9 Sajudis organized another rally on the delegates' return to Vilnius, this one attended by up to one hundred thousand. Demands burst forth for legalization of the Lithuanian tricolor, resignation of republican first secretary Ringaudas Songaila and second secretary Nikolai Mitkin, and "sovereignty" for Lithuania.[41] Relations between the republican party leadership and Sajudis remained tense; Songaila and Mitkin were sending "panicky characterizations of Sajudis" back to

[38] Alfred Erich Senn, *Gorbachev's Failure in Lithuania* (New York: St. Martin's Press, 1995), p. xv.
[39] *Vesti iz SSSR*, 11–2, 1988; *ELTA Information Bulletin*, no. 7, July 1988, p. 20.
[40] Senn, *Lithuania Awakening*, pp. 79–82; *ELTA Information Bulletin*, no. 8, August 1988, pp. 9–10.
[41] *ELTA Information Bulletin*, no. 8, August 1988, p. 15; Senn, *Lithuania Awakening*, pp. 86–92.

Moscow.[42] In response, Gorbachev dispatched Aleksandr Yakovlev to Vilnius and Riga in early August 1988 to investigate the situation. By this time, the leadership struggle in Moscow had sharpened, and Yakovlev viewed his Baltic visit in part as a forum for rebuffing public statements by Party Secretary Yegor Ligachev that openly questioned the direction reform had taken. Yakovlev shocked his hosts in Vilnius by publicly supporting the popular fronts against local party bureaucrats. Kazimiera Prunskiene later noted that "[i]n 1988 Sajudis divided time into 'pre-Yakovlev' and 'post-Yakovlev.'"[43] The visit constituted a major turning point in the fortunes of Sajudis, making it impossible for party officials to harass, censor, or ignore the movement any longer. On August 23, the 49th anniversary of the Molotov-Ribbentrop Pact, Sajudis organized a wave of demonstrations across Lithuania, attracting up to two hundred thousand people in Vilnius alone under a sea of recently legalized Lithuanian tricolors. A broad array of speakers, including some party officials, denounced the secret protocol that had consigned Lithuania to Soviet control and called for its publication and renunciation by the Soviet government. Senn writes: "*In just three hours* [emphasis in original] on August 23rd, 1988 Sajudis changed Lithuania."[44] As he described the changes in consciousness that had ripened over six weeks:

People who had been at both meetings . . . on July 9 and August 23, differed as to which they considered the more impressive. The meeting of July 9 had been more emotional, more spontaneous. . . . The meeting of August 23, more structured and organized, appealed more to the intellectuals. For many the discussion of the Molotov-Ribbentrop Pact was indeed something new, and several intellectuals indicated to me that . . . [it] had an especially great impact on them. . . . [After the August meeting] the public behavior of Lithuanians changed radically. . . . The public now spoke more freely of its concerns; it raised new demands.[45]

But even in August 1988 to utter the words "secession" or "independence" in public seemed "a daring act," with most Sajudis activists believing that

[42] Senn, *Lithuania Awakening*, p. 102.
[43] Quoted in Senn, *Gorbachev's Failure*, p. 25. On the role of internal Kremlin politics in shaping Yakovlev's Baltic visit, see Mikhail Gorbachev, *Zhizn' i reformy*, vol. 1 (Moscow: Novosti, 1995), pp. 403, 511. Subsequently, in his report to the Politburo on his trip, Yakovlev assured the Soviet leadership that "all the Balts are for *perestroika*, for the Union." Gorbachev contends that "this optimism calmed" the Politburo, "but it seemed to me to be excessive." If Gorbachev did indeed think that Yakovlev had oversold Baltic loyalty, he nevertheless did nothing in response.
[44] Senn, *Gorbachev's Failure*, p. 37.
[45] Senn, *Lithuania Awakening*, pp. 132, 136.

"it was unrealistic ... to think seriously about Lithuanian independence within the next ten to fifteen years."[46] At the end of September, the Songaila regime made a series of unsuccessful attempts to reestablish its control over the streets, targeting the unauthorized rallies of the dissident Lithuanian Liberty League. The move backfired, leading Sajudis to support the nationalist dissidents and to call for Songaila's resignation. His replacement by Algirdas Brazauskas, republican party secretary for ideology and a strong supporter of Sajudis, removed the last major obstacle restraining freedom of expression in Lithuania.

The strength of dissident movements and the weakness of the Popular Front delayed a discursive breakthrough in Latvia. It was not the Popular Front that organized the major demonstrations of the summer of 1988, but rather the dissident Helsinki-86. Participation in these demonstrations lagged well behind analogous demonstrations in Estonia and Lithuania, hovering in the forty to sixty thousand range, although the rhetoric at these meetings was considerably more radical than in Vilnius or Tallin.[47] These initiatives by dissidents were greeted with hesitancy and uncertainty by much of the population. Andrejs Plakans writes of the mood among Latvians at the time, "Public opinion during the summer of 1988 remained in turmoil, as these organizations tested the limits of the permissible. Although Latvian disillusionment with membership in the USSR was increasing, not all were prepared to say that their lot would be improved by totally separating from the larger system."[48] Only after Yakovlev's visit to Riga in August, the emergence of massive protests in Estonia and Lithuania, and the promotion of party first secretary Boris Pugo to Moscow and selection of a new leadership sympathetic to the aims of the front did the Latvian Popular Front begin to play a significant role in the republic. On October 7, on the eve of its founding congress, the front organized a major demonstration of one to two hundred thousand people on the occasion of Soviet Constitution Day under the slogan "For a Law-Governed State in Latvia." The meeting was addressed by Anatoly Gorbunovs, the newly elected chair of the republican Supreme Soviet, who, under fluttering red and white interwar Latvian flags legalized only the preceding day by the republic's legislature, lent his support to the movement and its aims.[49] The

[46] Senn, *Lithuania Awakening*, pp. 151–52.
[47] *Radio Liberty Baltic Area Report*, SR/9, August 26, 1988, pp. 7–10.
[48] Plakans, *The Latvians*, p. 172.
[49] Stockholm Domestic Service, in *FBIS*, October 11, 1988, pp. 52–54.

mood of the crowd was "euphoric," punctuated by "patriotic speeches and long-forbidden songs." In the words of one participant, "It was together-ness – a power one is suddenly aware of, Latvia's power."[50] The front's founding congress echoed themes that had already found expression across the Baltic: sovereignty within a confederal Soviet Union, the assertion of Latvian cultural rights, and the removal of bureaucratic domination and privilege. Latvian party first secretary Janis Vagris addressed the meeting, lending cautious support to the movement.[51] In November the flag of inter-war Latvia was raised above Riga castle for the first time, giving rise to mass expressions of separatist nationalism. By the end of the year, Vagris with-drew his support from the front as the local Russian population mobilized in opposition. In early January 1989 the front's registration as a public orga-nization was revoked, ultimately leading to a split within the Latvian Com-munist Party.

In the cases of the Balts, within an extremely short period new identity frames moved from the fringes of politics to its mainstream in a way pre-viously unimaginable. But even in these cases, where secessionist senti-ment was marginalized but widely shared on the eve of mobilization and emboldening supporters to express latent but suppressed sentiments was the dominant mode of mobilizing identity, the consolidation of a seces-sionist frame involved a considerable degree of persuasion. When the first public opinion poll on the issue was taken in November 1988, only 56 percent of Estonians supported secession from the USSR.[52] A survey in April 1989 again showed 56 percent of Estonians supporting complete independence, whereas 39 percent preferred a confederal arrangement within the USSR.[53] In late 1988 and early 1989, the leadership of the Estonian Popular Front persistently denied any separatist aims, calling for turning the Soviet Union into a union of sovereign states.[54] As one member of its leadership noted, "Naturally, the goal of every Estonian is an inde-

[50] Quoted in Dreifelds, "Latvian National Rebirth," p. 85.
[51] *Sovetskaia Latviia*, October 9, 1988, pp. 1, 4.
[52] *Vesti iz SSSR*, 22–3, 1988.
[53] *Vesti iz SSSR*, 7/8–4, 1989; Cynthia Kaplan, "Estonia: A Plural Society on the Road to Independence," in Ian Bremmer and Ray Taras, eds., *Nations and Politics in the Soviet Suc-cessor States* (Cambridge, UK: Cambridge University Press, 1993), pp. 215–16, 221; A. A. Semenov, "Russkoe i russkoiazychnoe naselenie natsional'noi-respubliki v period krizisa imperii (na primere Estonii)," N. Ukhneva and Kh. Krag, eds., *Leningradskaia konferentsiia po pravam men'shinstv* (Leningrad: Leningradskii uchenyi soiuz, 1991), pp. 121–33.
[54] *Sirp ja vasar*, in *FBIS*, Aug. 23, 1988, pp. 40–41.

pendent Estonia." But "we see the realization of this idea in the transformation of the Soviet Union into a union of states where every republic is sovereign."[55] Not until July 1989 did the Estonian Popular Front officially call on the Estonian Supreme Soviet to declare the Soviet occupation of Estonia illegal and invalid,[56] although the idea had been floated on many occasions before. Over 1989 and 1990 public opinion further consolidated around secessionist frames. Still, in September 1989 only 64 percent of Estonians favored independence. The spread of secessionist mobilization elsewhere in the USSR, the East European revolutions of fall 1989, and the republican elections of 1990 played critical roles in altering the opinions of those who earlier failed to identify fully with the independence objective. By January 1990 81 percent of Estonians favored independence; only 15 percent preferred a confederal arrangement within the USSR. By March 1990, when Lithuania declared independence from the USSR, the proportion of Estonians favoring secession had risen to 94 percent.[57] As these public opinion data show, processes of persuasion and bandwagoning under the influence of events outside Estonia were critical in the consolidation of a secessionist consciousness among approximately two-fifths of all Estonians.

A similar picture emerges among Latvians. Though the founding congress of the Latvian Popular Front called for the introduction of a separate Latvian currency and the right of Latvia to representation abroad, the movement continued to advocate a confederation within the Soviet Union until May 1989, when its leadership officially embraced the idea of an independent Latvia. Even then a significant portion of the front's council had second thoughts about independence.[58] A survey conducted in June 1989 revealed that only 55 percent of Latvians favored independence for Latvia. One year later the proportion of Latvians supporting independence had risen to 85 percent, and by March 1991 to 94 percent.[59] In other words, as the Baltic cases show, even for those groups for which prior structural facilitation was the strongest and emboldening was a dominant process within the mobilization of identity, a significant number of individuals less

---

[55] *Vestnik narodnogo fronta*, no. 10, 1988, p. 3.
[56] Stockholm Domestic Service, in *FBIS*, July 14, 1989, pp. 50–51.
[57] Jerry F. Hough, "Editor's Introduction," *Journal of Soviet Nationalities*, vol. 1, no. 1 (Spring 1990), p. 7.
[58] Dzintra Bungs, "People's Front of Latvia: The First Year," in *Report on the USSR*, vol. 1, no. 41 (October 13, 1989), pp. 25–27.
[59] Karklins, *Ethnopolitics and Transition*, p. 50.

committed to independence embraced secession only under the effect of event-generated influences.

## Emulation, Emboldening, Repulsion: The Rise of Georgian Separatism

As we move over time to examine secessionist politics among groups with less robust stores of symbolic capital over secession and with fewer propitious facilitating conditions than the Balts, identity politics was increasingly governed by event-generated influences. The emergence of secessionist consciousness among Georgians illustrates not only how events in the Baltic helped to crystallize analogous developments elsewhere, but also how events themselves could play a significant role in provoking a secessionist consciousness into being.

This is not to say that Georgians entered *glasnost'* without a significant reservoir of symbolic capital surrounding independent statehood. The kingdom of Georgia had an extensive history of independence before the late eighteenth century, when Georgian nobles voluntarily accepted Russian rule to avoid capture by Persian and Turkish forces. The Georgians also experienced four years of independent statehood from 1918 to 1921. A major revolt against Bolshevik rule occurred in 1924. Resentment of Muscovite dominance survived in Georgia in the ensuing years, though Stalin became a major symbol of identification with the Soviet Union for many Georgians. Although occasional dissident agitation for independence could be found in Georgia in the pre-*glasnost'* period, oppositional activity before *glasnost'* overwhelmingly focused on language and cultural issues rather than independence.[60] These concerns were magnified by Georgia's own minority problems. Efforts to assimilate minority peoples living on the territory of the republic to solidify claims to territory evoked continual confrontation. As the arbiter of these disputes, Moscow inevitably became embroiled in them and was often accused of using them to control the region. Georgia's minorities viewed Moscow as their only recourse for protection, whereas Georgians frequently saw Moscow's hidden hand behind their minority problems.

All this came to a head with the onset of *glasnost'*. In October 1987 a coalition of nationalist intellectuals and dissidents, some of whom had

---

[60] Ludmilla Alexeeva, *Soviet Dissent: Contemporary Movements for National, Religious, and Human Rights* (Middletown, CT: Wesleyan University Press, 1985), pp. 106–20.

178

recently been released from prison, organized the Il'ia Chavchavadze Society, named after Georgia's leading nineteenth-century nationalist activist and poet. The group called for allowing Georgians to perform military service within Georgia and for "defending the rights and interests of the Georgian people," but its demands fell well short of independence, focusing primarily on ecological and cultural issues.[61] Even so, the authorities refused to register the organization. In March 1988 the more radical wing of the nationalist dissidents split from the Chavchavadze Society, forming a separate movement known as the "Fourth Group" (later renamed the Society of Saint Il'ia the Just). For a while the "Fourth Group" worked along the edge of the limits imposed by the Soviet system. In May 1988, for instance, it organized a demonstration to mark the seventieth anniversary of Georgian independence. Only 100 people attended, and the meeting was broken up by the authorities.[62] But events in the Baltic transformed the Georgian political landscape, signaling the possibility of a new kind of politics. Encouraged by Baltic developments, a group of young nationalists from the "Fourth Group" established the National-Democratic Party of Georgia in late August 1988. The party openly proclaimed the reestablishment of Georgian independence as its goal and repudiated any form of cooperation with the Soviet state. The program adopted by the less radical Chavchavadze Society in October 1988 also reflected a strong influence from the Baltic. It called for the introduction of a republican currency, the transfer of most administrative functions from Moscow to the republic, the introduction of republican citizenship, and the use of the flag of the independent Georgian republic as the republic's official symbol.[63]

By fall 1988 the radicalization of Georgian nationalist movements under the influence of the Baltic example was paralleled by a growing gap between conservative republican Communist Party authorities and the society over which they ruled. The defining feature of Georgian politics during this period was the degree to which local Communist Party authorities resisted *glasnost'* – effectively excluding a mainstream politics that might have provided an alternative to more extreme nationalist

---

[61] See Elizabeth Fuller, "Independent Political Groupings in Georgia," *Radio Liberty Research Bulletin*, no. 527/88, November 25, 1988, pp. 1–8.

[62] *Vesti iz SSSR*, 10–26, 1988.

[63] Anatolii Sobchak, *Tbilisskii izlom, ili Krovavoe voskresen'e 1989 goda* (Moscow: Sretenie, 1993), p. 53.

movements. It was not, for instance, until June 1989 – after the April 1989 Tbilisi massacres – that the authorities allowed the organization of a Georgian Popular Front along the Baltic model as a way of coopting nationalist sentiment.[64] When multicandidate elections were permitted for the first time in March 1989, 57 percent of constituencies in Georgia still had only one candidate on the ballot – far above the average for the USSR as a whole.[65] As one observer noted, "the Georgian authorities' initial response to the creation of the Ilia Chavchavadze Society . . . was virtually indistinguishable from the tactics of threats, detention, and arrest employed against the Georgian human-rights movement during the late Brezhnev era."[66]

By fall 1988 a more militant mood could be detected within the population. After a year of stalling, Soviet defense ministry officials finally agreed to move a military firing range from the ancient Davitgaredzha monastery. But in late October the shelling continued, giving rise to generalized public outrage. Ten thousand angry students, with emotions raised to "fever pitch," demonstrated over the issue on the streets of Tbilisi.[67] Earlier that same month, a wave of unrest over alleged discrimination against the local Georgian population swept the Marneuli district of Georgia, populated by an Azerbaijani majority. Leaders of the "Fourth Group" rushed to the scene, seeking to utilize the occasion to focus resentment against Moscow and to mobilize secessionist sentiment. They were aided by the clumsy politics of republican authorities, who merely called on local Georgians to learn Azerbaijani. Demonstrations organized by the "Fourth Group" in Marneuli and Tbilisi, attracting up to three thousand participants, advocated the closure of Azerbaijani schools in the region and called for protection of the local Georgian population, linking these issues with calls for secession from the USSR.[68]

It is within this context that one must understand the explosions of nationalist mobilization which encompassed Georgia in November 1988 and April 1989. In both cases, radical nationalist movements sought to

[64] Darrell Slider, "The Politics of Georgian Independence," *Problems of Communism* (November–December 1991), pp. 64–65.

[65] Stephen Jones and Robert Parsons, "Georgia and the Georgians," in Graham Smith, ed., *The Nationalities Question in the Post-Soviet States*, 2d ed. (New York: Longman, 1996), pp. 298–300.

[66] Fuller, "Independent Political Groupings in Georgia," p. 5.

[67] AFP, in *FBIS*, September 26, 1988, pp. 63–64.

[68] *Vesti iz SSSR*, 21–2, 1988; *Ekspress khronika*, no. 42, October 1988.

utilize public moods of frustration and outrage with Moscow over other issues to refocus nationalist consciousness around demands for independence. The demands voiced by radical nationalists were at times far in front of the mood of the crowds they mobilized. In both November and April mobilization under secessionist banners petered out. What ultimately transformed public consciousness irrevocably was the backlash reaction to the violence unleashed by the regime on April 9 – a watershed event in Georgian politics.

The focus for mobilization in November 1988 was the draft USSR constitution – part of Gorbachev's democratization program – whose articles 108 and 119 gave the new USSR Congress of People's Deputies the right to strike down republican laws in conflict with all-union laws, as well as to approve or disapprove petitions for secession. The draft constitution was the source of considerable animosity and mobilization in the Baltic, and Georgian nationalists similarly sought to utilize the occasion to radicalize public opinion. On November 12 up to one hundred thousand people participated in a demonstration organized by the Chavchavadze Society, the National-Democratic Party, and the "Fourth Group" to protest the constitutional amendments. Under the flag of independent Georgia, these groups focused their criticism on "Russification" of the republic, citing the newly published draft constitution as an example and linking this with calls for an end to "colonization" of Marneuli district by Azerbaijanis. Already on the eve of the rally the Georgian Communist Party leadership, frightened by the public mood, discussed the possibility of introducing tanks and declaring martial law in the republic.[69] Ten days later a session of the republican legislature called to discuss the USSR constitutional amendments became the occasion for massive demonstrations of one to two hundred thousand in Tbilisi, at which demands for sovereignty mingled with calls for secession. Representatives of Sajudis and the Estonian Popular Front appeared at the demonstrations, and on November 23 the republican Supreme Soviet formally called for revisions in the draft constitutional amendments. The radical nationalists continued to press, calling on Georgian deputies at the forthcoming session of the USSR Supreme Soviet on November 29 to take a clear stand against the amendments. By this time, republican authorities had lost control over the streets, and on November 26 they panicked, sending two telegrams to

---

[69] Sobchak, *Tbilisskii izlom*, pp. 54, 122; *Vesti iz SSSR*, 21–2, 1988; Fuller, "Independent Political Groupings in Georgia," pp. 4–5.

Moscow begging for the introduction of martial law. On November 28, after another one-hundred-thousand-person demonstration, tanks began to enter the city, but could not make their way to the center due to barricades. Gorbachev dispatched former Georgian party boss Eduard Shevardnadze to Tbilisi with a message (broadcast over local television) assuring the Georgians that republican sovereignty would be respected. On November 29, after the USSR Supreme Soviet in Moscow altered the language of the constitutional amendments, a crowd of seventy thousand people in Tbilisi dispersed and demonstrations ceased, to the chagrin of the secessionist nationalists who had spearheaded the protests and had hoped to use them as a catapult into power.[70]

Unlike the Baltic, where the limits of the permissible and possible structured the expression of secessionist sentiment, in Georgia the population's commitment to independence in late 1988 and early 1989 was equivocal and context-driven, influenced to some extent by events in the Baltic, by alienation from local authorities, and by anger over state policies toward minorities residing within Georgia. Anatolii Sobchak, whose USSR Supreme Soviet commission studied these events in detail as part of its investigation into the April 1989 massacres, noted: "the majority of people were still not prepared to give them [the nationalists] their active support. . . . The nation still slept, and it was necessary to awaken it."[71] As Figures 4.4a and 4.4d indicate, despite continuing attempts by nationalist movements in the months following November 1988 to mobilize the population around secessionist frames, the protests remained small.

Not until April 1989 would the demand for secession again be raised at a demonstration attracting large numbers. The initial pretext for mobilization was relatively remote from secession. At the end of March 1989, in response to Abkhaz demonstrations calling for separation from Georgia and annexation to the Russian Republic, local Georgians in Abkhazia mobilized. When a bus carrying Chavchavadze Society supporters from Tbilisi to these demonstrations was attacked by a group of Abkhaz on April 1, injuring ten, the event provoked outrage throughout Georgia.[72] On April 4, the Chavchavadze Society began to organize demonstrations in

[70] *Vesti iz SSSR*, 22–2, 1989; Vadim Medvedev, *V komande Gorbacheva. Vzgliad iznutri* (Moscow: Bylina, 1994), p. 92; Yegor Ligachev, *Inside Gorbachev's Kremlin* (New York: Pantheon, 1993), p. 150; Gorbachev, *Zhizn' i reformy*, vol. 1, p. 515.
[71] Sobchak, *Tbilisskii izlom*, p. 49.
[72] *Atmoda*, November 13, 1989, pp. 4–5; *Zaria vostoka*, April 4, 1989.

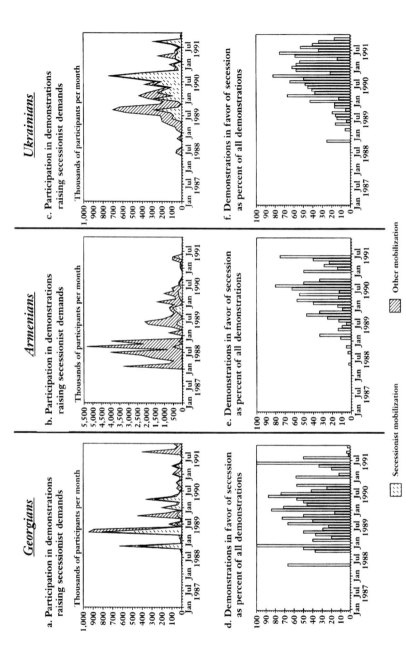

**Figure 4.4.** Demonstration mobilization in favor of secession from the USSR among Georgians, Armenians, and Ukrainians, 1987–91.

183

Tbilisi focused primarily on the situation in Abkhazia. By April 5 the crowds had grown to fifteen thousand people, and by April 6 to one hundred thousand. The Georgian party leadership believed that the removal of Abkhaz party first secretary Boris Adleiba, who supported Abkhaz claims for separation from Georgia, would calm public opinion, and on April 6 Adleiba was dismissed. According to eyewitnesses, when the demonstrators in Tbilisi learned of this, "there was clear excitement [in the crowd], and one could sense the joy. . . . [But] the meeting did not stop at this. The slogans changed sharply, and one even got the impression that passions grew even more heated."[73] Nationalist movements attempted to utilize the generalized anger surrounding the Abkhaz events, the animosity toward Moscow that it represented, and the growth of secessionist politics elsewhere in the USSR to shift the frame of discourse toward independence. Given that the Abkhaz had repeatedly sought reprieve from Georgian efforts at cultural assimilation through separatist activity aimed at joining RSFSR, the issue of Abkhazia was viewed by many Georgians as a larger metaphor for Georgia's relationship with Russia – an association that nationalists consciously attempted to foster. As Merab Kostava told the crowds assembled outside the House of Government on April 6 before the resignation of Adleiba, "Russia has an appetite for Abkhazia. . . . We should not separate the issue of Abkhazia from that of Georgian independence."[74] In the aftermath of Adleiba's removal, calls to liquidate Abkhazian autonomy altogether mingled with impassioned speeches for Georgian independence, pronouncements that the Georgian communists were unfit to rule, and even suggestions for direct overthrow of the government. Large crowds and similarly impassioned speeches continued on April 7 and 8. Certainly, for some attending these meetings Georgian independence was a sacred cause to which they were long committed. But for many of the participants these demonstrations, like those in November, were occasions to vent anger against the Soviet government for what they perceived as its insensitivity to Georgian national interests, against possible territorial aggrandizement by Russia at the expense of Georgia, and against a conservative republican party organization supported by Moscow that had undermined all efforts at dialogue with society over the previous two years. By April 8 "people had begun to grow tired. It was decided to continue for a couple of days, and then to disperse, in order to gather strength for the next attack, since now, after the change in

---

[73] Quoted in Sobchak, *Tbilisskii izlom*, p. 84.    [74] Quoted in Sobchak, *Tbilisskii izlom*, p. 86.

the leadership of the Abkhaz *obkom*, the sharpness of this issue, with which everything had begun, had fallen." In any case, nationalist movement leaders agreed among themselves that the entire protest campaign, including hunger strikes, would cease by April 14.[75]

Instead, the violent dispersal of a crowd encamped outside the House of Government in the early hours of April 9 transformed the situation. I examine the decision making surrounding the April 9 massacre in detail in Chapter 7. Let me simply note here that if, on the eve of the April 9 massacre, the degree of public support for independence was uncertain and equivocal, five months after the event 89 percent of Georgians believed that Georgia should be an independent country – significantly more than supported separate statehood in Estonia at the time.[76] A month after the massacre, in May 1989, the new republican party first secretary Givi Gumbaridze, in an attempt to come to grips with the new mood that encompassed the republic, declared the anniversary of Georgian independence in 1918 an official holiday and permitted demonstrations of up to half a million people in support of independence.[77] In February 1990 the communist-controlled Georgian legislature declared Georgia an occupied country. When the new nationalist government of Zviad Gamsakhurdia, whose Roundtable coalition easily won elections to the republican Supreme Soviet in October 1990, declared Georgian independence in 1991, it did so on April 9, in a symbolic reaffirmation of the transformative role played by the events of spring 1989.

The rise of secessionist sentiment in Georgia represents somewhat of an anomalous case in that elements of the type of emboldening characteristic of the Baltic were clearly present, yet event-generated influences – primarily in the forms of emulation of the Baltic successes, reaction to events in Marneuli and Abkhazia, and repulsion from the excessive use of force in the April 9 massacres – played critical roles in the process as well. In this sense, the rise of secessionist sentiment in Georgia departed from the Baltic pattern. As a comparison of Figures 4.3d through 4.3f with Figures 4.4a and 4.4d reveals, independence did not exercise the same degree of dominance over protest agendas in Georgia as in the Baltic. Unlike the banded patterns exhibited by the Balts, the role of secession as a demand within Georgian protest showed a greater element of upward sloping. This is reflective of the extent to which nonsecessionist issues

[75] Sobchak, *Tbilisskii izlom*, p. 106.    [76] *Vesti iz SSSR*, 19/20–2, 1989.
[77] *Zaria vostoka*, May 23, 1989, p. 1; *Vesti iz SSSR*, 9/10–1, 1989.

became the catalyst for the crystallization of widespread secessionist sentiment. As public opinion polls indicate, unlike the Baltic, where an initial breakthrough spread secessionist sentiment to a slight majority of the eponymous group and the remainder followed suit over the next year and a half under the influence of subsequent events, the generalization of a secessionist consciousness in Georgia was a more sudden affair produced in large part out of backlash effects from excessive government coercion against civilian populations. As the Georgian case shows, repulsion can be an extremely powerful shaper of identities – and in some respects, a more efficient persuasive force than either positive identification or bandwagoning.

## The Gradual Emergence of a Secessionist Consciousness Among Armenians

Armenians provide a good example of the growing role of event-generated influences in the crystallization of secessionist sentiment over the mobilizational cycle. As Figures 4.4b and 4.4e indicate, secessionist mobilization among Armenians appeared intermittently and was a secondary part of the larger mobilizational waves that engulfed Armenia during the early years of *glasnost'*. Central government actions and the larger context of the tide pulled secessionist issues onto the public agenda where they were largely absent before. In Ron Suny's words, in the course of two years Armenians "moved from being one of the most loyal Soviet nations to complete loss of confidence in Moscow."[78] Failure to resolve the Karabakh issue and the influence of tidal forces emanating from outside Armenia were the driving forces behind this transformation.

As former Prime Minister Nikolai Ryzhkov recalls, Moscow treated the members of the Karabakh movement as "nationalist-extremists" – a policy that, Ryzhkov believes, ultimately fed into the radicalization of Armenian nationalism.[79] The Karabakh Committee began as a mainstream movement led by leading members of the Armenian intelligentsia; more extreme secessionists, like Paruir Airikian, remained peripheral to it. Nevertheless, at the end of March 1988 the USSR government declared the Karabakh Committee illegal – a decision which meant little, since the movement

---

[78] Ronald Grigor Suny, *Looking toward Ararat: Armenia in Modern History* (Bloomington, IN: Indiana University Press, 1993), p. 238.
[79] Ryzhkov, *Perestroika*, p. 204.

never had legal status in any case. Signs of radicalization of the public mood were already evident by May 1988, when a wave of unrest swept through Armenia and Azerbaijan in the wake of the first trials of participants in the Sumgait pogroms. During these weeks, up to half a million people participated in demonstrations for transferring Karabakh to Armenia, for stiffer punishment of those implicated in the massacres, and for the release of prisoners of conscience. In the midst of this wave, Politburo member Yegor Ligachev publicly stated the regime's policy on Karabakh: no internal boundary changes would be considered. This produced a swell of indignation throughout Armenia. On May 28, the anniversary of Armenia's independence in 1918, the radical Association for National Self-Determination mobilized thirty to fifty thousand people, some carrying the tricolor of independent Armenia, in a demonstration calling for the day to be marked as a public holiday.[80] Thus, even at this time – before the rise of Baltic separatism on a mass scale – some degree of support for Armenian independence was evident, boosted in particular by frustration with Moscow's policies toward Karabakh.

In July 1988 a new wave of protest racked Armenia in the aftermath of the Nineteenth Party Conference and the disappointment of Armenians over the conference's failure to address the Karabakh issue. When Armenian protestors, attempting to close the Zvartnots airport outside Yerevan, clashed with Soviet soldiers, wounding thirty-six and killing one, the emotional chemistry of the population shifted still further in an anti-Russian direction.[81] In August 1988, under the influence of these events and developments in the Baltic, the Karabakh Committee endorsed a program that stopped short of independence but for the first time took the movement beyond the Karabakh issue. It called for democratization of Soviet politics, priority for Armenian-language schools, the right to display the (still illegal) flag of the independent Armenian republic, the performance of military duty on Armenian soil, economic sovereignty for the republic, and the right to separate diplomatic representation abroad in countries with significant Armenian populations.[82]

---

[80] *Vesti iz SSSR*, 10–11, 1988; AFP, in *FBIS*, May 31, 1988, p. 42.

[81] See Pierre Verluise, *Armenia in Crisis: The 1988 Earthquake* (Detroit, MI: Wayne State University Press, 1995), p. 93; *The New York Times*, July 11, 1988, p. A2.

[82] *The New York Times*, September 5, 1988, p. A1, A8. One sign of the Baltic influence on this program was the presence of a number of representatives of Estonian and Lithuanian popular fronts at Armenian demonstrations in August. *Vesti iz SSSR*, 16–4, 1988.

The first large-scale mobilizations by the Karabakh Committee in which some speakers overtly called for Armenian independence occurred in mid-September 1988 in the wake of a wave of violent attacks against Armenians in Azerbaijan. The threat of secession was explicitly used by the movement's leadership to prod republican authorities to call a special session of the republican Supreme Soviet to condemn Moscow's policy towards Karabakh.[83] Signs emerged that, under the influence of events in the Baltic secessionist sentiment was beginning to crystallize within the Armenian intelligentsia. As one Western correspondent who visited Yerevan at the time noted, a substantial number of Armenian nationalists had begun to "talk openly of full independence. Few think this is a realistic prospect in the short term . . . But separation is rapidly become a sort of litmus test."[84] Still, secession from the USSR was not openly embraced by the Karabakh Committee as a goal, and Armenian independence did not appear among the demands voiced at most of the major rallies of the time.

What with the Armenian earthquake, the declaration of martial law, and the arrest of Karabakh Committee leaders in December 1988, it was not until May 1989 that significant mobilization over secession materialized again, after mass secessionist sentiment had already appeared in neighboring Georgia. A major protest campaign emerged for the release of Karabakh Committee leaders and an end to martial law. In an attempt to win back popular support, the regime decided to make concessions, not only freeing the Karabakh Committee leaders, but also declaring May 28 – the anniversary of the 1918 declaration of Armenian independence – an official holiday and the tricolor of independent Armenia the national flag.[85] Most of the discussion at the three-hundred-thousand-person demonstration on that day focused around Karabakh rather than independence from the USSR, and the more radical Association for National Self-Determination, which openly advocated secession, drew only thirty thousand to its independence day demonstration.[86] Through mid-1989 independence remained almost an afterthought for Armenian nationalism and was never consistently voiced. To be sure, Armenian nationalism was strongly influenced by the Baltic example, but the Karabakh issue

[83] *Vesti iz SSSR*, nos. 17/18–1, 1988.
[84] *The New York Times*, September 25, 1988, p. A12.
[85] Suny, *Looking Toward Ararat*, p. 235.
[86] *Vesti iz SSSR*, 9/10–2, 1989; *Kommunist* (Yerevan), May 30, 1989, p. 3.

remained primary. Most important from the Armenian nationalist point of view, the territorial transfer of Karabakh appeared likely to require that Armenia remain within the USSR. Attempts to exit would have meant a loss of influence in efforts to transfer the territory.

In Figure 4.4e, the upwardly sloped character of the role of secessionist issues in protest agendas is evidence of event-generated influences at work in the emergence of a secessionist identity in Armenia. Only in fall 1989 – after mass mobilization over secession had spread to Western Ukraine and Moldova – did secessionist sentiment really began to solidify in Armenia. A survey taken in August 1989, for instance, indicated that only 17.3 percent of the population of the republic favored secession from the USSR.[87] But another wave of violence over Karabakh in September 1989 and continued frustration over Soviet policy toward Karabakh once again politicized the secession issue. This new wave of mobilization began with a two-hundred-fifty-thousand-person demonstration in Yerevan on September 15, at which Karabakh Committee members specifically threatened the republican Supreme Soviet that if its decisions at a forthcoming session did not sufficiently reflect the popular mood, "we will elect people to the Supreme Soviet who will demand Armenian independence."[88] Throughout October secessionist mobilization increased, usually joined with demands for creating a national Armenian army to protect the Karabakh Armenians, a boycott of USSR military service, and the introduction of republican citizenship. A survey taken in November 1989 found that 83 percent of Armenians considered themselves primarily citizens of the republic rather than the USSR, though the wording of the question was not an adequate test of opinion on secession.[89] Nevertheless, it did reflect what appeared to be a shift in the public's views on the independence issue. That shift gained further momentum on November 28, 1989, when the USSR Supreme Soviet voted to eliminate the USSR Special Administration in Karabakh and resubordinate the territory directly to the Azerbaijani government – a decision met with outrage within Armenia. On the following day – the anniversary of the establishment of Soviet power in Armenia in 1920 – a massive demonstration in favor of independence occurred, with two hundred fifty thousand people mobilizing in a

---

[87] *Ogonek*, no. 43, October 1989, pp. 4–5.
[88] *Vesti iz SSSR*, 17/18–1, 1989.
[89] *Sovetskii prostoi chelovek. Opyt sotsial'nogo portreta na rubezhe 90-x* (Moscow: Akademiia nauk, 1993), p. 22.

mourning march through Yerevan.[90] This event – which occurred at the height of the East European revolutions – represented a divide of sorts in the character of protest agendas. Subsequently, secessionist demands were regularly voiced at rallies and gained particular currency during the republican elections of spring and summer 1990, at a time when the Balts were issuing declarations of independence and secessionist protest was spreading to encompass new groups. With the victory of the Karabakh Committee's successor, the Armenian All-National Movement, in republican elections, opinion consolidated around the eventual introduction of Armenian independence. In August 1990 the new Armenian government formally declared its intention to become an independent state. By the time Armenians voted in a referendum on the issue in September 1991, after the collapse of authority in Moscow, 99 percent favored independence. As Lev Ter-Petrossian explained his republic's turn to independence, the Soviet Union was "no longer a reliable guarantor of our future. That is why we have to create our own guarantees of our existence."[91] Over the course of two years Armenian national consciousness had moved from a situation in which secessionist opinion was relatively marginalized (and indeed, largely unthinkable) to one in which it became nearly universal. Repulsion from Soviet policies toward Karabakh and the influence of events outside of Armenia were central in this shift, which differed from the Baltic pattern of consciousness change in the markedly larger role played by event-generated influences.

## Riding a Mobilizational Tide: The Ukrainian National Revolution

In early 1990 the Soviet state slipped into what was widely perceived by both its supporters and detractors as a generalized crisis. Not only had

---

[90] Suny, *Looking Toward Ararat*, pp. 236–37; *Vesti iz SSSR*, 21/22–2,1989. The same November 28 USSR Supreme Soviet decision that evoked a massive secessionist mobilization in Armenia also provoked the first large-scale demonstration in Baku in which secessionist demands were voiced – a demonstration in which two hundred and fifty thousand people participated. Moscow's decision left Azerbaijanis angry, since it sanctioned the restoration of the Armenian-dominated local Soviet in Karabakh and kept MVD forces in the region to protect the Armenian population. *Vesti iz SSSR*, 21/22–3, 1989. See also Audrey L. Altstadt, *The Azerbaidzhani Turks: Power and Identity under Russian Rule* (Stanford, CA: Hoover Institution Press, 1992), p. 207.

[91] *The New York Times*, April 15, 1991, p. A7.

Soviet control over Eastern Europe collapsed, but in the republican elections of late 1989 and early 1990 the Communist Party lost control over governments in the Baltic, Western Ukraine, Moldova, and Russia; its hold over the Transcaucasus, where elections had yet to take place, was tenuous at best. The economy also began to deteriorate seriously under the impact of strikes and ethnic unrest. If, in December 1989, public opinion surveys indicated that 52 percent of the Soviet population "fully approved" of Gorbachev's activities, by May 1990 that figure had dropped to 39 percent, and by July 1990 to 28 percent.[92] In May 1990, Yegor Ligachev, leader of the conservative opposition within the Politburo, addressed a letter to the Central Committee and to Gorbachev on what he viewed as the imminent breakup of the USSR. "The country," he wrote, "is in a depressed state. This is the question: Either everything that has been achieved by the efforts of generations will be preserved and developed, . . . or the Soviet Union will cease its existence and be replaced by dozens of states."[93]

The spread of nationalist contention throughout the USSR was a prime cause of this crisis. But the crisis of the Soviet state in its last years also had its own independent effect on collective understandings of nationhood. In most republics nationalist movements represented the primary opposition to the central government. Therefore, alienation from the center bred identification with the positions of nationalist movements. As one Ukrainian from Khar'kov, reflecting the popular mood in Eastern Ukraine that brought about an overwhelming vote in favor of independence throughout Ukraine in December 1991, later wrote: "Earlier, we had never paid much attention to nationality. But many, like myself, voted [for Ukrainian independence] because they did not believe in the leaders who had brought about the collapse of the union."[94] Not only repulsion, but positive identification under the influence of the example of others and strategic bandwagoning played critical roles in shaping public perceptions of nationhood in these circumstances.

The crystallization of secessionist consciousness among Ukrainians well illustrates the persuasive influence that example exerts on national identities, particularly among groups with weaker facilitating conditions. The impact of Polish-Lithuanian rule and the partition of Ukraine between

[92] *Gorbachev-Yel'tsin: 1500 dnei politicheskogo protivostoianiia* (Moscow: Terra, 1992), p. 281.
[93] Ligachev, *Inside Gorbachev's Kremlin*, p. 177.
[94] *Nesostoiavshiisia iubilei: Pochemu SSSR ne otprazdnoval svoego 70-letiia?* (Moscow: Terra, 1992), p. 537.

Austro-Hungary and the Russian Empire left deep cultural, religious, and political divisions in Ukraine along regional lines. Western Ukraine remained a hotbed of nationalist dissent, whereas Eastern and Southern Ukraine were under strong Russian cultural influence. Ukrainians from Galicia constituted the core leadership of the short-lived Ukrainian experiments in statehood that accompanied the collapse of the Russian Empire. Incorporated into the Soviet Union as a result of the Molotov-Ribbentrop Pact, Western Ukrainians (who had been under Polish rule from 1918 to 1940) fought a guerilla war of resistance well into the 1950s, and small-scale acts of opposition continued throughout Soviet rule. But independence was not part for the conceivable universe for the vast majority of Ukrainians – from West or East – in the post-Stalin years. Indeed, as John Armstrong showed, through their loyalty to the Soviet state Ukrainians (particularly those from the East) earned a reputation as the "younger brothers" of the Soviet state.[95] In the 1960s, under Ukrainian party First Secretary Petro Shelest', nationalist dissent manifested itself in agitation for cultural and economic autonomy. But in the early 1970s these strivings were efficiently suppressed by Shelest's successor, Vladimir Shcherbitskii, who kept a tight lid on nationalist expressions in the ensuing years.

With the onset of *glasnost'*, nationalist mobilization in Western Ukraine at first closely followed the contours of the permissible and the possible in a typical emboldening pattern. Initial mobilization in 1987 and 1988 by longtime dissidents was concentrated in the West and focused on issues of language policy and religious freedom for the then illegal Uniate Church. These actions occasionally raised secessionist demands, though mobilizations over the issue remained small.[96] The republican Communist Party apparatus strongly resisted the emergence of a popular front on the Baltic model, but in February 1989, on the eve of a visit by Gorbachev to Kiev, the Popular Movement of Ukraine (Rukh), organized by mainstream Ukrainian writers and cultural activists, was given official approval. Its initial program recognized the leading role of the Communist Party and proclaimed the movement's goals as democratization and the establishment of Ukrainian as the official language of the republic. But Rukh activists in Western Ukraine, often affiliated with the more radical

---

[95] John A. Armstrong, "The Ethnic Scene in the Soviet Union: The View of the Dictatorship," in Erich Goldhagen, ed., *Ethnic Minorities in the Soviet Union* (New York: Praeger, 1968), pp. 3–49.
[96] *Vesti iz SSSR*, 22–33, 1988.

Ukrainian Helsinki Union and under the strong influence of the Baltic example, organized a protest campaign to demand the resignation of Shcherbitskii after the First Congress of USSR People's Deputies, connecting this with the democratization of Ukrainian politics and utilizing the occasion to raise the issue of independence for Ukraine. In the summer of 1989 demonstrations attracted seventy to one hundred thousand participants in the city of L'vov, where local Communist Party officials, in an attempt to ride the wave of radicalized public opinion, openly endorsed the idea of Ukrainian sovereignty.[97] During this period Ukrainian activists from Western Ukraine maintained close contact with their Baltic counterparts and borrowed heavily from them in terms of tactics and discourse.

As Figures 4.4c and 4.4f indicate, in summer and fall 1989 secessionist demonstrations began to appear with greater frequency, though still a small portion of Ukrainian demonstrations and confined to a single geographic area of the republic. In September 1989 Rukh was finally permitted to hold its founding congress – a blow to Shcherbitskii and a sign of his pending removal. Demands for Ukrainian independence were voiced at the congress by delegates from the West, but the program adopted by Rukh was moderate in orientation, stopping far short of goals espoused by popular fronts in other republics and calling merely for guarantees of religious and political freedom, economic reform, and environmental protection.[98] Rukh's protest activities in the aftermath of the congress focused on reform of Ukraine's electoral laws, the legalization of the Uniate Church, and the recognition of Ukrainian as the state language of the republic. But as Figures 4.4c and 4.4f demonstrate, in 1990 Ukrainians experienced a major transformation in public attitudes toward secession. Mobilization over secession grew in a rising crescendo, coming to dominate the agenda of public protest. At the heart of this explosion was the geographic spread of secessionist sentiment from Galicia to other regions of the republic. As Bohdan Nahaylo described it, "What appears to have happened is that swiftly and almost imperceptibly, . . . a revolution occurred in the minds of Ukraine's inhabitants. Somehow, during a remarkably short period, the idea of Ukrainian independence, for so long depicted in the Soviet press as the hopeless cause of diehard nationalists in Western Ukraine, took hold throughout the republic."[99]

[97] *Vesti iz SSSR*, 12–3, 1989; 15/16–3, 1989.
[98] *Report on the USSR*, vol. 1, no. 38 (September 22, 1989), pp. 22–23, 27.
[99] Bohdan Nahaylo, "The Birth of an Independent Ukraine," *Report on the USSR*, vol. 3, no. 50 (December 13, 1991), pp. 1–2.

Two developments prepared the way for the spread of secessionist sentiment outside Western Ukraine: the East European revolutions of late 1989 and the republican elections of early 1990. Throughout the Cold War, large-scale revolt in communist-controlled Eastern Europe had given rise to heightened nationalist challenges within the Western portion of the USSR – an example of the ways in which nationalist contention flowed across state borders.[100] The effect of the collapse of East European communist regimes in fall 1989 on nationalist movements in Ukraine was particularly strong, leading to a sense that a momentum had built up against the Soviet state that could no longer be contained and to an immediate radicalization of demands. At a small demonstration in the Eastern Ukrainian city of Dnepropetrovsk in December 1989, for instance, Rukh actively utilized the example of East European rejection of communism to mobilize the populace against the regime; "the peoples of Poland, Hungary, East Germany, and Czechoslovakia have said no to communist dictatorship," their banners read. "The next word is ours, citizens!"[101] With the inauguration of the electoral campaign, Rukh nationalists directly brought the secessionist struggle into central and Eastern Ukraine. Borrowing a tactic utilized by the Balts in summer 1989, on January 21, 1990, the anniversary of the union of the Western Ukrainian People's Republic with the Ukrainian People's Republic in 1919, Rukh organized a human chain across Ukraine, from L'vov to Kiev, culminating in a secessionist rally of fifty to one hundred thousand in Kiev the following day (including Rukh activists bussed into the city for the occasion).[102] Similar but smaller demonstrations were organized that same month in Zhitomir, Khar'kov, Donetsk, Odessa, and Zaporozh'e, though in some localities in central and Eastern Ukraine nationalists were met with hostility by local residents.[103] Rukh activists described the human chain as an event marking "a genuine rebirth of the Ukrainian nation." As one activist observed at the time, "Spring has finally arrived in Kiev."[104]

The continued attempt to link the East European revolutions and Baltic secession with mobilization in Eastern Ukraine was evident a month later

---

[100] See Roman Szporluk, ed., *The Influence of East Europe and the Soviet West on the USSR* (New York: Praeger, 1975).

[101] *Ekspress khronika*, no. 51, December 17, 1989, p. 1.

[102] *Ekspress khronika*, no. 4, January 23, 1990.

[103] *Pravda Ukrainy*, January 12, 1990, p. 2.

[104] Bohdan Nahaylo, "Human-Chain Demonstration in Ukraine: A Triumph for 'Rukh,'" *Report on the USSR*, vol. 2, no. 5 (February 2, 1990), pp. 17–18.

at an eighty-five to one-hundred-thousand-person electoral rally in Kiev on February 25, at which Polish, Czechoslovak, Bulgarian, and Latvian flags flew alongside the Ukrainian national flag.[105] Election rallies throughout the republic provided numerous occasions to raise secessionist issues, although such demonstrations attracted no more than a thousand participants in eastern and southern provinces. But the electoral campaign also gave rise to a rash of local uprisings against provincial Communist Party authorities, with massive rallies venting frustration over economic and social issues and sweeping away local leaderships in eight non-Galician Ukrainian provinces. In elections in March, Rukh gained control of local governments in Galicia and performed well in Kiev, in all winning about a quarter of the seats to the republican legislature. Nevertheless, Rukh had failed up to that point to make significant inroads in other parts of the republic, in spite of the evident growing dissatisfaction with Communist authorities.

Buoyed by the electoral results and encouraged by the Lithuanian declaration of secession, by the end of March 1990 Rukh officials no longer spoke in muffled tones about independence; they openly linked their fate with that of the Balts, declaring independence as the movement's ultimate goal.[106] At the end of March Rukh held solidarity rallies throughout Ukraine (including ten cities in Eastern and central Ukraine) in sympathy with the Lithuanian decision to secede from the USSR, with yellow and blue Ukrainian flags flying alongside posters reading "Colonial Ukraine greets independent Lithuania!"[107] Russia's declaration of sovereignty in June transformed the Ukrainian political landscape, making it difficult for Ukrainian politicians to avoid movement in the same direction. When Shcherbitskii's successor, Vladimir Ivashko, abandoned his position for a promotion to Moscow, opinion within the Ukrainian legislature radicalized, leading to the passage of a declaration of sovereignty in July; though signaling Ukraine's intent to sign a new union treaty, the document also asserted the supremacy of Ukrainian laws over all-union laws on Ukrainian territory, as well as Ukraine's right to create its own banking system and armed forces.

The opening of the second session of the Ukrainian parliament in October coincided with the collapse of negotiations between Yeltsin and

---

[105] *Ekspress khronika*, no. 9, February 27, 1990; Radio Kiev, in *FBIS*, February 27, 1990, p. 90.
[106] AFP, in *FBIS*, March 22, 1990, p. 102.
[107] *Yezhednevnaia glasnost'*, April 2, 1990, pp. 1–2.

Gorbachev over plans for marketization and a further drop in Gorbachev's approval rating to 21 percent.[108] Deepening alienation from Muscovite authority in central and Eastern Ukraine flowed over into a split within the Communist majority in the legislature. The session became the occasion for a massive protest campaign focused around Ukrainian independence. Enormous demonstrations of one hundred to two hundred thousand in Kiev were accompanied by demands that Ukrainian Prime Minister Vitalii Masol resign, that military service for Ukrainian residents be performed inside the republic only, and that Ukraine refuse to sign a new union treaty. "This is a revolution," one Rukh activist observed at the time.[109] A wave of student strikes and demonstrations culminated on October 17 in what could be described as the "moment of madness" in Ukrainian politics, when the Ukrainian political world was turned upside down. Under great pressure from the street, the Ukrainian parliament agreed not to consider signing a new union treaty until after a new Ukrainian constitution had been approved, placed military service outside the republic on a voluntary basis, and accepted Masol's resignation. This marked a major shift in the Ukrainian political landscape, primarily because of the realignment within the Ukrainian government that it brought about. Ukrainian Supreme Soviet Chair Leonid Kravchuk, once an implacable enemy of Rukh, now emerged as leader of a new national communist fraction within the Rada supporting a far-reaching Ukrainian sovereignty and possibly independence.[110] This defection represented only a partial institutionalization of secessionist mobilization. The Ukrainian government increasingly paid allegiance to goals of ensuring Ukrainian sovereignty and independence. But the Ukrainian nationalist movement did not capture the state, as occurred in the Baltic, Georgia, and Armenia. Rather, through the mobilizational pressure that the nationalist movement generated and the force of the example of others, portions of the state

---

[108] *Gorbachev-Yel'tsin*, p. 281.

[109] Reuters, October 16, 1990.

[110] As late as the end of 1989 Kravchuk was authoring virulent, anti-Rukh pamphlets. One colleague who worked with Kravchuk for many years within the Ukrainian Central Committee apparatus (and who was even his superior at one time) observed that Kravchuk had the reputation of having "a solid Marxist-Leninist theoretical training" and "dedication to *nomenklatura* duty," but also "was fixated on public opinion, and above all on his closest surroundings." Aleksandr Kapto, *Na perekrestkakh zhizni. Politicheskie memuary* (Moscow: Sotsial'no-politicheskii zhurnal, 1996), pp. 96, 99.

previously associated with the Soviet regime came to accept the nationalist position on independence, thereby turning communists into nationalists.

But even after the split within the communist leadership of Ukraine, public attitudes had not yet fully consolidated around independence. Gorbachev's March 1991 referendum on the preservation of the USSR as a "renewed federation of sovereign republics" was conducted in Ukraine with an additional question added by the republican government on whether Ukraine should be part of a union of "sovereign states" on the basis of its sovereignty declaration, as well as a separate vote in Galicia directly posing the independence issue. Although 88 percent of Galicians voted for independence, Gorbachev's question received 70.5 percent support in Ukraine as a whole (with stronger support in the East and South), and the republican question received 80.2 percent. As one study notes, "it was possible for all political forces in Ukraine to interpret the results as they saw fit."[111] A public opinion poll in March 1991 found that 62 percent of Ukrainians believed that a republic should have the right to leave the USSR if the people of that republic freely chose a path of secession – considerably fewer than the 92 percent of Estonians who answered the same question in the affirmative.[112] The miners' strikes of March 1991 in Eastern Ukraine (with their demands for the resignation of the USSR government) and the August 1991 coup constituted further critical tipping points of opinion in Eastern and Southern Ukraine. In the December 1991 referendum on Ukrainian independence the East and the South recorded overwhelming votes for independence, with the exception of Russian-majority Crimea, where a bare majority of 54 percent favored independence. The bulk of this opinion in the East and South represented the combined effect of alienation from Moscow's economic policies, the influence of example, and bandwagoning behavior in the face of the multiple declarations of independence which followed the collapse of the August coup. But opinion toward secession in the East and South was highly unstable. In the December 1991 referendum 90 percent of the Ukrainian population voted in favor of separate statehood, but public opinion polls in the ensuing several years demonstrated sharp fluctuations in support for

---

[111] Taras Kuzio and Andrew Wilson, *Ukraine: Perestroika to Independence* (New York: St. Martin's Press, 1994), p. 159.
[112] *Mir mnenii i mneniia o mire*, no. 2, March 1991, p. 2.

an independent Ukraine, with at times as few as 56 percent favoring Ukrainian independence.[113] In Ukraine persuasion thus represented a less stable form of identity change, one clearly influenced by the events of the moment and the example of others.

## Summary and Conclusion

Through this process-tracing of six cases of successful secessionist mobilization, we have seen that the successful mobilization of identity always involves some mix of pre-existing structural facilitation, emboldening of supporters in the face of institutional constraints, and event-generated influences over the less committed. Each of these elements is fungible to some extent: Movements from groups with less robust facilitating structures can to some degree "substitute" event-generated influences in place of structural facilitation by taking advantage of the tidal effects produced by the earlier action of other groups or by precipitating other forms of event-specific influence. As a tide of nationalism emerges, increasing numbers of groups – each with fewer advantageous facilitating conditions than their predecessors – are drawn to engage in mobilization under the influence of the prior successful example of others and the efforts of early risers to spread contention laterally. In general, the emboldening of supporters tends to grow easier over time, as compliance systems grow taxed. Event-generated influences also grow increasingly salient, as repulsion, positive identification, and bandwagoning play more significant roles in affecting identities. In this sense, the rise of secessionist sentiment in the USSR was hardly a matter of opening Pandora's box. Rather, it depended very much on the ways in which the successful actions of one movement influenced subsequent actions, both within and across groups. The massive mobilizations in favor of independence from the USSR among Georgians, Armenians, Azerbaijanis, Moldavians, and Ukrainians would have been unthinkable without the influence of the prior successful example of Balts. And as we saw, even a significant portion of opinion among Balts was influenced by the successful actions of others.

Thus, as a tide proceeds, groups with declining levels of structural advantage are increasingly dependent on the power of tidal effects in the

---

[113] *OMRI Daily Digest*, January 10, 1995.

mobilization of identity. As we will see in the next chapter, the difference between the success and failure of national movements in significant part boils down to the question of who is better able to utilize tidal forces to their own advantage.

# 5

## Tides and the Failure of Nationalist Mobilization

I detest these absolute systems, which represent all the events of history as depending upon great first causes linked by the chain of fatality, and which, as it were, suppress men from the history of the human race. . . . [Chance] plays a great part in all that happens on the world's stage; although I firmly believe that chance does nothing which has not been prepared beforehand.

Alexis de Tocqueville, *Recollections*

In a study of the impact of the event on nationalism, it would be all too easy to fall into the seductive trap of focusing exclusively on successful nationalisms or on nationalisms which produced significant action. Yet, no serious analysis of nationalism can ignore an explanation of the ways in which nationalism fails as a mobilizational and political force. For Ernest Gellner it was the dog that failed to bark (that is, the failure of nationalist movements to emerge in some contexts) that provided what he considered the vital clue to understanding nationalism. Most potential nationalisms, Gellner argued, "must either fail, or, more commonly, will refrain from even trying to find political expression." They "fail to bark" primarily because industrialization assimilates them to dominant cultures, so that the group category never takes on significant meaning within the political realm. As Gellner wrote, "most cultures are led to the dustheap of history by industrial civilization *without offering any resistance*" [emphasis added].[1]

Gellner's understanding of the failure of nationalism was boldly developmentalist. Failures of nationalism were caused by long-term, secular forces of modernization undermining particular categories of belonging

[1] Ernest Gellner, *Nations and Nationalism* (Ithaca, NY: Cornell University Press, 1983), pp. 6, 43, 47.

while making others more important. What is absent within this teleological vision are the roles of opportunity and action in the constitution of failure. In this chapter, I develop an alternative basis for evaluating failures of nationalism. I begin with the proposition that, if one were to look for a context in which to test whether a particular nationalism failed or succeeded, tides of nationalism would have to be considered fruitful sites. Within the context of a tide nationalist movements have greater opportunities to engage in open expression and action supportive of nationalist goals due to the attenuation of institutional constraints and the supportive example of others. The failure or success of a particular nationalism cannot be judged without taking into consideration nationalism's larger relationship to order and the constraints authority imposes on society. Obviously, a nationalism forced to abide constantly behind tall fences cannot be judged to have fully failed. Failure and success require opportunities to fail or to succeed. They cannot be separated from the mobilizational context which makes the question even possible to ask. Thus, an adequate explanation of the failure of nationalism must necessarily be linked with the study of action, for not only does action alter the chances of nationalism's success, but it is the presence or absence of action which most observers use to identify nationalism's success or failure in the first place.

Viewed from this perspective, failures of nationalism are a more diverse set of phenomena than Gellner would have us believe. We have already seen that within a tide of nationalism the "barking" of one nationalism attracts and incites noise from other animals. Successful challenge to order evokes further challenge, and as order wears thin numerous nation-building projects emerge – at times with seemingly limitless imagination. But only a subset of these "barking" nationalisms gain enough resonance within their target populations to generate significant mobilization and to break through the institutional constraints to which they are subject. The "barking" of nationalism (the emergence of a nationalist movement or discourse) is only one dimension by which to judge nationalism's success or failure; even when nationalisms do bark, it is far from certain that they will bite or whether their bites will find their intended target.

In this chapter I attempt to explain why some nationalisms fail to produce significant mobilization and why, when others do, their efforts sometimes prove unsuccessful. Empirically, I accomplish this through an examination of the successes and failures of one particular set of nationalist frames – separatist nationalism – during the *glasnost'* tide of nationalism.[2] As the Soviet Union came undone, nationalist movements espousing separatist aims emerged within a broadening number of groups under the influence of the example of others. As we saw in the last chapter, nationalist movements among twenty-one different nationalities at some point in the cycle espoused demands for secession from the USSR at demonstrations attracting at least one hundred supporters. Even this, however, hardly captures the variety of separatist movements that emerged during this period, not to mention the multiple movements that appeared seeking secession from union republics and their successor states. Once dismissed as crackpots or dreamers, separatist nationalists of all sorts attempted to ride the nationalist tide generated by *glasnost'*.

Yet, only a small minority of these movements ever gained power. In some cases, independence came about in spite of efforts by nationalist movements to mobilize populations, as a result of external events imposing themselves on political reality and the strategic appropriation of independence agendas by nomenklatura elites. The aims of separatist movements were thus in some senses achieved, but not by separatist movements; these movements remained marginalized within their respective political realms and were incidental to the outcome. In other cases, the demand for separate statehood never became the basis for significant mobilization. As we will see, the ways in which pre-existing structural conditions and institutional constraints interact with tidal effects are critical to an explanation of these disparate outcomes.

## *Conceptualizing Outcomes Within a Tide of Nationalism*

What is meant by the failure or success of a particular nationalism begs clarification. I begin by differentiating failure from irrelevance. In view of the variety of demands that fall under the rubric of nationalism, we need to recognize that for some groups a particular frame of nationalism may simply be irrelevant for their circumstances. This does not mean that

---

[2] Again, I understand nationalism as collective discourse, mass mobilization, or state practice that challenges or upholds the territorial or membership boundaries of the state or the rules of cultural interchange underlying the conduct of state affairs. For purposes of this analysis, I define separatist nationalism as nationalism aimed at secession (in this case, from either the USSR or from its union republics or successor states) with the aim of establishing separate statehood, specifically excluding instances of irredentist struggle for unification of a nationality divided across political borders (for example, the Karabakh issue).

other nationalist frames are also irrelevant. As Gellner argued, in the modern world the insolvency of one form of nationalism is usually associated with the success of a rival form. For this reason, within a given population one can only judge the success or failure of specific nationalist frames, not nationalism in general. Moreover, there is a problem in talking about the failure of an irrelevant nationalism. For Soviet Jews in the 1980s, secession from the USSR was not considered an appropriate aim, largely because Jews were dispersed over the territory of the Soviet Union and identified with a distant, already existing national homeland. Emigration was the preferred choice of exit. We cannot say that separatist nationalism failed among Soviet Jews because no movement emerged espousing secession as a goal. Secession was not considered a relevant goal.

This points to a larger issue underlying Gellner's silent dogs: One must assume that there are dogs in the vicinity capable of barking if one expects to hear noise in the first place, even if in the end it does not occur. Gellner did not provide us with a sound basis for pursuing counterfactual analysis with respect to the failure of nationalism, for he did not equip us with criteria for identifying what we should reasonably expect from nationalism. The irrelevancy of a particular form of nationalism is an interesting question, but, I would argue, one which remains analytically distinct from the success or failure of nationalism. We should not expect all nationalist frames to be equally relevant to populations for the simple reason that cultural groups find themselves in varied relationships to state authority and to the state system which has emerged over the past several centuries. Not all groups find independent statehood an appropriate goal to pursue, and were it otherwise, the world would be a considerably more chaotic place. Usually, when a particular nationalist frame is irrelevant to a population, it is because of the ways in which states have coopted, inspired, or consolidated opposition to themselves: the particular constellation of cultural interests bound up with the state; the ways in which the state classifies populations and acts on the basis of those classifications; the ways in which state policies discriminate against populations on the basis of culture; and the relationships groups may have with alternative state authorities. There is a fine line between irrelevancy and failure to act. In the former a particular nationalist frame is never contemplated, even by the most radical of activists; in the latter it is considered desirable by at least some, however impossible it may, in reality, be. In this sense, any attempt to compare the outcomes of nationalist mobilization must begin by identifying the pool of groups whose activists might potentially hold a specific nationalist frame as a reasonable goal.

Gellner provided no criteria for identifying such a pool other than the mere existence of linguistic distinction. Indeed, on the basis of the number of languages in the world, he once calculated that there were eight thousand potential nationalisms, only eight hundred of which had become active in any sense. A more reasonable effort might distinguish the pool of potential nationalisms by the possibility, within a specific temporal context, that some activists could plausibly draw an analogy with the behavior of other groups espousing a particular nationalist frame. As a tidal perspective on nationalism would lead us to believe, analogy is one of the most powerful forces in the spread of nationalism; the inescapable urge of humans to compare themselves to others stretches the national imagination in directions in which it would otherwise be unlikely to wander. The pool of potential nationalisms emerges in relationship to the actions of others held to be in analogous positions. This is hardly a quality that can be determined with precision. There will always be ambiguity between the irrelevancy of a nationalist frame and the failure of a nationalist frame to generate action; as we will see, this ambiguity provides some insight into the process by which nationalist frames fail to generate action. Nevertheless, this is a more reasonable position than assuming that all groups are potential candidates for mobilization around a particular nationalist frame, or that linguistic differentiation (often the arbitrary product of the classificatory scheme of the linguist) is enough to make any nationalism imaginable.

Even after we have identified such a pool, there are still various criteria by which we might judge failure or success. There is a need to distinguish between mobilizational success (the wide resonance of nationalist action within society), issue success (the adoption of movement aims as the basis for state policy), and political success (gaining control over the state). Some nationalisms succeed both politically and mobilizationally, and certainly mobilizational success makes political success likely. The cases studied in the previous chapter were examples of nationalist movements that achieved both mobilizational and political success, though certainly there are cases of movements outside of tides that succeed mobilizationally but fail politically (Solidarity in Poland in 1980–81 was one) largely because, due to external factors, regimes are unwilling to abdicate or share power even after any pretense of popular support has dissipated. In the case of the collapse of the USSR under *glasnost'*, the absence of an external savior, the unraveling of institutional constraints, and the presence of multiple, reinforcing challenges all made political success a likely concomitant of mobilizational success.

More important for understanding the Soviet case is the fact that nationalist frames may fail mobilizationally yet succeed substantively. This was an outcome relatively common throughout the USSR – in fact, equally as common as the mobilizational success of nationalist movements. In these cases, in spite of the inability of nationalist movements to gain significant influence through mass mobilization, the nationalist ideas they espoused ultimately succeeded through their strategic appropriation by the politically powerful. This appropriation typically occurred through the influence of the nationalist actions of other groups, particularly as the coherence and viability of the USSR grew doubtful. Thus tidal forces are available for appropriation by a variety of political actors, not just nationalist movements. They can exercise significant influence in the ways in which state elites are forced to adjust to the impact of external events.

Thus, five possibilities are relevant to a discussion of mobilizational outcomes within a tide of nationalism: (1) irrelevancy (a particular frame is inappropriate and therefore unimagined); (2) failures of action (a potentially relevant frame does not become the basis for significant efforts to mobilize); (3) failures of mobilizational effect (efforts to mobilize around a particular frame fail to achieve sufficient resonance within target populations to allow a movement to overcome institutional constraints); (4) mobilizational failure but issue success (a challenging frame is strategically appropriated by the powerful even in the absence of effective mobilization); and (5) mobilizational success (a mobilizational frame gains sufficient resonance within target populations to allow a movement to break through institutional constraints, leading to capture of the state or control over its agenda). I will concentrate on the latter four, leaving the first for others to probe.

We have seen that within a mobilizational cycle the mobilization of identity is subject to conflicting forces across time. On the one hand, mobilization grows more difficult due to the diminishing levels of structural advantage possessed by later risers; on the other hand, mobilization simultaneously grows easier because of the thinning of institutional constraints and the growth of tidal forces generated by the actions of others. In this chapter I argue that groups differ in their capacity to utilize to their own advantage the tidal forces generated by the actions of others, largely because of the structural advantages they possess and the institutional

constraints they confront. The quotation at the beginning of this chapter by Tocqueville encapsulates the fundamental idea: Chance operates
because movements possess different capabilities for taking advantage of
the opportunities and influences chance presents. This is a very different
statement from saying that chance has no effect on historical outcomes
or that historical outcomes are merely structurally determined. In the last
chapter we saw that without tidal effects, historical outcomes would probably have been different given the structural conditions characteristic of
groups. Structure alone would not have been enough to allow movements
to overcome the institutional constraints they faced. Had Ukrainian
nationalism faced the Soviet state in temporal isolation from other
nationalisms, Ukrainian independence would probably never have
materialized.

In this chapter I enlarge on these findings, arguing that political opportunities and tidal effects without facilitating structural conditions are also
unlikely to be translated into successful action. Not only are tidal forces
(the example of successful mobilization by others) temporally rising during
a mobilizational cycle; they are also more or less equally available for
appropriation by all populations. Example does not discriminate among
those who would look to it. What does vary are the differential propensi-
ties and abilities of movements, and the groups they target, to take advantage of example. In cases of what I have called failures of mobilizational
effect, the target group's level of mobilization remains below the point at
which institutional constraints could be overcome despite the crescendo
of examples. In these cases tidal forces exercise some effect on elite behavior, manifest primarily in emulative attempts to mobilize, but low structural facilitation leads to weak resonance within target populations, making
it difficult for movements to take advantage of tidal forces and easier for
authority to marginalize challengers. Failures of mobilizational effect are
often rooted in a set of mutually reinforcing conditions of weak structural
facilitation and robust institutional constraints.

By contrast, in cases of what I call failures of action, failure occurs not
because regimes of repression directly limit action, but because structural
disadvantage cumulates to the point that action appears futile. In these
cases significant institutional constraints may or may not be in place, but
they are likely to be superfluous to the outcome. Rather, in these cases
nationalist mobilization fails because the structural disadvantages of target
groups are so great that even those who do believe in a particular goal lose
faith in the efficacy of collective action. Thus, although rooted in the same

set of causal factors, failures of mobilizational effect occur primarily at the level of the target group, whereas failures of action occur primarily at the level of the activists themselves. They fail to act not so much because they are directly constrained by institutions, but because they operate within a cultural and social environment overwhelmingly unreceptive to their aims. Failures of action can thus be understood in Gramscian terms as situations of cultural hegemony. By cultural hegemony, I mean a mode of dominance by one cultural group over another, reproduced by limiting the imagination of subordinate groups primarily through the cumulation of structural disadvantages, making challenge appear impossible and outlandish. For Gramsci, hegemony was a form of political control based not only (or even primarily) on coercion, but more significantly on the manufacture of consent within society to a particular conception of the world. Having monopolized political space, the Soviet government sought to create such a cultural hegemony within the nationalities sphere and even came to believe falsely in the efficacy of its efforts. In some locales, the attempt to create cultural hegemony operated less effectively, requiring the government to deploy occasional force to ensure the marginalization of challenging nationalisms. But elsewhere cultural dominance grew normalized and embedded in social reality to the point that force was no longer required to enforce it. Because in cases of the failure of action, attempts to mobilize around the frame in question are widely viewed by target populations as outlandish, the boundary between the irrelevancy of nationalism and the failure of nationalist action is often difficult to code. In failures of action, challenging nationalist frames appear irrelevant to the vast majority of group members, but due largely to the influence of the example of others these frames do find marginal expression in public and private discourse, and therefore are imaginable to some.

I first examine the structural conditions underlying cultural hegemonies of this sort, illustrating the ways in which the cumulation of structural disadvantage limits national imagination, even in conditions of relaxed institutional constraints and an explosion of contention by analogous groups. Subsequently, I show empirically how structure becomes advantageous primarily through the potential it provides for nationalist movements and their target groups to profit from the actions of others. This furnishes the backdrop for a discussion of the structural factors which help or hinder mobilizational success and whose absence contributes to failures of mobilizational effect. Finally, through a series of case studies I not only illustrate the interplay between structure, tide, and institutional constraint in the production of mobilizational failures, but also the process by which nationalist movements can fail yet nationalism nonetheless succeed.

## The Structural Underpinnings of Failures of Action

Statistical analysis of patterns of separatist mobilization in the USSR during its final years helps us to understand the ways in which pre-existing structural conditions shape the nonevent in nationalism. To carry out this analysis, my first task was to narrow the larger pool of forty-seven nationalities used in this study to a subset of groups from which one might reasonably have expected separatist mobilization, at least on the basis of the presence of action by groups in analogous circumstances. This primarily involved eliminating groups such as Jews, Germans, Bulgarians, Koreans, Kurds, and Uighurs which had external homelands (whether or not they currently constituted states), which were geographically dispersed without ethnofederal territories, or for whom emigration rather than territorial separation was the most likely exit option. Russian separatism, though a significant phenomenon during this period, had its own specific dynamics that differentiated it from non-Russian separatism due to the close association of Russians with the Soviet state. I deal with it separately in Chapter 8. In the end, I was left with a set of forty target groups that might possibly have been expected to engage in some separatist action. For each of these forty groups separatism was not necessarily apparent but was to some degree "imaginable" in that members of other groups in a situation analogous to their own in size and political status engaged in separatist behavior during the period under examination. Yet, for only twenty of these forty nationalities did movements materialize which succeeded in organizing at least one demonstration voicing separatist demands and attracting a minimal one hundred participants. Thus, our pool of potential separatist target groups divided roughly into three sets: (1) those whose movements failed to generate significant separatist mobilizational activity (failures of action); (2) those whose movements generated some significant separatist mobilizational activity, though not enough to break through the institutional constraints to which they were subject (failures of mobilizational effect); and (3) those whose movements generated significant separatist mobilizational activity and successfully transcended the institutional constraints to which they were subject (mobilizational success). Table 5.1 lists the classification of outcomes and relevant mobilizational activity for each of the forty groups. I analyze these outcomes by concentrating initially on the first category (failures of action), subsequently differentiating between all three.

Table 5.2 presents the results of a series of logit regressions predicting the probability of observing at least one separatist demonstration with a minimum of a hundred participants by nationalist movements of a particular nationality during the *glasnost'* period (that is, the probability of avoiding a failure of action).[3] Equations 1, 2, and 3 identify three factors systematically associated with failures of action: population size, the ethnofederal status of a group, and linguistic assimilation. The first two factors are highly correlated, and their effects cannot be separated. However, comparing the log likelihoods of Equations 1 and 2 and the number of mispredicted cases in each, population size is the better predictor of failures of nationalism. Even in the context of a tide of nationalism, when numerous other groups were swept up by separatist sentiment and the political order was coming undone, smaller and more linguistically assimilated groups were unlikely to be influenced to separatist action by the upsurge in separatism elsewhere. In Equation 1, each percentage point increase in the proportion of a nationality claiming as its native language the language of another group was associated with a 15.8 percent decrease in the odds of observing a nonzero separatist outcome relative to a zero outcome. Though perhaps more difficult to interpret because of its logged form, population size was similarly associated with robust decreases in the odds of a nonzero separatist outcome. Each unit of increase in population size (measured here in thousands of persons logged) was associated with a 219 percent decrease in the odds of a nonzero separatist outcome compared to the odds of a zero separatist outcome. Both population size and patterns of linguistic assimilation were closely linked with the federal system, and with the exception of one case (the Turkmen) union republican status was perfectly correlated with a nonzero separatist outcome in the logit regression. As Equation 2 shows, union republican status increased the odds of some separatist mobilization by over 1,800 percent. But union republican groups were not the only groups to engage in significant separatist mobilization. As Equation 3 shows, even when republican status is introduced into the logit analysis, both population size and

---

[3] The regression coefficients represent the change in the log-odds associated with a unit change in an independent variable (this has been exponentiated to an odds ratio, indicating the relative amount by which the odds of a nonzero separatist outcome increase or decrease when the value of the predictor variable is increased by one unit).

Table 5.1. *Mobilizational Parameters and Mobilizational Outcomes for Separatist Nationalism Among Forty Non-Russian Nationalities, 1987–92*[a]

| Group | 1989 population (thous.) | Ethnonationalist demonstrations, 1987–92 | Separatist demonstrations, 1987–92 | Participation in separatist demonstrations, 1987–92 | Outcome classification for separatist nationalism[b] |
|---|---|---|---|---|---|
| Ukrainians | 44,186 | 782 | 346 | 4,460,960 | Mobilizational success |
| Uzbeks | 16,698 | 58 | 6 | 36,650 | Failure of mobilizational effect |
| Belorussians | 10,036 | 45 | 6 | 177,500 | Failure of mobilizational effect |
| Kazakhs | 8,136 | 83 | 14 | 61,900 | Failure of mobilizational effect |
| Azerbaijanis | 6,770 | 235 | 73 | 4,525,367 | Mobilizational success |
| Volga Tatars | 6,649 | 69 | 55 | 104,383 | Failure of mobilizational effect |
| Armenians | 4,623 | 546 | 96 | 9,626,150 | Mobilizational success |
| Tajiks | 4,215 | 84 | 10 | 96,000 | Failure of mobilizational effect |
| Georgians | 3,981 | 394 | 192 | 3,062,902 | Mobilizational success |
| Moldavians | 3,352 | 153 | 82 | 1,858,858 | Mobilizational success |
| Lithuanians | 3,067 | 325 | 254 | 4,443,034 | Mobilizational success |
| Turkmen | 2,729 | 0 | 0 | 0 | Failure of action |
| Kirgiz | 2,529 | 33 | 4 | 6,100 | Failure of mobilizational effect |
| Chuvash | 1,842 | 2 | 0 | 0 | Failure of action |
| Latvians | 1,459 | 114 | 72 | 2,992,225 | Mobilizational success |
| Bashkirs | 1,449 | 9 | 6 | 4,450 | Failure of mobilizational effect |
| Mordvinians | 1,154 | 0 | 0 | 0 | Failure of action |
| Estonians | 1,027 | 69 | 53 | 1,256,499 | Mobilizational success |
| Chechens | 957 | 76 | 53 | 426,547 | Mobilizational success |
| Udmurts | 747 | 2 | 0 | 0 | Failure of action |
| Mari | 671 | 0 | 0 | 0 | Failure of action |

210

| | | | | | |
|---|---|---|---|---|---|
| Ossetians | 598 | 52 | 4 | 12,500 | Failure of mobilizational effect |
| Lezgins | 466 | 7 | 0 | 0 | Failure of action |
| Karakalpaks | 424 | 0 | 0 | 0 | Failure of action |
| Buriats | 421 | 0 | 0 | 0 | Failure of action |
| Kabardinians | 391 | 13 | 0 | 0 | Failure of action |
| Yakuts | 382 | 3 | 0 | 0 | Failure of action |
| Komi | 345 | 0 | 0 | 0 | Failure of action |
| Ingush | 237 | 43 | 0 | 0 | Failure of action |
| Tuvans | 207 | 3 | 2 | 800 | Failure of mobilizational effect |
| Gagauz | 198 | 27 | 11 | 7,650 | Mobilizational success |
| Kalmyks | 174 | 0 | 0 | 0 | Failure of action |
| Karachai | 156 | 19 | 0 | 0 | Failure of action |
| Karelians | 131 | 0 | 0 | 0 | Failure of action |
| Adygei | 125 | 1 | 0 | 0 | Failure of action |
| Abkhaz | 105 | 36 | 16 | 73,800 | Mobilizational success |
| Balkars | 85 | 11 | 0 | 0 | Failure of action |
| Khakass | 80 | 2 | 0 | 0 | Failure of action |
| Altai | 69 | 0 | 0 | 0 | Failure of action |
| Cherkess | 52 | 5 | 0 | 0 | Failure of action |

[a] Separatist mobilization is defined as mobilization raising demands for secession (in this case, from either the USSR or from its union republics or successor states) with the aim of establishing independent statehood. Instances of irredentist struggles for unification of a nationality divided across political borders (such as, for example, the Karabakh issue) were excluded. As explicated in the text, the success or failure of mobilization around separatist frames does not imply that mobilization around other nationalist frames also succeeded or failed.

[b] A failure of mobilizational effect is defined as a situation in which a potentially relevant nationalist frame did not become the basis for significant efforts at mobilization. A failure of action is defined as a situation in which efforts to mobilize around a particular frame materialized but failed to exercise sufficient resonance within target populations that might have allowed the movement espousing the frame to overcome the institutional constraints to which it was subject. Mobilizational success is defined as a situation in which a nationalist movement espousing a particular frame gained sufficient mobilizational resonance within target populations so as to break through the institutional constraints to which it was subject.

Table 5.2. *Logistic Regression of the Probability of a Nonzero Separatist Outcome by Nationality, January 1987–December 1992*[a]

| Independent variable | Equation 1 Coefficient | Equation 1 Odds ratio | Equation 2 Coefficient | Equation 2 Odds ratio | Equation 3 Coefficient | Equation 3 Odds ratio | Equation 4 Coefficient | Equation 4 Odds ratio |
|---|---|---|---|---|---|---|---|---|
| Ln population size (thousands), 1989 | 1.159 (2.71)** | 3.187 | – | – | 1.179 (1.68)* | 3.250 | 1.125 (2.66)*** | 3.080 |
| Dummy variable for union republic | – | – | 2.947 (2.46)** | 19.055 | -0.072 (-0.04) | .931 | – | – |
| Linguistic assimilation, 1989 | -0.172 (-2.20)** | .842 | -0.104 (-1.59) | .901 | -0.174 (-1.95)* | .841 | -0.121 (-2.18)* | .886 |
| Level of urbanization, 1970 | 0.068 (1.26) | 1.071 | 0.091 (1.89)* | 1.096 | 0.068 (1.26) | 1.071 | 0.086 (1.42) | 1.090 |
| Dummy variable for peoples of traditionally Islamic cultures | -1.553 (-1.27) | .212 | -0.824 (-0.74) | .439 | -1.568 (-1.21) | .208 | – | – |
| Years experience as independent state or as part of other state, 1918–40 | – | – | – | – | – | – | 0.193 (1.63) | 1.212 |

212

| | Equation 1 | Equation 2 | Equation 3 | Equation 4 |
|---|---|---|---|---|
| Constant | -7.455224 | -2.201726 | -7.550722 | -9.342581 |
| Number of observations (nationalities) | 40 | 40 | 40 | 40 |
| Number of correctly predicted observations | 35[b] | 32[c] | 35[d] | 36[e] |
| Observations eliminated due to complete determination | 0 | 0 | 0 | 0 |
| Pseudo $R^2$ | .5074 | .4368 | .5074 | .5560 |
| Likelihood ratio chi-square | 28.13**** | 24.22**** | 28.14**** | 30.83**** |
| Log likelihood | -13.658902 | -15.614316 | -13.658266 | -12.311426 |

*Significant at the .10 level    **Significant at the .05 level    ***Significant at the .01 level    ****Significant at the .001 level.

[a] Coefficients are the log-odds of a nonzero separatist outcome (with $z$-scores provided in parentheses), which have been exponentiated into odds ratios.

[b] In Equation 1 the Turkmen were overpredicted to be a nonzero separatist outcome, and the Abkhaz, Gagauz, Bashkirs, and Tuvans were underpredicted as zero separatist outcomes.

[c] In Equation 2 the Turkmen, Kalmyks, and Ingush were overpredicted to be nonzero separatist outcomes, and the Abkhaz, Gagauz, Bashkirs, Chechens, and Tuvans were underpredicted as zero separatist outcomes.

[d] In Equation 3 the Turkmen were overpredicted to be a nonzero separatist outcome, and the Abkhaz, Gagauz, Bashkirs, and Tuvans were underpredicted as zero separatist outcomes.

[e] In Equation 4 the Turkmen were overpredicted to be a nonzero separatist outcome, and the Abkhaz, Bashkirs, and Gagauz were underpredicted as zero separatist outcomes.

linguistic assimilation remain statistically significant. Though urbanization did not have a statistically significant relationship with the probability of a nonzero separatist outcome in Equation 1, it was marginally significant in Equation 2, when ethnofederal status was used in place of population size; each percentage point of urbanization was associated with a 9.6 percent increase in the odds of a nonzero separatist outcome compared to the odds of a zero separatist outcome. By contrast, in none of the equations was Islamic cultural background found to be a statistically significant factor in increasing or decreasing the odds of some separatist mobilization.

The logit regression in Equation 1 correctly predicts a zero or nonzero outcome in 88 percent of the cases – a fairly accurate level of prediction. Four nationalities (Abkhaz, Gagauz, Bashkirs, and Tuvans) were mispredicted to be likely failures of action, whereas one (Turkmen) was wrongly predicted as avoiding a failure of action. In Equation 4 I have introduced an additional variable representing the number of years in which a group experienced independent statehood or was part of another state from 1918 to 1940 as a refinement of the model suggested by the anomalous Tuvan case.[4] As the results show, though the variable for alternative state experience in the interwar period is not statistically significant, the fit of the model is slightly improved, yielding accurate predictions for 90 percent of the cases.[5]

Identifying the causal mechanisms underlying these correlations is more difficult. Was small population size associated with an absence of separatist action due to the influence of international norms concerning group size and self-determination, the relationship of the federal system to population size, recognition of the practical problems involved in creating separate states for small groups, or the power differential small groups would likely experience in attempting to contest the state's dominant national order? Each of these factors was a powerful enough reason to expect group size to limit the degree to which separatist frames might

---

[4] This continuous variable ranged from 0 to 22, with high scores for Balts, Moldovans, Tuvans, and Karelians representing their extensive interwar experience outside the Soviet state, low scores for Transcaucasians, Ukrainians, and Belorussians representing their short-lived experiments with statehood during the Russian civil war, and zero scores for others.

[5] The statistical insignificance of urbanization and prior independent statehood in Equation 4 is largely the result of the aggregated nature of the outcomes examined here. Both variables are significant in the ordered logit model examined below.

gain resonance. But there is a fundamental problem in trying to sort out competing causal stories for nonevents. Proceess tracing obviously is not available, and it is difficult to identify even a set of actors responsible for the absence of an event. Even if one could identify such a group, people usually do not reflect on their motivations for behaving in ways they consider normal; they do not write memoirs about why they did not engage in separatist activity.

The failure to act in this sense is better understood as an inertial state whose reproduction over time is supported by multiple, overlapping processes. Multiple structural conditions stack the deck against particular nationalist frames. Their cumulation makes it unlikely that nationalist movements espousing these frames could move out of a condition of marginalization and engage in effective action. This improbability becomes self-reinforcing, undermining a movement's coherence and creating within target populations a sense of the movement's eccentricity and exoticism. It is this domination based on consent and buttressed by the cumulation of structural disadvantage which allows us to speak of a cultural hegemony capable of operating even without institutional constraint.

A case study drawn from our sample illustrates more concretely how a situation of cultural hegemony can be established, undermining nationalist action by instilling a widespread sense of the impossibility that things could be otherwise and marginalizing those who imagine alternatives. Observers of the Buriat scene have frequently commented on the degree to which interethnic relations within Buriatiia have been marked by an absence of tension, even in the midst of the enormous tide of nationalism that swept the USSR during the *glasnost'* years. This contrasts sharply with the situation in the early twentieth century and during the Russian Revolution, when Buriats were centrally involved in political movements aimed at establishing an independent pan-Mongolian state.[6] But in the late 1980s and early 1990s, when analogous groups such as the Tuvans did engage in separatist action, such ideas were raised only tentatively by Buriats and did not constitute a basis for any significant separatist mobilization. The four hundred twenty-one thousand Buriats of the USSR had maintained a strong sense of distinctive identity – reinforced by racial differentiation from the dominant Russian settlers and by Soviet nationalities policies – despite a high degree of linguistic assimilation, brought on by the closing

[6] See Robert A. Rupen, "The Buriat Intelligentsia," *The Far Eastern Quarterly*, vol. 15, no. 3 (May 1956), pp. 383–98.

of Buriat-language schools in the 1970s and a massive influx of Russians into the region (demographically, Russians predominated as early as the 1920s). Yet, as Caroline Humphrey has observed, the vast majority of Buriats came to feel "at ease with, or perhaps resigned to, their close relations with the Siberian Russians."[7] Within our sample of forty groups, Buriats ranked slightly above average in linguistic assimilation (13.5 percent claimed Russian as their native language in 1989, compared with the 10.4 percent mean for the sample) and low in urbanization (only 24.4 percent in our 1970 data, well below the 32.7 percent mean for the sample). Moreover, overwhelmed by the Russian presence in their republic (in 1989 Buriats constituted only 24 percent of the population of Buriatiia) and politically dominated by the local Russian nomenklatura, Buriats found that the possibilities for successful separatism seemed remote and strategies of survival dictated accommodation to the existing social order.

Even among many Buriat nationalists the term "nationalism" came to be understood as pejorative, as the narrow promotion of ethnic Buriat political interests at the expense of others. The seemingly unchallengeable hegemony of Russians over the territory was the critical factor pushing toward limiting national imagination. Buriats experienced a cultural revival in the *glasnost'* period, and a small nationalist movement emerged aimed at resuscitating language use and Buddhist religious practice. In November 1990, shortly after the parade of sovereignties reached Buriatiia and the Russian-dominated local government declared sovereignty (in the process, unilaterally upgrading the status of Buriatiia to a union republic), a number of Buriat intellectuals organized a Buriat-Mongolian National Party (BMNP). The movement remained small, claiming two hundred members by July 1991. It officially limited its programmatic demands to Buriat "self-determination" and the recovery of Buriat lands separated from the republic by Stalin in the 1930s. The BMNP became the focal point for Buriat separatist aspirations to the extent that these existed, and by this time, under the influence of the tide, Buriat independence had become imaginable to some. As Jasper Becker recalled on visiting the region at the time, "It was strange to meet young and angry Buryiat Nationalists demanding the expulsion of all Russians but having to do this in Russian."[8] A survey of 304 Buriats conducted in 1995 found that 8.6

---

[7] Caroline Humphrey, "Buryatiya and the Buryats," in Graham Smith, ed., *The Nationalities Question in the Post-Soviet States* (2d ed.) (London: Longman, 1996), p. 124.

[8] Jasper Becker, *The Lost Country: Mongolia Revealed* (London: Hodder and Stoughton, 1992), p. 247.

percent believed that the Buriat Republic would be better off if it separated from Russia and created its own state (as did, curiously enough, 3.2
percent of Russians living in Buriatiia).[9] Separatist ideas were widely held
by the vast majority of Buriats to be outlandish, and social pressure, even
by fellow Buriats, against those advocating separatism was strong.[10] By
early 1992, the BMNP's fortunes further waned, as members began to
leave its ranks. As one study of interethnic relations in Buriatiia concluded,
the nationalists "enjoy no authority among the majority of inhabitants, in
that they are not numerous and they have no clear social programs."[11] In
short, the marginalization of Buriat separatism was a self-reinforcing
situation. In contrast to the situation seventy years earlier, by the 1980s
Russian political hegemony seemed insurmountable to most Buriats. The
weak structural position of Buriats in terms of group size, level of urbanization, linguistic assimilation, and lack of experience with independent
statehood stacked the deck against separatism, making a nationalism which
previously had been substantial appear to the vast majority of Buriats to
be impossible and absurd today.

Thus, the failure to act, even when a particular nationalism is imaginable to some and in the absence of the need to apply repression, is trace-
able to a situation in which multiple structural disadvantages reinforce a
widespread sense of a nationalism's impossibility and outlandishness. This
type of cultural hegemony operated with relative efficiency even in the
midst of a tide of nationalism and without resort to repression largely
because challenging movements faced a cumulative structural situation
which made dominant norms more attractive and alternatives less credible. One cannot point to a single cause of failures of action or a single
pattern of structural conditions associated with these cases. Rather,
various combinations of structural disadvantage, through their cumulation,
produced a sense of impossibility surrounding alternative national
orders.

This conclusion is supported by a Monte Carlo simulation of the probability of a failure of action on the basis of the structural characteristics
of target groups. Using the specification in Equation 4 in Table 5.2, I

---

[9] A. D. Karnyshev, *Mezhetnicheskoe vzaimodeistvie v Buriatii: Sotsial'naia psikhologiia, istoriia,
politika* (Ulan-Ude: Izd-tsvo Buriatskogo gosuniversiteta, 1997), pp. 157–58. Similar
results were repeated in a subsequent survey the following year.
[10] See, for instance, Becker, *The Lost Country: Mongolia Revealed*, pp. 241–42.
[11] S. S. Buiakhaev, *Etnopoliticheskaia i etnokul'turnaia situatsiia v Respublike Buriatiia* (Moscow:
Institut etnologii i antropologii, 1993), p. 11.

utilized the techniques developed by King, Tomz, and Wittenberg[12] to estimate a Monte Carlo simulation (based on a thousand sets of simulated parameters) of the average predicted probability that a nationality would engage in at least one separatist protest attracting a hundred participants or more under varying conditions of the independent variables. Monte Carlo simulation allows us, on the basis of a given empirical track record, to pinpoint likely tipping points characteristic of changes in the probability of outcomes assuming particular levels of the independent variables. It thereby provides us with the opportunity to explore a series of counterfactuals concerning the ways in which different combinations of independent variables might interact. On the basis of these Monte Carlo simulations, Figure 5.1 presents the average predicted probabilities of engaging in no separatist protest (a failure of action) associated with variations in population size, linguistic assimilation, urbanization, and prior state experience in the twentieth century. The heavy black lines in the figures represent the average predicted probabilities for zero and nonzero separatist outcomes at various values of an independent variable, holding all other variables constant at their means. Each of these figures describes a tipping process associated with the variable, where, holding other variables at their means, the average probability of a target nationality engaging in at least one separatist demonstration attracting a minimum of a hundred participants shifts from less than .50 to greater than .50. I have also shown in some of the figures how shifts away from the mean for particular variables alter the probability of a zero separatist outcome (these appear as broken lines in the figures and have been labeled according to the ways in which they deviate from the mean for all target groups in the sample).

As can be seen from Figure 5.1a, holding all other variables at their means, the tipping point for a failure of action in terms of population size was approximately five hundred sixty thousand; thus, according to the simulation model, nationalist movements from nationalities with fewer than five hundred sixty thousand on average had less than a .50 probability of engaging in some separatist protest, assuming average levels of other

[12] Gary King, Michael Tomz, and Jason Wittenberg, "Making the Most of Statistical Analysis: Improving Interpretation and Presentation," paper prepared for the Annual Meeting of the American Political Science Association, Boston, MA, August 1998. The simulations were computed using the CLARIFY program developed by Tomz, Wittenberg, and King, Version 1.2.1.

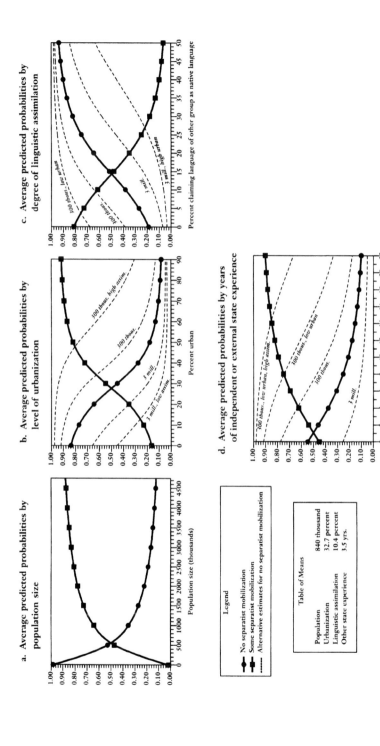

**Figure 5.1.** Average predicted probabilities for a failure of action (zero separatist outcome) for separatist nationalism in the USSR, 1987–92 (Monte Carlo simulation). Unless otherwise noted, all other variables held constant at their means.

219

variables, whereas nationalist movements from target groups over five hundred sixty thousand had more than a .50 probability of engaging in some separatist protest. Similarly, in Figure 5.1b, we see that the average probability that a nationality engaged in at least one separatist demonstration drops below .50 when less than 28 percent of a nationality's population is urbanized, assuming average values of other variables. As Figure 5.1c shows, on average target groups with more than 14 percent of their population claiming the language of another group as their native language had more than a .50 probability of engaging in no separatist protest, assuming average values of other variables. And less than a year of experience of independent or alternative statehood in the twentieth century was associated on average with less than a .50 chance of engaging in some separatist protest, holding other variables constant at their means (Figure 5.1d).

Of course, in real life ethnic groups do not exhibit uniformly average values for these other variables. What we have done with the Monte Carlo simulation is to perform a counterfactual experiment based on the real-life patterns demonstrated by the groups whose activities have been studied empirically. But the counterfactual experiment allows us to gain some leverage on why the nationalist movements of some groups fail to engage in separatist action whereas those of other groups do. It provides us with an empirically based understanding of how the cumulation of structural advantage or disadvantage alters the probability of separatist action in a context in which other groups are widely engaged in action. For example, in Figure 5.1b, simply altering the population size of a group to three million while holding other variables constant at their means lowers the degree of urbanization necessary for a .50 chance of avoiding a failure of action from 28 percent to 12 percent. A nationality of three million members with a low degree of linguistic assimilation would have been expected to engage in some separatist action irrespective of its degree of urbanization. Examples roughly analogous to this within our sample were the 4.2 million Tajiks and 2.5 million Kirgiz – both of whom engaged in some separatist action under the influence of tidal forces.

By contrast, a nationality of only three hundred thousand members with an average degree of assimilation and external state experience would have to have been relatively urbanized (at a minimum, 40 percent urban) to have been expected to engage in some separatist action during the tide of nationalism; this was a situation roughly analogous to that of the five hundred ninety-eight thousand Ossetians (53 percent of whom were urban in 1970), who did in fact engage in some separatist mobilization during the period examined here. At the same time, a group of three hundred thousand that was relatively assimilated linguistically would have to have been even more urbanized (68 percent) to have been expected to engage in some separatist mobilization – in actuality, a level of urbanization higher than that of even the most urbanized group in the sample (the Armenians). The one hundred seventy-four thousand Kalmyks, for instance, who had an average degree of urbanization (32.7 percent) and a relatively low degree of linguistic assimilation (7.5 percent), fell far below the 51 percent level of urbanization necessary to offset the other structural disadvantages they suffered in view of their small population size, lack of union republican status, and absence of twentieth-century experience with independent statehood. Even in the midst of a tide of separatist mobilization, the highly assimilated seven hundred forty-seven thousand Udmurts of Russia, 30 percent of whom claimed Russian as their native language in 1989, would have to have been twice as urban as they were (64 percent, as opposed to their actual 32 percent) to counteract their other structural disadvantages for separatist action. In Figure 5.1c, a relatively small nationality of three hundred thousand members with a low degree of urbanization was unlikely to engage in any separatist action irrespective of the degree to which it was linguistically assimilated, whereas it was likely that a highly urbanized group of three million, even if 40 percent of its members claimed the language of another group as their native language, would nevertheless engage in some separatist mobilization. Even the powerful effects of experience with independent statehood in the twentieth century were subject to trade-off. Thus, a group of three hundred thousand that was relatively less urbanized (such as the Tuvans) required a lengthy experience with independent or alternative statehood in the twentieth century (an experience which the Tuvans possessed) to overcome its other structural disadvantages for separatist action, whereas on average a population of three million with average levels of urbanization and assimilation did not require any experience with independent or alternative statehood to engage in some separatist mobilization during the years under discussion. By contrast, even twenty-two years of independent or external statehood was unlikely to counterbalance other structural disadvantages for a target group of three hundred thousand that was highly assimilated and relatively less urbanized (a situation that resembled the Karelians but for their above-average degree of urbanization).

These trade-offs between facilitating structural conditions show that there are no specific single structural conditions associated with failures of action. One can approximate similar probability curves for separatist action through quite different combinations of structural variables. Rather, it is the cumulation of structural disadvantages, not any particular structural disadvantage, which sustains situations of cultural hegemony. Thus, of the twenty target groups in our sample that experienced a failure of separatist action, four had two of the four structural disadvantages analyzed here (one being the mispredicted case of the Turkmen), ten had three of these structural disadvantages, and six had four of these structural disadvantages. By contrast, of the twenty target groups in the sample that engaged in some separatist action, six had none of these structural disadvantages, three had only one, nine had two (including the mispredicted case of the Abkhaz), and two (the mispredicted cases of the Bashkirs and Gagauz) had three.

Thus, the cumulation of structural disadvantage stacks the deck against collective action on the part of particular nationalisms. In these types of situations, although nationalist outcomes may be imaginable to some (particularly under the influence of the actions of others), such outcomes tend to appear impractical and outlandish to the overwhelming majority of members of the target group, undermining not only the conditions necessary for successful collective action, but belief in its efficacy as well.

### Exploring Anomalous Cases

The logit regressions in Equations 1 and 4 of Table 5.2 performed exceedingly well as a predictive apparatus. Nevertheless, an examination of the mispredicted cases (Abkhaz, Gagauz, Bashkirs, Tuvans, and Turkmen) provides insight into the ways in which outcomes are the product of an interaction between structural facilitation, institutional constraints, and tidal effects. Based solely on the model in Equation 1, for instance, one would have predicted a .13 probability that a group with the structural characteristics (population size, level of assimilation, and degree of urbanization) of the Abkhaz would have engaged in separatist mobilization, a .31 probability of some separatist mobilization for groups with features like those of the Gagauz, a .38 chance for groups like the Bashkirs, and a .44 probability for those similar to the Tuvans. Movements from these groups avoided a failure of action in spite of some of the structural disadvantages of their target groups. As we will see, the explanation lies primarily in the ways in which they came under particularly strong influence from the mobilizational activity of others. In the cases of the Abkhaz, Gagauz, and Bashkirs, this influence emerged from their close association with other groups swept up by separatist nationalism (the Georgians, Moldovans, and Volga Tatars, respectively). In the cases of the Abkhaz and Gagauz, the powerful impact of reference groups lowered the institutional constraints to which separatism was normally subject, as separatist movements enjoyed strong support from local state units (and even the USSR government as well). As the tide of nationalism spread, the nesting of interethnic conflict through the ethnofederal system, the presence of strong reference groups already involved in separatist protest, and the supportive role played by state institutions at the local or all-union levels unleashed separatist mobilization among some groups that, judging solely on the basis of the structural advantages enjoyed by other separatists, would otherwise have been unlikely candidates for separatism.

The one hundred and five thousand Abkhaz, for instance, were the smallest group in the USSR to engage in separatist action – one of the reasons why their actions were so poorly predicted by our statistical model. The Abkhaz exhibited a relatively low level of linguistic assimilation (4.8 percent claiming a language other than Abkhaz as their native language) and a somewhat above-average level of urbanization (34.9 percent). But the disadvantage of small size was mainly offset by a history that, at least since the 1930s, had associated Abkhaz nationalist aspirations with separation from Georgian rather than Russian domination. Abkhaz separatist mobilization emerged in late 1988 and early 1989 under the influence of the major waves of Georgian separatist mobilization in November 1988,[13] though it had clear roots in a long record of separatist efforts over the previous several decades. Tensions between Abkhaz and Georgians date from before Russian control over the region in 1810, intensifying particularly after the 1870s, when the Tsarist government brutally suppressed an Abkhaz revolt, sent two hundred thousand Abkhaz (half the Abkhaz population at the time) into exile abroad, and settled large numbers of Georgians, Mingrelians, and others in the region. Under the influence of Lavrentii Beria (a Mingrelian born in Abkhazia) a policy of Georgianization was pursued by the Soviet government during the Stalinist period. Abkhazia was incorporated directly into Georgia as an autonomous republic in 1931, the Georgian alphabet was introduced in place of Latin script in 1938, school curriculum was reoriented around Georgian language instruction, and a large in-migration of Georgians took place. The post-Stalinist period saw a reversal of these trends, with Abkhaz taught once

---

[13] *Vesti iz SSSR*, 5/6–36, 1989; *Report on the USSR*, vol. 1, no. 14 (April 1989), p. 30.

again in some schools and a nativization of the local party apparatus and government, leading to significant overrepresentation for Abkhaz relative to their proportion within the population. Nevertheless, Abkhaz remained a small minority within their republic (17 percent in 1979), with few opportunities for advancement except through assimilation. Formal appeals to Moscow to transfer Abkhazia to Russian control were made in 1957 and 1967. In June 1978, when debate over the wording of a new constitution unleashed a wave of mobilization over language issues among Georgians, twelve thousand Abkhaz demonstrated in the village of Lykhnyi against the "Georgianization" of Abkhazia, again appealing to Moscow to separate the territory from Georgia and allow it to join with the RSFSR.[14] Abkhaz separatism was thus already a well-established reaction to Georgian nationalism before the onset of *glasnost'*.

Inspired by developments in Nagorno-Karabakh and the growing activity of Georgian nationalists in early 1988, Abkhaz intellectuals sent a letter to the presidium of the Nineteenth Party Conference in June 1988 calling for the transfer of Abkhazia to direct rule from Moscow. Known as the "Abkhaz letter," the appeal was made only days after the Supreme Soviet of Armenia had adopted a resolution calling for Karabakh to be united with Armenia. The letter was forgotten and largely unknown within Abkhazia until after the massive secessionist demonstrations that rocked Tbilisi in November 1988. With this impetus, in December 1988 the authors of the appeal formed the Popular Forum *Aidgylara* (Unity), an Abkhaz national movement organized with the blessing of the local Abkhaz communist leadership (and some believe, under Moscow's influence). The main platform of the movement – a document which received wide circulation from official government organs in Abkhazia – called for raising the status of Abkhazia to that of a union republic, thereby taking it outside of Georgia and subordinating it directly to Moscow's authority. Abkhaz nationalism thus differed qualitatively from the separatism then growing elsewhere in the USSR in that it formed a countermovement to Georgian separatism. Abkhaz nationalists, for instance, specifically argued in favor of the preservation of the USSR and against the attempts of Georgian nationalists to undermine the Soviet state. Some have likened the Popular Forum to the various interfronts then emerging within the Russian-speaking populations of the Baltic and Moldova, viewing its

---

[14] See Darrell Slider, "Crisis and Response in Soviet Nationality Policy: The Case of Abkhazia," *Central Asian Survey*, vol. 4, no. 4 (1985), pp. 51–68.

appearance as part of a larger effort by Moscow to pressure Georgians to remain within the USSR. The close connection of Abkhaz separatism with official government organs is evident. A demonstration of thirty thousand Abkhaz held in Lykhnyi to mark the creation of the Popular Forum was officially authorized by the Abkhaz local government, and the appeal issued to the USSR authorities by the gathering was signed by many local Abkhaz officials, including the then first secretary of the Abkhaz obkom, Boris Adleiba (subsequently fired from his job by the Georgian authorities for his support of Abkhaz separatism).[15] Once Georgian separatism emerged as a force, Abkhaz separatism did not face significant institutional constraints since it enjoyed the support of local (and even USSR) state authorities, and only republican state authority stood in its way. Rather than mobilizing to capture the state, Abkhaz separatists began with significant encouragement from the state, utilizing mobilization largely as a means for contesting competing notions of state sovereignty and control emanating from rival segments of the state.

Similarly, separatist mobilization among the one hundred ninety-eight thousand Gagauz (Orthodox Christian Turks resettled to Bessarabia from Bulgaria after the Russo-Ottoman war of 1806–12, and the second smallest nationality after the Abkhaz to engage in significant separatist mobilization during the *glasnost'* period) had its roots in 1989 in the wake of large-scale demonstrations by Moldovans for declaring Moldovan the official language of the republic.[16] At the time, 91 percent of Gagauz claimed Gagauz as their native language, and only 5.5 percent had a knowledge of Moldovan as either a first or second language (the vast majority of Gagauz utilized Russian in their dealings with the official world, especially since it had become the language of instruction in schools by the 1960s). Thus, change in the legal regime governing language use was bound to have a significant impact on the daily lives of Gagauz. The Gagauz national movement *Gagauz Halki* (Gagauz People) first arose amid the ferment that gripped Moldova in late 1988 and early 1989, and Gagauz activists participated in the founding of the Moldovan Popular Front in May 1989. But in response to growing agitation among Moldovan nationalists

[15] M. Yu. Chumalov, ed., *Abkhazskii uzel: Dokumenty i materialy po etnicheskomu konfliktu v Abkhazii, vypusk 2* (Moscow: Institut etnologii i antropologii, 1995); S. M. Chervonnaia, *Abkhaziia – 1992: Postkommunisticheskaia vandeiia* (Moscow: Mosgorpechat', 1993), pp. 60–64.
[16] See Charles King, *The Moldovans: Romania, Russia, and the Politics of Culture* (Stanford, CA: Hoover Institution Press, 1999).

concerning language change, already in April 1989 Gagauz nationalists had begun to demand the creation of their own ethnofederal unit within Moldavia. These demands gained the support of local Gagauz Party and government officials within the Gagauz-populated districts of Moldavia. Gagauz mobilization accelerated in the wake of massive Moldavian nationalist demonstrations in summer 1989 calling for language change, republican sovereignty, and secession. The Gagauz were joined at the time by the Russian-speaking community of the republic, forming an alliance in opposition to Moldavian demands and enjoying support from the USSR government. Thus, Gagauz separatism resembled that of the Abkhaz in that it formed in direct opposition to separatist mobilization by the eponymous nationality of the union republic in which they resided, favored the preservation of the USSR, and enjoyed a high degree of state sponsorship – factors which offset the structural disadvantages of small size in separatist politics.

The language law adopted in Moldova in August 1989 recognized Moldovan as the state language and called for a gradual transition to the Latin alphabet, but also established Russian as the "language of interethnic communication" and Gagauz as the official language of Gagauz districts. Nevertheless, Gagauz attempts to establish their own federal unit within Moldova continued to be frustrated by the Kishinev government. After the December 1989 revolution in Romania and republican elections in Moldova (which, by April 1990, had brought to power a government under the influence of the Moldavian Popular Front), Gagauz demands for autonomy turned separatist. In August a group of Gagauz deputies and local officials unilaterally declared the formation of a Gagauz republic outside of Moldova. Gagauz separatism was thus in large part a reactive response to the emergence of Moldovan separatism.

Bashkir separatism, by contrast, gained impetus from the breakup of the USSR and from the Bashkirs' close and often tense relationship with their Volga Tatar cousins. A striking feature of Bashkir nationalists' campaign for independence, as one study concluded, was "the way in which it leaned on the campaigns waged by the Balts . . . [and] on Tatarstan's campaign for state sovereignty."[17] In 1989 the 1.4 million Bashkirs of the USSR (eight hundred and sixty-five thousand of whom lived in Bashkiria) constituted

[17] Mikhail Kryukov and Iver B. Neumann, "Bashkortostani Politics and the Possible Breakup of the Russian Federation," Report No. 177, Norwegian Institute of International Affairs, April 1994, pp. 29–30.

a minority within their own autonomous republic, comprising only 22 percent of the population and trailing demographically both Russians (39 percent) and Volga Tatars (28 percent). Tatar and Bashkir cultures have long been intertwined. Almost a third of Bashkirs claim Tatar as their native language, and the actual definition of who is a Bashkir and who is a Tatar remains contested. Despite (or because of) their cultural proximity, tensions between Tatars and Bashkirs have been a recurring theme of cultural politics in the Middle Volga throughout the twentieth century and were exploited by Moscow in its efforts to maintain control over the area. The first nationalist movements to appear in Bashkiria in the *glasnost'* era were in fact Tatar movements, and Bashkir movements were established in large part "as a countermove to the formation of Tatar organizations."[18] Though a Bashkir cultural organization was created in March 1989, it was not until December that a nationalist movement, the Bashkir National Center *Ural*, was founded. The movement's founding congress had a strong air of conventionality to it, even calling in its final resolutions for adherence to the Communist Party's policies in the nationalities sphere and for full cooperation with Party and Soviet organs.[19] The movement's chief demand was for upgrading the ethnofederal status of Bashkiria to that of a union republic – a goal Tatar nationalists had also proclaimed nine months earlier, and one which Bashkir party officials had raised explicitly at the Central Committee Plenum on nationalities issues in September 1989. Though it sought to move Bashkiria outside the authority of the RSFSR, it did not seek to transcend Moscow's authority over Bashkiria, aiming only at an administrative reordering rather than independent statehood. Indeed, in the Center's documents from this period quotes from Lenin frequently appear alongside diatribes against Tatar and Russian demographic dominance in Bashkiria.

In the wake of the republican and local elections of March 1990, which led to a drop in Bashkir representation within the local legislature, ethnic divisions within Bashkortostan accelerated. A heated contest ensued for chair of the legislature, with Murtaza Rakhimov, director of a large oil refinery in Ufa, emerging as the compromise candidate. The parade of sovereignties in summer and fall 1990 and Yeltsin's visit to Kazan' and Ufa (when he delivered his famous statement urging Russia's minorities to

[18] Kryukov and Neumann, "Bashkortostani Politics and the Possible Break-up," p. 11.
[19] See M. N. Gubloglo, ed., *Etnopoliticheskaia mozaika Bashkortostana: Ocherki, dokumenty, khronika*, vol. 2 (Moscow: Institut etnologii i antropologii, 1992), pp. 93–107.

"take as much sovereignty as you can swallow") led to a radicalization of demands by Bashkir nationalists to include Bashkir hegemony over the state and to declare Bashkir the state language. Four drafts of a declaration of state sovereignty circulated in the local press in late summer and early fall 1990, though the more radical draft proposed by the Bashkir National Center was never seriously considered by the authorities. Even it, however, envisaged only the creation of a "Bashkir Soviet Socialist Republic" in which Bashkirs would be the dominant political force.[20] In late 1990 and early 1991 Rakhimov actively participated in negotiations over a new union treaty, lobbying to obtain union republican status for Bashkortostan within a revamped USSR. Throughout this period the Bashkir National Center advocated the same goal.

In the aftermath of the collapse of the USSR and a major wave of separatist mobilization in Tatarstan in fall 1991, the Bashkir nationalist movement radicalized considerably. At the third congress of the Bashkir National Center at the end of December, independence was openly proclaimed as the movement's strategic goal. The movement embraced the creation of an alternative national legislature – a Bashkir National Congress – representing only the indigenous population and modeled on the Estonian National Congress established earlier (a similar idea had been proposed only months before in Tatarstan).[21] Bashkir nationalists even formally appealed to the United Nations to lend support to Bashkir "decolonization." "The only difference between the Bashkirs and the Estonians and Latvians," it was said, "is that the fate dealt to the latter groups was incomparably luckier."[22] Inspired in particular by the success of the Tatar referendum on independence in March 1992, Bashkir nationalists, jointly with local Tatar separatists, organized a short-lived protest campaign in opposition to the possibility that both republics might sign the Federation Treaty with Moscow. The largest of these pro-independence demonstrations attracted up to four thousand participants – some of them local Tatars who supported Bashkir independence from Moscow. Bashkir nationalists condemned Rakhimov for signing the treaty and declared their intention to struggle for the liberation of Bashkortostan from Russian

[20] See D. Zh. Valeev, *Natsional'nyi suverenitet i natsional'noe vozrozhdenie* (Ufa: Kitap, 1994), pp. 92–98; Gubloglo, ed., *Etnopoliticheskaia mozaika*, vol. 1, pp. 111–43.
[21] F. Kharullin, "Natsional'noe dvizhenie ili bor'ba za kreslo prezidenta?" in Gubloglo, ed., *Etnopoliticheskaia mozaika*, vol. 2, pp. 55–56.
[22] Appeal to the United Nations by the Bashkir National Center, in Gubloglo, ed., *Etnopoliticheskaia mozaika*, vol. 2, p. 154.

colonial rule.[23] But that struggle fizzled quickly as Rakhimov consolidated his control. In exchange for signing the Federal Treaty, Rakhimov obtained far-reaching concessions from Yeltsin for a power-sharing agreement, signed in February 1994. Having gained extensive autonomy from Moscow, Rakhimov then pursued a policy of Bashkirization of governmental and cultural spheres, in many respects appropriating the nationalist agenda. At the same time, the Bashkir nationalist movement withered; by 1994 the Bashkir National Center had slipped into inactivity, prompting one study to note that the movement "was not well-known and did not enjoy the support of the . . . [very] peoples whose interests they claim to defend."[24]

In each of the above three cases, the presence of strong reference groups in the context of a tide of mobilization gave rise to separatist mobilization where it otherwise would have been improbable. Tuvans, with a prior history of independent statehood from 1921 to 1944, were similarly influenced by tidal factors, explaining why a group whose structural characteristics would have led one to expect a failure of action engaged instead in some separatist mobilization. The two hundred seven thousand Tuvans were the only other people of the Soviet Union besides the Balts to have enjoyed a significant experience of independent statehood in the twentieth century. It comes as little surprise, then, that the tide of nationalism generated by the Balts should have eventually reached the distant hills of Tuva. Throughout its period of independence Tuvan sovereignty had been a questionable affair, since by the late 1920s what had originally been established as a buffer state between China and Soviet Russia had been transformed into a Soviet puppet state along the Mongolian model. Tuvan sovereignty had been recognized only by the USSR and Mongolia. But even a symbolic experience with independent statehood was enough to evoke some significant secessionist mobilization within the tide of nationalism that swept the Soviet Union in the late 1980s and early 1990s – even within one of the poorest and least urbanized populations of the USSR.

In late 1989 a Tuvan Popular Front *Khostug Tyva* (Free Tuva) was organized, in imitation of the Baltic fronts. It gained a small representation in the local legislature in the March 1990 elections (9 out of 130 seats). The

---

[23] *Ekspress khronika*, no. 15, April 6–13, 1992; no. 16, April 14–20, 1992; no. 17, April 21–27, 1992; Gubloglo, ed., *Etnopoliticheskaia mozaika*, vol. 2, p. 244.

[24] M. N. Gubloglo, ed., *Resursy mobilizovannoi etnichnosti* (Moscow: Institut etnologii i antropologii RAN, 1997), p. 227.

Popular Front at first came out solely in favor of upgrading the status of Tuva to that of union republic, but subsequently advocated a referendum on independence.[25] More radical elements openly called for the Russians to leave and for the creation of a Tuvan national guard. But the movement remained weak organizationally and engaged in only occasional, small protests. After the Popular Front's leader Kadyr-ool Bicheldei was elected to a seat in the RSFSR Congress of People's Deputies in March 1990 and moved to Moscow, the movement largely slipped into inactivity – reflective of the weak urban networks on which Tuvan nationalist movements could rely.[26] Separatist mobilization instead took on more diffuse and violent form. Violence between Tuvans and Russian settlers had occurred occasionally since at least the 1970s. By the late 1980s many Russians feared traveling to remote mountainous regions of the republic, particularly after several parties of Russian geologists and fishermen were murdered. In December 1989 Tuvan raiders on horseback engaged in occasional attacks on recently established Russian settlements, and a spree of ethnically motivated murders targeted the Russian settler community. This diffuse anti-Russian violence caused an exodus of three thousand Russians from the republic in the first six months of 1990 alone. By the summer of 1990 separatist violence had been transformed into a series of anti-Russian riots, sniper attacks on trucks transporting goods from Russia to Tuva, and the murder of Russians venturing to the countryside. According to reports, by July 1990 at least eighty-eight Russians had died from attacks in Tuva, and in August an additional eighty were killed, as raids by marauding bands on Russian settlements proliferated. Several thousand OMON police troops were dispatched to contain the revolt.[27]

Thereafter the situation remained tense but under control. In September 1991 the local government was forced to resign due to its support for the August coup, leading to new legislative and presidential elections. But by this time the Popular Front was practically nonexistent. A former

[25] Toomas Alatalu, "Tuva – A State Reawakens," *Soviet Studies*, vol. 44, no. 5 (1992), pp. 891–92.
[26] Jasper Becker, for instance, recalls the difficulties he had in even contacting the Tuvan Popular Front in 1991 during his visit to Tuva. See Becker, *The Lost Country: Mongolia Revealed*, p. 285.
[27] *Informatsionnyi biulleten' Aziia-Press*, no. 1, 1991, p. 9; Gail Fondahl, "Siberia: Assimilation and Its Discontents," in Ian Bremmer and Ray Taras, eds., *New States, New Politics: Building the Post-Soviet Nations* (Cambridge, UK: Cambridge University Press, 1997), pp. 217–18.

*obkom* secretary was elected the first president of Tuva, while Bicheldei, the former leader of the Front, was elected chair of the legislature. In 1992 its more radical members attempted to revive the Popular Front, demanding a referendum on Tuva's independence from Russia.[28] But the front was banned from participating in local elections in 1993, and its activity once again plummeted. The new constitution of the Tuvan Republic, reflecting the secessionist sentiment of a portion of the Tuvan populace, recognized the right of the republic to secede from Russia (contradicting the Russian constitution). Yet, a public opinion survey conducted in Tuva in 1994 found that only 27 percent of Tuvans supported the idea that Russia's republics in general should have the right to secede from Russia, and only 13 percent expressed the more radical position calling for Tuva to secede.[29] Tuva's prior history of independent statehood thus made independence more easily imagined by Tuvans within a tide of separatist actions emerging elsewhere, leading to a wave of secessionist mobilization in 1990 that otherwise would have been unlikely given the other facilitating conditions Tuvan nationalism possessed. But the incapacity of Tuvan nationalist organization, caused primarily by weak urban networks, ultimately led to marginalization of the movement, as local nomenklatura elites took advantage of political openings where Tuvan nationalists could not.

Finally, there is the anomaly of the absence of Turkmen separatism in spite of the predictions of our model to the contrary. At first glance this appears difficult to explain, particularly given Turkmenistan's union republican status, the small proportion of Turkmen who were linguistically assimilated (1 percent), and the relatively high level of urbanization among Turkmen (31 percent in 1970) in comparison with other Central Asian union republican nationalities. Thus, structurally the Turkmen appeared to be in a situation which should have produced some separatist action. Some nationalist movements did emerge among the Turkmen, but they produced no significant separatist mobilization. The *Agzybirlik* movement, created in September 1989, called for Turkmen independence from the USSR and claimed as many as a thousand members, though visitors to

---

[28] Marjorie Mandelstam Balzer, "From Ethnicity to Nationalism: Turmoil in the Russian Mini-Empire," in James R. Millar and Sharon L. Wolchik, eds., *The Social Legacy of Communism* (Cambridge, UK: Cambridge University Press, 1994), pp. 73–74.

[29] L. M. Drobizheva, A. R. Aklaev, V. V. Koroteeva, G. U. Soldatova, *Demokratizatsiia i obrazy natsionalizma v Rossiiskoi Federatsii 90-x godov* (Moscow: Mysl', 1996), p. 87.

Turkmenia found an attitude of indifference within most of the public to the appeals of the separatists.[30] Within four months of the movement's founding the authorities revoked its registration and closed it down for its separatist orientation, arresting its leaders and placing some under psychiatric care.[31] Throughout this period a regime of repression operated in Turkmenistan with the consistency and efficiency reminiscent of Brezhnev days, and an open media simply did not exist. *Agzybirlik* engaged in a significant demonstration for the first time only on August 27, 1991, using the occasion of the failure of the August coup and President Saparmurad Niiazov's wait-and-see attitude toward the putsch as an opening to take to the streets. The demonstration in Ashkhabad attracted five hundred participants and called for Niiazov's resignation and the dissolution of the republic's "obsequious" Supreme Soviet, but it failed to make a clear statement on separatism and therefore was not coded as a separatist protest in my sample. Within three days of the demonstration, Niiazov took measures against future disturbances of this sort, warning opposition organizers of severe consequences should they continue protests, and turning off their home telephone service.[32] After all the union republics with the exception of Russia and Kazakhstan had declared independence, Niiazov held a referendum on the issue in late October 1991, with 94 percent of the population voting in favor.[33] On the following day he declared the country's independence. Thus, although they did not engage in any significant separatist protest and mobilization played no role in bringing about independence, the Turkmen do not fully fit the cultural hegemony pattern found in other failures of action, in that the explanation rests in significant respect on government coercion, and eventually – under the influence of events beyond the republic – the Turkmen government itself embraced independence.

Overall, these anomalous cases point to some of the limits of a purely structural explanation of nationalism's failure or success. To be sure, the outcomes in these cases were strongly conditioned by structure; they

---

[30] See Marat Akchurin, *Red Odyssey: A Journey Through the Soviet Republics* (New York: Harper Collins, 1992), p. 335.

[31] David Nissman, "Turkmenistan: Just Like Old Times," in Bremmer and Taras, eds., *New States, New Politics*, p. 640; Akchurin, *Red Odyssey*, p. 354.

[32] *Ekspress khronika*, no. 36, September 3, 1991, p. 2.

[33] Ironically, only seven months earlier in the March 1991 referendum, 98 percent of Turkmen voters had, at least according to the official results, cast ballots in favor of preserving the USSR.

uphold Tocqueville's assertion that chance requires advanced preparation to do its work. Yet it is also clear that tidal influences played a key role in explaining the presence of separatist mobilization in a number of cases where its absence would otherwise have been expected judging simply by the structural conditions associated with separatist action elsewhere, whereas the continued vibrancy of institutional constraints helps explain cases in which structural conditions would have led one to expect separatist action but where it was nonetheless absent.

## Tide and Structure in Time and Space

I have argued that without tidal effects it is likely that the historical outcomes of nationalism in the former USSR would have been different given the structural preconditions characteristic of most groups, as structure alone would not have been enough to allow movements to overcome the institutional constraints they faced. Tide and structure were intertwined in the ways in which separatist action materialized across time and space. Separatist action accelerated at specific temporal junctures for certain groups and not for others, because groups possessing particular structural advantages were better positioned to take advantage of the temporally specific opportunities presented by the actions of others and declining institutional constraints.

This becomes evident when we examine the temporal dimension of failures of action – and specifically, the evolution of failures of action over time in relationship to particular pre-existing structural conditions. To accomplish such an analysis, I calculated the Kaplan-Meier product-limit estimates for the failure function (which, despite its name, refers to the probability over time that at least one event has occurred) associated with the first separatist demonstration in which a group engaged over the entire period of the tide.[34] Figure 5.2 presents these estimates for the sample of forty nationalities over the 1987–92 period, in each graph dividing the sample into two streams according to varying values of the variables we have analyzed so far: population size, status of ethnofederal unit, level of urbanization, linguistic assimilation, Islamic cultural background, and

---

[34] The Kaplan-Meier survival function estimates are calculated by taking the probability across all points in time that a case does not experience a failure event within a given population of cases. See D. Collett, *Modelling Survival Data in Medical Research* (London: Chapman & Hall, 1994).

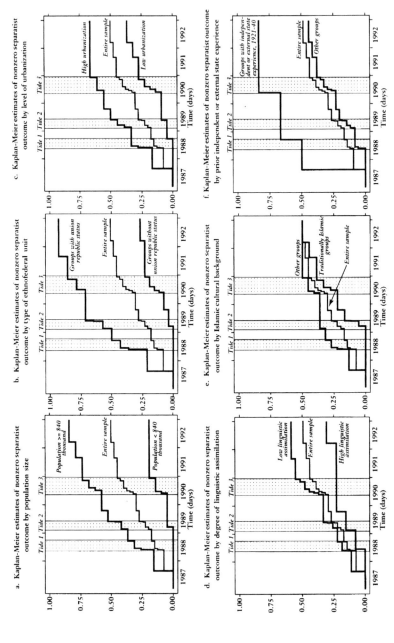

**Figure 5.2.** Kaplan-Meier estimates of the probability of a nonzero separatist outcome among forty non-Russian nationalities, 1987–92.

234

extended experience with independent statehood or as part of another state during the interwar period (1921–40).[35]

The cumulative probability of a nonzero separatist outcome for the entire sample (reproduced in each figure as a baseline) essentially shows three condensed periods of time in which separatist protest spread across multiple groups (visible as sharply upward increases, often with a jagged or steplike character to them): summer 1988, spring 1989, and May 1990 through November 1990. I have marked them in the figure and refer to them respectively as Tides 1, 2, and 3. Relatively little initial separatist action occurred outside of these three condensed periods – further proof of the tidal influences exerted on these cases. The first of these periods was connected with the first waves of separatism which swept across the Baltic. The second period followed the success of Baltic separatisms and coincided with the electoral campaign to the First Congress of People's Deputies. The third occurred in the wake of the collapse of communism in East Europe, the declaration of independence by Lithuania, and republican and local elections throughout the area and took place in the midst of the so-called parade of sovereignties, when ethnofederal units across the board went about unilaterally declaring their sovereignty vis-à-vis their formal superiors. This arguably was a stronger tide than the previous two because of the extent to which rebellion had spread and the degree to which state control had disintegrated by this time.

One of the conclusions suggested by this concentration of initial separatist action in discrete time periods is that predisposing structure gains much of its effect on action because it allows certain movements to take better advantage of the tidal influences generated by others. By bifurcating the sample into groups displaying contrasting values on a particular structural condition, we obtain some sense of the types of structural features most likely to facilitate or hinder action in each tidal period. As Figure 5.2a shows, the probability that a group with less than eight hundred forty thousand members would engage in at least one separatist demonstration

---

[35] This category included not only the Balts, but also the Moldavians, Tuvans, and Karelians. Here, I excluded groups with short-lived experiments in statehood during the Russian Civil War. Given that the preponderance of Ukrainians lived within the USSR during the interwar period, I did not include them among groups having extensive experience with independent or alternative statehood. In the case of population size, I used the sample mean for categorizing groups (which, because of the logged form of the variable, was actually closer to the median), whereas for urbanization and linguistic assimilation I used the tipping points identified earlier through Monte Carlo simulations.

remained low and relatively flat throughout the 1987–92 period. By contrast, the probability of a nonzero separatist outcome among groups greater than eight hundred forty thousand rose consistently throughout this period – a differentiation that appeared in 1987 and only widened over the course of the cycle (with the differences between the two failure functions statistically significant at the .001 level). Only groups with populations over eight hundred forty thousand were affected by the first wave of tidal influence in summer 1988, and almost all those affected by the second wave in spring 1989 were also large in size. By contrast, both large and small groups were influenced relatively equally by the third and more powerful tide in 1990. Similar patterns emerged according to the status of a group's ethnofederal unit (Figure 5.2b). Here also, an early differentiation in separatist activity occurred between groups with union republic status and those without (again, significant at the .001 level). But the gap between the two streams narrowed slightly in the 1990 period, as groups without union republican status began to engage more frequently in separatist action. Only groups with union republic status were affected by the first wave of separatist tidal influence in 1988–89, and almost all the groups influenced by the second tide of separatism also had union republic status. But groups with units lower than a union republic or without a federal unit were disproportionately affected by the third separatist tide in 1990.

A pattern of early differentiation also appears in 5.2f, comparing groups with or without extensive prior experience of independent statehood in the twentieth century (the difference between the two failure functions again being significant at the .001 level). The small number of groups in this category makes it difficult to generalize about the influence of tidal effects. Nevertheless, it should be noted that, aside from the initial burst of separatism associated with the Balts (which preceded the three tidal periods identified here), two out of the other three groups having significant experience with alternative statehood in the twentieth century did engage in separatist action in the *glasnost'* period, beginning their separatist action precisely during periods of tidal influence.

Different patterns of separatist activity between highly urbanized and less urbanized groups (Figure 5.2c) became evident early within the mobilizational cycle, growing sharper during the first and second tidal phases in 1988 and 1989. But groups that were less urbanized were strongly affected by the third period of tidal influence in 1990, allowing them to narrow slightly the gap between them and more urbanized groups (even so, the two failure functions were significantly different at the .05 level). Here again, some groups were able to utilize the stronger tidal influences emerging later in the cycle to overcome structural disadvantage. By contrast, in Figure 5.2d the differences between linguistically assimilated and unassimilated groups remained relatively minor until mid-1990, when tidal forces brought about an increase in the proportion of unassimilated groups that engaged in at least one separatist demonstration (overall, the difference between the two failure functions was significant at the .10 level only). During this latter part of the cycle, however, the pattern for assimilated groups remained entirely flat. Whereas linguistic assimilation was not a significant factor of differentiation between groups during the first two phases of tidal influence, during the third tide less assimilated groups proved considerably more capable of taking advantage of tidal influences than more assimilated groups. Linguistic assimilation only became a source of differential patterns of separatist mobilization in the context of the enhanced tidal influence of the latter portion of the mobilizational cycle.

Traditionally Islamic cultural groups show the reverse pattern: Islamic groups were considerably delayed in exhibiting separatist action in comparison with non-Islamic groups – a pattern already apparent during the first period of tidal influence in mid-1988. But the differences between these two sets of groups narrowed over time, particularly during the second and third phases of tidal influence in 1989 and 1990, as increasing numbers of traditionally Islamic groups came to press separatist demands under the influence of the example of others. In the end the two failure functions showed no statistically significant difference (though had one right-censored the sample in May 1989, the difference between the two streams would have been statistically significant at the .01 level). Thus, tidal forces provided traditionally Islamic groups with greater possibilities for engaging in a separatist politics that had previously been relatively slow to develop among them.

In sum, we have seen that much of what structure is about is endowing groups with advantages in profiting from the actions of others. Structure operated differentially during these three periods in large part because the tidal effects in these periods made structure advantageous in different ways.

## Tides, Structure, and Failures of Mobilizational Effect

I turn now to failures of nationalism attributable to insufficient mobilizational effect rather than to a failure to mobilize entirely. Of the twenty groups in our sample of forty which had nonzero separatist mobilizational outcomes, only in eleven cases (Estonians, Latvians, Lithuanians, Georgians, Moldovans, Armenians, Azerbaijanis, Ukrainians, Abkhaz, Chechens, and Gagauz) did nationalist movements prove successful in gaining control over segments of the state, allowing them to implement a separatist course of action. The degree to which this occurred as a result of the mobilizational challenges emerging from the street varied; as we saw, in two cases (the Gagauz and Abkhaz) movements for separation enjoyed strong support from local nomenklatura elites in reaction to separatist efforts by the union republican units within which they were embedded. By contrast, for nine nationalities movements espousing separatist nationalism experienced a failure of mobilizational effect. In these cases (Uzbeks, Belorussians, Volga Tatars, Kazakhs, Tuvans, Tajiks, Kirgiz, Ossetians, and Bashkirs) tidal forces did exercise some degree of influence on behavior, manifested primarily in emulative attempts to mobilize over separatist demands. Yet, the resonance of these efforts within target groups was insufficient to overcome the institutional constraints to which they were subject. In cases of a failure of mobilizational effect, nationalist movements which succeeded in "barking" failed in their attempts to "bite." The question which needs to be addressed, then, is why some nationalist movements never proved capable of moving beyond mere "barking," whereas other movements proved more potent in their efforts to harness popular support in remaking a national order.

Once again I look for an answer at the intersection between pre-existing structural conditions, institutional constraints, and the ways in which movements profited from the actions of others. On average successful separatist mobilizers engaged in 113 separatist demonstrations attracting an average of 2.9 million participants for the entire period. By contrast, unsuccessful separatist mobilizers engaged on average in only 12 separatist demonstrations for each nationality, attracting an average total of fifty-six thousand participants.[36] Thus, not only did those groups which attempted to mobilize around separatist frames but failed engage in markedly fewer separatist demonstrations, but those in which they did engage attracted significantly fewer participants. Yet, unsuccessful separatist movements were generally not subjected to any more severe government repression than successful separatists. It is true that repression against unsuccessful separatist movements was more consistent than that

---

[36] A simple t-test confirms the differences in the means between the two sets of groups at the .01 level.

applied against successful separatist movements. For unsuccessful separatists, 27 percent of separatist demonstrations experienced some form of government repression compared to 7.3 percent for successful separatists, but the severity of repression was markedly less: .8 arrests, injuries, or deaths per demonstration, compared to 5.5 per demonstration for successful separatists. It took relatively little repression to marginalize unsuccessful separatists, and governments that were successful in doing so used primarily consistent rather than severe repression (a theme I take up further in Chapter 7). A key difference between successful and unsuccessful separatist mobilizers was that the institutional constraints to which these movements were subject remained effective in the latter cases but deteriorated at a steeper pace in the former. The continued vibrancy of institutional constraints and the inability of movements to utilize tidal forces to their advantage in these latter cases allowed state elites to appropriate elements of the separatist agenda. Predominantly in those cases in which separatist movements emerged but failed (in contrast to cases in which separatist action did not materialize at all) do we find nomenklatura elites refitting themselves as separatist nationalists as the Soviet Union came apart.

Clearly, structure conditioned the ways in which movements confronted institutional constraints and rode tidal forces. But structure alone cannot account for outcomes. We saw earlier how successful secessionist movements effectively utilized tidal effects to their advantage. One of the critical differences between successful and unsuccessful separatist mobilizers was the capacity of the former to utilize the actions of others to their own advantage. Tables 5.3 and 5.4 confirm this. In the tables I compare the effects of cross-case influences on the weekly separatist mobilizational activity of successful separatist mobilizers with their effects on the weekly separatist activity of unsuccessful separatist mobilizers (in total, 20 groups over 308 weekly time periods).[37] In addition to the significantly more

---

[37] On fixed-efffects negative binomial cross-sectional time-series analyses, see A. Colin Cameron and Pravin K. Trivedi, *Regression Analysis of Count Data* (Cambridge, UK: Cambridge University Press, 1998), pp. 294–95; Jerry Hausman, Bronwyn H. Hall, and Zvi Griliches, "Econometric Models for Count Data with an Application to the Patents-R&D Relationship," *Econometrica*, vol. 52, no. 4 (July 1984), pp. 909–38. As the number of time periods in the two models was large and the number of cases small, as in earlier chapters I introduced a dynamic element into the models, allowing event-counts and participation rates to depend on prior event-counts and participation rates, to control for individual and random effects. Fixed effects models control for individual effects by absorbing this variation into a single parameter. For the linear model in Table 5.4, this was the intercept, whereas in the case of the negative binomial model in Table 5.3, it was the dispersion parameter.

Table 5.3. *Comparison of Conditional Fixed Effects Negative Binomial Regressions of Weekly Count of Separatist Protest Demonstrations among Successful and Unsuccessful Separatist Mobilizers (January 1987–December 1992)*[a]

| Independent variable | Successful separatists | | Unsuccessful separatists | |
|---|---|---|---|---|
| | Coefficient | Incidence Rate ratio | Coefficient | Incidence Rate ratio |
| Ln (separatist demonstrations + 0.5), t − 1 | 0.249 (9.22)**** | 1.283 | 0.369 (3.78)**** | 1.446 |
| Ln (separatist demonstrations + 0.5), t − 2 | 0.113 (4.17)**** | 1.119 | 0.322 (3.16)*** | 1.380 |
| Ln (separatist demonstrations + 0.5), t − 3 | 0.080 (2.95)** | 1.084 | −0.015 (−0.14) | .985 |
| Ln (separatist demonstrations + 0.5), t − 4 | 0.052 (1.92)* | 1.054 | 0.520 (5.64)**** | 1.682 |
| Ln (separatist demonstrations + 0.5), t − 5 | 0.062 (2.35)** | 1.064 | −0.146 (−1.21) | .865 |
| Ln (separatist demonstrations + 0.5), t − 6 | 0.092 (3.51)**** | 1.096 | 0.164 (1.55) | 1.179 |
| Number of separatist demonstrations by other nationalities, t − 1 | 0.032 (3.95)**** | 1.032 | 0.034 (1.41) | 1.034 |
| Number of separatist demonstrations by other nationalities, t − 2 | 0.002 (0.17) | 1.002 | 0.001 (0.04) | 1.001 |
| Number of separatist demonstrations by other nationalities, t − 3 | 0.009 (1.02) | 1.009 | 0.024 (0.94) | 1.025 |
| Number of separatist demonstrations by other nationalities, t − 4 | 0.009 (1.05) | 1.009 | −0.023 (−0.90) | .977 |
| Number of separatist demonstrations by other nationalities, t − 5 | 0.009 (1.02) | 1.009 | 0.030 (1.24) | 1.031 |
| Number of separatist demonstrations by other nationalities, t − 6 | 0.017 (2.02)** | 1.017 | 0.011 (0.51) | 1.011 |
| Constant | −0.6430937 | | 0.2663955 | |
| t × n | 3,388 | | 2,772 | |
| Number of nationalities | 11 | | 9 | |
| Observations per group | 308 | | 308 | |
| Log likelihood | −1,886.4325 | | −298.46457 | |
| Wald model chi² | 552.42**** | | 141.35**** | |

*Significant at the .10 level    **Significant at the .05 level    ***Significant at the .01 level    ****Significant at the .001 level.

[a] Z-scores for coefficients are in parentheses.

Table 5.4. *Comparison of Fixed Effects Regressions of Weekly Count of Number of Participants in Separatist Protest Demonstrations among Successful and Unsuccessful Separatist Mobilizers (January 1987–December 1992)*[a]

| Independent Variable | Successful separatists | Unsuccessful separatists |
|---|---|---|
| Participants in separatist demonstrations, t − 1 | 0.328 (19.02)**** | 0.099 (5.22)**** |
| Participants in separatist demonstrations, t − 2 | −0.087 (−4.78)**** | 0.045 (2.37)** |
| Participants in separatist demonstrations, t − 3 | 0.015 (0.87) | −0.008 (−0.43) |
| Participants in separatist demonstrations, t − 4 | 0.011 (0.62) | 0.006 (0.31) |
| Participants in separatist demonstrations, t − 5 | −0.015 (−0.84) | 0.065 (3.41)**** |
| Participants in separatist demonstrations, t − 6 | 0.018 (1.06) | −0.012 (−0.63) |
| Number of participants in separatist demonstrations by other nationalities (thousands), t − 1 | 11.207 (2.10)** | 0.145 (0.68) |
| Number of participants in separatist demonstrations by other nationalities (thousands), t − 2 | 17.350 (2.98)*** | −0.032 (−0.14) |
| Number of participants in separatist demonstrations by other nationalities (thousands), t − 3 | −8.892 (−1.52) | 0.014 (0.06) |
| Number of participants in separatist demonstrations by other nationalities (thousands), t − 4 | −2.185 (−0.37) | −0.224 (−0.96) |
| Number of participants in separatist demonstrations by other nationalities (thousands), t − 5 | 4.124 (0.71) | −0.044 (−0.19) |
| Number of participants in separatist demonstrations by other nationalities (thousands), t − 6 | −0.092 (−0.02) | 0.432 (2.03)** |
| Constant | 4,926.447 | 112.0044 |
| t × n | 3,388 | 2,772 |
| Number of nationalities | 11 | 9 |
| Observations per group | 308 | 308 |
| R-square within | 0.1057 | 0.0192 |
| R-square between | 1.0000 | 1.0000 |
| R-square overall | 0.1106 | 0.0209 |
| corr ($u_i$, Xb) | 0.0929 | 0.0999 |
| F statistic (12, 2751) | 33.15**** | 4.49**** |

*Significant at the .10 level    **Significant at the .05 level    ***Significant at the .01 level    ****Significant at the .001 level.

[a] T-scores for coefficients are in parentheses.

241

consistent pattern of recursion among successful separatists, the analysis shows that successful separatists were substantially better at utilizing the example of separatist actions by other groups to their own advantage than unsuccessful separatists. Thus, each separatist demonstration by another nationality was followed by a 3.2 percent increase in the incidence of separatist demonstrations by successful separatists in the next week and a 1.7 percent increase six weeks later, even controlling for the prior separatist activity of the group. However, no statistically significant relationship was found between the separatist action of unsuccessful separatist mobilizers and the prior separatist action of other nationalities. Similarly, every ten thousand participants in separatist demonstrations by other nationalities was associated with an increase of 112 participants in demonstrations by successful separatists a week later and an increase of 173 participants two weeks later (translating in weeks of peak cross-case influence to a robust twenty-five to forty thousand increase in the number of participants). By contrast, for unsuccessful separatist mobilizers one finds evidence of a very weak cross-case effect only, with every ten thousand participants in separatist demonstrations by other nationalities associated with four additional participants in separatist demonstrations six weeks later (translating overall to only six hundred to nine hundred additional participants in separatist demonstrations in peak influence weeks). If successful separatist movements could add forty thousand participants a week simply because of the temporally contiguous actions of others, and unsuccessful movements were able to add only nine hundred, then clearly part of the explanation for the success or failure of separatist mobilization was the differential ability of movements to take advantage of the example of others.

The structural advantages and disadvantages characteristic of target groups were central to the ways in which movements were able to ride tidal forces and weather the institutional constraints to which they were subject. This becomes evident as we examine the ways in which structure was systematically associated with mobilizational outcomes. In Table 5.5 I present the results of an ordered logit regression which attempts to predict, on the basis of the structural characteristics of a nationality, whether a group would experience a failure of action, a failure of mobilizational effect, or successful separatist mobilization during the *glasnost'* period.[38] I begin in Equation 1 with the specification used earlier for the

---

[38] The ordered logit regression model was appropriate in view of the ordinal nature of the three possible outcomes. Ordered logit uses maximum likelihood to find the best set of

Monte Carlo simulations, which included independent variables for population size, linguistic assimilation, urbanization, and the number of years in which a group experienced independent statehood or was part of another state during the 1918–40 period. In Equation 2, I test for the independent effect of Islamic cultural background on mobilizational outcomes.

As with any logit model, the fit of the model can be evaluated on the basis of how well the model predicts the observed distribution of outcomes across categories. In this case the fit in Equations 1 and 2 is relatively good, with the correct category predicted by the model in 80 percent (thirty-two out of forty) of the cases. All the variables with the exception of Islamic cultural background had statistically significant relationships with separatist mobilizational outcomes at the .10 level or lower controlling for the effect of other variables, and most were statistically significant at the .05 or .01 levels. We examined earlier a number of the mispredicted outcomes (specifically, those of the Abkhaz, Gagauz, Bashkirs, and Turkmen) and the reasons underlying these mispredictions. We saw that in these cases the influence of tidal effects and institutional constraints led to outcomes different from those one would otherwise have predicted, judging solely by the structural conditions affecting other groups. In addition, the cases of the Uzbeks, Volga Tatars, Kirgiz, and Chechens are mispredicted by the models in Equations 1 and 2, with the first two overpredicted as

regression coefficients that predicts values of the logit-transformed probability that the dependent variable falls into one category rather than another. It is based on a proportional odds assumption that the effects of the independent variables across the three categories of the dependent variable are the same. This was a reasonable assumption in view of the argument made above concerning the cumulative effects of structural advantage and disadvantage. The proportional odds assumption of ordered logit contrasts with the assumptions of multinomial and generalized ordered logit models. I assessed the goodness of fit of each through a likelihood ratio test. For each specification, low and insignificant chi-square values were produced, suggesting that the ordered logit model was no less appropriate than its most likely competitors. In addition to regression coefficients associated with each independent variable, ordered logit fits a set of cutoff points (in this case, marking the two cutoffs between the three levels of the dependent variable) such that for fitted values of the regression below the first cutoff the dependent variable is predicted to take on a zero value (no separatist mobilization), for fitted values between the first and second cutoffs the dependent variable is predicted to assume a value of one (separatist mobilization which was ineffective), and for fitted values greater than the second cutoff the dependent variable is predicted to assume a value of two (successful separatist mobilization). The raw regression coefficients are difficult to interpret, since they make sense only in relationship to the cutoff points. However, they can be exponentiated into odds ratios that indicate the effect of a one unit increase in the independent variable on the ratio of the odds of being in a higher category versus a lower category.

Table 5.5. *Ordered Logit Regressions of Mobilizational Outcomes of Separatist Nationalism (Failure of Action/Failure of Mobilizational Effect/Mobilizational Success) by Nationality, January 1987–December 1992*[a]

| Independent variable/equation | Equation 1 | Equation 2 | Equation 3[b] | Equation 4[b] |
|---|---|---|---|---|
| Ln population size, 1989 | 0.777 (2.86)*** | 0.814 (2.87)*** | 0.850 (2.76)*** | 0.872 (2.76)*** |
| Linguistic assimilation, 1989 | −0.108 (−2.52)** | −0.124 (−2.38)** | −0.103 (−2.32)** | −0.111 (−2.17)** |
| Level of urbanization, 1970 | 0.082 (2.23)** | 0.077 (2.03)** | 0.093 (2.16)** | 0.086 (1.85)* |
| Years experience as independent state or as part of other state, 1918–40 | 0.161 (2.57)*** | 0.139 (1.94)* | 0.172 (2.53)** | 0.159 (2.05)** |
| Number of persons of nationality confined to special prison settlements, 1953 (thousands)[c] | – | – | 0.022 (1.77)* | 0.023 (1.79)* |
| Dummy variable for peoples of traditionally Islamic cultures | – | −0.772 (−0.71) | – | −0.501 (−0.40) |
| Number of observations (nationalities) | 40 | 40 | 39 | 39 |
| Number of correctly predicted observations | 32[d] | 32[d] | 32[e] | 32[e] |
| Observations eliminated due to complete determination | 0 | 0 | 0 | 0 |

244

| Ancillary parameters | | | | |
|---|---|---|---|---|
| First cut point | 7.300206 | 6.740078 | 8.469877 | 8.010204 |
| Second cut point | 9.398054 | 8.869347 | 10.6621 | 10.22517 |
| Log likelihood | −24.325778 | −24.065644 | −21.185113 | −21.103955 |
| Likelihood ratio model chi$^2$ | 34.33**** | 34.85**** | 37.53**** | 37.70**** |
| Pseudo R-square | .414 | .420 | .470 | .472 |

*Significant at the .10 level  **Significant at the .05 level  ***Significant at the .01 level  ****Significant at the .001 level.

[a] Coefficients represent the change in the log-odds of the outcome being in a higher category versus a lower category associated with a unit increase in the independent variable, with z-scores in parentheses.

[b] Volga Tatars had to be dropped from Equations 3 and 4 due to missing information on the number of political exiles in 1953.

[c] *Source: Istoriia SSSR*, no. 5, 1991, pp. 154–65.

[d] In Equations 1 and 2 the Uzbeks and Volga Tatars were overpredicted to be successful separatist mobilizational outcomes, the Turkmen overpredicted to be a case of ineffective separatist mobilization, and the Kirgiz, Bashkirs, Chechens, Gagauz, and Abkhaz underpredicted to exhibit no significant separatist mobilization.

[e] In Equations 3 and 4 the Uzbeks were overpredicted to be a successful mobilizational outcome, the Turkmen and Ingush overpredicted to be cases of ineffective separatist mobilization, and the Kirgiz, Bashkirs, Abkhaz, and Gagauz underpredicted to exhibit no significant separatist mobilization.

successful mobilizational outcomes and the latter two underpredicted as failures of action.

The glaring anomaly of the mispredicted zero outcome for the Chechens (in reality they were the only group without a union republic aside from the Abkhaz and Gagauz to engage in successful separatist mobilization during this period) suggests that the regressions in Equations 1 and 2 are misspecified. As many have noted, the Chechens were an archetypal case of protracted opposition to the imposition of externally imposed state structures.[39] Over a period of two centuries Chechens engaged in broadscale resistance to Tsarist, Soviet, and post-Soviet Russian states. If the model seriously mispredicts the outcome in this case, it suggests that missing from this atemporal analysis is a sense of the iterative nature of nationalist conflict – the fact that the *glasnost'* cycle was not the first time in which nationhood in this part of the world was contested, but only one of a series of tides of nationalism (each unique in contour and outcome) which swept across the Eurasian region (and other parts of the world) over the past two centuries.

In an attempt to correct partially for this lacuna, in Equations 3 and 4 I include a variable that captures some of the iterative character of national contention: the number of persons of a particular nationality confined to special prison settlements as of January 1953. In 1952–53 Stalin's Ministry of State Security conducted a detailed census among the 1.8 million adults (including other family members, 2.8 million persons) who lived in special prison settlements, giving a finely grained breakdown of the nationality composition of this population.[40] These were primarily people who had been subjected to mass deportation: the so-called "punished peoples" of World War II; those deported from the Western territories of the USSR after World War II; and other repressed minorities dealt with in this fashion. These were the peoples most likely to have engaged in nationalist opposition to the Soviet state during the tide of nationalism that preceded the one studied here (that is, during and immediately after the Second World War). It is reasonable to assume that the nationality statistics for those confined to special settlements in 1953 are a fair representation of the nationality composition of the larger population of those repressed for reasons of nationalism by the Stalin regime in the 1940s and

---

[39] See the excellent analysis in Anatol Lieven, *Chechnya: Tombstone of Russian Power* (New Haven, CT: Yale University Press, 1998).
[40] See *Istoriia SSSR*, no. 5, 1991, pp. 154–65.

early 1950s.[41] The national composition of Stalin's victims shifted over time, the number of repressed among certain groups swelling while shrinking among others; admittedly, had a census been taken by the secret police in the 1930s, a different picture of the cultural background of the repressed would have emerged. These figures from the early 1950s are not a perfect control, but provide us with some sense of the extent to which the scope of mass repressions for reasons of nationalism during the late Stalin era was associated with separatist action in the late 1980s and early 1990s. As Equations 3 and 4 show, the data on the nationality background of those confined to special prison settlements by Stalin are marginally significant at the .10 level when controlling for the influence of other variables, and inclusion of this variable marginally improves the fit of the model (with the pseudo R-square value rising from .41 in Equation 1 to .47 in Equation 3).[42] Thus, while we see here indications that nationalist contention can be an iterative and protracted phenomenon, accounting for some of the patterns of separatist politics in the *glasnost'* era, the evidence for long-term continuity in patterns of separatist action is less than overwhelming.

In Figure 5.3 I have provided an interpretation of the substantive effects of independent variables on the probability of separatist mobilizational success through a second series of Monte Carlo simulations (again, on the basis of a thousand sets of simulated regression parameters). The average predicted probabilities for each of the three mobilizational outcomes is presented, utilizing the regression results from Equation 3 of Table 5.5 as the basis for the simulations. As earlier, the Monte Carlo simulation allows

---

[41] I did not adjust these figures for population size, given that there was only a .27 correlation between the 1959 population size of a nationality (logged) and the number of its members in special prison settlements in 1953. Although figures were also collected in 1951 and previous years on the nationality breakdown of the approximately 2.5 million prisoners in prison camps and labor colonies (representing yet another population of repressed persons in the Stalin era), the presentation of these figures in official documents contained information on only seventeen of the groups in our sample. Moreover, the prison camp and labor colony populations included a considerable criminal element as well. It is true that members of some groups were more likely to be punished by a term in prison camps or labor colonies rather than by exile to special settlements. Yet, for those seventeen groups for which information exists for both populations of repressed persons, the rankings of groups are almost identical (the data for the two populations by nationality have a .92 correlation). *Sotsiologisheskie issledovaniia*, no. 6, 1991, p. 26; no. 7, 1991, p. 8.

[42] Even without controlling for other factors, patterns of repression from the late 1940s and early 1950s account for only 9 percent of the variance in separatist outcomes during the *glasnost'* period.

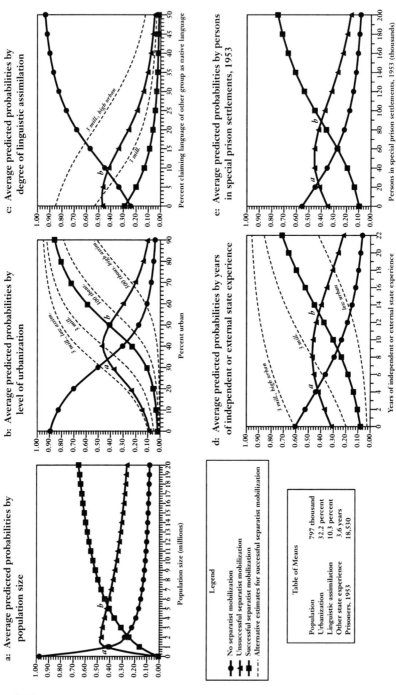

248

**Figure 5.3.** Average predicted probabilities for a failure of action, failure of mobilizational effect, or successful mobilization for separatist nationalism in the USSR, 1987–92 (Monte Carlo simulation). Unless otherwise noted, all other variables held constant at their means.

us to pinpoint probable tipping points for changes in the likelihood of each of the outcomes, assuming particular levels of the independent variables, and to explore a series of counterfactuals concerning the ways in which different combinations of independent variables interact. As before, the heavy black lines represent the average predicted probabilities for each of the three outcomes at various levels of the independent variable under examination, holding other variables constant at their means. In Figure 5.3a two tipping points emerge – labeled $a$ (below which failures of action were the most likely outcome) and $b$ (the breaking point for successful separatist mobilization as the most likely outcome). Assuming average levels of other structural variables, a failure of mobilizational effect would be the most likely outcome for nationalities of more than nine hundred thirty thousand but less than 5.8 million in size, while mobilizational success would be the most probable outcome for nationalities greater than 5.8 million in size. Thus, groups which had only average degrees of structural facilitation from other sources would have to have been fairly large (approximately six million) in order to have a good chance of engaging in successful separatist mobilization within the tide.

Figure 5.3b shows two tipping points for levels of urbanization where the probabilities of each of the outcomes shift, holding other variables constant at their means, with failures of mobilizational effect most likely when a group was greater than 33.6 percent urbanized and less than 49.8 percent urbanized. These tipping points were relatively high, so that (holding other variables at their means) groups with average levels of urbanization were likely to exhibit failures of action; only a handful of groups were more urbanized than the upper tipping point dividing likely failure from likely success. Here again we see that it was the cumulation of structural advantage – not any single advantage – which endowed groups with the capability of mobilizing successfully. Moreover, structural advantages were fungible, so that there was more than one way to accumulate the assets necessary for taking advantage of the openings offered by others. In Figure 5.3b I again show how shifts away from the mean for particular variables alter the probability of successful mobilization by providing alternative estimations. As before, these appear as broken lines and have been labeled according to the ways in which they vary from the mean. Thus, assuming no other structural advantages or disadvantages, within the Soviet context a nationality of three million members would have required significantly lower levels of urbanization (about 38 percent) than a group of eight hundred thousand (the mean population size of the sample) to be expected to achieve a successful separatist mobilizational outcome within the tide, whereas a group of three million with a relatively low level of linguistic assimilation would have required an even lower level of urbanization (28 percent, below the average level of urbanization for the sample as a whole) to be expected to achieve success. By contrast, assuming no other structural advantages, a group of three hundred thousand that was highly assimilated linguistically would likely achieve separatist mobilizational success within the tide only if 90 percent of its members were urban – far beyond the level exhibited by any group in the sample.

In Figure 5.3c we see that the absence of linguistic assimilation on its own – without other structural advantages – was not enough to propel a group toward a successful separatist outcome. Holding other variables at their means, a tipping point $b$, below which a failure of mobilizational effect was more likely than a failure of action, emerges, but no tipping point for mobilizational success. Yet, as the alternative simulations show, linguistic assimilation could have made the difference between likely success or likely failure when cumulated with other structural advantages. Even small differences in levels of assimilation would have produced a significant difference between likely success or failure for a group of three million members. At the same time, a highly urbanized nationality with at least three million members would have been likely to engage in successful separatist mobilization even at high levels of assimilation (that is, with up to 20 percent of its members claiming the language of another group as its native language), holding other variables constant at their means.

Figure 5.3d shows that within the context of the tide separatist mobilizational success was likely only if a group had more than thirteen years of experience with independent or alternative statehood in the twentieth century, assuming the presence of no other structural advantages or disadvantages. But as the alternative simulations show, a nationality with a low degree of urbanization but average levels of other variables, even if it had experienced twenty-two years of independent statehood in the twentieth century, still would have been unlikely to have become a successful separatist within the tide (a situation approximating that of the Tuvans). The alternative simulations also show that, assuming no other structural disadvantages, a highly urbanized nationality with over three million members would have been expected to become a successful separatist mobilizer within the tide even in the absence of any significant experience of alternative statehood in the twentieth century.

## Tides and the Failure of Nationalist Mobilization

One of the great advantages of these simulation models is that they allow us to change the conditions of history with some sense of what the consequences might have been and to see what might have happened under different circumstances based on the experience of others. Had Belorussians not been subjected to the type of strong assimilation policies pursued by the Soviet state but were in every other respect the same as they were in the late 1980s, according to our simulation model they would have been expected to exhibit a .75 average probability of successful separatist action in the *glasnost'* period (judging at least from the patterns exhibited by other groups) in comparison with the .22 average probability of success the model predicts for groups with their characteristics. Similarly, had Belorussians, by some accident of history in 1918 (German victory in World War I, Allied intervention in the Russian civil war, and so on), experienced twenty-two years of independent statehood in the interwar period like the Balts, the simulation model would have predicted a .83 average probability of successful separatist mobilization in the *glasnost'* period, even considering their high level of linguistic assimilation. At the same time, had Estonians not experienced twenty-two years of independent statehood in the interwar period but had been incorporated into the Soviet state like the Belorussians (an outcome entirely conceivable in 1918), and had they been subjected to a fierce and successful Russification campaign like the Belorussians or Karelians, given their other structural advantages one would have expected on average only a .14 chance of successful separatist mobilization on their part in the *glasnost'* period (as opposed to the .94 probability that the model predicted for groups like the Estonians).

Obviously, history is not available to be replayed. Yet, as these examples illustrate, the structural advantages and disadvantages which accrue to particular movements are rooted ultimately in historical counterfactuals. The outcomes of prior tides of nationalist contention, the assimilatory and modernizing policies of government, the classification schemes imposed by the state on populations, and the demographic fortunes enjoyed and suffered by groups – all these affect the capacity of nationalist movements to mobilize target populations and provide spatial meaning to Gellner's statement that nationalism is fated to prevail, but not any one nationalism. Structure in this sense is not a given characteristic of groups, but a set of advantages or disadvantages accumulated by contending actors in a protracted struggle to configure or reconfigure the nature of order. These advantages and disadvantages are shaped by the prior conscious actions of individuals, and only become advantageous or disadvantageous at those moments when order is put to the test.

## Tides and the Strategic Appropriation of Nationalism

I turn now to examine in detail several examples of the mobilizational failure of separatist nationalism – in particular, Belorussian, Uzbek, and Volga Tatar separatist movements. These cases were selected in view of the presence of significant separatist mobilizations among each of these target groups; two (the Uzbeks and Volga Tatars) were actually mispredicted by our structural model to be cases of successful mobilizational outcomes. In each of these cases separatist movements at times appeared to be gaining the upper hand, but ultimately failed mobilizationally and politically. Here, I seek not only to illustrate concretely how the structural, institutional, and tidal factors examined above intersect to explain why separatist mobilization failed in these cases, but also to explore the ways in which tidal forces ultimately brought about change in spite of the failure of separatist mobilization. Earlier, I drew a distinction between the mobilizational success of nationalism and its issue success, throwing out the possibility that a nationalist movement might fail mobilizationally, yet succeed substantively. As these cases show, once tidal forces have gained momentum to the point where they appear impossible to contain, they become an extremely powerful force for the remaking of identities through bandwagoning. The question facing societies in such situations is no longer whether nationalism will succeed, but rather who will control its success – nationalist oppositions or the state.

As we have seen, the failure of nationalist movements within a tide of nationalism is usually a multiply determined phenomenon in the sense that the weakness of pre-existing structural supports is compounded by the continued vibrancy of the compliance systems which movements face and their failure to utilize tidal forces to their advantage. This redundancy in causation (inadequate structural support, robust institutional constraint, weakened tidal influence) is visible in the failure of Belorussian nationalist movements to mobilize their target population around the separatist frames that had gained wide resonance elsewhere in the USSR. Although it is true that Belorussian nationalism has been relatively weak throughout most of the twentieth century, Belorussian nationalism was actually among the first to make themselves felt during the *glasnost'* tide. In spring 1987, when nationalist movements had yet to appear in the Baltic, informal nationalist movements sprang into existence in Minsk, and *glasnost'* gave birth to a small wave of activism within the Belorussian intelligentsia over the revival of Belorussian culture and language. These movements even enjoyed organizational support within the Belorussian Writers' Union. In November 1987, on the traditional *Dziady* (All Saints' Day) holiday, nascent Belorussian nationalist movements organized a demonstration to "pay tribute to the memory of our ancestors," attracting a crowd of two to three hundred.[43] In December 1987 thirty independent Belorussian groups began the formation of a consolidated nationalist organization – six months before the formation of the Baltic fronts. The discovery of mass graves of victims of Stalinism in Kuropaty Woods outside Minsk in May and June 1988 led to rapid politicization of the issue of Stalinist repression in Belarus, in some ways paralleling developments in the Baltic. Nationalist demonstrations attracted sizeable crowds of several thousands – analogous in resonance to the early Baltic demonstrations.[44]

From mid-1988 Belorussian nationalists patterned their activities on the Baltic model and made a clear effort to ride the tide of secession emerging out of the Baltic. An open appeal to Belorussian youth issued in July 1988, at the height of the Baltic national awakening, noted:

We are watched with hope and concern by the peoples of Estonia, Latvia, and Lithuania. They are waiting for us to join the formidable wave of national upsurge that is rolling over the Baltic region. In Belarus's joining this surge, there is the assurance of irreversibility of revolutionary changes in the Baltic republics as well as throughout the entire Soviet Union.[45]

Belorussian nationalist movements exhibited early successes in forcing republican authorities to enhance Belorussian language instruction in schools and universities. At the peak of their mobilizational capacity in February 1990, during the republican electoral campaign, Belorussian nationalists were able to turn out up to one hundred thousand participants in a mass demonstration espousing separatist demands.[46] The enormous environmental devastation of the Chernobyl accident in Belorussia also gave rise to widespread resentment of the regime's handling of the situation – a factor which, in a number of other republics, had provided an

---

[43] *Current Digest of the Soviet Press*, vol. 40, no. 1 (February 3, 1988), pp. 8–9.
[44] See *Vesti iz SSSR*, 12–34, 1988.
[45] Quoted in Jan Zaprudnik, *Belarus At a Crossroads in History* (Boulder, CO: Westview Press, 1993), p. 130.
[46] *Ekspress khronika*, no. 9, February 27, 1990.

opening for nationalist movements.[47] Taking all this into account, one might have expected Belorussian nationalism to have developed into a more substantial political force than it ultimately turned out to be.

Yet, in the end Belorussian nationalists failed in their efforts to generate the kind of sustained massive mobilization around secessionist frames characteristic of the Baltic, Transcaucasus, Moldova, and Ukraine. When the Belorussian population finally did mobilize in large numbers in spring 1991, it did so primarily as an independent trade union movement expressing outrage over price increases, not as a nationalist movement demanding independence. Moreover, in Gorbachev's March 1991 referendum on the future of the Soviet Union 83 percent of the Belorussian population voted in favor of preservation of the USSR, the highest proportion in favor in any union republic outside of Central Asia. How does one explain the failure of Belorussian nationalists to capitalize successfully on a nationalist tide which others, such as the Ukrainians, successfully rode?

Clearly, a major element of the explanation is the comparatively low degree of structural advantage enjoyed by the Belorussian nationalist movement. Belorussians, for instance, had the highest rate of linguistic Russification among all union republican peoples of the USSR. Assimilation had gone particularly far in urban centers, aided by a long-standing campaign of discriminatory practices against Belorussian-language school instruction.[48] Belorussian nationalists thus suffered two significant disadvantages relative to most of the successful nationalist movements of the time: a diminished linguistic base and a weakened set of urban networks. Add to this the historical weakness of Belorussian nationalism and the strength of identification with Soviet symbols, particularly among the older generation (Belorussia suffered the greatest destruction in the Second World War and became a center of partisan resistance to the Germans),[49] and it becomes clear that Belorussian separatists were bound

---

[47] Jane I. Dawson, *Eco-nationalism: Anti-Nuclear Activism and National Identity in Russia, Lithuania, and Ukraine* (Durham, NC: Duke University Press, 1996).

[48] In 1972–73 98 percent of urban schoolchildren in the republic attended Russian-language schools, and by 1987 only 23 percent of schoolchildren in Belorussia attended a Belorussian-language school. Roman Solchanyk, "More Concessions to Belorussian Language and Culture," *RFE/RL Research Report*, RL 482/88 (October 25, 1988), pp. 1–2.

[49] David Marples argues that Soviet national identity successfully supplanted Belorussian national identity as a result of the experience of the Second World War. David R. Marples, *Belarus: From Soviet Rule to Nuclear Catastrophe* (New York: St. Martin's Press, 1996), pp. 117–18.

to confront a formidable set of structural disadvantages in gaining a popular following. Our statistical model, for instance, would have predicted a .22 average probability of successful separatist action and a .41 average probability of a failure of mobilizational effect for separatist nationalism for a nationality with the structural characteristics of the Belorussians. Yet, as significant as these disadvantages were to the resonance of Belorussian separatism, some social base for separatism existed in Belorussia. As the large size of the February 25, 1990, demonstration indicated (it attracted up to one hundred thousand participants), a significant number of Belorussians could heed the mobilizational calls of Belorussian separatists given the proper circumstances. At that time, the recent collapse of communism in Eastern Europe, the opportunities for contestation afforded by the republican electoral campaign, and a degree of popular outrage over electoral manipulation by republican authorities boosted the Popular Front's following.

But Belorussian nationalists also faced consistent interference from the state in their efforts to gain a popular following. The generally repressive posture taken by the republican authorities toward manifestations of separatism in reaction to events in the Baltic eventually earned Belorussia the title of "the Vendée of the Soviet Union" among oppositional elites throughout the USSR. For example, when an initiative committee for creating a popular front organized an unauthorized demonstration in Minsk in October 1988, on the day before the *Dziady* holiday, republican authorities, fearing a repetition of events in the Baltic, unleashed tear gas and water cannons against a crowd of ten thousand, injuring up to a hundred and arresting eighty-six of the participants.[50] In January 1989 the authorities would not even allow Belorussian nationalist youth groups a place to meet in the republic, forcing them to convene their meetings in Lithuania, where Sajudis was happy to accommodate them. Similarly, when the founding congress of the Belorussian Popular Front was finally convened in June 1989, the event had to be transferred to Vilnius when the authorities refused to permit the meeting to take place in Belorussia.[51] In the highly manipulated republican legislative elections of 1990, Popular Front candidates captured only 25 out of 360 seats: Heavy-handed government control over the media and a high number of noncompetitive races in rural districts proved critical in marginalizing the nationalists. Ultimately, the

[50] *Vesti iz SSSR*, 19/20–8, 1988; *Ogonek*, no. 47, Nov. 1988, p. 31.
[51] Zaprudnik, *Belarus at a Crossroads*, p. 135.

Popular Front's failure to contest power effectively led it into decline, making it a still more inviting target for repression. As the Belorussian example illustrates, nationalist movements from groups with weaker structural supports not only faced a more difficult environment for mobilization, but were also more easily deterred by institutional constraints than groups with stronger structural supports.

But ultimately, an account of the failure of Belorussian separatist nationalism that focuses solely on weak structural supports within the Belorussian population is at a loss to account for how Belorussian separatist demands were eventually coopted by the very state agents who had so vigorously opposed them. As one observer has noted concerning the adoption in January 1990 of a language law declaring Belorussian the state language of the republic, in spite of the authorities' prolonged opposition "the government could not ignore the general trend occurring throughout the non-Russian republics of the Soviet Union," particularly the Baltic and Ukraine[52] (the law was subsequently rescinded in the post-Soviet period and Russian declared the official language of independent Belarus). Similarly, in July 1990 the communist majority within the republican legislature "had no choice but to accept the urgings" of Popular Front deputies to issue a declaration of state sovereignty, given the wave of such declarations then sweeping the Soviet Union (particularly the declarations of sovereignty by Russia and Ukraine).[53] Not to have declared sovereignty would have created a significant political opening for opposition mobilization given the pressures generated by the tide. Not pressure from nationalists nor pre-existing structural conditions, but the weight of events and the example of others proved powerful enough to cause nomenklatura elites to engage in nationalist actions which, only a short while earlier, they openly opposed. The Belorussian declaration of independence from the USSR in August 1991 after the collapse of the August coup (which had been supported by the Belorussian political leadership) was again a development made unavoidable by external events. Failure to recognize Belorussian independence and continued defense of the integrity of the USSR (a position the Belorussian leadership had taken up to that point) would have led to a gaping strategic opening for oppositional elites. Inde-

---

[52] Zaprudnik, *Belarus At a Crossroads*, p. 138.
[53] Zaprudnik, *Belarus At a Crossroads*, p. 151. As Popular Front leader Zenon Pozdniak noted, 95 percent of the sovereignty declaration was based on ideas formulated by the Front over the previous year and a half.

pendence was thus achieved in Belarus largely because of tidal influences emerging outside Belorussia, and in spite of the failure of Belorussian nationalists to mobilize their target population rather than because of their successes.[54]

The case of Uzbek separatism demonstrates that even the widespread presence of sentiment against Russian domination did not guarantee that nationalist movements would overcome marginalization. Like Ukrainian and Belorussian nationalisms, Uzbek nationalism faced a number of structural disadvantages. Uzbekistan was a Soviet creation of the 1920s formed around a language community and carved from territories previously belonging to several khanates and the Russian province of Turkestan. Uzbek nationalism was thus an entirely modern phenomenon fostered to a large extent by the ways in which Soviet authority chose to delineate political space in Central Asia. Just as significant were the facts that Uzbekistan on the eve of *glasnost'* was still a predominantly rural society and that the urbanization and industrialization that had taken place were mainly Russian-dominated processes. As of 1990 only 42 percent of the population of Tashkent consisted of Uzbeks, compared with 90 percent before World War II.[55] Compared to the target groups of successful separatists, Uzbeks suffered from weak urban networks to support a separatist movement.

Significant modernization took place in Central Asia during the Soviet period, including the creation of a native cultural intelligentsia. And by the 1980s national identities had for the most part consolidated around officially designated national categories. In this respect, Uzbek nationalism – like Belorussian nationalism – did not face a situation entirely bereft of structural support. Very little Russification occurred within the indigenous population, as might be expected within a society still relatively excluded from the modern sector. And of all the republics of the Soviet Union, the Central Asian republics most closely resembled a traditionally colonial model. As we saw in Chapter 1, many knowledgeable foreign observers predicted ex ante (largely on the basis of structural inequalities)

---

[54] The stability of attachments to national categories in these circumstances was questionable. A public opinion poll conducted in Belarus in March 1994 discovered that more than 55 percent of Belarusians were in favor of the restoration of the USSR, and 63 percent favored unification of the republic with Russia. Radio Moscow World Service, March 21, 1994, 01:00 UTC.

[55] James Critchlow, "Uzbekistan: The Next Nationality Crisis?," in *Report on the USSR*, vol. 2, no. 20 (May 18, 1990), p. 7.

that of all areas of the USSR Uzbekistan was a likely arena for the resonance of anticolonial mobilizational frames. As one of the poorest regions of the Soviet Union, and one suffering from enormous environmental devastation due to the excessive farming of cotton, there was no shortage of grievances in Soviet Uzbekistan, and resentment of Russian rule was widespread.[56] Public opinion surveys conducted in November 1989 showed that a larger proportion of Uzbeks (53 percent) considered themselves primarily citizens of their own republic (as opposed to citizens of the USSR) than did Ukrainians (46 percent).[57] Our model would have predicted that target groups with the structural characteristics of the Uzbeks would have had on average a .49 chance of separatist mobilizational success within the tide and a .37 chance of a failure of mobilizational effect. The structural advantages leaned toward success, although the probability of success was not that much greater than the probability of failure. The answer as to why these potential advantages were not better exploited by nationalist movements lies in the interaction between effective local compliance systems, the structural disadvantages facing separatists, and the tide.

Under the influence of the Baltic example, a group of Uzbek writers and scientists organized the *Birlik* (Unity) Movement in Tashkent in November 1988. As one of the founders recalled, the movement was established "imitating the Baltics or other places where we saw better examples, because we were not able to see one among us."[58] Initially, the movement focused on the issues of the Aral Sea crisis and the republic's cotton monoculture, but in the ensuing months, following trends around the USSR, the movement's attention shifted to the issue of making Uzbek the state language of the republic, and later, by fall 1989 and early 1990, toward republican sovereignty, alternative military service, and secession.

From the end of 1988 through spring 1990 *Birlik* organized a series of demonstrations attracting tens of thousands of followers. As Annette Bohr has observed, "At its height, the movement commanded a notable degree of popular support, particularly among the indigenous population – a fact which was implicitly recognized by the authorities when they dispatched *Birlik*'s leaders to the Fergana Valley in 1989 to help pacify the violent

[56] See James Critchlow, *Nationalism in Uzbekistan: A Soviet Republic's Road to Sovereignty* (Boulder, CO: Westview Press, 1991).

[57] Yu. A. Levada, *Sovetskii prostoi chelovek: Opyt sotsial'nogo portreta na rubezhe 90-x* (Moscow: Izdatel'stvo "Mirovoi okean," 1993), p. 22.

[58] Interview with Abdurakhim Pulatov, in *Umid/Hope*, vol. 1, no. 2 (Fall 1992), p. 39.

disturbances taking place there."[59] *Birlik* demonstrations in October 1989 for establishing Uzbek as the state language attracted up to fifty thousand participants.[60] By early 1990 the movement claimed a following of four hundred thousand, with formal membership cards issued to fifty thousand and divisions in six Uzbek provinces. In the republican legislative elections of February 1990, *Birlik* claimed to have helped elect fifty candidates, although only ten openly recognized themselves as representatives of the movement after the election.[61] Given the movement's growing support and the significant violence against Meskhetian Turks in the Fergana valley in summer 1989, a number of foreign experts were predicting that Uzbekistan would become the USSR's "next nationality crisis." As James Critchlow wrote in May 1990, "challenges to local political authority are becoming ever more insistent, both from dissident factions of the Uzbek élites and from the masses. With no remedy for the basic causes of unrest in sight, the question is not whether a revolutionary situation exists, but what will come first: a national revolution staged by the élites or a grass-roots upheaval with overtones of Islamic fundamentalism."[62]

Yet, as we know, neither of these materialized. Rather, through a skillful campaign of consistent repression, cooptation, and divide-and-conquer tactics, the government of Islam Karimov, which came to power in June 1989, successfully diffused all mobilizational challenges. *Birlik* was accused of fostering interethnic enmity and violence in the government-controlled mass media, and increasingly the government sought to restrict its activities. In October 1989, as *Birlik*'s mobilizational capacity was expanding, the Uzbek government adopted a law which introduced penalties of up to two months in prison for those violating public order and authorized the police to use whatever means necessary to prevent disturbances. In February 1990, on the eve of republican elections, a second decree introduced penalties for distributing materials or oral communication that threatened public order. A third decree, enacted days after the election, banned all public demonstrations.[63] During this period the police did not shy away

---

[59] Annette Bohr, *Uzbekistan: Politics and Foreign Policy* (London: Royal Institute of International Affairs, 1998), p. 12.

[60] *Vesti iz SSSR*, 19/20–8, 1989; *Yezhednevnaia glasnost'*, October 27, 1989.

[61] Aleksandr Verkhovskii, *Sredniaia Aziia i Kazakhstan: Politicheskii spektr* (Moscow: Panorama, 1992), pp. 33–34.

[62] Critchlow, "Uzbekistan: The Next Nationality Crisis?," p. 6.

[63] Gregory Gleason, " 'Birlik' and the Cotton Question," *Report on the USSR*, vol. 2, no. 24 (June 15, 1990), p. 21; William Fierman, "Political Development in Uzbekistan: Democratization?," in Karen Dawisha and Bruce Parrott, eds., *Conflict, Cleavage, and Change in*

from applying force against unauthorized *Birlik* demonstrations. In October 1989 more than two hundred activists were arrested for participating in unauthorized rallies in Tashkent, with some sentenced to minor terms of imprisonment.[64] In early March 1990 in the city of Parkent five thousand *Birlik* demonstrators protesting electoral fraud and the resettlement of Meskhetian Turk refugees to the area were fired on and beaten by MVD troops dispatched by the republican government to the city, injuring seventy and killing four. The Uzbek authorities utilized the incident to restrict further the activities of *Birlik*, branding the organization a threat to public order and refusing to issue permits for subsequent *Birlik* meetings.[65] In spite of the ban, on March 18 *Birlik* held a major unauthorized demonstration in Tashkent at which it protested rampant electoral fraud, expressed its support for Baltic independence, and put forth similar demands for independence for Uzbekistan. The demonstrators were attacked by police special forces, who beat and arrested up to fifty activists, including a number of the leaders of the movement.[66] Subsequently, police pressure on *Birlik* activists tightened even further. The coercive tactics of the regime and an emerging sense that *Birlik*'s fortunes were receding caused, in one activist's words, "a weakening of faith" in the movement, leading to a significant decline in activism through the rest of 1990 and 1991.[67] By 1991 a new wave of intimidation against the regime's opponents was being waged, including a law which introduced penalties of up to six years in prison for insulting the "honor and dignity" of the republic's president and other top-ranking officials. By this time, *Birlik* had been successfully pushed to the sidelines of politics, with interest in it definitely on the wane.

---

*Central Asia and the Caucasus* (Cambridge, UK: Cambridge University Press, 1997), pp. 370–71.

[64] *Vesti iz SSSR*, 19/20–8, 1989.

[65] Gleason, "'Birlik' and the Cotton Question," p. 21; *Svoboda* [Memorial Society], no. 7, 1990, p. 3.

[66] *Yezhednevnaia glasnost'*, March 19, 1990.

[67] The quotation is from an interview with Muhammad Salih, a leader of Birlik who split from the movement to form the rival Erk movement. See Annette Bohr, "Inside the Uzbek Parliamentary Opposition: An Interview with Muhammed Salih," *Report on the USSR*, vol. 2, no. 46 (November 16, 1990), p. 21. A survey conducted in 1991 showed that Uzbeks had relatively low interest by this time in nationality issues – considerably less than Ukrainians (57 percent as opposed to 74 percent). R. Kh. Simonian, "Ot natsional'nogo samosoznaniia k grazhdanskomu deistviiu," in V. A. Yadov, ed., *Massovoe soznanie i massovye deistviia* (Moscow: Institut sotsiologii RAN, 1994), p. 72.

The Karimov government also fostered splits within the *Birlik* leadership that severely weakened the movement. In fall 1989 Karimov initiated a series of conversations with prominent members of *Birlik*, helping to precipitate a split within the organization. One faction, denouncing the use of demonstrations as a movement tactic and openly favoring a less confrontational approach, created an alternative movement, *Erk* (Freedom), which defined itself as a parliamentary opposition.

Finally, as in Belarus, much of *Birlik*'s program was eventually adopted by the Karimov regime, particularly as events in other republics made the collapse of the union appear increasingly inevitable. In October 1989 Uzbek was declared the state language of the republic by the communist-dominated legislature. In June 1990 the Uzbek government adopted a declaration of sovereignty, following the lead of other federal units. By late 1990 and early 1991 the Karimov government was still distancing itself from Moscow as the prospects for maintaining the union waned. Still, the Uzbek government, like that of Belorussia, was about to put its signature on the new union treaty before the August coup intervened. Karimov at first appeared to support the coup, but withdrew his support as the operation collapsed, subsequently issuing a declaration of independence for Uzbekistan. Karimov soon shut down *Birlik* altogether and eventually imprisoned its leaders or forced them into exile abroad. In short, independence came to Uzbekistan as established elites adapted to changing circumstances outside the republic brought on by a tide of mobilization, not as a result of the actions of nationalist movements or mobilization by the population.

As a final example I turn to the Volga Tatars.[68] By a number of measures Volga Tatars might have been expected to exhibit significant mobilization around separatist frames during the *glasnost'* period. Given that population size was strongly associated with separatist activity, the 5.5 million Volga Tatar population, the sixth largest nationality within the USSR and far outnumbering the Balts, Georgians, or Armenians, should have been among the more active separatist mobilizers. Unlike the Uzbeks, the Volga Tatars in 1989 were among the most urbanized peoples of Russia (they had undergone extremely rapid urbanization in the years preceding

---

[68] I am grateful to Kate Graney for her aid in identifying material for this section. For a more detailed examination of how Tatar nationalism was shaped by larger tidal forces, see Katherine E. Graney, "Projecting Sovereignty: Statehood and Nationness in Post-Soviet Russia," Ph.D. dissertation, University of Wisconsin-Madison, 1999, Chapter 2.

*glasnost*') with the proportion of urban dwellers rising from 39 percent in 1970 to 63 percent in 1989. But Tatarstan had been under uninterrupted Russian control since 1552, when Ivan the Terrible conquered Kazan', and in the twentieth century Tatarstan experienced a significant Russian in-migration (in 1989 only 49 percent of the population of the Tatar ASSR was Tatar, whereas 43 percent was Russian). Nevertheless, Tatars managed to preserve a sense of cultural distinctiveness and a significant level of native-language usage. In 1989 83 percent of Tatars claimed Tatar as their native language – a greater proportion than, for instance, Ukrainians claiming Ukrainian (81 percent) and Belorussians claiming Belorussian (71 percent) as native languages. In the nineteenth century Kazan' had been a major center of the jadidist movement, and during the Russian Revolution Tatar nationalism – expressed in pan-Turkic and pan-Islamic idioms – was one of the most significant nationalist movements to emerge among the Muslims of the Tsarist empire. As a result of the threat which Tatar nationalism posed to Soviet control over the Middle Volga, the Soviet government in its early years pursued a particularly anti-Tatar policy. Tatars were granted only autonomous republican rather than union republican status, the boundaries of the Tatar ASSR were drawn so that they did not encompass large numbers of Tatars (in 1989 only 32 percent of Tatars lived within the Tatar ASSR), and official histories emphasized the brutality and exploitation of the Tatar/Mongol "yoke" vis-à-vis Russians.[69]

Thus, the structural legacy the Volga Tatars brought with them into the *glasnost*' period was mixed, with some factors leading one to expect significant separatist mobilization and other factors likely to disadvantage separatism. In our statistical model, when the variable on the number of prisoners in special settlements was added, the Volga Tatar case had to be dropped because official statistics did not differentiate between Volga Tatars and Crimean Tatars. But if we were to judge solely by the presence of other structural variables, our model would have predicted on average a .55 chance of successful separatism by nationalist movements from target groups with characteristics similar to those of the Volga Tatars and a .33 chance of a failure of mobilizational effect.

But it was the institutional constraints imposed by the ethnofederal system that proved to be the critical structural disadvantage undermining

[69] See Azade-Ayşe Rorlich, *The Volga Tatars: A Profile in National Resilience* (Stanford, CA: Hoover Institution Press, 1986); Ron Wixman, "The Middle Volga: Ethnic Archipelago in a Russian Sea," in Ian Bremmer and Ray Taras, eds., *Nation and Politics in the Soviet Successor States* (Cambridge, UK: Cambridge University Press, 1993), p. 430.

## Tides and the Failure of Nationalist Mobilization

Tatar separatist mobilization under *glasnost'*. Dissatisfaction with the Volga Tatars' second-rate status within the Soviet federal hierarchy was widespread and had become an obsession among Tatar elites and intellectuals. Since the 1920s the issue was repeatedly pressed as a Tatar demand whenever the opportunity arose.[70] Whereas nationalists from union republican groups smaller in size, less urban, or more assimilated than the Volga Tatars were proclaiming their republics' right to separate statehood in 1989 and 1990, Volga Tatar nationalist activity until 1991 focused almost exclusively on raising the status of the autonomous republic within the Soviet federal hierarchy to that of union republic, and on language demands. Like Bashkir nationalists, Tatar nationalists at times viewed the Soviet government as their potential ally in their struggle vis-à-vis the Russian republic (within which the Tatar ASSR was located). As in the Belorussian and Uzbek cases (though for different reasons), separatist mobilization within Tatarstan remained weak. It gained strength only in 1991, as it grew evident that the USSR was coming apart. In view of trends in support of secession within Tatarstan on the eve of the Soviet breakup, one might speculate that had the USSR lasted another year and tidal forces continued to operate, Tatar nationalism might have emerged as a much more potent force. Instead, in the specific context of Soviet collapse in 1991, the Tatar nomenklatura proved to be in a more advantageous position than nationalist movements to ride the tide of separatism accompanying the breakup.

The birth of the contemporary Tatar nationalist movement dates to June 1988, when, under the influence of the Nineteenth Party Conference and events in the Baltic, a group of Tatar intellectuals authored an appeal to the conference to raise the status of the Tatar ASSR to a union republic. This group subsequently evolved into a political organization: the Tatar Public Center, or TOTs. On October 15, 1988, the anniversary of the fall of the Kazan' Khanate in 1552, eight to nine hundred people gathered in the Kazan' Kremlin to commemorate the event. At first local party officials looked askance at the movement in view of its nationalist and anti-Muscovite orientation. Eventually, however, they gave permission for TOTs to hold its founding congress in February 1989, where it declared

---

[70] See, for instance, D. Iskhakov, "Sovremennoe Tatarskoe natsional'noe dvizhenie: Pod'em i krizis," *Tatarstan*, no. 8, 1993, p. 27; Marie Bennigen Broxup, "Tatarstan and the Tatars," in Graham Smith, ed., *The Nationalities Question in the Post-Soviet States* (2d ed.) (New York: Longman, 1996), p. 81.

its main goals to be raising the ethnofederal status of the Tatar ASSR, making Tatar the official language of the republic, and achieving Tatar "sovereignty."[71] As Mary McAuley observed, "All, at this time, shared a common aim: the acquisition of Union republic status. . . . None of the nationalists conceived of anything else."[72]

This demand was not confined to TOTs. It enjoyed significant support within official circles as well, even finding some resonance within the local Russian community. A poll conducted in 1989 indicated that 67 percent of the republic's inhabitants supported raising the status of the republic to a union republic, and beginning in fall 1989 official elites began to press the idea vigorously.[73] But whereas the local nomenklatura saw sovereignty vis-à-vis the RSFSR as a means for raising their status within the Soviet hierarchy, TOTs activists clearly took their cue from the Baltic fronts. Like their Baltic counterparts, they understood sovereignty as a necessary precondition for nationalizing society and moving toward eventual independence from Moscow. Soon after its formation TOTs established close contact with Baltic popular fronts. Much of the language about sovereignty within its initial platform – though falling short of calling for complete independence – was drawn from Baltic documents, and when the authorities in Kazan' refused to allow publication of the founding congress' proceedings, the movement's Baltic allies arranged publication.[74] Although TOTs was clearly spawned out of the tide of nationalism unleashed by the Balts, unlike the situation in the Baltic the federal system exercised a significant limit on the types of demands which seemed feasible and publicly acceptable. As one history of the movement notes, Tatarstan's "prolonged status as an autonomous republic sharply limited the horizons of political activity" of Tatar nationalist movements.[75]

Throughout 1989 and most of 1990 TOTs confined itself to publicist activity, occasional demonstrations, and a petition drive (gaining one hundred thousand signatures) aimed at upgrading the federal status of the republic. Interest in TOTs grew gradually during these years, and under the influence of events elsewhere, by early 1990 Tatar opinion began to move in a more radical direction. Reflective of this and of the continuing

[71] Graney, "Projecting Sovereignty," p. 88.
[72] Mary McAuley, *Russia's Politics of Uncertainty* (Cambridge, UK: Cambridge University Press, 1997), pp. 55–56.
[73] *Pravda*, September 22, 1989, p. 2.
[74] Graney, "Projecting Sovereignty," p. 88.
[75] Iskhakov, "Sovremennoe Tatarskoe natsional'noe dvizhenie," p. 30.

confusion over ends fostered by the federal system, in March 1990 more radical members of TOTs split from the organization to form the Ittifak National Party, which openly advocated independence for Tatarstan and a more militant nationalist program. More important for subsequent events, local officials proved skillful in outmaneuvering their nationalist competitors. As Kate Graney observed, "[i]n essence, as *glasnost'* and democratization progressed, and the Baltic sovereignty projects began to cast doubt on the future viability of the Soviet center, regional political elites began to try to co-opt the pro-sovereignty agenda which had spread from the Baltic states to Russia and its regions."[76] The selection of Mintimer Shaimiev as Tatar Communist Party First Secretary in October 1989 accelerated this process. Though a longtime party apparatchik, by March 1990 Shaimiev was already pressing Moscow to recognize that the Tatar republic had a special "treaty-based" relationship with Russia.[77] In view of this, the declaration by Yeltsin's government in June 1990 about Russian sovereignty vis-à-vis the USSR generated considerable indignation within Tatarstan. In response to this agitation and eager to prevent minority elites within Russia from being enlisted by Gorbachev against him in their power struggle, Yeltsin traveled to Kazan' in early August, urging the Tatars to "take as much sovereignty as you can swallow" and even implying that he would accept "whatever independence the Tatar ASSR chooses for itself."[78] As one of the leaders of TOTs later recalled, after Russia's sovereignty declaration and Yeltsin's speech in Kazan' "we opened our mouths wider in order to taste for real the promised freedom. . . . After all, what was there to fear if Russia had already declared sovereignty? The precedent was there."[79] Tatar nationalists were holding daily mass demonstrations at the time – some attracting up to thirty thousand participants – to pressure the Tatar government to respond boldly to Russia's sovereignty declaration. By the end of August the Tatar Supreme Soviet had issued its own sovereignty declaration which unilaterally raised Tatarstan's status to that of a union republic. Although unequivocally describing Tatarstan as a constituent republic of the USSR, the declaration made no mention whatsoever of the republic being within Russia. As one observer later noted,

[76] Graney, "Projecting Sovereignty," p. 90.
[77] See Edward W. Walker, "The Dog That Didn't Bark: Tatarstan and Asymmetrical Federalism in Russia," *The Harriman Review*, vol. 9, no. 4 (Winter 1996), pp. 11–18.
[78] Quoted in Walker, "The Dog That Didn't Bark," p. 12.
[79] Il'dus Sadykov, in *Ploshchad' svobody*, no. 16, July 1997, p. 11.

the local nomenklatura had "taken the initiative into its own hands and had begun actively to exploit the idea of republican sovereignty,"[80] with a view toward union republican status within the USSR rather than independence.

Shaimiev and the Tatar nomenklatura had unambiguously identified themselves with the Soviet government and had gambled on its continued coherence. As the fortunes of the Soviet government and the Communist Party waned, events began to play into the hands of the nationalist camp. The second half of 1990 was a period of intensive growth for the Tatar nationalist movement. By December some public opinion polls indicated that as many as 21 percent of the population of Tatarstan considered them-selves supporters of TOTs; other polls showed that a slightly larger proportion of the Tatarstani public (12 percent) trusted the nationalist movements than trusted the Communist Party (9.4 percent).[81] In Febru-ary 1991, as the USSR tottered on the brink of disintegration, TOTs held its second congress, at which its demands radicalized considerably, openly embracing full independence as a goal.[82] Tatar nationalists began for the first time to press unequivocally for independence at rallies and demon-strations. By contrast, Shaimiev continued his course aimed at union republican status within a renewed USSR. When Yeltsin, in an attempt to outmaneuver Gorbachev, appended an additional question about creat-ing a Russian presidency to Gorbachev's March 1991 referendum, the Tatarstan government announced that it would not include Yeltsin's ques-tion on the ballot, since, it argued, the RSFSR legislature had no author-ity in Tatarstan's territory. Shaimiev's subsequent decision not to bar Russian presidential elections in Tatarstan evoked the first sustained wave of separatist mobilization within the republic in May 1991, with approxi-mately fifteen thousand participating in a series of demonstrations orga-nized by TOTs and Ittifak, calling for a boycott of the elections and for Tatar independence.[83]

Shaimiev's open support for the August 1991 coup, and the declarations of independence by union republics that followed the collapse of the coup, created a major opportunity for Tatar nationalists. In September and

---

[80] Iskhakov, "Sovremennoe Tatarskoe natsional'noe dvizhenie," p. 29.

[81] Iskhakov, "Sovremennoe Tatarskoe natsional'noe dvizhenie," pp. 29, 31. The margin of error is not provided.

[82] At the time, the movement renamed itself VTOTs, adding the adjective "all-union" to its title in a symbolic affirmation of its hope to mobilize Tatars throughout the USSR.

[83] *Ekspress khronika*, no. 21, May 21, 1991; *Report on USSR*, May 31, 1991, p. 29.

October 1991 demonstrations calling for Tatar independence and Shaimiev's resignation mobilized up to fifty thousand participants, as the nationalist movement reached the peak of its support. Events came to a head in Kazan' in mid-October on the anniversary of Ivan the Terrible's seizure of Kazan' and the opening of a session of the Tatarstan Supreme Soviet. Armed Tatar nationalist demonstrators, calling for a declaration of complete independence and the overthrow of the Shaimiev government (and inspired by events then taking place in Chechnia), attempted to storm the building of the republican legislature, leaving seven demonstrators and sixteen police injured.[84] In the wake of the violence, public support for TOTs and other nationalist movements plummeted.[85] Yet, public opinion polls at the time showed that 86 percent of Tatars favored complete independence for Tatarstan[86] – precisely the kind of transformation in identities for which the nationalist movement had been agitating. Tidal effects, not mobilization, had done their work. The Shaimiev government proved skillful in outmaneuvering the nationalists by coopting their demands, decreeing at the end of October that a referendum on Tatarstani independence would be held in March 1992. In spite of heavy-handed efforts by Moscow to prevent the referendum and, failing that, to influence its outcome, 61 percent of the republic's electorate voted to recognize Tatarstan as "a sovereign state and a subject of international law." In the months that followed, Shaimiev consolidated his hold over Tatarstani politics, eventually negotiating a power-sharing treaty with the Yeltsin government that gave Tatarstan a wide-reaching autonomy within Russia. By contrast, nationalist organizations experienced multiple splits and a dramatic decline, as "the functions of organizer of national life and even the national movement itself partially transferred into the hands of state and parastatal structures."[87]

The failure of separatist mobilization in Tatarstan was structured in significant respects by the institutional constraints imposed by Soviet ethnofederalism. The Tatar ASSR's secondary status within that system exercised a limit on the political goals pursued by Tatar nationalists and raised the bar necessary to mobilize Tatars around secessionist frames. But

---

[84] *Ekspress khronika*, no. 43, October 22, 1991, p. 1.
[85] See F. Kh. Mukhametshin et al., *Tatarstan na perekrestke mnenii* (Kazan': Izdatel'stvo Verkhovnogo Soveta Respubliki Tatarstana, 1993), p. 47.
[86] *Ekspress khronika*, November 12, 1991, p. 2. The poll also showed that 24 percent of Russians favored Tatar independence – obviously the result of tidal effects.
[87] Iskhakov, "Sovremennoe Tatarskoe natsional'noe dvizhenie," p. 31.

this in itself is not a full explanation of the mobilizational failure of Tatar nationalist movements. Chechen nationalists faced similar obstacles in their campaign for independence, which also emerged late (1991) within the *glasnost'* cycle. Like the Tatars, even into 1991 Chechen nationalists pressed primarily for Chechnia to become a union republic within a renewed USSR and outside the Russian Federation.[88] And as in Tatarstan, the August coup and the support of the local nomenklatura for the State Emergency Committee presented Chechen nationalists with a significant political opening, which, in contrast to the Tatars, they utilized effectively to carry out a national revolution. The differences in the outcomes in Chechnia and Tatarstan have as much to do with those factors which allowed the Chechen nationalist movement to overcome many of the same structural disadvantages faced by the Tatars (an extremely robust system of symbolic capital emerging out of the 1944 exile experience and strong mobilizational networks inherent in the Chechen clan system) as they do with those factors which allowed the nomenklatura in Tatarstan to appropriate tidal forces in a way that the Chechen nomenklatura could not. The Zavgaev and Shaimiev governments faced different situations and displayed different approaches toward riding the nationalist tide then overwhelming the USSR. The Zavgaev government was permeated with clan divisions, making it easier for the Chechen nationalist movement to penetrate official institutions and to undermine them, whereas in Tatarstan the Shaimiev government's compliance system largely remained intact before and after the August coup. But more significant, unlike Shaimiev, the Zavgaev government's close association with Moscow made it incapable of presenting itself as an alternative to the nationalist movement, whereas Shaimiev effectively outflanked his nationalist opposition by riding the tide and assuming many of its demands as his own.

As these examples show, the tidal forces of nationalism can be harnessed by either governments or nationalist oppositions, and structure plays a central role in advantaging or disadvantaging one side or another. In all three cases, structural disadvantages crippled efforts by separatist movements to utilize tidal forces to their advantage and made the marginalization of challenges considerably easier to carry out. But as we have also seen, structural disadvantage alone is an inadequate explanation of these outcomes. In the Belorussian case, for instance, separatist nationalism appeared to be gaining ground in early 1990, and in the cases of the Uzbeks

[88] See Lieven, *Chechnya: Tombstone of Russian Power*, p. 58.

and Volga Tatars structure reasonably allowed for success or failure, even leaning toward expectations of success. Ultimately, in each of these cases separatist movements failed because of the ways in which structural advantages were put to use in challenging or upholding a particular national order and in utilizing the example set by others to one's own advantage. In the end, however, though separatist movements failed, in all three cases separatist nationalism prevailed: under the weight of tidal forces nomenklatura elites appropriated it toward their own ends. Thus, tides of nationalism are powerful forces potentially affecting not only the behavior of nationalist challengers, but of established elites as well.

## Summary and Conclusion

This chapter elaborated a notion of the failure of nationalism and demonstrated the ways in which structural advantage, institutional constraint, and tidal effects are implicated in its production. In distinguishing between the irrelevancy and failure of nationalism, I argued that the failure of nationalism implies the counterfactual of the imaginability of alternative outcomes. Based on the empirical patterns of mobilizational outcomes found among Soviet nationalities in the *glasnost'* era, I explored a number of those counterfactuals probabilistically, pointing to the ways in which changed government policies or historical circumstances could have altered the outcomes of separatist politics given what we know from the outcomes of other cases.

Evidence was presented concerning the systematic association of particular structural characteristics of target populations – population size, ethnofederal status, urbanization, linguistic assimilation, prior state independence, and previous levels of nationalist conflict with the state – with the probability of failure or success of separatist movements. The cumulation of structural disadvantage was shown to have led to situations of cultural hegemony, with the deck stacked against challenging nationalisms through the sense of impracticality and outlandishness which overwhelming structural disadvantage instilled, without resort to institutional constraint. The structural advantages and disadvantages of target groups were cumulative and fungible. Nationalisms could succeed or fail in the presence of a variety of combinations of structural factors, and much of what structural influence was about was in endowing groups with advantages in profiting from the actions of others. Indicative of the limits of structure, we saw that tidal influences were critical in explaining successful outcomes in a number of cases where failure would otherwise have been expected, whereas the continued vibrancy of institutional constraints helped to explain cases in which structural conditions would have led one to expect action but where action was nevertheless absent. Moreover, failure emerged out of an interactive process between structural advantage, institutional constraints, and tidal effects. Overall, without the effect of tidal forces, it is probable that the failure of separatist nationalism in the USSR would have been much more extensive than was actually the case. But even when separatist movements failed, separatist nationalism often succeeded in any case due to its strategic appropriation by dominant elites, largely under the burgeoning influence of tidal forces. Thus, I have shown that a tidal perspective is crucial for understanding the success and failure of nationalisms, because it allows us to explain how the chances of success facing a particular nationalism can be altered by taking advantage of the actions of others, it helps us to understand how pre-existing structural conditions come to be translated into actual patterns of nationalist action, and it explains how nationalist movements might fail yet nationalism nonetheless succeed.

# 6

## *Violence and Tides of Nationalism*

So great was the confusion of those years; so difficult was it at the moment when "humanity" was being re-evaluated, to determine the place madness was to occupy within it; so difficult was it to situate madness in a social sphere that was being restructured.

Michel Foucault, *Madness and Civilization*

Nationalism in and of itself is neither a social good nor a social evil. Rather, our moral judgments concerning nationalism emerge from what agents do in the name of the nation. Nationalism thus cannot be understood as only a "state of mind" or "political principle." It is also a way of comporting oneself, a motivated collection of actions and discourses, and, in the totality of acts that it involves, a repertoire of behaviors oriented toward a specific set of objects. Within this repertoire of nationalist behaviors, violence assumes a special place. Violence has been visibly prominent in the history of nationalism since its inception in the revolutions of the seventeenth and eighteenth centuries. It remains pronounced as well in the "ethnic cleansing" and civil wars which continue to rack portions of the planet.

Most generic theories of nationalism have had little to say about the relationship between nationalism and violence. They have been much more interested in issues of identity than in what is done in the name of the nation (as if action flowed logically from holding a particular identity position). This has not inhibited the growth of a large cottage industry focused on explaining nationalist violence. A review article by this author identified no less than thirteen major approaches to the subject spread across two generations of research.[1] As this plurality suggests, no single

---

[1] Mark R. Beissinger, "Violence," in Alexander J. Motyl, ed., *Encyclopedia of Nationalism*, vol. 1 (San Diego, CA: Academic Press, 2001), pp. 849–67. The introduction to this chapter draws in part from that article.

explanation for nationalist violence could possibly emerge, in large part due to the great variety of acts which fall under the rubric of nationalist violence (some of which often go unrecognized as violence). Extensive and largely separate literatures exist on genocide, state-sponsored terror against cultural groups, ethnic or racial riots, pogroms, vigilante violence, interethnic warfare, national insurrections, and nationalist-motivated terrorism. Where a tidal perspective on nationalism can potentially contribute to these disjointed conversations is in placing these disparate acts into a broader framework of contentious politics, in situating acts of nationalist violence within a larger repertoire of violent and nonviolent actions, and in gaining an understanding of the ways in which acts of violence can become part of their own causal structure and are influenced by the nationalist actions of others. In this sense, a tidal perspective on nationalist violence is not necessarily exclusive of other approaches; the spiraling of ethnic mistrust into violent intergroup conflict described by rational choice theories, for instance, is likely to be located within tidal phenomena, as is the mobilizational pull of cultural allegiance noted by culturalist theories. What a tidal perspective adds is not an alternative to these theories, but a way of thinking about individual acts of nationalist violence within a larger politics of contention.

In many respects nationalist violence is quintessentially a tidal phenomenon. Right-wing violence in Europe, for instance, has generally followed a cyclical pattern, influenced to various degrees by macroeconomic trends, specific state policies, and media representations of violence. As studies have suggested, the waves of right-wing violence against foreigners that swept Western Europe in the early 1990s were interrelated events fostered in part by a sense of connectedness and the cross-national discourses and linkages maintained by extremist groups with one another.[2] Terrorist violence is also temporally clustered and transnationally related; a cease-fire agreement by the IRA in the late 1990s, for instance, exerted influence on ETA to do the same, at least temporarily. Certainly, extremist nationalist or racist ideologies are central to explanations of genocide. But most scholars of genocide do not view them as sufficient explanations of the phenomenon. Warfare, a disintegrating social order, a heightened

---

[2] See, for instance, Tore Björgo and Rob Witte, "Introduction," in Tore Björgo and Rob Witte, eds., *Racist Violence in Europe* (London: St. Martin's Press, 1993), pp. 1–16; Simon Epstein, *Cyclical Patterns in Antisemitism: The Dynamics of Anti-Jewish Violence in Western Countries since the 1950s* (Jerusalem: The Vidal Sassoon International Center for the Study of Antisemitism, 1993).

sense of threat, and intense cultural challenge have been identified as critical contextual variables as well.[3]

A tidal perspective seems particularly relevant for understanding mobilized nationalist violence. Like other types of contentious events, mobilized nationalist violence is temporally clustered rather than randomly distributed over time, part of larger chains, waves, and cycles of violent and nonviolent challenges to authority. Those challenging a given national order have at times resorted to violence as a way of disrupting and undermining authority or intimidating those associated with or protected by authority. But nationalist violence is not only a way of contesting domination. It is also a way of institutionalizing domination. Those threatened by a potential reconfiguration of authority have at times utilized violence as a means for asserting and upholding group dominance. Indeed, for some types of nationalist violence it is often difficult to discern whether violence was initiated by those seeking to contest an existing order or to uphold it, given the conflicting claims about culpability propagated by the adversaries and the interactive chains of events that set violence in motion.[4]

In this respect, nationalist violence is intimately connected with questions of political order – and specifically, with the particular national order which states invariably seek to project on society. Yet, as a number of authors have observed, significant outbreaks of large-scale violence remain the exception in the politics of nationalism rather than the norm. Most nationalist conflicts do not produce widespread violence, and there is a much larger number of cases in which identity groups share political space in relative harmony or in which violence over nationalist issues has remained implicit and marginalized rather than overt and endemic. According to one group of Russian experts, for instance, in all, from 1988 through 1991, more than 150 different ethnic conflicts took place in the Soviet Union, only 20 of which caused human casualties.[5] One of the implications of this is methodological: nationalist violence cannot be adequately investigated in isolation from larger processes of contesting a national order. This has become increasingly recognized by scholars,

---

[3] See Christopher R. Browning, *The Path to Genocide* (Cambridge, UK: Cambridge University Press, 1992), pp. 86–121; Robert Melson, *Revolution and Genocide: On the Origins of the Armenian Genocide and the Holocaust* (Chicago, IL: University of Chicago Press, 1992), pp. 6–8.

[4] On this, see in particular Paul R. Brass, *Theft of an Idol: Text and Context in the Representation of Collective Violence* (Princeton, NJ: Princeton University Press: 1997).

[5] *Nezavisimaia gazeta*, January 10, 1992, p. 5.

although, as Laitin and Fearon have asserted, much work continues to suffer from the practice of sampling on the dependent variable.[6] It is precisely here that a tidal perspective is helpful, for it provides us with empirical grounding in the event itself as a method for sorting out competing causal claims about nationalist violence, for analyzing nationalist violence in relationship to other forms of contesting the boundedness of states, and for identifying temporal and spatial variation in the contexts in which nationalist contention assumes violent form.

But another implication is purely substantive. If large-scale nationalist violence is the rare exception, then truly exceptional circumstances are required for nationalist violence to materialize and proliferate. Before the initiation of waves of mobilized nationalist violence, violence usually remains outside the realm of the conceivable for most people. It is not unusual for victims to be aware of rumors about impending violence against them, often refusing to believe their veracity. As one survivor of the Sumgait pogroms of February 1988 later reflected, "it was all so far-fetched, so unheard of in our lives, that it was just impossible to take it seriously."[7] Large-scale nationalist violence emerges in circumstances which make the seemingly impossible thinkable – circumstances of great change and confusion in which it becomes increasingly difficult, as Foucault says, to situate madness. Not only is large-scale nationalist violence a rupture of the normal (in which behaviors normally regarded as deviant become accepted by a significant segment of society as normal), but large-scale nationalist violence also usually occurs in circumstances in which what was once understood as normal is no longer recognizable. Here, a tidal perspective on nationalist violence is fruitful, for it helps us to situate these "moments of madness" within the context of a larger unraveling of order, to identify conditions associated with its spread and proliferation, and to understand the ways in which violence brutally reconfigures reality.

This chapter does not aim to develop a generic explanation of nationalist violence; such a task, as noted earlier, is impossible given the variety of acts that would have to be explained. Rather, my purposes are to examine the emergence and evolution of the multiple waves of mobilized nationalist violence that accompanied the *glasnost'* tide of nationalism, to

[6] James D. Fearon and David D. Laitin, "Explaining Interethnic Cooperation," *American Political Science Review* 90 (December 1996), pp. 715–35.
[7] Samvel Shahmuratian, ed., *The Sumgait Tragedy: Pogroms Against Armenians in Soviet Azerbaijan.* Vol. I: *Eyewitness Accounts* (Cambridge, MA: Zoryan Institute, 1990), pp. 75–76.

demonstrate the importance of a tidal perspective to an explanation of these events, and to show the ways in which acts of violence came to constitute a significant causal role in the further production of violence and the disintegration of the Soviet state. My argument is that in the Soviet case violent nationalist mobilization was a tidal phenomenon par excellence. This does not mean that it was not heavily influenced by pre-existing structural conditions. Rather, it means that a knowledge of relevant pre-existing structural conditions alone would have been grossly insufficient for explaining why multiple waves of violence emerged within the context of a mobilizational cycle and grew sustained in some cases and not others. In general nationalist violence was concentrated during a particular phase of the mobilizational cycle – the latter portion of the tide. As we will see, this was due largely to the fact that prior waves of mobilization led to shifts of authority within political institutions that, in a limited number of cases, set in motion violent mobilizational processes across group boundaries. Strategic concerns generated out of a shifting political context were important in explaining the shift from nonviolent to violent modes of mobilization, largely by advantaging violent entrepreneurs over nonviolent entrepreneurs. But as we shall also see, segments of the Soviet state also seemed to sanction violence in certain circumstances, provoking, abetting, and directly generating violence as a strategy of contention. State authority at some level was almost always involved in encouraging or perpetuating nationalist violence, either through the signals and cues which state actors sent to violent entrepreneurs within populations or through the explicit organization of violence by state institutions themselves. Paralleling the institutionalization of nonviolent mobilization within the tide, over time the forms which violence assumed evolved away from mobilizational forms toward more organized forms of ethnic warfare. Nationalist violence grew partially institutionalized in emerging state structures precisely as these structures sought to validate claims to territorial control – a pattern characteristic of state breakdown in other contexts as well.[8]

Once initiated, violence exercised its own independent effect on subsequent events, altering cultural identities and wielding, in Sewell's words, "a transformative power that goes beyond such obvious political effects as

---

[8] See Youssef Cohen, Brian R. Brown, and A. F. K. Organski, "The Paradoxical Nature of State Making: The Violent Creation of Order," *American Political Science Review* 75 (December 1981), pp. 901–10.

redistribution of power or reshaping of political strategies."[9] As Feldman explains, "[n]ovel subject positions are constructed and construed by violent performances, and this mutation of agency renders formal ideological rationale and prior contextual motivation unstable and even secondary."[10] Thus, nationalist violence is fundamentally a tidal phenomenon not only because it materializes out of a tidal context, but also because of its capacity to become its own progenitor of subsequent actions, identities, and interests.

## The Limits of Structural Explanations of Mobilized Nationalist Violence

According to official police statistics, at least 1,314 people lost their lives and 12,750 people were injured in interethnic conflicts in the Soviet Union from January 1988 through May 1991, with 76 percent of the deaths and 57 percent of the injuries concentrated in the 1990–91 period. During these years more than seven hundred thousand people were forced to flee their homes, and property destruction from these conflicts cost tens of billions of rubles.[11] As one government journal put it in 1990, the USSR on the eve of its demise was convulsed by a series of "undeclared wars" of society against itself.[12] The inability of the government to control nationalist violence over the expanse of its territory was one of the critical factors leading to the collapse of the Soviet state, reinforcing perceptions of the frailty of Soviet power and its institutional sclerosis, impelling some groups toward secession, and provoking a sense of exhaustion and frustration within the military and police. With the collapse of the USSR in August 1991, nationalist violence accelerated even more dramatically. Estimates of the number of deaths from civil conflicts throughout this period ranged somewhere between one hundred and two hundred thou-

---

[9] William H. Sewell, "Collective Violence and Collective Loyalties in France: Why the French Revolution Made a Difference," *Politics and Society*, vol. 18, no. 4, 1990, p. 548.

[10] Allen Feldman, *Formations of Violence: The Narrative of the Body and Political Terror in Northern Ireland* (Chicago, IL: University of Chicago Press, 1991), p. 20.

[11] These figures were calculated from Radio Moscow, in *FBIS*, September 21, 1989, p. 45; *Pravda*, April 17, 1990, in *Current Digest of the Soviet Press*, vol. 42, no. 16 (1990), p. 11; Moscow TV, in *FBIS*, August 27, 1990, p. 114; *Krasnaia zvezda*, May 16, 1991, in *FBIS*, May 21, 1991, p. 47; *Report on the USSR*, May 31, 1991, p. 29.

[12] *Pravitel'stvennyi vestnik*, no. 29 (July 1990), p. 12.

sand, most of them ascribable to Russia's wars in Chechnia and the conflict in Tajikistan. Yet, as significant as the violence was, it was considerably less intense and widespread than many experts had anticipated – particularly when juxtaposed to the civil wars of Yugoslavia or Africa. Although areas such as Karabakh, Pridnestrovia, Abkhazia, and Ossetia will long remain zones of potential violent conflict, wars in these regions had eventually wound down by the mid-1990s through exhaustion or defeat, and a number of other zones of potential violent conflict – Northern Estonia, Crimea, Northern Kazakhstan, and Ajaria, for example – did not produce significant violence in spite of the expectations of some to the contrary.

There is no shortage of explanations for this explosion of violence or for its less than anticipated scope. Some have viewed it as an expression of deep-seated civilizational divides and cultural differences.[13] Others, drawing on frustration-aggression theory, have argued that ethnic violence is more likely to be initiated by economically backward groups as a result of anxieties generated from unequal status.[14] Some analysts have pointed to cultures of violence or nonviolence – that is, to socialized approaches to resolving problems which project themselves onto a variety of contexts, fostering continuity in the ways in which groups approach conflictual situations.[15] Still others have focused on the design of ethnofederal institutions in promoting or containing violence.[16] Each of these conditions may have contributed in specific cases to violent outcomes, but none holds systematically when viewed across the range of cases represented in the Soviet Union (or for that matter, elsewhere in the world).

This becomes clear when we examine the patterning of violent action across a large number of nationalities. Table 6.1 presents the results of an ordered logit regression of the outcomes of violent mobilization based on

---

[13] Samuel P. Huntington, *The Clash of Civilizations and the Remaking of World Order* (New York: Simon & Schuster, 1996); John Armstrong, "Toward a Framework for Considering Nationalism in East Europe," *East European Politics and Societies*, vol. 2, no. 2 (Spring 1988), pp. 280–305.

[14] See Donald Horowitz, *Ethnic Groups in Conflict* (Berkeley, CA: University of California Press, 1985), pp. 166, 247.

[15] See David Laitin, "Nationalist Revivals and Violence," *Archives Européennes de Sociologie*, vol. 36, no. 1 (1995), pp. 3–43.

[16] See, for instance, Valerie Bunce, *Subversive Institutions: The Design and the Destruction of Socialism and the State* (Cambridge, UK: Cambridge University Press, 1999), pp. 102–26.

Table 6.1. *Ordered Logit Regressions of Violent Mobilizational Outcomes (No Major Violence/Sporadic Violent/Intermittent Violence/Sustained Violence) by Nationality, January 1987–December 1992*[a]

| Independent variable/equation | Equation 1 | Equation 2 | Equation 3 | Equation 4 | Equation 5[b] | Equation 6[b] |
|---|---|---|---|---|---|---|
| Ln population size, 1989 | 0.711 (2.08)** | – | 0.745 (2.03)** | – | 1.115 (2.13)** | 1.408 (2.24)** |
| Proportion within federal unit of primary habitation, 1989[c] | 0.011 (0.60) | – | – | 0.035 (2.42)** | –0.011 (–0.48) | –0.020 (–0.83) |
| Dummy variable for union republic | – | 2.143 (2.41)** | 0.434 (0.36) | – | –0.263 (–0.16) | –0.501 (–0.30) |
| Linguistic assimilation, 1989 | –0.136 (–3.12)*** | –0.101 (–2.78)*** | –0.137 (–2.99)*** | –0.105 (–2.75)*** | –0.161 (–3.02)*** | –0.208 (–2.75)*** |
| Level of urbanization, 1970 | 0.054 (1.83)* | 0.059 (2.01)** | 0.055 (1.85)* | 0.058 (1.98)** | 0.091 (2.33)** | 0.073 (1.74)* |
| Dummy variable for peoples of traditionally Islamic cultures | – | – | – | – | – | –1.249 (–0.98) |
| Number of mass violent events in which nationality engaged, 1965–86 | –0.024 (–0.12) | 0.048 (0.24) | –0.051 (–0.24) | 0.166 (0.90) | –0.244 (–1.00) | –0.312 (–1.19) |
| Number of persons of nationality confined to special prison settlements, 1953 (thousands) | – | – | – | – | 0.002 (0.36) | 0.002 (0.47) |

| | | | | | |
|---|---|---|---|---|---|
| Number of observations (nationalities) | 47 | 47 | 47 | 47 | 40 | 40 |
| Number of correctly predicted observations | 28 | 30 | 31 | 27 | 25 | 26 |
| Observations eliminated due to complete determination | 0 | 0 | 0 | 0 | 0 | 0 |
| Ancillary parameters | | | | | | |
| First cut point | 5.186789 | 1.234059 | 5.114427 | 1.999241 | 8.217492 | 7.744193 |
| Second cut point | 7.11413 | 2.975208 | 7.0452 | 3.675495 | 9.787028 | 9.33169 |
| Third cut point | 8.795484 | 4.568056 | 8.712309 | 5.280934 | 11.57852 | 11.17921 |
| Log likelihood | -39.466153 | -41.834306 | -39.58172 | -41.805211 | -34.166964 | -33.687824 |
| Likelihood ratio model chi$^2$ | 37.92**** | 33.19**** | 37.69**** | 33.25**** | 32.87**** | 33.83**** |
| Pseudo R-square | .324 | .284 | .323 | .285 | .325 | .334 |

*Significant at the .10 level  **Significant at the .05 level  ***Significant at the .01 level  ****Significant at the .001 level

[a] Russians excluded from the analysis. Coefficients represent the change in the log-odds of the outcome being in a higher category versus a lower category associated with a unit increase in the independent variable, with z-scores in parentheses.

[b] Seven cases had to be dropped from Equations 5 and 6 due to missing information on the number of political exiles in 1953.

[c] Federal unit of primary habitation is defined as the unit in which the largest number of members of that nationality resided in 1989. *Source:* 1989 census data.

an analysis of information concerning 1,897 mass violent events over ethnonationalist issues that took place from January 1987 through December
1992.[17] Based on actual patterns of mobilization, I classified each of
forty-seven non-Russian nationalities according to four possible outcomes:
groups which experienced sustained nationalist violence (defined here as
those whose members engaged in one hundred or more ethnonationalist
mass violent events during this period); groups which experienced intermittent nationalist violence (those whose members engaged in ten to one
hundred ethnonationalist mass violent events); groups which experienced
sporadic nationalist violence (with records of ethnonationalist violence
ranging from one to ten events); and groups which experienced no ethnonationalist violence.[18] The independent variables chosen represented a
variety of possible causal linkages: prior patterns of conflict; the contours
of the federal system; civilizational differences (specifically, Islamic cultural
background and the degree of linguistic assimilation of a group); and levels
of urbanization and development. Variables controlling for population size
and the demographic dominance of a group within its ethnofederal unit
were included as well.

---

[17] I defined a mass violent event as mass political action whose primary purpose was to inflict
violence, either in the form of an attack on people or on property. A minimum size of
fifteen persons was used to distinguish these events from terrorist, criminal, or other small-
scale acts of violence. As explained in Chapter 5, the ordered logit model fits a set of cutoff
points (in this case, marking the three cutoffs between the four levels of the dependent
variable) such that for fitted values of the regression below the first cutoff the dependent
variable is predicted to take on a zero value (no ethnonationalist mass violence), for fitted
values between the first and second cutoffs the dependent variable is predicted to assume
a value of one (sporadic ethnonationalist mass violence, as defined above), for fitted values
between the second and third cutoffs the dependent variable is predicted to assume a value
of two (intermittent ethnonationalist mass violence), and for fitted values greater than the
third cutoff the dependent variable is predicted to assume a value of three (sustained ethnonationalist mass violence). The raw regression coefficients can be exponentiated into
odds ratios that indicate the effect of a one-unit increase in the independent variable on
the ratio of the odds of being in a higher category versus a lower category (which the proportional odds assumption of the model assumes to be equal across the four categories).
[18] Obviously, Russians were in a number of cases intimately involved in nationalist violence
in the former USSR, exhibiting the fourth highest level of violent nationalist mobilization
among the groups in the sample (217 events). However, by necessity they had to be
excluded from this analysis, since the Russian category actually included multiple communities in quite disparate locations and contexts; moreover, the inclusion of a variable
measuring linguistic assimilation in the specification made no sense vis-à-vis the dominant
nationality.

The analysis demonstrates the weak capacity of any and all the factors tested to predict levels of nationalist violence in a systematic fashion, confirming the "all-pervading unpredictability" that Hannah Arendt noted as a hallmark of the realm of violence.[19] No more than 66 percent of the observations were correctly predicted by any of the specifications. This is not to say that the "quiet" politics of nationalism was not related to violent outcomes. What stands out here is that the very same factors we saw earlier to be systematically associated with nonviolent mobilization – population size, linguistic assimilation, and urbanization – were also associated with violent mobilization. More than this, a number of the models of nationalist violence noted earlier find little systematic support in patterns of violent mobilization in the former USSR. It is true that the degree of linguistic assimilation of a group was negatively associated with nationalist violence, and one could interpret this as a sign of a cultural model of violent conflict. But one could also argue that this association is merely an indication that identity processes are important to mobilization more generally; linguistic assimilation was also strongly associated with nonviolent mobilization. The connection with violent conflict is thus less clear. And although there is a simple correlation between patterns of violence during the pre-*glasnost'* period (1965–86) and during *glasnost'*, this relationship disappears once one controls for population size, well known within the cross-national literature to be related to the frequency of mass violence within a society.[20] This is not to say that past violence had no effect on the incidence of violence within the *glasnost'* cycle; rather, because prior patterns of violence were also related to other factors influencing the frequency of violence under *glasnost'*, there is no way to differentiate its systematic effect. Moreover, there are definite limits to an explanation based on the continuity of violence over time. A prior history of intense conflict with the state – measured here by the number of persons of a nationality confined to special prison settlements in the late Stalin period – was not systematically related to patterns of nationalist violence (whether or not one controls for other factors). Based solely on patterns of violent mobilization and conflict in the 1940s, one would have anticipated that the Balts, Ukrainians, Chechens, and Germans would most likely have the highest levels of violent conflict with the Soviet state in the *glasnost'* period.

---

[19] Hannah Arendt, *On Violence* (San Diego, CA: Harcourt Brace and Company, 1970), p. 5.
[20] Douglas A. Hibbs, *Mass Political Violence* (New York: Wiley, 1973), p. 25.

Yet, during the 1987–92 period none of these groups were among those engaged in sustained violent conflict (the Chechen wars emerging only later). By contrast, the groups that displayed the highest levels of nationalist mass violence in the *glasnost'* period – the Georgians, Armenians, Azerbaijanis, Abkhaz, Ossetians, and Moldovans – were (with perhaps the exception of the Moldovans) not among those engaged in the most intense conflicts with the Soviet government in the 1940s. These temporal discontinuities raise questions about the capacity of civilizational and culture of violence arguments to explain nationalist violence. Even within specific spatial contexts one finds no consistency in patterns of violence in the USSR to enable one to speak consistently of a culture of violence applied extensively to a wide range of objects. When one examines, for instance, murder rates in the union republics in 1989, one finds no relationship whatsoever between the incidence of murder within a population and the propensity of that population to engage in violent mass mobilization.[21]

The fact that urbanization was positively associated with levels of nationalist violence defies the notion that less advantaged groups were more likely than the advantaged to engage in violent action. More urbanized groups in the USSR generally were the more advantaged populations economically, not the least advantaged. As Valery Tishkov concluded, it was "not the most deprived groups in terms of 'basic needs' who initiate[d] violence" in the former USSR, but rather groups "with titular status and with well-established cultural institutions."[22] Those groups which experienced significant nationalist violence during this period were relatively mobilized populations – often groups with close connections to state institutions. This is confirmed in Equation 4, which shows that groups that were majorities within their federal unit of primary habitation were more likely to engage in violence than were minorities (though due to this variable's strong correlation with population size, the effect disappears when controlled for population size).

[21] Murder rates here refer to both registered premeditated and attempted murders per one hundred thousand population aged fourteen years or older. Murder rates in Turkmenia and Kazakhstan were the highest in 1989, whereas Kazakhstan rated fourth among republics in that year in the frequency of mass violence and Turkmenia, last. Azerbaijan, Georgia, and Uzbekistan were areas of the greatest mass violence in 1989, but actually had below-average murder rates. *Prestupnost' i pravonarusheniia v SSSR. Statisticheskii sbornik, 1989* (Moscow: Iuridicheskaia literatura, 1990), p. 41.

[22] Valery Tishkov, "'Don't Kill Me, I'm a Kyrgyz!': An Anthropological Analysis of Violence in the Osh Ethnic Conflict," *Journal of Peace Research*, vol. 32, no. 2 (1995), p. 133.

In this sense, the character of Soviet ethnofederalism undoubtedly had an important impact in shaping the contours and dynamics of nationalist violence. It provided access to the state at the local level for eponymous ethnic groups – a factor which, as we will see, proved critical to the eventual production of violence. The inclusion of a variable controlling for the effects of a group having a union republican ethnofederal unit did improve slightly the accuracy by which outcomes were predicted, though it lowered the overall fit of the model. But here also, it is difficult to establish any systematic effects, especially given the close relationship between federal structure and population size. In the literature addressing cross-national variations in violence, the connection between population size and the frequency of violent events is well established even outside an ethnofederal context. This relationship between violence and population size could be attributable simply to the probability that violence might occur within any given number of people, to the effects of international norms concerning self-determination in fostering ethnic mobilization, or to the power advantages which size endows. Thus, whatever influence ethnofederalism had on the overall frequency of violence in the former Soviet Union is impossible to separate from processes which naturally occur outside an ethnofederal context, from other factors closely associated with ethnofederalism, and from the effects of ethnofederalism on mobilization (violent and nonviolent) more generally.

The point is that mobilized nationalist violence is generally a less structured and less predictable phenomenon than nonviolent nationalist mobilization because its initiation and multiplication are even more dependent than nonviolent mobilization on the contingencies and prior outcomes of the mobilizational process itself. It is not that structure does not matter in the production of violence. Different structural elements may contribute to violent outcomes in individual situations but still not leave a systematic trace across multiple cases. Moreover, as we have seen, structure exercises similar systematic influences on both violent and nonviolent processes of mobilization. Thus, although the conflict out of which violence emerges may be heavily structured by the past, the specific outcome of violence is not. Rather, nationalist violence unfolds out of conflict and is contingent and dependent on what takes place within conflictual situations. It is obvious that a more contextualized understanding of nationalist violence becomes necessary – one focused on how action within conflictual situations moves conflict toward violent results.

## Tides, the Institutionalization of Mobilization, and Nationalist Violence

This leads us to the question of why conflict should evolve into violence in some situations but not others. As we turn to more contextually sensitive modes of analysis, one of the conditions associated with triggering and intensifying nationalist violence becomes strikingly clear: the role played by shifting authority within state institutions, often itself the result of prior waves of mobilization. Figure 6.1 details the distribution over time for 2,173 mass violent events during the 1987–92 period for which information was available. As it shows, the most conspicuous leap in mass violence in the former Soviet Union occurred in the wake of the August 1991 coup and with the breakup of the Soviet Union, when the frequency of mass violent events increased exponentially, doubling by December 1991 and more than tripling by April 1992. But well before the waves of violence unleashed by the breakup of the USSR, a significant leap in mass violence had occurred in mid-1989, with violence gradually rising over the first half of 1990 and leveling off at a stable but high level until the explosions unleashed by the August 1991 coup. The vast majority of the mass violent events throughout this period were ethnonationalist in character. Although it is true that violent events over other issues also rose in the

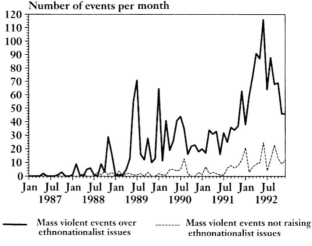

**Figure 6.1** Frequency of mass violent events in the former Soviet Union, 1987–92.

aftermath of the collapse of the Soviet state, they did not rise at any-where near the pace exhibited by ethnonationalist violence. Overall, mass violence was concentrated in the latter part of the mobilizational cycle, spilling over into the post-Soviet period and proliferating with great rapidity.

Not only did mass violence grow more frequent over the course of the cycle. It also grew more intense in terms of human and property damage. Figure 6.2 breaks mass violent events into low-intensity (five or fewer com-bined injuries or deaths), medium-intensity (six to fifteen injuries or deaths), and high-intensity (sixteen or more injuries or deaths) violence.[23] Nationalist mass violence began in early 1988 with a small number of rel-atively high-intensity events. The spread of violence in 1989 was mostly an explosion of low-level violence, but in 1990 medium-intensity violence grew significantly. High-intensity violence mushroomed after the breakup of the USSR.

The "rear-packed" temporal location of violent mobilization relative to nonviolent mobilization provides us with a conspicuous clue as to the dynamics triggering large-scale violent action. As we saw in Chapters 2 and 3, the period from mid-1989 through mid-1990, when violence first accelerated, was the very time when participation in nonviolent demonstrations began to decline sharply due to the institutionalization of nationalist contention within state institutions. Similarly, the exponential increase in violence that occurred after the collapse of the USSR followed the institutionalizing moments of August and December 1991. In this respect, the record of violent mass mobilization in the Soviet Union par-allels patterns of violent mobilization within other mobilizational cycles. As Della Porta and Tarrow noted in their study of political violence in Italy, in general within a cycle of mobilization "as mass mobilization winds down, political violence rises in magnitude and intensity."[24] Thus, the explosion of nationalist violence that occurred in the USSR might be rightly viewed as part of a phase within mobilizational cycles in which mobilization turns increasingly violent due to the political implications of the institutionalization of prior waves of mobilization.

---

[23] If no information on the number of human casualties was available, information on damage to property was used instead as a basis for classifying events.
[24] Donatella Della Porta and Sidney Tarrow, "Unwanted Children: Political Violence and the Cycle of Protest in Italy, 1966–1973," *European Journal of Political Research*, vol. 14 (1986), pp. 607–32.

## a. Low-intensity events (5 or fewer injuries or deaths)

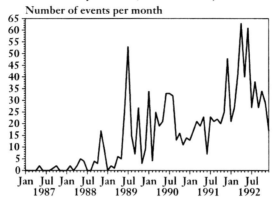

## b. Medium-intensity events (6-15 injuries or deaths)

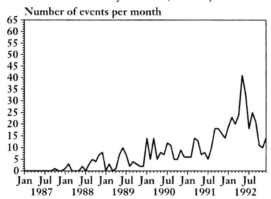

## c. High-intensity events (16 or more injuries or deaths)

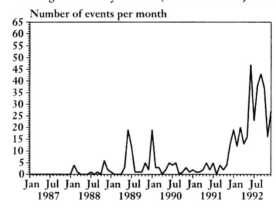

**Figure 6.2**    Intensity of mass violent events in the former USSR, 1987–92.

Della Porta and Tarrow explained the rear-packed location of violence within the Italian mobilizational cycle by reference to the growth of competition and differentiation within the social movement sector, the declining ability of movements to mobilize mass followings, and a growing demand for public order on the part of authorities. In a climate of demobilization, they argue, political violence becomes the only form of serious disruption possible, particularly for small competing groups that emerge as the social movement sector expands over the course of a cycle. There is little evidence that the sharp rise in the frequency and intensity of violence in the former Soviet Union in 1989–90 and at the end of 1991 can be traced to heightened competition by smaller factions within the social movement sector. In many cases violence was organized by mainstream nationalist movements or paramilitary groups loosely attached to them, and by the latter part of the mobilizational cycle governments themselves were playing an increasing role in the organization of nationalist violence.

A second critical clue for why violence multiplied is the fact that most of the violence was connected with a particular type of issue: the definition of interrepublican borders. As Figure 6.3a indicates, violence aimed at redefining or at preventing redefinition of interrepublican borders rose significantly in 1989–90, increasing exponentially in 1991–92 and largely accounting for the concentration of mass violence in the latter portion of the mobilizational cycle. By contrast, in spite of the widespread belief among experts that the breakup of the USSR would evoke a violent struggle between supporters and opponents of the Soviet order, violence by secessionist movements seeking to exit the USSR or by those seeking to prevent exit from the USSR (6.3d) remained minimal and almost entirely confined to the 1990–91 period.[25] For the most part, the issue of secession from the USSR was contested by supporters and opponents through non-violent means – even by nationalist movements that perpetrated significant violence over the issue of defining interrepublican boundaries. Georgian, Armenian, and Azerbaijani nationalist movements, for instance, while fomenting massive levels of violence over the definition of the borders of their respective republics, generally did not contest the issue of secession from the USSR through violence.[26] Although in a number of

---

[25] Violent mobilizations over other ethnonationalist issues were sporadic, bursting forth in the summer of 1989 and once again in the summer of 1990, but otherwise accounting for a small amount of the overall violence during this period.

[26] The Azerbaijani insurrection of December 1989–January 1990 stands out as an important exception.

288

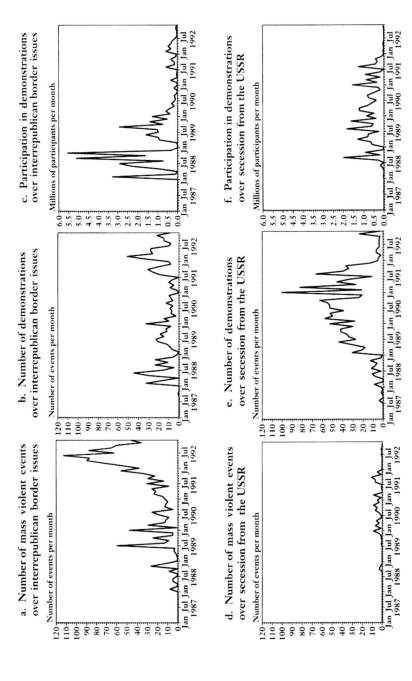

**Figure 6.3** A comparison of patterns of violent and nonviolent mobilization over interrepublican border issues and over secession from the USSR, 1987–92.

cases the Soviet regime violently repressed those agitating for secession from the USSR, in general these acts of repression did not precipitate retaliatory waves of violence – in sharp contrast to the way in which violence against those seeking alterations in interrepublican boundaries resulted in a growing spiral of retaliation. Even if we include government repression against demonstrations within our definition of violent events, little changes in the overall picture of the concentration of violence within a single issue area. In short, if a culture of violence operated in the former Soviet Union, it was confined to a specific set of issues.

The relationship of institutionalization with temporal patterns of proliferation of violence and the segregation of violence by issue area point to a lurking strategic underpinning to much of the nationalist violence that overtook the USSR. The essence of that logic did not reside in the issues associated with violence per se, but rather in the targets of mobilization associated with these issues – specifically, the way in which targets shifted over time in response to the institutionalization of prior action within the cycle, the differing vulnerabilities and strengths of targets, and the capacity of violent and nonviolent modes of mobilization to address these vulnerabilities effectively.[27] During much of Soviet history, interrepublican borders were treated as a trifling nuisance within what was otherwise a hypercentralized state; on several occasions (and even as late as the mid-1970s) the authorities even hinted that they would do away with interrepublican borders altogether, although the expected reaction by non-Russians always held them in check. During the *glasnost'* mobilizational cycle, the shifts in authority resulting from early mobilizations within the cycle strengthened the significance of interrepublican borders by nationalizing republican governments, thereby threatening adversely territorially concentrated minorities within the republics. In 1988 minorities with federal subunits lower than a republic and minorities without a federal subunit hardly mobilized at all in favor of revising interrepublican borders. From 1989 on the frequency of nonviolent and violent mobilizations among these peoples over this issue increased significantly, with major eruptions of violence following waves of nonviolent mobilization. Shifts in authority at the republican level politicized groups such as the Abkhaz, Ossetians, and Gagauz, not to mention the Russophone minorities in a number of the non-Russian republics, to seek self-

---

[27] For similar arguments within the social movement literature, see William A. Gamson, *The Strategy of Social Protest* (Homewood, IL: Dorsey Press, 1975), p. 82.

protection in a revision of interrepublican borders. This in turn unleashed a reaction from nationalized republican governments seeking to prevent alterations in boundaries and to consolidate their control over their territories.

We know of many cases around the world in which secession has erupted into civil wars of enormous magnitude, while internal boundary change has occurred peacefully. Why did those who sought exit from the USSR contest the issue nonviolently, while those who sought to challenge internal boundaries were drawn more to violent mobilization? A critical reason for this is that over time a nonviolent politics surrounding interrepublican borders grew less and less possible. As Figure 6.3 shows, the issue of inter-republican borders was at first contested in a predominantly nonviolent fashion. In 1988 and 1989, there were massive nonviolent mobilizations over the issue of changing or preventing change in interrepublican borders, particularly in the Transcaucasus. These mobilizations accounted for 65 percent of the number of people participating in all nonviolent demonstrations during this period. But beginning in mid-1989, participation in nonviolent demonstrations over these issues declined precipitously, even though efforts to mobilize people continued apace. During the 1990–92 period nonviolent mobilization over these issues was only one-fifth of the level it had been in 1988–89 and accounted for only 19 percent of all participants in nonviolent demonstrations. Thus, the rise of violence in the USSR in significant part was associated with the decline of nonviolent mobilizations contesting interrepublican borders.

This shift makes sense in strategic terms if we understand against whom the mobilizations were directed. For the most part, conflicts over interrepublican borders in 1988 and early 1989 were targeted against the USSR authorities and one's own republican or local government, seeking to force them to engage in policies aimed at bringing about a revision or maintenance of borders. These predominantly nonviolent mobilizations were particularly effective in undermining or coopting republican and local party elites and were of great concern to the USSR authorities. By mid-1989 the USSR government had repeatedly shown itself unwilling to consider any alteration of interrepublican borders or to defend effectively their inviolability. As we saw earlier, the Soviet leadership viewed internal boundary change through the prism of a "domino theory," fearing the encouragement one boundary change might give to other groups seeking to challenge boundaries.[28] Ironically, there had been regular border adjustments among republics in the Stalin and Khrushchev periods; between 1930 and 1970 thirty border changes were effected among the federal units of the USSR, including the transfer of Crimea from the Russian Federation to Ukraine. Even more extensive boundary manipulation occurred in the first decade of Soviet power. But during the Brezhnev period a discursive frame that essentially froze internal boundaries became ensconced. The Gorbachev leadership unanimously defended this policy, even after it was evident, as former Prime Minister Nikolai Ryzhkov wrote in his memoirs, that "the fire of the conflict would not die down"[29] and that the old frame had been transcended by developments on the ground. By making itself invulnerable to a nonviolent politics over internal borders, the USSR government undermined the possibilities for a nonviolent outcome over these issues and unwittingly channeled mobilization over interrepublican boundaries in a violent direction. This is not to say that violence might not have emerged in any case. Rather, the point is that the Gorbachev regime left little space for alternatives to violence to flourish.

At the same time, in 1988 and 1989, under pressure from the street, local and republican governments coopted these issues, in many cases openly supporting the positions of nationalist movements. As the logic of this situation began to sink in, the sense of mobilizing against the center or one's own republican or local government to seek change in interrepublican boundaries dissipated: The USSR government refused to review internal boundaries, and local and republican governments generally supported the boundary alterations being pushed by the nationalist movements of their eponymous group. Instead, mobilization was increasingly targeted against the opposing republic, local government, and ethnic group which supported or challenged existing boundaries. Most nonviolent forms of mobilization, however, were ineffective means for bargaining with other republics, local governments, and ethnic groups at a time when these populations were often equally mobilized over the issue and

<hr>

[28] On the decision taken in early 1988 not to consider any alterations in interrepublican borders, see Yegor Ligachev, *Inside Gorbachev's Kremlin* (New York: Pantheon Books, 1993), p. 172. As Ligachev reports, the Politburo in February 1988 reached the "unanimous and correct decision" that "it was impermissible to redraw national and territorial borders at that time. To violate that principle even once would open up a path for a multitude of bloody conflicts."

[29] Nikolai Ryzhkov, *Perestroika: istoriia predatel'stv* (Moscow: Novosti, 1992), pp. 203–4.

where the disruptive effects of mobilization were little felt. Armenians simply did not care whether Azerbaijanis in Azerbaijan went on a general strike for a month. A general strike in Azerbaijan had little effect on Armenians in Azerbaijan or Armenia or on the Armenian government (though the railroad blockades of 1990–91 did, since they cut off key supply routes to the republic). The ineffectiveness of nonviolent means of addressing problems thus increased the attraction to violence as a tool for contesting interrepublican borders, since, unlike nonviolent mobilization, violence could be directed against the vulnerabilities of these new targets (their ethnic compatriots living in proximity to the perpetrators) and potentially could alter radically the situation on the ground. As one group of Soviet specialists involved in containing mass disorders later noted, in most cases violent disturbances "began with what at first glance appeared to be peaceful meetings and demonstrations,"[30] but only subsequently shifted toward violence. This is not to say that the same segments of the population necessarily participated in both violent and nonviolent acts. Compared to participation in nonviolent demonstrations, where a disproportionate number of participants were recruited from the intelligentsia, participants in violent political action tended to be recruited disproportionately (though not exclusively) from the lower-middle stratum of society. The changing sense of possibilities and constraints associated with a shifting set of mobilizational targets undermined the basis for mobilization among one set of political entrepreneurs and enhanced it for another.

By contrast, mobilization in pursuit of secession from the USSR (which, not surprisingly, tended to focus on a single target – the USSR government) was overwhelmingly nonviolent during this period. Throughout these years the USSR government remained highly vulnerable to nonviolent forms of contention such as demonstrations and strikes. By vulnerability, I mean only that Soviet central elites cared a great deal about the disruptions caused by nonviolent forms of contention, and this was understood by those who challenged the state. Strikes and demonstrations interfered with the achievement of highly prized economic goals of the Soviet government. They punctured legitimating myths of the Soviet regime, such as the claim that it had "solved" the nationalities problem or represented the interests of "toilers." Even if they were located thousands of miles away from Moscow, demonstrations and strikes violated longstand-

[30] V. N. Grigor'ev and Yu. D. Rogov, *Fenomeny "perestroiki": Chrezvychainoe polozhenie* (Moscow: Verdikt, 1994), p. 41.

ing norms of behavior in Soviet politics, flaunted the weakness of the Soviet state by laying bare its inability to repress them, and created tensions within governing circles over how to deal with them. In a number of cases the Soviet regime was deeply involved in fomenting violent mobilization by groups seeking to separate from republics whose governments were themselves seeking secession. The hope was to utilize these conflicts to pressure republican governments to remain in the union. The Soviet government chose to deploy violence over the issue of interrepublican boundaries rather than to contest secession directly with violence (as Stalin so brutally had done in the late 1940s), hoping that republics seeking exit from the USSR would be driven back into the fold by the threat of territorial dismemberment.

At the same time, given the overwhelming concentration of coercive power in the hands of the Soviet government, violence targeted against it could only have been seen as a failing strategy, a perception reinforced by the bloody suppression of the Baku revolution in January 1990 (the one time after the Tbilisi massacres of April 1989 in which the Soviet regime did deploy massive force against secessionists, who were themselves attempting to press secession through a violent insurrection). This is not to say that violent entrepreneurs did not emerge over both sides of the issue of secession. In almost every context in which a secessionist politics emerged, so too did some degree of violence, but in most cases it remained marginalized and limited in scope, because the Soviet government hesitated to support violent entrepreneurs directly contesting secession and the effectiveness of the nonviolent tactics pursued by nationalist movements in support of secession in most cases marginalized proponents of violence within their ranks. Thus, in the Soviet case, in sharp contrast to many other cases of secession around the world which came to be disputed violently, violence was not a central part of the secession story. It was, however, a major part of the narrative of the post-Soviet transition and the consolidation of aspiring successor states.

## The State and the Origin of Waves of Nationalist Violence

So far, the argument has been confined to the countrywide level, explaining trends in overall patterns of violent and nonviolent nationalist mobilization. I now descend to the level of the event itself to understand what takes place to move violence from the unimaginable to the widely imagined.

As the above discussion points out, waves of mobilized nationalist violence in the former Soviet Union were usually initiated within an embedded milieu of intergroup competition. We have also seen that violence emerged within a context of shifting political authority. Both of these conditions, however, were associated as well with nonviolent mobilization and must therefore be considered necessary but insufficient for the emergence of large-scale violence. But, as the above discussion also implied, what was critical for switching mobilization onto the tracks of violence was the way in which entrepreneurs of violence were empowered relative to entrepreneurs of nonviolence – in part by the nationalization of local and republican governments and the ways in which opportunities to resolve issues nonviolently were structured.

Mobilized nationalist violence usually took place within a larger social setting in which the propensity for violent solutions to problems emerged more broadly than among those individuals who directly participated in violent action. Within a compressed period of time, the world of social norms was inverted, and violent action came to be considered "normal" by many where it once was considered taboo. The focus of explanation thus needs to be shifted to elicit those cultural, social, or political circumstances that advantaged entrepreneurs of violence and caused "ordinary" individuals to commit what, in times of normality, would have been considered the most "unordinary" of crimes. Mobilized nationalist violence is widely known as a fairly gruesome form of violence, in which neighbor violates neighbor and the sadistic instincts of individuals can come to the fore. Victims are not merely harmed or killed in a struggle for control over boundaries. Their bodies are mutilated; they are often tortured, taunted, and humiliated before being murdered; violence is focused against the person for what he or she represents rather than for what he or she has done. These acts do not aim merely to kill the physical body of the victim, but to engage in symbolic acts of desecration that demonstrate authority over boundaries through domination over bodies and the utter humiliation this produces. It is not unusual (particularly in pogrom violence) for women of all ages to be paraded naked before crowds, for victims to have ears, heels, nostrils, fingers, or limbs sliced, or even to be burned alive. Mocking of victims by crowds is common. Through such gross acts of dehumanization, perpetrators attempt to demonstrate symbolically their affirmation or rejection of the patterns of dominance under contestation.

What is more, this is violence which enjoys a significant degree of public support. One survivor of the Sumgait pogroms, at the time of the pogroms seven months pregnant, recounted how her attempts to escape a pursuing crowd were frustrated by her neighbors:

We lived on the second floor. We needed to cross over from our balcony to our neighbor's. . . . The balcony looked onto the street. At that time people were coming home from work, and many just stood there watching. I pleaded and begged: "Please, call someone, have someone come!" I even started shouting, "I'll throw down the children, . . . you catch them and take them somewhere, so at least the children will survive." Either they were afraid or . . . I don't know what. They looked as though they were watching a movie. Some of them started throwing stones at us. . . . [T]hese weren't the bandits, these were people from the other part of the building and from our entryway, they were just regular people, passersby.[31]

Even taking the diversity of motives underlying violent action into account, there is overwhelming evidence that violent orientations are much more widely shared in these microcontexts than simply among those who directly carry out violent acts. Indeed, who constitutes the participants in mobilized nationalist violence is subject to interpretation, since the range of behaviors involved is so great. In addition to many shades of direct participation, there are also multiple forms of indirect participation (such as verbal encouragement, driving participants to the scene of the violence, identification of potential victims, and so forth). At times neighbors do intervene to save neighbors. However, direct participants in violence usually attempt to intimidate and victimize those who sympathize with their intended victims, hide them, or in some way aid them, creating strong disincentives for those who reject violence to become involved. Those who do so anyway display extraordinary bravery in the face of considerable risk to their lives. Both those who participate directly in violent mobilization and those who attempt to protect victims are almost always minorities within their communities. The vast majority of inhabitants stay on the sidelines, though it is clear from descriptions that even among them a significant number sympathize with the perpetrators rather than the victims. In the Sumgait pogroms a female Azerbaijani doctor treating an Armenian female victim who had been raped, brutally beaten, and was covered with blood (the doctor shortly before had delivered the victim's infant niece) minimized the victim's wounds, telling her that "your people have been doing even worse things." Azerbaijani nurses treating victims in some cases told them that it would be proper to eliminate all Armenians, teased them that they might medically mistreat them, and directed them to go to

[31] Shahmuratian, ed., *The Sumgait Tragedy*, p. 319.

Yerevan for care.[32] Even the Hippocratic oath could not withstand the awful pull of sectarian violence.

Obviously, such inversions of public norms did not materialize out of thin air; contributory discourses of violence were prevalent and sub rosa well before the onset of violence.[33] But a specific chain of events became the occasion for their magnification and eruption into the public sphere. An important part of the explanation for this centers around the sense of license which the perpetrators felt – in particular from the cues and signals about violence emanating from government institutions. Certain practices and cues imparted a sense of empowerment among entrepreneurs of violence and made it appear to some segments of the public that even the state supported attempts to redress cultural differences through violent means, or that it would implicitly tolerate such attempts. Moreover, in some cases these perceptions of government support for violence were essentially correct – that is, government itself, in an attempt to consolidate its authority against groups challenging it, sanctioned the use of violence by societal members as a means for contesting boundaries. As we will see further below, what distinguishes conflicts in which nationalist violence grows sustained from those in which it does not is the role eventually played by the state as coordinator of nationalist violence. This role becomes possible in part because the state usually does play some part in the precipitation of violent mobilization in the first place.

The events which set off the Azerbaijani-Armenian conflict in 1988 provide a case in point. There is little doubt that an atmosphere of mistrust remained beneath the surface of interpersonal relations between Armenians and Azerbaijanis throughout the Soviet period,[34] largely the residue of earlier tides of nationalist contention. Major waves of violence broke out between Azerbaijanis and Armenians in 1905, 1918, 1920, and 1922. As we saw in Chapter 2, when borders were drawn in 1921, large minorities of both groups were located inside the titular republic of the other, with Karabakh Armenians being given their own autonomous province. Tension between Armenians and Azerbaijanis remained

---

[32] Shahmuratian, ed., *The Sumgait Tragedy*, pp. 39, 99, 131, 277.

[33] On this point, see Brass, *Theft of an Idol*.

[34] Victims of the Sumgait massacres report the anti-Armenian expressions that had circulated at some workplaces and neighborhoods for many years before the February 1988 events, and one longtime Russian resident of the town speaks of the "atmosphere of animosity, to put it mildly," that existed toward the Armenians throughout the twenty-six years she worked there. See Shahmuratian, ed., *The Sumgait Tragedy*, pp. 165, 247, 263.

throughout the Soviet period, with occasional reports of open friction. Karabakh Armenians constantly complained that they were being discriminated against in terms of economic investment and access to Armenian-language media. Minor outbreaks of interethnic violence occurred in Karabakh in 1963, 1968, and 1987, but for the most part Armenian demands were pressed peacefully, through petitions, letter-writing campaigns, and even occasional demonstrations.[35] Most Azerbaijanis and Armenians in Azerbaijan lived and worked together peacefully. As one Azerbaijani journalist later noted in October 1993, "No matter where you go and whom you meet in Azerbaijan, whenever you bring up the subject of war, the majority of Azerbaijanis will pause and reflect, 'Armenians used to be our friends.'"[36]

But public norms of interethnic cooperation were undermined in a matter of days in February 1988. As we saw in Chapter 2, a peaceful campaign to shift Karabakh to Armenian control emerged in 1987. In mid-February 1988 mass rallies and meetings erupted in Stepanakert, leading the local legislature to vote on February 20 to petition for transfer of the territory from Azerbaijan to Armenia, triggering further enormous rallies in Yerevan in support of the boundary change. On February 22 anti-Armenian pogroms broke out in the town of Gadrut in Nagorno-Karabakh, injuring sixteen and killing two.[37] Shortly thereafter, clashes occurred between Armenians and Azerbaijanis in the district of Askeran, where angry Azerbaijani mobs attempted to march on Stepanakert. When police, backed up by local Armenians, stopped the crowd, fifty people were wounded and two died (one shot by an Azerbaijani policeman).[38] The Azerbaijani identity of the victims remained unknown until USSR Deputy General Procurator Aleksandr Katushev revealed their names on February 27 in a television interview. Although other events, including alleged pogroms over a year before in December 1986 against Azerbaijanis living in the Kafan region of Armenia, played key roles in kindling the violence,

---

[35] Ronald Grigor Suny, *Looking toward Ararat: Armenia in Modern History* (Bloomington, IN: Indiana University Press), pp. 194–95; *Glasnost'*, January 1989, p. 11; V. Ponomarev, *Obshchestvennye volneniia v SSSR: Ot XX s"ezda KPSS do smerti Brezhneva* (Moscow: Aziia, 1990), p. 6.

[36] Svetlana Turyalay, "We Used To Be – Friends," *Azerbaijan International* [internet edition], February 1994.

[37] *Vesti iz SSSR*, no. 4–1, 1988.

[38] Radio Liberty, *Report on the USSR*, July 7, 1989, p. 16; *The New York Times*, March 11, 1988.

the Katushev revelations are generally believed to have been the spark that ignited the Sumgait massacres. On February 26 anti-Armenian rallies had begun to gather on the central square of Sumgait. Indeed, since February 21, immediately after the decision by the Karabakh legislature to seek a revision of boundaries, news about a forthcoming anti-Armenian demonstration organized by Azerbaijani refugees from Kafan was being spread at workplaces in Sumgait.[39] In his subsequent investigation of the Sumgait massacres, Deputy General Procurator Katushev noted that the Sumgait events were "connected in the closest way with the events in Nagorno-Karabakh," which "inflamed the situation in Sumgait" and allowed organizers to "make use of the extremely tense atmosphere."[40] As one survivor recalled the mood in the city on the eve of the killings, "At the bus stops, in the lines, everywhere people spoke only of Karabakh and the Armenians."[41]

A poor industrial suburb of Baku, Sumgait had been established in the 1940s by Azerbaijani refugees from Armenia. Housing was scarce, with thousands of recent arrivals living in makeshift shanties of cardboard, tin, and plywood on the edge of town. In late January and mid-February 1988 a large group of refugees from Kafan, apparently forced from their homes by local Armenian authorities, arrived in Sumgait and began to spread reports of atrocities committed against them.[42] By February 27 demonstrations had grown to "thousands" and were transformed into violent pogroms, with groups of fifty to two hundred people roaming the city in search of Armenian victims. This lasted for several days until order was finally restored by USSR troops. Sumgait was not the only city in Azerbaijan to be engulfed by anti-Armenian violence at the time. Similar but less intense events broke out in Baladzhary and Kirovabad, where

---

[39] As noted by a Georgian employee of the Sumgait Superphosphate Plant, in Shahmuratian, ed., *The Sumgait Tragedy*, p. 75.
[40] *FBIS*, August 23, 1988, p. 34.
[41] Shahmuratian, ed., *The Sumgait Tragedy*, pp. 204, 301.
[42] Audrey L. Altstadt, *The Azerbaijani Turks: Power and Identity under Russian Rule* (Stanford, CA: Hoover Institution Press, 1992), p. 197; *Ekspress khronika*, no. 9, February 26, 1991, p. 5. According to this latter source, about four thousand people fled Kafan at the time. What actually occurred in Kafan is an aspect of the Sumgait tragedy that remains clouded in mystery. It went unreported in both the official and unofficial press. Orators on the central square in Sumgait and participants in the pogroms claimed that Armenians in Kafan entered a dormitory for Azerbaijani girls and raped the residents. But this is disputed by Armenian sources, which claim that this was a fabrication spread by refugees to inflame the population.

martial law also had to be imposed.[43] In a context of shifting authority and ambiguous signals coming from political institutions, the microclimate of Sumgait became a conducive atmosphere for large-scale violence, providing an opportunity to exact revenge against Armenians by the Kafan Azerbaijanis, and for Azerbaijanis more generally to vent outrage over recent indignities. This is not to argue that all (or even a majority) of Azerbaijani inhabitants of Sumgait sympathized with the perpetrators of violence. Many Azerbaijani neighbors hid Armenians from rampaging mobs, and Azerbaijani soldiers entering the city were shocked by what they found. Nevertheless, violence was generalized to the point that it penetrated even within local political institutions. Local politicians found that they could not easily ignore the militant mood of the population.

One of the interesting aspects of the Sumgait events – and one typical of waves of mobilized nationalist violence in the former Soviet Union – was the ambiguous and even in some senses sympathetic role played by local authorities in the massacres. The 850-strong local police force disappeared entirely from the streets and refused to answer calls from frantic Armenians begging for protection. In a number of cases in which victims came across police and appealed to them for help, the police actually ran in the other direction. Video recordings of the events show that the militia stood by and watched the violence, making no effort to intervene. In a few cases police actually participated in looting Armenian apartments.[44] Regular soldiers and police units from Dagestan and Bashkiria had to be brought in to quell the disturbances because of the unreliability of local law enforcement organizations. Firefighters and ambulances refused to answer calls, and phone service was cut from Armenian apartments. The city Communist Party committee apparently helped to mobilize people to attend the anti-Armenian demonstration on February 27, which had among its audience a significant number of Party, Komsomol, and even Pioneer members.[45] The second secretary of the city party organization addressed the demonstration, attempting to cool passions but calling for the Armenians to "leave Azerbaijani soil freely." The first secretary also arrived and sat quietly through speeches calling for violent revenge against

---

[43] *Vesti iz SSSR*, no. 4–1, 1988; no. 5/6–1, 1988.

[44] Shahmuratian, ed., *The Sumgait Tragedy*, pp. 38, 45, 56, 86, 179–80, 224, 240, 261. See also material from the trials of participants, cited in *Moscow News*, no. 46, November 20–27, 1988, p. 12; no. 47, November 27–December 4, 1988, p. 15.

[45] Shahmuratian, ed., *The Sumgait Tragedy*, pp. 142–43, 318.

the Armenians. According to one eyewitness, the first secretary's presence and speech (in which he also called for allowing Armenians to leave the city freely) "only incited the crowd." As the bystander explained, "they had probably expected him to shut down the demonstration, which he didn't do. . . . I realized that the Azerbaijanis were afraid that would happen. And by trying to placate the crowd, . . . he merely further incited them." When the demonstration set off down the street, the communist boss of the city was at the head of the crowd. According to the party first secretary, he joined the crowd to cool their passions by surreptitiously leading them away from the center of the city, but at a certain point in time the crowd stopped following him and began searching for Armenian victims. Nevertheless, the impression given to participants was clearly one of sympathy with their violent demands. This contrasts with the first secretary's behavior the day before, when, according to one eyewitness, he met with the demonstrators from Kafan (then numbering only a few hundred), and told them explicitly that there was to be "no verbal abuse."[46] In short, state officials prevaricated. They sent signals that could easily be interpreted as sanctioning violence, and some parts of the state did give active support to anti-Armenian violence.

The ways in which a chain of events crystallized a violent mood within a significant segment of the population and local authorities encouraged violence through the cues and signals they sent were also salient features of the outbreak of nationalist violence in Abkhazia. We explored the historical roots underlying the Abkhaz-Georgian conflict in Chapter 5. That conflict was longstanding and took on a separatist character well before *glasnost'*. After the events of 1978, when Abkhaz demonstrations against "Georgianization" had raised the possibility of separation from Georgia, the Georgian Communist Party decreed the opening of an Abkhaz State University in Sukhumi as a concession to the Abkhaz.[47] However, in April 1981 several hundred Georgian students from Sukhumi conducted a demonstration in Tbilisi, complaining that the rights of Georgians in Abkhazia were being infringed and demanding the creation of a

---

[46] Shahmuratian, ed., *The Sumgait Tragedy*, pp. 77–78, 165–66, 221, 258, 299–300. One victim claims that the first secretary or someone in his office actually sent a crowd after him after the victim called the local party organization and appealed to the first secretary for help over the phone (pp. 185–86).

[47] See Darrell Slider, "Crisis and Response in Soviet Nationality Policy: The Case of Abkhazia," *Central Asian Survey*, vol. 4, no. 4, 1985, pp. 51–68.

Georgian-language university in Sukhumi[48] – a demand the authorities refused to meet. As we saw earlier, Abkhaz separatism began to heat up after the massive waves of Georgian mobilization in November 1988. On March 18, 1989 thousands of Abkhaz gathered in the village of Lykhnyi to call for separation from Georgia, a demand supported by the local communist leadership. Georgians living in Abkhazia mobilized in demonstrations against the Lykhnyi declaration, and when a bus carrying demonstrators from Tbilisi to these meetings was attacked by a group of Abkhaz on April 1, injuring ten, the event prompted an enormous wave of mobilization in Georgia, leading to the intervention of troops and ultimately to the April 9 Tbilisi massacres. Subsequently, local police and prosecutorial officials were accused of failing to investigate the Abkhaz disturbances properly, with several officials losing their jobs as a result.[49] For self-protection, some Georgian inhabitants of Abkhazia were already arming themselves with hunting rifles.

At the end of April 1989 twelve hundred Georgian students and three hundred Georgian instructors from Abkhaz State University announced they were leaving the university to set up a rival Georgian-language affiliate of Tbilisi University in Sukhumi. Unlike the response of the Georgian government eight years earlier, this time the request was quickly approved in May by a decree of the Georgian Council of Ministers. When Abkhaz complaints reached Moscow, a commission of the USSR Supreme Soviet examined the issue, advising the Georgian government not to establish the university affiliate for fear it would provoke a confrontation. Nevertheless, the Georgian side, now keen to display its autonomy from Moscow in the wake of the Tbilisi massacres and to demonstrate its control over Abkhazia, continued with its plans to hold entrance examinations to the new university on July 16. Local Georgians in Abkhazia even demanded that a formal rebuttal by the Georgian government to the Supreme Soviet commission be published in the Georgian-language newspaper in Sukhumi.[50]

Once again, the role played by local authorities in signaling acquiescence toward violence was key in sparking disorder. In addition to the signals encouraging confrontation noted above, in Sukhumi on July 12

[48] Ponomarev, *Obshchestvennye volneniia v SSSR*, p. 8.
[49] *Zaria vostoka*, in *FBIS*, June 7, 1989, p. 45.
[50] *Atmoda*, November 13, 1989, pp. 4–5.

Abkhaz authorities looked the other way while crowds of armed Abkhaz militants from the Popular Forum surrounded the building of the local Georgian-language newspaper, forcing it to shut down before a rebuttal to the Supreme Soviet commission's report could be published. Two days later, police ignored calls from desperate employees of the newly established Sukhumi branch of Tbilisi State University, where crowds of armed Abkhaz had surrounded their building and threatened to storm it; according to one account, the police even cut off the telephone connection and water supply to the building. That same night, several leading Abkhaz officials from the local party organization and government met with the armed extremists, but no measures were taken to break up the crowd. Rather, on the morning of July 15, police of Georgian nationality guarding the university building were removed from the area and replaced with police of Abkhaz nationality (dressed in white parade uniform shirts, to distinguish them from their gray-shirted Georgian colleagues). A police unit sent to Sukhumi from Tbilisi to help restore order was disarmed without intervention by the local police.[51] Reports circulated among local Abkhaz that USSR Minister of Education Yagodin had issued a decree forbidding the opening of a second university in Sukhumi, and groups of Abkhaz began to gather on the main square in anticipation of local party first secretary Vladimir Khishba's announcement of the decree.[52] At this point, the chain of events grows murky; Georgians claim that a group of armed Abkhaz fired on a peaceful Georgian demonstration in Rustaveli Park. Abkhaz claim that armed Abkhaz arrived on the scene only after several Abkhaz had been beaten by the Georgian crowd, which then produced arms and attacked the Abkhaz demonstration on the main square of the town.[53] Whichever version is true, the building of the Sukhumi affiliate of Tbilisi State University was stormed that evening by a crowd of five thousand Abkhaz, many of whom were armed. As *Izvestiia* later reported, the school was stormed "in spite of the close and, one would have thought, threatening proximity of the police forces of the autonomous republic."[54]

This set off open warfare between armed groups that soon encompassed the entire region, aided in part by the participation of local authorities in

---

[51] *Vestnik Gruzii*, no. 1, October 1989, pp. 13–14; *Atmoda*, November 13, 1989, pp. 4–5.
[52] *Yezhednevnaia glasnost'*, July 19, 1989.
[53] Compare *Yezhednevnaia glasnost'*, July 15, 1989 and *Atmoda*, November 13, 1989, pp. 4–5.
[54] *Izvestiia*, July 20, 1989, p. 3.

both Abkhazia and Western Georgia. Local police of Abkhaz nationality shot at unarmed Georgians, militia helicopters were used to transport Abkhaz combatants,[55] and the heads of the Ochamchira district procuracy office and the local militia led crowds directly to hidden stores of weapons and openly handed out Kalashnikovs to their compatriots (an act for which they were subsequently arrested and tried).[56] Many Georgians living in Abkhazia at the time had relatives in Western Georgia, where local police headquarters were "stormed" to obtain automatic weapons. But as USSR Minister of Internal Affairs Vadim Bakatin later noted, police in both Abkhazia and Western Georgia "offered very weak resistance to such raids," and "even facilitated them to some extent."[57]

The common strands running through these two cases are clear. Conflict was a longstanding assumption in each, and a series of precipitating events activated ethnic boundaries and crystallized violent orientations within a segment of society. But the state was not an innocent bystander to these conflicts. In almost every case of major mass violence in the former USSR, the state played a significant role in either organizing violence directly or in sending sympathetic cues to those who did, providing a sense of license to violent entrepreneurs. In Moldova, for instance, Russophone and Gagauz militants operated directly under the guidance of local party officials and were supported by Moscow as part of a plan to prevent secession by playing the interrepublican boundary card. As Anatoly Luk'ianov told a Moldovan delegation at the time, if Moldova signed the union treaty "there will be one Moldovan republic; if not, there will be three."[58] The Gagauz and Russophone self-defense forces were supplied with weapons by the Soviet military, and General Gennadii Yakovlev, the commander of the Soviet Fourteenth Army, eventually became Minister of Defense of the Transdniestr Republic. The Moldovan side was no less coordinated by the state. The call to create a group of Moldovan "volunteers" to protect the territorial integrity of the republic was adopted as a decree by Prime Minister Mircea Druk, who sympathized with the more radically nationalist wing of the Moldovan Popular Front. OMON troops subordinate to the republican government accompanied the "volunteers"

---

[55] *Atmoda*, November 13, 1989, pp. 4–5.
[56] *Vestnik Gruzii*, no. 1, October 1989, p. 15; TASS, in *FBIS*, August 8, 1990, p. 89.
[57] Moscow Domestic Service, in *FBIS*, July 19, 1989, p. 87.
[58] Quoted in Stuart Kaufman, "Russian Policy and Local Elites in Moldova's Civil War," paper presented at the annual convention of the American Association for the Advancement of Slavic Studies, October 1995, Washington, DC, p. 38.

and participated in the initial outbreak of violence.[59] In almost every case of major nationalist violence in the USSR during these years, police participation was axiomatic. Specialists from the MVD charged with investigating crimes committed during waves of mass unrest in Karabakh, Fergana, Osh, Baku, and Andizhan recall that very often "it was impossible to establish normal relations with employees of the local police, and even more to receive real help from them." Frequently "one met with not only a cold and guarded attitude, but even with open sabotage toward the activity of the investigating group, and often with opposition. . . . Among police employees there are nationalist-oriented people who openly sympathized with the perpetrators of pogroms and did not want to help expose them." Moreover, "in the depositions of victims appear the names of many police employees, who, according to the victims, sat together with the perpetrators of pogroms in cars, pointing out transport routes or houses that needed to be destroyed." The investigators found it necessary to hide the course of investigations from local police, even to the point of encoding documents. In one case in the Agdam district of Azerbaijan in fall 1988, local police removed evidence from the scene of the crime, tipped off nationalist groups as to the presence of the investigators, and stood by while two of the investigators were murdered. As one investigator, himself hurt during the incident, subsequently remarked, "These are not police, but just the opposite."[60]

By creating a hierarchy of groups in which smaller ethnoterritorial units were embedded inside larger ones, by consolidating ethnicities around these units, and by encouraging limited access to the state by ethnic groups, Soviet ethnofederalism inadvertently created the conditions for the explosion of violence that accompanied its breakup. Not that violence followed the lines of ethnofederal authority. Rather, ethnofederalism helped to foster violence by creating conditions in which state officials, in the chaotic and impassioned context of heightened contention, often sympathized with the aims of violent entrepreneurs within their populations or found it difficult to take a public stand against them. As authority shifted within the Soviet state, competition over defining the physical, human, and cultural boundaries of the state intensified, and the signals sent by local

[59] See Kaufman, "Russian Policy and Local Elites"; Pål Kolstø and Andrei Ekemsky, with Natalya Kalashnikova, "The Dniester Conflict: Between Irredentism and Separatism," *Europe-Asia Studies*, vol. 45, no. 6 (1993), pp. 973–1000.

[60] Grigor'ev and Rogov, *Fenomeny "perestroiki": Chrezvychainoe polozhenie*, pp. 143–45.

authority frequently gave the impression of support for the aims of those contesting the nation (and, in many cases, even for the use of violence as a means for doing so). Indeed, in a number of cases the state directly organized violence for these purposes.

Of course, once initiated, violence took on a dynamic of its own, feeding on the victimization it created. But as these cases demonstrate, it is not difficult to see how portions of the state might have assumed an interest in the ongoing production of nationalist violence, for as we have seen, the state at some level was usually involved in the rise of violent mobilization in the first place.

## From Mobilized to Organized and Sustained Violence

Waves of nationalist violence usually assume multiple forms, and each form represents a specific type of social relationship between the subjects and objects of action and the extent to which violence is integrated into a normalized social order. The differences among these acts are not merely a matter of the arbitrary or self-interested coding of violence. The vocabulary used to describe them reflects presumed differences in power relationships, in the targets and purposes of violence, and in the actors involved. In Figure 6.4 I provide a representation of many of the common forms nationalist violence assumes, classified by the degree to which state agents are typically involved and the extent to which they are mobilizationally or organizationally based.

If we think about violent nationalist action in terms of subject-object relationships, three broad families emerge. One set of actions – what might be called acts of dominant aggression – are typically perpetrated by members of dominant groups or the state against members of subordinate groups (pogroms, genocide, forced expulsion or "ethnic cleansing," vigilante violence, and state-sponsored terror). These acts tend to be planned and executed by (or at a minimum, encouraged by) state authority. They differ primarily in their scope, degree of organization, and the extent to which state authority is involved. Another set of violent nationalist acts – acts of national rebellion – are perpetrated by members of subordinate groups vis-à-vis members of dominant groups or the state (ethnic riots, terrorist action, and national insurrections). In these cases, nationalist violence and revolution share a certain kinship, and revolutionary analogies abound in the discourse of participants. These acts of violence share a common vocabulary because they share similar targets – the state and the

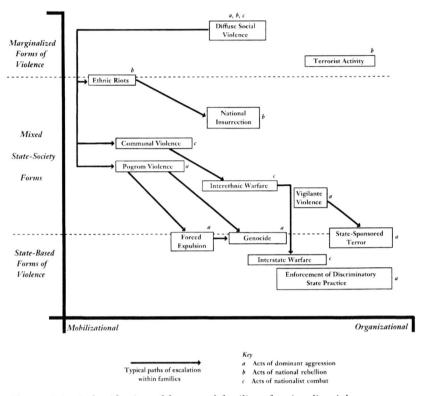

**Figure 6.4** A classification of forms and families of nationalist violence.

dominant cultural interests that underlie it. They diverge from one another primarily in their scope and degree of organization. A third set consists of acts of nationalist combat (communal violence, interethnic warfare, and interstate warfare) that necessarily involve two groups of perpetrators seeking to inflict damage on each other. Within each of these sets acts are related to one another in terms of similar subjects and objects of violence. In Figure 6.4 I sketch out some typical paths of escalation by which violence grows more intense and broader in scope within these families (a violent act within one family can incite violent acts within another as well). In general, the escalation of violence tends to involve greater degrees of organization, particularly as short-term mobilizational acts grow into sustained modes of violent action.

One of the interesting yet infrequently asked questions about nationalist violence is why it assumes the forms it does. For if we understand the forms which violence assumes as expressing subject-object relationships, then shifts in the forms of violence must logically be linked to underlying changes in authority relations and the nature of nationalist contention more generally. The forms assumed by nationalist violence are often sharply differentiated by time period, country, and even world region, pointing to distinctive repertoires of violence shaped by larger patterns of authority. One of the conspicuous features of the violence unleashed within the *glasnost'* mobilizational cycle (and one which distinguished it sharply from the Italian mobilizational cycle described by Tarrow) was the critical role forms of armed combat played within it. In the Italian mobilizational cycle, violence primarily took the form of marginalized terrorist activity, which grew in frequency as nonviolent mobilization wound down or became institutionalized in state structures. In the Soviet case the rise in violence in the latter part of the cycle did not take the form of terrorist actions. Rather, interethnic warfare came to predominate.

A closer examination shows that the forms assumed by nationalist violence evolved over the course of the cycle away from more mobilized forms of nationalist combat and toward more organized forms. Figure 6.5 details the evolution of the four most widespread forms of nationalist violence in the former Soviet Union: ethnic riots, communal violence, pogroms, and interethnic warfare.[61] These four categories account for 94 percent of the mass violent events in the former USSR during this period for which information was found. They include acts from all three families of nationalist violence: acts of dominant aggression, acts of national rebellion, and acts of national combat. As can be seen from Figure 6.5, within each type of nationalist violence more mobilized forms of violence (pogroms, riots, and communal violence) predominated in the 1988 and 1989 period. But beginning in late 1989 violent contestation evolved away from mobilized forms of violence and acts of dominant aggression or national rebellion

---

[61] I use the term pogrom to refer to mass-based mobilized violence by a dominant group against a subordinate group. As used in this study, a pogrom differed from genocide – a calculated and coordinated set of government policies aimed at the destruction of a culturally based group – largely by the degree to which it was coordinated by the state and the altered scale of action that this state coordination produces. I use the term ethnic riots for mobilized acts of violence by marginalized actors that were targeted against state institutions or collaborative social actors, distinguishing them from acts of terrorism, which are not mass-based or mobilized phenomena. I reserve the term communal violence for mass-based mobilized violence between members of two ethnic groups. By contrast, the term ethnic warfare describes protracted, armed combat between culturally based groups, differing from communal violence primarily in its duration and organization.

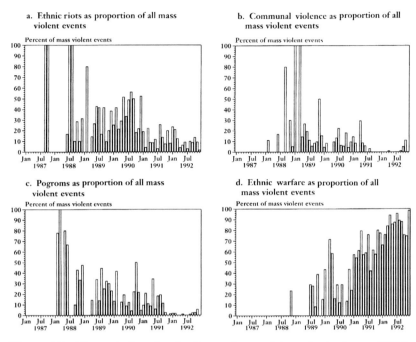

**Figure 6.5** The evolution of major forms of mass violence in the former USSR, 1987–92.

and toward more organized and sustained forms of nationalist combat – specifically, ethnic warfare. This shift occurred at the very time when the frequency of violence was growing at an unprecedented pace and nonviolent mobilization over the issues generating violence was rapidly decreasing. As one newspaper report about the Karabakh conflict noted in early 1992, "The meetings, strikes, and calls for peace long ago became an attribute of history; now everything is decided on the battlefield."[62] Eventually, with the breakup of the Soviet state nationalist mass violence shaded off into organized interstate warfare; where the line stood between the two was impossible to tell, much as it was difficult to draw the line between the paramilitary organizations carrying out many of these acts and the would-be states in whose name they were carried out.

Ethnic warfare emerged as the dominant form of nationalist violence largely as a result of the advantages which organization (public or private)

[62] *Ekspress khronika*, no. 6, February 4–11, 1992, p. 7.

provided in contesting interrepublican boundary issues – issues which, as we saw, contained within them a violence-generating logic. There was a moderately strong and statistically significant relationship (phi = +.57, significant at the .001 level)[63] between whether an act of violence concerned interrepublican borders and whether it assumed the form of ethnic warfare. In 82 percent of instances of mass violence in which interrepublican borders were not the issue of contention, violence did not assume the form of armed combat, whereas in 78 percent of cases in which interrepublican borders were the issue of violent contention, violence assumed the form of armed combat. The growing need for organization in the conduct of mass violence – resulting primarily from the sustained and unresolved nature of these conflicts – naturally pulled state authority (as well as numerous private entrepreneurs and criminals) into the production of nationalist violence.

In all, I have been able to identify thirty-two major waves of nationalist violence in the former USSR during the 1987–92 period, part of sixteen larger ethnonationalist conflicts involving violence during these years. Only in four of these conflicts (the Azerbaijani-Armenian conflict, the Georgian-Ossetian conflict, the Georgian-Abkhaz conflict, and the Moldovan-Transdniestr conflict) did violence become a self-sustaining strategy of contesting state boundaries, with relatively short waves of violence growing increasingly protracted over time.[64] In all other cases, violent mobilization remained short-lived. What distinguished conflicts in which mass violence grew sustained from those in which violence ceased to proliferate was the relationship of state institutions to the production of violence.

Normally, mobilized mass violence tends to be concentrated in short bursts and eruptions. Without sustained organization perpetrators find it difficult to maintain prolonged commitment to violent behaviors. Indeed, as eyewitness and participant descriptions of these events indicate, after a few days of mobilized violent acts (pogroms, communal violence, or ethnic riots) perpetrators are usually in a state of exhaustion, having had little sleep.[65] Moreover, in most cases state authority usually attempts to

---

[63] Phi is a measure of association (computed as chi-squared divided by n) used for measuring the strength of relationships in 2 × 2 contingency tables. Its value varies between −1 and +1.

[64] I am excluding here the Tajik civil war, which I do not categorize as nationalist violence per se. Also, in 1994 and 1995, after the time period analyzed here, the Chechen-Russian conflict grew into a sustained wave of violence.

[65] See Tishkov, "'Don't Kill Me, I'm a Kyrgyz,'" p. 138.

intervene in order to quell disturbances on its territory, as they violate the state's monopoly on the use of force, disrupt ongoing social life, and violate norms concerning violence. Clearly, mobilized acts of nationalist violence require organization. Informal leaders, often with connections to state authority at some level and usually cemented to followers through personal ties and bonds of charismatic authority, are conspicuous in their production. In the Osh valley violence in Kirgizia in 1990, for instance, perpetrators "were constantly asking for permission to execute a decisive act" from Ataman Tashaliev, a former Supreme Soviet deputy, who "issued commands that were followed with complete obedience."[66] The organizers of the Sumgait pogroms in Azerbaijan in February 1988 were recent refugees from the Kafan region of Armenia who had come to Sumgait looking for revenge for wrongs they had suffered among Armenians. Their most visible leader, an anonymous man dressed in an Eskimo dogskin coat and a mink hat, sat on the podium with local communist officials at the February 27 rally which unleashed the violence, claiming in his fiery speeches that his family and relatives had been victimized in Kafan and urging Azerbaijanis to take revenge. How and why this obviously well connected refugee was afforded a podium by the local party organization remains unclear. The same man later appeared leading mobs into action. According to one survivor, his entrance into the room "had such an impact on everyone that my neighbor's axe froze in the air. Everyone stood at attention for this guy, like soldiers in the presence of a general. Everyone waited for his word: continue the atrocities or not."[67] On the eve of the Sumgait massacres, a secretary was paid to compile lists of Armenian employees of certain institutions and their addresses, allowing the crowds to identify their victims with ease.[68] Emissaries were sent to factories, announcing to workers that "Everyone who wants to kill Armenians [should] come to the bus station on Saturday at ten." Even before the violence began, participants had developed a system of signals to communicate with one another about the location of potential Armenian victims. Word of these signals spread throughout the Azerbaijani population in advance of the attacks.[69] In the Fergana valley in June and July 1989 the

---

[66] Tishkov, "'Don't Kill Me, I'm a Kyrgyz,'" p. 141.
[67] Shahmuratian, ed., *The Sumgait Tragedy*, p. 125. See also pp. 76, 96, 154.
[68] *Moscow News*, no. 46, November 20–27, 1988, p. 12.
[69] Shahmuratian, ed., *The Sumgait Tragedy*, pp. 104, 190, 192. Azerbaijanis were told to keep the lights on in their apartments so Armenian apartments could be identified.

houses of Meskhetian Turks were identified in advance, and perpetrators "carefully studied approach and departure routes and enlisted a great deal of motor transport."[70] "Emissaries" were sent around to various villages of the region recruiting young people with stories (and even forged photographs) of how the Meskhetian Turks were about to attack or were already raping women and beating up old men and children. Arms were handed out in advance. Dump trucks delivered a steady supply of stones to the participants, and a supply of Molotov cocktails was specially organized. Trucks, buses, fire engines, and even diesel locomotives were enlisted for transporting participants. Within a few days, the crowds began to take on the appearance of organized military units, which moved around the countryside with great mobility.[71]

But with the emergence of sustained and militarized conflict came the need for more permanent forms of coordinating the conduct of violence. Prior to independence, republican and local governments obviously could not declare open warfare or initiate drafts to sustain a citizen army. They possessed no armed forces of their own other than police and local internal affairs troops (theoretically also subordinate to Moscow). In many cases, particularly in the early stages of militarization, local police units played a central role in waging battles or supplying those who did with weapons and support. But nonstate paramilitary units recruited on the basis of clan, family, or neighborhood attachments were also prevalent, and, as conflict grew prolonged, criminal organizations tended to join in the action, utilizing the opportunities created by disorder to loot with impunity. Criminal organization was often evident in mobilized acts of violence as well. Eyewitness accounts of the Sumgait events confirm that there were a number of Russians, Lezgins, and even an occasional Armenian in the crowds (the latter a criminal with two convictions) who utilized the occasion to loot apartments. News of the forthcoming pogrom traveled through the criminal underworld in advance of the event, aided by ties among former inmates.[72] In the Fergana valley violence, local law enforcement officials say that they recognized "many of their 'acquaintances' [in the crowd] – people against whom criminal proceedings have been instituted in the past and people with previous convictions."[73] Some

---

[70] *Izvestiia*, in *FBIS*, June 20, 1989, p. 51.
[71] *Novoe vremia*, no. 9, 1990, p. 34; *Literaturnaia gazeta*, June 14, 1989, p. 2.
[72] Shahmuratian, ed., *The Sumgait Tragedy*, pp. 28, 63, 124, 139, 140–41, 250.
[73] *Pravda*, June 20, 1989, p. 6, in *FBIS*, June 21, 1989, p. 55.

participants were apparently paid by organizers to engage in violent actions against Meskhetian Turks.[74]

But as the demand for the sustained organization of nationalist violence grew, criminal organizations ironically became significant providers of services to the state. These nonstate armed bands enjoyed a murky relationship with local and republican state authority and institutions of order, especially where nationalist movements had gained a pervasive influence. In a number of cases they were formally affiliated with the major nationalist movements of their respective groups. In some cases they actually became the basis for newly established defense ministries in the republics (as occurred, for instance, in Georgia under Gamsakhurdia), though at the same time continuing their private enrichment activities. On the one hand, in cases of sustained violence the state's claim to monopoly over the legitimate use of violence was challenged by the rise of paramilitary organization. On the other hand, given the military weakness of nationalist-dominated republican and local state governments and their attempts to mobilize all potential forces in support of their war efforts, the state's claims to territorial sovereignty required turning a blind eye to these alternative providers of violence, abetting them, and even institutionalizing them within state structures.

As the conduct of violence grew central to the imperatives of would-be states to establish their sovereignty and claims to territory, nationalist violence grew partially institutionalized in state structures as it grew increasingly criminalized. The state took on an interest and a significant role in organizing violence. It also free rode on the organized violence perpetrated by private actors. We usually think of individuals free riding on the state or other public organizations, but in this case, due to the weakness of the state, the reverse was true: Private actors provided public goods, though largely for private ends. In these situations of sustained mass violence we can talk not merely of the emergence of a culture of violence, but of an entire social system of organized violence, with individuals basing careers on their ability to organize violence, local economies oriented toward the provision of violence and managing its consequences, and social stratification increasingly the result of the divide between victimizers and victims. In purely Weberian terms, the state, as the sole organization making claims to a monopoly over the legitimate use of violence within its ascribed territory, could not but be involved in the production of

---

[74] *Sovetskaia Rossiia*, in *FBIS*, June 16, 1989, p. 49.

sustained nationalist violence, either by organizing this violence directly, aiding its conduct by others, or looking the other way while others went about the business of violent entrepreneurship.

Once permanent organization – whether private or public – became involved in the production of nationalist violence, the intensity of violence multiplied immensely, for permanent organization provided the possibility of deploying more powerful weapons against nationalist opponents. A key factor accounting for the exponential rise not just in the frequency of violence, but in its intensity as well in 1991–92, was the quantum leap in the availability and sophistication of weaponry utilized to contest the boundaries of nations during this period. Figure 6.6 divides mass violent events over the cycle into four streams according to the level of weaponry used. As it shows, significant leaps in mass violence were accompanied by the introduction of more sophisticated levels of weapon technology. Interethnic violence began in February 1988 as a "stone war," with most acts of violence carried out using stones, knives, pipes, axes, or fists. In fall 1988, summer 1989, and fall 1989 significant surges in the frequency of violence were accompanied by the introduction of new types of weapons, in particular, small firearms (and occasionally, automatic weapons). By the

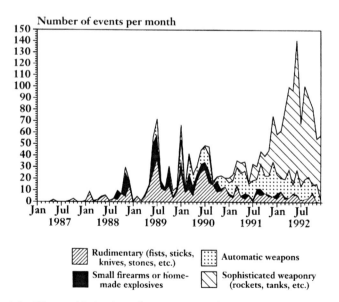

**Figure 6.6** The sophistication of weaponry used in mass violent events in the former Soviet Union, 1987–92.

first half of 1990 automatic weapons came to be used regularly alongside small firearms, accounting again for a significant surge in the number of events. By the end of 1990 the use of rudimentary weapons or small firearms had practically vanished, and in early 1991 sophisticated weapons (rockets, tanks, helicopter gunships, armored personnel carriers, artillery, flamethrowers, etc.) began to make their appearance for the first time alongside automatic weapons. As Figure 6.6 makes obvious, the huge increase in mass violence which accompanied the demise of the USSR was fueled almost entirely by violence involving sophisticated weaponry.

It would be a mistake to interpret the leaps in the frequency and intensity of violence that followed the introduction of new types of weaponry to mean that weapons created conflicts. On the contrary, as the evidence here shows, at moments when violence intensified, groups sought out more effective means to kill each other. Sophisticated weapons were not always utilized properly; there are accounts of the use of tanks to steal cattle,[75] and weapons were frequently aimed indiscriminately in the direction of opposing forces or at civilian populations.[76] Although machinery was not properly serviced and often broke down or left to rust, technology nevertheless profoundly influenced the ways in which nationalist contention was fought out. Modern sophisticated weapons are not only more destructive in terms of the damage they wreak; they also multiply considerably the incidence of violence due to their ability to strike targets at a distance. The concentration of violence toward the latter part of the mobilizational cycle in the former Soviet Union was in part due to the application of more sophisticated weapons technologies as conflict grew better organized, causing the incidence and intensity of ongoing violent conflicts to increase.

The obvious question which comes to mind is where did these weapons come from? This was not a society in which weapons traditionally were freely available to the population. The acquisition and use of these weapons by republican and local governments, nationalist movements, and paramilitary organizations cannot be understood outside the crumbling framework of Soviet institutions. Beneath the surface of leaps in the technology of violence lay deeper transformations in authority relations, in the

---

[75] *Nezavisimaia gazeta*, July 23, 1991, p. 3.
[76] Charles H. Fairbanks, Jr., "The Postcommunist Wars," *Journal of Democracy*, vol. 6, no. 4 (October 1995), pp. 17–34.

coherence of state institutions, and in the relationship of nationalist violence to the state.

Sporadic attacks on local police outposts for the purpose of seizing weapons began in fall 1988 in Azerbaijan, but not until the summer of 1989, with the onset of violence in the Fergana valley and Abkhazia, did the attacks assume major proportions. In Abkhazia and Southern Ossetia alone in 1989 almost ten thousand shotguns, 648 carbines, 511 assault rifles, 10 machine guns, and more than five tons of explosives were stolen from police arsenals.[77] As Figure 6.6 indicates, automatic weapons began to make their way into nationalist conflicts at this time, fueled by a large number of attacks on local police headquarters, army outposts, and peace-keeping forces in the first half of 1990. In many cases these attacks were staged, as local police willingly handed out weapons to the combatants. As we saw earlier, this was already the case in summer 1989 during the violence in Abkhazia. But as violence proliferated, the Soviet army became a favorite target of attack for those seeking more sophisticated weapons. According to the chief of the political department of the Yerevan garrison, by June 1990 attacks on military patrols in Yerevan had become "a normal phenomenon."[78] Paramilitary groups, often organized by the leading social movements of the republic,[79] seized large quantities of arms from local police and military storehouses, at times with the aid of accomplices within the Yerevan police. Arms thieves in Yerevan frequently had precise information about the protection of arms warehouses, as well as the number of weapons stored on these sites. In one case, for instance, "with the obvious complicity of officials of the militia," a paramilitary group entered the local Yerevan police headquarters and seized one hundred pistols with ammunition.[80] These developments and the more general spread of weapons throughout the country prompted Gorbachev to take measures in July 1990 to contain the growth of paramilitary organizations and the illegal possession of weapons. Individuals were given a fifteen-day period during which to surrender weapons voluntarily with impunity. Ironically, the most effective recovery of weapons occurred in Belorussia, Russia, and Kirgizia

---

[77] *Sovetskaia Rossiia*, in *FBIS*, July 31, 1990, p. 66.

[78] TASS, in *FBIS*, June 4, 1990, p. 108.

[79] Among the groups involved in such thefts were the military formation of the Armenian Pan-National Movement and the Republican Party Independent Army. *Krasnaia zvezda*, in *FBIS*, August 3, 1990, p. 70.

[80] *Sovetskaia Rossiia*, in *FBIS*, July 31, 1990, p. 66.

– only the latter being a site of significant interethnic unrest.[81] The Armenian Supreme Soviet actually suspended implementation of the decree on Armenian territory. In an implicit admission of the failure of this effort to contain the spread of weapons, Gorbachev extended the deadline for voluntary surrender of weapons for two additional months after the August 10 deadline expired, though without much success in reversing the flow of arms into nationalist conflicts.[82]

An illicit market had emerged by this time, with stolen weapons from various sites around the country being funneled into conflict hot spots. In May 1990 the KGB's elite Al'fa force engaged in a major operation known as "Trap," intended to capture peddlers and customers in the burgeoning weapons market.[83] Nevertheless, by December 1990 a Kalashnikov rifle was selling on the black market for seven to ten thousand rubles; an Israeli UZI could be bought for eighteen to twenty-five thousand rubles.[84] According to one source, 40 percent of all arms thefts in the USSR were committed in schools, where access could be gained to weapons used in civil defense training classes.[85] By the beginning of 1991, unraveling discipline within the Soviet armed forces led to wholesale dumping of the military's weapons on the black market. At this time, before the breakup of the USSR, sophisticated weapons clearly drawn from a modern military arsenal began to find their way onto the frontlines of ethnonational conflict. For the most part, these weapons fell into the hands of contestants through illegal sales on the black market. Open attacks on police and military units with the goal of seizing weapons were relatively rare during this period.[86]

With the collapse of central authority after the August 1991 coup, seizures of weapons from military and police units increased at a rapid pace. Again, in many cases these "seizures" were staged to cover up illicit sales of armaments. Then Armenian Minister of the Interior Ashot Manucharian, a leader of the Karabakh movement, openly admitted in an interview in October 1991 that often "stories of attacks with the goal of

---

[81] *Izvestiia*, in *FBIS*, August 13, 1990, p. 44.
[82] Armenpres, in *FBIS*, August 6, 1990, p. 86; TASS, in *FBIS*, August 13, 1990, p. 44.
[83] Mikhail Boltunov, *Al'fa ne khotela ubivat'* (Sankt-Peterburg: Shans, 1995), p. 334.
[84] *Sovetskaia Estoniia*, December 8, 1990, p. 3.
[85] *Sovetskaia Rossiia*, in *FBIS*, July 31, 1990, p. 66.
[86] Although I recorded over seventy attacks on police and military units or weapons storehouses with the aim of seizing weapons during the first eight months of 1990, only five such attacks could be found for the first eight months of 1991 – a pattern which also stands in marked contrast to the record after the breakup of the USSR.

seizing automatic weapons and military technology only camouflaged deals for weapons sales."[87] Similar accusations that MVD forces stationed in Tskhinvali were selling and renting sophisticated military technology to Ossetian rebels surfaced at about the same time.[88] At times with the complicity of local generals and perhaps even with official sanction from defense ministry officials in Moscow, "weapons seizures" were enacted as a way of arming groups favorable to Moscow or making a quick profit off the collapse of the Soviet state.[89] This was when large caches of weapons were sold to the Dudaev regime in Chechnia, only to be used against Russian troops when they invaded at the end of 1994. In sum, the disintegration of the authority of the Soviet state and the crumbling coherence of its institutions led to a situation in which sophisticated weapons became available for use in nationalist struggles, multiplying tremendously the frequency and intensity of nationalist conflict.

## Summary and Conclusion

As we have seen, mobilized nationalist violence in the former Soviet Union needs to be understood within the framework of waves, cycles, and tides of nationalist mobilization rather than as individual and isolated acts. Violence emerged as a phase within a larger cycle of mobilization and was shaped in part by the specific opportunities and vulnerabilities presented by targets of contention to those seeking to challenge them. These evolved over time, and because the Soviet government precluded a nonviolent politics over its internal boundaries and mobilization over this issue increasingly revolved around targets relatively impervious to a nonviolent politics, the strategic logic of contesting interrepublican borders pushed mobilization in a violent direction by advantaging entrepreneurs of violence at the expense of entrepreneurs of nonviolence.

We also saw that the state played a key role in triggering and sustaining violence – a phenomenon encouraged by the way in which state

---

[87] Quoted in *Ekspress khronika*, no. 52, December 17–24, 1991, p. 6.

[88] *Ekspress khronika*, no. 45, November 5, 1991, p. 1; Interfax, in *FBIS*, October 15, 1991, p. 67.

[89] In May 1992 a group of ten tanks and fifteen armored personnel carriers were supposedly dispatched to Dubossary with the goal of "defending military officers and their families," only to be "seized" by Transdniestr guards for use in their conflict with Moldova. When asked why his forces took no action to gain the return of the equipment, Major General Yurii Netkachev replied: "When women and children, your own dear ones, are perishing before your very eyes, it is impossible to restrain people." *Ekspress khronika*, no. 21, May 26, 1992, p. 2; ITAR-TASS, in *FBIS*, May 22, 1992, p. 48.

structures were identified with ethnicity within the Soviet ethnofederal system. Usually, at the beginning of waves of mobilized nationalist violence, specific chains of events crystallized widely shared moods of fear, revenge, outrage, and self-assertion which, when combined with a sense of license gained from supportive cues sent by state authority, erupted into violence. In other cases, the state itself directly initiated mobilized violence against ethnic groups or ethnicized segments of the Soviet state as part of its attempts to control challenges to its territoriality. Thus, within the context of "thickened" history social norms proscribing nonstate violence or violence between segments of a single state were set aside, and violent action came to be considered permissible and even moral by large numbers of people. Ultimately, the behavior emanating from the state – whether it made a concerted effort to suppress violent mobilization over its territory, or whether violent mobilization became institutionalized in and abetted by state structures – was central in prolonging violent mobilization beyond its initial outbreak and giving rise to sustained violent conflict.

When Ingush forces entered the town of Chermen in North Ossetia in November 1992, they reportedly took over the local mental hospital, where they are said to have executed two hundred patients of Ossetian nationality.[90] The paradox of nationalist violence is precisely this: These acts of seeming madness seek to reaffirm the boundaries of a contested social reality, and in the process blur the line that runs between sanity and insanity. Nationalist violence is largely a tale of worlds turned upside down and of ordinary people doing the most unordinary things. As one Armenian schoolteacher from Sumgait recounted:

The person who injured and insulted me most painfully . . . was the oldest in the group. He looked around 48. I know that he has four children and that he considers himself an ideal father and person, one who would never do such a thing. Something came over him then, you see, even during the investigation he almost called me "daughter," he apologized, although, of course, he knew that I'd never forgive him.[91]

The same teacher recounts how the director of her school dismissed class early so that teachers could attend anti-Armenian rallies in the town center. The school director spoke at the rally, calling openly for violence against Armenians.

---

[90] Interfax, in *FBIS*, November 4, 1992, p. 21.
[91] Shahmuratian, ed., *The Sumgait Tragedy*, p. 121.

Right then in our group – there were nine of us – the mood changes, and the subject of conversation and all school matters were forgotten. Our director of studies, for whom I had great respect, he's an Azerbaijani . . . Before that I had considered him an upstanding and worthy person . . . So he tells me, "Lyuda, you know that besides you there are no Armenians on the square? If they find out that you're an Armenian they'll tear you to pieces. Should I tell them you're an Armenian?" . . . When he said it the first time I pretended not to hear it, and then he asked me a second time. I turned to the director . . . and said that . . . I should be on my way.[92]

In these moments of madness when the normal constrictions of the social world are overturned, people's lives are transformed, and behaviors that seem so patently taboo and irrational within the context of an anchored, normalized order come to be embraced as normal and rational by those swept up by these events. As these transformed lives attest, mobilized nationalist violence is fundamentally a tidal phenomenon in that it is not merely an expression of pre-existing structural conditions. The interaction emerging from the tidal context of mobilization is central to its initiation and multiplication. But nationalist violence is also a tidal phenomenon in the sense that violent action radically alters social reality and thereby powerfully constitutes a central element of its own causal structure.

[92] Shahmuratian, ed., *The Sumgait Tragedy*, p. 143.

# 7

## *The Transcendence of Regimes of Repression*

Socialism rests on the shoulders of the KGB, on our shoulders.
  A KGB officer to Yuri Orlov during his interrogation in 1977[1]

All states attempt to marginalize challenges to their national orders. The USSR was no exception in this regard. But since the days of the Russian Civil War successive Soviet leaders proved ruthless in wielding the state's coercive instruments to normalize control over a multinational population. The Soviet state gained a reputation as one of the most repressive states in modern history – a reputation earned in significant respects for its repression of challenging nationalisms. Until the late 1980s that repression appeared from all angles to be extraordinarily efficient, even to the point that large numbers of Soviet citizens and outside observers came to believe in the impossibility of Soviet collapse.[2]

  In the end, coercion did not save the Soviet state. But the sense that it could have lingers in the debates over who is responsible for Soviet disintegration. One of the frequently cited puzzles of the Soviet collapse is why force was not deployed with greater vigor against the state's opponents – particularly against separatist nationalists. Some attribute this simply to a lack of will on the part of Gorbachev. Jerry Hough, for instance, has decried Gorbachev's failure to impose a Tiananmen-type crackdown on Soviet society, which he believes to have been a viable solution to the disorders unleashed by *glasnost'* but was irrationally rejected by

---

[1] Yuri Orlov, *Dangerous Thoughts: Memoirs of a Russian Life* (New York: William Morrow and Company, 1991), p. 218.
[2] For an argument that the collapse of the USSR was unlikely because of the efficiency of Soviet coercion, see Alexander J. Motyl, *Will the Non-Russians Rebel?: State, Ethnicity, and Stability in the USSR* (Ithaca, NY: Cornell University Press, 1987).

Gorbachev.[3] In a number of localities nomenklatura elites did not shy away from using force against nationalist challengers and in some instances were successful in marginalizing them. None, however, deployed the type of massive shootings of thousands that took place in Beijing on June 3 and 4, 1989, when Chinese armed forces were ordered to use any means necessary (including gunfire aimed directly at crowds) to clear the central square of the capital of prodemocracy protestors.[4]

Other observers of *glasnost'*, such as Archie Brown, have on the contrary pointed to the ways in which government repression not only undermined democratic norms, but also proved counterproductive to holding the Soviet Union together. As he noted, "in the new climate of raised expectations and aroused civic courage," the harsh use of force frequently "produce[d] the opposite effect from that intended by the Soviet authorities."[5] In a number of instances (Vilnius in September 1988, Tbilisi in April 1989, Kishinev in November 1989, Baku in January 1990) the use of force against nationalist challengers became a cause of further mobilization against the Soviet state. The implication of Brown's position is that the attempt to blame Gorbachev for his failure to deploy massive force against secessionist challengers is misplaced, since the large-scale use of force would only have proved counterproductive to the goals of both democratic transition and holding the USSR together – the latter primarily because of the backlash effects which force would have generated.

There are, of course, the larger ethical questions implied by these arguments: Is severe violence justified as a means for ensuring the survival of the state under any circumstance, and is it the business of scholars to advocate that a regime that could survive only by deploying such violence utilize murder to prop itself up? But simply looking at the issue from the instrumental angle of how a government deploying repression against opponents can or cannot be challenged successfully, Hough and Brown outline two contrasting positions on the use of force for preserving the

---

[3] Jerry F. Hough, *Democratization and Revolution in the USSR, 1985–1991* (Washington, DC: Brookings Institution Press, 1997), pp. 251–54.

[4] The actual casualty toll from the Tiananmen Square events is unknown, but most estimates of the number of civilians killed range in the low thousands, with the additional number of injured running into the many thousands and even tens of thousands. In addition, thousands were arrested throughout China in the ensuing crackdown. See Amnesty International, *China: The Massacre of June 1989 and Its Aftermath* (London: Amnesty International Publications, 1990); Timothy Brook, *Quelling the People: The Military Suppression of the Beijing Democracy Movement* (New York: Oxford University Press, 1992).

[5] Archie Brown, *The Gorbachev Factor* (Oxford: Oxford University Press, 1996), p. 265.

USSR and for demobilizing nationalist challenges. As is true of much historical controversy, the debate is counterfactual, since a major crackdown against nationalist challengers on the scale of Tiananmen Square never took place. Two related questions emerge from this debate which are central to an understanding of Soviet collapse: Why severe violence against nationalist challengers never occurred, and what would have been the consequences had it been attempted?

This chapter addresses these two questions from the point of view of a tidal understanding of nationalism, attempting in the process to elaborate a framework for analyzing the broader relationship between repression and mobilization. The counterfactual nature of the debate should not deter us from seeking ways to evaluate these positions. The issue is not one of answering the question with certainty; certainty is never attainable in social scientific reasoning in any case, and as Weber contended, "empirical science would be in a bad way if those lofty problems to which there is no answer had never been raised."[6] Rather, the issues are probability and credibility. Here, I draw on the criteria proposed by Tetlock and Belkin for evaluating counterfactual arguments: (1) the clarity of the argument; (2) its logical consistency; (3) its historical consistency (altering as few well-established historical facts as possible); (4) its theoretical consistency (with causal mechanisms consistent with well-established theoretical generalizations); (5) its statistical consistency (supported by well-founded statistical generalizations); and (6) its projectability (with testable implications for other observations which have actually occurred).[7] These criteria could sensibly apply to any social scientific argument; they provide reasonable yardsticks for assessing whether the deployment of large-scale force could have saved the USSR in the late 1980s and early 1990s.

In terms of theoretical consistency, however, there is a problem: What theory are we to believe? The issues of when and why government repression proves effective in marginalizing challengers have long been concerns within social scientific inquiry. But several decades of initial research

---

[6] Max Weber, "Critical Studies in the Field of Cultural Logic," quoted in Alexander Demandt, *History That Never Happened*, 3d ed. (London: McFarland and Company, 1993), p. 135.

[7] Philip E. Tetlock and Aaron Belkin, "Counterfactual Thought Experiments in World Politics: Logical, Methodological, and Psychological Perspectives," in Philip E. Tetlock and Aaron Belkin, eds., *Counterfactual Thought Experiments in World Politics: Logical, Methodological, and Psychological Perspectives* (Princeton, NJ: Princeton University Press, 1996), pp. 3–38.

provided an abundance of evidence for, as one review of the literature put it, "all conceivable basic relationships . . . except for no relationship" between government coercion and mobilization.[8] Many argued for an inverted U-shaped relationship, that is, that both severe and low-level government coercion are associated with diminished levels of mobilization (the former by raising the costs of action to unacceptable levels, the latter by allowing for the cooptation of opponents), whereas mobilization escalates under moderate levels of repression. Others showed evidence that in some circumstances severe levels of repression generated backlash effects and thereby escalated mobilization.[9]

The connection of these two traditional perspectives with the Hough and Brown positions should be obvious. But in recent years a number of studies have questioned the assumptions of this debate along several fronts. First, the idea that the amount of government repression is the most critical factor in determining patterns of mobilization has come under challenge. Lichbach's rational choice analysis, for instance, focused attention on the consistency of incentives emerging from both repression and concessions rather than on the amount of repression in determining the effect of repression on opposition activity.[10] The forceful demobilization of populations is not only about the physical costs imposed by force on oppositions; it also concerns the ways in which government actions affect the beliefs and commitments of large numbers of individuals. In this regard, as Lichbach's analysis implies, the severity of force is not the only relevant factor and indeed may be less significant an influence on mobilization than the consistency of government action and the relationship of repression to other acts of government.

Second, the meaning of "effective" repression has been rethought in line with a clearer understanding of how backlash processes operate. The effects of a specific act of repression on mobilization can fluctuate across time. Opp and Ruehl, for example, differentiated between the short-term and long-term effects of repression, providing evidence that, although repression may depress mobilization in the short run, in the long run it

---

[8] E. Zimmerman, "Macro-Comparative Research on Political Protest," in Ted R. Gurr, ed., *Handbook of Political Conflict: Theory and Research* (New York: Free Press, 1980), p. 191.

[9] For a review of these contrasting arguments, see Mark Irving Lichbach, "Deterrence or Escalation? The Puzzle of Aggregate Studies of Repression and Dissent," *Journal of Conflict Resolution*, vol. 31, no. 2 (June 1987), pp. 266–97.

[10] Lichbach, "Deterrence or Escalation? The Puzzle of Aggregate Studies of Repression and Dissent."

can elevate mobilization by activating micromobilizational processes – a finding confirmed in Rassler's study of the Iranian revolution.[11] The effectiveness of repression in demobilizing populations should be judged not by its immediate effects but rather by the ways in which it activates or undermines mobilizational processes over time, leading overall to heightened or dampened patterns of action.

Third, repression is never cost-free to governments. Not only does it take a toll on a regime's legitimacy, but it also requires institutional resources, and those resources are not inexhaustible. As the scholarly literature on revolutions has come to emphasize, in generating and applying resources for repression, the cohesion of state institutions (particularly, of those institutions called on to carry out repression – the army and the police) is critical for explaining the effects of repression.[12]

Fourth, recent studies have observed that what should be at issue in evaluating the effectiveness of repression "is not the simple correlation between government coercion and rebellious behavior, but the partial correlation, after pertinent factors that impinge on this dynamic and complex relationship are taken into account."[13] Clearly, numerous factors besides repression influence mobilization, and one cannot evaluate the impact of repression without controlling for the effect of these other factors, which in essence affect the mobilization/repression relationship. For one thing, target groups display varying capabilities for generating mobilization in the face of repression.[14] Moreover, the openness or closedness of state institutions has a bearing on the ability of regimes to carry out repressions without generating backlash effects. Gupta, Singh, and Sprague have provided tentative evidence that government coercion against protestors within an established democracy is more likely to generate backlash mobilization than under an authoritarian regime. This is so, they speculate,

[11] Karl Dieter Opp and Wolfgang Ruehl, "Repression, Micromobilization and Political Protest," *Social Forces*, vol. 69 (1990), pp. 521–47; Karen Rassler, "Concessions, Repression, and Political Protest in the Iranian Revolution," *American Sociological Review*, vol. 61 (February 1996), pp. 132–52.
[12] Theda Skocpol, *States and Social Revolutions: A Comparative Analysis of France, Russia, and China* (Cambridge, UK: Cambridge University Press, 1979).
[13] Dipak K. Gupta, Harinder Singh, Tom Sprague, "Government Coercion of Dissidents: Deterrence or Provocation?" *Journal of Conflict Resolution*, vol. 37, no. 2 (June 1993), p. 302.
[14] See Jack A. Goldstone, "Is Revolution Individually Rational? Groups and Individuals in Revolutionary Collective Action," *Rationality and Society*, vol. 6, no. 1 (January 1994), pp. 139–66.

because democratic governments are expected to operate according to fixed legal rules that limit their ability to impose severe sanctions and channel political conflict into institutional channels, so that violence against protestors challenges the legitimacy of the democratic process.[15] But one suspects that other reasons might lead this to be true as well. Within either an established democracy or a democratizing society, access to mass media (and their penchant for exhibition of acts of violence) and competition among political elites provide opportunities for challengers to politicize acts of repression and to form alliances across groups to pressure elites and institutions carrying out repression.

Finally, there is evidence that the relationship between government repression and mobilization is bounded temporally – that is, that similar coercive acts against the same group can suppress protest within one temporal context but incite it within another. Opp, for instance, has noted that political events themselves altered the incentives to protest in the face of possible repression in Leipzig in October 1989, making participation more likely.[16] The mechanisms which transform one pattern of reaction to repression into another have not been fully teased out. Nevertheless, it is clear that the relationship between repression and mobilization is not a constant. Demobilization through repression, for instance, is generally easier to accomplish prior to the emergence of a mobilizational cycle (that is, before multiple, interrelated challenges have developed) or at the end of a cycle (when institutionalization or exhaustion naturally tend toward demobilization). Thus, in evaluating the potential role of force in preventing the Soviet collapse, one cannot mechanically assume that the same types of repressions that were once effective in marginalizing nationalist challenges in the USSR in 1953, 1965, or 1985 could have been applied with equal effect in 1989 or 1990; norms about the use of force, the scale of dissenting action, and the expectations of successful challenge in the face of repression were fundamentally transformed by intervening political events. The phase within the mobilizational cycle at which the Soviet regime might have attempted to repress nationalist challenges is also relevant for evaluating the prospects for successful demobilization by force.

---

[15] Gupta, Singh, and Sprague, "Government Coercion of Dissidents: Deterrence or Provocation?"

[16] Karl-Dieter Opp, "Repression and Revolutionary Action: East Germany in 1989," *Rationality and Society*, vol. 6, no. 1 (January 1994), pp. 101–38.

In this chapter I evaluate the possibilities for alternative outcomes to the Soviet collapse through the forceful defense of the Soviet order against a rising tide of nationalist contention. I do so on the basis of an empirical examination of patterns of failure and success in the Soviet government's efforts to marginalize nationalist dissent through repression during the *glasnost'* period. These efforts have been widely judged as failures. To a large extent, this is an accurate assessment, though the reality of the record of demobilization through repression during this period was more mixed than has often been made out in retrospect. In some circumstances force remained an effective instrument in marginalizing challengers and helped to maintain traditional nomenklatura elites in power, in spite of the increasing examples of successful challenge by others. But in a whole series of republics efforts to impose force failed dramatically, and a marked shift took place in the relationship between repression and mobilization over the course of the cycle. Eventually, a failed effort by the leadership of the military and secret police to reimpose order and prevent the breakup of the USSR became the immediate cause of the collapse of the Soviet state. Understanding the causal factors behind these outcomes not only provides us with a tool for sorting out the otherwise unanswerable counterfactuals regarding the use of force and the breakup of the USSR; it also furnishes us with an opportunity for reconstructing theory concerning the effects of repression on government challengers.

My attempt to elucidate why force failed to save the USSR begins by thinking about the expectations which government repression seeks to instill. By a "regime of repression," I have in mind a set of regularized practices of repression and the internalized expectations about the ways in which authority will respond punitively toward challenging acts that result from these practices. Repression exercises its effect in part because it functions as habitus. That is, part of the effect of repression occurs because individuals "have internalized, through a protracted and multi-sided process of conditioning, the objective chances they face"[17] in challenging authority and what types of penalties they would most likely suffer on the basis of prior punitive responses of authority to challenge. These expectations about the likelihood and severity of costs are maintained and reproduced through state practice – that is, the predictability of response by government to challenging acts is maintained by example. The repeated

---

[17] Pierre Bourdieu and Loïc J. D. Wacquant, *An Invitation to Reflexive Sociology* (Chicago: University of Chicago Press, 1992), p. 130.

example of government repression (or its absence) generates a sense of regularity and predictability because this behavior is in fact based on a set of practiced repertoires of repression. These repertoires are often encoded in legal systems and in the standard operating procedures or standing orders guiding the behavior of state institutions charged with upholding order – the police, legal institutions, and the army. Thus, regimes of repression rely heavily for their effect on the regularities produced by institutions and involve a set of shared expectations about behavior among both repressor and repressed. All states – even democratic ones – seek to establish some type of regime of repression in this sense; the challenge within a democratic setting has always been how to establish and enforce expectations about the acceptable limits of dissenting behavior without undermining opportunities for legitimate expression.

The notion of a regime of repression focuses our attention on the consistency, regularity, and predictability with which repression occurs, the internalized discipline that emerges as a result, and the institutional resources necessary to produce such patterning. But these are not the only dimensions by which repression can be judged. Repression has a physical dimension as well; it inflicts real costs on oppositions, and the severity of those costs is usually measured by the injuries, deaths, and arrests suffered by government opponents. These physical costs can undermine mobilization by undermining movement leadership and damaging mobilizational networks, making them less capable of operating with effect. Generally, the more severe the repression, the more damage it inflicts on mobilizational networks. The ability of mobilizational networks to weather and recover from repression depends not only on the extent of the damage, but also on the thickness of mobilizational networks. Movements suffer repression differentially, with some more capable of withstanding repression than others. These two dimensions of repression – the physical and the internalized – are intertwined in the ways in which repression mobilizes or demobilizes groups.

But a regime of repression not only constrains the repressed; it also constrains the repressor. For one thing, because regimes of repression rely on the regularities produced by institutions, they are limited physically by institutional capabilities. More than that, state officials themselves internalize a sense of the limits of acceptable repression. Thus, the type of severe repression that became characteristic of the Stalinist period – with its tens of millions of victims – required certain types of individuals and institutions to carry out. It would have appeared as a gross violation of internalized expectations within the Soviet elite about the proper bounds of exercising repression by the Brezhnev or Gorbachev eras. By the 1970s and 1980s this level of severity was in essence off the scale of conceivable government responses to challenge, a measure appropriate for elites and institutions inhabiting an entirely different historical context. Not even the most radical of Gorbachev's critics imagined such a possibility in their arguments for imposing order. Yet, the types of measures that Gorbachev's critics did imagine might save the USSR undoubtedly would have been judged within the context of Stalinism as acts of weakness.

A regime of repression is not only a central element in understanding how groups break through repressive orders. It also constitutes an important benchmark by which to understand governmental repertoires of repression and the boundaries of acceptable force, leading us toward an explanation of why elites choose particular modes of suppressing challenge. As I argue below, the kind of severe force imposed in Tiananmen Square was not possible in the USSR in the *glasnost'* period for a number of reasons. But one key reason was that, unlike China in 1989, it lay outside the boundaries of acceptable force on the part of state officials themselves – in large part because elites had internalized a certain sense of how order should be created. When the prospect of massive bloodshed loomed as a possibility through a conjuncture of circumstances, elites in a position to impose severe violence quickly shrank from such a position in view of its normative consequences. The failure of the Soviet regime to defend itself through severe force was partially a matter of Gorbachev's personal commitment to nonviolence. As I detail below, Gorbachev altered the long-standing regime of repression characteristic of the Brezhnev era by attempting to establish a legal framework to regulate revolt. This attempt faltered badly, in large part because in a context of burgeoning contention rules could not be enforced with any consistency. In the wake of this failure, as Gorbachev later recalled, he contemplated using force to prevent the disintegration of the USSR. However, he rejected this idea in favor of other ways of preserving the union without bloodshed.[18] But the "Gorbachev factor" (as Archie Brown called it) does not provide us with a full explanation of the failure of the Soviet state to defend itself through severe force for, as we will see, it was not only Gorbachev but the vast majority of his conservative critics as well who eschewed a Tiananmen-type crackdown. This lack of commitment to the use of severe violence as

---

[18] *RFE/RL Newsline*, vol. 2, no. 53, March 18, 1998.

a tool for reimposing order stands in marked contrast to the Russian record in the postcommunist period. Yeltsin's use of severe force as a strategy for dealing with revolt – both in the October 1993 events and in the various wars in Chechnia – exceeded considerably that which was acceptable to any of the major actors of the communist regime during the *glasnost'* or, for that matter, Brezhnev eras. Ironically, the norms of postcommunist transition have justified more severe applications of force than those of Brezhnevian bureaucracy.

Thus, rather than focus solely on Gorbachev, I root an explanation for the failure of the Soviet state to defend itself against rebellion through severe violence in the fact that the "forces of order" in the USSR in the late 1980s and early 1990s conceived of how order should be created in a particular way, through the predictability of repression and the thickness of institutional presence rather than the harshness of force. This is not to argue that repression exceeding the boundaries of the conventional is impossible. If this were so, one could never explain the rise of a Stalin or other modern despots. But acts of severe repression that break with widely shared expectations about violence require leaders not bound by a sense of the normal. Such leaders were absent within the Soviet elite during the *glasnost'* period. As Georgii Shakhnazarov, Gorbachev's chief domestic political advisor, observed, "The paralysis of will which is now ascribed only to Gorbachev in reality was characteristic of his colleagues as well."[19]

I also argue below that even if leaders could have been found for such an enterprise, the window for success was relatively narrow – a matter of months in late 1988 and early 1989. As we saw in Chapter 2, nationalist mobilization could have been shut down easily in 1987 and 1988 (and was at times, particularly if it violated the parameters of the acceptable). But at that time acts of nationalist contention were not widely recognized as the fundamental threat to the state they ultimately came to be. By late 1988 and early 1989, however, this was no longer true. In the wake of the failure of Gorbachev's effort to regulate revolt by law, a more concerted effort to crack down on challenging nationalist mobilization emerged but backfired, leading unintentionally to the Tbilisi massacres of April 1989 and the enormous political backlash engendered by those events. I argue that from mid-1989 on, in the wake of Tbilisi and as the tide of nationalism gained in scope, the success of a violent crackdown against nationalist movements

[19] Georgii Shakhnazarov, *Tsena svobody: Reformatsiia Gorbacheva glazami ego pomoshchnika* (Moscow: Rossika, 1993), p. 212.

would have been improbable even if a leader capable of wielding violence on such a scale could have been found. For one thing, multiple mobilizational challenges encompassed the country both in its political center and in key non-Russian regions, and fear that the regime could successfully employ repression was fading among significant numbers of people. The context of regime liberalization also undermined efforts at large-scale repression. In the wake of Tbilisi a transnational alliance of opposition movements aimed at undercutting the regime's ability to repress emerged out of the shifting institutional milieu of democratic transition and the political opening created by the misapplication of force. Finally, the institutions of order were severely taxed and significantly compromised by the tide of nationalist mobilization that engulfed the USSR during these years. All this not only raised the bar in terms of the severity and frequency of repression required to alter public expectations about the probability of successful demobilization by force. It also made it harder for elites to imagine the successful deployment of repression as a way of controlling the streets and saving the Soviet state. The failure of a regime of repression occurs when government repertoires of punitive response to challenge no longer exercise their intended effect. That is, they either generate challenges rather than depress them, or they have no effect on mobilization whatsoever. There is considerable evidence that, in multiple locations of the USSR after mid-1989, this is precisely what occurred, making the reimposition of control a much more difficult task. As I argue, in the transformed context of the tide neither Brezhnevism nor Stalinism was a credible answer to the problem of recreating order, the former because it was no longer possible, the latter because it was no longer imaginable.

## The Brezhnevian Regime of Repression

An understanding of the relationship between repression and mobilization in the *glasnost'* era requires a knowledge of the preceding regime of repression. Fortunately, this was subjected to extensive investigation by two leaders of the Soviet human rights movement, Ludmilla Alexeeva and Valery Chalidze, in an unpublished report written under contract to the U.S. Department of Defense in 1985.[20] Based on an analysis of over two

---

[20] Ludmilla Alexeeva and Valery Chalidze, "Mass Unrest in the USSR," Report No. 19, Office of Net Assessment of the Department of Defense (August 1985). The following discussion is drawn primarily from pp. 335–77 of that report.

thousand demonstrations, strikes, and mass disturbances of all sizes known to the human rights movement during the post-Stalinist period, Alexeeva and Chalidze identified the outlines of what appeared to be standard operating procedures governing the Soviet state's response to mass protests and disturbances. These evolved over time, but nevertheless contained a certain consistency.

In the Stalin era, the NKVD carried out most mass repressions in reprisal for rebellious actions, usually with little involvement of the local party hierarchy. These were characterized by great brutality and the application of overwhelming and often arbitrary force. By the Khrushchev era, local party officials were charged with maintaining public order, and a clearer procedure on how to deal with disturbances developed. Under the guidance of local party organizations, the local militia and KGB were the first to take action. If these forces proved insufficient, troops from the local garrison were to be called in. Should further force be warranted, with the permission of Moscow special crack units could be summoned to the scene. In all cases in which severe force was inflicted against rebellious populations in the Khrushchev years, it was carried out by these special forces.

According to Alexeeva and Chalidze, the regime's use of force against rebellion shifted with the overthrow of Khrushchev. Of the nine cases that occurred after Stalin's death in which the authorities opened fire with live ammunition on participants in mass disturbances, almost all occurred in the late 1950s and early 1960s[21] and only one during the Brezhnev era (this took place in Dneprodzerzhinsk in June 1972, when antipolice rioters, provoked by police brutality against members of a wedding procession, stormed local police headquarters; no deaths were reported in that incident). In the Brezhnev and immediate post-Brezhnev years the authorities displayed a reticence to deploy severe violence against participants in mass actions, although mass actions on a large scale occurred on a significant number of occasions. Special forces units were summoned at least twenty-one times from 1965 through 1985 to quell mass demonstrations and disturbances, but this was accomplished without the type of brutal violence characteristic of the Stalin and Khrushchev years.

How, then, did the Brezhnev regime demobilize challenges without deploying the kind of severe force against rebellion applied in the past? As Alexeeva and Chalidze detail, most probably in reaction to the bloody

---

[21] These were Tbilisi (1956), Temir-Tau (1958), Kaunas (1960), Krasnodar (1961), Aleksandrov (1961), Murom (1961), Novocherkassk (1962), and Kemerovo (1962).

suppression of the Novocherkassk rebellion in June 1962,[22] the rise of the human rights movement in the mid-1960s, and the growing exposure of the USSR to the outside world, Khrushchev's successors issued new instructions to party officials, police, and special forces units charged with suppressing rebellion. For one thing, special battalions were established among the MVD troops for suppressing demonstrations and riots. By the late 1960s these forces had been equipped with fire trucks, armored transport, electrically charged night sticks, and grenades with compressed tear gas. Indicative of the existence of standard operating procedures for dealing with unrest, these troops underwent periodic training in the art of dispersing demonstrations and containing mass disorders. Secret decrees in 1970 and 1973 laid down rules for the use of force by the police. Though allowing the use of firearms by special battalions, these decrees specifically noted that shooting was to occur only in exceptional circumstances as a last resort and only in places where bystanders could not be hurt.[23] However, after the issuance of this decree no instances of the use of firearms by special battalions occurred. As Alexeeva and Chalidze observe, the post-Khrushchev leadership displayed "greater flexibility and caution" in their tactics for repressing disturbances in comparison with the Khrushchev years, especially in instances of nationality conflict.

In the Brezhnev era the police developed tactics aimed at eliminating public acts of challenge without the use of severe force against crowds. Mass repressions against demonstrations were rare; rather, before or after a demonstration, the organizers were regularly targeted. They would typically be fired from their jobs, expelled from school, arrested (in some cases subsequently released, and less often sentenced to prison terms), or on rare occasions placed in prison psychiatric hospitals. Prison sentences could be substantial, and prison conditions were oppressive. But such punishment

---

[22] In June 1962 in the city of Novocherkassk troops were ordered to fire automatic rifles directly into a crowd of demonstrators protesting price rises, killing twenty-four and wounding thirty. Subsequently, seven participants in the protests were executed and ninety-eight sentenced to terms in prison camps. The Soviet government attempted to cover up the massacre, though knowledge of it circulated widely within the dissident movement. The number of casualties did not become public knowledge until the *glasnost'* era, however, leading to public belief that the scope of the repressions was actually much higher. See *Literaturnaia gazeta*, no. 25, June 21, 1989, p. 13.

[23] For mention of the 1970 and 1973 decrees, see Anatolii Sobchak, *Tbilisskii izlom, ili Krovavoe voskresen'e 1989 goda* (Moscow: Sretenie, 1993), p. 141; *L'Unita*, in *FBIS*, October 19, 1988, pp. 65–67.

was reserved for a handful of activists who engaged in repeated challenges and was not applied more broadly to participants in mass actions. More often, proactive measures were taken by the KGB to prevent demonstrations before they occurred by detaining or harassing organizers, particularly in cases of demonstrations which regularly took place on symbolic dates. Potential participants in small acts of protest were often summoned to Komsomol meetings at their schools or at work on the eve of the action and warned about possible consequences if they acted. Meeting places were frequently blocked off in advance. These types of preventative measures for suppressing demonstrations grew more significant over time. When demonstrations did occur, loudspeakers were often utilized by the police to drown out the voices of speakers. Police provocateurs mingled with the crowds, at times provoking fights, and when possible participants were secretly photographed. Police harassment and certainly roughness during arrest were common, though open beatings of participants were rare, occurring with greater frequency in demonstrations by minority groups such as Crimean Tatars or Meskhetian Turks. In rare instances the demands of demonstrators were satisfied by the authorities.[24]

Clearly, the most important feature of repression in the late Soviet period was not the severity of violence but its regularity, predictability, and efficiency. Of 195 demonstrations in the USSR with more than 100 participants that I studied for the 1965 through 1986 period, only for 20 demonstrations (10 percent) were serious prison sentences handed out to some participants. In the vast majority of cases (76 percent) no known sanctions were imposed on participants. Yet, some degree of police harassment (ranging from blocking the path of demonstrators to serious beatings) occurred in at least 67 percent of all cases – most often in the form of the temporary detention or arrest of key organizers. Deaths of demonstrators were practically unknown during this period. Numerous planned actions were prevented from taking place through proactive measures by the police. Institutional capacity to repress in this manner invariably exceeded the mobilizational challenges which institutions faced, and the

---

[24] Examples in which the authorities gave in to the demands of protestors in the Brezhnev era include protests in Georgia in 1978 and 1981 over language and cultural issues, in Ukraine in 1967 over detention of demonstrators at the Shevchenko monument, and in Almaty in March 1981 over the burial of Kazakhs killed in Afghanistan in a mass grave without proper burial rites. Alexeeva and Chalidze, "Mass Unrest in the USSR," p. 376.

consistency of repression created a sense of hopelessness and fatigue among consistent challengers.[25] The Brezhnevian regime of repression, like its Stalinist and Khrushchevian predecessors, was extremely efficient, but, unlike Stalin and Khrushchev, Brezhnev generally did not rely on severe violence to marginalize challenges. Rather, the predictable, consistent, and efficient application of low level and moderate coercion proved extremely effective.

It was this regime of repression which Gorbachev inherited on assuming power in 1985. Indeed, it is striking how many of the above-mentioned tactics were applied by the police in dealing with unwanted demonstrations during the Gorbachev era. Moreover, in the early Gorbachev period (1985–86) the relationship between regime and opposition displayed much the same consistency of response as was characteristic of the previous two decades. This is important to keep in mind in evaluating arguments about the role of force in preventing the collapse of the USSR, for when conservatives in the USSR talked about reintroducing "order," few conceived of this as involving the type of brutal violence displayed during the Stalin or even Khrushchev years. Tiananmen Square was not part of the usual repertoire by which authority enforced order in the late Soviet period. Rather, "order" was understood as the type of predictability and effect from consistent, low level or moderate coercion against challenging acts characteristic of the Brezhnev era.

## Glasnost' and the Legal Regulation of Revolt

Beginning in 1987 an attempt was made to alter the Brezhnevian regime of repression in line with the new parameters of liberalization. The Soviet government began to allow some small-scale demonstrations, which Gorbachev believed would aid him in challenging the power of entrenched bureaucrats. In spite of its reputation for liberality, however, the Gorbachev regime never exhibited a total tolerance of challengers. From the very beginning it sought to discriminate between challenging acts viewed as supportive of its goals and those that violated the spirit of *perestroika*. From January 1987 through May 1988 at least 277 demonstrations with a hundred participants or more took place in the country. A total of 2,144

[25] This point is made by Alexeeva and Chalidze in explaining the decline in Crimean Tatar and Meskhetian Turk protest over the Brezhnev era. See Alexeeva and Chalidze, "Mass Unrest in the USSR," p. 378.

arrests, injuries, or deaths occurred at these demonstrations – an average of 7.7 per demonstration. In all, 30 percent (84) experienced some form of government repression, a marked drop from the 67 percent of demonstrations repressed in the Brezhnev era, but still a significant proportion. Moreover, the policy of discriminating between demonstrations supportive of *perestroika* and those that were not was followed with a good deal of consistency. Figure 7.1 presents information on arrests, injuries, and deaths at protest demonstrations during the 1987 through 1992 period. As one can see from Figures 7.1b and 7.1c, through mid-1988 the proportion of demonstrations which experienced repression rose at approximately the same pace as the number of demonstrations, peaking in May 1988.

Indicative of the attempts by the Soviet government during this period to introduce a law-based state, an effort was made in 1987–88 to establish new legal norms regulating revolt. Article 50 of the 1977 Soviet Constitution supposedly guaranteed Soviet citizens freedom of assembly, including the right to conduct street demonstrations and meetings. However, this right existed on paper only. Until 1987 no procedure for authorizing demonstrations existed in the Soviet Union. In April 1981, for instance, an attempt by four Jewish refuseniks to submit a formal application to the local government in Novosibirsk to hold a demonstration in the city center "provoked panic among city officials." The police cordoned off whole neighborhoods in response, and two of the would-be organizers were immediately granted permission to emigrate.[26] The idea of introducing legal regulation as a gatekeeper for demonstration activity was borrowed directly from the experience of Western Europe and North America. In the West the regularization of protest had given rise to local regulations governing the place, process, and manner in which public acts of protest could be carried out, thereby imposing a frame within which challenging acts occurred. In the Soviet case the intention was to move from a situation in which all demonstrations were banned to one in which the authorities could exercise a legal discretionary power over the types of groups permitted to demonstrate. Thus, law was to be harnessed to the purposes of the regime, marginalizing serious opponents while mobilizing civic activism for the goal of institutional reform.[27] At least this was how the

[26] Ludmilla Alexeyeva, *Soviet Dissent* (Middletown, CT: Wesleyan University Press, 1985), p. 195.

[27] See the interview with the USSR Ministry of Justice Boris Kravtsov in *Izvestiia*, July 22, 1988, p. 6.

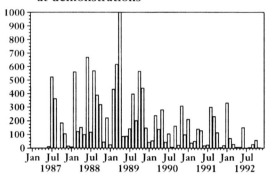

a. Number of arrests, injuries, and deaths
   at demonstrations

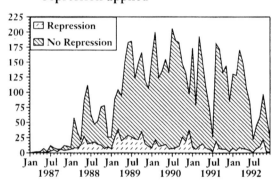

b. Number of demonstrations at which
   repression applied

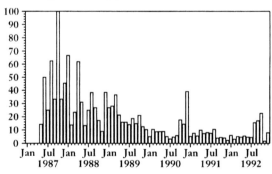

c. Percent of demonstrations at which
   repression applied

**Figure 7.1.** Government repression at protest demonstrations, 1987–92. (April 1989 data point in Figure 7.1a reduced to improve visibility.)

regulatory process was sold to politicians and explained to the public at the time.

The impetus for regulation was a series of demonstrations that violated the authorities' conception of the acceptable. In late August 1987, after the troublesome wave of demonstrations in downtown Moscow by Crimean Tatars, the Moscow City Soviet formally banned demonstrations in the city center and established rules for holding meetings elsewhere in the city. According to the new rules, registration and approval by the Moscow City Soviet were necessary seven days in advance in order to conduct a demonstration in the capital, and in general demonstrations were barred from Red Square and from other areas adjacent to the Kremlin.[28] These regulations provided authorities with a legal tool for limiting demonstrations by groups openly challenging the government or that were considered otherwise worthy of discrimination. As the Moscow official in charge of issuing permits noted, "We approve those actions which correspond to the interests of the people and the goals of strengthening and developing the socialist order."[29] Even as late as the summer of 1988 the actual details of the Moscow regulations had not been published, leading legal scholars to complain about the arbitrariness with which they were being applied.[30] Following the lead of Moscow, other cities soon passed regulations each with their own peculiarities. By the end of 1987, as one Soviet correspondent noted, the extent to which citizens were capable of exercising their right to demonstrate "depends to a large extent on the specific position of specific officials in the localities."[31]

The platform produced by the Nineteenth Party Conference called for new laws to protect citizens' right to assembly, and in July 1988, "for the purpose of strengthening and developing the socialist system," the Presidium of the USSR Supreme Soviet introduced new guidelines governing demonstration activity (subsequently passed as law by the Supreme Soviet in October 1988). These guidelines reinforced the decision-making authority of republican and local governments over whether to permit particular demonstrations, giving them broad discretion "with regard to local conditions." Demonstrations were legal only if the organizers applied to the local authorities for permission to hold a demonstration at least ten

[28] *Radio Liberty Research Report*, RL 357/87, September 4, 1987, p. 7.
[29] *Sobesednik*, no. 3, January 1988, p. 7.  [30] *Trud*, June 22, 1988, p. 2.
[31] *Literaturnaia gazeta*, no. 50, December 9, 1987, p. 10.

days in advance, and local authorities had the power to ban demonstrations if the activities violated Soviet laws or "threaten public order and the safety of citizens." The guidelines established standard penalties for holding unauthorized demonstrations. Violators were liable to fines of up to two thousand rubles or imprisonment for up to two months (up to six months for repeated violations)[32] – obviously an enormous weakening of the penalties formerly meted out for engaging in illegal challenging acts. The intention was to make enforcement of these laws consistent, so that harsh punishment would be unnecessary. The guidelines were soon followed by a series of laws passed by republican legislatures to enforce them. Moreover, recognizing that "the militia's strength is inadequate" for enforcing the new laws, the Soviet government issued a decree in July 1988 expanding and upgrading MVD special forces battalions. These were to remain under all-union control, largely for dealing with cases in which local authorities had lost control (as had already occurred by this time in Armenia and parts of Azerbaijan).[33] These special forces units, the infamous OMON, were to play a consequential role in the events precipitating the collapse of the USSR. Earlier, in November 1987, the Ministry of Internal Affairs had decreed the creation of special units for policing demonstrations under the jurisdiction of local police units in major cities as an additional means for beefing up enforcement of legal regulations governing demonstration activity.[34]

But an explosion of challenging acts outside this legal framework was unleashed in the wake of the Nineteenth Party Conference, with its freewheeling debates. As Figure 7.1b indicates, a sharp rise in the number of demonstrations occurred after the conference, particularly in the Baltic and Georgia. The vast majority of these protests were unauthorized, but the very scale of action made it difficult to apply legal sanctions.[35] As Figure 7.1c shows, throughout this period a further decline occurred in the regularity with which repression was applied against demonstrations. Thus, in all from June through December 1988 at least 457 demonstrations with a hundred participants or more took place, with a total of 2,328 arrests,

---

[32] *Izvestiia*, July 29, 1988, p. 2.
[33] *L'Unita*, in *FBIS*, October 19, 1988, pp. 65–67. The quotation is from Major-General Viacheslav Ogorodnikov, then first deputy chief of the Main Administration for the Maintenance of Public Order of the USSR Ministry of Internal Affairs.
[34] TASS, in *FBIS*, September 1, 1988, p. 27.
[35] On the ways in which this undermined legal regulation of protest in Moscow, see Bill Keller, "In Moscow, Tolerance of Protests," *The New York Times*, June 8, 1988, p. A12.

injuries, or deaths (an average of 5.1 per demonstration) and with 20 percent (93) of all demonstrations experiencing some government repression. Overall, the total number of arrests, injuries, and deaths inflicted by the government remained relatively stable throughout the country as a whole in comparison with the previous period. In 1988 the police deployed tear gas against crowds on more than a thousand occasions, and by July 1988 more than a thousand police and soldiers had been left injured and six dead in attempts to repress unauthorized demonstrations and disorders.[36] In short, the capacity of the state to enforce a regulatory regime that relied on law to discriminate between types of challenges was increasingly taxed by the explosion in protest activity, particularly as the number of groups mobilizing grew.

Local authority functioned as the gatekeeper for what was permissible, a power exercised with considerable variation. As a group of legal experts noted in October 1988:

> One consequence is that strange picture whereby officially sanctioned rallies were held in the Baltic republics, for instance, on the most acute political problems; special operations detachments in Moscow broke up a rally devoted to the Czechoslovak events of twenty years ago; and the Leningrad authorities have long turned a blind eye to rallies held by "Pamyat," whose slogans and calls directly contravene not only the Constitution but Soviet criminal legislation.[37]

In many localities, the Brezhnevian regime of repression continued to function, with local governments refusing to grant permission for any demonstrations and repressing attempts to organize challenges with great consistency. By contrast, in places where nationalist movements had already begun to exercise influence over local governments, legal regulation of protest hardly functioned at all. The Estonian government, for instance, refused altogether to implement the USSR decree on regulating demonstrations.[38] A Latvian law was not passed until July 1989, in this case banning events which challenged the "fundamentals of the state and social system" of the Latvian government (as opposed to the Soviet government, obviously leaving room for the possibility of banning attempts by local Russians to mobilize against secession).[39]

---

[36] TASS in *FBIS*, July 5, 1989, p. 70; UPI, July 30, 1988 (19:55 GMT).
[37] *Sovetskaia kul'tura*, in *FBIS*, October 28, 1988, p. 69.
[38] *Sovetskaia Estoniia*, May 19, 1989, p. 1.
[39] *Sovetskaia Latviia*, November 2, 1989, p. 4.

But the fundamental problem with the government's attempts to regulate challenging acts through law at the very moment when these acts were exploding was the sheer inability of many republican and local governments to enforce the regulations. In Lithuania, for instance, regulations banning unauthorized rallies issued in August 1988 were simply outstripped by events; after the massive public backlash to police actions in September 1988 that brought about the demise of the Songaila government, the regulations remained unenforced.[40] In many localities a growing gap appeared between the regulatory intentions of the authorities and their ability to carry out those intentions in practice. In places where republican and local authorities were reluctant to grant any permits for demonstrations to opposition groups, applicants took matters into their own hands, thereby undermining the process of regulation.

In many major urban centers significantly more applications for holding demonstrations were rejected than were granted. In Leningrad, for instance, thirty applications were made for conducting demonstrations in the first nine months of 1987, only eleven of which were approved by local authorities. In most cases those who were refused decided to demonstrate in any case.[41] With such massive violations of the regulations, the impossibility of enforcing punishment against violators was apparent. The following description of developments in Georgia, drawn from the report of the parliamentary commission established to investigate the April 1989 Tbilisi massacres, is fairly typical of what occurred in late 1988 in those large urban centers where street challenges were expanding:

the holding of unauthorized rallies had become a general rule in the republic largely because the authorities did not authorize the holding of any rallies. Having failed to obtain permission to hold official rallies, representatives of the public and informal organizations opted for holding unauthorized rallies. . . . Following the adoption of the well known legislative acts on the procedure for holding rallies and demonstrations in August 1988, the republic's local organs of power received 33 applications for permission to hold sundry mass events, but local Soviet executive committees gave permission for only 6 such events. Despite this, 28 unauthorized rallies were held, and the holding of such rallies became the general rule from then on.[42]

[40] *Vozrozhdenie* [Vilnius], no. 5, February 1989, pp. 1, 6.
[41] *Sobesednik*, no. 3, January 1988, p. 7.
[42] *Izvestiia*, in *FBIS*, January 9, 1990, p. 71.

Throughout 1988 and 1989, the proportion of unauthorized rallies increased steadily. In the first six months of 1988, 246 unauthorized demonstrations took place in Moscow, undoubtedly a large proportion of the total number of demonstrations in the city.[43] In the following four months, the number of unauthorized demonstrations in Moscow had climbed to 398.[44] Out of the 724 "mass events" that took place in Ukraine in the first nine months of 1989, 338 (47 percent) were unauthorized.[45] There were even times when the authorities were forced to suspend existing legislation regulating demonstrations because they realized that enforcement incited rather than contained protest. Such was the case in Moscow (and in a number of other cities) during the first session of the Congress of People's Deputies in May 1989, when, following an attack by the militia on a Democratic Union demonstration of two thousand people, the Congress suggested that the Moscow City Soviet set aside Luzhniki Stadium as a free gathering spot for demonstrators during the remainder of the Congress's sessions.[46] A public opinion poll of twenty-five hundred respondents across the USSR, conducted by the Academy of Social Sciences in 1989, found that 41 percent of the Soviet population believed that unauthorized demonstrations were "perfectly or partially permissible."[47]

In short, by late 1988 and early 1989 it was evident that Gorbachev's effort to introduce a legal regulatory regime as a gatekeeper for challenging acts had already failed in many parts of the country. In retrospect the idea of utilizing law as a means to regulate protest in the Soviet Union was probably doomed to failure, given what we know to have been the attitude of Soviet citizens to law and the widespread subversion of rules characteristic of this society. The gap between legal regulations and their enforcement only grew larger over the ensuing months. In April 1989, at the very time of the Tbilisi events, the Soviet criminal code was amended to punish calls for overthrow of the political system with up to seven years in prison, deliberate acts of inciting ethnic hatred with up to ten years in prison, and insulting state organs and "public organizations" (a codeword for the Communist Party) with up to three years in prison. These repre-

---

[43] TASS, in *FBIS*, August 5, 1988, p. 45. According to the report, only ninety-three unauthorized meetings had taken place over the last six months of 1987. The figures refer to demonstrations of all sizes.
[44] *Moskovskie novosti*, no. 46, November 1988, p. 14.
[45] *Radianska Ukraina*, in *FBIS*, November 30, 1989, p. 69.
[46] *Izvestiia*, in *FBIS*, May 28, 1989, pp. 39–42.
[47] *Sobesednik*, in *FBIS*, June 29, 1990, p. 6.

sented considerable reductions in the penalties meted out for these crimes, but were still potentially significant penalties had they been enforced. But in the context of the broadening contention of the tide, they were not enforceable. In 1990, as the Soviet state slipped further into disarray, additional laws were passed banning movements that kindled ethnic hostility or strife, punishing those who publicly insulted the USSR president, and establishing a legal process for secession from the USSR (actually intended to make secession difficult if not impossible by requiring that a republic first gain a two-thirds vote within the republic in favor of secession, go through a five-year waiting period, and obtain the approval of the USSR Supreme Soviet and Congress of People's Deputies). None of these laws was enforceable in the context of the tide, and none was taken seriously by those challenging the Soviet state.

But what was significant was not merely the failure of the attempt to impose legal regulation of revolt, but also the fact that the imagined alternative to its failure was not Stalinism but Brezhnevism, not severe violence against opponents violating the bounds of the acceptable, but an attempt to enforce order through the regularity of institutions and to recapture the lost predictability of the well-ordered party-state. At this time, for instance, the notion that a state of emergency should be declared in particular regions of the country began to be raised by Gorbachev's critics as a means for gaining back control over the streets. Yet, as challenges accelerated, institutional repertoires that were effective in demobilizing challenges in the 1970s proved incapable of doing so within the altered institutional environment and tidal context of the late 1980s.

## First Attempts to Reestablish Order

The first attempts to impose a crackdown on unauthorized challenging acts occurred in Armenia and Azerbaijan. These set the tone for many of the measures taken in late 1988 and early 1989 to strengthen enforcement of the legal regime governing demonstrations and ultimately for the authorities' fateful reaction to events in Tbilisi in April 1989. Shortly after the Sumgait pogroms, a state of emergency was declared in a number of locations in Azerbaijan, but sizeable acts of protest continued in Yerevan. On March 22, on the eve of the announcement of the Soviet government's decision about Karabakh's status, up to sixty thousand army troops were introduced into Yerevan to establish order and to aid in "neutralizing" the Karabakh Committee; they patrolled the city and cordoned off Opera

Square, the main site of Karabakh Committee demonstrations. The Armenian and Azerbaijani governments issued new regulations governing demonstrations that required application to the local authorities ten days in advance and threatened one to two years of imprisonment for repeat offenders. Paruir Airikian, leader of the radical nationalist Association for Self-Determination and a longtime advocate of Armenian independence, was arrested and charged with "spreading deliberately false fabrications discrediting the Soviet state and social system" – a throwback to the Brezhnev years. The republican government officially banned the Karabakh Committee, and several demonstrations attempting to protest the crackdown attracted small numbers and were forcibly broken up.[48] Gorbachev publicly denied Armenian demands for transfer of Karabakh, but in an effort to deflate the Karabakh issue offered instead a series of measures for economic development of the territory and improved access to Armenian-language media. An appeal by the Karabakh Committee for the population to remain at home in protest fell largely on deaf ears. In short, the Soviet government appeared successful in its initial efforts to shut down the Armenian protests in March 1988 – even to the point where the military withdrew from Yerevan a few days later.

But control proved elusive, in large part due to the altered institutional environment of *glasnost'*. Less than a month after the Karabakh Committee was declared illegal, a massive mourning procession commemorating the victims of both 1915 and the Sumgait pogroms and expressing support for unification of Karabakh with Armenia was tolerated at Matenadaran, the memorial monument to the Armenian genocide. Several subsequent demonstrations in early May were quickly broken up by the police. When outrage over the first sentencings of those convicted of crimes during the Sumgait pogroms touched off a protest march of eighty thousand in mid-May, troops cordoned off Opera Square and prevented the crowd from entering, but otherwise did not interfere. Analogous protests in Baku at the time caused the Soviet government to introduce tanks and troops to protect Armenian neighborhoods. In Yerevan in particular, control over unauthorized demonstrations by the Karabakh Committee (which now called itself "the Committee of the Karabakh Movement of Armenia," since the ban on the Karabakh Committee was still nominally in force) broke down completely after new republican Communist Party leaders

---

[48] *Kommunist* (Yerevan), March 25, 1988, p. 2; *Vesti iz SSSR*, 5/6–1, 1988; AFP, in *FBIS*, March 28, 1988, p. 54.

were selected in Armenia and Azerbaijan on May 21. Huge unauthorized demonstrations once again filled Opera Square. With unrest in Karabakh continuing and the atmosphere surrounding the forthcoming Nineteenth Party Conference encouraging the pressing of Armenian demands, republican authorities displayed little capacity or desire to control the situation. Organizers of demonstrations during this period were arrested on one occasion only (and in that instance, fined a mere fifty rubles). The legal regulatory regime established at the end of March never functioned.

Throughout the summer and fall of 1988 Moscow exhibited inconsistent efforts to control the situation. In his memoirs, Gorbachev reports the debates within the Politburo in early June 1988 over how to react to the unrest in Armenia and Azerbaijan. One faction, represented by Gromyko and Ligachev, called for introducing the army into both republics to regain control. Another, represented by Yakovlev and Gorbachev, favored upgrading the federal status of Karabakh, granting it autonomous republic status within Azerbaijan, though this solution, he observes, was made impossible by the attempts by the Karabakh Committee to force unification. The only option left to the Soviet leadership, Gorbachev contends, was to introduce troops and try to maintain the status quo – essentially the Ligachev position. Ultimately, this was the strategy adopted. The problem with this strategy was not that it could not be implemented, but that it did not resolve the underlying issues feeding mobilization and left unresolved the issue of "what next?" According to Gorbachev, when he posed this question to his colleagues, he received no coherent answer.[49] So long as the Karabakh conflict was the only conflict requiring military intervention, it could be managed, but as the number of situations that crept out of control proliferated in 1989, institutional resources were stretched thin, and the role played by the military itself came under attack.

At the end of the Nineteenth Party Conference in June 1988, when Gorbachev once again renounced the possibility of altering republican boundaries, a new wave of protest ensued in Armenia and a general strike paralyzed the republic. On July 4, to convince reluctant airport employees to join the general strike, a column of ten thousand demonstrators descended on the Zvartnots airport, successfully shutting down the facility. In response, soldiers and MVD special forces were deployed to take back control of the airport. The crowd was disorderly, throwing stones

---

[49] Mikhail Gorbachev, *Zhizn' i reformy*, vol. 1 (Moscow: Novosti, 1995), pp. 507, 509.

and bottles at the soldiers. When negotiations with the crowd broke down, the MVD troops were ordered to clear the airport, which they did with a degree of brutality, seriously injuring thirty-six and killing one. This repression gave rise to a backlash, as hundreds of thousands of Armenians filled the streets of Yerevan and strikes shut down industry in protest. Many of the wounded were not even taken to the hospital, but directly to Opera Square, where they were displayed before the mass demonstration then in progress.[50]

By the middle of July, the Karabakh government had petitioned once again to be united with Armenia, and this was again rejected by the Soviet government. To contain the growing unrest Moscow introduced troops into Yerevan, forcibly exiled independence advocate Paruir Airikian by bundling him onto a plane to Addis-Ababa, began to expel Karabakh Committee members from the Communist Party, and initiated a wave of arrests in Karabakh. The general strike in Armenia was successfully broken by threatening to dismiss enterprise directors who tolerated worker absences. But unauthorized mass demonstrations continued to be held on a weekly basis by the Karabakh Committee, with little attempt by the authorities to rein them in. The large size of the demonstrations and the backlash generated by the violence at Zvartnots apparently dissuaded the authorities from attempting a full-scale crackdown, and only occasional fines were imposed on the organizers of unauthorized demonstrations. By September the republican authorities had initiated consultations with the Karabakh Committee in an effort to coopt the movement rather than repress it.[51] At the same time, the Soviet government imposed a state of emergency in Karabakh in an attempt to quell the violence.

But by November 1988 order had broken down on a much larger scale when violence between Armenians and Azerbaijanis accelerated. A state of emergency was imposed in a number of cities in Azerbaijan, and military units had to be brought in to protect Armenian communities under attack from Azerbaijani crowds. General Aleksandr Lebed' recalls being ordered to Baku with his troops and told not to use weapons under any circumstances, but rather, through the very presence of the troops, to "convince and persuade." As Lebed' remarked, "it was unclear whom I was supposed

---

[50] The demonstrator killed was shot at close range with a plastic bullet. For detailed accounts, see Yuri Rost, *Armenian Tragedy* (New York: St. Martin's Press, 1990), pp. 52–55; *Izvestiia*, July 17, 1988, p. 6; *Radio Liberty Research Bulletin*, RL 312/88, July 11, 1988, p. 2.
[51] *Vesti iz SSSR*, 17/18–1, 1988.

to convince and what I was supposed to persuade them of."[52] Despite the troops' presence, the unrest continued. Special forces units were called in to clear Lenin Square, the site of anti-Armenian rallies. The situation in Armenia was similarly deteriorating, with attacks on Azerbaijanis accelerating. With the Karabakh Committee increasingly resembling an alternative government, Moscow decided to declare a state of emergency in Yerevan as well and to seize back control over the streets by imposing a curfew. This effort gained new momentum after the disastrous earthquake that struck Armenia on December 7. Shortly afterward, Gorbachev ordered the arrest of several hundred Karabakh Committee activists, many of whom were flown to Moscow and kept in custody for six months without a trial. Under the command of General Al'bert Makashov (later to become infamous for his extreme Russian nationalism) a ban on demonstrations was strictly enforced in Yerevan. Attempts to organize protests against the repression met with further repression from special forces units, with numerous demonstrators wounded and arrested.[53] In addition, Karabakh was placed under a special form of administration under the direct supervision of the USSR government in a concerted effort to pacify the region.

The declaration of emergency in Armenia in December 1988 was relatively successful in temporarily quashing the Karabakh movement, in large part because the mobilizational networks necessary to challenge repression had been damaged by the earthquake, but also because of the regularity with which violations of the emergency regime were repressed by General Makashov.[54] Still, "the attempt of the old authorities to rule without the nation," as Ron Suny called the crackdown,[55] could not be maintained indefinitely, particularly as mobilization spread to other republics. In May 1989, within a very different political context altered by the Tbilisi massacres, the Soviet government released the Karabakh Committee activists, and control over the streets of Yerevan quickly evaporated. Yet, as Figure 7.1 indicates, early 1989 was a time when the

[52] Aleksandr Lebed', *Za derzhavu obidno . . .* (Moscow: Moskovskaia pravda, 1995), p. 230.
[53] *Krasnaia zvezda*, in *CDSP*, vol. 40, no. 51 (Jan. 18, 1989), p. 7; Rost, *Armenian Tragedy*, pp. 77–90.
[54] For examples of repressed demonstrations in Yerevan and Baku during this period, see *Vesti iz SSSR*, 2–1, 1989; 4–1, 1989; 5/6–1, 1989; 7/8–2, 1989; *Ekspress khronika*, no. 11, March 12, 1989.
[55] Ronald Grigor Suny, *Looking toward Ararat: Armenia in Modern History* (Bloomington, IN: Indiana University Press, 1993), p. 234.

regime took a tougher stance toward unauthorized protests more generally. This was true not only in Armenia and Azerbaijan, but in Moldova,
Ukraine, Belorussia, and Georgia as well. The breakdown of control
that had characterized the Armenian-Azerbaijani conflict in 1988 was no
longer to be tolerated. From December 1988 through March 1989 47
percent of all demonstrations in these six republics experienced some
degree of government repression (compared to only 15 percent for
these republics from May through November 1988). The Baltic, by contrast, remained largely unaffected by the tougher stance, while Central
Asia still slept. This was a time when the number of demonstrations in the
USSR as a whole was climbing sharply despite the demobilization in
Armenia and Azerbaijan. Protest was spreading laterally and exponentially,
but as Figure 7.1c shows, in the first three months of 1989 the proportion
of demonstrations experiencing some form of government repression kept
pace with the rapid proliferation of protest activity overall. Indeed, it was
the fear that the breakdown of order which had plagued Armenia and
Azerbaijan would spread to Georgia that precipitated the violent crackdown in Tbilisi in April 1989, with repercussions that were far from
intended.

## The "Tbilisi Syndrome"

More than any other event, the violent crackdown on April 9, 1989, in
Tbilisi defined the incapacity of the Soviet regime to marginalize nationalist challenges by force during the remaining years of its existence. In
Chapter 4 I explore in detail the events that led up to the wave of secessionist mobilization that washed across Georgia in April 1989 and the ways
in which the Tbilisi events transformed Georgian national consciousness.
Here, I am concerned more with the issues of why a crackdown was
attempted in the first place and why the events in Tbilisi so dramatically
undermined the capacity of the Soviet state to intervene forcefully in subsequent contexts.

One of the striking aspects of the Tbilisi events is just how quickly a
decision was reached in Moscow to use force against the demonstrators.
This contrasts markedly with the situation in November 1988, when secessionist demonstrations of analogous size had rocked the Georgian capital.
At that time the Georgian Communist Party leadership, frightened by the
radicalizing public mood, discussed the possibility of introducing tanks and
declaring martial law in the republic. Several telegrams were dispatched

to Moscow requesting the introduction of troops.[56] Instead, Gorbachev sent former Georgian Party boss Eduard Shevardnadze to Tbilisi to defuse the situation peacefully. But in April 1989, under the influence of events in neighboring Armenia and Azerbaijan, a greater propensity to use force was evident among decision makers in Moscow. Egged on by separatist demonstrations in Abkhazia, huge demonstrations of one hundred thousand assembled in Tbilisi on the square outside the Georgian House of Government beginning on April 6, and under the direction of nationalist leaders, radicalized in a secessionist direction. The offices of the leaders of the Georgian Communist Party were located only five hundred yards from the square, and descriptions indicate that the psychological pressure of the demonstrations on the Georgian Communist leadership was intense. As the demands of the orators radicalized, Communist Party leaders came to believe, as they had earlier in November, that they were about to be overthrown. From April 6, the first day of large-scale partic-ipation in demonstrations, the republican party leadership once again began to send telegrams to Moscow requesting help in putting down the demonstrations. Little attempt was made to negotiate with the demon-strators. A proposal by the Patiashvili leadership on April 7 to their nation-alist opponents to end the demonstrations was rejected out of hand, but no further negotiations were conducted. Moreover, Patiashvili specifically declined recommendations from Moscow that Shevardnadze and Razu-movsky be dispatched to Tbilisi to help negotiate a peaceful end to the protests, as in November 1988, arguing that he fully controlled the situa-tion. Ironically, as we saw in Chapter 4, the organizers of the protests were planning to end their campaign within a few days in any case because of fatigue and the uncertain commitment of the public. But on the evening of April 7 the republican party leadership, with the approval of Moscow,[57]

---

[56] Sobchak, *Tbilisskii izlom*, pp. 54, 122.

[57] Where this approval came from has never been conclusively determined, since the orders were given orally. However, it is clear that there was approval from someone in Moscow, and evidence points most clearly to Central Committee Secretary Viktor Chebrikov (who oversaw both the police and nationalities policy within the Central Committee Secretariat, was in constant direct contact with Patiashvili, and briefed Gorbachev and Shevardnadze on events on their return from London) and Defense Minister Dmitry Yazov. A short meeting of Politburo members at Vnukovo Airport on April 7, where they were gathered to meet Gorbachev on his return from London, did not approve such measures, but instead sanctioned the use of troops to guard government facilities and a negotiated settlement to the crisis. The direct involvement of the military in the decision making seems clear, as Yazov's representative, General Kochetov, was present in Tbilisi and since Yazov was

unanimously supported a plan to gain back control over the streets forcibly. In short, neither Moscow nor the local republican authorities displayed much patience with the protests.

The reason for this impatience appears to have been the belief that quick action was needed to contain the spread of nationalist revolt, and the justification for this, at least in the conversations that took place within the decision-making rooms, was the necessity of avoiding a Sumgait-type situation. The example of the events of 1988 in Armenia and Azerbaijan heavily colored the thinking of both central and republican authorities. Yegor Ligachev, for instance, recalled that at the April 7 meeting of a group of Politburo members which approved transfers of special forces police units from Russia and military troops in Armenia to Georgia, "everyone mentioned Sumgait, where the authorities didn't act and where dozens of peaceful citizens died. . . . The leitmotif of all the speeches . . . was to prevent ethnic conflict and more victims. We had to learn a lesson from Sumgait – not to be late again."[58] Patiashvili similarly recalled that "we constantly feared a repeat of Sumgait," and that the Sumgait example was used in the Georgian context by particular forces within the party to "provoke active measures against the population."[59] General Rodionov, who commanded the forces that carried out the operation, had played a critical role in the crackdown in Armenia and Azerbaijan only several months earlier. He was known in Moscow as someone who believed that the time had come to impose law and order. General Kochetov, the first deputy minister of defense who on April 7 was dispatched by Moscow to aid in overseeing the operation, arrived in Tbilisi from Armenia, where he had been observing the implementation of the state of emergency there. There were obvious differences between the mobilizations in Tbilisi in April 1989 and the pogroms of Sumgait in February 1988. The demonstrations on the square outside the House of Government threatened the republican government and contained an anti-Abkhaz strain, but primar-

---

reprimanded by Gorbachev after the events for using military force without his consent. Ligachev's role still remains clouded; many subsequently accused him of ordering the crackdown, but he strongly denied the accusations.

[58] Yegor Ligachev, *Inside Gorbachev's Kremlin* (New York: Pantheon Books, 1993), pp. 153–54. Ligachev chaired the session, as Gorbachev at the time was returning from London. The meeting only included those members of the Politburo who were also Central Committee Secretaries. Another meeting of the group apparently was held in the Central Committee Secretariat on April 8, though less is known about that meeting. See Nikolai Ryzhkov, *Perestroika: Istoriia predatel'stva* (Moscow: Novosti, 1992), pp. 215–16.

[59] *Izvestiia*, September 14, 1991, p. 3.

ily this was a national revolution, not a pogrom. Sumgait in this sense was little more than a codeword in party discourse for the need to engage in decisive action to turn back the growing tide of nationalist protest and disorder spreading throughout the USSR. In conversations with officials from the Central Committee in Moscow, republican party leaders gained the distinct impression that their efforts to restore order had the unequivocal support of their superiors.[60] The successes of the authorities in shutting down massive demonstrations in Armenia and Azerbaijan since December 1988 gave Moscow renewed belief in its ability to squelch protest forcefully – through the regular and efficient operation of law enforcement institutions, not through severe force.

But so strong was the appeal of the demonstrators within the population that the Georgian police were not considered fully reliable to carry out a crackdown. According to the original plans, twenty-five hundred city policemen were supposed to participate in clearing the square, but only five hundred were available for the assignment since large numbers of local police failed to appear for work. Moreover, most of the republic's MVD forces, including internal troops, were deployed at that time in Stepanakert to enforce the state of emergency in Karabakh or in Abkhazia to contain ethnic clashes there. Because of the inadequacy of local law enforcement forces, on the eve of the crackdown Moscow dispatched an additional two thousand special forces units to Tbilisi. But this was not considered sufficient for the operation and it was suggested that regular army forces be used in a supporting role. Generals Rodionov and Kochetov at first balked at the idea. The army, they argued, should not be used as a police force. But the republican leadership saw no alternative, and the plan that ultimately received approval from the Ministry of Defense in Moscow called for using about five hundred soldiers in the second echelon, largely for psychological effect on the protestors through a massing of force. Yet, on Moscow's orders General Rodionov, a military commander, was placed in charge of the operation, including command of the participating MVD forces. The action was to take place at about 4 A.M. on the morning of April 9, primarily because this was when the number of demonstrators on the square would be the smallest. The plan was to clear the square and then introduce a state of emergency, including restrictions on press freedoms.[61]

---

[60] Sobchak, *Tbilisskii izlom*, pp. 96–98, 100–11.
[61] Sobchak, *Tbilisskii izlom*, pp. 18–19, 92–93, 95–96, 108, 133, 136; *Zaria vostoka*, July 22, 1989, p. 4.

## The Transcendence of Regimes of Repression

At noon on April 8, in a last-ditch attempt to intimidate the protesters, a show of force was mounted on the streets of Tbilisi. Military helicopters flew overhead and tanks were paraded through the ranks of the demonstrators, but these were blocked by the crowds and traffic. According to subsequent investigations, the show of force had the opposite effect to what was intended. On previous nights, only about a thousand demonstrators remained on the square overnight. A crowd that size could have been handled easily. But that evening, expecting a crackdown and believing that they could halt the operation simply by sitting on the ground, ten thousand protestors appeared on the square, among them a large number of women. As the commission subsequently investigating the events concluded:

the whole city knew of the forthcoming use of force and that the troops were meant to use force against the participants in the rally and disperse them. Therefore, family members and friends of the hunger strikers made their way to the square, reasoning that the larger the number of people, the less likely it would be that force would be used.[62]

Suggestions to put off the operation because of the size of the crowd were rejected by Patiashvili only a short time before the operation began.[63]

Because of the noise of the crowd, as the operations began in the early hours of April 9, the warnings to clear the square that were delivered over a police megaphone could not be heard. No one thought of using the powerful public address system located in the square. Moreover, because the size of the crowd far exceeded what the police expected, a gap appeared in the police lines as special forces attempted to surround the crowd on three sides and push them out of the square. To fill the gap, a squadron of soldiers was deployed from the second echelon. A significant number of the fatalities were due to suffocation from the crush created as demonstrators were pushed off the square without sufficient room to exit. The crowd then rioted. To defend themselves and to clear the square, the special forces used rubber truncheons and tear gas (including some unauthorized gases with poisonous substances), while the soldiers, who were not specially equipped for crowd control, brutally began to beat the demonstrators with the sharpened edges of their sapper shovels. By the time the square was cleared, 19 people had died (16 of these women), 290

---

[62] *Izvestiia*, December 30, 1989, p. 2.　　[63] *Zaria vostoka*, July 22, 1989, p. 4.

had been wounded (183 seriously), and several thousand had been poisoned from the close range use of tear gas and other poisonous chemical substances. The Georgian Communist Party leadership observed the massacre from the window of the House of Government, but made no effort to interfere.[64]

In terms of the severity of violence deployed against demonstrators, the Tbilisi events exceeded the Novocherkassk events of 1962; many more people were injured in Tbilisi than in Novocherkassk, and the number of deaths was approximately the same. In contrast to Novocherkassk, troops did not fire directly into the crowd, and the police, the military, and the party leadership had not intended to inflict such massive injury. But more significantly, unlike Novocherkassk, Tbilisi became a watershed in the capacity of the Soviet government to apply force against populations with impunity. As Yegor Ligachev later pointed out, although the Tbilisi events were neither the first nor the last instances in which significant force was used against populations in the *perestroika* period, "none had political reverberations equal to those of the Tbilisi Affair."[65] Not only was the severity of force used subjected to heavy criticism, but the military for the first time was vilified for acting as an instrument of repression against the population. As the Kazakh writer Olzhas Suleimenov observed about what by 1990 had come to be called the "Tbilisi Syndrome" within party and military circles:

The post-Tbilisi criticism affected the army. It tried to avoid participating in internal conflicts. It was in a certain way "pulled out of the game." And this position of being a sideline observer ... stimulated action by ... forces in society. In Fergana, soldiers who were standing on guard patiently bore spits and insults, but did not shoot into the air. In Kishinev women lay down in front of tanks that were on parade, and the tanks turned back. In Nakhichevan the people destroyed border installations, and not a single shot. And so it came to be widely believed that the army would not attack unarmed people.[66]

As Figure 7.1a indicates, repressive measures against demonstrators were fairly common through April 1989, at which time they peaked and began to decline, particularly in 1990. Moreover, as Figure 7.1c shows, even though the regularity of repression against demonstrators had dropped significantly in comparison with the Brezhnev years, until Tbilisi the

[64] Sobchak, *Tbilisskii izlom*, pp. 138–45; *Izvestiia*, December 30, 1989, p. 2.
[65] Ligachev, *Inside Gorbachev's Kremlin*, pp. 146–47.
[66] *Rabochaia tribuna*, February 25, 1990, p. 1.

Soviet regime still engaged in repression against demonstrators in a significant proportion of cases. But after April 1989 a very small proportion of demonstrations were subjected to repression. Not only did Tbilisi undermine the Soviet state's first concerted efforts to defend itself against the tide of nationalism and make the regime more reluctant to use significant force against challengers, but because of what occurred in the wake of Tbilisi mass beliefs about the effectiveness of repression and expectations that troops would engage in severe repressive actions also began to alter dramatically.

The significant effect of April 1989 on both institutions and populations was due not so much to the events themselves or the backlash they produced within Georgia. Rather, it was because of the broader institutional environment within which large-scale repression occurred, which by spring 1989 had grown conducive to politicizing the issue. For one thing, the rise of independent media coverage – because of the end of censorship over government-owned media and the emergence of a vast informal press sector – spread word about the violence quickly within the Soviet population. Local and national newspapers gave detailed descriptions and photographs of the atrocities, despite the imposition of military censorship that accompanied the state of emergency declared after the events.[67] Press freedom altered significantly the content and flow of public information about acts of government repression.

Just as important was the fact that the incident preceded the opening of the new USSR Congress of People's Deputies, where, because of limited competitive elections, a visible opposition appeared for the first time within Soviet legislative institutions. Even before the first sessions began, newly elected deputies accused Moscow of a massive cover-up in the tragedy. Immediately after the Congress opened its first session on May 25, Latvian deputy Vilen Tolpezhnikov marched up to the podium out of turn and proposed a minute of silence in memory of the victims of Tbilisi – a request agreed to without a vote. The fact that this was done by a Latvian deputy demonstrates how an alliance of forces attempted to utilize the Tbilisi example as a way of undercutting the regime's repressive capacity. In effect, Tbilisi became an instrument of tidal politics, as other groups sought to utilize the opening afforded by the misuse of force to prevent force from being used against them. From the beginning of the new legislature's sessions, Tbilisi became the subject of heated parliamentary

[67] *Nedelia*, April 17–23, 1989, p. 8.

debate, and eventually a parliamentary commission was appointed to investigate the incident. Actually, even before the sessions of the parliament opened, the USSR Procuracy had begun a criminal investigation into the incident (the charges were abruptly dropped in March 1991, when conservative forces held sway within the government). The Tbilisi example became a symbolic weapon utilized by a broad array of nationalist movements in their attempts to undermine the regime's ability to exercise force against them. Shortly after the events, the chair of the Estonian Supreme Soviet called for opening criminal charges against the organizers of the massacre and for taking measures to ensure that similar occurrences did not repeat themselves "anywhere in the USSR."[68] At a 1989 counterdemonstration to the official celebration of November 7 in Kishinev, Moldavian Popular Front demonstrators called upon "the army of Kabul and Tbilisi" to "repent and restructure yourself."[69] Speakers at a demonstration in Volgograd in June 1990 warned that the Tbilisi events stood as an example of how the regime was planning to utilize extreme force against the population, citing as an illustration how troops then withdrawing from Eastern Europe were being redeployed to the city (and, according to rumor, were to be reorganized as special KGB forces).[70] Uzbek nationalists described the violence unleashed against demonstrators in Parkent in March 1990 as "yet another Tbilisi" – though the number of casualties was but a fraction of those at Tbilisi.[71]

The animosity and reproach suffered by the Soviet regime as a result of the Tbilisi fiasco made it significantly more difficult to commit force to put down unrest, emboldened nationalist movements to contest the use of force against them, created the basis for cross-national alliances of nationalist movements against the use of force, and accelerated processes of institutional disarray within the police and the military on the eve of the Soviet collapse.

## The Shifting Mobilization/Repression Relationship

I turn now to identifying the ways in which the Tbilisi events systematically altered the effectiveness of repression in demobilizing challenging

---

[68] *Sovetskaia Estoniia*, May 19, 1989, p. 1.
[69] Vladimir Socor, "Mass Protests and 'Exceptional Measures' in Kishinev," in *Report on the USSR*, vol. 1, no. 46 (November 17, 1989), p. 24.
[70] *Press-Reliz Agentsva "DS-Inform"*, no. 13, June 6, 1990, p. 1.
[71] *Svoboda* [Memorial Society], no. 7, 1990, p. 3.

acts in the USSR. I begin with the models of mobilization developed in Chapter 3, since, as noted earlier, an accurate assessment of the impact of repression on mobilization can only be made on the basis of a proper assessment of the role played by other factors in raising or lowering levels of mobilization; one of the shortcomings of much of the prior work on this subject has been the failure to control for the influence of other processes relevant to the mobilization/repression nexus.

Tables 7.1 and 7.2 present the results from introducing government repression against demonstrators into the demonstration model analyzing the frequency of attempts by nationalist movements to contest, and into the participation model analyzing levels of mass participation in these attempts developed in Chapter 3. These longitudinal regression models seek to explain weekly levels of mobilization over 237 weekly time periods stretching from January 1987 through August 1991 for fifteen non-Russian nationalities, for a total of 3,555 observations.[72] A series of variables representing different dimensions of government efforts to apply force vis-à-vis challengers were added to these models: (1) a variable representing the regularity of repression;[73] (2) the severity of repression, measured as the total number of arrests, injuries, and deaths per week inflicted on demonstrators at demonstrations by a nationality (this variable was lagged over a period of six weeks prior to the week being analyzed, to allow examination of the changing impact of repression on mobilization over time); and (3) a dummy variable measuring periods in which a state of emergency was

---

[72] Again, the demonstration model is a negative binomial regression whose coefficients can be exponentiated into incidence rate ratios (or the likely percent increase or decrease expected in the number of demonstrations from a unit change in the independent variable), and the participation model is an ordinary least squares regression, with panel corrected standard errors.

[73] This potentially ranged from 0 to 100, with 100 representing a completely repressive response to all demonstrations and zero representing a completely nonrepressive response. Several different methods of capturing the regularity of repression were tested. In the end, the index was a combination of two variables: one representing the proportion of demonstrations by a nationality occurring from January 1987 through the week prior to the one in question at which some degree of government repression was applied; the other representing the proportion of demonstrations by a nationality during the year prior to the week in question at which some degree of government repression was applied. Given the pre-*glasnost'* record of repression against demonstrations, it made interpretive sense to start each group with scores of 67 percent before any demonstrations for the group had occurred (the average proportion of demonstrations repressed across all groups during the Brezhnev era). In practice, scores ranged from 6 to 71, with a mean of 42 and standard deviation of 20.

Table 7.1. *Negative Binomial Regression of Effects of Government Repression on Weekly Count of Protest Demonstrations by Nationality, Controlling for Other Causal Processes (January 1987–August 1991)*[a]

| Independent variable | Equation 1 Jan. 1987–Aug. 1991 | | Equation 2 Jan. 1987–March 1989 | | Equation 3 April 1989–Aug. 1991 | |
|---|---|---|---|---|---|---|
| | Coefficient | Incidence rate ratio | Coefficient | Incidence rate ratio | Coefficient | Incidence rate ratio |
| Ln (demonstrations + 0.5), t − 1 | 0.456 (12.02)**** | 1.578 | 0.504 (6.06)**** | 1.656 | 0.384 (9.12)**** | 1.468 |
| Ln (demonstrations + 0.5), t − 2 | 0.122 (3.21)**** | 1.130 | −0.036 (−0.41) | .996 | 0.119 (2.82)*** | 1.126 |
| Ln (demonstrations + 0.5), t − 3 | 0.068 (1.77)* | 1.070 | 0.006 (0.07) | 1.006 | 0.070 (1.66)* | 1.073 |
| Ln (demonstrations + 0.5), t − 4 | 0.081 (2.12)** | 1.084 | 0.001 (0.01) | 1.001 | 0.098 (2.27)** | 1.103 |
| Ln (demonstrations + 0.5), t − 5 | 0.043 (1.14) | 1.044 | −0.103 (−1.14) | .902 | 0.057 (1.34) | 1.058 |
| Ln (demonstrations + 0.5), t − 6 | 0.025 (0.68) | 1.025 | −0.050 (−0.60) | .951 | 0.039 (0.94) | 1.039 |
| Ln population size (thousands), 1989 | −0.001 (0.01) | .999 | 0.036 (0.30) | 1.037 | 0.080 (1.07) | 1.083 |
| Dummy variable for union republican status | 0.350 (1.72)* | 1.419 | 1.653 (2.77)*** | 5.224 | 0.116 (0.51) | 1.123 |
| Linguistic assimilation, 1989 | −0.011 (−2.04)** | .989 | −0.007 (−0.60) | .993 | −0.018 (−2.75)*** | .983 |
| Level of urbanization, 1970 | 0.011 (2.28)** | 1.010 | 0.031 (2.60)*** | 1.031 | 0.013 (2.14)** | 1.013 |
| Dummy variable for period of electoral campaign | 0.213 (2.50)** | 1.237 | 0.500 (2.68)*** | 1.648 | 0.030 (0.23) | 1.030 |
| Political liberalization (ln week) | 0.465 (3.72)**** | 1.592 | 1.159 (4.24)**** | 3.187 | – | |
| Dummy variable for period after institutionalizing outcome | −0.442 (−5.23)**** | .643 | – | | −0.216 (−2.49)** | .805 |
| Regularity of repression against demonstrations | −0.018 (−4.33)**** | .982 | −0.026 (−3.10)*** | .974 | −0.008 (−1.62) | .992 |
| Arrests, injuries, and deaths of demonstrators (hundreds), t − 1 | −0.007 (−0.31) | .993 | −0.092 (−0.37) | .912 | −0.007 (−0.33) | .993 |
| Arrests, injuries, and deaths of demonstrators (hundreds), t − 2 | 0.003 (0.14) | 1.003 | −0.065 (−0.25) | .937 | −0.003 (−0.16) | .997 |
| Arrests, injuries, and deaths of demonstrators (hundreds), t − 3 | 0.012 (0.64) | 1.011 | −0.083 (−0.29) | .921 | 0.005 (0.27) | 1.005 |
| Arrests, injuries, and deaths of demonstrators (hundreds), t − 4 | −0.072 (−0.95) | .931 | 0.225 (1.04) | 1.252 | −0.158 (−0.95) | .854 |

356

| | Model 1 | | Model 2 | | Model 3 | |
|---|---|---|---|---|---|---|
| Arrests, injuries, and deaths of demonstrators (hundreds), t − 5 | 0.040 (2.49)** | 1.040 | 0.133 (0.53) | 1.143 | 0.028 (1.71)* | 1.029 |
| Arrests, injuries, and deaths of demonstrators (hundreds), t − 6 | 0.028 (2.31)** | 1.029 | 0.178 (0.56) | 1.195 | 0.022 (1.71)* | 1.023 |
| Dummy variable for declaration of state of emergency | −0.327 (−2.04)** | .721 | −1.248 (−3.78)**** | .287 | −0.385 (−1.89)* | .680 |
| Mass violent events involving nationality, t − 1 | 0.034 (3.91)**** | 1.035 | 0.022 (0.68) | 1.022 | 0.041 (4.39)**** | 1.042 |
| Mass violent events involving nationality, t − 2 | −0.025 (−1.84)* | .975 | 0.021 (0.62) | 1.021 | −0.020 (−1.40) | .980 |
| Mass violent events involving nationality, t − 3 | −0.004 (−0.30) | .996 | −0.012 (−0.31) | .988 | 0.002 (0.14) | 1.002 |
| Mass violent events involving nationality, t − 4 | −0.023 (−1.42) | .977 | −0.010 (−0.20) | .990 | −0.014 (−0.86) | .986 |
| Mass violent events involving nationality, t − 5 | 0.011 (0.87) | 1.011 | −0.003 (−0.06) | .997 | 0.017 (1.33) | 1.017 |
| Mass violent events involving nationality, t − 6 | −0.017 (−1.24) | .983 | −0.035 (−0.70) | .966 | −0.004 (−0.26) | .996 |
| Number of demonstrations by other nationalities, t − 1 | 0.004 (2.42)** | 1.004 | 0.011 (1.13) | 1.011 | 0.004 (2.21)** | 1.004 |
| Number of demonstrations by other nationalities, t − 2 | −0.007 (−3.20)**** | .993 | −0.015 (−1.70)* | .986 | −0.006 (−2.99)*** | .994 |
| Number of demonstrations by other nationalities, t − 3 | −0.002 (−0.89) | .998 | 0.003 (0.37) | 1.003 | −0.002 (−1.05) | .998 |
| Number of demonstrations by other nationalities, t − 4 | 0.005 (2.34)** | 1.005 | −0.012 (−1.36) | .988 | 0.005 (2.44)** | 1.005 |
| Number of demonstrations by other nationalities, t − 5 | −0.001 (−0.09) | .999 | 0.004 (0.37) | 1.004 | −0.001 (−0.14) | .999 |
| Number of demonstrations by other nationalities, t − 6 | −0.002 (−0.76) | .998 | 0.001 (0.04) | 1.001 | −0.001 (−0.63) | .999 |
| Constant | −3.049169 | | −7.945852 | | −1.375798 | |
| t × n | 3,555 | | 1,665 | | 1,875 | |
| Log likelihood | −3,161.9234 | | −807.38733 | | −2,278.2308 | |
| Wald model chi² | 1,101.43**** | | 394.14**** | | 470.60**** | |

*Significant at the .10 level  **Significant at the .05 level  ***Significant at the .01 level  ****Significant at the .001 level

Note:  n = 15 nationalities (excluding Russians); t = 237 weeks.

$^a$ Z-scores in parentheses.

Table 7.2. *Regression of Effects of Government Repression on Weekly Count of Participants in Protest Demonstrations by Nationality, Controlling for Other Causal Processes (January 1987–August 1991)*[a]

| Independent variable | Equation 1 Jan. 1987–Aug. 1991 | Equation 2 Jan. 1987–March 1989 | Equation 3 April 1989–Aug. 1991 |
|---|---|---|---|
| Participants in demonstrations, t − 1 | .2707354 (5.96)**** | .2942792 (3.61)**** | .1307264 (2.51)** |
| Participants in demonstrations, t − 2 | .0645816 (1.37) | .0295424 (0.32) | .0832464 (1.59) |
| Participants in demonstrations, t − 3 | .0566325 (1.20) | .0291631 (0.31) | .1056463 (2.02)** |
| Participants in demonstrations, t − 4 | .0058475 (0.12) | −.0369993 (−0.19) | .0515693 (0.98) |
| Participants in demonstrations, t − 5 | .0574465 (1.22) | .0077027 (0.08) | .0976912 (1.87)* |
| Participants in demonstrations, t − 6 | .0216999 (0.47) | .0632609 (0.70) | −.0402468 (−0.77) |
| Ln population size (thousands), 1989 | 2,506.8 (2.51)** | 4,702.5 (3.70)**** | 4,659.2 (2.95)*** |
| Thousands of participants in demonstrations, 1965–86 (squared) | 8.30 (3.09)*** | 11.9 (2.23)** | 4.93 (2.18)** |
| Linguistic assimilation, 1989 | −406.5 (−4.02)**** | −465.5 (−2.53)** | −368.0 (−3.26)**** |
| Dummy variable for peoples of traditionally Islamic cultures | −4,230.5 (−1.57) | 20,527.3 (3.99)**** | −18,674.7 (−3.95)**** |
| Dummy variable for period of electoral campaign | 8,121.4 (1.14) | −87.2 (−0.01) | 3,393.0 (0.32) |
| Dummy variable for period after institutionalizing outcome | −29,588.1 (−3.66)**** | — | −16,197.1 (−2.52)** |
| Regularity of repression against demonstrations | −673.3 (−5.08)**** | −2,861.1 (−5.67)**** | −4.40 (−0.02) |
| Arrests, injuries, and deaths inflicted on demonstrators (hundreds), t − 1 | −2,798.6 (−1.75)* | −1,077.0 (−0.06) | −2,920.4 (−1.90)* |
| Arrests, injuries, and deaths inflicted on demonstrators (hundreds), t − 2 | −1,025.1 (−0.67) | 12,221.4 (0.63) | −2,248.6 (−1.52) |
| Arrests, injuries, and deaths inflicted on demonstrators (hundreds), t − 3 | −1,146.2 (−0.75) | −22,733.0 (−1.17) | −1,919.0 (−1.31) |
| Arrests, injuries, and deaths inflicted on demonstrators (hundreds), t − 4 | −1,070.3 (−0.70) | 6,041.7 (0.31) | −1,954.4 (−1.34) |
| Arrests, injuries, and deaths inflicted on demonstrators (hundreds), t − 5 | 10,543.4 (6.96)**** | 20,014.1 (0.96) | 10,754.5 (7.38)**** |
| Arrests, injuries, and deaths inflicted on demonstrators (hundreds), t − 6 | 5,229.9 (3.42)**** | −4,206.6 (−0.17) | 7,326.6 (5.10)**** |

| | | | |
|---|---|---|---|
| Dummy variable for declaration of state of emergency | −28,393.6 (−1.20) | −168,202.8 (−2.26)** | 7,376.2 (0.38) |
| Dummy variable for period of heightened Armenian/Azerbaijani conflict | 30,487.7 (1.76)* | 18,398.2 (0.84) | 46,395.9 (2.02)** |
| Mass violent events involving nationality, t − 1 | 3,141.6 (1.06) | 1,964.1 (0.16) | 4,877.5 (2.00)** |
| Mass violent events involving nationality, t − 2 | −4,888.1 (−1.56) | −8,888.6 (−0.68) | −2,276.1 (−0.92) |
| Mass violent events involving nationality, t − 3 | 695.4 (0.22) | 9,416.9 (0.71) | −151.5 (−0.06) |
| Mass violent events involving nationality, t − 4 | −5,012.7 (−1.60) | −10,332.8 (−0.78) | −4,221.4 (−1.70)* |
| Mass violent events involving nationality, t − 5 | 892.2 (0.29) | 3,597.1 (0.28) | 73.8 (0.03) |
| Mass violent events involving nationality, t − 6 | −1,681.8 (−0.56) | −10,326.7 (−0.98) | 986.9 (0.41) |
| Participation by other nationalities (hundreds of thousands), t − 1 | 668.0 (2.15)** | 115.3 (0.36) | 876.2 (1.89)* |
| Participation by other nationalities (hundreds of thousands), t − 2 | −175.3 (−0.52) | −309.2 (−0.98) | 56.8 (0.12) |
| Participation by other nationalities (hundreds of thousands), t − 3 | −612.9 (−1.80)* | −703.9 (−2.26)** | −608.0 (−1.26) |
| Participation by other nationalities (hundreds of thousands), t − 4 | −339.2 (−1.00) | −355.2 (−1.15) | −833.4 (−1.72)* |
| Participation by other nationalities (hundreds of thousands), t − 5 | −265.4 (−0.79) | −375.5 (−1.20) | −458.5 (−0.96) |
| Participation by other nationalities (hundreds of thousands), t − 6 | 358.3 (1.16) | −361.3 (−1.24) | 864.6 (1.89)* |
| Constant | 22,799.58 | 133,505.8 | −17,796.28 |
| t × n | 3,555 | 1,665 | 1,875 |
| Log likelihood | −63,247.58 | −176,031.3 | −27,435.52 |
| Wald model chi² | 434.75**** | 133.75**** | 382.54**** |

*Significant at the .10 level     **Significant at the .05 level     ***Significant at the .01 level     ****Significant at the .001 level

*Note*: n = 15 nationalities (excluding Russians); t = 237 weeks.

[a] Coefficients represent OLS regression parameters, with panel-corrected standard errors.

declared against mobilization by members of a particular nationality. After analyzing the results for the sample as a whole, I divided the sample into pre-Tbilisi and post-Tbilisi time periods: January 1987 through March 1989 and April 1989 through August 1991 (the week of the Tbilisi events was excluded from this part of the analysis).

The analysis confirms much of what this chapter has noted up to this point.[74] It shows, for instance, that in the period prior to Tbilisi, the regularity of repression was a much more significant factor in containing mobilization than the severity of repression. For the January 1987 to March 1989 period, the number of arrests, injuries, and deaths of demonstrations had no statistically significant relationship with either the number of demonstrations or participation in these demonstrations. By contrast, each additional unit of variation in our index for the regularity of repression during this period produced a 2.6 percent reduction in the expected incidence of protest and a decline of 2,861 participants in demonstrations by a nationality per week. The patterns confirm that during the early Gorbachev period, as in its Brezhnevian predecessor, successful demobilization of populations through forceful means occurred primarily through the regularity and predictability of repression rather than its severity.

From April 1989 on, however, the effect of regular repression diminished enormously – for the demonstration model, declining to 0.8 percent per unit of the index, and for the participation model to a meager 4.4 participants per unit of the index (even here, in neither model was the regularity of repression statistically significant at the .10 level). After Tbilisi, the regularity of repression no longer exerted a systematic influence on

---

[74] In terms of the other variables in the models, little changed as a result of the introduction of the repression variables. For the demonstration model, the influence of electoral campaigns on demonstrations grew statistically significant in the first period, whereas the effect of institutionalizing outcomes grew statistically significant in the second period (these results uphold the interpretations given in Chapter 3). Moreover, cross-case influences on demonstrations appeared weaker in the early period of the cycle. Besides this, all the patterns of statistical significance and sign direction found in Table 3.4 in Chapter 3 remained fundamentally the same, while a few variables adjusted slightly up or down in their estimated coefficients and levels of statistical significance. A fixed-effects model was also tested, with analogous results. For the participation model, however, more significant changes occurred. Urbanization and time dependence (a dummy for liberalization) had to be removed from the specification due to multicollinearity. And in the second half of the cycle, an additional cross-case influence appeared for the sixth week of the lagged variable for participation by other nationalities. Otherwise, the results remained substantively identical.

mobilization, losing much of the potency it had exercised in the preceding period. Thus, populations and activists reacted differently to repression before and after Tbilisi; not only did repression occur with less regularity after April 1989 when viewing the record for the country as a whole, but even in those contexts in which repression was carried out with regularity, its effects were generally diminished in comparison with the immediate past.

The analysis also indicates a serious deterioration in the demobilizing capabilities of the regime through the declaration of states of emergency – a technique used on numerous occasions throughout the *glasnost'* period for dampening mobilizational challenges when they escaped local control. In all, thirteen states of emergency were introduced in the Soviet Union from January 1987 through August 1991, although in other instances of unrest significant force was applied without formally declaring a state of emergency.[75] As a result of the political backlash to the Tbilisi massacres, the effects of the regime's efforts to subdue serious unrest through declarations of emergency diminished precipitously and grew less systematic. Yet, as we saw in Chapter 6, it was at precisely this time that a significant rise in violent nationalist mobilization appeared. That there was a direct connection between the regime's political difficulties in deploying force against challenging mobilization in the wake of the Tbilisi affair and the outbreak of massive waves of nationalist violence in the summer of 1989 is doubtful. But at least one Politburo member, Yegor Ligachev, has argued that the hesitation of the authorities to commit force to put down the Fergana valley violence in June 1989 was due to the attacks on the armed forces' behavior in Tbilisi unleashed at the First Congress of People's Deputies in early June.[76] Prior to April 1989, a state of emergency aimed at quelling unrest by a particular nationality could be expected to lead to a 72 percent decrease in the incidence of protests by that group during the weeks in which it remained in effect, with the relationship highly significant at the .001 level. In the period following the Tbilisi events, that effect was more than halved (32 percent), and the relationship was only marginally significant. The effect of states of emergency on participation in demonstrations changed from a statistically significant, strongly negative

[75] A. Domrin, "Gosudarstvenno-pravovoi institut chrezvychainogo polozheniia: postanovka problemy," in *Mezhdunarodnaia zhizn'*, nos. 5–6, 1993, pp. 169–70.
[76] Ligachev, *Inside Gorbachev's Kremlin*, p. 158.

relationship before Tbilisi to a mildly positive, statistically insignificant one after Tbilisi, signaling a serious deterioration in the regime's law enforcement capability.

Equally important were the systematic backlash effects that appeared after Tbilisi among many groups in response to instances in which the regime did deploy large-scale repression. Although backlash mobilizations occurred occasionally prior to Tbilisi (Armenia in July 1988 and Lithuania in September 1988 are two examples), backlash mobilization as a response to repression was not widespread. But after Tbilisi, backlash mobilizations grew significantly in frequency and intensity. Figure 7.2 provides information on the temporal patterning of demonstrations protesting acts of regime repression, as well as participation in these demonstrations. As can be seen, the Tbilisi events in April 1989 marked a major shift upward in both the frequency and resonance of backlash mobilizations, in spite of the sharply curtailed use of force by the regime characteristic of the post-Tbilisi period. Thus, fewer attempts to impose order on challenging groups in the post-Tbilisi period generated increased protest over those efforts.

As Table 7.1 shows, in the post-Tbilisi period one can observe statistically significant increases in the number of demonstrations in the fifth and sixth weeks following repression (at a rate of 2.9 and 2.3 percent respectively in the incidence of demonstrations per week for every hundred arrests, injuries, or deaths of demonstrators). Substantively this is a relatively small effect, in that even six or seven hundred arrests, injuries, or deaths inflicted by the government at demonstrations by a nationality in a week would have been associated with only a 17 to 20 percent increase five weeks later in the total weekly incidence of demonstrations by that nationality. But what is more significant is the effect repression had on rates of participation. Again, as Table 7.2 makes clear, this was concentrated in the fifth and sixth weeks following repression, producing an additional eleven and seven thousand participants in these weeks respectively per hundred weekly arrests, injuries, or deaths of demonstrators (though only after producing a short-term decline of three thousand participants in the week immediately following repression). Thus, six or seven hundred arrests, injuries, or deaths of demonstrators in a week would have produced a short-term decline of eighteen to twenty-one thousand participants in protest demonstrations in the week following repression, but five weeks later would have led to a massive increase of an additional sixty-six to seventy-seven thousand participants in demonstrations. What is inter-

a. **Number of demonstrations protesting acts of regime repression**

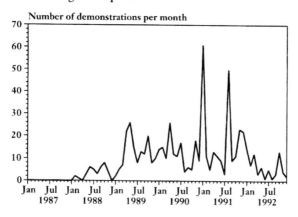

b. **Participation in demonstrations protesting acts of regime repression**

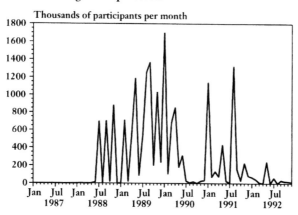

**Figure 7.2.** Backlash mobilizations against acts of regime repression, 1987–92.

esting here is that the relatively few demonstrations generated by repression produced enormous mobilizational turnouts within specific populations. Indeed, over the entire period examined here, backlash demonstrations against regime repression on average mobilized 43 percent more participants per demonstration than ethnonationalist demonstrations in general and 60 percent more participants per demonstration than demonstrations in favor of secession from the USSR. The symbolic power of a widespread sense of unjust repression was one of the most robust mobilizers throughout this period, far exceeding the mobilizational resonance of other nationalist or secessionist messages.

Not all groups, however, engaged equally in backlash mobilizations. Much as pre-existing structural conditions facilitated earlier timing with the cycle and higher levels of mobilization overall, so too did facilitating structure increase significantly the likelihood that movements would be capable of mobilizing in the face of repression. To demonstrate this, I divided the event sample into demonstrations at which protest against government repression was specifically raised as an issue (that is, backlash mobilization) and all other demonstrations. Table 7.3 compares the results of longitudinal analyses of the number of demonstrations per week for the fifteen nationalities of our sample for these two types of protests. As the results show, the same pre-existing structural conditions associated with other forms of mobilization were also closely associated with backlash mobilization. The effects of population size, ethnofederal status, linguistic assimilation, and urbanization were even more dramatic on the incidence of backlash mobilization than on the incidence of protests that did not seek to contest government repression.[77] These findings help considerably in understanding why the transcendence of the Soviet regime of repression was such an uneven process across the territory of the USSR. Groups differed structurally in their ability to generate mobilization in the face of repression. Equally striking were the contrasting relationships of institutionalizing outcomes to backlash mobilization and mobilization over other issues. Whereas institutionalizing outcomes had a sharply negative effect on both the incidence and resonance of mobilization over other issues, they had a positive relationship with the incidence and resonance of backlash mobilization. Thus, having a foothold in one level of the state hierarchy (which was the case for a number of nationalist movements after the republican and local elections of 1990) enhanced the capabilities of nationalist movements to protest against the use of force against them – in these cases, against force perpetrated by the central authorities.

To sum up, we have seen that the Tbilisi events roughly marked the beginning of a systematic shift in the ways in which movements and

---

[77] As one might expect, the amount of repression (the number of arrests, injuries, and deaths of protestors) was positively related to backlash mobilization, as were declarations of states of emergency – largely in contrast to the pattern for other types of demonstrations, whereas the regularity of repression acted with equal consequence in deterring activists from organizing demonstrations across both sets of cases.

Table 7.3. *Comparison of Negative Binomial Regressions of Weekly Count of Protest Demonstrations Protesting Government Repression and Protest Demonstrations Not Protesting Government Repression, by Nationality (January 1987–August 1991)[a]*

| Independent variable | Demonstrations protesting Government Repression | | Demonstrations not protesting Government Repression | |
| --- | --- | --- | --- | --- |
| | Coefficient | Incidence rate ratio | Coefficient | Incidence rate ratio |
| Ln population size (thousands), 1989 | 0.805 (5.71)**** | 2.237 | 0.183 (2.72)*** | 1.201 |
| Dummy variable for union republican status | 1.566 (2.44)** | 4.787 | 0.818 (2.90)*** | 2.267 |
| Linguistic assimilation, 1989 | −0.046 (−2.26)** | .955 | −0.016 (−2.23)** | .984 |
| Level of urbanization, 1970 | 0.039 (3.67)**** | 1.040 | 0.018 (3.59)**** | 1.018 |
| Dummy variable for period of electoral campaign | 0.133 (0.55) | 1.143 | 0.248 (2.66)*** | 1.282 |
| Dummy variable for period after institutionalizing outcome | 0.421 (2.33)** | 1.522 | −0.526 (−6.12)**** | .591 |
| Regularity of repression against demonstrations | −0.033 (−6.62)**** | .967 | −0.029 (−18.47)**** | .971 |
| Number of arrests, injuries, and deaths inflicted on demonstrators (hundreds), t − 1 | 0.070 (3.44)**** | 1.072 | −0.015 (−0.31) | .985 |
| Number of arrests, injuries, and deaths inflicted on demonstrators (hundreds), t − 2 | 0.079 (3.92)**** | 1.082 | −0.054 (−0.73) | .948 |
| Number of arrests, injuries, and deaths inflicted on demonstrators (hundreds), t − 3 | 0.078 (3.78)**** | 1.081 | 0.001 (0.35) | 1.001 |
| Number of arrests, injuries, and deaths inflicted on demonstrators (hundreds), t − 4 | 0.005 (0.06) | 1.005 | −0.050 (−0.75) | .951 |
| Number of arrests, injuries, and deaths inflicted on demonstrators (hundreds), t − 5 | 0.089 (5.21)**** | 1.093 | 0.003 (0.11) | 1.003 |
| Number of arrests, injuries, and deaths inflicted on demonstrators (hundreds), t − 6 | 0.077 (3.87)**** | 1.080 | 0.032 (2.04)** | 1.033 |
| Dummy variable for declaration of state of emergency | 0.467 (1.67)* | 1.594 | −0.706 (−3.89)**** | .493 |
| Constant | −11.83759 | | −2.851433 | |
| t × n | 3,645 | | 3,645 | |
| Log likelihood | −855.40699 | | −3,201.1277 | |
| Wald model chi² | 161.18**** | | 416.61**** | |

*Significant at the .10 level     **Significant at the .05 level     ***Significant at the .01 level     ****Significant at the .001 level

*Note:* n = 15 nationalities (excluding Russians); t = 243 weeks.

[a] Z-scores in parentheses.

365

populations responded to repression. In the wake of Tbilisi, the regularity of repression and declarations of a state of emergency grew less effective in containing challenge, whereas backlash effects from repression emerged with greater consistency. But in some contexts, regular repression continued to be effective in marginalizing opponents – primarily because these groups lacked the pre-existing structural conditions (strong identity processes, robust mobilizational networks, and so forth) necessary for recovering quickly from the damage done by repression and for generating significant backlash mobilization. Overall, the picture which emerged in the aftermath of Tbilisi was one of serious deterioration in the institutional capacity of the Soviet regime to impose order on its population as it had traditionally done in the past and an enormous multiplication in the severity of the mobilizational challenges the Soviet regime faced.

## Why Severe Force Was Not Seriously Contemplated

The reasons why a Tiananmen-type massacre was not considered appropriate and would not have been a feasible solution for saving the USSR once a tide of nationalism had gotten under way should now be clearer. Long before the Tbilisi massacres – and well before Gorbachev came to power – the use of severe force as a strategy for maintaining order had been erased from the Soviet elite's understanding of appropriate ways to behave toward opposition. The roots of the failure of the Soviet state to defend itself through severe force thus run much deeper than Gorbachev or the Gorbachev years; they are to be found instead in widely shared assumptions that emerged in the Brezhnev era about how order was to be created, which colored the way in which an entire generation of Soviet officials approached the issue. As Timothy Brook noted, the Tiananmen massacres were merely "one more entry in the register of our common barbarity" in a century that "witnessed so many spectacular slaughters that the killing of a few thousand civilians . . . does not fall outside what we are capable of imagining." But whereas Mao's heirs, still believing that power derived from the barrel of a gun, did not wince at shooting thousands of their opponents openly in the central square of the Chinese capital in an act that Brook called "historically and morally unambiguous,"[78] scenarios involving such severe violence lay outside the boundaries of appropriate force for those who sought to restore order in the USSR during the

[78] Brook, *Quelling the People*, pp. ix, 3.

*glasnost'* period. Instead, to the forces of order in the USSR during these years of open disorder, restoring order meant not severe force against opponents, but reclaiming a lost sense of predictability and regularity in the expectations governing the relationship between regime and opposition in the wake of Gorbachev's failed experiment of regulating revolt by law. Rather than emerging from a single act of absolute domination, order was fundamentally understood as an institutional patterning of behavior – ironically, in a period when the institutions charged with enforcing order were increasingly incoherent themselves and incapable of producing patterned behavior.

When one looks in detail at the plans laid by those involved in the August 1991 coup that toppled Gorbachev in a failed attempt to save the Soviet state from imminent disintegration, it is impossible to escape the conclusion that a Tiananmen-type massacre was not an acceptable possibility among those defending the Soviet state and that even the opposition to Gorbachev viewed order largely as resting on the effectiveness and weight of institutions rather than on severe force. KGB chief Vladimir Kriuchkov, the main organizer of the coup, had lobbied Gorbachev to engage in a show of force against hundreds of thousands of protestors in Moscow during the Revolution Day counterdemonstration in November 1990 and had long pushed Gorbachev to introduce a state of emergency in the country, though without success. Yet, Kriuchkov tells us in his memoirs that "it was not force nor the striving for violence that were the main factors behind the political and practical activities of the GKChP [State Emergency Committee]. . . . [F]or members of the GKChP the main thing was to avoid a forceful confrontation, bloodletting, and victims, and as soon as a real danger of this arose, the State Emergency Committee quickly ceased its activity." Kriuchkov goes so far as to claim that this position against severe violence, and on ending the coup should bloodshed begin, was openly discussed and "categorically specified" by the group before the decision to dispatch troops to Moscow was taken,[79] though this hardly seems believable in view of the extensive preparations made to storm the Russian White House. Judging from Kriuchkov's actions, it seems plausible, however, that, at least when he initiated the coup, he did not believe it would necessitate the use of severe force against civilian populations. Rather, it seems, the action was imagined largely in Brezhnevian

---

[79] Vladimir Kriuchkov, *Lichnoe delo, chast' vtoraia* (Moscow: Olimp, 1996), pp. 130–31, 180–84.

terms: relying heavily on the weight and regularity of institutions, confining repression to surgical arrests of opposition leaderships, consistently shutting down demonstrations, and expecting populations to submit in the face of the presence (as opposed to the use) of overwhelming force.

On the eve of the introduction of a state of emergency, for instance, Kriuchkov compiled a list, containing only several dozen names, of those whom he thought it necessary to "intern." The list handed to the KGB and the military on August 19 called for "administrative arrest" of a total of eighteen people (with former Politburo liberals Aleksandr Yakovlev and Eduard Shevardnadze, whom Kriuchkov and fellow hardline plotter Aleksandr Tiziakov believed were foreign agents, at the top of the list). Only seventy others were mentioned as eventual targets.[80] In the end, only several of those on the list were actually apprehended. It is said that the KGB staff ordered two hundred fifty thousand pairs of handcuffs and the printing of three hundred thousand arrest forms on the eve of the coup.[81] But it is not clear that such a large number of arrests was actually contemplated by the GKChP leadership, and certainly there is no evidence that massive violence against protestors was considered. Even extremists, such as Colonel Viktor Alksnis, although calling for large-scale arrests, eschewed mass violence against the regime's opponents: He told an interviewer in the midst of the coup, "[u]nfortunately, there will have to be arrests. I personally like the Polish version best, where people were interned for a certain period without a sentence, under good conditions."[82] The only victims of the entire August 1991 coup were three youths who were killed and several others who were wounded in the early hours of August 21 when a crowd, mistakenly believing an attack on the White House was taking place, attempted to block the movement of a column of armored cars through a Moscow underpass.[83]

Tiziakov's plan of action, already written in April 1991 and in significant respects the blueprint for what occurred in August 1991, did call for "shooting those responsible on site without a trial" in instances of widespread interethnic violence. And Tiziakov also started compiling his own lists of would-be victims for the time of reckoning when a state of emer-

---

[80] V. Stepankov and Ye. Lisov, *Kremlevskii zagovor* (Moscow: Ogonek, 1992), pp. 91, 110.
[81] See *The New York Times*, August 25, 1991, p. A1; David Remnick, *Lenin's Tomb: The Last Days of the Soviet Empire* (New York: Random House, 1993), p. 443.
[82] Vienna ORF Television Network, in *FBIS*, August 21, 1991, p. 18.
[83] A few additional casualties occurred in the Baltic in connection with the seizure of facilities by Soviet troops in Lithuania and Latvia.

gency was to be imposed. But his plan for "introducing order" was not Stalinism but Brezhnevism revived. It involved, in the words of those who investigated the August 1991 events, the restoration of "a strong state" and the "return of society to the system which existed prior to 1985."[84] He called for removing Gorbachev as General Secretary, abandoning the system of Soviets, introducing direct party rule at the local level, reestablishing censorship over the mass media, and prosecuting those who engaged in strikes and demonstrations, threatening them with fines of up to three thousand rubles or imprisonment for up to three years for attempts to organize public protest (hardly more severe punishment than was currently the law). Obviously, this was not rule by terror, but a bureaucrat's conception of the well-functioning party-state – an attempt to restore order through re-establishing the predictability of repression rather than through severity.

Some of the most macho rhetoric during the meetings of the GKChP emanated from Prime Minister Valentin Pavlov. At a meeting of the coup plotters on August 18 at which Kriuchkov discussed his plans to "arrest a little more than a dozen," Pavlov noisily interjected that it was necessary instead to "arrest a thousand." Even this was a relatively small number given the vast scale of organized opposition to the Soviet state in disparate parts of the country at the time, as well as the fact that many opposition movements had been preparing for a seizure of power by party conservatives since at least the fall of 1990. On August 19, Prime Minister Pavlov (who, according to his account, suffered an attack of high blood pressure at the time, but who, according to several others, spent much of the August coup in a drunken stupor and was on this occasion apparently particularly well oiled) phoned Defense Minister Dmitri Yazov demanding that he organize the arrest of thousands of striking coal miners who had begun to protest the seizure of power, a suggestion Yazov simply could not take seriously.[85] As David Remnick observed, the leaders of the coup might have had certain Stalinist impulses, "but not the same core of cruelty, the willingness to flood the city in blood."[86]

After failing to arrest Yeltsin and the core of the Russian leadership the day before, the GKChP on August 20 did make extensive preparations under the leadership of Defense Minister Yazov to storm the Russian

---

[84] Stepankov and Lisov, *Kremlevskii zagovor*, pp. 129–31, 167.
[85] Stepankov and Lisov, *Kremlevskii zagovor*, pp. 91, 110, 132.
[86] Remnick, *Lenin's Tomb*, p. 485.

White House in the early hours of August 21 – which would have led to massive bloodshed on a scale not unlike that of Tiananmen Square. Called "Operation Thunder," the plan was to use army and internal troops to create a wedge through the barricades and the crowd of fifty thousand that would allow KGB special forces units to enter the building, disarm its occupants, and seize Yeltsin, placing him under arrest. According to the KGB's information, inside the White House were five thousand armed defenders, and the military and KGB officers in charge of the operation estimated that any attempt to take the building would lead to large numbers of civilian casualties – certainly in the thousands. "Operation Thunder" failed because it was never carried out. It could not be carried out because the military and police commanders asked to design and execute the plan found the severe casualties it would have involved unacceptable. Many of these same officers – Generals Grachev, Lebed', Gromov, and Karpukhin – had been intimately involved in prior violent actions by the military and police against civilian populations in Tbilisi, Baku, and Vilnius. But those events paled in scope to the bloodshed that would have occurred in the storming of the White House in August 1991. Recognizing this, each of these generals – the leaders of the KGB special forces, military, and internal troops involved in the operation – refused to carry out the plan even before the signal to attack had been given. When word of this reached Defense Minister Yazov, he understood that the coup was finished and called off the plan.

In short, it was not merely Gorbachev who, to his credit, failed to use large-scale violence to defend the Soviet state. Neither did his opponents who favored tougher measures to salvage the Soviet order. To be sure, the GKChP was a hastily concocted exercise. Nevertheless, in contrast to Mao's heirs its leaders instinctively shied away from imposing order through bloodshed, and when pushed to the decision to do so, retreated. As Anatoly Lukianov, sometimes called the ideological inspiration for the coup, tells us in his memoirs, the purpose of the GKChP was to "restore elementary order in the country," and the military and political leadership "understood perfectly that it was impossible to allow bloodshed" and were "very sorry" for the small amount of blood that nonetheless flowed.[87] One cannot imagine Deng Xiaoping issuing a similar apology. In China in June 1989 there was also some dissent within both the Communist Party

[87] Anatoly Liuk'ianov, *V vodovorote rossiiskoi smuty (razmyshleniia, dialogi, dokumenty)* (Moscow: Kniga i biznes, 1999), pp. 63, 67.

hierarchy and the military leadership over the use of severe force against civilian protestors.[88] The key differences between China in June 1989 and the USSR in August 1991 were not in the presence or absence of dissent within the military over the use of force, but rather in the normative boundaries of what leaders found acceptable in the use of force, in the capacity of leaders to enforce their will on institutions, and in the degree of unity and resolve of leaders to commit to a forceful imposition of order. As Timothy Brook observed, in China government leaders ordered soldiers to use severe force against civilians "because they could not imagine any other way of reestablishing authority."[89] By contrast, in the waning years of the USSR government leaders failed to order the use of severe force against civilians because that way of reestablishing their authority was to them unimaginable.

## Why Force Could Not Have Saved the USSR

Returning to our counterfactual, there are several reasons why it was improbable that force could have saved the USSR once a tide of nationalism had emerged. As the statistical analyses presented earlier show, regular repression and states of emergency lost much of their dampening effects on dissent after mid-1989, and attempts to root out nationalist opposition by force generated significant backlash mobilizations in many locations. The regime of repression had failed in multiple contexts, and reestablishing order would have necessitated a very significant institutional capacity. It is clear, however, that from mid-1989 on the institutional capacity of the Soviet regime to engage in a violent crackdown was rapidly deteriorating. The police and the military were simply incapable of meeting the challenges of imposing order when confronted with a tide of nationalism involving multiple, simultaneous, interacting waves of mobilization. They were quite literally overwhelmed.

In many instances, local police themselves were pulled into the rising tide of revolt – as in Leningrad in April 1989, when three hundred police demonstrated in Palace Square in favor of legal reform and improved

---

[88] On the military resistance to the order to use severe force against civilians in China, see Andrew Scobell, "Why the People's Army Fired on the People: The Chinese Military and Tiananmen," *Armed Forces & Society*, vol. 18, no. 2 (Winter 1992), pp. 193–213; Chu-yuan Cheng, *Behind the Tiananmen Massacre: Social, Political, and Economic Ferment in China* (Boulder, CO: Westview, 1990), pp. 133–34.
[89] Brook, *Quelling the People*, p. 8.

working conditions,[90] or as in Kiev in November 1990, when the city police force demonstrated to demand that they be relieved of the unpleasant assignment of having to police street demonstrations but against independence (most demonstrations, at that time were secessionist in orientation).[91] In Chapter 6, we saw evidence of the widespread involvement of local police organizations in carrying out acts of interethnic violence. But if local and republican law enforcement institutions were often unreliable, all-union institutions were not capable of filling the gap. In addition to the enormous waves of protest that had engulfed the Baltic, Transcaucasus, Moldova, and parts of Russia and Ukraine, from the summer of 1989 multiple violent conflicts raged across the southern tier of the USSR. Already at this time the USSR Ministry of Internal Affairs began to complain about a shortage of internal troops to keep nationalist revolts in check.[92] By then, thirty-six thousand internal troops were available for use as peacekeeping forces where nationalist mobilization had escaped the control of local authorities. In view of the swelling need, their number was increased by an additional twenty-seven thousand. It was common practice to send students from police academies, as well as regular army troops, into emergency situations, usually with no experience or training in these matters. To enforce the state of emergency declared in Azerbaijan and Armenia in January 1990, for instance, five thousand regular army troops were dispatched, in addition to six thousand additional internal police troops.

Law enforcement organizations were, in the words of two specialists from the MVD, "practically powerless" against the wave of nationalist unrest that swept the USSR and "were not always able even to defend themselves."[93] Police and army units were frequently poorly armed and ill prepared for dealing with mass disorders, and in cases of mass violence often could do nothing but stand by and watch the course of events. In some cases they were forbidden by their superiors to use weapons in spite

---

[90] *Vesti iz SSSR*, 7/8–38, 1989; *Chas pik*, no. 38, November 12, 1990, p. 2.

[91] *Yezhednevnaia glasnost'*, November 13, 1990, p. 5.

[92] *Report on the USSR*, vol. 1, no. 30 (July 28, 1989), p. 46. Signs of the overstretching of Soviet police forces were evident even before summer 1989. As we saw, one of the reasons why army troops were called in to Tbilisi in April 1989 in the first place was because most of Georgia's republican MVD forces were located in Stepanakert and in Abkhazia at the time.

[93] V. N. Grigor'ev and Yu. D. Rogov, *Fenomeny "perestroiki": Chrezvychainoe polozhenie* (Moscow: Verdikt, 1994), pp. 10, 50, 62, 64–65, 67–68, 96–102.

of the fact that their own lives were in danger. For the first two years in Karabakh internal troops were equipped with handmade shields that, according to the commander of these forces, "fall apart at the first blow."[94] Troops sent into Baku in January 1990 had no tear gas, rubber bullets, or clubs; most of the bulletproof vests they were given proved defective, and the riot shields supplied to them were described as "useless."[95] From what we know about how Soviet institutions operated, these examples do not seem farfetched. But it is also hardly surprising that the military sometimes made use of inappropriate weapons such as tanks, automatic weapons, or sapper shovels to protect themselves against rioting crowds.

In the wake of Tbilisi, the use of the army as a tool to contain ethnic revolt grew heavily politicized, and particularly as authority shifted to the republics, actions by the central government's institutions of order to quell nationalist unrest became embroiled in controversy. The repeated dislocation of the armed forces to hot spots in the Transcaucasus, Central Asia, and Moldova came to be known widely within the military as "the Southern Variant" – a term which General Aleksander Lebed' sarcastically called "the completely brilliant invention of the military thinking man." As Lebed' described the repertoire that "the Southern Variant" represented:

They give you a certain number of airplanes and you are free to choose whatever you want to put in them: an artillery division, anti-aircraft division, any configuration of armored transport, and any quantity of weapons. Then, you fly wherever they send you and do whatever is necessary so that things are OK. But what that means and how to achieve it is your problem. If everything goes well, you won't have to fill out a report. But if something goes awry, if something seems wrong to the mysterious political "rudders," then the investigations begin.

Lebed' concluded:

Then I believed and now I believe that this was not the army's affair – to be involved in internal disorders. . . . In general, placing police functions on the army was a great humiliation for the army. The army was not prepared psychologically for this kind of activity, and whenever it was forced to do it, it led to one result only: enormous bitterness and the undeserved outrage of the crowd against the army.[96]

Similarly, General Yevgenii Shaposhnikov argued that

---

[94] *Krasnaia zvezda*, in *FBIS*, November 13, 1989, p. 67.
[95] Helsinki Watch, *Conflict in the Soviet Union: Black January in Azerbaijan* (New York: Human Rights Watch, 1991), p. 31.
[96] Lebed', *Za derzhavu obidno*, pp. 288, 249.

the main mistake of the military leadership . . . [during this period] was its tacit consent to dragging the army into all kinds of conflicts within the country. Even without this the state of the army evoked criticism within public opinion, but on top of this were added police functions. . . . [All this led to] a lowering of the prestige of military service and the authority of the Armed Forces. The decisions of the political leadership of the country to utilize military units for punitive actions in Tbilisi, Baku, and Vilnius to a large degree brought about these destructive results.[97]

The declining morale of those charged with keeping order was a constant theme at the time. By injecting themselves into interethnic conflicts, peacekeeping troops and law enforcement officials became targets of attack from both sides of hostilities. In a number of cases, republican governments under the control of nationalist movements complained about efforts by peacekeeping troops to collect weapons from the population without their approval, portraying this as interference in their sovereign affairs.[98] Moreover, the weapons that the military and police carried became prized resources for those who sought to contest boundaries violently. Laws passed to protect the militia and to ban activities aimed at promoting hostility and ethnic violence remained on paper only. Draft evasion became a common phenomenon, even among Russians, in part because of the fear of being sent into combat on "peacekeeping" missions. Mothers of Russian soldiers began conspicuous protests seeking to remove their sons from dangerous peacekeeping operations, unwilling to see them die for the sake of preserving order among warring ethnic groups. By December 1990, service in military units stationed in the Transcaucasus had to be put on a voluntary basis only.[99]

Over the course of 1990 discipline within the armed forces began to unravel in a more serious way. As General Shaposhnikov tells us in his memoirs, Defense Minister Yazov became obsessed with issues of discipline within the military: "It was strikingly evident that practically any conversation with him on any issue – from improving military preparedness to technical supply, from the training of pilots to supplying housing for the summer contingent – always ended in criticisms and reproaches concerning the state of military discipline."[100] Not a single military or police

[97] Yevgenii Shaposhnikov, *Vybor*, 2d ed. (Moscow: Pik, 1995), pp. 65–66, 71.
[98] Grigor'ev and Rogov, *Fenomeny "perestroiki,"* pp. 85–86; Armenpres, in *FBIS*, August 6, 1990, p. 86.
[99] Moscow Television, in *FBIS*, December 6, 1990, p. 97.
[100] Shaposhnikov, *Vybor*, p. 33.

institution remained unaffected by the pressure of the mobilizational tide. Even the elite KGB special forces Al'fa unit, which had been dispatched over the previous several years to various "hot spots" of nationalism around the country, had by early 1991 grown "tired."[101]

Most of the officers who commanded key units during the August 1991 coup – Generals Varennikov, Achalov, Grachev, Lebed', Gromov, Samsonov, and Karpukhin – had been intimately involved in putting down nationalist unrest in various parts of the country in the past three years. One suspects that this is why Defense Minister Yazov and KGB chief Kriuchkov chose them to command critical operations during the August coup. But given the effect many of these earlier actions had on morale within the police and the military, it does not seem accidental that many of these same officers, when called on to use force against a civilian population of their own nationality on an even larger scale for the sake of preserving the USSR in August 1991, refused to carry out their superiors' orders. Over the course of 1990 and 1991 a significant erosion of support for using force as a tool for saving the Soviet state occurred both within the Russian public at large and within the institutions of order.

The extent of this erosion is seen in the public reactions to the events in Baku in January 1990 and Vilnius in January 1991. In December 1989 and January 1990, a national revolution was in process in Soviet Azerbaijan until army troops intervened in a bloody massacre. It began in fall 1989, when a new wave of mobilization and violence overtook Karabakh, provoking massive demonstrations in both Armenia and Azerbaijan to protest Soviet policy toward the region. By the end of December, inspired in part by the tearing down of the Berlin Wall, followers of the Azerbaijani Popular Front began attacking Soviet installations in Nakhichevan on the border with Iran (in some instances burning them to the ground). With Armenian-Azerbaijani violence in Karabakh escalating into full-scale warfare, on January 11 Popular Front activists seized power in the towns of Lenkoran and Jalalabad, and on January 12 in Baku radical nationalists within the Popular Front began organizing armed detachments in factories. Ostensibly the detachments were to protect Azerbaijanis on the border areas with Armenia, but in fact at rallies that day calls were issued for the resignation of the republican government and expulsion of all Armenians. During the following several days, massive anti-Armenian

---

[101] Mikhail Boltunov, *Al'fa ne khotela ubivat'* (Sankt-Peterburg: Shans, 1995), pp. 333–34.

rallies in Baku produced an orgy of violence against the remaining Armenian community in the city, killing 56 people and wounding 112. Twelve thousand USSR MVD special forces were stationed in the city at the time, but for reasons still not fully clear they did not intervene immediately to stop the murders.[102] Apparently, in a number of instances, troops were barricaded in their quarters by crowds, and the republican party organization itself was paralyzed into inaction by internal discord and splits. Unrest began to spread to numerous towns and cities across Azerbaijan. In the meantime, Popular Front radicals organized barricades in Baku and armed themselves in anticipation of eventual intervention by Moscow. Demonstrations in Baku on January 16 and 17 were openly secessionist, with several foiled attempts by crowds to break into the republican Central Committee building. In the meantime Gorbachev dispatched advisor Yevgenii Primakov and Central Committee Secretary Andrei Girenko to investigate the situation; they reported "extremely alarming information" about the spreading scope of the revolt, including the fact that local authorities had already been swept aside in eighteen districts within the republic. On January 19 the Popular Front gained control over the republican television studio, only to have the power station feeding the studio destroyed by a bomb planted by KGB special forces units.[103] Late that evening, a large number of troops began to arrive in the city, and a state of emergency was declared. Due to a shortage of troops available to put down the spreading unrest throughout the Transcaucasus, Defense Minister Yazov was forced to call up army reserves.[104] Reports indicate that it was these troops in particular who were responsible for many of the atrocities that subsequently occurred. As they entered the city, the troops encountered significant resistance from barricaded crowds and armed bands of Popular Front supporters, some of whom fired at the troops with automatic weapons from cars that quickly disappeared down the streets (Yazov subsequently claimed that the rebels were aided by the republican Ministry of Internal Affairs). In response, frightened and poorly trained army reservists went on a rampage, firing indiscriminately at civilians and crushing cars and buses with their armored vehicles. In the end, 121 civil-

---

[102] Some see in this a provocation to incite disorder and justify a military intervention on the part of the authorities. This, however, is flatly denied by Gorbachev, and no firm evidence has ever surfaced supporting the provocation argument. For Gorbachev's account of these events, see Gorbachev, *Zhizn' i reformy*, vol. 1, pp. 518–20.

[103] See *Ekspress khronika*, October 22, 1991, p. 6.

[104] TASS, in *FBIS*, January 19, 1990, p. 52.

ians were killed and more than 700 wounded (additionally, 21 soldiers were killed and 90 wounded in the fighting).[105]

The foiled revolution of January 1990 constituted a turning point in the development of secessionist politics in Soviet Azerbaijan, although the state of emergency, which remained in effect throughout most of 1990, allowed local party elites loyal to the center to maintain a shaky control up through the August 1991 coup. In terms of the number of victims, "Black January" – as it came to be called – constituted the most violent government crackdown on dissent during the *glasnost'* period. For many of the army officers involved, it demonstrated once again the senselessness of deploying army troops to fulfill police functions. Though it evoked a number of formal investigations by human rights and legal institutions, the crackdown did not engender the same type of reaction as occurred surrounding Tbilisi – perhaps because the victims were Muslim, perhaps because of the pogroms against Armenians which accompanied the uprising. A public opinion survey in early 1990 in Leningrad revealed that 56 percent of the population believed it was necessary to use the army to put down the revolt against Soviet power in Azerbaijan and only 26 percent disagreed – and this in a city that within several months would come under the political control of Democratic Russia.

But the effect on morale within the military of the events in Baku and the mounting wave of nationalist violence was nonetheless conspicuous – not because of moral qualms about the deaths of Azerbaijanis, but because within Russia itself (as well as Ukraine) public opinion shifted sharply against placing the lives of Slavic soldiers on the line for the sake of policing interethnic conflicts. In early January 1990, as significant nationalist unrest began to encompass Azerbaijan, three hundred military servicemen stationed in Batumi refused to obey the reassignment of their division to Nakhichevan, abandoning their unit and engaging in a sit-down protest in front of the local theater, where draftees were already demonstrating in protest against military service in the Soviet army.[106] The mobilization of reserve troops for service in Azerbaijan evoked a wave of protest in neighboring Stavropol' and Krasnodar krais. In the village of Donsk in Stavropol' krai, women lay under the wheels of the bus that was about to

---

[105] For the report by the independent soldiers' rights group *Shchit* on the events, see *Soglasie*, no. 31, July 30–August 8, 1990, pp. 5–6. See also Helsinki Watch, *Conflict in the Soviet Union; Chernyi ianvar'. Baku – 1990: Dokumenty i materialy* (Baku: Azerneshr, 1990).
[106] *Ekspress khronika*, no. 3, January 16, 1990.

take their sons off to Azerbaijan, and in the towns of Ipatov and Svetlograd strike committees formed in protest against the mobilization order. In the town of Blagodar five thousand people rallied and sent a letter to the USSR Supreme Soviet to protest mobilization. In Stavropol' a large-scale demonstration on the city's main square condemned the mobilization of citizens for military service in the Transcaucasus as a "criminal" act. In Krasnodar, fifty thousand people attended rallies outside the regional Communist Party headquarters demanding that all local soldiers be brought back immediately and that Soviet troops be removed entirely from Azerbaijan, Armenia, and Nagorno-Karabakh.[107] Similar rallies took place in L'vov and Kiev. Again in June 1990, mounting interethnic violence set off a wave of demonstrations in Russia and Ukraine against the dispatch of troops. In Zaporozh'e, for instance, 350 parents demonstrated against "sacrificing our children for the sake of the imperial ambitions" of Moscow in the Transcaucasus.[108] In Cheliabinsk, a demonstration occurred under the banner "Do Not Send Our Ural Boys to the Hot Spots of the Country!"[109]

This shifting willingness to die for the sake of preserving a motherland coming apart at the seams and increasingly condemned as a failing empire explains in large part the public reaction to the attempted crackdown in Lithuania in January 1991. After the new Lithuanian government declared independence in March 1990, General Valentin Varennikov presented a plan to the Politburo for proclaiming a state of emergency in the republic, imposing presidential rule, introducing three regiments, isolating the nationalist leadership, and eventually establishing a puppet government. Preparations for this scenario proceeded, but by April Gorbachev chose to impose an economic blockade rather than pursue a military response.[110] But by fall 1990, the liberal wing of the Communist Party had exited, the parade of sovereignties had gutted much of central authority, talks between Yeltsin and Gorbachev on economic reform had broken down, and pressure had built from conservatives for a more forceful response. Gorbachev came to the conclusion that only force could prevent a Baltic exit from the USSR and (as a result) the eventual collapse of the country. He began to lean heavily toward a hawkish position. The central government was reor-

[107] *Ekspress khronika*, no. 4, January 23, 1990.
[108] *Ekspress khronika*, no. 26, June 26, 1990; *Yezhednevnaia glasnost'*, June 24, 1990.
[109] *Ekspress khronika*, no. 24, June 12, 1990, p. 2.
[110] A. S. Cherniaev, *Shest' let s Gorbachevym* (Moscow: Kultura, 1993), pp. 337–40.

ganized, and many of those who eventually carried out the August 1991 coup were placed at the center of power. In December 1990, in protest against the growing strength of conservative forces within the government, Foreign Minister Eduard Shevardnadze resigned, warning in his speech about the coming "onset of dictatorship."[111]

By this time, a forceful crackdown against secessionist Lithuania and Latvia was being prepared. Gorbachev subsequently denied responsibility for the bloody events in Vilnius in January 1991, but there is little doubt from the sequence of events and from the public statements he made at the time that he was well aware of the plan to utilize force to push Lithuania (and the rest of the Baltic) more firmly back into the Soviet fold.[112] The crackdown developed pretty much according to Varennikov's plan. A false crisis was precipitated – utilizing the Lithuanian government's announcement of a price rise as an excuse to mobilize demonstrations by local Russians and Poles, who demanded the resignation of the Lithuanian government. The republic was portrayed by Kremlin controlled media as having slipped into chaos, justifying the imposition of a state of emergency. Local Russians and Poles appealed to Gorbachev to impose presidential rule, and preparations were made for a puppet government. The day before the crackdown, Gorbachev dispatched a telegram to the Lithuanian parliament demanding that it cease its efforts to restore a "bourgeois order" in the republic. General Varennikov himself arrived in Vilnius, and troops started patrolling the city. They first seized the Press House and then turned their attention to controlling parliament and other communication centers. Crowds of largely unarmed Lithuanians mounted a blockade of the parliament building and the republic's broadcasting tower. Fearing the loss of life that might ensue in a direct assault on the parliament, the military chose instead to move first on the television tower, where 13 people were killed and 165 wounded when KGB special forces Al'fa units stormed the facility in the early hours of January 13.[113] Having carried the scenario so far, Gorbachev abruptly cut it off in the wake of the first bloodshed (and denied any responsibility for these acts).

The Vilnius events touched off a massive wave of protest in other republics in solidarity with the Lithuanians, as opposition movements

---

[111] For the best account of these events, see Brown, *The Gorbachev Factor*, pp. 269–79.
[112] For extensive evidence of Gorbachev's participation in these events, see Alfred Erich Senn, *Gorbachev's Failure in Lithuania* (New York: St. Martin's Press, 1995), pp. 127–41.
[113] Senn, *Gorbachev's Failure in Lithuania*, pp. 127–38.

sought to exploit the occasion to undermine further the Soviet regime's ability to repress them, demonstrating the type of backlash such acts could be expected to generate. More than 64 demonstrations protesting the Vilnius events and involving over half a million participants occurred in various parts of Russia, Ukraine, Georgia, and Moldova in the weeks following the failed crackdown. In Moscow alone, Democratic Russia mobilized one to two hundred thousand people at a demonstration on January 20 calling for Gorbachev's resignation under the banner "Today – Lithuania, Tomorrow – Russia!" Dozens of flags representing nationalist movements from around the country fluttered over Moscow's Manezh Square, and a minute of silence was marked in memory of the victims of Tbilisi, Baku, and Vilnius.[114] The Vilnius events further solidified a cross-national front of resistance to the use of force against the USSR's various opposition movements, making it difficult for the regime to apply force within any single context without confronting significant disruption elsewhere.

More significant still was the effect these events had on the military's attitude toward the use of the army to crush secessionist revolt. As General Shaposhnikov, a key actor in causing the failure of the August 1991 coup, recalled, "After Vilnius and the television scenes that I saw of our soldiers beating civilians with the butts of their automatic rifles, I understood that a decisive and final end had to be put to this."[115] Similarly, for Sergei Goncharov, a KGB special forces officer, Vilnius was, in his words, "the last straw" and a key link in the refusal of his unit eight months later to storm the Russian White House. Others, such as General Pavel Grachev, believed that the army learned a somewhat different lesson from the Vilnius events: The politicians' cowardice in pushing the blame away from themselves and onto the shoulders of the military for the consequences of violent crackdown was a good reason for any military officer to hesitate in carrying out orders to crush oppositions violently.[116]

Over the course of 1990 and 1991 attitudes within the population and the military toward the use of force against nationalist revolts markedly altered. In early 1990 56 percent of Leningraders believed it was necessary to use the army to put down the revolt in Azerbaijan. A year later in the aftermath of the attempted crackdown in Vilnius in January 1991 only 14 percent of Leningraders believed the use of the army to keep the Baltic

[114] Radio Rossiia, in *FBIS*, January 22, 1991, p. 106; *Izvestiia*, in *FBIS*, January 22, 1991, p. 107.
[115] Shaposhnikov, *Vybor*, p. 19.     [116] Senn, *Gorbachev's Failure in Lithuania*, pp. 138–39.

republics in the USSR was justified and 77 percent expressed their opposition to such actions. But perhaps most significant, whereas 82 percent of
the military officers in the January 1990 sample expressed support for the
crackdown in Baku, by January 1991 62 percent of the military officers in
the sample opposed forceful measures by the army in the Baltic.[117] It is
true that pockets of support for a violent crackdown against nationalist
dissent remained within the military and helped to precipitate the August
1991 coup – some of these officers having been involved in the events of
January 1991. The military hardliners were most visible in organizations
such as *Soiuz*, the parliamentary group formed to defend the integrity of
the USSR. But the larger pattern of evidence indicates a massive erosion
of support within the military over the course of 1990 and early 1991 for
the use of the army in repressing nationalist revolts, paralleling trends
within society at large.

Equally important to the deterioration of the Soviet Union's institutional capacity to repress was the fact that many people had simply stopped
believing in the capacity of the regime to repress successfully. The credibility of the Soviet state's regime of repression had evaporated in multiple
republics. According to participants in the demonstrations defending the
television tower in Vilnius in January 1991, for instance, no one expected
that troops would actually fire into the crowd. As one participant recalled,
the appearance of troops on the streets of Vilnius was thought by most
Lithuanians to be "an empty threat."[118] The last efforts by the regime to
crack down on opposition movements prior to the August 1991 coup
occurred in February and March 1991 in Moscow, when Gorbachev
attempted unsuccessfully to ban demonstrations by Democratic Russia and
to remove Yeltsin as chair of the RSFSR Supreme Soviet. This led to a
direct confrontation for control over the streets of Moscow when Democratic Russia called a massive demonstration in Yeltsin's support for March
28. In an attempt to break the back of the opposition, on March 25 Prime
Minister Valentin Pavlov banned all demonstrations in Moscow from
March 26 to April 15 and instructed the Moscow city government, the
KGB, and the MVD to enforce the order.[119] But RSFSR and city authorities refused to comply with the ban. Police indicated that the March 28

---

[117] *Ekho Litvy*, February 15, 1991, p. 4. The surveys were conducted by the Center for the
Study and Forecasting of Social Problems. The sample sizes are not given in this source.
[118] *Lietuva 1991.01.13: Dokumentai, liudijimai, atgarsiai* (Vilnius: Spaudos Departmentas,
1991), pp. 83, 118. I am grateful to Pranas Ciziunas for his translation of these materials.
[119] Vremia, in *FBIS*, March 26, 1991, p. 73.

demonstration would be stopped by force if necessary, and a large number of troops were moved into the city – in all, up to fifty thousand men. Police barriers were erected on Manezh Square, the intended site of the rally, and water cannon were deployed in various parts of the city to disperse the expected crowds. But these blatant threats of force had no effect whatsoever on the huge turnout, which numbered several hundred thousand by most accounts. A survey of 891 participants conducted by the All-Union Center for the Study of Public Opinion directly at the demonstration discovered that, even though the regime had unambiguously threatened that force would be used to break up the protest, 54 percent of those attending thought it highly unlikely or impossible that the regime would actually resort to force against them, and only 14 percent thought it likely. A quarter of the demonstrators believed that the use of force by the regime to stop a large demonstration was "impossible."[120] Aside from preventing the crowd from entering Manezh Square, the regime's threats to enforce the ban on the demonstration remained empty.

Two weeks before the August 1991 coup, KGB Chair Vladimir Kriuchkov and Defense Minister Dmitry Yazov assembled a small group of KGB and military advisors to evaluate the prospects and consequences of introducing emergency rule throughout the country. The expert group (which included General Grachev as the representative of the military) came to the conclusion that emergency rule was not advisable, was unenforceable, and would probably stimulate further disorder in the country.[121] The evidence we have seen in this chapter – statistical, historical, theoretical – indicates that they were correct on all counts. In the end, Kriuchkov and Yazov decided to ignore the advice of their experts and to act in any case. Plans by Gorbachev to sign a new union treaty on August 20 and ultimately to fire Kriuchkov and Yazov from their jobs forced their hand. But it was abundantly clear to the KGB and military experts that the institutional capacity to enforce a major crackdown against opponents had long ago disintegrated. Not only was discipline within the military and police crumbling, but the mobilizational challenges that the institutions of order confronted had grown overwhelming in scope, and threats of force no longer enjoyed credibility within a significant portion of the population. Thus, after mid-1989 it is unlikely that force could have saved the

---

[120] I am grateful to Yuri Levada and Aleksei Levinson for providing me with the results of this survey.
[121] Stepankov and Lisov, *Kremlevskii zagovor*, p. 84.

USSR even if it had been deployed with greater severity, for Soviet institutions of order were simply overcome by the tide of nationalism they were charged with repressing.

## *Summary and Conclusion*

We have seen in this chapter that the severity of repression is only one dimension by which to understand the repression/mobilization relationship, and perhaps not even the most important dimension. Rather, by introducing the notion of a "regime of repression," I have attempted to show how the patterning of repressive practice and the expectations internalized as a result influence the ways in which challenging movements and their target populations behave in the face of possible repression. Over the *glasnost'* period, with its massive upsurge in mobilization across multiple groups, the consistency of repressive response to challenge declined, and repressive actions lost much of their demobilizing effect, as movements and populations came to believe in the improbability of an effective repressive response to challenge. Thus, whereas severe repression may in a single moment inflict great damage on mobilizational networks and thereby undermine the physical capacity of groups to contest, the patterning of repression across time and internalized expectations about the possibilities for successful challenge that result are equally important in explaining how repression mobilizes or demobilizes in its wake.

The notion of a regime of repression also helps us understand better the supply side of repression: why state officials and institutions systematically choose particular types of repressive responses over others. A regime of repression operates as repertoires of behavior on the part of the state, and these repertoires – encoded in the operational rules guiding state institutions – assume a particular strategy toward demobilization and constitute an important benchmark by which to understand the boundaries of acceptable force on the part of the state. As we saw, Soviet elites eschewed the type of severe force deployed in China in June 1989 as a means of defending the Soviet state, in large part because it lay outside their understanding of how order should be created. When faced with the choice of imposing massive bloodshed in defense of the Soviet state, they retreated.

Finally, the notion of a regime of repression focuses us on the types of institutional capacities required for states to enforce demobilization across time. The collapse of the USSR was due as much to the multiple waves of mobilization that enveloped it as it was to the crisis of institutions these waves precipitated. The institutions of order were no longer capable of dealing with the mobilizational challenges they faced, as the mobilizational tide undermined discipline and morale and stretched institutional resources to the limit. By contrast, a single-minded focus on the severity of repression as a causal element of demobilization seriously exaggerates the institutional capacity of the Soviet state to enforce order through severe repression. This is not to underestimate the damage a single moment of severe repression can inflict on an opposition. But order functions in large part by reproducing itself over time – in patterned action rather than isolated episodes. As such, order requires institutions capable of dealing with challenges with regularity and consistency.

The critical issue raised by a violently imposed order is not just the harshness with which governments shoot, beat, or arrest, but, perhaps more important, what happens after they shoot, beat, or arrest. Does violent repression become internalized by challengers as part of a larger set of expectations about likely state responses to challenge, or does it become an opportunity for subsequent challenge to the state itself? As we have seen, the answers to these questions vary across both time and space, and the tidal context of mobilization is critical to the ways in which force mobilizes or demobilizes. As the Soviet experience shows, whereas a particular level of repression against a group might demobilize in one period, the same level of force may generate backlash effects within this same group in a temporal context in which challenge has gained a sense of momentum or grown normalized. We have also seen that even within the same temporal context, groups exhibit varying capacities to generate mobilization in the face of repression. In this respect, the notion of a regime of repression helps us to understand one of the more significant anomalies of Soviet collapse: why some groups previously deterred by force from mounting major challenges against the state to the point that they viewed successful challenge as nearly impossible came to believe under the influence of the *glasnost'* tide of nationalism in the impossibility that they might be deterred by government repression and acted accordingly.

# 8

Russian Mobilization and the
Accumulating "Inevitability"
of Soviet Collapse

Struggles over words . . . consist in trying to carry out what musicians call inversions of the chord, in trying to overturn the ordinary hierarchy of meanings in order to constitute as a *fundamental* meaning, as the root note of the semantic chord, a meaning that had hitherto been secondary, or, rather, *implied*, thus putting into action a symbolic revolution which may be at the root of political revolutions.
  Pierre Bourdieu, *In Other Words: Essays Towards a Reflexive Sociology*

Three Decembers tell the basic story behind the final years of the Soviet state. In December 1989 the Soviet Union was a deeply troubled country. By that time, the Soviet economy was in a state of marked decline, secessionist revolts had spread to the Baltic, Georgia, Western Ukraine, Moldova, Armenia, and Azerbaijan, nationalist violence had become an entrenched aspect of life in multiple regions of the country, and the Soviet Union's East European communist allies – under the impact of tidal effects emanating from the USSR – had been overturned with astounding rapidity. The possibility that the Soviet Union could fall apart and strategies for preventing this from happening had already been discussed on several occasions within the Politburo. Opinion polls showed that 53 percent of the Soviet population allowed the possibility that some republics might leave the USSR.[1] But whereas the prospect of a few republics leaving had grown conceivable and even increasingly acceptable to the public, the notion that the country would totally disintegrate and disappear from the map still seemed implausible to the vast majority of Soviet citizens and foreign observers alike.

By contrast, by December 1990 the perception that the existence of the Soviet state was directly under threat was nearly universal. By that time,

---

[1] Yu. A. Levada, *Est' mnenie! Itogi sotsiologicheskogo oprosa* (Moscow: Progress, 1990), p. 289.

separatist governments had come to power in multiple regions of the USSR, and the authority of the Soviet government had been confounded by a concatenation of sovereignty declarations – including that of the RSFSR. Lithuania declared its independence in March 1990. Estonia, Latvia, Moldavia, Georgia, and Armenia made clear their intentions to secede. Azerbaijan had been prevented from doing so only by bloody military intervention. Ukraine was sending signals that it too might not participate in a renewed Soviet Union, or would do so only if allowed to retain its own currency and army. The Soviet and Russian governments were at constant loggerheads over the reach of their respective sovereignties. The economy was in a state of collapse, and plans for introducing market reforms had foundered over the issue of the division of powers between center and republic. In December 1990 the USSR Congress of People's Deputies approved the idea of a referendum on the future of the country (eventually conducted in March 1991). Public opinion surveys reveal that by December 1990 27 percent of the Soviet population had come to believe that the disintegration of the USSR was "inevitable"[2] – an astounding figure given that this was still eight months before the August coup and a year before the Belovezhskoe agreement formally ending the Soviet state. Yet, even though the country's survival seemed increasingly in doubt, surveys showed that 73 percent of the Soviet population approved of efforts to preserve the country in revised form.[3]

By December 1991, however, belief that the Soviet Union should be preserved had been seriously undermined, and the sense that there was no alternative to its demise was widespread. When the USSR Supreme Soviet formally met in December 1991 to vote on whether to abolish itself and accept the dissolution of the Soviet Union, hardly any deputies bothered to attend.[4] As noted at the time by *Rossiiskaia gazeta*, the newspaper of the Russian parliament, "The former union is no more. And much more important, no one needs it."[5] A demonstration in Moscow called by a variety of political movements to protest the termination of the Soviet

---

[2] Cited in Vera Tolz, *The USSR in 1990: A Record of Events* (Boulder, CO: Westview Press, 1992), pp. 807–8. Even so, 53 percent continued to believe that the disintegration of the country was "impossible."

[3] See Matthew Wyman, *Public Opinion in Postcommunist Russia* (New York: St. Martin's Press, 1997), p. 159. This roughly paralleled the result in Gorbachev's March 1991 referendum.

[4] *International Herald Tribune*, December 27, 1991, p. 1.

[5] *Rossiiskaia gazeta*, December 12, 1991, p. 1.

Union attracted only three to ten thousand participants.[6] Although nostalgia for the USSR (particularly within the older generation) subsequently developed among many Russians and non-Russians after the USSR ceased to exist, numerous public opinion polls in December 1991 and January 1992 showed clear majorities of Russians supporting the creation of the Commonwealth of Independent States in place of a renewed Soviet state.[7] As one journalist noted, even the communists within the Russian parliament "participated quite wholeheartedly, with very few abstentions and naysayers, in the nearly unanimous ratification of the Belovezhskoe treaty," and the lowering of the Soviet flag over the Kremlin on December 25 "was mostly met with malicious indifference."[8] The once unthinkable and impossible had become the conventional and inevitable.

This chapter traces how a sense of inevitability came to envelop the disintegration of the Soviet state. Central in bringing this about (though a story largely ignored in this study so far) was the pivotal role played by Russian mobilization. Indeed, the Soviet state was brought down as much by what Roman Szporluk perceptively termed the "de-Sovietization of Russia,"[9] that is, the growing alienation of Russians from a state with which they had, in the past, routinely identified, as by pressure by non-Russians for independence. Russian nationalism was long understood as the linchpin of Soviet power, and the capacity of successive Soviet rulers to tap into it was said to have been largely responsible for the Soviet state's ability to incorporate non-Russian territories, weather Hitler's invasion, and become a global superpower. Soviet communism was widely viewed as Russian communism, and Leninist ideology was said to have powerfully resonated

---

[6] *Kommersant'*, December 9–16, 1991, p. 18; *Nezavisimaia gazeta*, December 12, 1991, p. 2; TASS, in *FBIS*, December 11, 1991, p. 46.

[7] One poll of 998 inhabitants of 22 regions of Russia taken by the Center for Comparative Social Research in December 1991 found that 62.4 percent of those surveyed believed the creation of the Commonwealth was a positive factor. *Rossiiskaia gazeta*, December 26, 1991. Another poll of 1,005 inhabitants of Russia living in 14 cities found a similar percentage (64 percent) supporting the agreement that put an end to the USSR and only 11 percent opposed. *Nezavisimaia gazeta*, December 18, 1991, p. 2. See also Wyman, *Public Opinion in Postcommunist Russia*, p. 166.

[8] Sergei Roy, "This Is the Way the Empire Ends," *Moscow News*, no. 45, November 24, 1999, and no. 46, December 1, 1999, from Lexis-Nexis News Service.

[9] See, in particular, the series of essays by Szporluk on this subject reprinted in Roman Szporluk, *Russia, Ukraine, and the Break-up of the Soviet Union* (Stanford, CA: Hoover Institution Press, 2000).

with embedded elements of Russian political culture. By all these measures of traditional common sense, Russians should have been expected to defend the coherence of the Soviet state. Indeed, one of the reasons why earlier tides of nationalism in Eurasia had failed to undermine Russian control over non-Russian territories was precisely the way in which Russians had come to the defense of the realm. Yet, in the late 1980s, when the Soviet state liberalized and Russian dominance was under attack, not only did Russians by and large fail to come to the defense of the Soviet state; many actually joined in the attacks, even coming to identify themselves as victims of Soviet "imperial" domination. In the end, in the specific context of December 1991, Russian public opinion overwhelmingly acquiesced to – and to some extent, even embraced – the Soviet state's demise.

Most studies of the role of Russian mobilization in the breakup of the Soviet state analyze the Russian case in isolation from other waves of mobilization[10] or focus attention on the role played by Boris Yeltsin in channeling Russian mobilization in an anti-Soviet direction.[11] Without underestimating the role played by Yeltsin or Russian social movements, there is a need as well to recognize that both were deeply affected by the broader tide of contention of which they were a part. We have already seen in previous chapters how, riding the tide of nationalism that had emerged, in 1989 and 1990 mass secessionist sentiment had crystallized among non-Russians in disparate parts of the country, nationalist movements espousing secession had risen to power, the coherence of institutions had been compromised, protracted violent disorders had emerged along the Soviet Union's southern tier, and law enforcement institutions were overwhelmed and demoralized, rendering the successful application of force increasingly unlikely. All this had a profound effect on Russians, both in the non-Russian republics and within Russia itself. Russians, too, came to understand themselves in radically different terms in the ways in which they borrowed from, allied themselves with, or struggled against the tide of nationalism that was washing across the country. Russian mobilization therefore needed to be treated separately in this book, not so much because

[10] See, for instance, Michael Urban (with Vyacheslav Igrunov and Sergei Mitrokhin), *The Rebirth of Politics in Russia* (Cambridge, UK: Cambridge University Press, 1997); M. Stephen Fish, *Democracy from Scratch: Opposition and Regime in the New Russian Revolution* (Princeton, NJ: Princeton University Press, 1995).

[11] See Jerry F. Hough, *Democratization and Revolution in the USSR, 1985–1991* (Washington, DC: Brookings Institution Press, 1997).

it stood outside the tide of nationalism, but rather because of the close association of Russians with the Soviet state, which defined structurally the ways in which Russians mobilized for or against the state and were distinguished from other groups.

It was this association which made Russian opinion the structural pivot on which perceptions of the likely survival or collapse of the Soviet state ultimately rested. But as we will see, it also led to the trifurcation of Russian mobilization into nationalist-conservative, liberal, and labor-economic streams, each of which comprehended its relationship to the Soviet state and to non-Russian nationalisms in different terms. Key to the eventual outcome of Soviet collapse was the way in which Russian liberals forged an alliance with non-Russian separatists against the Soviet regime and subsequently against the Soviet state, even borrowing the sovereignty and anticolonial frames championed by non-Russians and using these as a wedge to force a far-reaching decentralization of power. Russian liberals did not define themselves as nationalists. They saw themselves as struggling primarily against the communist regime, not for the nation. Yet, over the course of 1990 they adopted many of the tropes of national liberation then extant elsewhere in the USSR, coming to advocate a brand of liberal nationalism in which Russian sovereignty and self-determination were seen as necessary parts of the democratization process. In 1990 and 1991 this defense of Russian sovereignty against an overbearing and imperial all-union government became the dominant theme of Russian mobilization. Institutional contingencies – specifically, the republican and local elections – were critical in extending the influence of this anticolonial frame to Russia. By contrast, those defending the integrity of the Soviet state, for reasons we will explore, failed to generate effective countermobilization of their own. In 1990 most Russians (including the Yeltsin leadership) still hoped for the creation of a Union of Sovereign Republics that would draw Russians, Ukrainians, Belorussians, and others into a common state. By the end of 1990, however, this possibility had grown increasingly remote in view of the tangled negotiations over a new union treaty, the spread of secessionist sentiment in Ukraine, and sharpened conflict between the Soviet and Russian governments over the proper bounds of their authority. As I argue below, with the emergence of sovereignty as a dominant theme in Russia, by late 1990 structural conditions conducive to Soviet collapse had cumulated to the point that perceptions of its "inevitability" began to take on mass proportions. Much of the history of the final year of the Soviet state is the story of actors across the political spectrum coming to grips with the transformed structural situation wrought by the tide. To be sure, the Novo-Ogarevo agreement put a temporary halt to conflict by accepting the partial breakup of the Soviet state and what was fundamentally a confederal arrangement among those who would remain. But as we will see, it is unlikely that the agreement would have resulted in a workable, stable solution to the crisis of the Soviet state, even if the August coup had not intervened. In the wake of the coup, when union republics declared their independence with astounding speed one after another, the possibilities for an agreement to create a rump Soviet state quickly evaporated, particularly as Ukraine moved to assert its independence and Russian liberals sought to substantiate their sovereignty through a leap to the market. Ironically, those who killed Gorbachev's attempts to create a rump Soviet state in late 1991 – the Russians, Ukrainians, and Belorussians – were precisely those who, prior to the intervention of the tide, should have been most expected to support the union. Instead, republican legislatures and mass opinion overwhelmingly supported the decision to end the Soviet state. The USSR was not murdered by an individual or a cabal; rather, it expired, succumbing to a generalized sense – even among its most likely supporters – that, having exhausted itself in the face of uncontainable nationalist revolt and failed reform, it could not be salvaged in usable form.

### *Russians and the Tide of Nationalism*

Russian mobilization against the Soviet state was a central part of the politics which brought about the dissolution of the USSR. Yet, as one can see from Figure 8.1, within the cycle as a whole Russian mobilization resembled somewhat the pattern of a late riser. It is true (as we saw in Chapter 2) that Russian and Russian-dominated movements centered in Moscow and Leningrad (the Democratic Union, *Pamiat'*, the Group for Trust, Civic Dignity, the Federation of Socialist Clubs, *Miting-87*, and others) played critical roles in 1987 and 1988 in staking claim to the new political space of the streets, and Russians were dominant in the institutional politics that brought about liberalization. But although Russians constituted 52 percent of the Soviet population, they accounted for only 30 percent of the demonstrations and only 21 percent of the participants in demonstrations in 1987. During 1988 Russian mobilization increased and diversified geographically, particularly in connection with the Nineteenth Party Conference, when abuses in the delegate selection process unleashed

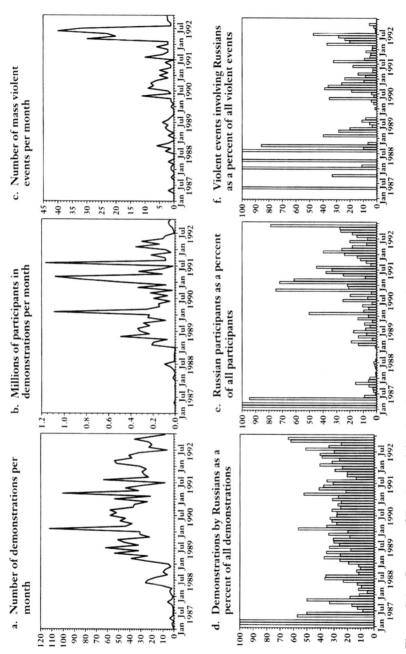

**Figure 8.1.** Patterns of Russian mobilization, January 1987–December 1992.

391

a wave of small demonstrations in provincial cities. But in total this mobilization represented only 17 percent of the demonstrations and only 0.6 percent of the participants in demonstrations throughout the USSR in 1988. Only three demonstrations by Russians in 1988 attracted more than twenty thousand participants, all of these occurring in the city of Kuibyshev in June and July 1988.[12]

The first wave of Russian protest to attract a significant following was nationalist in character and occurred in early 1989 outside of Russia proper. In summer and fall 1988 the Russian-speaking community of Estonia had begun to organize sporadic counterprotests against the growing nationalist influence over the republic, and by the end of the year countermovements to popular fronts had appeared in all three Baltic republics: Intermovement and the somewhat more moderate United Council of Labor Collectives in Estonia; Interfront in Latvia; and *Yedinstvo* (Unity) in Lithuania (which included significant participation from Lithuania's Polish minority as well). Though calling themselves "internationalist," these countermovements represented the interests of Russians and others who had migrated to the Baltic during the years of Soviet occupation, as well as of compactly settled minorities. In early 1989 the Baltic republics adopted a series of language laws that declared Estonian, Lithuanian, and Latvian the official languages of their respective republics. This, along with the growing secessionist bent of Baltic nationalist movements, provided a focal point for the countermobilization of Russian speakers, provoking a wave of demonstrations and strikes in February and March 1989 that typically attracted fifty to sixty thousand participants in each of the Baltic republics.[13]

A second major wave of Russian protest, concentrated within Russia itself, emerged in spring 1989 in connection with elections to the USSR Congress of People's Deputies. This wave bore a strong liberalizing character, defining itself as a diverse set of movements for speeding the pace of democratization and reform. It too had been influenced by the Baltic example – not as a reaction against Baltic nationalisms, but rather gaining inspiration from them, primarily in the spread of the popular front as an

---

[12] The first two were part of a successful protest campaign to oust the local party boss; the third was an ecological demonstration. *Vesti iz SSSR*, 12–38, 1988; 14–26, 1988; *Obshchina*, no. 22, November 13, 1988, p. 25.

[13] *Vesti iz SSSR*, 3–3, 1989; 4–6, 1989; 5/6–4, 1989; *Ekspress khronika*, no. 8, February 19, 1989.

organizational form for mobilizing populations against the party-state. In February and March 1989, these groups became the core for organizing electoral rallies in seventeen major Russian cities in support of candidates favoring accelerated democratization, with the largest (attracting forty thousand participants), in support of Yeltsin's election, taking place in Moscow the day before balloting.[14] This wave gathered massive strength in May with the opening of the Congress, as demonstrations involving tens and hundreds of thousands were held on a daily basis in Moscow. A transnational alliance was evident at these rallies; the May 28 demonstration organized by Memorial and the Moscow Popular Front, for instance, which attracted one hundred fifty thousand people, was addressed not only by liberal leaders Andrei Sakharov and Yuri Afanas'ev, but also by representatives of the Estonian Popular Front and the Ukrainian Uniate Church (then in the midst of a campaign for legalization); the June 6 meeting, in which fifty thousand participated, condemned both Tbilisi and Tiananmen Square massacres.[15]

A third wave of Russian mobilization, emerging in July 1989, predominantly economic in character, was vastly larger than the first two. Labor unrest had been growing throughout the USSR in 1988 and early 1989. The overwhelming majority of time lost to strikes in Soviet industry occurred in the non-Russian republics, as a series of general strikes in support of nationalist movements paralyzed the Transcaucasus.[16] Strikes over economic issues had also grown more frequent, though usually these were confined to a single enterprise, lasted only a few days, and were focused narrowly on issues of wages and work conditions. The miners' strikes of July 1989 were qualitatively different, due in large part to the broader scope for challenge that emerged from the Congress of People's Deputies in June. Beginning in a single mine in the city of Mezhdurechensk in Kemerovo province, the strike quickly spread to shut down the entire city within several days and the entire province within a week. By the time the strike ended after nine days, strike action had spread to the Donbass region of Ukraine, the Vorkuta region of Komi province, the Karaganda region of northern Kazakhstan, and elsewhere – in all encompassing more than five hundred thousand workers. As Peter Rutland noted, "The situation in these

---

[14] TASS in *FBIS*, March 30, 1989, p. 43.
[15] *Vesti iz SSSR*, 9/10–9, 1989; *Press-Reliz "Glasnost'*," June 7, 1989.
[16] Elizabeth Teague and Philip Hanson, "Most Soviet Strikes Politically Motivated," *Report on the USSR*, vol. 2, no. 34 (August 24, 1990), pp. 1–2.

towns took on a carnival atmosphere. Social roles were turned upside down as the authority of officials evaporated. People were exhilarated, and felt they were behaving as they had never behaved before."[17] None of these actions was framed in specifically nationalist terms. The demands focused instead around the lack of consumer goods, raising wages, and improving benefits and working conditions. But as Stephen Crowley observes, from the beginning they contained a political element as well. Strikers saw themselves as challenging domination by a faceless and exploitative bureaucratic system, so that enterprise independence from ministerial control also figured centrally among the demands.[18] Much as nationalist movements sought autonomy from a dominating center, so too did miners seek the economic sovereignty of the enterprise.

Thus, by mid-1989 three streams of Russian mobilization had emerged – nationalist-conservative, liberal-intellectual, and labor-based economic – raising distinct sets of issues and reflecting the multiple relationships of Russians to the Soviet state. Russians were the dominant nationality of the Soviet Union and had the most to lose from overturn of the prevailing national order; they also constituted a disproportionate share of the intelligentsia and the working class relative to most other nationalities[19] – the former most likely to be attracted to ideas of liberalization, the latter (due to their vulnerable position at a time of growing economic insecurity) most likely to protest the regime's economic policies. The relationship of each stream to the larger tide of nationalism then sweeping the country was varied. The nationalist-conservative stream – which included not only those who sought to preserve the Soviet system, but also those who criticized it for undermining Russian dominance – emerged on a mass scale specifically in opposition to non-Russian nationalisms. The liberal stream, dominated by intellectuals seeking to overturn the continuing legacies of

---

[17] Peter Rutland, "Labor Unrest and Movements in 1989 and 1990," *Soviet Economy*, vol. 6, no. 3 (1990), p. 354.

[18] Stephen Crowley, *Hot Coal, Cold Steel: Russian and Ukrainian Workers from the End of the Soviet Union to the Post-Communist Transformations* (Ann Arbor, MI: University of Michigan Press, 1997), pp. 25–45. For other accounts of the strike, see Simon Clarke and Peter Fairbrother, "The Origins of the Independent Workers' Movement and the 1989 Miners' Strike," in Simon Clarke et al., *What About the Workers? Workers and the Transition to Capitalism in Russia* (London: Verso, 1993), pp. 121–44; Theodore H. Friedgut and Lewis Siegelbaum, *The Soviet Miners' Strike, July 1989: Perestroika from Below* (Pittsburgh: Carl Beck Papers in Russian and East European Studies, 1990).

[19] See Darrell Slider, "A Note on the Class Structure of Soviet Nationalities," *Soviet Studies*, vol. 37, no. 4 (October 1985), pp. 535–40.

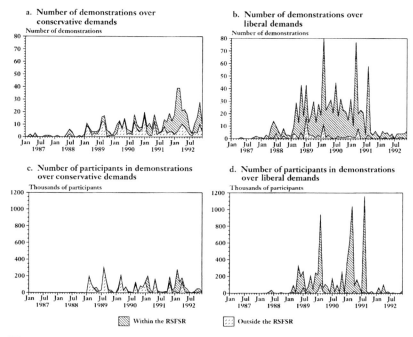

**Figure 8.2.** Russian mobilization over conservative and liberal demands within and outside of the RSFSR, 1987–92.

totalitarianism, allied itself with non-Russian nationalisms against the Soviet regime and borrowed freely from them. The labor-based economic stream, although conditioned by the non-Russian mobilization that had preceded it, tended to view the tide as incidental to its actions and frequently displayed apprehension toward those who sought in one way or another to involve it in tidal politics.

Each of these streams occurred within relatively distinct geographic zones. Nationalist-conservative demands gained large-scale resonance within the Russian-speaking communities of the Baltic and Moldova, but as Figure 8.2 indicates, through the end of 1991 did not find a major following within the RSFSR proper.[20] This occurred only in 1992, after the

---

[20] In Moscow and Leningrad some large-scale nationalist-conservative mobilization did take place. The Leningrad party organization in particular was a sponsor of the nationalist-conservative movement. But in both cities nationalist-conservative mobilizations paled in size and significance compared to those advocating liberalizing demands.

breakup of the USSR, when nationalist-conservative mobilization by Russians within the RSFSR increased significantly (largely in connection with Gaidar's program of shock therapy), while nationalist-conservative demonstrations by Russian speakers outside of Russia declined. By contrast, liberal mobilization was dominant within the large cities of the RSFSR. As Figure 8.2 indicates, relatively little mobilization in support of liberalizing demands emerged from the Russian community outside the RSFSR. But even within the RSFSR, liberal mobilization was overwhelmingly a phenomenon of Moscow and Leningrad, where the bulk of the Russian intellectual elite was concentrated, with smaller echoes in cities of lesser size. Mobilizational turnouts at demonstrations expressing liberalizing demands were on average six times as great in Moscow and Leningrad as in other cities in Russia with more than five hundred thousand inhabitants, accounting for 78 percent of the total number of Russian participants in liberal demonstrations.

Labor-based economic mobilization was also urban in character. It gained significant resonance within the RSFSR and in Russified zones of the non-Russian republics, but was distinctly a phenomenon of Russians and Russian speakers in the coal-mining regions of Western Siberia, Komi, Eastern Ukraine, and Northern Kazakhstan. Various explanations have been proffered for why coal miners, as opposed to workers in other industries, were particularly prone to unrest during this period. Though coal mining is known in many countries to be among the more strike-prone industries, and though the discontent of Soviet miners was well known prior to *glasnost'*, in the Brezhnev era the automobile industry had experienced more labor protest than coal, with demands similarly focused around shortages of consumer goods, wages, and working conditions.[21] Generally, with the exception of the coal industry, strike action over economic issues in the *glasnost'* period tended to remain localized and diffuse, held in check by worker dependence on factory management for goods and services and the absence of effective trade union organization. The larger context of the mobilizational cycle played a critical role in the eruption of coal miner activism. As Crowley observed, miners in large cities displayed markedly higher levels of activism than those in isolated communities, in large part

---

[21] On the strike in Tol'iatti in May 1980 involving seventy thousand automobile workers, as well as other instances of labor revolt in the USSR prior to *glasnost'*, see Betsy Gidwitz, "Labor Unrest in the Soviet Union," *Problems of Communism*, November–December 1982, pp. 33–34.

because of their "exposure to intellectual critiques and condemnations of communism and expressions of alternative political and economic arrangements."[22] But the specific conditions of the Soviet coal industry – its high rate of accidents and hazardous work conditions, its declining share of investment and rate of productivity, and the deteriorating housing and social infrastructures of mining towns – were critical to the social explosion as well. At the beginning of 1989 the coal industry had been placed on full economic accounting as part of the economic reforms then slowly taking place throughout Soviet industry. However, the price set by the state for a ton of coal was only half the cost of its extraction. Add to this the shortages of basic consumer items that had grown rampant in summer 1989 (in particular, soap, a necessity for miners) and it is not difficult to see why the coal industry served as the institutional frame for class-based challenge to the Soviet state.

Each of these three streams of Russian mobilization thus enjoyed a significant following within specific and largely separate microcontexts. In this respect Russian mobilization differed substantially from that of other groups at the time, for it was unusually divided. Not only was there a plethora of movements, but these movements stood for quite distinct and in some instances opposing frames. Again, this division was an expression of the varied relationships of Russians to the Soviet state. It played a critical role in the politics leading to the Soviet collapse, for rather than generating a nationalist backlash among Russians to non-Russian mobilization, as many observers had traditionally predicted, the tide of nationalism instead drove a wedge more deeply among Russians, politicizing and polarizing existing cleavages. Of the three streams, the liberal stream was best positioned to take advantage of the tide. Class-based labor movements were reluctant to spread their revolt more widely across Soviet industry primarily because they viewed themselves as local movements, not national ones. Labor protest expressed a particular trope of alienation from the Soviet state that appealed within Russified company-town contexts. In 1989 and early 1990, protesting workers did not seek connection with the liberal intelligentsia in Moscow and Leningrad, and unlike Solidarity in Poland in 1980, there was no serious attempt to generate sustained national organization.[23] In contrast to Russified working-class contexts,

---

[22] Crowley, *Hot Coal, Cold Steel*, p. 35.
[23] See Boris Kagarlitsky, *Farewell Perestroika: A Soviet Chronicle* (London: Verso, 1990), p. 184; Rutland, "Labor Unrest and Movements in 1989 and 1990," p. 350.

relatively unassimilated non-Russians were disproportionately attracted to nationalist rather than labor paradigms. In all, at 665 strikes during the 1987–91 period, 81 percent of the person-days lost by Russians to strikes were lost at strikes raising economic demands, whereas only 10 percent were incurred at strikes raising nationalist demands. By contrast, only 2 percent of the person-days lost to strikes carried out by non-Russians occurred at strikes raising economic demands and 93 percent were lost at strikes raising nationalist demands. Outside of highly Russified regions such as the Donbass, northern Kazakhstan, and Belorussia, nationalism trumped class as the most significant frame for mobilization in the non-Russian republics (though as we saw in Chapter 5, nationalism also failed to generate significant resonance in many places). Industrialization had been a Russian-dominated process and had produced a Russian-dominated industrial elite and working class, while the operation of ethnofederal institutions in the non-Russian republics over six decades had instilled a sense of the primacy of ethnicity over class. By contrast, class, not nation, had long been the salient narrative of rebellion within Russian culture against a culturally similar but overpowering state. Where cultural difference with authority had been effaced or did not exist, culture could not offer a basis for effective resistance to authority; class, by contrast, did.

The July 1989 strikes sent a shock wave through Soviet political society and demonstrated the seemingly enormous political potential of the Russian worker as a force for or against change. The miners' strikes, and the liberals' consequent belief that reform had a mass base, influenced the formation of the Interregional Group of Deputies as a formal opposition at the end of July. The strikes affected the Interregional Group's tactics, for the faction's leadership concluded that the course of *perestroika* would be determined, in Gavril Popov's words, "not by the readiness of the party apparatus to introduce particular legislation or even the capacity of the deputy-democrats to fight for it, but by the actions of the masses," with legislative institutions understood as a base by which to mobilize this force.[24] In December 1989 a portion of the Interregional Group, led by Popov and Andrei Sakharov, appealed for a two-hour countrywide work stoppage to force abrogation of Article 6 of the Soviet Constitution on the leading role of the Communist Party. The appeal fell largely on deaf ears, gaining its most successful response in Western Ukraine but only sporadic

[24] Gavriil Popov, *Snova v oppozitsii* (Moscow: Galaktika, 1994), pp. 67–68, 74.

398

support elsewhere.[25] In the wake of the July 1989 strikes representatives of alternative social movements traveled to the Kuzbass, Donbass, and Karaganda to enlist worker participation, but found instead a guarded attitude toward outside political entrepreneurs. In 1989 and 1990 Rukh activists similarly met hostility from Donbass miners, some of whom chased them away from their microphones.[26] Nationalist-conservatives at first displayed a negative attitude toward Russian labor activism, viewing it as a disruptive force. But they too soon contemplated its potential power and engaged in efforts to lure the Russian working class into an antireform alliance. As one nationalist-conservative wrote in August, the miners' strikes had become "a rallying point for those basic forces of the people that have not yet realized visible benefits from restructuring."[27] But nationalist-conservatives found little support among the miners; their antimarket stance and general support for the central Soviet state clashed with the miners' sense of exploitation by the center and desire for control over local enterprise. Over time, as workers grew frustrated with Moscow's failure to keep its promises and to reverse the slide into economic chaos, the miners' demands radicalized, so that by fall 1990 and spring 1991 many miners in the Kuzbass, Donbass, and Vorkuta regions openly advocated the dismantlement of the central Soviet state – including, in the case of the Donbass, Ukrainian independence.[28] Thus, tidal effects and the growing disorganization of the Soviet state pushed the workers' movement to identify with the aims of Russian liberal politicians and their sovereignty paradigm, and in Ukraine, even with the separatist aims of non-Russian nationalists.

Throughout this period Russian nationalist-conservatives failed to generate a countertide of the own. As Pal Kalstoe noted, "From the very beginning the interfronts were on the defensive. They did not set the political agenda but instead only reacted to initiatives from the popular fronts . . . , and often very lamely."[29] Their base of support was considerably older than the nationalist movements they opposed, and as Anatol Lieven quipped, pensioners (especially, elderly women) were simply "not the stuff of which

---

[25] *Ekspress-khronika*, December 17, 1989.     [26] APN, July 16, 1990.

[27] *Literaturnaia Rossiia*, in *CDSP*, vol. 51, no. 43 (November 22, 1989), pp. 8–9.

[28] On the radicalization of the miners' movement, see Crowley, *Hot Coal, Cold Steel*, pp. 141–44; Walter Connor, *The Accidental Proletariat: Workers, Politics, and Crisis in Gorbachev's Russia* (Princeton, NJ: Princeton University Press, 1991), p. 299.

[29] Pal Kolstoe, *Russians in the Former Soviet Republics* (Bloomington, IN: Indiana University Press, 1995), p. 113.

successful counter-revolutions are made."[30] Despite the emergence of umbrella organizations in Russia for coordinating the activities of nationalist-conservative movements, relatively little cooperation occurred across republican boundaries; each "internationalist" movement was run by separate local nomenklatura groupings that looked to Moscow and the state, not to each other, for aid and guidance. Within Russia nationalist-conservatives also proved inept in conducting an electoral campaign and performed poorly in the March 1990 elections.[31] In the Baltic the mobilizational base of the nationalist-conservatives deteriorated over time. The Russian-speaking community contained within it various strands of opinion, and the antireform stance of nationalist-conservative movements – often expressed in hyperbolic terms – drove many local Russians in the opposite direction. Even in November 1988 public opinion surveys showed that 10 percent of non-Estonians in Estonia favored secession from the USSR. Eventually by March 1991, up to a third of non-Estonians sup-ported Estonia's exit from the USSR, whereas a slightly higher proportion of non-Latvians supported Latvian independence.[32] Thus, the pressure of the tide gradually pushed a portion of local Russian opinion in the Baltic further toward acceptance of independence. One of the striking patterns in Figure 8.2 is the massive decrease of participation in protest demonstrations among Russian nationalist-conservative movements in the non-Russian republics in 1990 and 1991, as the breakup of the Soviet state grew imminent. Logically, one would have expected the reverse trend, for Russian resistance to the tide to grow more significant over time. Yet, precisely the opposite occurred. In some areas of the USSR, the Russian-speaking diaspora lost its will to exercise a collective voice through disruption well before the Soviet collapse. And as Figure 8.1 shows, mass violent mobilization did not become a major element of the mobilizational repertoire of Russians in the non-Russian republics until after the demise of the USSR, and even here, was almost entirely confined to Moldova.

[30] Anatol Lieven, *The Baltic Revolution: Estonia, Latvia, Lithuania and the Path to Independence* (New Haven, CT: Yale University Press, 1993), p. 197.
[31] See Yitzhak M. Brudny, *Reinventing Russia: Russian Nationalism and the Soviet State, 1953–1991* (Cambridge, MA: Harvard University Press, 1998), pp. 243–45.
[32] *Vesti iz SSSR*, 22–3, 1988; Rein Taagepera, *Estonia: Return to Independence* (Boulder, CO: Westview, 1993), pp. 141, 194; Rasma Karklins, *Ethnopolitics and Transition to Democracy: The Collapse of the USSR and Latvia* (Washington, DC: The Woodrow Wilson Center Press, 1994), p. 101.

By contrast, Russian liberals embraced the tide of nationalism, borrowed heavily from it, and ultimately used it to ride to power. The pivotal events in this process were the 1990 republican and local elections and the waves of mobilization that accompanied them, which fundamentally tipped the balance between the regime and its liberal Russian opposition.

## From the Streets to Dvoevlastie

As noted in Chapter 4, the politics of revolution and the politics of secession share a number of similarities. For one thing, the dissolution of the state, like the overthrow of a regime, is among the most radical of demands in politics. Both involve forms of mobilizational politics that revolve around the overthrow of the dominant forces underlying state power in their differing guises and dimensions. As Valerie Bunce has pointed out, the difficulty in distinguishing the Soviet regime from the Soviet state meant that the overthrow of the Soviet regime could not be easily disentangled from the end of the Soviet state.[33] This same fusion also made a transnational alliance between Russian liberals and non-Russian separatists feasible, for in 1988 and 1989 Russian liberals primarily defined themselves in opposition to the Soviet regime, whereas non-Russian separatists defined themselves in opposition to the Soviet state.

Beginning in 1990 the positions of Russian liberals increasingly converged toward those of non-Russian separatists. As we saw in Chapters 2 and 3, the peak of mobilizational fervor in the USSR coincided with the period in which the politics of the street came to be institutionalized within the state – the republican and local elections in the first half of 1990. As a *Pravda* editorial described the mood within Russia at the time, "A radicalization of public awareness is taking place, distrust of official political structures and administrative bodies is gaining strength, and criticism of the 'Partocracy' and rally-applied pressure demanding the resignation of local bodies have become pointed and embittered."[34] This was, in the minds of party reformers, the "critical wave" of mobilization that conditioned the Soviet collapse, largely by ushering in an alteration in the ways in which Russians related to the Soviet state and transforming the balance

---

[33] Valerie Bunce, *Subversive Institutions: The Design and the Destruction of Socialism and the State* (Cambridge, UK: Cambridge University Press, 1999).
[34] *Pravda*, March 26, 1990, pp. 1–2.

between the regime and its Russian liberal opposition.[35] A shift in the Russian public's evaluation of Soviet institutions occurred at the time, the beginning of a tipping process that ultimately undermined Russian belief in the future of the Soviet state. In May 1990, for the first time, Gorbachev's popularity sank below that of Yeltsin among Muscovites, and within the USSR as a whole Gorbachev's approval rating plummeted from 52 percent in December 1989 to 28 percent by July 1990.[36]

But what made this period so critical in terms of the disintegrative end point of the Soviet state was not merely the transformed consciousness which accompanied the electoral mobilization, but even more the way in which these waves of mobilization were, within multiple contexts, institutionalized within the Soviet state. As David Remnick wrote at the time, "In 1990, nationalist consciousness was transformed from a range of popular movements to a central fact of political power."[37] Opposition movements formally assumed power in Estonia, Latvia, Lithuania, Russia, Moldova, Armenia, and Georgia, while in Ukraine they gained control over Western Ukrainian local governments and a significant minority representation within the republican legislature.[38] Elections in these cases institutionalized the politics of the street, returning it to the state via the legislative floor. Indeed, the behavior of parliamentary deputies, who only a short time before were leading demonstrations, often differed little from street politics. It bore the same disorder, shouts and noise, and sense of sharpened lines of conflict. As one description of the debates within the Ukrainian Supreme Soviet in November 1990 noted, "the hall became a rally square."[39] But in institutionalizing street politics at the republican and local levels, a fragmented state emerged in which the authority of ethnofederal units quickly became the center of dispute.

In some republics governments had already come under the de facto control of nationalist movements well before the 1990 republican elections. On gaining control, these movements spearheaded attempts to assert

---

[35] See Vadim Medvedev, *V komande Gorbacheva. Vzgliad iznutri* (Moscow: Bylina, 1994), p. 107.

[36] *Gorbachev–Yel'tsin: 1500 dnei politicheskogo protivostoianiia* (Moscow: Terra, 1992), p. 281; *Demokraticheskaia Rossiia*, no. 3, September 1990, pp. 12–13.

[37] *The Washington Post*, December 20, 1990, p. A1.

[38] In Moldova and Russia, opposition movements did not gain a majority of seats in the republican legislatures, but were able to broker arrangements with independent deputies to control these legislatures.

[39] *Pravda*, December 1, 1990, p. 5. On the similarities between parliaments and crowds, see the work of Scipio Sighele, as discussed in J. S. McClelland, *The Crowd and the Mob: From Plato to Canetti* (London: Unwin Hyman, 1989), p. 178.

republican sovereignty vis-à-vis the center. In November 1988 the Estonian Supreme Soviet adopted a "Declaration About the Sovereignty of the Estonian SSR" which affirmed that, in accordance with Article 76 of the Soviet constitution, the republic's sovereignty was "integral and indivisible" and declared the supremacy of republican laws on the territory of Estonia.[40] As the quotation at the beginning of this chapter indicates, at the core of all revolutions lies a struggle over words in which implied meanings overturn established understandings. The notion of "sovereignty" (in Russian, *suverenitet*) was one of the critical struggles over words within the *glasnost'* revolution; later, after sovereignty became an established fact and a number of republics had exited the state, the struggle among those remaining would turn around the disputed meaning of "union" (*soiuz*) and "independence" (*nezavisimost'*). Sovereignty had long been part of the Soviet political vocabulary; the Soviet constitution had described union republics as "sovereign," though in reality the hypercentralization of the Soviet state had limited their empirical sovereignty. The Estonian government never actually declared sovereignty for Estonia in 1988, since according to the Soviet constitution the Estonian S.S.R. already was a sovereign entity. Rather, its declaration "about" sovereignty (often mistranslated as a declaration "of" sovereignty) subverted authority by giving new understanding to words whose meaning had previously been appropriated by others. As Rein Taagepera notes, "What was revolutionary was that . . . [a union republic] dared to propose an interpretation of the constitution rather than meekly accept however Moscow chose to construe it."[41] The Estonian declaration was subsequently pronounced unconstitutional by the USSR Supreme Soviet, though the republican authorities, in line with their interpretation of sovereignty, simply ignored the central government's decision. In fall 1988 the authors of the Estonian declaration did not necessarily interpret sovereignty as independent statehood; sovereignty could just as well imply a far-reaching autonomy. The ambiguity of the term was an ally in gaining acceptance for new meanings. But as the tide of nationalism developed and others joined the Estonian revolt, "sovereignty" increasingly came to be deployed by Estonians as a signifier for separate statehood.

The Estonian declaration is generally viewed as the beginning of the so-called war of the laws in the Soviet Union – a prolonged hit-and-run battle between institutions of the ethnofederal hierarchy over whose laws

---

[40] For the text, see Taagepera, *Estonia: Return to Independence*, p. 146.
[41] Taagepera, *Estonia: Return to Independence*, p. 145.

would have precedence. This struggle reached its crescendo in 1991 and was eventually responsible for tearing apart the Soviet state. In the wake of the Estonian declaration and as their governments came under nationalist control, other republics adopted similar resolutions. In May 1989 the Lithuanian Supreme Soviet passed an analogous resolution about sovereignty, as did Latvia in July 1989. In October 1989, the Azerbaijani Supreme Soviet asserted the superiority of its laws over those of Moscow, and in November 1989, only days after the USSR Supreme Soviet pronounced the Baltic and Azerbaijani declarations illegal, the Georgian Supreme Soviet declared its right to veto all-union laws and to republican control over all land, water, and natural resources on its territory. In January 1990 the Armenian Supreme Soviet similarly appropriated the right to veto laws passed by the all-union government.

In this respect, the Russian "declaration about sovereignty" in June 1990 fit the larger mold that had been established. It was not an original act. Rather, it borrowed heavily from the language of prior declarations about sovereignty. What was significant about the declaration was not the act but the actor. This was Russia – supposedly the bulwark of the union – asserting its autonomy vis-à-vis the union. Its declaration about sovereignty was an unambiguous sign of the ways in which the tide of nationalism had affected the thinking of cultural groups closely affiliated with the Soviet state. In 1988 the idea that Russia might declare its sovereignty vis-à-vis the all-union government seemed an absurdity. By spring 1990 it was already taken for granted by all political actors. As a liberal Jewish intellectual recounted in May 1990: "If you had told me two years ago I would be out on the street at demonstrations shouting '*Ross-i-ya, Ross-i-ya*,' I would have thought you were crazy."[42] But by May 1990, even before the Russian declaration of sovereignty was passed, public opinion polls showed that 43 percent of the RSFSR public believed that Russia should receive political and economic independence (up to and including exit from the USSR), whereas another 35 percent favored a federal arrangement granting the Russian government much expanded economic and political rights, but leaving the final say over most questions with the central Soviet government.[43]

---

[42] John Morrison, *Boris Yeltsin: From Bolshevik to Democrat* (New York: Dutton, 1991), p. 19.
[43] John Dunlop, "Russia: Confronting a Loss of Empire," in Ian Bremmer and Ray Taras, eds., *Nations and Politics in the Soviet Successor States* (Cambridge: Cambridge University Press, 1993), p. 42. The survey was conducted by the All-Union Center for the Study of Public Opinion among 1,517 persons in twenty regions of the RSFSR.

## Russian Mobilization and the "Inevitability" of Soviet Collapse

The significance of a Russian declaration of sovereignty had long been clear to the Kremlin. As Prime Minister Ryzhkov told his colleagues in the Politburo at a meeting to discuss the situation in the Baltic in November 1989, "we should not fear the Baltic, but Russia and Ukraine. This would smell like total disintegration. And then we would need another government, another leadership for the country, and already another country."[44] The Russian declaration about sovereignty became the tipping point in the development of sovereignty claims, setting off a wave of further declarations by union republics, autonomous republics and provinces, national districts, and even cities and islands in what came to be known as the "parade of sovereignties." The parade of sovereignties universalized a situation of dual power (*dvoevlastie*) in which relations between lower-level and higher-level institutions of territorial governance throughout the ethnofederal hierarchy grew ambiguous and contested. The currency of the term *dvoevlastie* to describe the final acts leading to the Soviet collapse – a term which had its origins in the revolutionary processes of early twentieth century Russia – speaks to some of the underlying similarities between revolution and secession. In much the same way as Lenin gained control over the Petrograd Soviet in 1917 and used it as a base from which to subvert authority by asserting the predominance of the Soviets, so too did opposition movements in 1989 and 1990 gain control over segments of the Soviet state, using them as a base from which to challenge the Soviet government by asserting sovereignty over it. In both cases, previously secondary meanings became the instrument through which challengers overturned authority.

Many interpret the declaration about Russian sovereignty as the invention of Boris Yeltsin. But a more accurate assessment would show that by spring 1990, under the influence of the tide of nationalism, sovereignty had become a widely shared political goal across the Russian political spectrum, and that the real issue was not whether a declaration would be adopted by the Russian government, but which version of a sovereignty declaration would be embraced. Long before the 1990 elections, the rising tide of nationalist mobilization in the non-Russian republics had begun to influence the ways in which Russian politicians, primarily nationalist-conservatives, construed their interests vis-à-vis the all-union government. At the First Congress of People's Deputies in June 1989 the nationalist Russian writer Valentin Rasputin, lashing out against the "Russophobia"

---

[44] *Soiuz mozhno bylo sokhranit'* (Moscow: Aprel'-85, 1995), p. 76.

that he said had by then encompassed the Baltic, Georgia, and other republics, raised the possibility that Russia, too, might think about leaving the union. Rasputin did not advocate the breakup of the USSR, but merely meant to illustrate that Russians could also claim suffering and discrimination at the hands of the center – according to Rasputin, even more severe than those seeking exit.[45] But by July 1989 demands for Russian sovereignty began to emerge more regularly from Russian nationalists, particularly in Leningrad. The issue was even discussed in the Politburo, with Gorbachev rejecting the idea on the basis that it would "take the core out of the Union." Vadim Medvedev warned the Politburo that "the RSFSR is backbone of the Union. To make Russia sovereign is the golden daydream of the Balts."[46] Gorbachev claims in his memoirs that

long before Yeltsin the Baltic separatists pointed to the necessity of the "sovereignization" of Russia and favored the creation of a Russian Communist Party. They understood that this was the key moment: If Russia bit for this and Russian nationalism began to seethe, the union would end. The proponents of Ukrainian independence similarly poured oil on the fire. . . . In short, there was an attempt to "acquire" Russia, after which all the rest would become, so to speak, a simple affair.[47]

To the extent that such a strategy of instigating Russians toward a sense of *ressentiment* was operative, it proved exceedingly successful. By the time of the September 1989 Central Committee Plenum on nationalities issues, the idea of upgrading the powers of the RSFSR and creating a separate Russian Communist Party had gained widespread support within party circles and was openly championed by the conservative wing of the Politburo. The irony is that the demands of Russian nationalist-conservatives for sovereignty unwittingly helped to pave the way for Russia's eventual exit from the USSR.

Gorbachev remained skeptical toward these demands, viewing them as an attempt by his opponents to undermine reform by moving the bulk of the party's membership and resources from his control. At first, as a com-

[45] *Pervyi s"ezd narodnykh deputatov SSSR, 25 maia–9 iiunia 1989 g. Stenograficheskii otchet,* vol. 2 (Moscow: Politizdat, 1989), pp. 458–59.
[46] *Soiuz mozhno bylo,* p. 64.
[47] Mikhail Gorbachev, *Zhizn' i reformy,* vol. 1 (Moscow: Novosti, 1995), p. 521. For specific examples of such behavior, see Roman Szporluk, "Dilemmas of Russian Nationalism," *Problems of Communism* (July–August 1989), p. 32.

promise, he allowed the creation of a separate Bureau for the RSFSR in December 1989, but as pressure mounted from liberals in early 1990 for legalizing a multiparty system, nationalist-conservatives were prodded into taking further action. At its February 1990 Plenum the party's Central Committee formally voted to permit party competition, recognizing what had in fact already become an unofficial reality. Almost immediately afterward, conservatives began to engage in concrete efforts to create a separate Russian Communist Party, culminating in a conference establishing the party in June. This proved to be the final undoing of the CPSU, for as Gorbachev later noted, the hijacking of the Russian Communist Party by Russian nationalists provoked a mass exit of the liberal Russian intelligentsia from the CPSU, associated the CPSU unambiguously with the opponents of reform, and confirmed the confederalization of the party itself.[48]

Ironically, the push for Russian sovereignty by Gorbachev's conservative critics coincided with significant pressures emanating from the republican electoral process driving Russian liberals in the same direction. Partially competed elections had taken place for the new USSR Congress of People's Deputies in March 1989, and in July 1989, at the end of the legislature's first session, a small opposition faction, known as the Inter-Regional Group of Deputies, formed. The size of the faction varied over time, but at its height consisted of 388 affiliated deputies out of a total of 2,250. These were overwhelmingly Russian, 77 percent elected from the RSFSR (and only 17 percent of these from autonomous republics).[49] But contingents of independent deputies from the Baltic, Ukraine, Kazakhstan, Belorussia, Georgia, and Armenia also participated in or allied themselves with the group. The faction played its most active role during the Second Congress of People's Deputies in December 1989, when it championed proposals for repealing Article 6, defended the sovereignty of union republics in amendments to the Soviet constitution, and advocated a far-reaching decentralization within the framework of the USSR.[50] The Inter-regional Group of Deputies represented an attempt by Russian liberals to

[48] Gorbachev, *Zhizn' i reformy*, vol. 1, pp. 538–39.
[49] The figures come from a faxed list of those participating in the faction. See also *Informatsionnyi biulleten'*, September 15, 1989, p. 1.
[50] See, for instance, the interview with Georgian deputy Revaz Salukvadze about the tactics of the Baltic and Georgian opposition deputies within the legislature, in *Zaria vostoka*, June 20, 1989, p. 2.

forge a cross-national alliance of opposition movements within institutions and at the all-union level, much as the popular fronts had promoted similar alliances across republics for the politics of the street. In fall 1989, before the republican elections, most Russian and many non-Russian participants still thought of the Interregional Group as a long-term strategy through which they might ultimately win power from the Soviet regime within the frame of the Soviet state. As Gavril Popov, one of its leaders, later recalled, "we had prepared for the role of being in the opposition for many years to come. I thought that for three or four years we would attempt to awaken the masses from the tribune of the parliament, creating our organizations, structures, and newspapers so that we could have better chances of winning the next elections in five years." But the predetermined rhythms of institutions intervened. By law elections to republican and local legislatures were to take place every five years in the Soviet Union. As these regularly scheduled elections neared in early 1990, it became evident to the leaders of the Interregional Group that, as Popov later put it, "there was a different tactical option – to transfer the center of struggle to a different level, where our chances of a favorable balance of forces were better."[51] In the context of the elections, Russian liberals began to focus on an entirely new set of demands – Russian sovereignty vis-à-vis the all-union government. Popov observed:

elections in the republics inevitably strengthened the forces of national liberation and forced communist-nationalists themselves – in the chase for votes – to promote slogans of national rebirth. Even in Russia, this aspect – an emphasis on the rebirth specifically of Russia – came to play an important role. . . . We chose a path of struggle for power which already contained the outcome of a rejection of the USSR . . . [M]uch of this we did not foresee, and it only became clear in subsequent years. . . . What would have happened had we not decided to attempt to gain power in the republics and localities but remained the same opposition that we had been at the union level? What would have been the path of development of the country then? I do not know the answer, but it is a complicated question.[52]

Thus, in the first half of 1990, under the rising influence of the tide, growing factionalism within the party, and the opportunities presented by

---

[51] Popov, *Snova v oppozitsii*, pp. 67–68, 74, 77–78.
[52] Popov, *Snova v oppozitsii*, pp. 78, 81. For an analogous view on electoral sequencing as critical to the outcome of Soviet collapse, see Juan J. Linz and Alfred Stepan, "Political Identities and Electoral Sequences: Spain, the Soviet Union, and Yugoslavia," in Stephen R. Graubard, ed., *Exit From Communism* (New Brunswick, NJ: Transaction Publishers, 1993), pp. 123–40.

the republican and local elections, Russian political actors from all parts of the political spectrum were pulled toward various forms of specifically Russian self-assertion vis-à-vis all-union institutions. John Morrison notes that "[b]y the time the March 1990 elections came round, all candidates for seats in the Russian Federation Congress of People's Deputies were to some extent running on a 'Russia first' ticket."[53] For liberals, "Russia first" meant that republican institutions should become a vehicle for undermining the excessive centralization and controls of the Soviet regime. Thus, asserting "sovereignty" for liberals was mainly a vehicle for foisting a far-reaching decentralization of authority onto a recalcitrant central government that had only partially liberalized and which had been dragging its feet in enacting further political and economic reforms. For Russian nationalist-conservatives, by contrast, sovereignty meant gaining the same type of self-respect won by the language of self-determination then so vociferously championed by non-Russian challengers, finding a language to counter demands for secession, asserting the dominance of Russians within Russia, and gaining a more powerful political base from which to undermine Gorbachev's reforms.

When Yeltsin came to champion the notion of Russian sovereignty in spring 1990, he was thus riding a larger tide of nationalism precisely as it was sweeping through Russia. Prior to March 1990, there is little evidence that Yeltsin viewed Russian sovereignty vis-à-vis the USSR government as a significant issue. He had, it is true, defended Baltic claims to independence in December 1989, though he had also opposed the exit of Lithuanian communists from the Communist Party, calling instead for providing "maximum independence of republican communist parties, but within the structure of the CPSU."[54] During his initial electoral campaign in Sverdlovsk at the end of January 1990, he did not raise the idea of sovereignty, but called only for using Russian governmental structures "to nudge the center" more quickly along the path of reform. He advocated instead a bizarre reorganization of the RSFSR into seven constituent republics to further decentralization and gain greater attention for regional problems.[55] Yet, on the eve of the election in March, Yeltsin called for "strong republics that would themselves decide what functions to give to

[53] Morrison, *Boris Yeltsin*, p. 141.    [54] *Gorbachev–Yel'tsin*, pp. 164, 169.
[55] *Soiuz mozhno bylo*, p. 93. Non-Russians within the RSFSR would have found this particularly odious, and later Yeltsin was quick to point out that in January 1990 he did not understand the sovereignty issue in the same way that he did by summer 1990.

the president and which to keep for themselves" – clearly viewing Russian sovereignty as a means for stripping the overbloated Soviet state of much of its power.[56] Thus Yeltsin transformed himself during the 1990 elections into a proponent of Russian sovereignty.

When the new RSFSR Congress of People's Deputies met in May 1990, all factions favored the passage of a declaration about sovereignty, and a Russian declaration about sovereignty would have occurred no matter who controlled the Congress. As it happened, largely because of defections from the communist camp, on his third try Yeltsin was elected chair of the Congress by four votes, thus assuring that the liberals' more expansive understanding of sovereignty would be dominant. But even if Aleksandr Vlasov, Yeltsin's chief rival and the candidate supported by Gorbachev, had been elected chair and his sovereignty program advocating "fully fledged economic and political sovereignty" accepted, much of the "parade of sovereignties" would probably have occurred in any case. Vlasov's sovereignty declaration also emphasized the damage that Russia had suffered from a rapacious Soviet government "even more than others" and called for "the exclusive right" for Russia to control "all the natural wealth and all of the accumulated economic, scientific-technical, and intellectual potential" on its territory, even suggesting that Russia might pursue an independent foreign policy.[57] As John Morrison observes:

It is clear, in retrospect, that Gorbachev would have faced serious problems handling the RSFSR in 1990, with or without Yeltsin's personal role. As it happened, the parliamentary challenge came from the left, who narrowly succeeded in getting Yeltsin elected. If a few votes had gone the other way, the winning candidate might have been Ivan Polozkov, a party conservative whose capacity to undermine Gorbachev became clear, when he and his allies seized control of the founding congress of the new Russian Communist Party in June. Even if the old RSFSR leadership of Vorotnikov and Vlasov had been reappointed, their campaign promises to increase republican sovereignty would have led to increased friction with the central government. To some extent, Yeltsin skillfully jumped aboard a train that was ready to leave the station.[58]

The liberals' declaration about sovereignty, which Yeltsin presented and which was backed by deputies from Moscow, Leningrad, and Sverdlovsk, was explicit in drawing on the tide's antiimperial master frame. Yeltsin, for

---

[56] *Gorbachev–Yel'tsin*, p. 173.
[57] *Pervyi s"ezd narodnykh deputatov RSFSR, 16 maia–22 iiunia 1990 goda. Stenograficheskii otchet, tom 1* (Moscow: Respublika, 1992), pp. 261–82.
[58] Morrison, *Boris Yeltsin*, p. 148.

instance, openly criticized "the longstanding imperial policy of the center" in undermining the rights of the union republics, even more so Russia, thereby implying that Russians too were victims, not janissaries, of empire. He put forth a radical and open-ended program for "full-blooded political sovereignty," in which Russia, through the new union treaty Gorbachev was advocating, would decide the extent of the powers exercised over it by the USSR government, would have full control over property, enterprises, and wealth on its territory, and would engage in its own relations with other republics and foreign affairs.[59] There were some who interpreted this as a demand for secession similar to those emanating from the Baltic, Transcaucasus, Ukraine, and Moldova, but there is little evidence that Yeltsin advocated Russian statehood outside of a revamped USSR. From late 1989 on he had been a consistent proponent of a voluntary state, opposing the use of force to keep the Balts and others in the USSR against their will. But he was also consistent in describing Russia as part of a remade Soviet state, even if Russia were to take on attributes of state sovereignty normally reserved for central authority. Both nationalist-conservatives and liberals talked about an "independent" Russia as if independence and secession were not necessarily identical. On the eve of his election, Yeltsin made clear in response to the accusations of his opponents that he "never advocated Russia's secession," but rather favored "a situation in which the republics are strong and that this strengthens our Union."[60] In the end Russia's declaration about sovereignty passed overwhelmingly by a 907 to 13 vote on June 12. Its most controversial clause asserted the predominance of republican laws over all-union laws on the territory of the RSFSR, making it similar to the declarations about sovereignty that had preceded it. The declaration also recognized the RSFSR as a constituent unit of the USSR and indicated that disagreements between the republic and the union should "be resolved by a process established by the Union agreement."[61] In the wake of the declaration, Russian public opinion further consolidated around the liberal notion of Russian sovereignty, so that by September 1990, in the midst of the parade of sovereignties, 48 percent of the inhabitants of Russia believed that the Russian

---

[59] *Pervyi s"ezd narodnykh deputatov RSFSR, tom 1*, pp. 567–72. As Vorotnikov remarked on the speech, many of Yeltsin's points "on a number of positions coincide with our own project." V. I. Vorotnikov, *A bylo eto tak . . .* (Moscow: Sovet veteranov knigoizdaniia, 1995), p. 382.

[60] *Pervyi s"ezd narodnykh deputatov RSFSR, tom 2*, p. 381.

[61] *Pervyi s"ezd narodnykh deputatov RSFSR, tom 4*, pp. 476–78.

government should have the right to revoke decisions of the Soviet government on its territory, whereas only 22 percent opposed the idea.[62]

The Russian declaration about sovereignty gave rise to a flood of sovereignty declarations by ethnofederal units at all levels. But even before the passage of the Russian declaration, the Ukrainian and Uzbek legislatures were scheduled to debate drafts of their own sovereignty statements, and Moldova undoubtedly would have done the same with or without the Russian declaration. Moreover, even if Russia had never issued a sovereignty declaration, a milder version of the "parade of sovereignties" probably would have occurred – especially in view of the fact that the union treaty was to be renegotiated, providing incentives for units to assert their sovereignty and to upgrade their status unilaterally. But the Russian declaration about sovereignty did have a powerful impact in pushing events at a quicker pace and further than might otherwise have been the case. By the end of 1990 all union republics and nearly all autonomous republics and provinces had declared their sovereignty. Furthermore, the Russian declaration legitimated and normalized more radical interpretations of sovereignty, so that even loyal republican governments such as Kazakhstan found it necessary to proclaim the precedence of republican laws over all union laws on their territories. In effect, this gutted the powers of the central government, even where secession was not being contemplated, and made a utopian conception of confederation the only politically acceptable alternative to total collapse of the Soviet state. Over the course of 1990 the "war of the laws" intensified, as all levels of government began to take unilateral action to substantiate their claims to "sovereignty." Many republican governments insisted that they had to approve all Soviet laws or presidential decrees before they could take effect on their territories. The power of the center had so deteriorated by October that the USSR Supreme Soviet was forced to pass a law declaring that its laws had precedence throughout the USSR. Only a few hours later, the RSFSR Supreme Soviet responded by rescinding that law, asserting that all-union laws had effect on Russian territory only after ratification by the RSFSR Supreme Soviet, and within several days Ukraine and Belarus did the same. And by concluding numerous "interstate agreements" among themselves that recognized each other's sovereignty, the republics harnessed the power of

---

[62] Dunlop, "Russia: Confronting a Loss of Empire," p. 43. The survey was conducted by the All-Union Center for the Study of Public Opinion among 1,458 respondents in twenty-five population points of Russia.

numbers behind the new conception of republican sovereignty, making it exceedingly difficult for a reversal of republican sovereignty to take place.

Yet, in the immediate aftermath of the Russian declaration, both Gorbachev and Russian liberals began an ill-fated attempt to form a left-center alliance. These efforts centered around negotiations over the direction of economic reform. Yeltsin's game plan was that Gorbachev would ultimately choose to jettison the central planners who controlled the government bureaucracy and opt instead for radical proposals to speed the transition to the market. These would involve a far-reaching devolution of economic powers to the republics, as envisioned in the sovereignty declarations, and ultimately result in the renegotiation of the union treaty on a confederal basis. This was not entirely far-fetched. Prime Minister Ryzhkov and his government were then under widespread criticism for their failure to arrest the decline of the Soviet economy and to commence serious economic reforms.[63] Moreover, in June negotiations over a new union treaty, which Gorbachev then naively believed could be concluded within three or four months, had begun. Yeltsin's model – again, drawn from the experience of the tide – was the Polish Roundtable, with the ultimate goal of Russian democrats becoming junior partners in a coalition with the reformist wing of the party that would control the Soviet state.[64]

But with the creation of the Russian Communist Party in June and the eviction of the Democratic Platform from the CPSU in July, the party was transformed into a predominantly conservative organization, making this strategy less feasible. Gorbachev seriously contemplated the possibility of such a coalition. He and Yeltsin established the Shatalin-Yavlinskii commission to develop an alternative economic program to that of Ryzhkov and his assistant Leonid Abalkin. But the left-center coalition foundered over their polar visions of center-republican relations. The Five Hundred-Day Plan presented by Shatalin in August was hardly a realistic blueprint. Still, within the context of the times – with price increases looming, rampant shortages of food and basic consumer goods, and production in a tailspin – it was taken by liberals and many Western economists as a refreshing approach to decades of stalled economic reforms sabotaged by

---

[63] Ryzhkov's popularity declined sharply in spring and summer 1990, even before the open controversy over the Five-Hundred-Day Plan. See *Demokraticheskaia Rossiia*, no. 3, September 1990, pp. 12–13.

[64] Popov, *Snova v oppozitsii*, pp. 99–100, 131, 198–99; Morrison, *Boris Yeltsin*, pp. 161–62, 164.

the bureaucracy. In accord with the Russian declaration about sovereignty and those of Ukraine, Uzbekistan, Belorussia, and others, it devolved nearly all economic functions to the republics, leaving only defense, energy, communications, transport, and foreign policy in the hands of the all-union government. Ryzhkov argued that the Shatalin plan spelled an end to the USSR as an integral state. He announced in September that he would resign rather than accept it. Shatalin defended the plan as the only feasible alternative to collapse. As he put it at the time:

Let us look at what is really happening in our lives now. The Baltic republics, Russia, Ukraine, and Belorussia have adopted declarations about sovereignty. In some places they intend to introduce their own money and establish customs barriers. Will this lead to a strengthening of "the united family of fraternal peoples," as we recently used to call it? . . . So what happens next? Do we introduce troops throughout our entire territory, from the Baltic to the Pacific? In the first place, there are not enough troops, and in the second place, I think that the troops already won't fire on the people. And so the disintegration [of the union] is taking place, and the central authorities are quickly losing control of the levers of management. And this is understandable to anyone who does not watch life just through an office window. This is why we believe that the only way of saving the state is to strengthen an economic union of the sovereign republics. This, I repeat, is our only chance: in place of the breakup that is now taking place, to move to create [something new].[65]

Gorbachev found the rapid transformation to the market envisioned by the Shatalin plan attractive, but he objected that the plan already assumed a confederal outcome to the negotiations over the union treaty and feared that, as a result, it would exercise a disintegrative effect on the union by pushing others toward or even beyond a confederal position.[66]

To pressure Gorbachev to accept the Five Hundred-Day Plan, Yeltsin had it passed as law by the RSFSR Supreme Soviet and continued to lobby Gorbachev to fire Ryzhkov and establish a coalition government. But ten days after the RSFSR legislature adopted the Shatalin plan, Gorbachev publicly rejected it, refusing to fire Ryzhkov and instructing Academician Abel Aganbegian to forge a compromise between it and the Ryzhkov proposal. Yeltsin's strategy of establishing a coalition government around radical market reform had failed. Moreover, the Soviet government still retained control over almost all the enterprises and resources of Russia, making Russian sovereignty a mere piece of paper and rendering it impos-

---

[65] *Trud*, September 15, 1990, p. 2.    [66] Gorbachev, *Zhizn' i reformy*, vol. 1, p. 576.

sible for the Russian government to implement reforms on its own. Yeltsin began to assume a much more confrontational stance toward Gorbachev, threatening to take his supporters to the streets if Gorbachev did not deal more forthrightly with Russia's demands. On the November 7 anniversary of the Bolshevik Revolution, one hundred fifty thousand supporters of Democratic Russia mounted a counterdemonstration on the streets of Moscow to mourn the victims of communist oppression, calling for genuine sovereignty for Russia and for the resignation of the Soviet parliament and Gorbachev.[67] The war of the streets resumed, though now largely as a bargaining chip deployed by republican governments vis-à-vis the center.

The collapse of the proposed left-center coalition meant the failure as well of Gorbachev's efforts to renegotiate the union treaty, for without Russia this was impossible. Yeltsin announced in November that, contrary to the urgings of Gorbachev, Russia would not sign a new union treaty until its sovereignty had been recognized by the Soviet government and an agreement reached on the conduct of economic reform and control over economic resources. At the core of the Soviet-Russian conflict was not only the intense personal rivalry between Gorbachev and Yeltsin, but also a fundamental divide over what a revamped USSR should look like – federal or confederal. This division materialized relatively quickly in 1990, within the course of several months, due to the combined effects of the tide and the republican electoral process. By the end of 1990 neither a federal nor a confederal plan would likely have arrested the disintegrative process then overtaking the Soviet state – the former because it was no longer attractive to key players (particularly Russia and Ukraine), the latter because it was unlikely to be a stable or manageable form of government and implied, by this time, at a minimum the partial breakup of the country. Yeltsin's position reflected the first of these truths, and Gorbachev's the second. Gorbachev believed that even the partial breakup of the country – specifically, the exit of the Baltic states – would unleash much wider processes of secession, leading to unpredictable results. This may not have been true in early 1989, but it clearly had become true by late 1990. By then, any decision to allow the partial breakup of the country would have been difficult to contain, since secessionist movements were firmly in power not only in the Baltic, but also in Moldova, Armenia, and Georgia,

[67] *Ekspress khronika*, no. 46, November 13, 1990.

and the Ukrainian government was rapidly moving in a separatist direction. It seems obvious why not just the partial breakup of the country, but its total disintegration began to appear increasingly imminent to the Soviet elite and public by fall 1990. Just as Ryzhkov had warned in 1989, once the tide of nationalism had overtaken Russia and Ukraine, the probability that a solution (whether negotiated or coerced) could have been found to prevent a mass exodus of republics grew increasingly remote.

## The Accumulating "Inevitability" of Disintegration

The Russian declaration of sovereignty was a critical tipping point in the accumulating sense of inevitability surrounding Soviet disintegration. Nevertheless, one would be hard-pressed to point to one factor that made the total breakup of the Soviet state appear unavoidable. The interrelationships across cases meant that there were many turning points and contributing actions along the way. Russian sovereignty, for instance, would have been unimaginable outside the context of the tide, and its import in pushing toward disintegration was magnified by the simultaneous presence of other nationalisms pushing in the same direction. Over the course of 1990 the momentum of events and the cumulative effect of the altered structural conditions produced by the tide began to press with increased force in the direction of total disintegration. By late 1990 this sense of ascendant structural advantage emboldened advocates of secession, breeding a new sense of certainty in the achievement of independence. As one Ukrainian nationalist leader told David Remnick at the end of 1990, "there are no forces that will ultimately be able to hold back the fall of the empire. ... This has become an inevitable process at this point."[68] It was also in 1990 that nomenklatura elites, sensing the current of history, began their strategic appropriation of independence agenda – as we saw in Chapter 5, in many cases successfully refitting themselves as nationalists.

A sense of confluence toward a final outcome was by this time growing increasingly apparent to the public as well. It was most demonstrably expressed in the stalled negotiations over a new union treaty, which began in November with the publication of a first draft prepared by Gorbachev's staff. The draft was a nonstarter. It relegated few powers to the republics and failed to take into account the republican sovereignty declarations of

---

[68] *The Washington Post*, December 30, 1990, p. A1.

the previous six months, thereby incurring the rejection not only of Russia, but also of Ukraine, Uzbekistan, and Kazakhstan. As one commentator portrayed the "inevitability" of the failure of the negotiations in January:

The situation with the Union agreement has clearly reached an impasse. And it could not have been otherwise. The draft proposed by the Center was knowingly unacceptable, since it accorded with the republican declarations about sovereignty like water and fire. It was entirely natural that almost all republics, including those which in principle are in favor of a Union agreement, have in one form or another removed this teacup from their lips.[69]

There was already talk of the major republics – Russia, Ukraine, Belorussia, and Kazakhstan – gathering together to reach their own settlement on the future of the Soviet state.[70] A second draft of the treaty published in March also elicited little support; it too failed to break with a federative model, no longer seen as reasonable by almost all republics. Negotiations over the new union treaty had by this time reached a dead end. Kravchuk, for instance, is said to have insisted that Ukraine retain the right to its own armed forces, to declare war, to conduct its own space program, to have its own currency, and, "if the necessity should arise, to annul immediately one or another of the powers delegated to the Union."[71] Clearly, a coherent state could not have been crafted on this basis.

By November 1990 the growing realization that the Soviet state was reaching a "dead end" bred a more serious threat to Gorbachev's power from the political right. Rumors of a military coup and of suspicious troop movements had been rife in Moscow for months. But the potential threat from the military was most directly brought home to Gorbachev at a meeting with military deputies on November 13, when officers vented their anger over the disorder that had overtaken the country, repeatedly interrupting his speech and heckling him from the floor. The following day, members of the USSR Supreme Soviet dropped their regularly scheduled business and demanded that Gorbachev appear before them to answer for the chaotic state of the country in what came to be known as the "parliamentary uprising." Gorbachev addressed the group, but was given a cold reception and bluntly told to present a concrete program to pull the country out of crisis. Members of the conservative parliamentary faction

---

[69] *Nesostoiavshiisia iubilei: Pochemu SSSR ne otprazdnoval svoego 70-letiia?* (Moscow: Terra, 1992), p. 416.
[70] *Gorbachev–Yel'tsin*, p. 296.
[71] *Nesostoiavshiisia iubilei*, p. 442.

*Soiuz* called for Gorbachev's resignation in the event that he fail to take more forceful measures. The Russian left had also begun to talk about Gorbachev's resignation in frustration over his refusal to accept the Five-Hundred-Day Plan. In one sleepless night Gorbachev decided to reorganize his government, centralizing power further in the hands of the president, upgrading the role of the Federation Council representing the leaders of the republics, and vowing in his presentation of the plan to parliament on November 17 to prevent the breakup of the country and to enforce order.

This was the beginning of Gorbachev's "turn to the right" – a period lasting from November 1990 through March 1991 in which, on the basis of a center-right coalition, he attempted to save the Soviet state through a more confrontational stance. This involved a major shake-up of the Soviet government, as Gorbachev surrounded himself with conservatives, many of whom later played key roles in the August 1991 coup. As Gorbachev told the Soviet population in his annual New Year's message, "there is no cause more sacred" than the preservation of the USSR, and 1991 would resolve "the fate of our multiethnic state."[72] His strategy for saving the Soviet state – to the extent that it was coherent – was to pursue a version of the Varennikov plan for gaining back control over Baltic governments, to remove the Yeltsin threat in Russia, and to demonstrate popular support for preserving the USSR, thereby undermining the core challenges, generating pressure on recalcitrant republican governments, and using this transformed situation to negotiate a new union treaty. The first two prongs of this strategy quickly backfired. As we saw in Chapter 7, the botched attempt to impose presidential rule in Vilnius on January 13 (killing thirteen civilians, and cut short by Gorbachev after the first bloody encounter) drove public opinion in Russia still further against efforts to preserve the Soviet state forcefully. The vivid images of tanks in the streets of Vilnius running over civilian protestors led to a wave of protest in the Baltic, Russia, Ukraine, Georgia, Moldova, and elsewhere in solidarity with the Lithuanians and sharpened conflict between the Russian and USSR governments. Yeltsin hinted that perhaps Russia should obtain its own army and police to protect itself from the predations of the center. He issued a joint statement with the leaders of Latvia, Lithuania, and Estonia recognizing each other's sovereignty and "expressing their readiness to render concrete support and help to one another in the event

[72] TASS, in *FBIS*, January 2, 1991, p. 26.

that a threat to their sovereignty emerges."[73] In February Gorbachev and his conservative allies began to move more decisively against Yeltsin, orchestrating a call by a group of 274 deputies for an extraordinary session of the Russian Congress of People's Deputies to discuss Yeltsin's removal. This precipitated intensified conflict between the USSR and Russian governments, as Yeltsin in turn called openly for Gorbachev's resignation. The battle spilled over into the streets, as both sides sought to demonstrate popular support through demonstrations and counterdemonstrations. On February 22 Democratic Russia convened a huge rally of four hundred thousand in support of Yeltsin and demanding Gorbachev's removal.[74] On February 23 (Soviet Army Day) *Soiuz*, the military, and the Moscow city Party Committee organized a large counterdemonstration of thirty to one hundred thousand (many of whom were soldiers ordered to attend the rally), at which calls for preservation of the union mingled with demands for Yeltsin's resignation.[75]

This intensification of conflict coincided with the March 17 referendum on the future of the USSR, which Gorbachev hoped would legitimate efforts to contain secessionist revolts and pressure republics to sign on to a federative state. Democratic Russia openly called for its followers to vote "no" in the referendum, believing this would send a strong signal of opposition to Gorbachev. Yeltsin took a more circumspect position, merely calling on the Russian electorate to vote its conscience. At the same time, Yeltsin added a question to the ballot in Russia asking voters to approve the creation of an elected Russian presidency. Opposed by Gorbachev, the introduction of a Russian presidency was intended to insulate Yeltsin from the attacks of the communists, provide him with enhanced powers by which to assert Russian sovereignty, and place him on an equal footing with his rival (in fact, in a superior position, since Gorbachev had never run in a competitive election). On March 10, Democratic Russia convened a demonstration of several hundred thousand in Moscow at which support for Yeltsin and Russian sovereignty accompanied calls for Gorbachev's resignation and appeals to vote down the March 17 referendum.[76] In 1991 these waves of liberal mobilization overtly linked Russian

---

[73] Quoted in *Soiuz mozhno bylo*, p. 131.

[74] *Ekspress khronika*, no. 9, February 26, 1991; Radio Moscow, in *FBIS*, February 25, 1991, p. 38.

[75] Moscow TV, in *FBIS*, February 25, 1991, p. 56.

[76] *Yezhednevnaia glasnost'*, March 11, 1991.

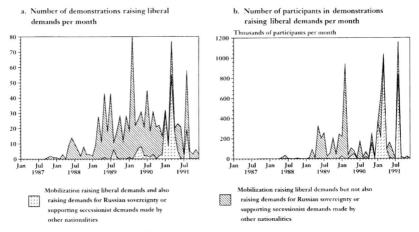

a. Number of demonstrations raising liberal
   demands per month

b. Number of participants in demonstrations
   raising liberal demands per month

Mobilization raising liberal demands and also
raising demands for Russian sovereignty or
supporting secessionist demands made by
other nationalities

Mobilization raising liberal demands but not also
raising demands for Russian sovereignty or
supporting secessionist demands made by
other nationalities

**Figure 8.3.** Russian liberal mobilization in support of Russian sovereignty or the
separatist demands of other nationalities, 1987–91.

democratization with demands for Russian sovereignty and support for the
secessionist efforts of other groups. Figure 8.3 portrays the growing weight
of such demands within Russian liberal mobilization, as Russian liberals
increasingly focused their opposition not merely against the Soviet regime,
but against the Soviet state as well.

Though the March 17 referendum produced a majority vote in favor
of preserving the USSR (76 percent of those participating voted "yes"), it
did not resolve the issue of the future of the country, nor did it provide a
clear signal about where public opinion stood. For one thing, the wording
of the question – "Do you consider necessary the preservation of the
Union of Soviet Socialist Republics as a renewed federation of equal
sovereign republics, in which the rights and freedoms of a person of any
nationality will be fully guaranteed?" – was ambiguous. It was not clear
what was being "renewed"and how rights and freedoms would be "guaranteed." "Equal sovereign republics" could be interpreted as implying
a state based on the superiority of republican over all-union law, while
"federation" implied precisely the opposite. In Kazakhstan the question
was worded differently, asking voters if they considered it necessary "to
preserve the USSR as a Union of equal sovereign states," more directly
suggesting confederation rather than federation; the question won
overwhelmingly, though the votes were counted at the all-union level as
part of the overall positive vote. In Ukraine, a parallel question was placed

on the ballot asking voters whether they agreed that Ukraine should participate in a "Union of Soviet sovereign states on the basis of Ukraine's
Declaration About State Sovereignty" – implying a confederation. This
question was approved by 80 percent of those participating, as opposed to
the all-union referendum question, which was approved by only 70
percent. If one counts not only those who voted "no," but also those who
boycotted the referendum (a position advocated by some nationalist movements) or who did not vote for other reasons, then at most only 61 percent
of the eligible electorate expressed approval of the all-union question,
irrespective of how the question was interpreted by voters. Moreover, six
republics – Estonia, Latvia, Lithuania, Moldova, Georgia, and Armenia –
did not participate in the vote, so the level of actual support for the question was probably closer to 58 percent.[77] Ironically, the highest rates
of support for the referendum question occurred in Central Asia; in
Turkmenistan, for example, 96 percent of eligible voters voted "yes,"
91 percent in Tajikistan, 89 percent in Uzbekistan, and 88 percent in
Kyrgyzstan. Yet, only 54 percent of eligible voters in Russia voted "yes."
In general, the more authoritarian the republican context, the stronger the
vote in favor of the referendum question – suggesting that in some localities the results may have been rigged, particularly since many of these
same republics produced overwhelming votes in favor of independence
only six to nine months later.[78]

Conflict between the Russian and Soviet governments reached its peak
on March 28, as the Russian Congress of People's Deputies met to discuss
Yeltsin's removal. Democratic Russia planned a rally in support of Yeltsin.
Gorbachev and his aides, fearing that Yeltsin's removal might lead to the
storming of the Kremlin by huge crowds,[79] banned all demonstrations in
Moscow and introduced large numbers of troops to enforce the order. As
we saw in Chapter 7, this had little effect on the huge turnout of several
hundred thousand, as few believed the government would attempt to
disperse them by force. Ultimately, the communists lacked the votes to
oust Yeltsin and retreated in disarray, with a group of 170 deputies, led by

---

[77] This becomes evident when one adds the total number of eligible voters by republic
reported in the official results and published in *Pravda*, March 27, 1991, p. 2.

[78] Thus, in October 1991 94 percent of Turkmen voters participating in the republican referendum on independence voted in favor of independence; in December 1991 99 percent
of Azerbaijani and 98 percent of Uzbekistan voters participating in referenda on independence voted for independence.

[79] V. Stepankov and E. Lisov, *Kremlevskii zagovor* (Moscow: Ogonek, 1992), p. 75.

Colonel Aleksandr Rutskoi, breaking ranks with the communists and forming a new parliamentary group, Communists for Democracy. The Congress even approved new emergency powers for Yeltsin and scheduled Russian presidential elections for June.

Having failed to oust Yeltsin (and indeed, having only strengthened him), Gorbachev did one more about-face, proposing a "round table" with those leaders of the republics willing to participate in a renewed USSR. This became the basis for the meeting of nine leaders of the union republics with Gorbachev at the Novo-Ogarevo estate outside Moscow on April 23. The so-called "9 + 1" agreement it produced was little more than a promise to stop open conflict and accelerate efforts to complete a new union treaty. But it marked a shift in Gorbachev's stance toward the negotiations and an attempt to forge a pact with a subset of republics around the creation of a rump Soviet state. For the first time, Gorbachev recognized in the "9 + 1" talks that the treaty would be an agreement among "sovereign states," thereby acknowledging the legitimacy of republican sovereignty declarations. In return, the other parties were obliged to put an end to civil disobedience, strikes, and calls for the overthrow of the existing order. But the agreement also formally recognized the right of the six republics not participating (Estonia, Latvia, Lithuania, Moldova, Georgia, and Armenia) to decide their own fates, thereby sanctioning the partial breakup of the USSR.[80]

The "9 + 1" agreement set in motion a series of negotiations that produced a draft treaty to create a rump Soviet state, which five republics – Russia, Kazakhstan, Uzbekistan, Tajikistan, and Belorussia – were scheduled to initial on August 20 had the coup not intervened. Three more republics – Azerbaijan, Turkmenistan, and Kyrgyzstan – indicated their willingness to sign at a later date. But the Ukrainian government refused even to debate the treaty until it had finished rewriting its own constitution; its representatives attended the negotiations as observers only. The comments of both Ukrainian Supreme Soviet Chair Leonid Kravchuk and Prime Minister Vitol'd Fokin indicated that the draft treaty was considerably at odds with the Ukrainian declaration about sovereignty and unacceptable in its final, negotiated form.[81] Even had the August coup not intervened, without Ukraine's participation the agreement most likely

---

[80] For the text of the agreement, see *Nesostoiavshiisia iubilei*, pp. 443–46.
[81] David Marples, "Radicalization of the Political Spectrum in Ukraine," *Report on the USSR*, vol. 3, no. 35 (August 30, 1991), pp. 30–33.

would have collapsed. In August the Coordinating Council of Democratic Russia made clear to Yeltsin that it opposed Russia's signature on the treaty unless Ukraine, Kazakhstan, and Belorussia all signed as well.[82] As Sergei Shakhrai, Yeltsin's advisor for legal affairs, noted rhetorically at the time, "what kind of Union could this be without Ukraine, just as one might ask what kind of union it could be without Russia?"[83] It appears that Yeltsin probably would not have signed the treaty on August 20 and intended to call for additional changes to the draft, possibly waiting to decide whether to sign until September, when Ukraine would have given a clearer indication of its position.[84] Even after the treaty had been signed, republican leaders still needed the approval of their legislatures, and this would have been problematic in some cases. Democratic Russia's Coordinating Council, for instance, claimed that elements of the treaty contradicted Russia's declaration about sovereignty.

Although the Novo-Ogarevo negotiations produced an agreement for creating a rump Soviet state, it is highly doubtful that they would have produced a working government. Though creating what was referred to in the treaty as a "federal" government, the document actually established something closer to a confederation – one whose center was likely to have been consumed by conflicts over authority with its constituent parts, and whose constituent parts themselves remained at loggerheads with one another. According to the final draft, not only was each republic considered "a sovereign state" (the name of the country was to be changed to the Union of Soviet Sovereign Republics), but each also retained the right to suspend all-union laws on its territory if those laws contradicted republican laws; these conflicts were to be resolved by a constitutional court, though on what legal basis remained unclear. Most of the finance of the central government was to take place through the republics, which would decide, on the basis of negotiation with the all-union government, what they would pay into the central government's coffers (a position that Gorbachev had rejected at the time of the Shatalin Plan). The treaty

---

[82] *Nesostoiavshiisia iubilei*, pp. 464–66.

[83] Interfax, in *FBIS*, August 19, 1991, p. 50.

[84] Gorbachev, *Zhizn' i reformy*, vol. 2, p. 553–54. In Yeltsin's meetings with Nazarbaev in Kazakhstan on the eve of the coup, the two leaders agreed to additional changes in the treaty that would have cut back on the powers of the center still further, created an economic zone across the territory of the union, and clarified the role of the former autonomous republics as signatories of the agreement. Interfax, in *FBIS*, August 19, 1991, p. 51.

transferred nearly all economic property to the republics, including subsoil wealth, and it gave each state forming the union the right to a share of the gold, diamond, and foreign currency reserves of the union. Almost all the powers of the central government were placed under the joint authority of the republics and the center; thus, defense, the secret police, the protection of state secrets, foreign policy and international trade, and economic and social policy were all to be jointly managed, though the exact nature of this shared authority was, according to the document, to be decided later "by agreements, special understandings, and the adoption of basic legislation by the union and the republics and their corresponding republican laws." Each of the states forming the union was considered a full-fledged member of the international community, with the right to establish its own diplomatic relations. Moreover, republics could secede from the union if they so desired and if they followed a legal process, which remained undefined in the agreement.[85] Even who was allowed to sign the treaty was unclear; this had been one of the most contentious issues at the negotiations, as the autonomous republics of Russia, against Russia's opposition, sought to upgrade their legal status within the union.[86] Thus, the treaty left most of the major questions of governance unresolved and, as one commentator rightly noted at the time, was likely to "become the source of new frictions and conflicts," ultimately "strengthening the process of the collapse of the federal state."[87]

It is obvious why the Novo-Ogareva process did not produce a workable governing arrangement. Given the altered structural situation brought about by the tide, little incentive existed for republics to compromise their interests. The negotiations were extremely difficult, and on almost all major points the embattled Gorbachev was forced to cave in to republican demands or to find vague language to patch over differences. As Valery Boldin, Gorbachev's chief of staff, described the June 3 negotiations, "Some forty republican leaders were present at the meeting, each with his own views, his own approach, and his own demands. Virtually no solutions had been found on issues brought up by each member in the text of the draft; bitter wrangling was commonplace. On matters of

---

[85] For the text of the July 23 draft of the treaty, see *Izvestiia*, August 15, 1991, pp. 1–2.

[86] Georgii Shakhnazarov, *Tsena svobody: Reformatsiia Gorbacheva glazami ego pomoshchnika* (Moscow: Rossika, 1993), pp. 235–36.

[87] *Nesostoiavshiisia iubilei*, p. 458.

substance, no one was prepared to back down." At the next meeting on June 17 "[t]he leaders of the former autonomous republics objected to any restriction of their rights. They considered themselves to be sovereign republics and demanded to be treated as such during the drafting of the treaty.... More squabbling ensued, before someone proposed that the discussion be suspended until the next meeting."[88] As another witness to the negotiations observed, the conflicts were "very intense, even at the last meeting before the signing of the Treaty."[89] Given the variety of ideological positions represented within the republican leaderships – from the radical reformist leadership of Yeltsin to the conservative party elites of Central Asia – and the unresolved conflicts between Russia and its autonomous republics, it seems probable that even had the treaty been signed, serious conflicts would have emerged within the group shortly afterward. Thus, in spite of the Novo-Ogareva agreement the USSR on the eve of the August coup was on a trajectory not merely toward partial dismemberment, but in all probability toward total dismemberment or, at a minimum, an unstable and conflict-ridden form of government whose future was highly dubious.

## The Denouement

It was the conservative reaction to Gorbachev's concessions to the republics at Novo-Ogarevo that pushed the Soviet state to its final, tumultuous conclusion. The immediate motivation for the August 19 coup was to forestall the scheduled signing of the union treaty the following day, which the coup organizers rightly understood as sanctioning the partial breakup of the USSR and, most likely, its eventual total disintegration. In its "Appeal to the Soviet People," its principal statement justifying the seizure of power, the State Emergency Committee condemned what it called "extremist forces" who, playing on "national feelings," had "adopted a course of destroying the Soviet Union" and had left the country "ungovernable."[90] As Vice-President Gennadii Yanaev, the committee's formal chair, noted at the press conference following the emergency declaration:

---

[88] Valery Boldin, *Ten Years That Shook the World* (New York: Basic Books, 1994), pp. 275–78.

[89] Yuri Baturin, "Chess-Like Diplomacy at Novo-Ogarevo," *Demokratizatsiya*, vol. 2, no. 2 (Spring 1994), p. 212.

[90] TASS, in *FBIS*, August 19, 1991, p. 10.

a real threat of disintegration has arisen, the breakup of a single economic space, a single space of civil rights, a single defense and a single foreign policy. Normal life in these circumstances is impossible. In many regions of the USSR, as a result of multinational, interethnic clashes, there is bloodshed, and the breakup of the USSR would entail the most serious internal and international consequences. Under these circumstances, we have no other choice but to take decisive measures in order to stop the slide of the country toward catastrophe.[91]

In its first act, the State Emergency Committee ordered that "structures of power and administration and paramilitary formations acting contrary to the USSR Constitution and USSR laws" be disbanded and prohibited the holding of street demonstrations and strikes.[92] Judging from the actions of the committee, the plan (to the extent to which it had been thought through) was to declare a countrywide state of emergency (with or without Gorbachev's approval),[93] to assert control first over Moscow and Leningrad through a massive military presence, then to declare presidential rule in the Baltic republics, Moldova, Georgia, and key cities of Russia on August 21, dissolving these republican and local governments. Legal backing for these actions (and for Gorbachev's removal from power) was to be supplied at a USSR Supreme Soviet session on August 26. The coup plotters mistakenly believed that the Ukrainian and Kazakhstani leaderships would acquiesce to their actions; on the contrary, both Kravchuk and Nazarbaev opposed the coup from the beginning, though they did not rush to condemn it publicly.[94] The failure of the first stage – gaining control over Moscow and Leningrad – and the consequent unraveling of the coup on August 21, even before the coup leaders could move against other republics, explains to a large extent why so little action occurred outside these two cities. Though a state of emergency was declared in Leningrad on August 19, troops never entered the city, as the regional military commander General Viktor Samsonov (under the

[91] *Pravda*, August 20, 1991, pp. 1–2.
[92] Moscow Central Television, in *FBIS*, August 19, 1991, p. 12.
[93] The plotters attempted first to gain Gorbachev's support for the state of emergency. Gorbachev, however, refused. He remained isolated at his vacation estate in Foros throughout the entire period.
[94] Moscow Central Television, August 19, 1991; Stepankov and Lisov, *Kremlevskii zagovor*, pp. 28–29, 114–17; Popov, *Snova v oppozitsii*, p. 162. General Varennikov was assigned the task of getting Kravchuk to declare a state of emergency in Western Ukraine. Kravchuk declined, replying that, according to the law, emergency rule could not be introduced in a republic without first obtaining the approval of the republic's Supreme Soviet. The following day, a column of thirty thousand troops began to march toward Kiev, but remained outside the city.

prodding of Sobchak, who pointedly reminded him of the consequences suffered by the military from the Tbilisi events) promised that troops would not be introduced into the city despite orders from his superiors to the contrary, and that under no circumstances would troops attack civilians. By August 20 the Leningrad emergency committee had fallen apart, and demonstrations of up to three hundred thousand against the coup encompassed Palace Square.[95] Although there were troop movements in many areas in preparation for the second stage of the operation, the only significant military action (and the only casualties) outside of Moscow and Leningrad occurred in the Baltic, where broadcasting stations and communications networks were seized in preparation for the planned assault on Baltic governments.[96] Strikes in protest of the coup broke out in many places, but outside Moscow and Leningrad demonstrations involving more than fifty thousand were rare (occurring only in Kishinev and Sverdlovsk)[97] – in part because many preferred to wait and see whether the regime would enforce its ban on demonstrations, in part because outside of Moscow the State Emergency Committee did so little to warrant major street action.

The plotters represented the key institutions of power within the Soviet state – the army, the police, the party apparatus – and operated according to the old rules of the political game, when institutions still had coherence and the key political resource was control over them. The very presence of the army, it was thought, would be enough to ensure control of the streets, so no concrete plans were laid ahead of time for marginalizing street challenges. There were many reasons for the quick failure of the August coup: its hasty organization; the failure to control the media fully; and political divisions within institutions, particularly the army and the police. But the regime's inability to control the streets also played a critical role. From the beginning on the morning of August 19, crowds openly disobeyed the ban on demonstrations. In Moscow, they clambered on top of tanks and armored transports, preventing them from moving further, fraternizing with the troops, and enjoining them to refuse orders to fire on civilians. Indeed, late in the night several regiments defected, arriving

[95] A. Veretin, N. Miloserdova, G. Petrov, *Protivostoianie* (Sankt-Peterburg: Ekopolis i kul'tura, 1992), pp. 51–54, 84–86; David Remnick, *Lenin's Tomb: The Last Days of the Soviet Empire* (New York: Random House, 1993), pp. 468–69; *Megalopolis Express*, August 20, 1991, p. 35.
[96] For reviews of events outside of Moscow and Leningrad, see *Putch: Khronika trevozhnykh dnei* (Moscow: Progress, 1991); *Krasnoe ili beloe? Drama Avgusta-91* (Moscow: Terra, 1992).
[97] *Ekspress khronika*, no. 35, August 27, 1991; Rompres in *FBIS*, August 21, 1991, p. 81.

at the Russian White House to aid in its defense. The first day, in part due to heavy rain, demonstrations were relatively small, consisting mainly of activists. In the afternoon, a crowd of fifteen to twenty thousand gathered outside the Russian White House, where they erected barricades using trolley buses, steel rods, and concrete blocks. That night, only five thousand remained, though no attempt to storm the building occurred.[98] Still, as one eyewitness observed, that day "set the scene for the defeat of the bungling junta. The politically aware among the population realized their strength, and I saw little evidence of doubt among those on the barricades whether democracy would prevail."[99] On August 20, huge crowds of one to two hundred thousand gathered outside the Russian White House, and fifty thousand responded to the call to remain overnight to defend against attempts to storm the building.[100] In the face of this opposition and the bloodshed which would have accompanied the planned assault, a number of key military commanders refused to act, leading on August 21 to the collapse of the coup.

The failure of the coup brought about the collapse of the party's central institutions and a paralysis of all-union state organizations, including the military and the police. In retaliation for the party bureaucracy's supporting role in the coup, Communist Party property in many parts of the country was nationalized, the Central Committee Secretariat was surrounded by an angry mob and forced to shut down, and in some republics Communist Party activity was suspended (Russia) or declared illegal (Moldova, Estonia, and Lithuania). Gorbachev subsequently blamed the coup leaders for the collapse of the USSR, claiming that the coup derailed the treaty process and drove republics to exit.[101] Although the Novo-Ogarevo process probably would not have halted the breakup of the Soviet state, the vacuum of power and centrifugal forces generated by the failed putsch precipitated one last powerful tidal surge, as republican governments one after another – many under the control of nomenklatura elites – moved into the void to declare independence or to assert their control over property, resources, and powers previously held by the center.

---

[98] *V Avguste 91-go: Rossiia glazami ochevidstev* (Moscow: Limbus-Press, 1993), p. 30.
[99] Iain Elliot, "Three Days in August: On-the-Spot Impressions," *Report on the USSR*, vol. 3, no. 36 (September 6, 1991), p. 64.
[100] *Report on the USSR*, vol. 3, no. 35 (August 30, 1991), p. 46.
[101] *Soiuz mozhno bylo*, pp. 328–35.

Already on August 20, the second day of the coup, when a military incursion seemed possible at any moment, the Estonian government had declared its full independence from the Soviet Union. Latvia followed suit the next day.[102] What ultimately dealt the final deathblow to the USSR was Ukraine's declaration of independence on August 24, setting in motion a rush to exit among republics that had previously considered signing the treaty. As we saw earlier, even before the coup public opinion in Ukraine and the Ukrainian government had been moving in the direction of independence. The emotional backlash surrounding the coup provided the impetus for the Ukrainian Supreme Soviet to adopt an independence resolution by a large majority, setting December 1 as the day for a republicwide referendum on the issue. Within a week of Ukraine's decision, Belarus, Moldova, Azerbaijan, Kyrgyzstan, and Uzbekistan had all declared their independence. In a number of these cases nomenklatura elites did so to protect their interests in the wake of the collapse of the center. In Belorussia, for instance, conservative party apparatchiki teamed up with Belorussian nationalists to pass an independence resolution in the Belorussian parliament.[103] The alliance removed Supreme Soviet chair Nikolai Dementei for his support of the coup, electing Stanislav Shushkevich, the first deputy chair, in his place. Uzbek President Islam Karimov similarly announced on August 30 that his republic was seeking independence. He subsequently changed the name of the Uzbek Communist Party to the Popular Democratic Party of Uzbekistan, while his government cracked down on opposition *Birlik* politicians who had spearheaded earlier attempts to press independence from below.[104] Perhaps the most bizarre case of apparatchiki refitting themselves as nationalists occurred in Azerbaijan. There, on August 30 First Secretary of the Azerbaijani Communist Party and President Ayaz Mutalibov, who had been responsible for the crackdown on the Azerbaijani independence movement after the repressed revolution of January 1990, declared his republic independent and announced that he was "a genuine anticommunist" and had been a "secret Muslim" for years. Mutalibov resigned from his party post, called

---

[102] Lithuania and Georgia had already declared their independence in March 1990 and April 1991 respectively.

[103] Walter Stankievich, "The Events behind Belorussia's Independence Declaration," *Report on the USSR*, vol. 3, no. 38 (September 20, 1991), pp. 24–26.

[104] *The New York Times*, September 1, 1991, p. A6; September 9, 1991, p. A6; September 18, 1991, p. A7.

an emergency party congress in September to dissolve the Azerbaijani Communist Party, and nationalized the party's property (which in essence meant simply transferring property from his former party organization to his government). He then ran in an uncontested election for president on September 8, which he, of course, won overwhelmingly.[105] In September Tajikistan and Armenia declared independence, the latter in the wake of a long-scheduled referendum on secession in which 99 percent of those participating voted for independence. With only Russia, Kazakhstan, and Turkmenistan remaining,[106] it was obvious by mid-September that the Soviet government had become little more than a legal fiction.

## The Termination of the Soviet State

As Gorbachev himself notes, by this time he was "devilishly tired,"[107] exhausted by the upheavals of the previous four years and by the difficult negotiations he had conducted with the republics, now no longer relevant to the transformed situation. On August 27, as republics one after another were declaring independence, he called in his aide Georgii Shakhnazarov and asked him to focus on reviving negotiations over a new union agreement. Shakhnazarov replied, "Are you sure that you will be able to revive all that, at least in the near future?" Gorbachev responded, "Sure or not sure, that's not the issue. If we sit and fold our hands, we'll lose in the end. The country will be dragged under by the devil." Shakhnazarov observed that "the situation now is entirely different. The republics will want to snatch up even more rights." Gorbachev retorted, "Of course, and we, from our side, should explain to them that without the union not one of them can survive." Shakhnazarov and his team consulted with Yeltsin's advisors, who noted that the union treaty was not high on Yeltsin's agenda and that it had "lost its timeliness." Shakhnazarov came away with the impression that Yeltsin had returned to the idea of replacing the union with a series of bilateral treaties between Russia and the republics or with a four-sided agreement between Russia, Ukraine, Belorussia, and Kazakhstan, as floated back in January. Only the Central Asian states and Belorussia expressed interest in resuming negotiations. But soon

---

[105] *The New York Times*, September 4, 1991, p. A10.
[106] On October 28 Turkmenistan declared its independence after a referendum produced an overwhelming vote in favor.
[107] Gorbachev, *Zhizn' i reformy*, vol. 2, p. 587.

430

thereafter, Gorbachev met with Yeltsin and persuaded him to renew talks about creating a rump Soviet state.[108]

In early September Gorbachev reopened the negotiations – this time on a self-avowed confederal basis. The chances of success were minimal. As a result of the coup, Gorbachev was, as his aide Cherniaev later put it, "politically denuded."[109] Power in Moscow had fallen into the hands of Yeltsin, who did not shrink from demonstrating his dominance by embarrassing Gorbachev publicly. Yeltsin issued a series of decrees subordinating all-union ministries to the Russian government and assuming the power to remove and appoint local leaders in the Russian provinces. The Soviet state existed nominally, with its army, currency, and diplomatic embassies. But it controlled nothing, as effective power had slipped into the hands of the republics. This devolution was represented in the reorganization of central state institutions proposed by Gorbachev in early September, modeled on the institutions envisioned in precoup drafts of the union treaty. It created a State Council consisting of the leaders of the republics that was to be the main policy-making body of what remained of the Soviet state and serve as the forum for renegotiating the treaty. The first act of the State Council was to recognize the independence of the Baltic states. Since the USSR Supreme Soviet had been dominated by conservative forces, Gorbachev attempted to create an alternative legislature; each republic was to dispatch twenty deputies from its legislature to an all-union Soviet of Representatives of People's Deputies. But when the sessions of that body opened in October, it was immediately paralyzed by the absence of delegations from Ukraine, Georgia, Armenia, and the Baltic, while Moldova and Azerbaijan allowed their deputies to attend only as observers.[110] The center had little to offer republics in exchange for handing power back to the center. If the Novo-Ogarevo talks prior to August could not produce a workable government, such an outcome was even less likely after the coup, when the center was eclipsed by the republics. From the beginning there were sharp differences. As Gorbachev noted, "in the end we came to an agreement not to fix in detail the division of powers in the agreement, but only to foresee 'spheres of joint management'" – once again "putting off until some future time the formation of a relatively clear managerial structure that was so necessary for pulling

[108] Shakhnazarov, *Tsena svobody*, p. 281–82.
[109] A. S. Cherniaev, *Shest' let s Gorbachevym* (Moscow: Progress, 1993), p. 491.
[110] Medvedev, *V komande Gorbacheva*, pp. 220–21.

the country as quickly as possible out of the crisis."[111] By November there was still no agreement over what the treaty should produce – a confederation or merely an international community of states along the lines of the European Union.

In the end the decision to terminate the USSR was unanimous among republican governments. But two factors in particular were critical in the materialization of that consensus: the position of Ukraine, where aversion to Muscovite control, even in Russified Eastern Ukraine, had grown dominant, and Yeltsin's impatience to pursue market reform. Even in negotiations over creating an economic community, Ukraine balked at becoming a member, though the three-year agreement recognized the signatories as "independent states consisting of the former subjects of the Union of Soviet Socialist Republics," allowed them to establish their own currencies, and focused mainly on coordination of legal regimes and the conduct of negotiated joint policies.[112] In November, the Ukrainian parliament allowed Prime Minister Fokin to initial the agreement, subject to parliamentary scrutiny after the independence referendum in December. Gorbachev had hoped that the creation of an economic community would become the basis for a broader state-building process, but the Ukrainian government never displayed interest in such an outcome. Throughout this period the insistence of the Ukrainian government and parliament that Ukraine establish its own armed forces made Ukraine, in Marshal Shaposhnikov's words, "the pioneer and motor of processes of dissociation in the defense sphere."[113] In October the Ukrainian parliament authorized the creation of a four-hundred-thousand-strong army from among units of the Soviet military stationed on Ukrainian soil. At the October 11 meeting of the State Council Kravchuk formally announced what was already widely expected, that Ukraine would not participate in negotiations over a new union treaty. Opinion polls in Ukraine in October and November consistently showed robust majorities in favor of independence, even in the Russified East and South.[114] It was in fact Ukraine, not Yeltsin, that took the initiative in calling the Belovezhskoe Forest meeting that formally dissolved the USSR. The idea had emerged within the Ukrainian government as early as October.

[111] Gorbachev, *Zhizn' i reformy*, vol. 2, p. 589.
[112] *Soiuz mozhno bylo*, pp. 211–27.  [113] Shaposhnikov, *Vybor*, p. 144.
[114] *Report on the USSR*, vol. 3, no. 46 (November 15, 1991), p. 57.

Gorbachev refused to treat any of these acts as definitive signs of Ukraine's defection from the union. In response to Kravchuk's announcement, Gorbachev authored a letter in the name of the State Council to the Ukrainian Supreme Soviet calling on it to reverse its decision about independence, since "We cannot imagine a Union without Ukraine."[115] Such appeals had no effect (and even possibly a negative effect) within the charged atmosphere of the Ukrainian referendum and presidential election. The Ukrainian government boycotted meetings of the State Council called to negotiate a new treaty. Gorbachev's hope was to pressure Ukraine through the example of other republics – to create a reverse tide of sorts – that would push Ukraine back to the negotiating table. As Marshal Shaposhnikov noted, "Though the Ukrainian position was that the leaders of Ukraine did not want to participate in any form in a Union, nevertheless, in discussing the question of the union agreement, the reckoning apparently was that if all the republics would sign an agreement, then Ukraine would be forced to join."[116] The issue of Ukrainian participation in a rump Soviet state was settled once and for all on December 1, when the referendum produced an overwhelming vote of 90 percent in favor of independence, with solid majorities voting "yes" even in the highly Russified provinces of the East and South. Immediately afterward, Poland, Canada, Hungary, and the United States indicated their willingness to recognize Ukrainian statehood.

It is difficult to determine the degree to which the impending exit of Ukraine influenced Yeltsin's decision to seek independence. Long before August, Yeltsin had indicated that Russia would not sign a union treaty without Ukraine, and there is no doubt that Ukraine's failure to participate strengthened the resolve of those who believed that Russia should declare independence. Without Ukraine, the chances of approval for a union agreement within the Russian parliament were minimal. Already in September Yeltsin's advisors were divided into two camps: those favoring an economic union among the republics and the creation of a renewed Soviet state on a confederal basis; and those favoring independence and a rapid, Polish-style transition to the market. As plans for Russia's economic reforms took shape, the latter position gained strength. But even had the former position triumphed, it is unlikely that a rump Soviet state would

---

[115] *The New York Times*, October 23, 1991, p. A5.
[116] Shaposhnikov, *Vybor*, p. 120.

have survived for long, since its confederative structure would have been highly unstable. Gorbachev was well aware of this. As Shakhnazarov told him in early September, there was not a single successful confederal arrangement in the world, and confederation could only be a temporary affair leading either to a federal arrangement or a series of independent states. Gorbachev grew angry, resenting Shakhnazarov's lecture and replying that he too had studied in a university and knew this without the professor's help. Gorbachev's gamble was that the instability of confederation would work in his favor, eventually leading back to a federal state as republics realized they had more to gain from cooperation than divorce.[117] He therefore insisted that the agreement create not "a union of states" but a "union government," for the former formula would have ruled out the eventual emergence of a substantial state out of the instability of confederation and led instead to the breakup of the country.

But the inertia toward disintegration was strong. Would Azerbaijan have remained a member of the confederation if its members (particularly Russia) refused to defend Azerbaijani borders from the Armenian insurrection? By November Azerbaijan stopped attending meetings of the State Council due to the escalation of the Karabakh conflict. Would market transition have been possible under conditions of confederation, with the difficult decisions of price increase, unemployment, and monetary and fiscal control that would have affected republics differentially? Ukraine was already introducing its own currency, and it was obvious that any attempt at serious reform would require the kind of state a weak confederation could not provide. The Bolsheviks could justify control over Central Asia and the Transcaucasus ideologically as part of their efforts to spread revolution. But what would have justified Russian participation in a state which, without Ukraine, would have united them primarily with sixty million relatively impoverished Muslims? Confederation was not a viable solution to the problems faced by the republics, and federation had long been out of reach, even before August.

Russian public opinion in the aftermath of the coup favored the preservation of the union, but the meaning of "union" was rapidly diluting as possibilities for constructing a rump Soviet state receded. Even before the coup, Russians had been divided over whether the union should be a confederal or federal entity, with majorities in Moscow and Leningrad favoring the former and majorities in the Middle Volga and North Caucasus

---

[117] Shakhnazarov, *Tsena svobody*, pp. 287–88.

supporting the latter.[118] By October 1991 one in four Russians had come to believe that there should be no union at all; those who favored preservation of the union were equally divided among those who wanted an economic union only, those who wanted an economic and political union (federal or confederal), and those who favored a union with central control over military affairs.[119] Thus, although the August coup and the massive exit of republics that followed did not entirely undermine Russian belief in the desirability of some kind of union, they tipped Russian opinion toward a much looser understanding of what union actually meant.

Throughout September Yeltsin publicly stood behind Gorbachev's efforts to revise the union treaty along confederal lines, though each leader interpreted this differently – a union of states or a path toward the eventual creation of a rump Soviet state. In the first revisions to the draft treaty in September, Yeltsin compromised more than Gorbachev.[120] But beginning in October, in connection with the development of plans to foster a rapid transition to the market via shock therapy (freeing prices and a tight monetary policy), Yeltsin's position toward the treaty began to harden, and his interest in it waned.[121] Logically, the leap to the market meant that Yeltsin would not have wanted Russia's hands tied by any kind of center or by obligations to pursue consensual policies agreed on with other republics – most of which were considerably more conservative in their approach to market reform. Indeed, when Yeltsin set out the details of his economic program at the end of October, it was viewed by Gorbachev and others as a violation of the economic community agreement that Yeltsin had just signed. Not only did Yeltsin obtain for himself special powers during the transitional period, but he also spoke of eliminating eighty all-union ministries (which, by this time, had been subordinated to Russian government oversight), including the USSR Ministry of Foreign Affairs. Gorbachev rightly viewed the plan as nothing less than an end to the Soviet state.[122]

With Ukraine clearly set on a course toward independence, and Russia eager to take an independent path to the market, it became evident that the negotiations over a renewed Soviet state were leading nowhere. At the

---

[118] Opinion elsewhere in Russia was evenly divided. See Wyman, *Public Opinion in Postcommunist Russia*, p. 163.
[119] Wyman, *Public Opinion in Postcommunist Russia*, pp. 164–65.
[120] Shakhnazarov, *Tsena svobody*, p. 288.
[121] See Hough, *Democratization and Revolution*, pp. 464–70.
[122] Gorbachev, *Zhizn' i reformy*, vol. 2, pp. 591–92.

November 4 meeting of the State Council, Gorbachev sought to reverse the impending failure by beginning the meeting with a forty-minute lecture, broadcast to the entire country, concerning the unacceptability of Yeltsin's unilateral approach to economic transition, the necessity of co-ordinating actions across the republics, and the dangers of the imminent disintegration of the Soviet state. The logic undoubtedly was to generate pressure on Yeltsin to commit to the treaty process. Yeltsin walked into the session fifteen minutes into the speech in a sign of disrespect to the treaty process. The speech elicited an icy, two-minute silence from those republican leaders present.[123] As Cherniaev recalled, "We in Gorbachev's close circle left the meeting with full certainty that specifically on that day . . . things would unravel very quickly with respect to the Union."[124]

Indeed, at the November 14 meeting of the State Council, at which representatives of only seven republics were present, a dead end was reached almost immediately. Yeltsin and Shushkevich expressed the view that the union should be understood merely as a community of states, not a union government.[125] Gorbachev protested, threatened to resign, and began to pack up his papers, saying that "if there is no state, I won't participate." He insisted that the agreement concern the creation of a coherent state and not merely an international community of states. After four hours, the awkward situation was temporarily diffused when the experts emerged with the formula of "a confederal democratic state exercising power" – which seemed to favor Gorbachev's interpretation.[126] As Shushkevich later wrote, "At Novo-Ogarevo Gorbachev literally forced us leaders of the republics to agree to a 'mild,' meaningless formulation of a Union treaty. It led to nothing other than irritating the heads of these states and their Supreme Soviets."[127] At the news conference following the meeting, one republican leader after another proclaimed in front of the television cameras that "there will be a union,"[128] but what type of union was still unclear. Gorbachev may have engineered what he thought was a consensus, but the artificiality of that consensus quickly became apparent.

[123] Andrei S. Grachev, *Final Days: The Inside Story of the Collapse of the Soviet Union* (Boulder, CO: Westview, 1995), pp. 89–92.
[124] Cherniaev, *Shest' let*, pp. 515–16.
[125] The word *soiuz* in Russian contains considerable ambiguity, meaning either "union" or "alliance." As Gorbachev noted, behind its interpretation "stood the question of whether we will be one country or whether we will divide into several states." Gorbachev, *Zhizn' i reformy*, vol. 2, p. 593.
[126] Medvedev, *V komande Gorbacheva*, p. 221; Grachev, *Final Days*, pp. 106–19.
[127] *Ogonek*, no. 49, December 2, 1996, p. 10.    [128] *Soiuz mozhno bylo*, pp. 250–51.

One day later, on November 15, Kravchuk contacted Yeltsin and Shushkevich about holding a meeting after the Ukrainian referendum to discuss the future of the union. It was this invitation that led to the Belovezhskoe Forest meeting.[129] About this same time Gorbachev also came to the conclusion that the end of the Soviet state was near. He invited Marshal Shaposhnikov, his defense minister, to the Kremlin late one evening for a conversation; he told his guest that the USSR was on the verge of falling apart entirely and it was necessary "to do something." After discussing various alternatives, the most suitable, according to Gorbachev, was for the military to seize power, put a new government in place, stabilize the situation, and then step aside. When Shaposhnikov mentioned that this sounded uncannily like what had just been attempted in August, Gorbachev said that he was not proposing anything, but just thinking aloud, and the conversation abruptly ended.[130] In the last two weeks of November Yeltsin moved aggressively to assert Russian control over oil, gold, diamonds, and the printing of Soviet currency. He cut off funding to all-union ministries and authorized the Russian State Bank to take over all operations of the Soviet State Bank by the beginning of the year, while the Soviet government, then deep in debt, stood on the verge of bankruptcy. As a Yeltsin spokesman noted at the time, "de facto there is no Union anymore. There is only what we agree with other republics to leave in the center – foreign affairs, defense, interior, rail transport – and for the most part this is funded by Russia."[131]

At the final meeting of the State Council on November 25, Gorbachev prematurely announced to the press that the leaders of the republics had convened to initial a draft of the treaty, which would then be sent to the republican parliaments for ratification. Again, only seven republics were in attendance, with representatives of Ukraine and Azerbaijan absent. Shortly after the meeting began, Yeltsin intervened, stating that "there are several formulations here with which we did not agree." Specifically, Yeltsin objected to the statement that the union was to be a "confederal democratic state" as opposed to "a confederation of democratic states," noting that preliminary discussion in the Russian parliament had indicated no support for a single state, whether unitary or confederal. Yeltsin also observed that "signing the agreement without Ukraine is a useless act."

---

[129] Leonid Kravchuk, *Our Goal – A Free Ukraine* (Kiev: Globus, 1993), p. 25.
[130] Shaposhnikov, *Vybor*, pp. 137–38.
[131] *The New York Times*, November 25, 1991, p. A3.

Gorbachev objected that the issue had been debated for four hours at the last meeting and a consensus reached. Yeltsin insisted that this had only been an "exploratory conversation." Significantly, he was supported by Niiazov, Karimov, and Shushkevich, all of whom argued that their legislatures needed to comment further on the draft (a step likely to kill the treaty). Only representatives of Kazakhstan and Kyrgyzstan expressed approval for the agreement.[132] Gorbachev lost his patience, and after a short, angry speech in which he accused the republican leaders of treachery and political intrigue, he abruptly rose and left. As Yeltsin described the mood of those remaining, "We were left alone in the room, and precisely then, as a heavy, oppressive silence hung over the room, we suddenly realized that it was over. We were meeting here for the last time. The Novo-Ogarevo saga had drawn to a close."[133]

One week later, the Ukrainian referendum settled the fate of what remained of the union. The Belovezhskoe Forest meeting of the three Slavic leaders – Yeltsin, Kravchuk, and Shushkevich – on December 8 merely confirmed what had already been obvious since the collapse of the August coup – that nothing was left of the union to save. But the secrecy and atmosphere of intrigue that surrounded the meeting gave rise to accusations of a plot by the three leaders to kill what was left of the Soviet state. The location of the meeting, a hunting lodge at Viskuli, was chosen in part so that the conversation could take place in private, without Gorbachev's participation, and during the meetings the estate was guarded by a special security division to ensure, as Yeltsin later put it, "the utmost secrecy."[134] Gorbachev, who was scheduled to meet with Yeltsin, Kravchuk, Shushkevich, and Nazarbaev on December 9 to discuss whether there was a way out of the impasse, was well aware that the meeting at Viskuli was to take place. He had met with Yeltsin the day before his departure for Belorussia, at which time Yeltsin duplicitously pretended that he would act as Gorbachev's agent for sounding out the intentions of Kravchuk and for persuading him to participate in some kind of agreement. Ukraine, Gorbachev said, could agree to all the treaty's statutes or only some of them. Yeltsin even told Gorbachev that an international community of the three Slavic states would be proposed at the meeting and probed

[132] *Soiuz mozhno bylo*, 257–258; Grachev, *Final Days*, pp. 119–22; Shakhnazarov, *Tsena svobody*, pp. 300–1.
[133] Boris Yeltsin, *The Struggle for Russia* (New York: Random House, 1994), pp. 110–11.
[134] Yeltsin, *The Struggle for Russia*, p. 112.

Gorbachev's opinion on the idea (which, of course, was negative).[135] The conversation was meant by Yeltsin to set the stage for a final answer as to whether a rump Soviet state could be created. Yeltsin brought a copy of the draft union agreement with him to Viskuli and put it on the table in front of Kravchuk, saying: "I want you to know that these three questions are not mine, they are Mr. Gorbachev's. Yesterday I had a talk with Gorbachev, and I put these questions on his behalf. Gorbachev needs these answers, though I am also interested in knowing them. Question number one – do you agree with this draft agreement? How do you feel, should it be modified or amended to enable you to sign it?" Kravchuk later argued that, at that moment, the fate of what was left of the Union rested in Ukraine's hands. "[H]ad I stated Ukraine would sign the Union Treaty, Yeltsin would have signed it also." Instead, he answered in the negative to all the questions.[136] These answers were no surprise whatsoever to Yeltsin or Shushkevich; they would not have attended the meeting had they expected different answers. As Yegor Gaidar, present at Viskuli as part of the Yeltsin team, recalled, "all the participants knew full well the inevitability of the decision that they were taking."[137] The parties then sat down to discuss the creation of a new international community of states, a Commonwealth of Independent States. The final document was a significantly revised version of a draft that had been prepared back in February, when the three states plus Kazakhstan had explored a four-sided agreement outside the union treaty negotiations. It began by stating that the three states – which had participated in the founding of the USSR in 1922 – "declare that the USSR as a subject of international law and geopolitical reality has ceased its existence."[138] At the last minute, it was mentioned that Nazarbaev should be brought into the agreement. A frantic attempt to contact the Kazakhstan president found him at the airport in Moscow. He refused to fly to Belorussia, his feelings hurt for being left out of the meeting in the first place. But Nazarbaev was, as he put it at a news conference afterward, "a pragmatist."[139] He quickly accepted the "inevitability" of the decision at Viskuli and moved on, embracing his new role as president of independent Kazakhstan.

---

[135] Grachev, *Final Days*, pp. 136–37; *Soiuz mozhno bylo*, pp. 289–90.
[136] Kravchuk, *Our Goal – A Free Ukraine*, pp. 25, 107–8.
[137] Yegor Gaidar, *Dni porazhenii i pobed* (Moscow: Vagrius, 1997), p. 149.
[138] For the text of the agreement, see *Soiuz mozhno bylo*, pp. 302–6.
[139] Yeltsin, *The Struggle for Russia*, pp. 115–16; Shaposhnikov, *Vybor*, p. 126; Dmitrii Valovoi, *Kremlevskii tupik i Nazarbaev* (Moscow: Molodaia gvardiia, 1993), p. 148.

After signing the document, the three leaders then called Shaposhnikov, Gorbachev's minister of defense, and asked him to become the commander-in-chief of the combined Commonwealth forces (the agreement called for keeping the strategic nuclear forces of the USSR under a single command). As Shaposhnikov recalled, "In actual fact hardly any union structures at that time remained except, perhaps, for the USSR President and a few ministers, including myself." He agreed. He explained his decision to Gorbachev the next day in the following words: "I'm tired, Mikhail Sergeevich, of living in uncertainty. . . . The Commonwealth is at least some kind of certainty, but that which is occurring today long ago ceased to be a Union." Yeltsin, Shaposhnikov noted in his memoirs, "is often accused of having destroyed the USSR. In my mind, this is unfair. The Union realistically had begun to fall apart long before the Belovezhskoe meeting."[140] Just how plain this was to the overwhelming majority of the Russian political elite at the time was evident on December 12, when the Russian parliament ratified the Belovezhskoe accord by a vote of 188 to 6, with 7 abstentions, debating the issue for only one hour. The agreement was ratified by similarly lopsided votes in Ukraine and Belarus. Russian public opinion also accepted the "inevitability" of the decision. Thus, by December 1991 Russians favored an end to the USSR by a three-to-two majority, with only the older generation (over sixty) displaying any significant dissent.[141]

The signers of the Belovezhskoe agreement had left membership in the Commonwealth open to other republics of the USSR. Within days Armenia and Kyrgyzstan announced their intention to join. A meeting of the leaders of the Central Asian states on December 13 in Ashkhabad also expressed their support. The two groups of states – Slavic and Central Asian, along with Azerbaijan, Armenia, and Moldova – were brought together on December 21 in Alma-Ata, where the result was repeated, only on a larger scale. Gorbachev was left as president of nonexistent country. On December 25, as he officially announced his resignation, the Soviet flag was lowered over the Kremlin, and the Russian tricolor raised in its place. There were, no fireworks, no celebrations in the streets. In the non-Russian republics the euphoria had, in many places, occurred well before the legal termination of the Soviet state, whereas in Russia public opinion in 1992 consistently indicated that two-thirds of Russians were sorry the

[140] Shaposhnikov, *Vybor*, pp. 125–28, 132.
[141] Wyman, *Public Opinion in Postcommunist Russia*, p. 166.

union had disintegrated, but only little over a quarter favored not recognizing the breakup.[142] The Soviet Union was not toppled by a cabal; it exhausted itself over an extended period of time, and at the moment of its final disintegration its demise was accepted as inevitable almost universally – at the very least, out of a sense of a lack of alternatives among its remaining supporters.

## Summary and Conclusion

The central theme of this chapter – the ascending sense of inevitability which enveloped the disintegration of the Soviet state during its final two years – chafes against many of the dominant narratives of Soviet collapse. These tend to revolve around whether the USSR was destroyed by Gorbachev's naiveté or Yeltsin's ambitions, or around the assertion that the breakup of the USSR was objectively predetermined by some essential quality of the Soviet state – imperial, totalitarian, or ethnofederal. I have shown that these factors were only parts of the larger causal story, and not even necessarily its central element. Rather, the critical actors who brought about the demise of the Soviet state were themselves transformed by the broader tide of nationalism that swept through Soviet society during these years.

Explanations of Soviet collapse which ignore the causal role of the event are at a loss to explain how that which had almost universally been considered unimaginable and impossible at the onset of *glasnost'* came to be widely accepted as inevitable by the Soviet state's end. Rather than treating inevitability as an objective, timeless quality, I showed instead how an accumulating sense of the inevitability of Soviet disintegration developed out of the structural change wrought by the tide, and how the influence of the tide on Russians in particular was a critical structural pivot in the emergence of these perceptions, primarily because of the traditionally close association of Russians with the Soviet state. This relationship was altered by the combined effects of the tide of nationalism and the republican elections of 1990. But in the end it was not the Baltic, Transcaucasian, or Moldovan governments (governments of non-Russian groups that had mobilized for the right to separate nationhood) that took the final decision to abolish the Soviet state – or even, for that matter, the

---

[142] Wyman, *Public Opinion in Postcommunist Russia*, pp. 166–67.

governments of Central Asia. Rather, the decision was adopted by the Russian, Ukrainian, and Belorussian governments – governments of cultural groups traditionally closely associated with Soviet power. Moreover, within the elites and publics of these groups there was widespread support of – and at a minimum, acquiescence to – the decision due in large part to the widespread sense of "inevitability" that surrounded it. This is unambiguous testimony to the ways in which a tide of nationalism washed across the Soviet lands, inverting long-standing meanings and overturning conventional hierarchies of authority.

# 9

Conclusion: *Nationhood and Event*

There is a tide in the affairs of men,
Which, taken at the flood, leads on to fortune;
Omitted, all the voyage of their life
Is bound in shallows and in miseries.
  William Shakespeare, *Julius Caesar*

The streets and city squares no longer echo with rebellious slogans and impassioned speeches. Where enormous crowds once surged, shoppers now traverse, hardly cognizant that they tread on spaces where the fate of nations was once contested. Though it has been merely a decade since the Soviet collapse, the human flood that once washed across these lands has been largely swallowed back into the oceans of everyday routine. For most, the *glasnost'* revolution has become a hazy, distant past – another epoch, another country, another world – submerged in the inexorable currents of time.

To be sure, new waves of mobilization were stirred in the initial aftermath of the Soviet collapse. Chechen and Volga Tatar nationalists demanded the right to the same national states that Estonians, Russians, and others gained when the USSR disintegrated. The breakup of the Soviet state intensified violent conflicts in Karabakh, Abkhazia, Ossetia, and Moldova. Crimean Russians overwhelmingly voted for separation from Ukraine and reunification with their Russian homeland; Crimean Tatars demonstrated for the opportunity to return to the same territory, their once expropriated homeland. Tajiks and Georgians fought civil wars among themselves. Within Russia "shock therapy" evoked new outbreaks of protest from the now predominantly communist opposition and precipitated the violent breakdown of Russian political institutions in October 1993. But in spite of these and other mobilizations triggered by the Soviet collapse, the breakup of the USSR generally set in motion a gradual trans-formation from a "noisy" phase of nationalism to a "quiet" phase, as mobilization declined sharply and politics migrated from the streets to institutions. Though many of the disorders unleashed by *glasnost'* continue to live with us, by 1992 protest in the former USSR had begun to taper off sharply, and by the mid-1990s (with the exception of Chechnia and the continuing conflicts in the Balkans) most of the interethnic wars that emerged out of the collapse had been stilled, either through exhaustion, stalemate, or victory.

Numerous structural factors pushed toward the demobilization of nationalist challenges over the 1990s. The first and most obvious was the institutionalization of nationalist contention within the state, in part through the achievement of independence. In the Baltic, Transcaucasus, Moldova, and Ukraine, nationalist movements gained control over the state, undermining the rationale for further mobilization. The major target of mobilization during the *glasnost'* era – the Soviet state – no longer existed. The popular fronts that spearheaded independence drives soon split and fell into disarray after independence, losing their cohesive purpose with the demise of their adversary and splintering with the new and divisive issues intrinsic to the exercise of power. Where nomenklatura elites successfully repackaged themselves as champions of new nations, their rivals remained marginalized, losing adherents because of their inability to succeed and often disintegrating as organizations. Thus, for different reasons both victory and defeat were associated with the eventual decline of nationalist movements as politics moved from the streets back to the government office.

The international community of states also exercised powerful material and normative effects on demobilization. Until fall 1991, when the disintegration of the Soviet state became a fait accompli, Western leaders did everything in their power to keep the USSR from breaking apart. President Bush traveled to Kiev only two months before the August 1991 coup, where he lectured Ukrainian leaders about the foolishness of pursuing secession from the USSR – his infamous "chicken Kiev" speech. The prime minister of Lithuania Kazimiera Priunskene was forced to enter the White House through a back door when visiting Washington in December 1990 for fear of sending the wrong signal to Moscow about American desires to see the USSR dissolve. The United States liked dealing with its familiar and predictable superpower rival and feared the instability that its collapse might entail. But once the breakup of the USSR became established fact, Western powers moved quickly to assure successor states that they would not recognize the validity of further claims to independent statehood beyond those of the union republics. No states within the world community recognized the sovereignty claims of separatist movements within the union republics.[1] The union republics became the frames through which billions of dollars of aid, loans, and debt relief were channeled in a massive attempt to "build" new states and new economies. Efforts were made to pacify ongoing zones of conflict through the negotiation of cease-fire agreements. Membership in the European Union was made conditional on the existence of fixed political boundaries, an absence of outstanding territorial conflicts, and respect for minority rights. The general effect was to discourage the pressing of further claims to independent statehood, dampen irredentist urges, and demobilize separatist challenges to the former union republics.

Third, what Gellner called the "cultural equipment" of states – their coercive, material, and normative power – pushed toward demobilization, though with considerably less effect than their Soviet predecessor. Clearly, post-Soviet states were weak states, often with uncannily little ability to make their decisions stick and with incomplete control of the territories over which they claimed sovereignty. But it is also true that these were not entirely new states. They were in many cases fragments of an old state, including in most instances old police and KGB organizations. There was no need to invent repertoires of repression anew in many instances. In a number of republics Brezhnevian modes of dealing with dissent were maintained throughout the *glasnost'* period, so that the Gorbachev years naturally flowed into the oppressive practices of a Niiazov, Karimov, Aliev, or Lukashenka. And though the inertial norms of Brezhnevian bureaucracy could not sanction a bloodbath for the sake of preserving Soviet power, the new norms of post-communist transition could: Boris Yeltsin demonstrated less restraint in storming the Russian White House in October 1993 for the purpose of promoting market reform than did the members of the State Emergency Committee in August 1991 for saving socialism. Whereas the State Emergency Committee rejected waging a bloody war to salvage the USSR, the Yeltsin government did not shrink from twice bombing the city of Groznyi to rubble for the sake of preserving the integrity of the Russian Federation.

---

[1] The sole exception that proves the rule was the recognition of Chechnia by Taliban-controlled Afghanistan.

Fourth, exhaustion played a powerful role in dampening nationalist contention throughout the former Soviet region. As noted above, the weakness of newly established states did not mean they refrained from attempts to overwhelm internal nationalist challengers forcefully (as Russia tried to do unsuccessfully in Chechnia) or to buy them off with tax breaks, side payments, or financial incentives (as Russia did with more success in Tatarstan). Rather, it meant that, given the institutional frailty and limited resources of these states, the outcomes of such efforts were fraught with more than the usual degree of uncertainty and often stretched fiscal and human resources to the limit. Stalemate and exhaustion were the modal outcomes of nationalist conflicts in the post-Soviet era rather than clear-cut victory for newly established states or those who would challenge them. As we saw, late risers within tides of nationalism come with considerably fewer facilitating advantages relative to early risers. Many of the nationalist movements challenging the post-Soviet states were late risers within the *glasnost'* tide, mobilizing only as the collapse of the Soviet state grew imminent. In this sense, new states were not the only contenders suffering weaknesses in the post-Soviet period; so too were most of the nationalist challengers to states. Thus, neither states nor nationalist challengers possessed the capability for waging protracted cultural conflict. Both were compelled to restrain their ambitions.

Fifth, what Hendryk Spruyt has termed "mutual empowerment" – the tendency of states to seek support for themselves through supporting structurally similar peers[2] – created powerful incentives toward cooperation among post-Soviet states. As in post-colonial Africa, the internal weakness of post-Soviet states and the potential for the proliferation of disputes across boundaries fostered a common interest in minimizing challenges to external borders. Mutual survival dictated cooperation. The juridical character of most external state borders came to be quickly recognized and settled, even if actual control over territories was incomplete. With the sole exception of the Moldovan conflict in 1992–93, Russia, for instance, proved reluctant to aid its co-ethnics in its so-called near-abroad due to its desire for "normal" relations with its neighbors, its own internal weaknesses, and the external constraints imposed by major international donors. Even in Moldova Russia soon forced a truce on its Pridniestr clients. For the sake of normality, Russia "betrayed" the interests of its

[2] Hendryk Spruyt, *The Sovereign State and its Competitors* (Princeton, NJ: Princeton University Press, 1994), pp. 167–71.

co-ethnics abroad – or at least so it seemed to Russian separatists in Crimea and Kazakhstan. The triadic brew of nationalizing state, national minority, and national homeland which some expected would lead to a foaming reaction of disorder[3] fizzled, in significant part because the Russian national homeland, consumed with its own weighty problems and interested in the advantages of stability, never played its expected, catalyzing role. This same desire for normalcy in relations with other states led Kazakhstan, Kyrgyzstan, and China to reach a mutual understanding to combat the significant Uighur insurrection in Xinjiang, whose supporters within the Uighur diaspora were harassed and repressed by newly independent Central Asian governments.[4]

Finally, mobilization declined in part due to the growing sense of immutability surrounding the newly established status quo. As opportunities for contention dissipated, economic transitions took precedence, and the obligations of everyday life grew ascendant, belief in the effectiveness of collective action was undermined. As we have seen, institutional arrangements can gain a degree of acceptance precisely because they cannot be changed, and control over opportunities to challenge exercises a profound effect on national imagination. The post-Soviet state system gained in legitimacy as it gained in longevity. Thus, as the prospects of a revival of a rump Soviet state receded, the number of persons identifying themselves as citizens of the post-Soviet states climbed steadily, as diehards who continued to identify themselves as citizens of the defunct Soviet state declined, dropping sharply by the second half of the 1990s. For most citizens of the former Soviet Union the cataclysmic changes of the *glasnost'* revolution brought unwelcome effects. Families and villages were suddenly divided by state borders; collapsing economies and marketization brought about impoverishment, hyperinflation, and unemployment; crime, corruption, and disarray infected the frail frames of newly established states. Many observers initially expected that the triple transition of post-Soviet politics would lead to a social explosion, but in fact the opposite occurred: A sense of passivity and helplessness set in. As is true in the aftermath of many revolutions, the heady days of the street eventually gave way to disillusionment, cynicism, and despair. Public opinion polls showed a proliferation of materialistic values over idealism. Even as economies crashed

---

[3] Rogers Brubaker, "National Minorities, Nationalizing States, and External National Homelands in the New Europe," *Daedalus*, vol. 124, no. 2 (Spring 1995), pp. 107–32.

[4] *OMRI Daily Digest*, April 19, 1996, and April 30, 1996.

and wages went unpaid, the number of those protesting dwindled – due in large part to a declining sense of efficacy.[5]

Viewed in light of what came before and after, the *glasnost'* tide of nationalism was thus an unusual period of history. It was, as I have argued, a period of "thickened history" – one in which the pace of events accelerated, in which action came to play an increasingly significant role in its own causal structure, and in which the seemingly impossible, under the daily onslaught of challenge and change, became the seemingly inevitable. In contrast with what occurred before and after, during *glasnost'* challenges to the state multiplied and fed off of one another, overwhelming the capacity of the state to contain them and ultimately evoking large-scale structural change in the character of the state system. The tectonic changes in the global political order introduced by *glasnost'* were no less sweeping than those ushered in by the French Revolution, World War I, or decolonization. The *glasnost'* tide of nationalism fundamentally reconfigured political space and political power across more than a sixth of the world's surface, brought an end to the seventy-year history of communism in Europe, terminated the Cold War division of international politics, and gave birth to a new hegemony of global capitalism.

But more than that, the *glasnost'* tide of nationalism led to a major upsurge in nationalist mobilization worldwide.[6] Aside from the cross-national spread of national contention within the Soviet Union itself, the socialist bloc – a family of states sharing common institutional characteristics, ideologies, and modes of domination – was first to be affected by the tide. The success of secessionist movements in the Soviet Union also encouraged nationalist challengers farther afield in such places as northern Italy, Tibet, Scotland, Slovenia, and Quebec. Throughout 1990 and 1991 Slovenian leaders made constant reference to events in Lithuania, positing a fundamental analogy between Baltic independence from the USSR and Slovene independence from Yugoslavia. They even issued a "declaration of sovereignty" modeled on those of the Baltic. Lithuania was one of the first states to recognize Slovenian claims to independence, as Gorbachev, sensing the same analogy, was one of the most vocal support-

---

[5] Deborah Javeline, "Who Protests in Russia," United States Information Agency Opinion Analysis, December 8, 1998.
[6] Ted Robert Gurr, "Ethnic Warfare on the Wane," *Foreign Affairs*, vol. 79, no. 3 (May/June 2000), pp. 52–64.

ers of Yugoslav territorial integrity.[7] Jacques Parizeau, then leader of the
Parti Quebecois, hailed the collapse of the Soviet Union as proof that
Quebec's separatists were "visionaries" and "prophets" and were no longer
"rowing against the current of history." If sovereignty worked in the Baltic,
Parizeau contended, "it will be no less difficult in Quebec."[8] In the wake
of the Soviet collapse the Dalai Lama predicted that similar forces would
soon sweep across China as well.[9] The nationalist contention unleashed
by *glasnost'* became a transnational phenomenon that flowed across cultural and political boundaries, as actors consciously attempted to link
themselves with and to foster the success of analogous groups.

Although the *glasnost'* tide represented an unusual period of rapid,
cross-cultural diffusion of nationalist mobilization, it was not the first (nor
the last) such period in modern history. Over the twentieth century alone
the Eurasian political landscape was periodically contested through similar
upsurges in nationalist mobilization across multiple groups – each with
differing scope and outcome. Certainly, much nationalist contention
occurs outside of tides. But since the nationalist revolutions of the late
eighteenth and early nineteenth centuries, transnational upsurges in
nationalist mobilization have been central to the ways in which large-scale
structural change in the state system has occurred. During the century
from 1815 to 1914, for instance, nationalist conflict periodically spread
across cultural and political borders in Europe in concentrated bursts.[10] In
1820–21 significant nationalist rebellions broke out in Italy, Greece, and
the Danubian principalities; from 1830–33 in Poland, Belgium, Bosnia,
Italy, the Danubian principalities, Albania, Hungary, Bulgaria, Serbia,
Montenegro, Switzerland, and the Basque lands; in 1848 in Italy, Hungary,
the German principalities, Serbia, Poland, Wallachia, Greece, and Ireland;
in 1875–76 in Croatia, Bosnia-Herzegovina, Crete, Bulgaria, Serbia,
Montenegro, and Macedonia. In interwar Europe, the success of Mussolini's march on Rome in 1922 brought about a rash of right-wing nation-

[7] AP, March 23, 1990; UPI, January 9, 1991; *The Independent* (London), January 16, 1991,
p. 11.
[8] *The Guardian*, September 3, 1992, p. 23; *The Toronto Star*, August 27, 1991, p. A11.
[9] UPI, July 22, 1992; *The New York Times*, September 5, 1991, p. A16.
[10] Sandra Halperin, "The Spread of Ethnic Conflict in Europe: Some Comparative-
Historical Reflections," in David A Lake and Donald Rothchild, eds., *The International
Spread of Ethnic Conflict: Fear, Diffusion, and Escalation* (Princeton, NJ: Princeton University Press, 1998), pp. 151–84.

alist challenges across the continent seeking to refashion the political map of Europe and mutually supportive of one another. Similarly, after World War II decolonization diffused within and across empires, so that prior decolonizations accelerated the decolonization rate of remaining dependencies.[11] Tides of smaller scope and scale have been operative as well; to cite a contemporary example, the overthrow of the Suharto regime and the success of the East Timorese rebellion in Indonesia in the late 1990s encouraged additional challenges to Javanese dominance and Indonesian sovereignty over other parts of the archipelago, even flowing over state boundaries to encourage the dormant Moro insurrection in the neighboring Philippines.

In each of these cases, particular structural preconditions and institutional contingencies made the emergence of a tide of nationalism possible. In the preceding chapters we saw evidence that the emergence of a tide of nationalism in the Soviet Union under *glasnost'* was facilitated by specific features of the Soviet state: its institutional and ideological crises; its fusion between state and regime; its submerged sense of ethnic grievance across multiple groups; its overreach abroad. As I argued, the large multinational state encompassing several distinct, compactly settled, cultural entities has been particularly susceptible in its moments of institutional crisis to generating tides of nationalism, when multiple groups simultaneously contest the national order interactively. Yet, as we have seen, although these features made the Soviet state more vulnerable to experiencing a tide, they did not necessitate the emergence of the tide, nor do they tell us much about the specific actions that constituted the tide, why some groups succeeded and others did not, or how the politics of the tide played itself out. Rather, it was the forging of connections between acts of mobilization which was the critical process involved in the actual production of a tide of nationalism. This capacity to forge connections between acts of mobilization across time and space varied considerably from group to group. In the Soviet case certain features of target groups – their level within the ethnofederal hierarchy, their size, their patterns of linguistic usage, their degree of urbanization – facilitated the making of such linkages. We explored some of the causal mechanisms underlying differential abilities to take advantage of the opportunities afforded by the

---

[11] David Strang, "From Dependency to Sovereignty: An Event History Analysis of Decolonization 1870–1987," *American Sociological Review*, vol. 55 (December 1990), pp. 846–60.

tide. Those with higher level units within the ethnofederal hierarchy not only possessed greater mobilizational resources, but also avoided some of the institutional constraints which the ethnofederal hierarchy imposed on those with lower units. Large population size endowed groups with power advantages and allowed them to tap into international norms that traditionally favored the self-determination claims of large groups and disfavored those of small groups. Linguistic assimilation not only undermined collective identity within target populations, but also disrupted the cohesiveness and will to act among nationalist activists by making success seem less likely. Urbanization created thicker networks of activists and larger pools of potential followers for nationalist movements. The structural advantages and disadvantages possessed by target groups were cumulative and fungible in that nationalisms could succeed or fail in the presence of a variety of combinations of structural factors. Yet, as we also saw, even in the presence of all these structural advantages, it is doubtful that any single nationalist movement would have succeeded in gaining independence from the Soviet state had it mobilized in spatial or temporal isolation from others. The interaction across cultural and political boundaries was critical to the outcome of Soviet disintegration, just as the inability to take advantage of the example of others was a central part of the explanation of failure. As I argued, much of what structural influence was about was endowing movements with advantages in profiting from the actions of others, that is, in providing them with a capacity to generate and ride the tide of nationalism.

Within the literature on nationalism more generally, the recursive role of action in social affairs – its ability to function as both cause and effect – has been insufficiently appreciated. Theories of nationalism have tended to emphasize structure over agency, viewing nationalism as a logical externalization of a particular social interest or identity position embedded by prior history or emerging out of the impact of broader social forces (such as industrialization). Such a perspective is inadequate in a number of respects. For one thing, it relies on a deterministic understanding of causation which, even in the study of the natural world, is no longer held to be fully true. In the study of human affairs, such a perspective is even more problematic, since human actions are not independent of one another across time and space. Rather, the fact that, because of our reflective capacities, human action can be made more or less likely by prior human action, both within and across spatial contexts, injects a significant degree of contingency into historical outcomes. As John Stuart Mill recognized, the

451

principal difficulty in applying his method of agreement and difference developed for assessing natural experiments to the study of human affairs is "the extensive and constant reaction of the effects upon their causes," rendering politics "a subject matter whose properties are changeable."[12]

One of the greatest challenges to social scientific explanation in general is the fact that the phenomena we study are not the temporally and spatially "independent" observations many pretend they are, but are rather interdependent observations whose manifest pattern has been influenced by previous outcomes across time and space. The challenges posed by the spatial interdependence of actions are known within cross-cultural anthropology as "Galton's problem" – the lack of independence across cases due to varied processes of intergroup and intersocietal influence.[13] Assessments of the gravity of "Galton's problem" for social scientific explanation vary; some believe the issue is a limited one, whereas others see it as a more pervasive phenomenon, accelerating in particular as globalization forges connections across spatial contexts. In studying policies, ideas, or acts of contention in any single context or across contexts, the scope of the challenge posed by the lack of independence across cases is considerable. But the temporal interdependence of observations is no less a challenge to social scientific explanation, for if, as Adam Przeworski has put it, "the world nurtures successes and eliminates failures," then the outcomes we observe at any specific moment in time are hardly a random sample, but rather are in significant part the products of a selection process and of the outcomes of prior contentions.[14]

[12] John Stuart Mill, *Philosophy of Scientific Method* (New York: Hafner Publishing Company, 1950), p. 344.
[13] The issue is named after Sir Francis Galton, who in 1889 criticized the analysis of Edward Tylor that claimed to show correlations between economic and familial institutions in a wide variety of societies and explained them from a functionalist standpoint. Galton questioned whether these customs were independent of one another, speculating that they may have ultimately derived from a common source. For a sample of discussions concerning "Galton's problem" in the social sciences, see Raoul Naroll, "Galton's Problem: The Logic of Cross-Cultural Analysis," *Social Research* (1965), pp. 428–51; Adam Przeworski and Henry Teune, *The Logic of Comparative Social Inquiry* (New York: Wiley-Interscience, 1970), pp. 51–53; Arend Lijphardt, "The Comparable Cases Strategy in Comparative Research," *Comparative Political Studies*, vol. 8, no. 2 (July 1975), pp. 171–72; Marc Howard Ross and Elizabeth Homer, "Galton's Problem in Cross-National Research," *World Politics*, vol. 29, no. 1 (October 1976), pp. 1–28; John H. Goldthorpe, "Current Issues in Comparative Macrosociology: A Debate on Methodological Issues," in Grete Bochmann et al., eds., *Comparative Social Research*, vol. 16 (Greenwich, CT: JAI Press, 1997), pp. 9–12.
[14] Adam Przeworski, in Atul Kohli et al., "The Role of Theory in Comparative Politics: A Symposium," *World Politics*, vol. 48 (October 1995), p. 18. Przeworski concludes that a

## Conclusion: Nationhood and Event

The interdependence of human action across time and space renders deterministic, linear, or atemporal explanations of social and political phenomena problematic. As John Goldthorpe has noted:

the assumption that nations can be treated as units of analysis, unrelated to each other in time and space, is one required by the logical methods of comparison that are favored in case-oriented research no less than by statistical methods. . . . The scarcely disputable fact that situations and events occurring at one time tend to have been influenced by situations and events occurring earlier clearly breaches the assumption of the independence of cases – as built into Mill's or any other logical method.[15]

This lack of independence between observations is usually viewed as a nuisance rather than an opportunity in social science research – a "problem" to be controlled for or excluded when possible rather than a process worthy of its own investigation.[16] In studying nationalism, however, as I have argued throughout this book, the interdependence of human actions across time and space cannot be understood as a hindrance to explanation or as simply a methodological issue whose effects are to be controlled; it is rather a substantive issue central to the process of explanation of the phenomenon itself.

As we have seen through the example of the Soviet collapse, the event played a critical causal role in the disintegration of the Soviet state. For one thing, the emergence of a tide of nationalism was heavily dependent on the contingent outcomes of events, as repression could easily have shut down challenges in early phases of the mobilizational cycle. Moreover, over time event-specific influences grew more prominent in the production of nationalist mobilization. Early risers tended to enjoy strong facilitating structural advantages, but as the tide developed this gave way to

great deal of comparative political research suffers from selection bias due to the effects of endogeneity in human affairs.

[15] Goldthorpe, "Current Issues in Comparative Macrosociology," p. 10. Goldthorpe had in mind states rather than nations per se, mirroring the unfortunate tendency in much social science discourse to confound the two, though the statement applies equally to the study of nationalism.

[16] See, for instance, the discussion of endogeneity in Gary King, Robert O. Keohane, Sidney Verba, *Designing Social Inquiry: Scientific Inference in Qualitative Research* (Princeton, NJ: Princeton University Press, 1994), pp. 185–96. On attempts to deal with "Galton's problem" through sampling techniques or statistical controls, see Raoul Naroll, "Galton's Problem," in Raoul Naroll and Ronald Cohen, eds., *A Handbook of Method in Cultural Anthropology* (New York: Columbia University Press, 1974), pp. 974–89; G. P. Murdock and D. White, "Standard Cross-Cultural Sample," *Ethnology*, vol. 8 (1969), pp. 329–69.

action by movements characterized by structural preconditions less conducive to action, causing late risers to depend to a greater degree than early risers on the successful examples of those who preceded them. This was the "chronological unfairness" of history noted by Herzen. By riding the tide of nationalism some degree of structural disadvantage could be mitigated. Understanding the power of numbers, movements also pursued a conscious strategy of spreading revolt laterally, just as the state sought to contain the "domino effects" that contention potentially exerted from one case to another. But the recursive power of nationalist action emerged not only from its ability to influence action across spatial contexts. We have seen systematic evidence that successful prior action made subsequent action more likely and set in motion powerful bandwagoning effects within target populations. The outcome of the contention embodied in the event injected a significant contingency into the politics of nationalism, as those less committed tended to associate with winning identity positions. As the detailed case studies of secessionist politics showed, for most individuals emulation and conformity were more powerful forces than invention in the formation of national imagination. Through the prevention or production of events and through control over their outcomes, both the state and nationalist movements sought to generate (in Kuran's terminology) "reputational cascades," attracting adherents by enhancing the reputations of those who identified with them and lowering the self-esteem of those who failed to do so.[17]

The individual event constituted a powerful potential site for the constitution of identities due not only to the influence of the outcome of contention on cultural identities and loyalties and on the possibilities for subsequent contention, but also to the cultural transactions that took place within the event itself. As Max Weber observed, beliefs about nationhood often crystallize suddenly and dramatically, as a result of changed circumstances that evoke significant alterations in behavior.[18] This sudden transformation in identities potentially associated with the event is rooted in part in the ways in which order limits the possibilities for and the imagination about alternative national bindings. Through the actions and discourses that enter into the event, nationalist movements seek to embolden

[17] Timur Kuran, "Ethnic Norms and Their Transformation Through Reputational Cascades," *Journal of Legal Studies*, vol. 27 (June 1998), pp. 623–59.
[18] H. H. Gerth and C. Wright Mills, eds., *From Max Weber: Essays in Sociology* (New York: Oxford University Press, 1946), p. 174.

those who fear expressing a particular identity position due to the restrictions of compliance systems and to persuade those less committed to identify with or defect to it. Movements sought that crowds took on the symbolic mantle of nations, so that victory for the crowd would be interpreted as a victory for the nation, or violence against the crowd would become the violation of the nation. As we saw, violence was one of the most powerful forces mobilizing identities, whether through the backlash effects that at times emerged from government repression or the outrage and sense of rupture brought on by interethnic violence. As Stanley Tambiah commented on the role of violence in the constitution of identities in South Asia: "What was previously seen as an effect now serves as a cause."[19]

As we have also seen, the outcome of the event is constitutive of structures. Even in "normalized" times, the constant and predicable flow of the stream of social life gradually alters the bed and changes the shape of the banks. But the most dramatic erosions occur at flood time, when the torrent overflows its channel, dragging rocks and trees, submerging normally dry land, and spewing its debris far downstream. The structures which influence human affairs are established, altered, and potentially transformed through the rhythms and flows of human action – by the physical effects which action inflicts on reality, as well as by the sense of expectation which the patterning of action establishes. As the Soviet case shows, the generative effect of action on structure is most pronounced in periods of diminished and deteriorating institutional constraint, when action multiplies and potentially transforms institutions. These remade institutions not only establish new rules and constraints with which actors must contend, but also place into motion day-to-day practices that alter the distribution of resources and shape the structural conditions that facilitate subsequent action. The *glasnost'* revolution marked the beginning of a difficult transition to a new way of life, a new politics, new nations, and in so doing it altered – for better and for worse – the life chances of hundreds of millions. Such institutionalizing moments alter the path of history; they are structure-creating, pushing history onto new tracks previously unimaginable.

Finally, the clustering and linkage of events characteristic of tides produce, as Sidney Tarrow has argued, "general outcomes that are more

---

[19] Stanley Tambiah, *Leveling Crowds: Ethnonationalist Conflicts and Collective Violence in South Asia* (Berkeley, CA: University of California Press, 1996), p. 223.

than the sum of the results of an aggregate of unconnected events." The historical outcomes wrought by tides depend "less on the balance of power between and the resources of any pair of opponents than on the generalized structure of contention and the responses to it of elites, opponents, and potential allies."[20] States can literally be overwhelmed by events. They may indeed enjoy preponderant force over any individual challenger or challenge and support from the international community of states, and yet eventually become relatively powerless to contain the spread of contention and the unraveling of order. Such an outcome, as we have seen, can be made more or less likely by the presence of particular facilitating structural pre-conditions, but there is nothing inevitable about its materialization. Instead, it emerges, as Tarrow argued, out of the multiplicity of interactions within cycles of contention that "make their endings far less similar than their beginnings."[21]

It is thus not difficult to explain why the Soviet collapse was so poorly anticipated by foreign observers and Soviet dissidents alike. The critical issue is not whether structural preconditions determined Soviet collapse and therefore made it potentially predictable by social scientific reasoning. The USSR was certainly vulnerable to being overwhelmed by a tide of nationalism, just as structural preconditions have made and continue to make tides of nationalism possible in other contexts as well. But this did not necessitate that events unfold in the way they did. Rather, the critical issue is why, in spite of the presence and widespread knowledge of those conditions which made eventual collapse possible, the disintegration of the USSR still seemed so utterly unimaginable, even to those who eventually brought it about. In contrast to those who would merely lay the blame at the feet of Sovietology and stop there, I see the explanation as rooted more deeply in the ways in which order creates a sense of its own timelessness and in the way in which order can, as Tarrow noted, potentially be overwhelmed by events. As Dennis Wrong has noted, "the rule of expectations . . . is basic to the achievement of social order."[22] A sense of permanence and immutability is part of the modern state's desired modality of rule. To produce their effects, the large-scale institutions of the modern state rely

---

[20] Sidney Tarrow, *Power in Movement: Social Movements and Contentious Politics*, 2d ed. (Cambridge, UK: Cambridge University Press, 1998), pp. 142–43.

[21] Tarrow, *Power in Movement*, 2d ed., p. 160.

[22] Dennis H. Wrong, *The Problem of Order: What Unites and Divides Society* (Cambridge, MA: Harvard University Press, 1995), p. 44.

on the regularity and predictability inflicted by rules and on the marginalization of those who would disrupt rules, patterning behavior and instilling a sense of normality and absence of alternative. This includes as well conscious attempts to manipulate expectations about the persistence of order, for without such expectations, obedience and compliance grow senseless (this is in part what primordialist claims to state community are all about, for by portraying the existing or coveted state community as a transhistorical entity, primordialists seek to manipulate expectations about its future persistence or materialization). Thus, effective order generates a sense of its own permanence, mesmerizing even those who oppose it and those who make their careers studying it into believing in its timelessness and immutability.

Sovietology was a victim of such expectations (though certainly not the only victim). In the aftermath of Stalin's death and the development of a sense of "normalcy" within Soviet society, the focus of scholarly research shifted toward issues of governance and away from issues of rule.[23] In the extensive scholarly debates over the Soviet future in the 1970s and 1980s, nearly every possibility was assiduously considered – but revolution, breakdown, and disintegration of the Soviet state were almost invariably dismissed as unlikely or impossible. As Theodore Draper noted, "If 'normal' social science expectations cannot cope with 'abnormal' times, they fail us when we need them most."[24]

As I have shown through this book, for the study of nationalism there is a particular need to understand the politics of "abnormal" times. "Every nation has several moments which may be called great," Merab Kostava, the Georgian nationalist leader, told hundreds of thousands of Georgians massed outside the House of Government in the late hours of April 8, 1989, the night of the fateful Tbilisi massacre that turned Georgian politics upside down and played such a critical role in shattering the Soviet state's coercive capacities against its opponents. "For Georgia that time has come now."[25] Like most nationalists, Kostava championed the timelessness of the nation. But as the above quotation implies, he also recognized that nationalism is not a constant but a contingency, and that the actions of

---

[23] Compare, for instance, Merle Fainsod's classic *How Russia Is Ruled* (Cambridge, MA: Harvard University Press, 1953) with Jerry Hough's rewrite *How the Soviet Union is Governed* (Cambridge, MA: Harvard University Press, 1979).

[24] Theodore Draper, "Who Killed Soviet Communism?" *The New York Review of Books*, June 11, 1992, p. 8.

[25] *Ekspress khronika*, no. 15, April 10, 1990.

nationalist activists and their followers are a central aspect in the recognition of the nation as potent category of meaning. The role of action within nationalism is twofold: Not only is its presence or absence generally taken as a sign of nationalism's success or failure, but action is also meant to alter the chances of nationalism's success by challenging normalized practices, ongoing modes of causation, and established systems of authority.

The way in which pre-existing structural conditions, institutional constraints, and action itself conspire to imbue some nationalisms with force and to deprive others of the same provides new meaning to Gellner's insight that "Nationalism as such is fated to prevail, but not any one particular nationalism."[26] For if it is in and through action that particular nationalisms succeed or fail, and if the occasions and outcomes of action are themselves highly contingent and dependent in part on the actions of others, then nationhood in its concrete manifestations is indeed permeated with a tremendous degree of arbitrariness and uncertainty. As Michael Mann described the event-dependent conjunctures surrounding the rise of nations in late-eighteenth and early-nineteenth century Europe:

> Though the nation's rise seems inexorable when viewed teleologically from the twentieth century, in this period it advanced contingently . . . Had Louis XVI compromised, had the Brissotins foreseen that war would destroy them, had the French troops at Valmy run away (as they were expected to do), had the Directory not produced a consummate general who proved an insensitive conqueror and who made one terrible decision to invade Russia . . . these, and other "might have beens" might have stemmed the national tide.[27]

Contrary to Mann, I do not mean to imply that with the failure of any specific nationalism, other nationalisms would not have emerged; nationalism is a ubiquitous feature of a world of states (as Gellner noted, like gravity: "an important and pervasive force, but not, at *most* times, strong enough to be violently disruptive").[28] The objects at the center of nationalist contention – the configuration of the state's territorial boundedness, its membership, its rules of cultural intercourse – are enduring objects of politics in a world of rationalized political authority. But the dependence of nationhood on the conjuncture and outcome of the event injects a

---

[26] Ernest Gellner, *Nations and Nationalism* (Ithaca, NY: Cornell University Press, 1983), p. 47.
[27] Michael Mann, *The Sources of Social Power*, vol. 2 (Cambridge, UK: Cambridge University Press, 1993), p. 246.
[28] Ernest Gellner, *Encounters with Nationalism* (Oxford: Blackwell, 1994), p. xi.

deeper set of contingencies into nationalism than even Gellner's theory recognized. For the outcomes of nationalist politics are dependent not only on which configuration of nationhood states and their opponents choose to champion and whether the rise of industrial civilization leads some losers, in Gellner's words, to history's dustheap even before offering resistance. Those who do offer resistance still must confront the eventful contingencies involved in the politics of contention. Even improbable nations can sometimes succeed due to their linkages with other successful nationalisms and the ability of politicians to ride nationalism's tidal force.

If most nationalist movements that do succeed could never have done so in isolation from the contiguous example of the successes of others, if much of the structural facilitation that successful nationalist movements possess consists of their ability to take advantage of the actions of others, if some degree of structural disadvantage can be mitigated by riding the tide of nationalism generated by the actions of others, if nationhood often materializes suddenly and unexpectedly for large numbers of people, and if the failure of nationalisms can be ascribed in part to the inability or absence of opportunity to take advantage of actions by others, then there is an additional set of dependencies involved in the rise of nations that inheres in the sequence of, connections between, and outcomes emerging from events. One might go still further and observe that at any concrete moment, the specific constellation of recognized claims to nationhood in the world should not be understood as simply the result of the imaginings of intellectuals and bureaucracies or as merely the consequent manifestation of structural, secular forces. It is rather a reflection of the concrete ways in which a politics of contention has played itself out within the conjuncture of the event. For when a mighty superpower routinely accepted as a cornerstone of the international community can vanish entirely from the historical stage within a compressed and tempestuous period of time, and when unimaginable and seemingly impossible nations can be transformed into the allegedly inevitable and preordained possessors of nation-states, such outcomes must at least in part be ascribed to the vulnerability of the modern multinational state to being overwhelmed by events and to the ways in which the contention inherent in the event lies implicit within nationhood itself.

# Appendix I

## *Procedures for Applying Event Analysis to the Study of Soviet Protest in the Glasnost' Era*

Event analysis is a method of tracking systematically over time the rise and fall of particular types of occurrences and the features associated with them. It first emerged in the social sciences in the 1960s as part of the behavioral revolution and was primarily used for cross-national studies of collective violence, wars, and military coups. Charles Tilly's work marked a turning point in applications of the method to the study of collective action, refocusing it toward analysis of temporal trends and linkages and purging it of some of the narrow behavioralist orientation that characterized early applications.[1]

In addition to allowing systematic analysis of temporality in social and political relationships, one of the chief advantages of event analysis is its great flexibility.[2] Events can be segmented by their particular characteristics. They can be aggregated at almost any meaningful level of space or time. It is a misnomer to speak of a single methodology of event analysis. Although certain common practices have emerged to ensure methodological rigor, the method has been operationalized differently in practically every application. Standardization of categories, definitions, and approaches across objects of analysis has remained elusive. Even the events

---

[1] Charles Tilly, Louise Tilly, and Richard Tilly, *The Rebellious Century, 1830–1930* (Cambridge: Harvard University Press, 1975); Charles Tilly, *From Mobilization to Revolution* (Reading, MA: Addison-Wesley, 1978); Charles Tilly, *The Contentious French* (Cambridge, MA: Belknap Press, 1986); Charles Tilly, *Popular Contention in Great Britain, 1758–1834* (Cambridge, MA: Harvard University Press, 1995).
[2] For a useful review of approaches, see Sidney Tarrow, "Contentious Event Analysis: Eventful History, Event Histories, and Events-in-History," in Dieter Rucht, Friedhelm Neidhardt, and Ruud Koopmans, eds., *Acts of Dissent: New Developments in the Study of Protest* (Berlin: Sigma Press, 1998), pp. 33–64.

460

that scholars have taken as objects of study have varied widely. Researchers must ultimately make decisions about which forms of action deserve to be analyzed, what features of those actions are worthy of attention, what sources should be used to gain information about these events, and how one should organize the process of recording information. In a well-formulated study, both theory and context must interact to inform these choices.

Although other modes of collective action existed in the protest repertoires of Soviet citizens, demonstrations, mass violent events, and strikes comprised the most salient forms of collective action during the *glasnost'* period. The rise of the demonstration, the strike, and the mass violent event was closely linked with the liberalization of politics under *glasnost'*. In the repressive atmosphere of the 1960s and 1970s, these forms of contention were relatively rare; less confrontational forms of contention, such as the petition and the hunger strike, were more frequently deployed by dissident groups. Ideally, in this study information on other acts of contention (such as petitioning, hunger strikes, and terrorist actions) should have been collected to obtain a more complete picture of how protest repertoires evolved over time. However, given the sheer volume of events and the fact that the focus of analysis was not protest repertoires per se but rather nationalism, there were good theoretical and practical justifications for omitting them. Also, although I collected information on strikes, I chose not to make them a central part of the investigation for several reasons. The great variation in the units of analysis to which the descriptions of these events refer – ranging from small enterprises and shops within enterprises to entire regions and republics – made a simple event count difficult to interpret. Moreover, information on the number of enterprises participating and, better yet, the number of participants (both more meaningful measures of strike mobilization) was sporadic in press sources and had to be estimated from other information. Finally, my analyses of strike activity led me to conclude that this information changed little substantively in the arguments made in the book. I therefore confined the discussion mainly to demonstrations and mass violent events.

Event databases for demonstrations and mass violent events were constructed over a six-year period from July 1989 through June 1995. The data were based on a multiple-source media sample of protest events, described in detail in Appendix II. Over 150 different news sources were examined by myself and a team of assistants for accounts of these events. The sources included not only Western newspaper, wire service, and U.S.

government sources, but also a wide variety of émigré publications, central and local Soviet newspapers, and unofficial *samizdat* sources, including Russian-language newspapers of opposition political movements throughout the former Soviet Union, source material drawn from unofficial libraries and archives in Moscow, unofficial wire services, and source material drawn from Radio Liberty's *Arkhiv samizdata* in Munich. Accounts of these events were first assembled in the form of a file archive containing all the various media descriptions for each event and organized by the date and place of the occurrence. This archive was then analyzed and coded. Certain sources, because of their richness, could not easily be placed in the archive. Instead, they were coded concurrently with the materials from the archive for each event.[3] An initial pilot coding of the first one hundred files allowed for adjustment of data categories and for ironing out difficulties in the coding process. The coding of all material, involving the combination and at times reconciliation of diverse accounts of an event and their entry directly into the databases, was accomplished by myself and an assistant knowledgeable in Russian for each event entered. Thus, the coding of each event was essentially reviewed by two pairs of eyes, and I was involved in the coding of every event. This practice was followed in large part because of the difficulties involved in combining and reconciling information from disparate sources and in relying on coding teams for Russian-language material. Although it minimized issues of coder reliability, it obviously placed a heavy burden on the researcher.

For the purposes of this study, a demonstration was defined as an event that met the following five criteria: (1) it was a voluntary gathering of persons with the purpose of engaging in a collective display of sentiment for or against public policies;[4] (2) it involved a minimum of one hundred persons; (3) it was bounded by space and time (that is, occurred in a specific location during a limited time period); (4) the number of participants was not restricted by the organizers of the event (that is, it was not a conference, convention, or other restricted organized meeting);[5] and (5) it did not have as its primary purpose the infliction of violence by its participants (that is, was not a mass violent event). The Russian vocabulary for events of this type is rich, including such terms as *demonstratsiia* (demonstration),

---

[3] These included *Vesti iz SSSR*, *Ekspress khronika*, and *Yezhednevnaia glasnost'*.

[4] Demonstrations that failed to materialize because they were intercepted by the police before action could be initiated were not counted. For an example, see *Radio Liberty Research Bulletin*, RL 258/88, June 17, 1988, p. 2.

[5] For this reason, meetings held inside a building were excluded from analysis.

*miting* (meeting), *protest* (protest), *manifestatsiia* (manifestation), and *panakhida* (funeral procession). Most Russian words used to describe demonstrations are of foreign origin – indicative of the extent to which such behavior was learned from analogous behavior abroad, particularly in the late nineteenth century. Actions which did not involve voluntary participation but which were mobilized by the political authorities and were ritual in character (official May Day or Revolution Day parades) were excluded from the analysis, for such events were not voluntary, and participation was not open to anyone who desired to participate. Mass demonstrations sponsored or encouraged by the political authorities that were voluntary and nonritual in nature were included.

Like all events, demonstrations are unique in time and space. However, multiple events sometimes do occur in the same city on the same day, requiring rules for how to treat them. For instance, on May 28, 1989 four separate and largely unrelated demonstrations took place in Moscow. A thousand Armenians gathered to commemorate the independent Armenian republic of 1918–20;[6] a hundred Crimean Tatars gathered outside the Bulgarian embassy to protest the treatment of Turks in Bulgaria;[7] one hundred and fifty thousand Muscovites participated in a demonstration sponsored by the Moscow Popular Front and Memorial concerning the First USSR Congress of People's Deputies, then in session;[8] and a thousand Muscovites participated in a demonstration sponsored by the more radical Democratic Union calling for democratization of the USSR.[9] These events took place in separate locations and were organized by disparate movements with different purposes in mind. In such cases, every effort was made to count these occurrences as independent events. In large demonstrations, particularly those organized by coalitions of groups, sometimes a portion of the participants broke off from the main crowd and held separate marches or protests. Sometimes small groups that held separate demonstrations later joined large crowds. In instances when either of these conditions was detectable, these cases were considered parts of one large, related event rather than a series of separate events.

[6] *Vesti iz SSSR*, 9/10–2, 1989; *Yezhednevnaia glasnost'*, May 29, 1989.
[7] *Ekspress khronika*, no. 23, June 4, 1989.
[8] *Vesti iz SSSR*, 9/10–9, 1989; *Report on the USSR*, vol. 1, no. 29 (July 21, 1989), p. 26; *Yezhednevnaia glasnost'*, May 29, 1989.
[9] *Vesti iz SSSR*, 9/10–9, 1989.

Table AI.1. *Size of Protest Demonstrations in the Former USSR, 1987–92*

| Number of participants | No. of events | Percent |
| --- | --- | --- |
| <100 | n.a. | n.a. |
| 100–999 | 2,560 | 38.4% |
| 1,000–4,999 | 2,035 | 30.5% |
| 5,000–9,999 | 781 | 11.7% |
| 10,000–19,999 | 402 | 6.0% |
| 20,000–29,999 | 208 | 3.1% |
| 30,000–49,999 | 211 | 3.2% |
| 50,000–99,999 | 189 | 2.8% |
| 100,000–199,999 | 122 | 1.8% |
| 200,000–499,999 | 118 | 1.8% |
| Greater than 500,000 | 37 | 0.6% |
| TOTAL | 6,663 | 100% |

I chose to impose a minimum size of a hundred participants for the demonstrations analyzed in this study because of the inconsistency with which small events were covered in the media sources used to construct the event data. Media coverage of events before and after a mobilizational cycle is likely to be radically different from media coverage of events during a cycle. Before and after a cycle, small events tend to receive greater coverage, whereas during a cycle, when it is not uncommon for protest events to attract tens and hundreds of thousands of participants, small events tend to be covered poorly. In a study of 321 demonstrations by Soviet ethnic groups from 1965 to 1978, David Kowalewski found that most demonstrations during those years were small, with 58 percent having less than a hundred participants, and most having less than fifty.[10] Similarly, as Table AI.1 indicates, during the 1987–92 period the bulk of protest demonstrations were small. Given the sheer number of demonstrations during the *glasnost'* period and the poor coverage of smaller events by the media, and in view of the political insignificance of smaller events generally, the size minimum made sense.

I defined a mass violent event as a mass political action whose primary purpose was to inflict violence in the form of an attack on people or

[10] David Kowalewski, "Protest for National Rights in the USSR: Characteristics and Consequences," *Nationalities Papers*, vol. 8, no. 2 (Fall 1980), pp. 179–94.

property. A minimum size of fifteen persons was used to distinguish these events from terrorist, criminal, or other small-scale acts of violence. In constructing the study, I recognized the possibility that demonstrations and mass violent events might overlap. Violent events can (and often do) involve nonviolent mass demonstrations, and nonviolent mass demonstrations can (and at times do) evolve into violent mass mobilization. In such cases, the relevant dimension of these events was included in both the demonstrations data and the mass violent event data. All mass violent events analyzed in this study fell into six categories: riots, pogroms, brawls, communal violence, armed combat, and insurrections. A riot was defined as mob violence against established social or political authority (in the form of property or the institutions of the state). The term pogrom was limited to ethnically based mob actions with clearly defined aggressor and victim groups. Brawls were defined as street fights among groups or individuals. Communal violence referred to mass violence between members of different ethnic or other culturally based groups. Armed combat referred to sustained mass armed struggle between two groups. Insurrection was defined as a mass revolt against the state with the aim of seizing power. The Russian words used to describe mass violent events include the terms *besporiadki* (disorders), *pogrom* (pogrom), *drak* (fight), *volneniia* (disturbances), *stychki* (clashes), *boi* (battles), and *miatezh* (insurrection).

In all, forty categories of information were collected and coded for each demonstration and thirty categories for each mass violent event. The complete codebook for the data is available from the author on request. The following is a list of the more important categories for which information was coded.

**Sources (SOURCE1, SOURCE2, SOURCE3).** Published sources of information used in compiling the data.

**Starting date (STARTDATE).** The beginning date of a demonstration. Events for which a specific date could not be determined from the source material were excluded from the analysis.[11] In rare cases when the precise date of an event was not available but the month in which the event occurred was known, such events were included at the beginning, end, or

[11] For examples of events excluded on the basis of these criteria, see *Radio Liberty Research Bulletin*, 350/88, August 5, 1988, p. 13; *Zaria vostoka*, January 4, 1989, p. 2.

middle of the month, whichever seemed the most probable from the source description.

**Duration of event (DURATION).** The number of days which an event lasted. In essence, this functioned as a multiplier in the analysis. Since a one-day demonstration hardly represented the same mobilizational effort as a seventeen-day continuous occupation of a square, in the analyses performed in this book I weighted the event-count by the duration of events. All protests that occurred on a particular day were considered to have lasted a day in duration, even though in most cases they lasted for only several hours.

**Location of event (PLACENAME, PROVINCE, REPUBLIC).** The city, town, or village in which the event occurred, as well as the province and republic in which this was located. Events for which a specific place could not be determined from the source material were excluded from the analysis.[12] In the few cases in which the event stretched across a geographic unit (such as the "human chain" of protest organized across the Baltic on August 23, 1989),[13] this was indicated by including the end points of the protest action within a specific province or republic.

**Population size of event location (PLACESIZE).** The population of the city, town, or village in which the event occurred, according to data from the 1979 Soviet census (the last currently available at the time the study began), in thousands. If an event location had a population of less than fifty thousand (and therefore was not reported in census data), the location was examined in various atlases to differentiate between locales of less than ten thousand in size and those ranging between ten thousand and fifty thousand in population.

**Type of event (EVENTTYPE) [mass violent events only].** All mass violent events were classified into six categories: pogroms, riots, brawls, communal violence, armed combat, and insurrections.

---

[12] For an example of an event excluded on the basis of these criteria, see *Report on the USSR*, vol. 1, no. 8 (February 24, 1989), p. 49.
[13] *Vesti iz SSSR*, 15/16–5, 1989; *Atmoda*, August 28, 1989, p. 1.

**Estimates of number of participants (EST1PARTIC, EST2PARTIC, EST3PARTIC) [demonstrations only].** The number of participants in the demonstration, at the moment of its largest size. The number of participants in a demonstration can fluctuate drastically over the course of an event. Crowds of ten thousand, for instance, may gather on a square in the morning; by evening, the same demonstration may have tens or hundreds of thousands of participants. The variables here all reflect reported information on the peak number of participants mentioned in descriptions of the event. In all, specific information on the number of participants was available for 68 percent of the demonstrations recorded. Since estimating the size of crowds is an art rather than a science, divergent estimates were recorded whenever available.[14] Extreme deviant estimates were eliminated in cases of multiple figures. In those cases in which multiple estimates existed but did not diverge, they were not recorded. Two divergent crowd estimates were recorded for 15 percent of demonstrations, and three divergent estimates were recorded for 3 percent of demonstrations. The phrase "several" (*nemnogo*) was always interpreted to mean "3."

**Size category (CATGPARTIC) [demonstrations only].** A categorical variable ranging from one to ten and reflecting a range of number of participants. The following categories were used: (1) 100–999 participants; (2) 1,000–4,999 participants; (3) 5,000–9,999 participants; (4) 10,000–19,999 participants; (5) 20,000–29,999 participants; (6) 30,000–49,999 participants; (7) 50,000–99,999 participants; (8) 100,000–199,999 participants; (9) 200,000–499,999 participants; and (10) 500,000 or more participants. For those events which had precise estimates in their sources, this range was determined simply by averaging these estimates. But in the 32 percent of demonstrations for which no precise size was given in sources, a size category was estimated based on two types of information. If the number of participants was listed in a source as being in the hundreds (*sotni*), the thousands (*tysachi*), or the many thousands (*mnogotysachnyi*), these were generally assigned size categories 1, 2, and 3 respectively.[15] In those cases (a relatively small proportion of the sample) for which information on the size of a demonstration was still missing, a search was made in the

---

[14] On the controversies that estimates of crowd sizes produced in the USSR at the time, see *Izvestiia*, in *FBIS*, March 12, 1990, p. 76.

[15] In a few instances the term "many thousands" was given a higher size category when it appeared to merit this from the context reported in the description.

database for the closest similar events in time that occurred in the same city, were organized by the same group, and put forward the same demands. The size category of that event was used as the basis for the size category of the demonstration in question. Given the size and scope of the database, analogous events were almost always available for comparison. In the very rare cases when no information whatsoever was available, a size category of "1" was assigned.

**Participation score (PARTIC) [demonstrations only].** This figure was used for final calculation of participation rates in demonstrations. For those events which had precise estimates in their sources, it was calculated by averaging these estimates. For those events which had no precise estimate but only a size category, the low end of the range of the size category was used. The variable was weighted by the duration of a demonstration.

**Estimated participants in mass violence (TOTALPART) [mass violent events only].** Accounts of participation in mass violence differ significantly from those of demonstrations, justifying a separate count for these types of events. Only in 21 percent of all mass violent events recorded were specific group sizes given in sources.

**Nationality of participants (NATPART1, NATPART2).** The nationality of the bulk of participants. In some instances, a second nationality was in evidence, in which case this information was also recorded. If the demonstration was clearly nonnational in character and the participants recruited from multiple groups, the variables were coded as "pan-national in character." The nationality of participants was almost always self-evident from the social movement that organized the event or the demands put forth.

**Demonstration demands (DEMAND1, DEMAND2, . . . DE-MAND5) [demonstrations only].** The issues over which the demonstration occurred. These were either voiced in speeches at the event, implicit in the nature of the event itself, listed in a formal list of demands presented by the demonstrators, displayed on placards or banners, or implied by the behavior of demonstrators at the event. In all, 491 different demands were coded, with every attempt made to keep these categories as specific as possible. This allowed for flexibility in responding to the changing character of demands over the course of the cycle. These 491 demands were subsequently aggregated into broader categories of protest (secessionist, antisecessionist, and so forth). Only for two demonstrations was nothing known about the demands of demonstrators.

**Ostensible causes of mass violence (CAUSE1, CAUSE2, CAUSE3) [mass violent events only].** Mass violent events did not have formal "demands" in the same way as demonstrations. Yet, obviously there were issues or causes that stood behind them. An effort was made to classify the ostensible causes of violent events. These causes are "ostensible" in the sense that they are mentioned in sources. Multiple causes (up to three) were assumed to exist, and in cases where more than three were mentioned, those mentioned in more authoritative sources (or, in the absence of a more authoritative source, mentioned with greatest frequency) were selected. I made no attempt to differentiate between primary, secondary, or implicit causes of violence, accepting only those causes mentioned in sources as valid for coding purposes. Some effort was made to link events that deserved to be considered as a single wave of violence.

**Organizer of event (ORGAN1IZER, ORGAN2IZER, ORGAN-3IZER) [demonstrations only].** Up to three social movements that acted as organizers of a demonstration were recorded.

**Social groups associated with participants (PARTCAT1, PARTCAT2) [mass violent events only].** As noted in sources, information on other social characteristics (besides nationality) of the participants.

**Target of event (NATTARGET, LOC1TARGET, LOC2TARGET, ETHTARGET, ENTTARGET, PROPTARGET, OTHTARGET).** Recorded the targets of mobilization. These were categorized as central Soviet state or party institutions; republican state or party institutions of the republic in which the organizers were located; local (defined as federal units below the union republican level) state or party institutions of the local political unit in which the organizers were located; republican state or party institutions of another republic; local state or party institutions of another local unit; an ethnic group; enterprise management; property; or other target.

**Degree of coercion by authorities (VIOLEVEL) [demonstrations only].** A categorization summarizing the coercive measures taken by the authorities against demonstrators. The following coding was used: (0) no known coercion; (1) physical harassment of demonstrators by police or summoning of participants to police before or after event; (2) low-level coercion (sporadic arrests and/or injuries, defined as less than ten); (3) substantial coercion (defined as ten to seventy-five arrests or ten to forty injuries); and (4) major violence by authorities (defined as more than seventy-five arrests or more than forty injuries).

**Number of arrests (ARRESTNUM).** The number of participants detained by the police or subjected to sanctions by the authorities in any way (either before, during, or after the event). For demonstrations information on arrests appeared systematically in sources; for mass violent events it was reported sporadically.

**Punishment of those arrested (SANCTIONS) [for demonstrations only].** A four-level categorization of the sanctions imposed by the state against those arrested, coded in the following way: (0) no known sanctions imposed (quickly released); (1) fines imposed, or participant fired from work or expelled from city; (2) minor imprisonment (less than sixty days); (3) major imprisonment (sixty days or more).

**Number of injured at event (INJUREDNUM, DEMINJURED, POLINJURED).** The number of injuries (both to participants and to law-enforcement personnel) as a result of the event. For demonstrations, an attempt was made to separate injuries to participants and to police, although this was not always possible. Also, reported injuries in sources sometimes consisted of only those injured participants who subsequently asked for medical assistance rather than all participants who were actually injured at the event.[16]

**Number of deaths at event (DEATHSNUM, DEMDEATHS, POLDEATHS).** The number of deaths (both among participants and law-enforcement personnel) as a result of the event. For demonstrations, an attempt was made to separate participant deaths from police deaths.

---

[16] See Radio Kiev, in *FBIS*, November 9, 1989, p. 89, for a case in which many of the injured at a demonstration were not counted because they did not ask for medical assistance.

## Appendix I

**Degree of intensity of mass violence (VIOLEVEL) [for mass violent events only].** A five-point interval scale adapted from other studies of mass violence[17] that reflected the human and property damage inflicted by mass violence.

**Technological level of weaponry (WEAPONLEV) [mass violent events only].** The sophistication of weaponry was classified into four levels, based on the highest level of weaponry utilized in an event: (1) rudimentary (fists, sticks, knives, stones, and so forth); (2) small firearms and homemade explosives; (3) automatic weapons; and (4) sophisticated weaponry (rockets, tanks, helicopter gunships, armored personnel carriers, and so forth).

---

[17] See Seymour Spilerman, "Structural Characteristics of Cities and the Severity of Racial Disorders," *American Sociological Review*, vol. 41, no. 5 (October 1976), pp. 773–74.

# Appendix II

## *Sources for the Compilation of Event Data in a Revolutionary Context*

Most event analyses of mobilizational cycles have been conducted within a West European or North American context. Constructing event data for a revolutionary context like the Soviet Union during *glasnost'* presents problems different from those found in relatively more open polities or those in which the national frame of the state is not under open contestation.

The USSR was a polity which had experienced massive violent repressions and extensive restrictions on freedom of expression. In the period prior to *glasnost'*, police records could be expected to reflect the mentality and biases of a security apparatus charged with extirpating all acts of dissidence, although an apparatus which ultimately failed in its mission. Moreover, in the aftermath of regime change these records themselves have been at the center of controversy, since they could be utilized as weapons for political compromise and intrigue (not to mention their continued security value to postcommunist governments). Party archives have been opened throughout much of the former Soviet Union, but for the most part KGB and police records covering the post-Stalin period have not. By the end of 1990 Soviet researchers working with the USSR Ministry of Internal Affairs were provided with daily reports on major acts of mass protest; these reports covered a small part of the mobilizational cycle, were usually presented in index form, and failed to differentiate between types of events. Only in the city of Minsk were independent scholars provided access to the local police records of protest actions[1] – though Minsk

[1] See Larissa Titarenko and John McCarthy, "The Evolution of Protest Form During the Transition from Communism in Minsk, Belarus, 1990–1995," *Mobilization*, vol. 6, no. 2 [forthcoming 2001].

was not a major site of the nationalist upheavals that overtook the Soviet Union.

Even if police records from the *glasnost'* era were available, they would still raise reliability issues. Not surprisingly, police estimates of the number of participants in demonstrations differed significantly from those found in media sources, with the gap larger during the early part of the mobilizational cycle.[2] Moreover, in some cases police estimates of crowds so differed from those of multiple and independent Western eyewitnesses (not to mention those of social movement activists) as to be implausible. Descriptions of repressive police actions against demonstrators are likely to be even more biased. During this period the police at times provoked demonstrators in order to incite violence and justify repression. As evident from the behavior of top-level police officials (such as KGB chief Vladimir Kriuchkov or MVD chief Boriss Pugo), the police also engaged in systematic disinformation efforts not only toward society, but also toward their own superiors.

Alternatively, event analysis can be constructed on press-based sources. But press-based sources within a revolutionary context such as this also present special problems. The explosion of events that characterized the *glasnost'* mobilizational cycle made it difficult for any single media source to cover events consistently over the course of the cycle. The example of the newsletter *Vesti iz SSSR*, published from 1978 through 1990 by Kronid Liubarskii, demonstrates well the inability of any single source to encompass the record of protest mobilization in a period of "thickened" history. After his forced emigration from the USSR, Liubarskii was approached by several human rights organizations about establishing a central collection point for information about the human rights movement in the USSR. This project eventually turned into *Vesti iz SSSR*, a bimonthly newsletter based in Munich on the human rights movement in the Soviet Union. Relying on established networks of dissidents throughout the USSR, *Vesti* reported systematically on any act of protest that came to the attention of the human rights movement during the late 1970s and early 1980s. *Vesti* was well situated to report on protest events in the early part of the *glasnost'* cycle and became an outstanding news source on mobilizational acts of all kinds. But in January 1990 Liubarskii ceased reporting on mass events and focused instead on bringing individual cases of human rights abuse to light. As Liubarskii explained:

[2] See Table AII.3.

The geography of events has broadened, their scale and tempo increased. Over the last few years the editor has tried to keep up with events, attempting to give, albeit in a condensed form, a full picture of what was going on in the country. The bulletin has been constantly expanding. More and more often the quantity of information has made it impossible to process the news quickly, meaning that we have had to put out double issues and forgo the periodicity that we started out with. ... It has become clear that to continue publication on the previous basis was simply physically impossible. In any case the point of doing so has to a great extent disappeared. A significant proportion of such information about events in the USSR has started appearing in numerous other publications, both *samizdat* and official, as well as in the foreign press.[3]

Much as the quickened pace of events within "thickened" history overwhelms the ability of government to take their measure, it also overtakes the media's capacity to cover them, making it impossible for any single source to provide accurate coverage of what transpires.

Moreover, the Soviet Union under *glasnost'* was a transitional society. The shift from repression to contestation, which involved an explosion in the possibilities of public expression, also made it difficult to base an analysis of mobilization on any single press source or set of sources. Because of the continued legacies of censorship, in the early stages of the mobilizational cycle foreign, émigré, and underground (*samizdat*) publications were the most accessible and reliable sources of information about protest events. These, of course, contained their own biases, but they did afford extensive coverage of events which, for political reasons, were not covered in the official media. By the latter stages of the cycle, however, protest actions were regularly reported in the official media and in the burgeoning independent press sector that had emerged. Indeed, throughout *glasnost'* the press (like the rest of the polity) underwent radical change. Whereas studies of protest mobilization in advanced industrial societies deal with an institutionalized press, making a single-source or several-source study feasible, these conditions are absent in contexts where an independent press emerges concurrently with mobilization.

Figure AII.1 portrays some indicators of the development of an independent press sector in the Soviet Union during the *glasnost'* years drawn from the holdings of the *Arkhiv samizdata* (Samizdat Archive) at Radio Liberty[4] and a recurrent survey of the independent press conducted by the

---

[3] *Vesti iz SSSR*, no. 1, 1990, pp. 1–2. Eventually, Liubarskii closed *Vesti* altogether and emigrated back to Russia.

[4] The data are based on Part 2 of the catalogue to the archive, published in *Materialy samizdata*, no. 13 (November 4, 1991), pp. 143–55.

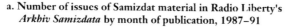

a. Number of issues of Samizdat material in Radio Liberty's
*Arkhiv Samizdata* by month of publication, 1987–91

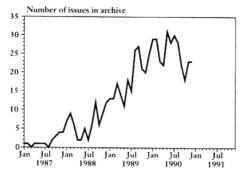

b. Number of independent publications in existence
in USSR, 1987–91 (SMOT Samizdat Census)

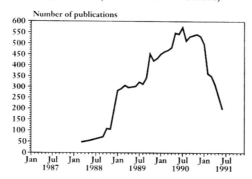

**Figure AII.1.** Development of an independent press sector in the Soviet Union,
1987–91.

unofficial trade union SMOT.[5] It shows how the evolution of the independent press sector followed broadly the patterns of the mobilizational cycle. An independent press sector in the Soviet Union emerged by the end of 1987, before the first major explosions in protest activity in early 1988, but did not develop on a significant scale until early 1989, well after the first large waves of mobilization. The organization of demonstrations and the organization of publications are both elite-led activities obviously influenced strongly by the openness of the political order. But although

[5] The data come from an examination of the full press run of *Informatsionnyi biulleten' SMOTa* from 1988 through 1991.

both followed much the same general trajectory, closer examination reveals that on a monthly basis independent press activity and press coverage of demonstrations varied independently of each other (that is, trends in the demonstration data are not a mere reflection of the rise of independent media).[6] The heyday of the independent press was in 1989 and 1990, when hundreds of publications burst into existence, many of them fly-by-night operations run by social movements. The number of independent publications peaked at about the same time as the number of demonstrations in the mobilizational cycle (mid-1990). Much like the fluidity within the social movement sector, the independent press sector was highly unstable, with publications appearing with great irregularity and, in many cases, disappearing as quickly as they had appeared. By early 1991 the number of independent press publications began to decline sharply – due in part to financial and organizational difficulties, in part to a vexing shortage of paper. On the eve of the breakup of the USSR in June 1991, there were fewer independent press publications than had been in existence in January 1989, with a shift away from party and social movement publications and toward commercial publications. Although not covered in these figures, the drop in independent publishing activity did not alter significantly after the breakup of the USSR. This shake-out within the independent press and the growing institutionalization of the press developed well after the institutionalization of protest mobilization in the wake of the 1990 elections. Moreover, the organization of protest demonstrations continued apace despite the decline in independent publications.

Thus, although scholars studying protest in advanced industrial societies prefer a single set of newspaper sources available throughout the entire period under study to ensure consistency in coverage, the reality is that in a revolutionary society like Gorbachev's USSR, this is impossible. In a revolutionary society the best strategy available to a researcher may well be a "blanketing" strategy, utilizing multiple sources and multiple types of information whenever they are available. In the Soviet Union, for

---

[6] For example, when one controls for time (representing the general trend of political liberalization during this period) and corrects for serial correlation of error terms, there is no statistically significant relationship between the number of issues in the *samizdat* archive and the number of demonstrations per month. Even without controlling for time (that is, liberalization), the number of issues in the archive would account for only 14 percent of the total variation in the demonstration data in any case. Monthly levels of participation in demonstrations and monthly trends in the development of the independent press sector varied entirely independently of one another.

# Appendix II

Table AII.1. *Coverage of Demonstrations and Mass Violent Events in the Former USSR by More Commonly Used Sources*

| Source | Dates of coverage | Proportion of events analyzed during period that contained some coverage by source | |
| --- | --- | --- | --- |
| | | Demonstrations | Mass violent events |
| *Foreign Broadcast Information Service, Daily Report* (English language, U.S. government publication) | 12/1/86–12/31/92 | 34.8% | 52.7% |
| *Vesti iz SSSR* (Russian language, émigré publication, Munich) | 12/1/86–12/31/89 | 61.9% | 51.3% |
| *Ekspress khronika* (Russian language, samizdat) | 11/1/88–12/31/92 | 42.9% | 48.9% |
| *Yezhednevnaia glasnost'* (Russian language, samizdat) | 5/1/89–5/31/91 | 32.2% | 10.2% |

instance, coverage of protest events by any single source was confined to a particular part of the cycle. As Table AII.1 indicates, even the best sources of information reported on only a fraction of the events we know about in the periods that they covered, and most covered only limited parts of the mobilizational cycle.[7] Of the events studied for this book, only 43.3 percent of demonstrations and 33.3 percent of mass violent events were reported on in more than one source; this highlights the lack of duplication in press coverage across sources for a significant number of events and the need to use multiple and disparate types of sources in order to gain a reasonably accurate record of what occurred. In those cases in which duplication of reporting occurred, disparate news sources often added significant information about an event that otherwise would have been lost, allowing for a greater consistency of analysis across events. For this

---

[7] Indeed, some of the best sources were forced to shut down publication for short periods in the middle of the mobilizational cycle. As a result of staff conflicts, for instance, *Yezhednevnaia glasnost'* ceased publication for several months in early 1991.

project, over 150 different news sources were examined, including not only Western newspaper, wire service, and U.S. government sources, but also a wide variety of émigré publications, central and local Soviet newspapers, and unofficial *samizdat* sources, including Russian-language newspapers of opposition political movements throughout the Soviet Union, source material drawn from unofficial libraries and archives in Moscow, unofficial wire services, and source material drawn from Radio Liberty's *Arkhiv samizdata* in Munich. Sixty of these sources were examined in their full press runs during the period under investigation.

We can get some idea of the gains in accuracy obtained from a multiple-source media sample by comparing the sample used in this study with others based on a subset of sources. Philip Roeder based an examination of nationalist mobilization in the early *glasnost'* period (September 1985–August 1989) on a reading of *The New York Times* and Radio Liberty's *Report on the USSR*. Excluding Russians within the RSFSR from his analysis, he found a total of 84 demonstrations with over ten thousand participants, 45 of which had over one hundred thousand participants.[8] By contrast, the multiple-source media sample used for this study includes 386 events with at least ten thousand participants that fit these criteria during the same period, 150 of which had at least one hundred thousand participants. For some kinds of analysis one might not care about missing so many large demonstrations, particularly if one is interested in tracking protest over years and decades rather months or weeks.[9] But if we are interested in comparing patterns of mobilization among subgroups of a population or analyzing the rise and fall of mobilization over time, a two-source sample such as Roeder's would be grossly inadequate. Table AII.2 presents a comparison by nationality between the Roeder sample and the multiple-source sample used in this study. As is evident, patterns of demonstrations with over one hundred thousand participants by nationality are not that radically different with the exception of the Georgians, whose mobilization is underestimated in the Roeder sample. When we examine demonstrations with ten thousand or more participants, however, the samples are drastically dissimilar. If we were interested only in patterns

[8] See Philip G. Roeder, "Soviet Federalism and Ethnic Mobilization," *World Politics*, vol. 43 (January 1991), pp. 196–232.
[9] Roeder was primarily interested in generalizing about the impact of education and the Soviet federal system on overall patterns of mobilization, although his sample of nationalities was too small and the time period examined too limited to draw firm conclusions.

Table AII.2. *A Comparison of Coverage of Demonstrations in Two-Source and Multiple-Source Media Samples, September 1985–August 1989*

| | Number of events covered | | | |
|---|---|---|---|---|
| | Greater than 100 thous. participants | | Greater than 10 thous. participants | |
| Nationality | Two-source sample[a] | Multiple-source sample | Two-source sample[a] | Multiple-source sample |
| Armenians | 25 | 102 | 30 | 175 |
| Azerbaijanis | 9 | 18 | 19 | 27 |
| Lithuanians | 4 | 7 | 9 | 50 |
| Latvians | 3 | 7 | 7 | 17 |
| Georgians | 2 | 10 | 4 | 25 |
| Estonians | 2 | 4 | 4 | 11 |
| Moldavians | 1 | 1 | 6 | 17 |
| Uzbeks | 1 | 0 | 1 | 3 |
| "Exclave" Russians | 0 | 0 | 3 | 17 |
| Belorussians | 0 | 0 | 1 | 5 |
| Ukrainians | 0 | 1 | 0 | 39 |
| Kazakhs | 0 | 0 | 0 | 0 |
| Kirgiz | 0 | 0 | 0 | 0 |
| Tajiks | 0 | 0 | 0 | 0 |
| Turkmen | 0 | 0 | 0 | 0 |

[a] Data based on a reading of *The New York Times* and Radio Liberty's *Report on the USSR*, as presented in Philip G. Roeder, "Soviet Federalism and Ethnic Mobilization," *World Politics*, vol. 43 (January 1991), pp. 196–232.

of very large demonstrations among subgroups of a population, then a single- or two-source sample might be sufficient for some purposes. Most studies of mobilization, however, do not confine themselves to events with over one hundred thousand participants. Such a restriction would limit severely the types of questions one could ask.

Another dimension of the Soviet milieu which obviously would affect any effort to engage in event analysis is the multinational and multilingual character of Soviet society. Numerous Russian-language publications from all regions of the Soviet Union (including official and unofficial publications from nearly all the union republics and from remote regions of Russia) were used in this study, as well as occasional materials in Ukrainian, Belorussian, and Romanian. However, in a country in which

127 different ethnic groups were officially recognized by the state, it is obvious that a considerable amount of important source material appeared in languages that would be inaccessible to any researcher or, for that matter, research organization, causing potential problems of coverage bias. To some degree, this problem was offset by the extensive ties within the dissident community across national groups. During the *glasnost'* period a single information space existed for dissemination of news about protest actions. Widely recognized informational collection points for news about protest acts throughout the Soviet Union operated in much of the period studied and published regular accounts of events (for instance, Radio Liberty's *Report on the USSR, Vesti iz SSSR, Ekspress khronika, Yezhednev-naia glasnost'*, and *Informatsionnyi biulleten' SMOTa*). A number of these publications maintained their own extensive networks of native corre- spondents throughout the country who reported systematically on protest events. Other groups throughout the USSR attempted to create similar networks over large portions of the country, but many of these existed for a short time only.[10] Unofficial archives of ephemeral material also appeared and acted as collection points for social movement publications. This study benefited from access to the archives of the Moscow Library for Infor- mation Exchange (MBIO), which attempted to act as a repository for un- official publications from the entire territory of Russia, as well as a less complete record of publications from other republics as well. The collec- tion is housed at the Russian State Humanities University. I also worked extensively with unofficial publications collected at Radio Liberty's *Arkhiv samizdata*, then located in Munich and now part of the Open Media Research Institute's holdings in Prague. In addition, archivists at Radio Liberty's *Arkhiv samizdata* kept ongoing files of newspaper clippings and wire service reports on early protest events that covered a broad scope of sources. A number of Russian-language newspapers reported on pro- test events throughout the USSR with some regularity, although these operated primarily in the middle and latter parts of the cycle.[11] Some of the more significant events of the period (such as the August 1991 coup)

---

[10] Examples of such publications utilized in this study include: *Informatsionnyi biulleten' KAS-KOR, Sibirskoe Informatsionnoe Agentsvo [SibIA]* (Novosibirsk), *Center for Democracy Bulletin, EKhO, Khronika Matsne* (Tbilisi), *Sluzhba yezhednevnykh novostei, DS-Inform*, and *Agentsvo novostei i informatsii*.

[11] Examples of such newspapers that were utilized in this study are: *Nasha gazeta* (Kemerovo), *Tartuskii kur'er* (Tartu), *Atmoda* (Riga), *Soglasie* (Vil'nius), *Panorama, Svobodnoe slovo, Neza-visimaia gazeta*, and *Kommersant'*.

received book-length treatments which provided systematic chronological accounts of protest events throughout the USSR.[12] Several organizations also compiled chronologies of events, some of which proved useful in providing supplementary information.

The following is a listing of press sources used in compiling the event data.[13] Sources marked with an asterisk (*) were examined systematically during the relevant period of their publication; other sources were consulted occasionally or appeared as clippings in file collections used by the author.

## Western News Sources and Publications

    AFP Wire Service
    AP Wire Service
\*    *Arkhiv samizdata* (Radio Liberty)
    *The Boston Globe*
\*    *Center for Democracy Bulletin*
    *Central Asia and Caucasus Chronicle*
    *Chronicle of Human Rights*
    CMD Wire Service
\*    *Current Digest of the Soviet Press* (after 1991, *Current Digest of the Post-Soviet Press*)
    DPA Wire Service
\*    *Foreign Broadcast Information Service, Daily Report: Soviet Union*
    *Foreign Labor Trends: USSR* (US Department of Labor)
    *Le Monde*
    NCA Wire Service
    *Newsweek*

---

[12] See, for instance, *Putch: khronika trevozhnykh dnei* (Moscow: Progress, 1991); *Krasnoe ili beloe? – Drama Avgusta-91: Fakty, gipotezy, stolknovenie mnenii* (Moscow: Terra, 1992).

[13] In addition to some of the news sources cited below, a number of books and reports proved useful for compiling information on the pre-*glasnost'* record of mobilization. These included: Ludmilla Alexeeva and Valery Chalidze, "Mass Unrest in the USSR," Report No. 19, submitted to the Office of Net Assessment of the U.S. Department of Defense (OSD/NA 85-2965), August 1983; Ludmilla Alexeeva, *Soviet Dissent: Contemporary Movements for National, Religious, and Human Rights* (Middletown, CT: Wesleyan University Press, 1985); V. Ponomarev, *Obshchestvennye volneniia v SSSR: Ot XX s"ezda KPSS do smerti Brezhneva* (Moscow: Aziia, 1990); Vadim Belotserkovsky, "Workers' Struggles in the USSR in the Early Sixties," *Critique* (Winter/Spring 1978–79), pp. 37–50; Betsy Gidwitz, "Labor Unrest in the Soviet Union," *Problems of Communism* (November–December 1982), pp. 25–42.

*Radio Free Europe Background Reports*
\* *Radio Free Europe Baltic Area Report*
\* *Radio Liberty Research Bulletin*
\* *Report on the USSR* (Radio Liberty)
Reuters Wire Service
\* *RFE/RL Daily Report*
*The Baltimore Sun*
*The Financial Times*
*The Guardian*
*The London Independent*
*The London Times*
*The Los Angelos Times*
\* *The New York Times*
*The Wall Street Journal*
*The Washington Post*
*The Wisconsin State Journal*
UPI Wire Service


## Official Soviet or Post-Soviet News Sources and Publications
\* *Bakinskii rabochii* (Baku)
*Chelovek i zakon* (Moscow)
*Dnestrovskaia pravda* (Tiraspol')
*Ekonomika i zhizn'* (Moscow)
*Gudok* (Moscow)
\* *Izvestiia* (Moscow)
\* *Kazakhstanskaia pravda* (Alma-Ata)
\* *Kommunist* (Yerevan)
\* *Kommunist Tadzhikistana* (Dushanbe)
*Komsomolets Uzbekistana* (Tashkent)
*Komsomol'skaia pravda* (Moscow)
\* *Kuranty* (Moscow)
*Kuzbass* (Kemerovo)
*Leningradskaia pravda* (Leningrad)
*Leninskaia smena*
*Literaturnaia gazeta* (Moscow)
*Molodezh Estonii* (Tallin)
*Molodezh Gruzii* (Tbilisi)
\* *Moskovskie novosti* (Moscow)

*Moskovskii komsomolets* (Moscow)
Novosti Wire Service
*Pravda* (Moscow)
*Pravda severa* (Severoural'sk)
\*     *Pravda Ukrainy* (Kiev)
\*     *Pravda vostoka* (Tashkent)
*Rabochaia gazeta* (Moscow)
Radio Vil'nius (shortwave broadcasts to North America)
\*     *Rossiiskaia gazeta* (Moscow)
*Rossiiskie vesti* (Moscow)
*Sobesednik* (Moscow)
*Sotsialisticheskaia industriia* (Moscow)
\*     *Sovetskaia Belorussiia* (Minsk)
\*     *Sovetskaia Estoniia* (Tallin)
\*     *Sovetskaia Kirgiziia* (Frunze)
*Sovetskaia kul'tura* (Moscow)
\*     *Sovetskaia Latviia* (Riga)
*Sovetskaia molodezh* (Riga)
\*     *Sovetskaia Moldaviia* (Kishinev)
*Sovetskaia Rossiia* (Moscow)
TASS Wire Service
*Trud* (Moscow)
\*     *Turkmenskaia iskra* (Ashkhabad)
*Uchitel'skaia gazeta* (Moscow)
*Ural'skii rabochii* (Sverdlovsk)
Vesti (television news program, Moscow)
Vremia (television news program, Moscow)
\*     *Zaria vostoka* (Tbilisi)

## Émigré News Sources and Publications
\*     *Chronicle of Current Events*
\*     *ELTA Information Bulletin*
\*     *Glasnost'*
\*     *News from Ukraine*
\*     *Russkaia mysl'* (Paris)
\*     *The Samizdat Bulletin*
*Turkistan Today*
\*     *Vesti iz SSSR*

## Unofficial Soviet, or Post-Soviet, News Sources and Publications

\*     *Agentsvo novostei i informatsii* (Moscow)

     *Almanakh*

\*     *Al'ternativa* (Moscow)

\*     *Atmoda* (Riga)

\*     *Baltiiskoe vremia* (Riga)

\*     *Belorusskaia tribuna* (Minsk)

     *Cheliabinskii Esdek* (Cheliabinsk)

\*     *Demokraticheskaia gazeta* (Moscow)

     *Demokraticheskaia platforma*

\*     *Demokraticheskaia Rossiia* (Moscow)

     *Den'* (Moscow)

\*     *Diena* (Riga)

     *Domostroi*

\*     *DS-Inform* (Moscow)

\*     *EKhO*

\*     *Ekspress khronika* (Moscow)

     *Ekspress (Zheleznodorozhnogo raiona Moskvy)*

     *Golos* (Kiev)

     *Golos izbiratelia* (Moscow)

\*     *Info-20* (Murmansk)

     *Informatsionnyi biulleten' Aziia-Press*

\*     *Informatsionnyi biulleten' KAS-KOR* (Moscow)

     *Informatsionnyi biulleten' Smolenskogo narodnogo fronta* (Smolensk)

\*     *Informatsionnyi biulleten' SMOTa* (Moscow)

     *Informatsionnyi biulleten' ural'skikh Sotsial-demokratov* (Sverdlovsk)

     *Informatsionnyi biulleten' "Vozrozhdenie"* (Nizhnii Tagil')

     Interfax Wire Service

     *Istoriko-Literaturnyi Klub, Informatsionnyi biulleten'*

     *Izvestiia OSTK*

     *Kauno aidas* (Kaunas)

     *Khronika matsne* (Tbilisi)

\*     *Kommersant'* (Moscow)

     *Moskovskie vedemosti* (Moscow)

\*     *Nabat* (Khar'kov)

\*     *Nasha gazeta* (Kemerovo)

     *Nevskii kur'er* (Leningrad)

\*     *Nezavisimaia gazeta* (Moscow)

\*     *Novosti Sotsial-Demokratii* (Moscow)

       *Obshchaia gazeta* (Moscow)
       *Obshchina* (Moscow)
\*    *Panorama* (Moscow)
       *Posleslovie* (Tambov)
       Postfaktum Wire Service
       *Pozitsiia* (Moscow)
       *Rech'*
       *Russkii vestnik*
       *Saratovskii listok* (Saratov)
\*    *Sibirskoe Informatsionnoe Agentstvo* [*SibIA*] (Novosibirsk)
       *Sibirskii kur'er* (Novosibirsk)
       *Slovo* (Apatity)
       *Smena*
       *Sodeistvie*
\*    *Soglasie* (Vil'nius)
       *Soobshchaet informatsionnoe rabochee agentsvo*
       *Svoboda*
\*    *Svobodnoe slovo* (Moscow)
       *Svobodnyi Ural*
       *Tartuskii kur'er* (Tartu)
\*    *The Baltic Independent* (Riga)
       *Trudovoi Tiraspol'* (Tiraspol')
       *Ural'skaia respublika*
       *Vechernii Yekaterinburg* (Sverdlovsk)
       *Vestnik Gruzii* (Tbilisi)
\*    *Vestnik Interdvizheniia* (Tallin)
       *Vestnik narodnogo fronta* (Tallin)
       *Vestnik rabochego dvizheniia*
\*    *Vozrozhdenie* (Vil'nius)
       *Vozrozhdenie Rossii*
\*    *Yedinstvo* [Interfront] (Riga)
\*    *Yezhednevnaia glasnost'* (Moscow)

The single information space concerning protest actions that existed during the *glasnost'* period soon began to disintegrate in the wake of the breakup of the USSR. Over the course of 1992, media sources grew less diversified in their reporting; their coverage increasingly came to mirror the new patterns of state authority that the *glasnost'* tide of nationalism had brought into being. Moreover, language became a greater barrier to the

Table AII.3. *A Comparison of Published Police Statistics on Demonstrations with Coverage in a Multiple-Source Media Sample*

| Location | Dates | Number of demonstrations | | | Number of participants (thous.) | | |
|----------|-------|--------|--------|---------|--------|--------|---------|
| | | Police | Sample | Percent | Police | Sample | Percent |
| USSR | 1/1/88–12/31/88 | 2,328 | 665 | 28.6% | | | |
| USSR | 1/1/88–8/2/88 | 600 | 390 | 65.0% | | | |
| Latvia | 1/1/88–12/31/88 | 83 | 37 | 44.6% | 220 | 924 | 420.0% |
| Moscow | 5/26/88–6/10/88 | 40 | 8 | 20.0% | 2 | 3 | 150.0% |
| USSR | 1/1/89–12/31/89 | 5,300 | 1,496 | 28.2% | 12,600 | 30,047 | 238.5% |
| Ukraine | 1/1/89–9/30/89 | 724 | 226 | 31.2% | | | |
| Ukraine | 10/1/89–10/20/89 | 125 | 31 | 24.8% | | | |
| Uzbekistan | 1/1/89–10/30/89 | 200 | 32 | 16.0% | | | |
| USSR | 1/1/90–2/23/90 | 1,500 | 289 | 19.3% | 6,400 | 5,100 | 79.7% |
| USSR | 2/25/90 | 311 | 61 | 19.6% | 982 | 888 | 90.4% |
| Moscow | 1/1/91–3/31/91 | 180 | 19 | 10.5% | 1,000 | 1,735 | 173.5% |
| RSFSR | 3/15/92 | 73 | 22 | 30.1% | 35 | 17 | 49.4% |

*Sources for police statistics:*
*Kommunist* (Yerevan), December 24, 1989, p. 1; TASS, August 2, 1988; Radio Moscow World Service, in *FBIS*, June 13, 1988, p. 62; *Brianskii rabochii*, February 9, 1989, p. 3; *Pravda*, March 26, 1990, p. 1; *Radianska Ukraina*, in *FBIS*, November 30, 1989, p. 69; Reuters, October 30, 1989; *Pravda*, in *FBIS*, March 26, 1990, p. 59; *Demokraticheskaia platforma*, June 1990, p. 1; *Izvestiia*, in *FBIS*, April 4, 1991, p. 51; Interfax, in *FBIS*, March 16, 1992, p. 58.

sharing of information on protest acts across new state boundaries. Thus, it would be considerably more difficult to create a protest event sample for the entirety of the former Soviet Union after 1992 with the same rigor that was followed in this study.

Obviously, as is true of any event analysis, coverage of the actual number of protest demonstrations that took place was incomplete. Nevertheless, coverage was quite substantial. As Table AII.3 shows, according to published police statistics in 1989 there were 5,300 demonstrations of all sizes throughout the entire Soviet Union. The multiple-source media sample includes information on 1,496 of these, or 28.2 percent of those reported by the police. Coverage of demonstrations recorded by the police in 1988 was the same. According to published police statistics, there were 2,328 protest demonstrations throughout the Soviet Union in 1988; information was found for 665 of these, or 28.6 percent. The nearly identical proportion of events noted in the police statistics that were covered by the multiple-source media sample for these two years is striking. Considering that the police statistics also included demonstrations and instances of picketing that were less than a hundred in size (as noted in Appendix I, likely to be a large proportion of all events), the coverage of demonstrations with a hundred or more participants in the multiple-source media sample can be said to be extensive – and certainly well beyond the normal standards of collection for this type of study. But as Table AII.3 shows, the proportion of events recorded by the police that were also covered in the multiple-source media sample dropped in early 1990. Whether due to a significant rise in the number of demonstrations with less than one hundred participants, an explosion in the number of events that outstripped the capacity of the media to report them, or a decline in media attention to protest, the multiple-source sample covered only 19.3 percent of the events recorded by the police for the first fifty-four days of 1990 (still a respectable figure). The regional statistics in Table AII.3 suggest that the proportion of events recorded by the police which were also covered in the multiple-source media sample was lower in areas of the Soviet Union where participation in demonstrations was lower (such as in Uzbekistan) or where there was an explosion of small demonstrations (as implied by the statistics on demonstrations and participation rates for Moscow during the first three months of 1991).[14] The shifting proportions of events recorded by the police that were also in the multiple-source media sample would seem to be due at least in part to the size limit imposed for the sample. But variations in media attention cannot be entirely ruled out, and a definitive answer obviously would require detailed analysis of police records, when and if they become available.

[14] Even so, as Titarenko and McCarthy's comparison of their police data for Minsk for 1990–92 with the sample used in this book indicates, temporal trends in the multisource media sample are similar to those found in the police record.

# Index

489

# Index

Bunce, Valerie, 401
bureaucracy, 57, 58, 62, 171
    appropriation of state resources by, 8, 99
Buriat-Mongolian National Party (BMNP), 216–17
Buriats, 211, 215–17
Bush, George, 444

Canada, 35
Carribean, 33
causation, 6–7, 37, 41–42, 103, 200, 214–15
    evolution of, 103, 130, 143–44
    probabilistic notion of, 6–7
    *see also* structure/agency debate
censorship, lifting of, 59–60, 75
Central Asia, 2, 254, 257, 347, 373, 442
Chalidze, Valery, 72n, 330–32, 334n25
Chebrikov, Viktor, 348n57
Chechens, 210, 213, 238, 243, 246, 268, 281, 443
    comparison with Volga Tatars, 268
Chechnia, 277, 317, 309n64, 329, 445n1, 446
Cherkess, 211
Cherniaev, Anatolii, 94n100, 96, 431, 436
Chernobyl, 58, 253
China, 371n88, 447, 448
Chong, Dennis, 154–55
"chronological unfairness," 103, 124–25, 129, 145–46, 454
Chuvash, 210
Civic Dignity, 390
class, 30, 79, 393–94, 396, 397–98, 399
coal-miner strikes, 30, 87–88, 393–94, 396–97
cognitive dissonance reduction, 20n39
Commonwealth of Independent States, 387, 387n7, 439, 440
Communist Party Central Committee
    February 1990 Plenum, 407
    January 1987 Plenum, 59
    June 1889 Plenum, 93
    October 1987 Plenum, 66, 80
    September 1989 Plenum, 93, 227, 406
Communist Party of the Soviet Union, 59–60, 98–101, 407, 409, 413
    effects of mobilization on, 67, 97–99, 107, 112–16, 124, 225, 226, 299–300
    federalization of, 99–100

Nineteenth Party Conference, 81–83, 82n65, 105, 170, 172, 173, 187, 224, 263, 337, 338, 344, 390
Twenty-Eighth Party Congress, 99
Communist Party membership (effects on mobilization), 110, 123, 126–27
Communists for Democracy, 422
confederation, 412, 420, 421, 423–24, 432, 434–35, 437
conformity, 29
Connor, Walker, 21, 33
contagion, 109
Crete, 449
Crimea, 52, 277, 291
Crimean Tatars, 60–62, 61n26, 68, 73, 333, 334n25, 337, 443, 463
Critchlow, James, 259
Croatia, 35, 449
cross-sectional time-series analysis, 41, 129–34, 239, 355–66
crowds, 22–23, 101
Crowley, Stephen, 394, 396–97
cultural equipment of the state, 20, 445
cultural hegemony, 39, 207, 215–17, 222
culture of violence, 277, 282, 289
Czechoslovakia, 27, 158n12

Dąbrowski, General Henryk, 162
Dagestan, 299
Dalai Lama, 449
Danubian principalities, 449
Davitgaredzha monastery, 180
de Certeau, Michel, 1, 21
decolonization, 448, 450
Della Porta, Donatella, 285, 287
Dementei, Nikolai, 429
Demichev, Petr, 61
Demirchian, Karen, 65, 66, 67
demobilization of nationalist contention, 443–48
Democratic Platform, 413
Democratic Russia, 90, 380, 381, 415, 419, 423
Democratic Union, 341, 390
democratization, 30, 49, 63, 86
demonstrations, 44, 54n8, 60, 85, 87, 89–91, 104–07, 292–93, 461–65, 462n4, 476n6
    comparison of types of demands within, 76–79

491

# Index

# Index

Moscow Library for Information Exchange (MBIO), 480
Moscow City Soviet, 337, 341
Moscow Association of Voters, 90
Muiznieks, Nils, 160
murder rates, 282n21
Mussolini, Benito, 449
Mutalibov, Ayaz, 429–30
"mutual empowerment," 446–47

Nagorno-Karabakh, 64–68, 66n45, 67n46, 97, 132, 186–90, 224, 277, 296–98, 308, 343–46, 350, 375, 443
Nahaylo, Bohdan, 193
Nakhichevan, 375
nation, 18–19
  crowds and, 22–23
  definition of, 18
  naturalization of the, 18, 19
  as punctuated plebiscite, 25, 457–58
national insurrections, 306, 465
National-Democratic Party of Georgia, 179
nationalism, 8–11, 18–34, 202n2, 451, 457–59
  and analogy, 75, 204
  chronotopic character of, 123–24
  and conformity, 29
  constructivist theories of, 10, 11, 112
  definition of, 18, 202n2
  developmentalist theories of, 11, 112, 116
  eventful approach to, 11, 34
  failure of, 37, 39, 200–70
  instrumentalist theories of, 10, 38, 155
  irrelevancy of, 202–03, 205
  noisy politics of nationalism, 26–27, 26n48, 32, 45, 107, 116–17, 150, 151, 443
  primordialist theories of, 10, 38, 155, 457
  quiet politics of, 26–27, 26n48, 32, 45, 69, 102, 116–17, 150, 281, 443
  recursive capacity of, 11, 27, 451–55
  role of action within, 458
  ritual and, 19
  stakes of, 19
  structure/agency debate and, 9–11, 34, 45
  transnational character of, 31, 32, 206

nationalist elites, 21, 38
nationalist mobilization
  and institutional contingencies, 86–91
  and pre-existing structural conditions, 37, 38, 49, 103–46, 156–59, 238, 242–47, 275
  cross-case influences on, 31, 32–33, 36, 41, 63–64, 68–69, 73–74, 124–29, 133, 142–43, 158n12, 160–62, 206, 239–42, 357, 359, 448–49
  historical precedents, 449
  institutionalization of, 38, 132, 140, 285, 289, 401–02, 444
  over time, 104–07
  spread to socialist bloc, 448
nationalist violence, 39–40, 67, 74, 88, 271–319
  acts of dominant aggression, 305
  acts of nationalist combat, 306
  armed combat, 465
  communal violence, 307n61, 465
  criminal elements in, 310–12
  effects on non-violent nationalist mobilization, 133, 357, 359
  entrepreneurs of, 294–96, 310
  ethnic riots, 307n61
  ethnofederalism and, 277, 283, 304–05
  explanations of, 271–72
  forms of, 305–09
  and institutionalization of mobilization, 275, 285, 287, 294
  interethnic warfare, 307–09, 307n61
  interrepublican borders, 287–93, 309
  national insurrections, 306, 465
  and national order, 273–74
  as phase within mobilizational cycle, 39, 88, 284–87
  and pre-existing structural conditions, 275, 277–83
  relationship with paramilitary organizations, 287, 312, 314–15
  right-wing in Europe, 272
  role of state in sanctioning, 273, 299–300, 303–05, 309–13, 317–18
  social system of, 312–13
  state as coordinator of, 273, 296
  symbolic dimension of, 294–96
  tidal perspective on, 272–76
  as unimaginable, 274
  and weapons, 313–17

Index

# Index

Yazov, Dmitrii, 348n57, 369–70, 374, 375, 376, 382
*Yedinstvo* (Unity), 392
Yeltsin, Boris, 60, 64, 83, 101n118, 196, 227–28, 265, 329, 381, 388, 389, 393, 445
  attempted removal of, 421–22
  and August 1991 coup, 369–70
  intensified conflict with Gorbachev, 418–22
  left-center coalition and, 414–15
  and March 1991 referendum, 419–20
  and market reform, 432, 433–35
  popularity of, 402

  and Russian sovereignty, 405, 406, 409–12, 409n55, 413, 414–16
  speech in Kazan', 227–28, 265
  union treaty negotiations, 430–41
  and use of severe force in postcommunist period, 328–29, 445
Yerevan, 342–45, 346
Young, Crawford, 2n3, 6
Yugoslavia, 33, 277, 448–49

Zavgaev, Doku, 268
*Zholtoksan* (December) movement, 73n58
Zolberg, Aristide, 91
Zvartnots airport, 187, 344–45